Inside the Index and Search Engines: Microsoft® Office SharePoint® Server 2007

Patrick Tisseghem
Lars Fastrup

PUBLISHED BY
Microsoft Press
A Division of Microsoft Corporation
One Microsoft Way
Redmond, Washington 98052-6399

Library of Congress Control Number: 2008923627

Printed and bound in the United States of America.

1 2 3 4 5 6 7 8 9   QWT   3 2 1 0 9 8

Distributed in Canada by H.B. Fenn and Company Ltd.

A CIP catalogue record for this book is available from the British Library.

Microsoft Press books are available through booksellers and distributors worldwide. For further information about international editions, contact your local Microsoft Corporation office or contact Microsoft Press International directly at fax (425) 936-7329. Visit our Web site at www.microsoft.com/mspress. Send comments to mspinput@microsoft.com.

Microsoft, Microsoft Press, Microsoft Dynamics, Access, Active Directory, BizTalk, Excel, InfoPath, IntelliSense, Internet Explorer, MSDN, OneNote, Outlook, PowerPoint, SharePoint, Silverlight, SQL Server, Visio, Visual Studio, Win32, Windows, Windows Live, Windows PowerShell, Windows Server, and Windows Vista are either registered trademarks or trademarks of Microsoft Corporation in the United States and/or other countries. Other product and company names mentioned herein may be the trademarks of their respective owners.

The example companies, organizations, products, domain names, e-mail addresses, logos, people, places, and events depicted herein are fictitious. No association with any real company, organization, product, domain name, e-mail address, logo, person, place, or event is intended or should be inferred.

This book expresses the author's views and opinions. The information contained in this book is provided without any express, statutory, or implied warranties. Neither the authors, Microsoft Corporation, nor its resellers, or distributors will be held liable for any damages caused or alleged to be caused either directly or indirectly by this book.

Acquisitions Editor: Ben Ryan
Developmental Editor: Devon Musgrave
Project Editors: Rosemary Caperton and Lori Merrick
Editorial Production: Waypoint Press
Technical Reviewer: Randall Galloway; Technical Review services provided by Content Master, a member of CM Group, Ltd.
Cover: Tom Draper Design

Body Part No. X14-65798

Contents at a Glance

Table of Contents

What do you think of this book? We want to hear from you!

Microsoft is interested in hearing your feedback so we can continually improve our books and learning resources for you. To participate in a brief online survey, please visit:

www.microsoft.com/learning/booksurvey

What do you think of this book? We want to hear from you!

Microsoft is interested in hearing your feedback so we can continually improve our books and learning resources for you. To participate in a brief online survey, please visit:

www.microsoft.com/learning/booksurvey

Acknowledgments

Writing a book while you have a full-time job during the day is very stressful, not only personally, but also for the family. That's why I want to thank, above all, my wife Linda and my two lovely daughters, Laura and Anahi, for their support once again during these past eight months. Lars was one of the students in my first SharePoint 2003 developer class in the summer of 2003. Since then, we have been close friends, and the choice of him as a co-author for this book was obvious due to his expertise in this domain. I would like to thank him for all of his efforts. Without him, the book would be totally developer-focused. He made sure that there are plenty of administrator-focused topics in the book. I also would like to thank Karine and the whole U2U team for their support; the people at Microsoft Press; the editors Lori, Steve, Jennifer, Randall, and Rosemary; Mike Fitzmaurice for his continuous support (even out there in the Antartic), and all of my students who have inspired me a lot during the many trainings in different countries I have led the past 2 years.

—Patrick Tisseghem

This is my first SharePoint book project, and before anything, I would like to thank my buddy Patrick Tisseghem for offering the opportunity to co-author this book. It has been a challenging and rewarding experience working with you on this project as it takes a lot to keep up with your standard of work. But your easygoing nature is very compatible with mine and I truly like working with you. I especially enjoyed our first review session at my place in Denmark, where our shared interest in a good single malt whisky also concluded the night very nicely. My acknowledgment also goes to the people at Microsoft Press for accepting and trusting me as an author. I would foremost like to thank my primary contacts, Lori Merrick, Rosemary Caperton, Steve Sagman, Randall Galloway, and Jennifer Harris, for your patience and competent approach to reviewing my chapters. I am impressed with the quality your work has added to the final result. Finally, I would also like to thank Microsoft and the SharePoint Search team for building and delivering a product that adds great value to the market. This product has played an important role in my professional career and has helped me build a great professional network and a valuable technical skill set. I can hardly wait to see what you come up with in the next version.

—Lars Fastrup

Introduction

Over the past decade, we have seen a large investment from Microsoft in the Enterprise Search space, and there's more to come. At the time of this writing, we have support for search in Windows SharePoint Services 3.0 and in Microsoft Office SharePoint Server 2007, there is the new release of Microsoft Search Server 2008, and community tools are available for extending the search infrastructure and the search user experience. There is also a wealth of Microsoft partners who are active in the Enterprise Search space, filling the niches; selling helpful add-ons that enrich the experience for administrators, users, and developers; and delivering consultancy services around of all this.

We (Lars Fastrup and Patrick Tisseghem) decided to team up in the summer of 2007 to write this book. We were, and still are, convinced that the time is right to have a dedicated book covering all aspects of the indexing and search infrastructure that is available when you deploy Microsoft Office SharePoint Server 2007 within an organization. Lars has spent most of his professional career working in the Enterprise Search space on a highly successful third-party product named Ontolica Search. Patrick is the author of *Inside Microsoft Office SharePoint Server 2007* (Microsoft Press, 2007), he educates people about SharePoint development, and he is very passionate about the options for customizing and extending the search infrastructure with custom solution components.

Target Audience

The result is a book covering a wide range of topics for both administrators and developers. And as you'll notice while reading through these chapters, very often there is a thin line in the world of SharePoint between what administrators have to do and what developers have to do. Both must know about each others' tasks to a certain degree.

This book is of course based on a lot of information that is contained in the Microsoft Software Developer Kit (SDK) for both Windows SharePoint Services 3.0 and Office SharePoint Server 2007. It is good to have this resource available while you go through the content. An online version is available from the Microsoft Developer Network (MSDN) at *http://msdn2.microsoft.com/en-us/library/bb931736.aspx*, or you can download the full documentation at *http://www.microsoft.com/downloads/details.aspx?FamilyId=6D94E307-67D9-41AC-B2D6-0074D6286FA9*. Administrators can get more background information on the Microsoft Technet site at *http://technet.microsoft.com/en-us/library/cc263630.aspx*.

Code Samples

The language used in the book is C#, and sample code is available only in C#. All of the examples are wrapped in single Microsoft Visual Studio 2005 or Microsoft Visual Studio 2008 projects and can be downloaded from the book's companion Web site at the following address:

http://www.microsoft.com/mspress/companion/9780735625358/

Microsoft Press provides support for books and companion content at the following Web site:

http://www.microsoft.com/learning/support/books/

Questions and Comments

If you have comments or ideas regarding this book or the companion content, or if you have questions that are not answered by visiting the preceding Web sites, please send them to Microsoft Press via e-mail to

mspinput@microsoft.com

Please note that Microsoft software product support is not offered through the preceding address.

Chapter 1
Introducing Enterprise Search in SharePoint 2007

After completing this chapter, you will be able to

- Describe the role of Microsoft in the Enterprise Search space.
- Distinguish between the search features supported in the various Microsoft Enterprise Search products.
- See how Federated Search is supported in Microsoft Search Server 2008.
- Understand the index and search architecture of the Microsoft Office SharePoint Products And Technologies at a high level.
- Describe the administrative and developer-oriented topics covered in this book.

The Importance of Search and the Role of Microsoft

"Knowledge is of two kinds: we know a subject ourselves, or we know where we can find information upon it." Samuel Johnson's thinking in the eighteenth century is obviously still very relevant in the world we are living in today. The amount of information that is stored in digital format is enormous, and growing more every day. As humans, it has become almost impossible for us to be knowledgeable in the many subjects that govern our lives without some support of software tools that help us in the quest to find the right information at the right time. This is true for all the things we carry out in our private occupations, but it is even more important within organizations, where there is a growing need for sophisticated software support that enables information workers to find the required piece of corporate information as fast as possible and regardless of where that piece of data is stored.

The past decade has seen a lot of investment from Microsoft in search-related technologies, with a focus on three search spaces: the Internet, the desktop, and internal corporate networks, known collectively as the *enterprise*. On the Internet, Microsoft delivers its search experience through Live Search (*http://www.live.com*), shown in Figure 1-1. Although Live Search is facing tough competition from search engines such as Google and Yahoo, the latest figures show a growing market share. This is due to one of the strongest features of Live Search: its integration with the other Microsoft online services.

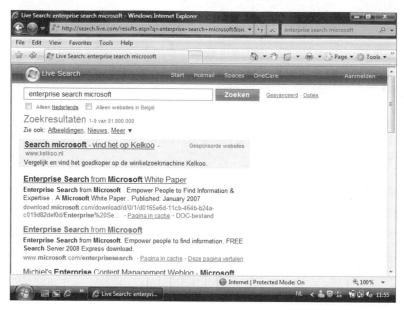

FIGURE 1-1 Microsoft Live Search

Search support in the desktop space is where Microsoft has a very strong position, with indexing and search technologies in the latest client operating systems, such as Microsoft Windows Vista, as shown in Figure 1-2.

FIGURE 1-2 Desktop search from the Start menu in Windows Vista

Many users see the search capabilities of Windows Vista, displayed on the Start menu, as shown in Figure 1-2, and in Microsoft Windows Explorer, as shown in Figure 1-3, as one of the best new features of the operating system. All of the data that is stored on a laptop or PC is indexed in the background in a nondisruptive way, and when it's needed, users can quickly find the data without being too worried about the place where they stored that data. The integration of all the support for search in popular software products such as Microsoft Office Outlook 2007 is definitely beneficial for information workers who want, for example, to find information that is stored in the many e-mail messages that are typically part of their mailboxes.

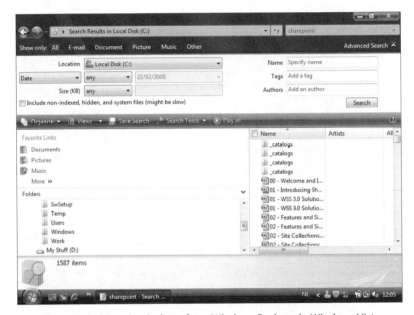

FIGURE 1-3 Searching the desktop from Windows Explorer in Windows Vista

The Internet and the desktop search space are beyond the scope of this book. Our focus will be on the support that Microsoft provides for indexing and searching of data stored within internal corporate networks. Support for searching within this area appeared more than ten years ago, with technologies such as the Windows Indexing Service, which was included in early versions of Internet Information Server (IIS) and is the precursor to the Microsoft SharePoint Products And Technologies: Microsoft Site Server 3.0. Support for search on corporate networks was initially concentrated on the indexing of data stored in database systems such as Microsoft SQL Server, but it has now been expanded to data that is stored within a multitude of various types of data storage systems.

Although support in these search spaces started as fairly separate efforts, today Microsoft is putting a lot of effort into the development and concentration of all of the search-related technologies into a single core search technology that is integrated within the majority of a company's products but customized to its own audiences. Clearly, employees should not be limited to support only for searching data that resides within the corporate database systems or shared folders. Information workers can be empowered with support to find information that comes from many places: the outside world, the local file system, and the data stores (whatever form they have) within the company. This uniting of the search spaces into one is also known as *Enterprise Search*.

> **More Information** You can learn more about Enterprise Search at *http://www.microsoft.com/ enterprisesearch*.

Enterprise Search is not just about indexing and searching information, however. Microsoft wants to go a step further and make the search results also actionable. In short, there are three important design goals: to enhance the end-user search experience, to include people's expertise in the search results, and to make sure that the results are returned as quickly as possible, in the most relevant order. And all of this must of course be manageable for the administrators.

The Search User Experience

The search for information ought to be a natural experience for users working in Microsoft desktop and server products. Without leaving a comfort zone such as Microsoft Office Outlook, Microsoft Office Word, or a document workspace in Microsoft Windows SharePoint Services, a user should be able to enter search queries, have the queries executed behind the scenes, and have the results flow into the same work environment, where they can be immediately processed. The search results should also provide information from various locations, including public places on the Internet like blogs and Wikis, shared folders containing Microsoft Office system documents on the intranet, and documents located on an external hard disk connected to the user's laptop. In other words, the user should be able to search in many locations from a single place.

The context in which the search is executed is equally important and should be reflected in the display of the search results. A salesperson operating in the North American region should not see the same search results as a salesperson working in the European region. Most companies capture and store contextual information such as details about the work environment and the responsibililities of the employees already and make it available in some form. Search engines should be able to pick up the information and adapt the search results accordingly. Users should also be able to see only the items in the search results that they are allowed to see based on access control lists (ACLs) that are associated with the containers storing the information. In some instances, the security information is associated with the individual piece of information itself. In all cases, a trimming of the search results should take place and should be transparent to the user and to the administrators who are responsible for the management of the search infrastructure.

Simply displaying search results to users is not enough. Search results should be action-able, with the actions again depending on context. Search results displayed after the execu-tion of a search in Microsoft Office Outlook offer different actions to the user compared to the search results that the user gets in a portal created with Microsoft Office SharePoint Server 2007. But again it is not only the context of the host application that is important, but also the user in question, and all of the profile information can also have an effect on the type of actions that can be performed on the search results as a whole or on an individual search item.

People in the Organization

In addition to the data that companies have stored in the various silos of information spread across the corporate network is another important asset: people. People have skills, people know about things, people can refer to other people who can help, people might have re-sources that they can share. It's extremely useful for a company to be able to index all of that expertise and to allow employees to search for it. There's a lot of momentum these days around Internet sites that provide support to join and maintain social, collaboration, and sharing networks—examples are sites such as, Del.icio.us, Facebook, and LinkedIn. Many other similar sites are available, and new ones are popping up almost every day. The cores of these sites are the people who visit them, and we use these sites to find out more about other people. More and more companies are looking at how to take advantage of this type of software internally to set up social networks within the company.

The collection and management of people information is not always easy, however. Different approaches are possible, from formal line-of-business (LOB) systems that store human re-sources information to loosely coupled collaboration sites and personal or professional blogs. Blogs, for example, can be hosted within the company and also exposed and used as an important image-building activity to the outside world. Whatever approach you take, make sure that the information on these sites and within these back-end systems is indexed and made searchable. The crawler, an important part of the index architecture that is responsible for the actual indexing of the content, should be able to absorb every piece of information that it can find about a person and make that information available to the search engines. All of this must of course be compliant with legal rules, including, for example, the rules dealing with privacy protection of personal data.

Search engines should display these types of results with the proper actions that can be im-mediately executed by the users. Figure 1-4, for example, shows the results of a query con-taining items that represent people and the actions that the user can immediately perform on one of the individual result items.

FIGURE 1-4 Actions that can be performed on a search result after the execution of a People query in Office SharePoint Server 2007

Enterprise Ready

The amount of information that is available in an enterprise can range from normal levels to terabytes of data. The places where this data is stored can be very diverse, often involving Microsoft as well as non-Microsoft platforms or software products. Indexing all of this information can be a daunting operation when it comes to the infrastructure that is required. Scalability, manageability, and extensibility are important factors that many IT managers are looking for when they have to select the indexing and search infrastructure for the company.

Microsoft supports indexing and searching for information at all levels: from very small organizations to very large ones. This is evident in the range of search-related products and technologies that we'll look at later in this chapter. The core architecture, however, is common, which makes it ready for an enterprise that wants to start small and over the years to grow at its own pace. The indexing and search infrastructure will scale accordingly, without the need to make disruptive IT decisions.

Management of the indexing and search infrastructure should be easy and transparent but also granular so that administrators have a lot of freedom and flexibility in the decisions they have to make. Because the out-of-the-box functionality does not always match the needs of a business from both the indexing and the searching perspectives, a large degree of extensibility should be available. Microsoft Enterprise Search products provide this extensibility. Developers can build tools, customize the administration and the end-user experience, extend the indexing architecture, and integrate the search experience in any type of custom application that is operated by the information workers in the company. Looking at the indexing and searching infrastructure from a developer angle is at the heart of this book, with the majority of the chapters covering extensibility and customization options.

Microsoft Enterprise Search Products

As mentioned, Microsoft has been in the search space for more than a decade now with various products and technologies. Instead of looking back at what was there in the past, let's have a quick look at what is available at the time of this writing. As will be the case in the rest of this book, we'll concentrate on the search infrastructure that is delivered with the Microsoft SharePoint Products And Technologies. And as you'll notice, this is already more than enough to fill a good-size book.

Microsoft Windows SharePoint Services 3.0

Not a lot of computer book writers would include Windows SharePoint Services in the list of products that include search technology. Things have changed with the latest version of Windows SharePoint Services 3.0, however.

Windows SharePoint Services 3.0 is a site-provisioning engine, enabling organizations to quickly set up a Web-based infrastructure for collaborating, storing, and managing content and documents. The installed infrastructure offers all of the needed ingredients to make this happen, allowing you to scale from a small team with a limited amount of users and content toward supporting large organizations with thousands of users and millions of documents. Many see Windows SharePoint Services 3.0 as a development platform because of its rich application programming interfaces (APIs) and extensibility options, as shown in the following illustration.

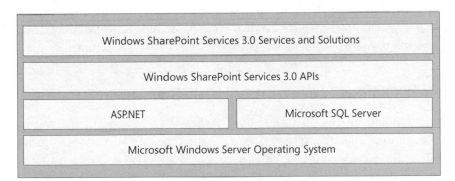

Windows SharePoint Services 3.0 is a server-side software layer, and thus it requires either Microsoft Windows Server 2003 or Microsoft Windows Server 2008. The platform relies heavily on the Web application development layer that is part of the Microsoft .NET Framework named ASP.NET. Microsoft .NET Framework 2.0 is required at a minimum, although many of you probably have already upgraded to version 3.0 or version 3.5. Content that users store, manage, and collaborate on in SharePoint sites is always stored in a Microsoft SQL Server database. This database is called the *content database*.

The Windows SharePoint Services 3.0 APIs consist of thousands of classes that you as a developer can communicate with in your custom applications and solutions that integrate or run on top of the platform. The product teams within Microsoft have created services and solutions also based on these APIs, and many of them are delivered out-of-the-box as Features. As you progress through the chapters of this book, you'll encounter and work with many of these Features.

Windows SharePoint Services 3.0 also has support for indexing and searching. The provided infrastructure is based on the same architectural components as are delivered with Microsoft Office SharePoint Server 2007, which we will cover in more detail in a moment. This support in Windows SharePoint Services 3.0 is very different from its predecessor. Windows SharePoint Services 2.0 relied heavily on the Microsoft SQL Server full-text search capabilities. No real indexing of content took place, and the search queries entered by users were directly executed as full-text queries against the data that was stored in the SQL Server content databases. Search in Windows SharePoint Services 3.0 is more in line with the Office SharePoint Server 2007 search infrastructure. This is good news for administrators and definitely also for developers who need to customize, extend, or communicate with the search engine. As a result of this unification, they can work with the same classes in the object model as the classes they communicate with when working in portals created with Office SharePoint Server 2007.

What has not changed, however, is the scope of the search queries. Users executing a query in a site will see only matching results that are stored within that site and when available, within the subsites under it. Note that the inclusion of the subsites is an expansion of the behavior found in the earlier version of Windows SharePoint Services. The administrator user experience is still quite limited, and administrators do not have the option to index content not found in the SharePoint sites. No external non-SharePoint content sources can be crawled with the Windows SharePoint Services 3.0 indexing infrastructure.

Microsoft Office SharePoint Server 2007

Windows SharePoint Services 3.0 is a free layer of software that is included in the licensing model of your server operating system. This is not the case with Microsoft Office SharePoint Server 2007, which is basically a bundled collection of additional services and solutions that is installed and that runs on top of the Windows SharePoint Services 3.0 platform, as shown on the opposite page.

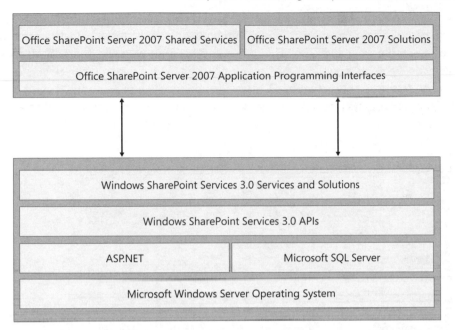

If you study the licensing model of Office SharePoint Server 2007, you'll notice two basic options: the Standard Version and the Enterprise Version. Office SharePoint Server 2007 consists of a core license for every server where you install it and client access licenses (CALs), which must be purchased for every employee who accesses the SharePoint sites or portals. The standard licenses allow the user to benefit from the standard set of services and solutions.

> **More Information** Full information regarding the available licensing options can be found on the Microsoft Web site, at *http://www.microsoft.com/sharepoint*.

The most important services and solutions that you'll encounter in this book are:

- **Collaboration and publishing portals** Office SharePoint Server 2007 is essentially the unification of Microsoft SharePoint Portal Server 2003 and Microsoft Content Management Server 2002. Portals come in two types: collaboration and publishing portals. Collaboration portals are created for the internal management, sharing, and collaboration of content; publishing portals are created to display this content to the outside world. Publishing portals are public Internet sites; collaboration portals are intranet sites. Both have the publishing infrastructure enabled, which requires that the content that is created and managed follows a controlled publishing life cycle. Content is created by content authors, and a workflow typically is started to allow other people to review the work and possibly approve it. Once approved, the content, which is typically delivered as a page on the site, is upgraded from a minor, or draft, version to a major version. Content that has a major version is visible to everyone visiting the site. Figure 1-5 displays a new press release page in a publishing portal in edit mode. Notice on the Page Editing toolbar at the top the different buttons that can be used to control the life cycle of this page.

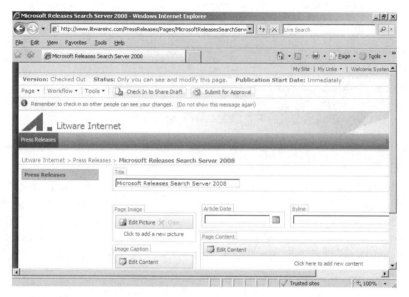

FIGURE 1-5 Content management in a publishing portal

Content management is an important new feature included in Office SharePoint Server 2007. It consists of much more than simply having content created, approved, and published. Microsoft covers with this release the full Enterprise Content Management domain, including services and solutions that help you to convert documents from one format to another, enforce information management policies, audit and log changes, build and deliver complex workflows that integrate with the business processes you have running within your organization, the archiving of content, and much more.

■ **People management**   Another main feature that is delivered as standard functionality with Office SharePoint Server 2007 is related to people management. Users in a Windows SharePoint Services 3.0 environment are identified by an account name, a display name, and an e-mail address. Office SharePoint Server 2007 adds more substance to this and can associate a user profile, enriching the information related to these individuals. User profile information can be used in SharePoint sites to create a more dynamic and adaptive user experience, which can be useful when it comes to displaying search results or trimming results based on information that is part of the user profile. In addition, users can become members of one or more *audiences*. An audience is basically a collection of people that match up with the membership conditions defined by the administrator for the audience. An example might be all people working in the same department. These audiences can be used to target information and personalize the experience of the user through the filtered display of parts of SharePoint pages and the content they contain. User profile information also plays an important role in the personal sites that can be created per user, exposing parts of the user profile information to other users visiting the public part of these personal sites.

■ **Index and search engine**   You'll find the same core components that are part of the index and search infrastructure of Windows SharePoint Services 3.0. The infrastructure has a lot of important additional features, however. First and foremost is that administrators can direct the crawler to index more than just SharePoint content. It is possible to index and make searchable basically any type of data, stored anywhere, on any platform. Administrators have dedicated administration pages where they can configure and fine-tune the indexing and the search experience; details will be described in Chapter 5, "Search Administration." Office SharePoint Server 2007 also comes with a dedicated place for end users to execute and review the results of simple and complex queries. This dedicated place is called the Search Center, and both administrators and developers can customize it to a certain degree, as you'll learn later.

The preceding services and solutions are all familiar to readers who have experience with the earlier versions of SharePoint Portal Server and Content Management Server. The new versions, however, have been upgraded and dressed up with important new features. Office SharePoint Server 2007 also introduces completely new services and solutions that can be accessed by users when the required enterprise CALs are purchased. Here's a list:

■ **Business Data Catalog (BDC)**   As mentioned earlier, the index engine included in Office SharePoint Server 2007 can index nearly everything that is available within your organization. One of the key technologies that makes this possible is the Business Data Catalog (BDC). The BDC is a new shared service that acts as a middle layer between SharePoint and the business data that is often locked away in LOB systems such as Microsoft Dynamics CRM, SAP back-end systems, AS 400 mainframe systems, and the like. The BDC is able to expose this data in a unified way to front-end user interface components that are part of the default installation of Office SharePoint Server 2007. Developers can also build custom solution components that take advantage of the object models exposed by the BDC. Figure 1-6 shows an example of a page that contains a number of Business Data Web Parts that are connected to each other and provide a master-detail user experience containing data that comes from an external LOB system. The business data can also be crawled by the index engine if the required definitions are part of the model of the business data that is stored in the BDC metadata store. The items will be stored, along with items coming from other content sources, in the index file, and users are able to search for that data.

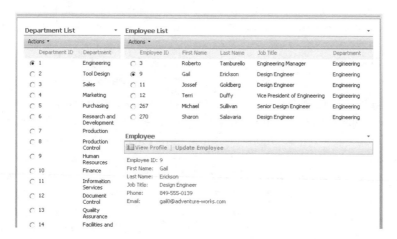

FIGURE 1-6 Business data displayed to users via the Business Data Web Parts

- **Microsoft Office Excel Services** This new service will not be covered in this book, but it is a very important part of the solution support that is made available in Office SharePoint Server 2007 in the space of business intelligence. Users are able to upload, store, and manage Microsoft Office Excel 2003 and Excel 2007 spreadsheets in SharePoint document libraries and make these spreadsheets available in ways that were not possible before. Spreadsheets, or snapshots of the data contained within the spreadsheets, can be rendered as pure HTML pages in the browser, viewable by anybody, without additional installations on their desktops. Solution components, such as Web Parts, can pick up the data made available in the spreadsheets and display this information to users, possibly connecting multiple Web Parts to provide a dashboard-like user experience, as shown in Figure 1-7. Excel Services also comes with the Excel Services Web service, which can be used by every platform and every development environment. Through this Web service, you can send new data to the spreadsheet, let it calculate internally the results using simple or complex formulas, and then return these results back to the application that initiated the call to the Web service.

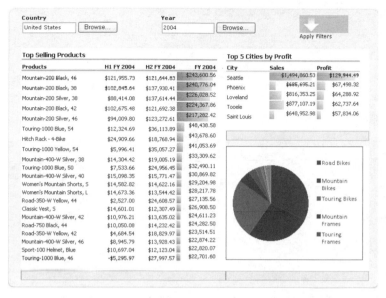

FIGURE 1-7 Dashboard page displaying data from Excel spreadsheets

- **Forms Services**   Microsoft Office InfoPath 2007 is a young product in the Microsoft Office system family, but it's extremely useful if within your organization you need to capture and display data using electronic forms. All of the data that is created and maintained within InfoPath forms is in XML format, which makes it a perfect medium for delivering data-capturing user interfaces to the various components that are in place to support the business processes within your organization. Examples of these components are SharePoint lists and document libraries, workflows that are running on top of the Microsoft Windows Workflow Foundation, and processes that are under the control of Microsoft BizTalk Server. With Forms Services, you are now able to deliver these electronic forms in the browser, avoiding the need for users to have the Office InfoPath rich client on their desktops to work with the forms. Having the electronic forms delivered in the browser, as shown in Figure 1-8, opens doors to new types of solutions that support information workers in their daily tasks.

Note   Microsoft Office Forms Server 2007, the software that makes this all happen, is also licensed as a stand-alone product.

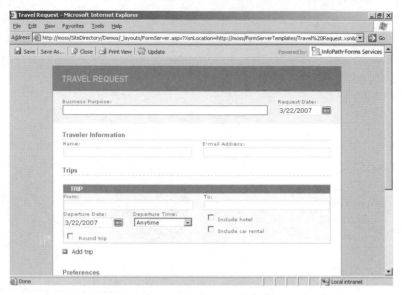

FIGURE 1-8 An InfoPath electronic form displayed in the browser

Microsoft Search Server 2008

There is a new member in the Microsoft family of Enterprise Search products, and it comes in two flavors: Microsoft Search Server 2008 Express Edition and Microsoft Search Server 2008.

Note   At the time of this writing, this product has not yet been released, but a release candidate is available for download at the following Microsoft site: *http://www.microsoft.com/ enterprisesearch.*

Microsoft Search Server 2008 can deliver a stand-alone index and search infrastructure within your corporate network. It uses the same components that are part of the index and search architecture included in Office SharePoint Server 2007 but expands the infrastructure with a number of new features. Search Server also isolates the infrastructure from the Microsoft SharePoint Products And Technologies. In other words, you do not need to install Windows SharePoint Services 3.0 or Office SharePoint Server 2007 within your organization to be able to index and search for content.

Let's have a closer look at Microsoft Search Server 2008 Express Edition, since it is brand new and quite exciting. Because it is so new and not yet released, we do not have a dedicated chapter in this book for this new product. However, the configuration, administration, and customization is similar to what you'll learn for Office SharePoint Server 2007. Most of the techniques learned in this book can be applied in a Search Server 2008 installation.

Installing Microsoft Search Server 2008 Express Edition

Search Server Express is, like all of the other Microsoft Express Editions, a free version of the product. Compared to the full version of the product, the Express Edition does of course have a couple of limitations related to the availability and the load-balancing options that are supported. There is essentially no limit to the number of documents that Search Server 2008 Express can index. However, if you decide to use Search Server 2008 Express Edition in combination with Microsoft SQL Server 2005 Express Edition, the maximum size of the database will be limited to 4 GB. As a result, the indexing capability of Search Server 2008 Express Edition is limited to approximately 400,000 documents, depending on the size and type of the documents. If you decide to make use of an existing Microsoft SQL Server 2005 database, you basically have no limit on the number of documents that can be indexed with Search Server 2008 Express Edition.

The installation is easy and can be done on any machine running Windows Server 2003 within your corporate network. Figure 1-9 displays the wizard that you'll see during the installation of Search Server 2008 Express Edition.

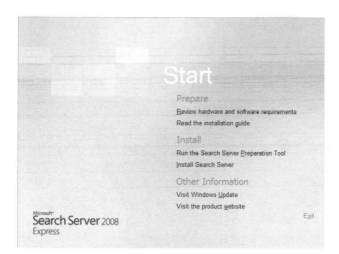

FIGURE 1-9 The start page when installing Search Server 2008 Express Edition

To ensure that you have the proper requirements to continue the installation, the wizard invites you to run the Search Server Preparation Tool. This tool verifies that Service Pack 1 for Windows Server 2003 is installed, together with .NET Framework 2.0 and the Windows Workflow Foundation Runtime Components. An installation of .NET Framework 3.0 of course includes both and also does the job. The tool also prepares the IIS Web Server for its role on the machine.

You can opt for one of two modes during the installation:

- **Basic Installation**   Installing using this option is straightforward. The installation wizard will try to use default settings wherever possible. The index and search infrastructure that is installed uses Microsoft SQL Server 2005 as its underlying database storage system. A basic installation installs Microsoft SQL Server 2005 Express Edition.

- **Advanced Installation**   The advanced installation process provides more configurable options; you will select this option if you have a Microsoft SQL Server 2005 installation that you want to use. The existing database that you'll specify during the installation can be on the same machine as the one you use to install Search Server 2008 Express Edition, or it can reside on a separate computer.

At the end of the installation, the wizard starts the SharePoint Products And Technologies Configuration Wizard, as shown in Figure 1-10.

FIGURE 1-10 The SharePoint Products And Technologies Configuration Wizard

This wizard performs a number of configuration tasks, such as the creation of the configuration and content database that will be used, as well as the creation of the Search Administration site that can be used to perform the administration tasks for the Enterprise Search infrastructure. When you have completed the wizard, this administration site is opened in your favorite Web browser, as shown in Figure 1-11.

FIGURE 1-11 Administration site for Search Server 2008

Adding Content Sources

It's too early in this book to really dive into all of the details regarding the administration tasks that are involved at this level. Let's restrict ourselves to the creation of a content source that is going to be used to index a local file share. In the section "Federated Search" later in this chapter, we'll configure the Search Server for a Federated Search scenario.

The administration site shown earlier in Figure 1-11 provides a different user experience for administrators from the one they're familiar with in the context of Office SharePoint Server 2007. This is not always a good thing, of course, but we have to acknowledge that here the presentation of the administrative tasks is clear and easy to use thanks to the new Administration Bar. A close-up of the Administration Bar is shown in Figure 1-12.

FIGURE 1-12 The new Administration Bar in Search Server 2008

Let's assume that there is a network folder that contains important documents that have to be included in an index so that users are able to search for it. To define this location, you have to create a content source. The Content Sources link in the Administration Bar redirects you to a page similar to the one shown in Figure 1-13, where you'll find the current content sources.

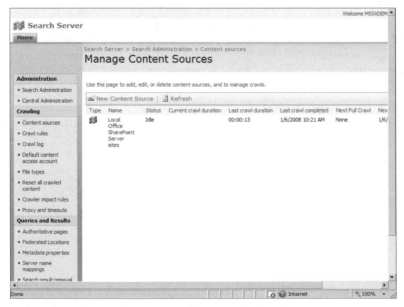

FIGURE 1-13 Managing locations that have to be indexed

The toolbar contains a New Content Source button for the creation of a new content source. Clicking this button displays the Add Content Source page, where you can enter the title of the new content source, the type of the content source, the start addresses, and the configuration of the crawling. You can add different types of content sources, as shown in Figure 1-14. Unlike the content source types supported in Office SharePoint Server 2007, there is no content type here for crawling business data. But you can create content sources that crawl SharePoint sites, Web sites, file shares, and Microsoft Exchange Server public folders.

FIGURE 1-14 Creating a new content source of type File Share

Because this is a new content source, you'll have to start a full crawl to have all of the documents from that file share included in the index. A log is maintained during the crawling. Figure 1-15 shows the different Microsoft Office system documents that are registered in the crawl log as successfully crawled items.

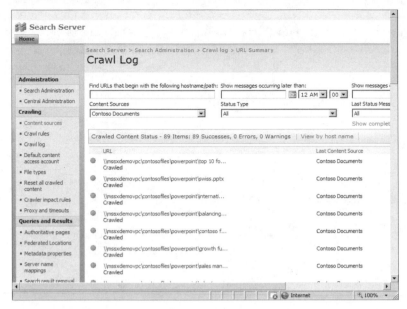

FIGURE 1-15 Reviewing the crawl log

If you navigate back to the home page of the Search Administration site, you'll find informa-tion about the recent actions completed. These items are displayed by the different Web Parts that make up the dashboard page. Figure 1-16, for example, displays a Web Part that shows an overview of the recently completed crawls.

Recently completed crawls

Content Source	Type	Finished	Duration	Success	Error
Local Office SharePoint Server sites	Incremental	1/6/2008 11:01 AM	00:00:21	6	0
Contoso Documents	Full	1/6/2008 11:01 AM	00:01:07	89	0
Local Office SharePoint Server sites	Incremental	1/6/2008 10:41 AM	00:00:13	6	0

⏮ ◀   Page 1 of 4   ▶ ⏭

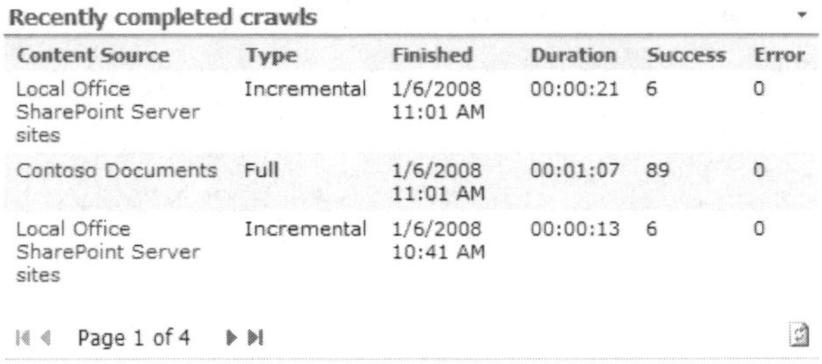

FIGURE 1-16 One of the Web Parts making up the dashboard that is the home page of the Search Administration site

Now that the content source is in place, we can start querying the resources that are included in the content index.

The End-User Search Experience

The Installation Wizard in Search Server 2008 Express Edition not only installs and configures an administration site, it also installs a Search Center site, which is a highly customizable site dedicated to searching. You'll learn about Search Center in the following chapters. The home page of the Search Center can be easily accessed via the Search Administration site. The Search Center is a simple site with a home page waiting for a search query to be entered by the visitor, as shown in Figure 1-17.

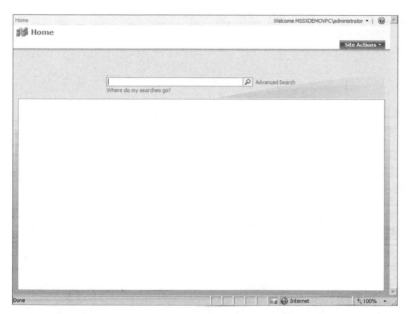

FIGURE 1-17 The Search Center home page, where users enter a search query

The results of a query on the keyword *contoso* are displayed in Figure 1-18. Notice that the page is split into two columns. The first column shows the search results that match the items in the local content index. The second column shows the results of the same query that have then been executed using the Internet search engine Live Search. This is already an excellent example of the power of the new functionality that is delivered with Search Server 2008: Federated Search. We'll have a closer look at Federated Search in the next section, but in short, it is the aggregation of search results that are delivered by other search engines such as Live Search.

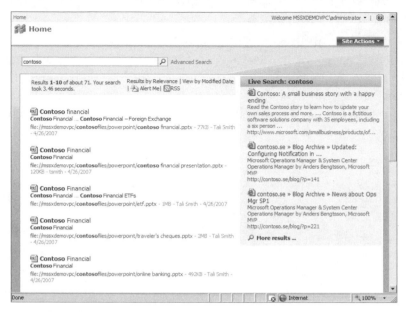

FIGURE 1-18 The search results page, containing items from the local content index and results from Live Search, illustrating the integration of Federated Search results

Federated Search

Figure 1-18 illustrates the integration of Federated Search within the search results returned by the search engine in Search Server 2008. Federated Search is an important extension. As mentioned earlier, the index engine of Office SharePoint Server 2007 is capable of crawling any type of content source. This crawling can be configured to use custom protocol handlers and possibly to use the BDC as the middle layer for the retrieval of that data. But maybe other index engines are already in place within your corporate network or outside of it in the Internet space that have done a good job of crawling data and building indexes that can be used to support users in their mission to search for the information they need. The index and search engine that is part of Office SharePoint Server 2007 is not directly capable of communicating with these other types of index and search engines.

Search Server 2008 solves this problem with the introduction of Federated Search. Federated Search support enables you to display search results for additional content that is not crawled by your Search Server. With Federation Search, the query can be performed over the local content index, or it can be forwarded to an external content repository, where it is processed by that repository's search engine. The repository's search engine then returns the results to the Search Server, which formats and renders the results from the external repository within the search results page together with the results from the Search Server's own content index.

To be able to connect to the external content repository, Search Server 2008 includes the concept of *Federated Search Connectors*. These connectors use the Open Search standard to communicate with the external search engines. Federated Search Connectors are config-ured with federated location definition (.fld) files, which are basically XML files containing the details of the external location and how to access it. Let's go through a small example illustrating the configuration of Search Server 2008 to allow users to see search results from Wikipedia together with the results that are coming from the local index file.

More Information   A number of sample connectors are available for download from the Microsoft site (*http://www.microsoft.com/enterprisesearch/connectors/federated.aspx*). One of these allows for the connection to Wikipedia. Other sample definition files for connecting to news, resources, media, and other types of data repositories are also available online.

To configure Federated Search, you'll have to go back to the Search Administration site that is part of Search Server 2008. In the Administration Bar, you'll find a Federated Locations link, under the header Queries And Results. Figure 1-19 shows the page displaying the list of cur-rently defined federated locations.

FIGURE 1-19 Managing federated locations

You have two options for creating a new federated location: create one from scratch, or import a location. The toolbar on the page displayed in Figure 1-19 provides a New Location button, which will display a page where you can enter detailed information defining the new location. The reason for the large quantity of data that must be provided is obvious. You're going to access external locations, and these other systems might define their queries and return their search results in a variety of ways.

It's much easier to import the details of a new location via a small XML file. Notice the Online Gallery link in the text in Figure 1-19. If you navigate to that site, you'll be able to download an .fld file. Many are available. We'll use the .fld file for Wikipedia. The .fld file is an XML file containing the definition of the external search location; it follows the syntax of the Open Search standard. To import the file, you click the Import Location button on the toolbar in the Manage Federated Locations page.

The Import Federated Location page, shown in Figure 1-20, demonstrates how simple it is. You browse for the downloaded .fld file and import it by clicking the OK button.

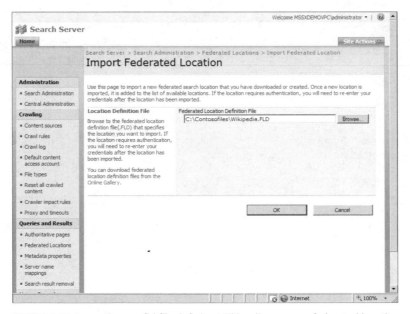

FIGURE 1-20 Importing an .fld file defining Wikipedia as a new federated location

You have the option to edit the details of the location after a successful import of the .fld file if needed. When you've finished, you'll have one additional entry in the Manage Federated Locations page, as shown in Figure 1-21.

FIGURE 1-21 Wikipedia defined as a new federated location

The end-user search experience does not automatically include search results from Wikipedia. Additional customization work at the level of the search results page is required.

Adding a Federated Source to the Search Results Page

The work at the level of the search administration is sufficient for the Wikipedia search services to be contacted by our search page, but unless we configure the search results page to include the results, nothing will really happen.

The customization of the search results page is all about adding and configuring Search Web Parts. Navigate again to the Search Center site, and enter a query so that you end up in the search results page. If you switch this page to edit mode from the Site Actions menu, you'll be able to modify the properties of the various Web Parts that are already placed on the page. Chapter 3, "Customizing the Search User Interface," covers the Search Web Parts, their configuration options, and the options to programmatically manipulate them in depth. Figure 1-22 shows the page with one Web Part that you won't find in the Search Center site included in an Office SharePoint Server 2007 installation: the Federated Results Web Part. By default, there is already such a Web Part on the page, which is configured to display the results generated with the default federated location Live Search.

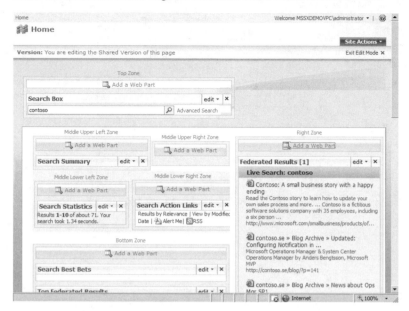

FIGURE 1-22 The search results page in edit mode

Add an additional Web Part by clicking the Add A Web Part button. The Add Web Parts dialog box, shown in Figure 1-23, displays a list of the Search Web Parts that are possible candidates to be included in the Web Part page. Select Federated Results, and then apply your choice by clicking the Add button.

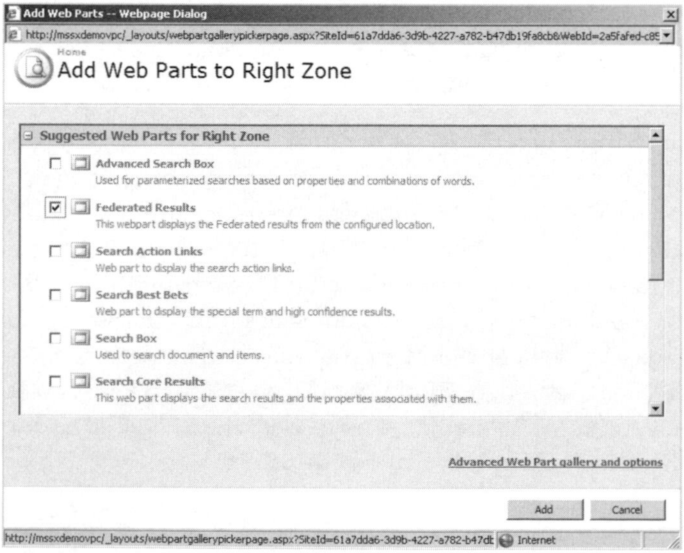

FIGURE 1-23 The list of Search Web Parts

To configure the Web Part, open the tool pane by clicking Edit and then clicking Modify Shared Web Part in the top-right corner of the Web Part. By default, the Location Properties group is expanded. You'll see a drop-down list with the locations that are defined within the Search Administration site. Figure 1-24 shows the tool pane with the Wikipedia option selected.

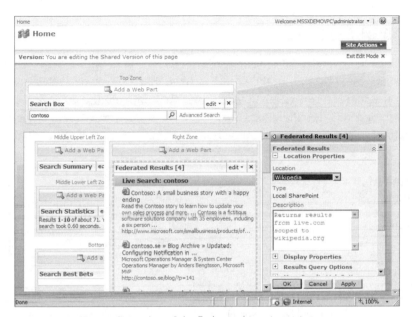

FIGURE 1-24 The configuration of the Federated Results Web Part

Click OK to apply your changes and see the results, as shown in Figure 1-25.

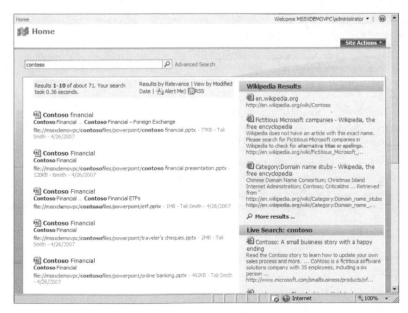

FIGURE 1-25 The search results of the Wikipedia federated location displayed in the search results page together-er with the search results that are part of the local content index and possible other Federated Search results

Nice work! If you have followed along, you have completed one of the many small walk-throughs that are part of this book. Each of these examples demonstrates in a hands-on way a specific configuration or programming task.

Comparison of Features

Table 1-1 completes this overview of the Enterprise Search products with a matrix comparing the features supported by each of the products. Note that at the time of this writing, Microsoft announced an Enterprise Search feature pack to complete the index and search infrastructure included in Office SharePoint Server 2007. This feature pack will include support for Federated Search; the table lists this feature as being included in Office SharePoint Server 2007.

TABLE 1-1 Feature Matrix

Product Feature	Search Server 2008 Express Edition	Search Server 2008	Office SharePoint Server 2007 (Enterprise)
A Search Center site to empower users to quickly find the information they need through a familiar, Web-style search interface and easy-to-use query syntax. Support for the reconfiguration of the layout of the Search Center elements without writing any code.	X	X	X
No preset document limits, allowing you to scale your search infrastructure to meet your evolving needs—however big or small they are—using the same search platform across a breadth of server hardware and SQL Server database configurations.	X	X	X
Extensible search experience by using powerful development tools (including Visual Studio and SharePoint Designer) and building of customized query/results experiences and search-enabled applications on the SharePoint platform—from altering the appearance of your search site using XSLT to enabling contextual actions that you can take on search results.	X	X	X
Relevance tuning with the retrieval of the most-relevant results across a diverse set of third-party LOB systems and content repositories from a single search query. Use of a ranking engine developed in collaboration with Microsoft Research and Windows Live Search.	X	X	X

Product Feature	Search Server 2008 Express Edition	Search Server 2008	Office SharePoint Server 2007 (Enterprise)
Continuous propagation indexing, improving the freshness of your search results with an index that incrementally updates itself as it crawls your information. Newly crawled content is propagated to the query servers so that people can search it sooner, without having to wait for all content to be crawled.	X	X	X
Federated Search Connectors, allowing for the federation of your searches to indexes in other data repositories, applications, and services using the Open Search standard. Quickly import or export your federated locations using packaged federated location definition (.fld) files.	X	X	X
Indexing connectors that allow the indexing of content on file servers, Web sites, Windows SharePoint Services, Office SharePoint Server, Exchange Server public folders, and Lotus Notes repositories.	X	X	X
Security-trimmed results, ensuring that users find only information they should have access to by automatically trimming search results based on the identity of the user at query time. Access control lists (ACLs) for content on file shares, SharePoint sites, and Lotus Notes databases are automatically captured at index time.	X	X	X
Unified administration dashboard to review common administrative tasks, monitor system and crawl status, and configure your search settings in a single, configurable view.	X	X	X
Query and results reporting with a possible review of most common searches, queries with no results, top destination pages, query volume, clickthrough rates, and most-clicked best bets. Recognize not only the most-popular searches but also the least successful, and improve searches by adding new best bets and content sources.	X	X	X
Streamlined installation, making it easy to get an Enterprise Search infrastructure running in your environment quickly.	X	X	

Product Feature	Search Server 2008 Express Edition	Search Server 2008	Office SharePoint Server 2007 (Enterprise)
High availability and load balancing, allowing you to grow your search infrastructure to meet your needs using a variety of front-end and back-end server topologies. Configure multiple query and clustered database servers to manage performance and ensure reliability.		X	X
People and expertise searching to find expertise and enable connections between people by using dynamically updated personal profiles and social networking information—integrated with LDAP, Active Directory, or any structured repository of people information. Sort your results by relevance or social distance, or pick results from a faceted list of titles and roles.			X
Business Data Catalog, which makes it easy for users to connect to, find, and act on information locked away in structured LOB systems (such as SAP or Siebel) by securely integrating the information into search results using a declarative framework. Configure actionable dashboards and mash up interfaces of this data without writing any code.			X
Integrating search with your collaboration portal, content management, workflow, electronic forms, and business intelligence activities by taking advantage of SharePoint's business productivity infrastructure.			X

High-Level Overview of the Search Architecture

All of the Enterprise Search products described earlier in this chapter share a common index and search architecture. The scope and richness depend on the product and the version that you are deploying within your corporate network. Some products offer additional features, such as the support for Federated Search included in Microsoft Search Server 2008. These features are not, or are not yet, available in the other products. The following graphic illustrates the common components at a high level without tying them to a specific product. In this section, we'll review the core components that are part of this architecture.

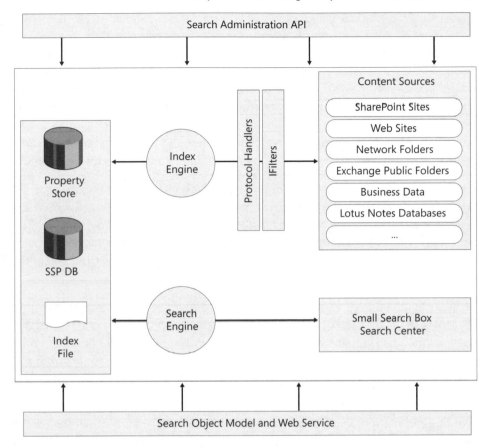

Index Engine

The index engine, or crawler, is responsible for building a content index file, for collecting custom metadata, and for storing the access control information associated with the content that is indexed. It's important to remember that within a Windows SharePoint Services 3.0 installation, the crawler is restricted to indexing SharePoint content only—that is, SharePoint sites, lists, and document libraries. There is no option to crawl content in addition to SharePoint content. If this option is a requirement, you'll have to install Office SharePoint Server 2007, which will extend the Windows SharePoint Services 3.0 search infrastructure. Keep in mind that even while you are running only Windows SharePoint Services 3.0, the index engine will use the same technologies, such as content sources, protocol handlers, and *IFilters* to crawl the content.

A *content source* is basically a location that you want the crawler to access. By default, you have a number of content sources that can be indexed because the required protocol handler is installed. Think of a protocol handler as the door that opens the location for indexing. *IFilters*, on the other hand, are used to index the content of a resource within that location, such as an Office Word 2007 document. Windows SharePoint Services 3.0 comes with a protocol handler named STS3, and by default you'll have common *IFilters* installed for indexing Microsoft Office system documents and text-based files. Office SharePoint Server 2007 and Search Server 2008 have additional protocol handlers and *IFilters* that will be installed. These, together with the creation and management of content sources, are discussed in Chapter 5.

It is of course possible to download or purchase additional protocol handlers and *IFilters* to support the crawling of other types of resources. An example is the crawling of Adobe PDF files that are enabled if you download and install the Adobe PDF *IFilter*. Chapter 5 covers the installation and configuration of additional *IFilters*, and Chapter 9, "Advanced Search Engine Topics," covers the creation of custom protocol handlers and *IFilters* if you don't find the one you're looking for.

The index engine does a bit more than just crawl content. It also collects custom metadata that is part of the lists and document libraries in the SharePoint sites or that is part of the business data that is retrieved via the BDC from LOB systems that are operating within your corporate network. In addition, access control information that has been applied to the containers storing the data by the administrators is also retrieved and used to trim the results for the user.

All of this information, together with the configuration information about the content sources, the crawl schedules, possible rules, and more, is stored in a Microsoft SQL Server database. The property store (shown in the preceding illustration of the search architecture) is the dedicated table for the storage of the metadata that is crawled by the index engine. As you'll learn later in this book, administrators must follow a number of steps to make this metadata available as possible criteria that can be incorporated by users when constructing their queries. The crawled metadata can also be used in various other scenarios.

The content index is a physical file that resides on one of the servers within your server farm. Chapter 7, "Search Deployment Considerations," contains more information and best practices for designing the topology of all of this.

Search Engine

The second core component in the search architecture is the search engine. Its role is to accept queries that are entered by users in one of their SharePoint sites. The search engine is also able to respond to queries that are delivered to the engine in a programmatic way. Users can use the dedicated controls that are part of a SharePoint installation, such as the small Search Box, or they can navigate to a dedicated site called the Search Center, where they can enter more complex, possibly highly customized queries to the search engine. Examples of the programmatic approach are custom Windows-based applications or add-ins in the Microsoft Office system products that allow users to make use of the SharePoint search infrastructure that is available within the organization. Queries that are submitted first go through layers of word breakers and stemmers before they are executed against the content index file that is available. *Word breaking* is a technique for isolating the important words out of the content, and *stemmers* store the variations on a word. An example of such a variation is *running* for the word *run*.

As mentioned, when working with the Windows SharePoint Services 3.0 search infrastructure, users are limited to the context of the site in which they are submitting the query. Only content belonging to that site and content stored in the possible subsites is returned as part of the search results. Chapter 10, "Searching with Windows SharePoint Services 3.0," covers all of this in more depth.

Search Object Models

Two object models will be covered extensively in the book. These object models can be accessed directly by developers when they are building solution components that run on the machine where SharePoint has been installed or when the components are running in the context of SharePoint, as is the case, for example, when building and delivering the custom search functionality with Web Parts.

The two search object models are:

- **Search Administration API**   This object model is new for SharePoint developers. It is covered in depth in Chapter 8, "Search APIs." All of the operations that administrators undertake within their administration environment (that is, the administration site of the SSP) are exposed by means of numerous managed types that can be used to create tools, add-ons, or new applications to support the administrators in their daily tasks.

- **Search Object Model and Web Services**   Developers can also use the classes delivered with the search API to construct and execute a search query in code. Chapter 8 covers the various techniques developers can use to accomplish this. If the application that executes the query is running outside the context of SharePoint and remotely on, for example, client desktop machines, the execution of the search queries will be handed over to the Search Web service that is part of an Office SharePoint Server 2007 installation.

Overview of Search Topics Covered in This Book

This book covers administration topics as well as development topics. As you read through the chapters, you'll often notice that there is a thin line between administrators and developers in the world of SharePoint. Administrators do have to know a bit about some of the development topics—for example, the customization of the search results using Extensible Stylesheet Language (XSL). XSL is used to transform the search results, which are returned in XML format by the search engine, into the display that is rendered in the browser. Developers, on the other hand, definitely will have to learn some of the administrative tasks and possible configurations for the index and search engine. We don't see major problems in the real world that would prevent both audiences from adapting to and learning a bit about both areas.

We'll conclude this chapter with a quick review of topics for administrators and topics for developers that will be covered in subsequent chapters.

Topics for Administrators

The following topics are covered in detail in the next chapters in this book and will help you in your job as administrator of the index and search infrastructure included in Office SharePoint Server 2007:

- **Managing the index file**   This important part of the administration tasks is covered in depth in Chapter 5. You'll learn how to create and manage the different types of content sources—always keeping in mind best practices for securing, scaling, and ensuring that all of the information is indexed with the best performance that is possible. Crawl rules, the inclusion and exclusion of file types, crawl schedules, and configuration of content access accounts will be no secret anymore after you have read Chapter 5.

- **Managing and configuring the end-user search experience**   An administrator is also typically involved in the management and the configuration of certain aspects of the end-user search experience. These can be simple tasks, such as the configuration of the small Search Box in the portals or SharePoint sites, or the more advanced configuration steps that need to be performed, for example, to enhance the display of the search results. As mentioned, knowing a bit about XSL and XML may come in handy when performing administration tasks at this level. But this task is not only about customizing Search Center or the small Search Box. Often administrators must create and manage search scopes that can be used by users to limit the search results or that can be picked up by developers who are building custom solutions that will integrate or replace the end-user search experience. Chapters 3 and 5 cover these topics.

- **Managing metadata**   A very important task that also has a big impact on the search end-user experience and the richness that users will see in the pages where they can enter and execute their search queries is the management of the metadata that is collected during the crawling of the content. Again, Chapters 3 and 5 cover the main details of the management of metadata, but you'll also learn how to manage metadata that was collected during the crawling of business data in Chapter 6, "Indexing and Searching Business Data." This task is all about managed properties that can be exposed in the Advanced Search pages of the Search Center sites or that can be part of the display of the details of a search result item.

- **Administering and configuring search usage reports**   There's always room for improving the way indexing is done and for making the end-user search experience richer and more effective. Usage reports can be a big help to accomplish this. If you are looking for answers regarding the administration and configuration of the search usage reports that are part of the Office SharePoint Server 2007 search infrastructure, look no further. We're devoting one complete chapter to this topic. You'll find a lot—maybe even all—of the answers to your questions in Chapter 4, "Search Usage Reports."

- **Configuring Business Data Catalog applications**   Most of the time in corporate networks, there is an abundance of data that is very important for information workers. Unfortunately, most of this data is critical for the enterprise and is often locked away in arcane, hard-to-use, and secured back-end systems. The BDC technology included in Office SharePoint Server 2007 can be used to unlock this data so that it can be accessed by the masses. Administrators again play a vital role here in the importing, management, and securing of the application definitions. An *application definition* is basically a model of the business data that we intend to get access to. These definitions are typically created by developers, but using the appropriate tools, administrators can also be made responsible for this operation. Administrators will absolutely be involved in the management of the metadata that is crawled and the way this metadata is exposed and capitalized on in the end-user search experience. Chapter 6 is dedicated to this one topic.

- **Monitoring performance**   Introducing new functionality, new types of content sources that have to be crawled, new scopes and metadata, and various other changes done by administrators and developers to the indexing and search infrastructure can have an important effect on the overall performance. Administrators have the task of ensuring that end users get the best performance they can get when searching or querying the content index. Choosing the best topology or deployment of the different components that are part of the index and search architecture is crucial and is well-covered in Chapter 7.

- **Administering protocol handlers and** *IFilters*   Office SharePoint Server 2007 comes with a decent set of protocol handlers and *IFilters* that help the index engine build up the content index that is needed to support the end-user search experience. Chapter 9 covers the details of creating custom protocol handlers and *IFilters*. This is of course meant for the developers, but once they have completed their part of the work, administrators will come in to install, configure, and manage these new protocol handlers and *IFilters*.

Topics for Developers

We have included a lot of developer topics in this book because we feel that the degree of extensibility and customization that is possible is definitely one of the strong points of the index and search infrastructure that is delivered with Office SharePoint Server 2007.

Here is a list of topics covered in the various chapters:

- **Advanced configuring of the end-user search experience**   Basic configurations are often done by administrators. More complex configurations, such as the replacement of the XSL that is used to render the search results in the Search Center, often is the work of a developer who has good skills in XSL or who has the right development environment to come up with the desired result. Chapter 3 is basically a mix of topics that cover high-level customization and is targeted for administrators as well as developers. It also delves deeper in the different APIs that are exposed by the Search Web Parts that make up the end-user search experience. There's also an interesting little section covering the use of the SharePoint *Delegate* control, which is responsible for the display of the small Search Box. Chapter 10 also covers a number of topics that deal with the customization of the end-user search experience from a developer angle, but in a pure Windows SharePoint Services 3.0 server farm.

- **Creating custom search components for users**   The end-user search experience might not meet all of the requirements of a business. There might be a requirement for custom search components that are integrated with the out-of-the-box components or that completely replace them. Chapter 8 is definitely not a chapter for administrators. In that chapter, you'll learn how to programmatically prepare, execute, and process the results of a query in the various ways. As a developer, you are not restricted to applications or solution components that run on the SharePoint machine. Executing search queries can be accomplished in Windows-based applications, add-ins for the Microsoft Office system desktop products such as Microsoft Office Outlook, and even mobile applications and the like. The search engine is accessible remotely through a Web service that is covered in detail in Chapter 8.

- **Building helpful tools to support the administrators in their work**   A big portion of Chapter 8 covers the brand-new administration object model. The new classes can be useful if there is the need to build additional support for administrators to either automate or facilitate their work.

- **Creating Business Data Catalog components**   If a lot of business data is locked away in back-end systems, be it traditional database systems like Microsoft SQL Server or Oracle or enterprise LOB systems such as Microsoft Dynamics or SAP, developers will have the task of creating the application definition files. The BDC also exposes two object models that are discussed, along with the creation of application definition files, in Chapter 6. For example, the run-time object model of the BDC is covered so that you can create your own custom SharePoint solution components that communicate directly with the business data retrieved.

- **Integrating with the search engine**   You'll want to read Chapter 9 if you're looking for programming techniques to build protocol handlers, *IFilters*, and custom security trimmers. The latter is useful if there is a need to filter the results that are shown to users based on additional security or context information.

Summary

This chapter introduced the importance of a good infrastructure for indexing and searching data. We've looked at what Microsoft offers, and you've learned about a new product called Microsoft Search Server 2008. The rest of this book will take you through the topics that matter to administrators and developers who want to learn more about the best practices and techniques for managing, configuring, customizing, and extending this infrastructure.

Chapter 2
The End-User Search Experience

After completing this chapter, you will be able to

- Use the small Search box to execute simple search queries.

- Understand the difference between the Search Center With Tabs and the Search Center Lite.

- Work with the information on a Search Results page.

- Construct and execute advanced search queries.

- Work with People Search in Microsoft Office SharePoint Server 2007.

A lot of good work was done to create a better end-user search experience in Microsoft Windows SharePoint Services 3.0 and Microsoft Office SharePoint Server 2007. This chapter describes the various components that make up this end-user experience and explains the functionality that is available by default, without customizations by administrators or developers. You'll first get an overview of what you can do with the small Search box that is available in most of the SharePoint sites, reviewing the basic functionality and covering in more detail the keyword syntax that you can use to express your search queries. The next section describes the Search Center, which is designed to provide a richer, more powerful, and also more customizable end-user search experience. Customization of the Search Center will be discussed in Chapter 3, "Customizing the Search User Interface."

Introducing the End-User Search Experience

Finding the correct information in the correct format is vital to information workers. According to our observations, a typical information worker spends about 30 percent of his or her time trying to find the pieces of data that are needed to support or complete a variety of daily tasks. Consider, for example, a developer who is stuck on a programming task. Most developers know that a quick search on the Internet often results in dozens of solutions to the problem. Perhaps the developer's organization has built an internal knowledge base over the years that can be searched as well. Salespeople also need access to information to react to customer requests. They are often overstressed and in definite need of a good intranet where they can execute a search in a rich, focused, and customized way. They want to get the results they need, filtered so that the exact information is included and ranked so that the most appropriate results appear at the top of the list. But finding information is not only about searching for documents or information in Web pages. How many times have you looked inside your organization for somebody who can help with one of your tasks? You know the expertise is there, within the company, but who has it? An intranet that has support for People Search boosts the productivity not only of the individual but also of the team as a whole.

The SharePoint platform, consisting of Windows SharePoint Services 3.0 and Office SharePoint Server 2007, delivers an infrastructure loaded with features that can deliver the end-user search experience that information workers need in the real world. If an organization uses only Windows SharePoint Services 3.0 as its collaboration and document management platform, the end-user search experience is still powerful, but limited. These limitations are described in the next section. For full search support, Office SharePoint Server 2007 must be installed on top of Windows SharePoint Services 3.0. As you'll learn in this chapter and the next chapter, dedicated sites for users searching for information can be created and fully customized to their different needs and requirements.

The small Search box is part of the end-user search experience everywhere in SharePoint, in Windows SharePoint Services 3.0 sites as well as Office SharePoint Server 2007 portals. The Search Center is a type of search-committed site available only with a server farm that includes an Office SharePoint Server 2007 installation.

The Small Search Box

Users who have worked with the earlier version of Windows SharePoint Services and with Microsoft SharePoint Portal Server 2003 will be familiar with a user interface control called the small Search box that is used for entering and executing their search queries. The small Search Box control is also available in Windows SharePoint Services 3.0 and Office SharePoint Server 2007. It comes in different flavors, and master pages make it available in many places within your SharePoint portals and individual sites. Chapter 3 covers the internals of the infrastructure in place for the small Search box and also describes how to create and deliver your own custom small Search box. In this chapter, we'll focus on the end-user experience.

When users navigate to the home page of a collaboration portal or a collaboration site, such as a team site, workspace, or Wiki site, they'll find the small Search box in the upper-right corner of the page, as shown in Figure 2-1.

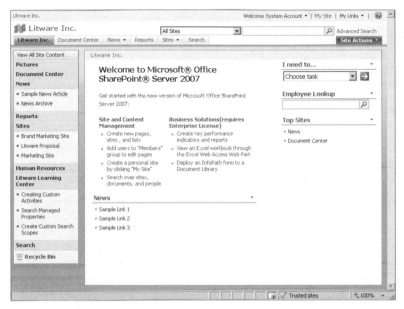

FIGURE 2-1 The small Search box at the top of the home page of a collaboration portal

By default, the small Search box consists of the following components:

- **Scope Picker**   The Scope Picker, shown in Figure 2-2, is a drop-down control displaying a list of search scopes. You'll learn more about search scopes in Chapter 3 and in
  Chapter 5, "Search Administration." In short, a search scope can be used to limit the
  quantity of results returned by the search engine based on some criterion. For example,
  an administrator can create and expose a search scope that enables a user to get only
  documents by a specific author in the results. The Scope Picker can display contextual
  search scopes as well as scopes created by an administrator either at the global level or
  at the local level. (See the sidebar "Two Types of Search Scopes.") An example of a contextual search scope is *This Site: Litware Inc*. Contextual search scopes are not explicitly
  created by administrators but are added automatically when needed by SharePoint.

FIGURE 2-2 The Scope Picker

- **Search box**   The next control in the small Search box is the text box that is used to
  enter the query. End users can formulate their search queries only using the keyword
  syntax. The keyword syntax is discussed in more detail in the next section. Chapter
  8, "Search APIs," covers a second type of syntax for formulating the search query:
  the Enterprise Search SQL query syntax. That syntax, however, is not exposed to end
  users directly.

Two Types of Search Scopes

In a SharePoint server farm, a Shared Services Provider (SSP) is responsible for the maintenance of one index file. As part of this index file, thousands or even millions of items can be collected from various locations and made available to the search engine. End users often find it useful, if not essential, to be able to limit these results. Administrators can create a *shared search scope* in the administration site of the SSP (explained in more detail in Chapter 5). These shared search scopes can become part of a display group at the level of the site collection. Display groups are an administrative layer between the Scope Picker and the search scopes. A Scope Picker is associated with a display group and as a result will display all of the scopes that are part of the display group.

The SSP is not the only level where administrators can create search scopes. If the scope is needed only within a single site collection, it is actually better to define a second type of search scope, often referred to as a *local search scope*. This search scope is created by the administrator in the site collection and can be part of display groups only of that particular site collection.

- **Go Search button**   To the right of the Search box is a small button with a magnifying glass that the end user clicks to start execution of the search query. The execution of the query is not the responsibility of the small Search box. Actually, the small Search box redirects the user to one of the Search Results pages that are available, and while doing this, it passes the selected search scope and the query to this page for further processing.

Note Depending on the configuration of the site collection and the availability of a Search Center in the site collection, the results page that the user is redirected to is the one that is part of the Search Center or the results page that is part of the Office SharePoint Server 2007 set of common pages. In the first case, the Search Results page of the Search Center takes full responsibility for the execution of the search query. The user ends up in the Search Center site and can then further refine the search results. The second option is the Microsoft ASP.NET page osssearchresults.aspx. This ASP.NET page is physically located in the C:\Program Files\Common Files\Microsoft Shared\Web Server Extensions12\ Templates\Layouts folder. This folder is quite important in Windows SharePoint Services 3.0 because it contains the pages that are common to all the site collections that are hosted on the front-end Web Server. Typically, these are pages that have to do with administration tasks, but the folder is very often also used by developers to host custom pages, often referred to as *application pages*.

- **Advanced Search link**   The last part of the small Search box is shown on the right in Figure 2-3. Users can click the Advanced Search link to navigate to the Advanced Search page. The options that are available on the Advanced Search page are discussed in detail later in this chapter.

FIGURE 2-3 The Advanced Search link in the small Search box

As mentioned earlier, the small Search box is displayed on the home page of a collaboration portal. But this is not the only place where you'll encounter the small Search box. If you navigate to the home page of a team site, as shown in Figure 2-4, you'll encounter a similar small Search box. Although this too is called a small Search box, behind the scenes, the implementation is very different compared with the one encountered on the collaboration portal. You'll also notice that its appearance is somewhat different. The internal architecture and the rendering process of the various types of small Search boxes will be covered in Chapter 3.

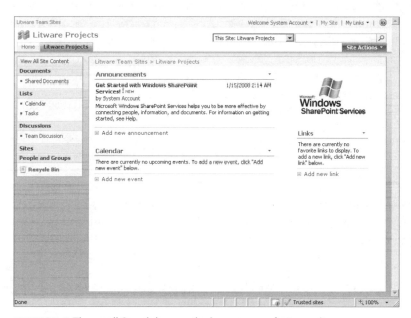

FIGURE 2-4 The small Search box on the home page of a team site

The end-user search experience in a collaboration site (such as the team site shown in Figure 2-4) does not by default provide the full search functionality that is delivered and maintained by the SSP that is part of the SharePoint server farm. For an end user working in a Windows SharePoint Services 3.0 site, the search experience is different from the search experience in a collaboration or publishing portal provisioned by Office SharePoint Server 2007. The small Search box available on a team site (or other Windows SharePoint Services sites) does not have the option to select search scopes other than the contextual search scope *This Site: Name of Site*. When entering a search query, the user is able to get only search results emerging from the site itself or the subsites under it. And last, as you can see in Figure 2-4, the small Search box does not display a link to an Advanced Search page. By default, there is no advanced search option in Windows SharePoint Services 3.0 sites.

> **Note** The preceding limitations on the end-user search experience are removed when Office SharePoint Server 2007 is deployed within the server farm. Administrators responsible for Windows SharePoint Services 3.0 sites can add a Search Center Lite to the site collection to enhance the end-user search experience, as described in the section "The Search Center" later in this chapter.

Keyword Query Syntax

When working with the small Search box, you express your query in the keyword syntax. The maximum length of the query cannot exceed 1024 characters. The keyword syntax is one of the two possible syntaxes you can use to construct a search query. The second option is the formulation of the query using the Enterprise Search SQL query syntax. The SQL syntax allows for the formulation of more complex search queries, but as already mentioned, this type of syntax is not exposed directly to the end users. Developers, however, have the power to create custom versions of the small Search box and translate the user's entries into a query that is formulated using the SQL syntax.

Are search queries formulated with the keyword syntax limited only to simple queries? Not at all! The keyword syntax is quite powerful. Here is a list of the various options that are available to construct a query:

- **Enter a single word** This is of course the simplest form of a keyword syntax query. You simply type a word like **marketing** and then click the Go Search button to navigate to the Search Results page, where you can review the results of the query.

> **Note** By default, the search engine does not make a distinction between *marketing* and *Marketing* unless administrators perform an additional configuration in the thesaurus file.

- **Enter multiple words** Another option you have in the small Search box is to input a collection of words—for example, **marketing manager**. A query containing multiple words is basically an AND query. The search engine returns only the search results that contain both the word *marketing* and the word *manager*.

> **Note** Readers familiar with SharePoint Portal Server 2003 know that the earlier version treats multiple-word queries differently from Office SharePoint Server 2007. In SharePoint Portal Server 2003, using multiple words for a query resulted in an OR-like query. Using the preceding example, if you entered **marketing manager** as the query, you got search results that contained only *marketing*, together with search results that contained only *manager*, and also search results that contained both words. As you'll discover later in this chapter, you can enter an OR-like query by navigating to the Advanced Search page and formulating your query there.

- **Enter a phrase**   A phrase is also a collection of two or more words, but when searching for a phrase, you enclose the words in quotation marks, as in **"marketing manager"**. The quotation marks communicate to the search engine that the words should be considered as one complete search term. The search results should contain only those results where the exact combination of text is found.

- **Use a prefix**   The last search option is prefix matching. Prefix matching lets you specify just the beginning of the word; you then let the search engine figure out the rest. The search results should include exact matches for the text and matches that include the text. A common use of prefix matching is wildcard searching, as in *marke**. Wildcard searching, however, is not supported at the level of keyword syntax search queries. In the Enterprise Search SQL query syntax, you can use the CONTAINS operator to formulate a query for wildcard searches. This is an option for developers building custom search components, because they can provide end users with additional support for using wildcards in their search queries. Do remember that by default—that is, without this customization by the developer—an end user who types in a part of a word will get the search results that exactly match that part. If there are no results, the search engine will try to help with the reformulation of the query. The Search Results page helps users by displaying the Did You Mean ... feature, as shown in Figure 2-5.

FIGURE 2-5 Searching for a part of a word and the Did You Mean ... feature

 Note The Did You Mean ... feature is available only when the search results are displayed in a page that is part of the Office SharePoint Server 2007 Search Center. In Windows SharePoint Services 3.0 sites, the Did You Mean ... feature is not available.

These various options for entering search queries are not the only ones available for keyword search queries. You can also explicitly include or exclude a search query. Excluding a word or phrase can be accomplished by typing a minus sign (–) in front of the word or phrase. This is basically the expression of a NOT operator for the query. You make it clear to the search engine that you do not want any results that contain the excluded word or phrase. The query *marketing –manager*, for example, will return the search results including the word *marketing* but excluding the results that also have the word *manager* in them.

Explicitly including a word or phrase is done by adding a plus sign (+) in front of the word or phrase. Because multiple words in a keyword query are always translated as an AND-like query, the inclusion prefix is not really required. The query *marketing +manager* returns the search results that contain the word *manager* and also the word *marketing*. The difference with the phrase query (enclosing the terms *marketing* and *manager* in quotation marks) is that you'll get not only the exact phrase combination but also the results containing both words in different locations or combinations in the indexed resource.

Another option you have as a user is the inclusion of property filters in the formulation of the search query. As you'll learn in Chapter 5, it is possible for administrators to expose custom managed properties.

Managed Properties

Managed properties are a new concept for administrators configuring and customizing the search experience. The details of how to use managed properties are described in Chapter 3 and Chapter 5. In short, a managed property represents one or more crawled, or indexed, properties in the search user interface. When, for example, SharePoint content is crawled, all of the custom metadata that is defined at the level of lists and document libraries is collected as well. The custom metadata is stored as crawled properties in the database. Crawled properties are not directly exposed in the search user interface unless they are mapped to a managed property.

Many properties are immediately available by default. And the good news for end users is that these properties can be used in a keyword syntax query in a very easy way by making use of the pattern *<property name>:<value>* in the query. End users can also add an inclusion or exclusion sign in front of the property. Assume, for example, that you are interested only in documents authored by Pat Coleman. The results should match the term *marketing*. The query returning you these results, shown in Figure 2-6, can be formulated as *marketing author:coleman contenttype:document*. The *author* property is self-explanatory. The *contenttype* property allows users to filter the results based on a specific content type. The sidebar "Content Types" briefly explains these content types.

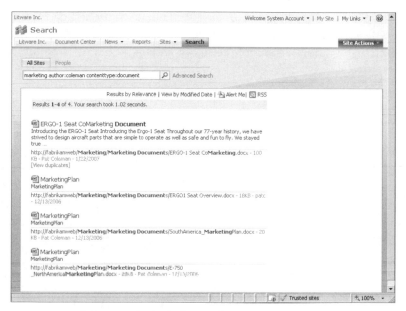

FIGURE 2-6 Using properties in the keyword syntax query

Content Types

Content types are extremely important in Windows SharePoint Services 3.0 as a new way of defining the underlying schema for either an item in a list or a document in a document library. Think of a content type as a packaged definition of the metadata that you want to associate with the content, as well as the definition of the behavior in the form of workflow templates, information management policies, and possibly event handlers hooked up with the type of content. Windows SharePoint Services 3.0 comes with a predefined hierarchy of content types (*document*, *event*, and *task* are examples) that is extensible either by adding new content types in the browser or by delivering them as Features. With Features, you can make your own custom content types available as reusable components in many places within your SharePoint environment. In Chapter 3, you'll learn how to make use of the Windows SharePoint Services 3.0 Features Framework while extending the end-user search experience. *Inside Microsoft Windows SharePoint Services 3.0* (Microsoft Press, 2007), authored by Ted Pattison and Daniel Larson, contains an excellent overview of content types from a developer perspective.

Recall the earlier discussion of wildcard searching. As mentioned, using wildcards within keyword syntax queries is not supported at the level of the individual words in the query. However, if you use property matches (as explained earlier), you will be able to benefit from wildcards. Take, for example, the following search query: *marketing author:fi*. This will return all of the items that were authored by somebody whose name (either first name or last name) begins with the letters *fi*. The wildcard (*) can be appended to the property filter value, as shown in Figure 2-7, but it is not needed for the search engine.

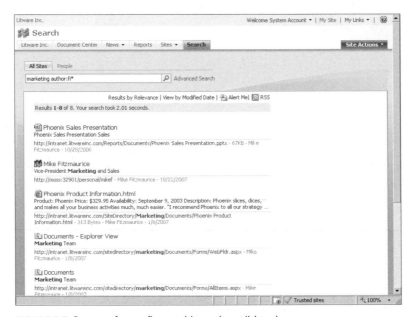

FIGURE 2-7 Support for prefix matching using wildcards

Just be aware that the use of wildcards in property filters is supported only for prefix matching and not for infix or suffix matching. An example of an infix matching term is *author:f*tz*. An example of a suffix matching term is *author:*tz*. Neither query will return any search results. Developers building custom search components can use the Enterprise Search SQL query language to provide this behavior if it is requested by users.

One more remark should be made regarding the use of properties in keyword queries. The remark is related to AND and OR searches. As mentioned earlier, by default, users will execute AND-like queries when formulating their queries with multiple words. This general rule is not always applied when you work with property filters in the query. If you use the same property more than once in your query, the search engine will combine the elements using an OR operator. A query like *author:fitzmaurice author:coleman* returns the items created by either Mike Fitzmaurice or Pat Coleman, and if an item exists that was authored by both of them, this will be returned as well. But when you combine different properties, all of these elements will be combined using the AND operator. The query *contenttype:document author:barker* returns all of the documents created by Rob Barker. Documents authored by someone else are not returned, and items that Rob created in addition to documents are not returned either.

Search scopes can also be included in the keyword query using the *<scope name>:<value>* syntax pattern. The use of this filter is dependent on the configuration of the core Web Part that is available on the Search Results page and is somewhat restricted to the programmatic execution of your query. Users should not directly use the search scope filter in the small Search box. By default, the Search Results page defaults automatically to the All Sites search scope, and any inclusion of a search scope filter will be ignored.

A last possible property filter is a string expressed in the pattern *<collapsed results type>:<value>*. Again, this is a property filter that is not immediately practical for end users performing search queries. You'll encounter this filter briefly in the section "The Search Center" later in this chapter. You use this property filter to either display or not display the duplicates for a search result item. The internal algorithm that identifies an item as a duplicate for another item is a bit unclear and not documented. But it is clear that duplicates are identified by their content and that a certain similarity must exist above some threshold. As mentioned, it is not documented what this threshold is. The query *marketing duplicate:http://moss.litwareinc.com*, for example, will show the duplicates matching the specified URL displayed in the search results. Documents with similar content where, for instance, the date or the name of the file is different will be considered duplicates. Hiding or making duplicates visible is also a setting that you can configure for the Web Part showing the search results.

A Closer Look at the Search Results Request

Let's have a closer look at the request that is sent by the user to the Search Results page before we close the topic of the small Search box. This is not a direct concern for end users, but it is important for administrators and developers to understand the process.

The query entered by the user in the small Search box is executed when the user clicks the Go Search button that is part of the control. The small Search box does not execute the query itself. It passes the selected search scope (if available) and the keyword query to the Search Results page that is associated with the small Search box at the level of the site collection. The passing is done simply by redirecting the user to the Search Results page (a normal HTTP GET request) and by using a query string that includes the parameter values that are provided by the user. All of this information is then processed by one of the Web Parts on the Search Results page, as you'll see in Chapter 3.

Say that you enter the query **marketing contenttype:document** in the text box and you select All Sites as the search scope. After you click the Go Search button, the search box redirects you to the Search Results pages as follows:

http://moss.litwareinc.com/searchcenter/Pages/Results.aspx?k=marketing%20 contenttype%3Adocument&s=All%20Sites

A number of parameters can be part of the query string; Table 2-1 summarizes them.

TABLE 2-1 Search URL Parameters

URL Parameter	Description	Sample
k	The value is the keyword query. Only one *k* parameter is allowed in the query string.	*?k=marketing*
s	Specifies the search scope. This parameter can contain multiple values, separated by colons (encoded as *%2c*).	*?s=All%20Sites*
v	Specifies how the sorting is going to be done on the search results. You can use *relevance* as the value if you want the results to be sorted by relevance. Another possible value is *date* if the results need to be sorted by date.	*?v=date*
start	Specifies which results page number to show. Typically, a large number of search result items are returned, and by default the Search Results pages display the results in *chunks* (also known as *pages*). The value of the *start* parameter passes the number of the page to be displayed.	*?start=3*

The Search Center

The Search Center plays an important role in the overall end-user search experience within SharePoint. The main goal of the Search Center is to provide an alternative to the small Search box discussed in the preceding section. The Search Center consists of a complete site template that delivers a rich out-of-the-box end-user search experience that can also be customized, as you'll learn in Chapter 3.

Note The Search Center is not available in a pure Windows SharePoint Services 3.0 deployment. You must install Office SharePoint Server 2007 to allow end users to work with these types of sites. Support for the Search Center is provided by the standard licensing of Office SharePoint Server 2007.

There are two versions of the Search Center:

- **Search Center With Tabs**   This version of the Search Center can be included only in a site collection where the Microsoft Office SharePoint Server Publishing Infrastructure Feature has been activated. A full description of the publishing infrastructure is provided in Chapter 3. In short, this Feature enables the content management infrastructure in the site collection. An example of a site collection that is ready for a Search Center With Tabs is a collaboration portal. In fact, if you provision a collaboration portal, you'll automatically get a Search Center With Tabs as part of the list of provisioned sites within that site collection. The Search Center With Tabs has a tab-based interface, as shown in Figure 2-8, which is fully customizable. The Customers tab in Figure 2-8 is an example of a custom tab.

FIGURE 2-8 A Search Center With Tabs that is part of a collaboration portal

- **Search Center Lite**   This version of the Search Center does not require the Microsoft Office SharePoint Server Publishing Infrastructure Feature to be activated at the level of the site collection. You can therefore very quickly add a Search Center Lite to a site collection that contains only collaboration sites. Examples of collaboration sites are team sites, Wikis, blogs, and document and meeting workspaces.

Creating a Search Center With Tabs in a Collaboration Portal

Collaboration portals include by default a Search Center With Tabs. As an administrator, you can add one or more additional Search Centers (both Search Centers With Tabs and Search Centers Lite). This can be interesting for an organization that has one central enterprise portal and that has the need to deliver search experiences for different departments that are independent from one another. You could have a Search Center for the marketing department and a Search Center for the human resources department. Providing multiple Search Centers does not mean that end users will see them all. Administrators can configure the access control for each of the Search Centers. For example, one of the Search Centers could be configured to allow only employees from the marketing department to see it. A second Search Center could be configured for only employees from the human resources department. The user interface security trimming that is part of the Windows SharePoint Services 3.0 core functionality ensures that every employee sees only the Search Centers he or she has access to.

An additional Search Center With Tabs is added to the portal just as with any other new site. On the Site Actions menu, select the Create Site option. In the page that is rendered in the browser, you can specify the title and a description for the page. Another section in the page shows you a list of possible sites you can create. Figure 2-9 shows the tabbed list box that includes a tab named Enterprise. When you click this tab, you'll see a list of templates that are associated with this category. Select the Search Center With Tabs list item, specify whether you want to inherit the security information from the parent site, and click Create to have SharePoint provision the additional Search Center.

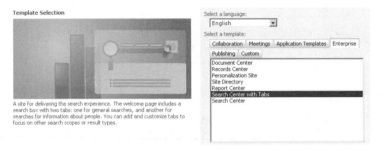

FIGURE 2-9 Creating an additional Search Center With Tabs for the collaboration portal

The Search Center Lite in a Publishing Portal

A *publishing portal* is a collection of sites that can be accessed by external visitors. By default, a Search Center Lite is provisioned in the out-of-the-box site definition for a publishing portal. This Search Center Lite is hidden by default, however. If you have administrative rights in the publishing portal, you can make the Search Center Lite visible to the user by performing a small configuration at the level of the navigation control. Here's how: You first navigate to the root site of your publishing portal. On the Site Actions menu, select Site Settings, and then select Modify Navigation. The page that is now rendered in the browser contains a section called Navigation Editing And Sorting, as shown in Figure 2-10.

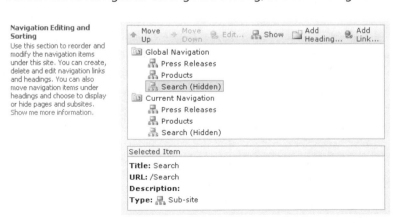

FIGURE 2-10 Tuning the navigation control to make the Search Center Lite in a publishing portal visible

This section shows the nodes that are part of the top navigation bar, also referred to as the *global navigation*. As you can see, the search node is marked as a hidden node. It is easy to change this. You simply select the Search (Hidden) node in the list and click Show on the toolbar. You then apply the changes by clicking OK at the bottom of the page.

As a result of your configuration, the top navigation bar now displays the link to the Search Center Lite, and users can navigate to it when they want to execute a search query. Figure 2-11 displays the Search Center Lite, which is part of a publishing portal.

FIGURE 2-11 A Search Center Lite that is part of a publishing portal

You must perform a couple of additional actions to give the newly added Search Center Lite the look and feel of the publishing portal and to have it display the global navigation.

Changing the look and feel is done by switching the master page of the created Search Center Lite from the default master to the master page that defines the look and feel of the other sites in the portal. You can do this from the Site Actions menu when the Search Center Lite is the site in your browser. Select Site Settings, and in the section titled Look And Feel, click Master Page. The Site Master Page Settings page that is rendered, shown in Figure 2-12, includes a list of candidate master pages that you can switch to. Note that you should make the switch to another master page in the Site Master Page section and not in the System Master Page section. The latter section gives you the option to switch to another master page for the administration pages within the portal. After you apply the changes by clicking OK, your Search Center will display itself nicely as an integrated subsite within the portal.

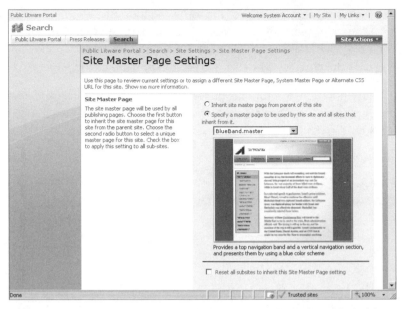

FIGURE 2-12 Switching within the Search Center Lite to the look and feel of the portal

The Search Center Lite can also display the top navigation bar with all of the top-level subsites in the portal. On the Site Actions menu, click Site Settings. In the Look And Feel section, click the Navigation link. The Site Navigation Settings page includes a section named Global Navigation, as shown in Figure 2-13. Here you have the option to display the same navigation items as the parent site. Apply the changes, and you'll get a full top navigation bar in the Search Center Lite.

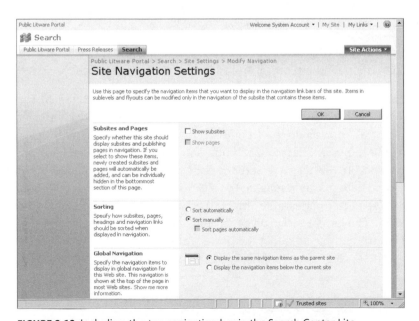

FIGURE 2-13 Including the top navigation bar in the Search Center Lite

> **Note** You are not restricted to only the Search Center Lite in the publishing portal. A publishing portal has by default, just like the collaboration portal, all of the publishing features activated. This means that you can also add a Search Center With Tabs to the site collection. The Search Center Lite is available by default within the site collection because of the portal's nature. Publishing portals target Internet visitors, and most of the time, there is no need for a customized tab-based search experience. But if you need to create one, you simply follow the steps in the preceding section, "Creating a Search Center With Tabs in a Collaboration Portal."

Creating a Search Center Lite for Collaboration Sites

Site administrators can easily add a Search Center Lite to a site collection that does not have the publishing infrastructure activated. Assume that you have a site collection with a number of collaboration sites. To add a Search Center Lite, on the Site Actions menu, you select the Create option. The Web Pages group includes a Sites And Workspaces link that takes you to a page where you fill in the title and the description of the site that is going to be created.

Farther down on the same page, all of the available site definitions are listed, as shown in Figure 2-14. When you click the Enterprise tab, you'll see, in addition to the other Office SharePoint Server 2007 templates, the two templates mentioned earlier: Search Center With Tabs and Search Center. The latter template is for the Search Center Lite.

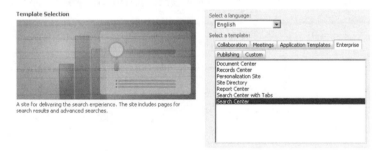

FIGURE 2-14 Creating a Search Center Lite

Finish your work on the page, and then click Create to provision the new site. After a couple of seconds, a Search Center Lite will appear as part of your site collection, as shown in Figure 2-15.

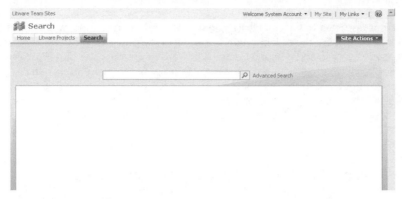

FIGURE 2-15 The Search Center Lite

Notice that the site does not have an infrastructure based on tabs; it contains a Search box for entering the search query. The execution is done by clicking the Go Search button, and just as with the small Search box discussed earlier in this chapter, you are redirected to the Search Results page that is part of the set of pages provisioned with your Search Center Lite. The Search Results page has Web Parts on it that display the results returned by the search engine. Figure 2-16 shows the Search Results page; notice that it contains results from many different locations. The search experience in a site collection that contains only Windows SharePoint Services 3.0 sites has been enhanced with the Search Center Lite, and the results of your search are similar to the results you'll get when you execute the same query in the Office SharePoint Server 2007 portals.

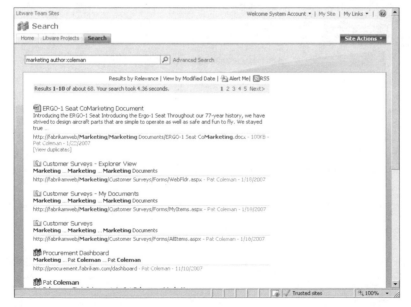

FIGURE 2-16 Search results in the Search Center Lite

> **Note** In the rest of this chapter, we'll concentrate on the Search Center With Tabs.

The Search Tabs

Figure 2-17 shows a Search Center With Tabs with the two tabs that are available by default. This tab-based infrastructure is of course extensible, as you'll discover in Chapter 3.

FIGURE 2-17 The two default search tabs

The two available tabs are

- **All Sites**   This tab is selected by default and is connected to a Search page containing a Search box that is configured to work with the All Sites search scope. All search results returned when executing a search from this page belong in one way or another to this search scope.

- **People**   This tab brings users to the people.aspx page, which contains a special version of the Search box. This Search box is dedicated to entering and executing a People Search query.

The Search Page

The All Sites tab is associated with the Search page (presented as the default.aspx page). This is basically the home page of your Search Center. It contains a Search Box Web Part that is similar to the small Search box discussed earlier in this chapter. The difference is that this Search Box Web Part by default does not display the Scope Picker (the drop-down list of search scopes). The Scope Picker can, however, become part of the user experience after a small configuration at the level of the Search Box Web Part. The search query is constructed using the keyword search syntax as described earlier, and the execution is started by clicking the Go Search button that is part of the Search Box Web Part. Similar to the small Search box, the entered query is passed to the Search Results page for execution.

The People Search Page

The page associated with the People tab is people.aspx. This page contains a different type of Search Box Web Part than the one available in the Search page described earlier. This Web Part allows you to formulate your query using the keyword syntax, but it also gives you the option to expand a small pane by clicking the Search Options link, as shown in Figure 2-18. The Search Options pane is useful when the user knows some of the property values that are part of the user profiles. (For more information about user profiles, see the sidebar "User Profiles.")

FIGURE 2-18 Working with Search Options on the People Search page

User Profiles

Office SharePoint Server 2007 includes the option to create and maintain user profiles for SharePoint users. A *user profile* is a collection of properties that describe the user. It includes properties that identify the user, such as first name, last name, account, e-mail address, and so forth. A user profile can also contain properties that are of interest to other employees within the organization. Examples are department, office, job responsibilities, and skills. These types of properties are often used when executing a people search. Assume, for example, the following common situation within a company.

Tracy and Dave have a presentation for a customer tomorrow about the benefits of introducing SharePoint within their organizational infrastructure. Tracy will do the sales pitch, while Dave will be responsible for the technical part of the presentation. Unfortunately, the day before the presentation, Dave must stay home because of illness. Tracy is now desperate to find somebody with similar skills to help her deliver the presentation to the customer. Luckily, she can navigate to the enterprise portal and execute a People Search using SharePoint as a value for the Skills property. She quickly finds somebody who is ready to help her. In situations like this, you realize the benefit of investing time and energy in the proper population of the user profile information. The investment is seen as the creation of the user profiles and the population of the property values. The creation of user profiles is typically automated based on the accounts of the users within the Microsoft Active Directory directory service. You have a couple of choices for the population of the property values. The information that is part of an account in the Active Directory can supply a good quantity of values. Users can be responsible for maintaining part of their public user profile information. And last but not least, external line-of-business (LOB) systems that store human resources data within the company can be connected to the SharePoint environment through the Business Data Catalog (BDC). Once administrators set up and configure the connection in the BDC, the data itself can be used to populate the values of the properties that are part of the user profiles.

For end users, the Search Options pane is also an easier way to create a keyword query that includes a property filter. Not all end users are familiar with the expression of property filters. Clicking the Search Options link and entering a value for the department, as shown in Figure 2-18, is often a lot easier. When the query is executed, the value in the Search Options pane is translated as *department:"Sales"*.

Some properties in the Search Options pane accept a single value; others can accept more than one value. Depending on the type of the value stored in the property, there is a small lookup button associated with the text box. In Figure 2-18, this is the case for the Responsibilities and Skills text boxes. Clicking on the associated lookup button will display a dialog box containing all of the possible values that you can enter for that property, as shown in Figure 2-19.

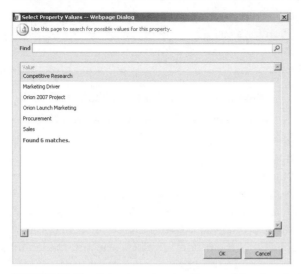

FIGURE 2-19 The dialog box showing the possible values for the Responsibility property in the user profile

The Search Options pane is extensible. Administrators can expose additional properties by configuring the People Search Box Web Part, as you'll see in Chapter 3.

The Advanced Search Page

When we examined the small Search box earlier in this chapter, we covered the various options that are available when formulating a keyword syntax query. Often in the real world, this option is not directly available to end users who feel uncomfortable with this kind of syntax or who might not be aware of the possibilities at all. This category of users will benefit from the extra options made available on the Advanced Search page. Here they can formulate the more complicated queries easily and, more important, without learning about the keyword syntax. The Advanced Search page is a good place to navigate to as an end user when you need to construct queries that heavily depend on metadata, item types, and possibly the language if you are working within a multilingual environment.

You access the Advanced Search page, shown in Figure 2-20, by clicking the link in the small Search box or the Search Box Web Part that is displayed on one of the Search pages or Search Results pages.

The Advanced Search page contains a single Web Part called the Advanced Search Web Part. You'll find a full explanation of the different configuration options in Chapter 3. Using this Web Part, the end users construct the search query.

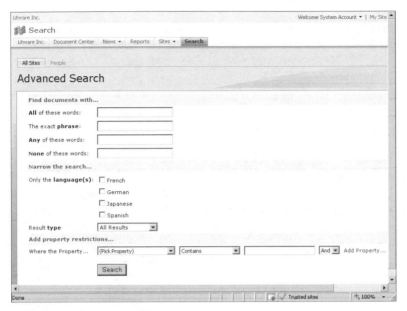

FIGURE 2-20 The Advanced Search page

As shown in Figure 2-20, you'll notice that without customizations, the Advanced Search Web Part offers the user three areas to work with:

- **Find Documents With**   This is the area where the keywords are entered. Although you do not explicitly make use of the OR and AND operators, by entering the search words in the corresponding text boxes, you construct a query making use of these operators behind the scenes. In the first text box, labeled All Of These Words, you enter all of the words that must be in the search results. In the second text box, labeled The Exact Phrase, you enter a phrase—for example, **marketing manager**. No quotation marks are needed here for the entered phrase. The items in the search results will contain both words, in the order in which you entered them in the text box. The third text box, labeled Any Of These Words, gives you the option to enter an OR-like query. You enter the listing of words that can but don't have to be there in the items that are part of the search results. If one of the words is part of a search result item, that is sufficient. The last text box, labeled None Of These Words, allows for the exclusion of one or more words. Items in the index containing one of these words will not be part of the list of the search results.

- **Narrow The Search**   This section of the Advanced Search Web Part can be used to narrow the search to one or more languages. By default, a number of languages are available. This list can be changed, as you'll learn in Chapter 3. Selecting one or more of the language options limits the search results to items that are authored in these languages.

Note The search engine includes an automatic language detection algorithm. During the crawling, the language that the document was created in is assigned to a managed property named *"detectedlanguage"*. The value of this property is verified if a condition on the language in the query is included.

You'll also find a drop-down list populated with result types to select from. By default, all types of results will be returned, but you can narrow the results to, for example, only Microsoft Office PowerPoint presentations, as shown in Figure 2-21.

■ **Add Property Restrictions** The last area that is part of the Advanced Search Web Part is one that you can use to apply property restrictions to the query. This is one of the most powerful options in the Advanced Search page. Using this option, you can create a query with one or more conditions. Each condition consists of three parts: the name of the property, the operator to be used, and the value. When you opt for multiple conditions, you can combine them using either an AND operator or an OR operator.

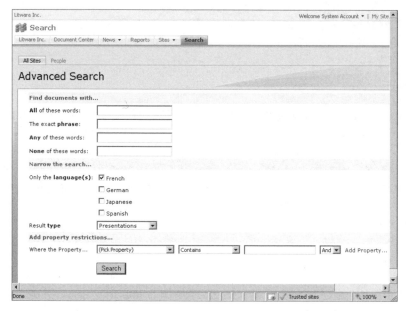

FIGURE 2-21 Configuring a query that will return only items of file type .pptx authored in the French language

Figure 2-22 shows an example of how you can use the Advanced Search page. The query formulated in the Advanced Search Web Part will return all of the Microsoft Office Word documents authored by either someone named Jesse or someone named Pat. All result items should include the word *marketing*, but the word *Fabrikam* is not allowed in the search results. Figure 2-23 presents the results when executing the query.

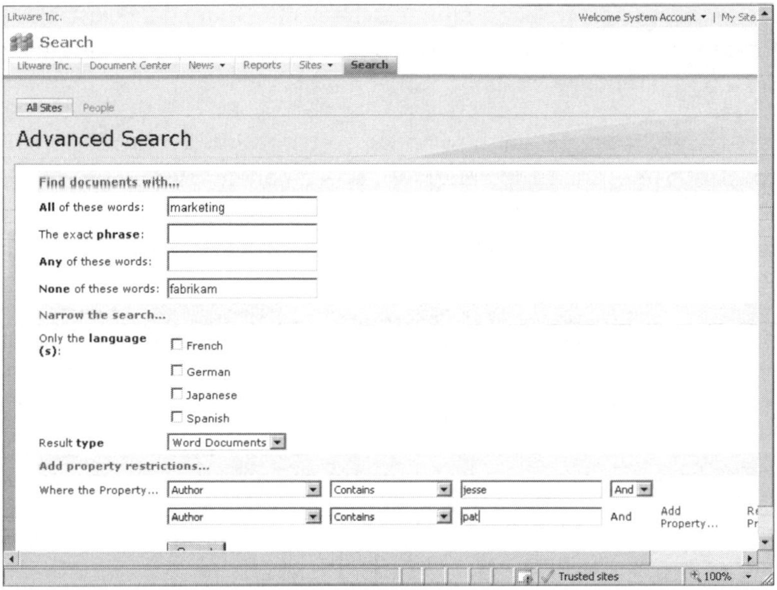

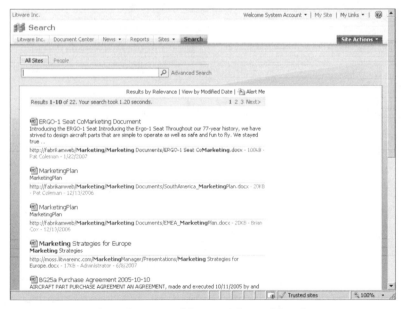

FIGURE 2-22 An example of a query constructed from the Advanced Search page

FIGURE 2-23 Search results returned from an Advanced Search page

The Search Results Page

A very important page within the Search Center is, of course, the Search Results page, presented as results.aspx. The Search Results page comprises many Web Parts that together make up the user experience for reviewing the search results. Figure 2-24 illustrates what a typical Search Results page displays to a user without any customization except the definition of a keyword and a best bet by the administrator in the site collection.

By default, the search results are paged showing ten search results per page. A small Web Part delivers information about the number of results that can be reviewed and how much time it took the search engine to execute the search query. Links to the other pages containing other parts of the search results are also part of this Web Part.

> **Note** The number of results as shown in Figure 2-24 is an estimate. For large result sets, the count is often an estimate because security trimming makes predicting the exact result count difficult. This is why the Web Part uses the phrase *of about*. When the count is exact, the word *about* is omitted from the text.

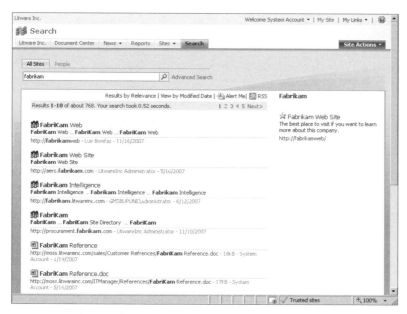

FIGURE 2-24 The Search Results page

Above this Web Part showing the statistical information and the paging links, you'll notice a Web Part that allows the user to perform some actions on the search results. The first two actions have to do with the sorting of the search results. The results can be sorted by relevance or by modified date. The search engine uses a complex relevance ranking algorithm to make sure that the results that match the query the best are displayed at the top of the list of search results. Later in Chapter 5, you'll learn more about this relevance ranking algorithm and how you can influence it as an administrator. Results By Relevance is the default sorting. With a click on View By Modified Date, you change this and ask the Web Part showing the search results to order the search results so that the newest additions are shown at the top of the list.

Users often want to be notified when new content that matches a search query they executed is indexed. Search-based alerts are by default activated within Office SharePoint Server 2007. This enables users to click the Alert Me link displayed in the Search Results page and configure the settings for the alert, as shown in Figure 2-25.

The first section on the page shows the title for the alert. You can change this title if needed. Next, depending on your role within the site collection, you enter the user names or e-mail addresses for the persons you want to have SharePoint send the alerts to. Creating alerts for other people is a new functionality in Windows SharePoint Services 3.0 that is welcomed by a lot of people.

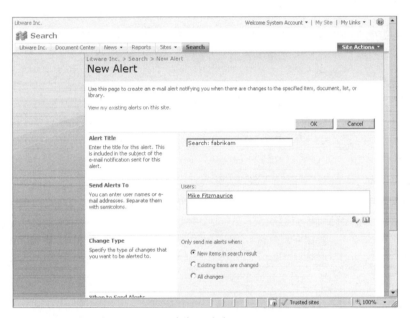

FIGURE 2-25 Creating a new search-based alert

The last two settings are all about the configuration of the alerts. The first one defines the change type. SharePoint can send the alerts when new items become part of the search results, when existing items that have been included in the search results are changed, or, if you don't want to be that specific, for all changes that happen within the search results. The second configuration is a decision that you have to make regarding the time the alerts will be sent to you. You can specify a daily summary or a weekly summary.

Alerts employ a *push-based model* for notifying the user: you create an alert and you receive e-mail messages with information about the changes. SharePoint in this case is notifying you by pushing mails to your mailbox. Really Simple Syndication (RSS) feeds follow a *pull-based model*: you subscribe to an RSS feed and *you* decide when you want to pull and review the changes within your RSS feed reader. The Search Results page gives users the option to subscribe to the RSS feed, translating the search results into an RSS stream.

The central piece on this page is of course the Web Part showing the search results. There is a detailed explanation in Chapter 3 of how this Web Part works internally and how you can, as an administrator and a developer, customize the workings of it. For now, let's analyze in more detail the information contained within a single search result item such as the one displayed in Figure 2-26.

Blue Yonder Airlines Budget Projections.xml
Blue Yonder Airlines Budget Projections.xml Blue Yonder Airlines Budget
Projections.xml xml 0 Barbara Decker 1321 **Sales** en-us
http://fabrikamweb/**Sales**/Blue Yonder Account Management Site/Blue Yonder
Airlines Budget Projections.xml - 1KB - System Account - 1/18/2007

FIGURE 2-26 An individual search result item

This search result item contains a title that can be used to navigate to the item itself. An icon showing the type of the item precedes the title. Next, a description is displayed. This description contains the keywords of the query in bold. Up to ten of these keywords can be highlighted. The description is not necessarily the first block of text from the resource. The search engine tries to locate the three most relevant sentences from the document relative to the search terms. This is also known as a *dynamic summary*. (The earlier version of SharePoint, SharePoint Portal Server 2003, showed a static description containing the first 300 characters.) Under the description, you'll find the raw URL for the item along with an indication of the size, the author, and the date of the last modification.

The last item in the Search Results page shown in Figure 2-24 is a Web Part that shows the best bet results. Administrators can associate the URLs of resources as best bets for a certain keyword; this process will be fully explained in Chapter 5. A *best bet* is basically an important match that occurred, and the Web Part highlights this to the user.

The People Search Results Page

The last page in the Search Center that we'll look at in this chapter is the People Search Results page, which displays the results of a people-related search query. Figure 2-27 shows an example of this page. A couple of the Web Parts on it might need some explanation.

To start with, the results by default are sorted by *social distance*. Social distance refers to the distance between two people based on their position within the organization and their common interests. For example, a manager performing a people search will likely prefer having people from the manager level pop up in the first ranks of the search results. The same goes for a clerk who is performing a search. You can switch the sorting to a relevance sorting again, just as with the normal search results.

An individual person in the search results, as shown in Figure 2-28, is represented by a picture, the name, and other information that is part of the user profile of that person. The name is a hyperlink, and when clicked, it brings you to the personal site of the person. On the personal site, you can learn more about that person, review the resources that he or she is sharing, and consult public sections of the user profile information and possibly a lot more information that is shared by that person. *Presence information*, a collection of parameters that provide more information about your online status, your whereabouts, and your contact information, is integrated within the people search results, giving you access to instant messaging, Active Directory information, e-mail options, and possibly also real-time collaboration if that is supported within the organization.

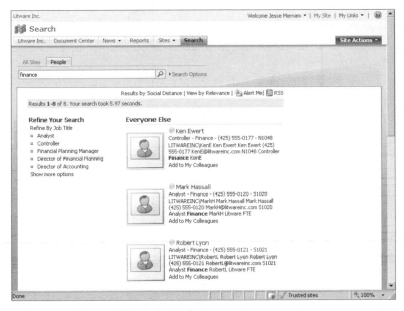

FIGURE 2-27 The People Search Results page

FIGURE 2-28 An individual search result item in the People Search Results page

Every people search result item also has an Add To My Colleagues link. This is part of the social networking support in Office SharePoint Server 2007. A page in your personal site is linked to this action, and you can finish the work here by first setting the privacy policy and by next associating the new colleague with an existing or a new group, as shown in Figure 2-29.

Users navigating to your personal site will see the colleagues that you have configured for public display.

Returning to the People Search Results page, you can again be notified when changes occur within these search results by creating a search-based alert or by subscribing to the RSS feed. Search result statistics and paging of the search results are supported just as on the Search Results page.

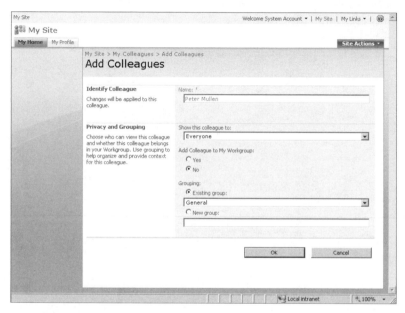

FIGURE 2-29 Adding a new colleague

The last piece of information you'll find on the People Search Results page is something very useful in the real world: the option to refine your search. As a user, you'll probably not find the perfect search result immediately. The Web Part showing the Refine Your Search options is an excellent way to further your search. Depending on what your search terms were, you'll be presented with different drill-down options here. For example, in Figure 2-27, shown earlier, you are able to refine your search by job title.

Summary

Finding the correct information is often crucial in the daily work of information workers. In this chapter, you've learned about the out-of-the-box end-user search experience delivered in Windows SharePoint Services 3.0 and Office SharePoint Server 2007. End users have two basic ways of executing a search query: they can use the small Search box or navigate to a dedicated Search Center. Both of these methods were discussed in this chapter, along with the various options you have as an end user working with the small Search box and the Search Center. In Chapter 3, you'll learn how to configure and customize the end-user search experience.

Chapter 3
Customizing the Search User Interface

After completing this chapter, you will be able to

- Understand the site definitions underlying the Search Center.

- Understand the architectural components of the Search Center.

- Master the configuration options for the Search Center from an administrator point of view.

- Deploy new functionality to the Search Center by using custom Features.

- Understand the different Search Web Parts from a developer angle and the customizations that can be made programmatically.

- Replace the small Search box with a custom-built control that allows users to enter a search query at the top of Microsoft Office SharePoint pages.

The Search Center plays an important role in the overall end-user search experience within Microsoft Office SharePoint Server 2007. In Chapter 2, "The End-User Search Experience," you learned about this experience and how to work with the different components that make up the Search Center. You might have the impression that the Search Center functionality delivered out of the box is more than enough. However, in a lot of real-world scenarios, you'll need to customize and configure the end-user search experience based on specific business requirements. This chapter covers the different options that are available for both administrators and developers. The first section gives you more insight into the architectural components that support the Search Center. The second section covers the numerous configuration options for administrators, as much of the customization of the end-user search experience can be accomplished without developing custom solution components. We conclude the chapter with developer-focused topics. Developers can enrich the end-user search experience with custom extensions for the Search Center, custom Extensible Stylesheet Language (XSL) files for rendering the search results, and optionally custom controls that replace the small Search box controls on the pages within the SharePoint sites.

Search Center Site Definitions

Microsoft Office SharePoint Server 2007 adds plenty of new site definitions on top of the definitions that are part of Microsoft Windows SharePoint Services 3.0. The sidebar "What Is a Site Definition?" provides more background information if you are not familiar with the concept of site definitions. Of the many site definitions available, two are related to searching. These two definitions, one for the Search Center Lite and one for the Search Center With Tabs, are used within SharePoint site collections to provide a better end-user search experience, as you saw in Chapter 2. A Search Center replaces the small Search box rendered at the top of the pages with a dedicated site containing search-related infrastructure pieces that are instantly usable. Many of these pieces can be customized by administrators and developers, as you'll discover while progressing through this chapter.

What Is a Site Definition?

A *site definition* is a core component of the Windows SharePoint Services (WSS) 3.0 provisioning engine. It is a collection of physical files making up the definition of a new template for a site. All of the site definition files are available, each in its own folder, in the 12\TEMPLATE\SiteTemplates folder that is part of the WSS system folder. Each site definition must be made available on every front-end Web Server that is part of the server farm.

> **Note** In a typical SharePoint installation, the WSS system folder is C:\Program Files\ Common Files\Microsoft Shared\Web Server Extensions.

The whereabouts of a site definition and the possible configurations defined are communicated to Windows SharePoint Services 3.0 via small XML files that are prefixed with *WEBTEMP* and are located in the 12\TEMPLATE\<*culture*>\XML directory, where the <*culture*> folder is the locale identifier (12\TEMPLATE\1033\XML for US English). The configuration information for a site definition is expressed in Collaborative Application Markup Language (CAML) and defined within the manifest file of the site definition. This file is named ONET.XML and can be found in the XML subfolder of the site definition. It's not a bad idea to browse through these files to become familiar with the concept of a site definition.

The two search-related site definitions are:

- **SRCHCEN** This is the site definition for the Search Center With Tabs. Sites based on this site definition can be added only to site collections where the Office SharePoint Server Publishing Infrastructure Feature is activated. This Feature enables the content management infrastructure that is required by the Search Center With Tabs. A collaboration portal by default contains a Search Center With Tabs as part of the provisioned sites within that site collection.

> **Note** A *collaboration portal* is a collection of sites that are internally faced within the organization. In mainstream IT talk, a collaboration portal is often referred to as the company's *intranet*. Publishing portals are externally faced, or in other words, are the Internet site of the company. Publishing portals do not contain a Search Center With Tabs by default. They have a hidden Search Center Lite as part of the provisioned sites.

- **SRCHCENTERLITE**   This folder contains the files that make up the template for the Search Center Lite. Site instances based on this folder are ideal candidates to augment the search experience in a site collection that consists solely of pure Windows SharePoint Services 3.0 sites (such as a group of team sites, workspaces, and maybe a blog or a Wiki site). Within these types of site collections, there is often no need for a publishing (or in other words, content management) infrastructure. The Search Center Lite does not require the Office SharePoint Server Publishing Infrastructure Feature to be activated within a site collection and is therefore easily added to the previously mentioned site collections. You can use the Search Center Lite to replace the small Search box that is by default available at the top of pages to site users.

Figure 3-1 displays the contents of the folder for the Search Center With Tabs site definition. The SRCHCEN folder contains a number of files and folders that make up the architecture for a site based on this site definition. Let's briefly review the contents. This is important information for developers who are researching the techniques for creating a custom Search Center site definition or for customizing existing site definitions. We'll look at this in more detail in the section "Extending the End-User Search Experience Through Code" later in this chapter.

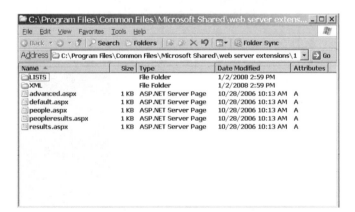

FIGURE 3-1 The SRCHCEN site definition folder

To start, there is a LISTS\Tabs folder that contains the schema and the Microsoft ASP.NET pages that are required for the two list instances that are part of a Search Center With Tabs. These two list instances store the tabs that are displayed to the user. The definition for the Tabs list template is part of the CAML that you can review when you open the ONET.XML file located in the XML subfolder. In addition, you'll find the definition of the default Search Center With Tabs configuration. The *Configuration* element in ONET.XML contains the CAML for provisioning the two instances of the Tabs list, as well as the set of Features that will be activated at the level of the site collection and at the level of the site itself. The *Configuration* element is further connected to a *Module* element. A *Module* element is used to provision pages based on page template files within the virtual file system that is maintained for a site. These page template files are located in the root folder of your site definition folder. A page template file basically contains the skeleton of what a page instance will be for the user. During the provisioning of the pages, instances of the Search Web Parts are added to each page. The definition of the Web Parts is done declaratively by means of the *AllUsersWebPart* XML element.

The site definition folder for the Search Center Lite, shown in Figure 3-2, does not contain a definition for a Tabs list, and no page template files are available for supporting people searches. In general, you'll find the ONET.XML file of the Search Center Lite containing the same types of elements described earlier.

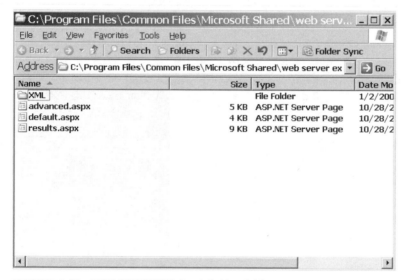

FIGURE 3-2 The SRCHCENTERLITE site definition folder

Architecture of the Search Center With Tabs

A Search Center With Tabs, as shown in the following illustration, is built from a number of components that are part of the Windows SharePoint Services 3.0 core infrastructure, the Microsoft Office SharePoint Server 2007 publishing infrastructure, and the application programming interfaces (APIs) used to communicate with the search engine that is under the control of the Shared Services Provider (SSP) in the server farm. We'll review each component briefly here and continue with deeper coverage of the configurations and customizations that can be performed by administrators and developers in subsequent sections.

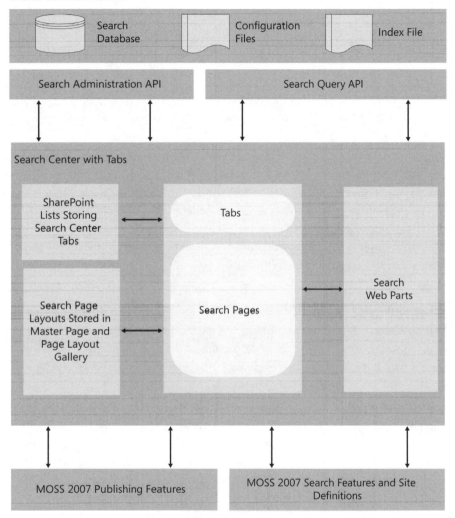

The Search Center With Tabs consists of the following important components:

- **Site definitions**   As described earlier, the site definition for a Search Center With Tabs contains the schema definition of what a site will look like, its initial functionality, and how it will behave when provisioned.

- **Search Features**   A number of search-related Features are installed and activated when you start working with Office SharePoint 2007. Some Features are part of the

Office SharePoint Server Standard Site Feature. Others are packaged independently, such as the search-related Web Parts that are advertised within a site collection when you activate the Office SharePoint Server Search Web Parts Feature.

- **Tab lists**   The Search Center With Tabs provides two lists. One is a list of the tabs that will be displayed on the Search pages. The other is a list of the tabs that will be shown on the Search Results pages.

> **Note** Under the hood, search tabs are displayed by an embedded Web control on the Web Part pages. That makes them an exception to the rest of the functionality rendered on the page, which is rendered by several Web Parts, as you'll see in a moment.

- **Search page layouts**   A Search Center With Tabs is a publishing site. The pages you use in the Search Center With Tabs are all based on page layouts that are stored in the Master Pages And Page Layouts Gallery. As its name implies, this gallery is also used for the storage of the master pages. Each site collection has exactly one gallery as part of its infrastructure. Page layouts will be discussed in detail in the section "A Closer Look at the XSL" later in this chapter. For now, consider them as templates for the pages that are part of the Search Center With Tabs.

- **Tabs**   Tabs displayed in the Search Center are ordinary items in lists. Each tab is connected to one Search page.

- **Search pages**   Pages in a publishing site are stored in the Pages document library, which is part of the publishing infrastructure of the site. The Search Center With Tabs comes with a number of search-related pages that are all based on the Search page layouts and stored in this Pages library.

- **Search Web Parts**   This is a collection of Web Parts that are available on the default Search pages. Note that the Search Web Parts are independent of the publishing infrastructure and that they can also be added on pages in collaboration sites such as a team site or workspaces, as you'll learn in the section "Configuring Search Web Parts" later in this chapter. We'll look at all of the available Search Web Parts from an administrative angle as well as a developer one.

- **Search Administration API**   This is a layer of classes that are used internally by the different building blocks that make up the Search Center. The Search Administration API is used to retrieve the configuration settings of the search experience that administrators have made in the administration site of the SSP. An example is the retrieval of shared search scopes and managed properties that must be shown to the end user in the Search Center. Chapter 8, "Search APIs," provides full coverage of the Search Administration API.

- **Search Query API**   Another layer of classes is used to execute the search query entered by the user. Chapter 8 contains sections discussing this API in detail.

- **Shared Services Provider**   Chapter 5, "Search Administration," provides detailed information about the role of the SSP within the server farm, especially as it relates to indexing content and providing an infrastructure for executing search queries. For now, suffice it to say that Search Centers require Office SharePoint Server 2007 and the SSP that is part of the server farm.

The Tabs Lists

Two list instances in the Search Center With Tabs are provisioned based on the schema definition that is part of the site definition discussed earlier in this chapter. Assuming that you are working within a collaboration portal, you can navigate to each of these list instances. In the Search Center, on the Site Actions menu, click View All Site Content to navigate to the page that displays a list of all the lists and libraries. On this page, you can click the links for each of the list instances storing the tabs:

- **Tabs In Search Pages**   This list contains items that represent the tabs that will be displayed on the Search pages and the Advanced Search page.

- **Tabs In Search Results**   Tabs displayed on the pages showing search results are stored as items in this list.

Figure 3-3 shows one of the items available in the list. It stores the details for the All Sites tab that is shown to the user.

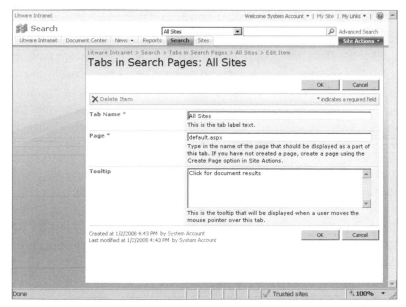

FIGURE 3-3 A definition of a tab for the Search Center

This tab contains the following metadata:

- **Tab Name**   The name of the tab as it will appear in the Search Center.

- **Page**   The page that is connected to the tab. This is typically a page based on the page layout for a Search page.

- **Tooltip**   A description of the page that will be displayed as a Tooltip when the user moves the mouse pointer over the tab.

Search Page Layouts

Four page layouts are available for the Search Center With Tabs, as summarized in Table 3-1.

TABLE 3-1 Page Layouts Available in the Search Center With Tabs

Page Layout	Description
Search Page (Searchmain.aspx)	Pages based on this page layout are typically associated with the tabs within the Search Center. By default, they contain the Search Box Web Part.
Search Results Page (SearchResults.aspx)	Page layout containing the various Search Web Parts that deliver the search results experience.
People Search Results Page (PeopleSearchResults.aspx)	People search results are displayed on pages based on this page layout, by combining a slightly different set of Web Parts than are used in the Search Results Page layout.
Advanced Search Page (AdvancedSearchLayout.aspx)	Page layout for the Advanced Search page, displaying the Advanced Search box as the single Web Part on the page.

Each page layout in the publishing sites is associated with a content type. The common content type for all of the Search page layouts is the Welcome Page content type, which is part of the Page Layouts Content Types group and is provisioned by default with collaboration portals. The Welcome Page content type has the Page content type as its parent. The Page content type is an important system content type that is part of the core of the publishing infrastructure; it is available when you activate the Office SharePoint Server Publishing Infrastructure Feature. The Page content type is part of the Publishing Content Types group.

The provisioning of the Search page layouts is defined within the PortalLayouts Feature. You can find this Feature in the 12\TEMPLATE\FEATURES\PortalLayouts folder on every Web front-end server. We'll come back to this feature when we look at the developer angle for customizing the Search Center in the section "Extending the End-User Search Experience Through Code" later in this chapter.

Search Web Parts

Office SharePoint Server 2007 comes with a nice collection of search-related Web Parts. These Web Parts are used on the pages that are part of the Search Center, but you can also easily add them to other types of pages on publishing sites as well as nonpublishing sites. An example of a nonpublishing site is a team site or a document workspace.

Let's briefly review each Web Part. Later in this chapter, you'll learn how they can be configured by administrators and also how developers can programmatically access them. The set of Web Parts made available by the Office SharePoint Server Search Web Parts Feature consists of:

- **Advanced Search Box**   This Web Part is available on the Advanced Search page and can be used for parameterized searches based on properties and combinations of words.

- **People Search Box**   The People Search page contains this Web Part, which allows users to enter a people-related search query with the option of using the Search Options pane for including property filters that are people-related.

- **People Search Core Results**   You'll find this Web Part on the People Search Results page. It is responsible for displaying the search results for a people-related search query.

- **Search Action Links**   This Web Part is available on both the Search Results page and the People Search Results page. It is configured to display hyperlinks to actions that can be performed on the search results.

- **Search Best Bets**   Best bets and high confidence results are displayed by this Web Part, which you'll typically find on the Search Results page.

- **Search Box**   This important Web Part is available on the Search page and the Search Results page, making it possible for users to enter a keyword syntax query. The execution of the search query is not the responsibility of Search box. The query and the additional parameters that the user has provided are passed to the Search Results page, where they are picked up for execution.

- **Search Core Results**   This is probably the most interesting Web Part, since it is the one that displays the results after the execution of the search query. One of the primary tasks that this Web Part is responsible for is the transformation of the incoming search results into the HTML displayed to the user in the body of the Web Part.

- **Search High Confidence Results**   This Web Part shows the keyword, high confidence, and best bets results to the user. You'll find it on the Search Results page. This Web Part and the Search Best Bets Web Part, described earlier, are actually the same Web Part but configured differently.

- **Search Paging**   Search results can be numerous. The execution of a search query can result in hundreds, even thousands, of items that are displayed to the user. To navigate through the entire search results in a user-friendly manner, the technique of paging is used. By default, a page contains 10 search results. The Search Paging Web Part gives the user the option to navigate to other pages, making the rest of the search results available.

- **Search Statistics**   This Web Part in the list of search-related Web Parts displays information to the user about the number of search results and the time it took to execute the query.

- **Search Summary**   This is a small Web Part that shows the summary of the query and, when needed, the Did You Mean... feature.

Now that we've covered all of the main building blocks, let's have a closer look at the options that you have as an administrator to configure the Search Center With Tabs.

Administrative Tasks in the Search Center

Let's assume that you have the role of an administrator whose responsibility it is to configure the Search Center (or possibly multiple Search Centers) in a collaboration portal. You will most likely get requests from end users to make changes to the configuration of these sites in order to optimize their search experience. This optimization typically consists of the following common tasks. We'll look at each of these tasks in more detail in the following sections.

- Extra custom pages can be added to the Search Center to expose additional functionality.

- Custom tabs can be created that allow the user to access the custom Search pages.

- The end-user experience for expressing a search query in the Search page can be customized by configuring the Search Box Web Part. In the case of a people-related search, the configuration will be done using the People Search Box Web Part.

- The search results are rendered using different Search Web Parts, of which the Search Core Results Web Part is the most important. Administrators can configure each of the Web Parts separately.

- One of the most common configurations is the customization or complete replacement of the XSL that is used to transform the search results into the HTML that end users see. Administrators will typically make only the smaller changes to this XSL; developers are called in when the XSL needs heavy customizations or needs to be completely replaced with custom XSL.

There are some additional configuration tasks for the administrator at the level of the site collection. You'll find a discussion of these tasks in Chapter 5.

Creating Custom Pages for the Search Center

As you saw earlier in this chapter, an out-of-the-box Search Center comes with a collection of pages that are created based on a set of Search-related page layouts. These page layouts are provisioned when you create a collaboration portal. The initial collection of pages can, however, be extended with additional Search pages, Search Results pages, Advanced Search pages, and people-related Search pages. The extra pages you make available can be based on the four page layouts we've looked at, or as you'll learn later in this chapter, you can also create your own custom search-related page layouts and use those for the creation of the extra pages in the Search Center. Let's go with the former option first and check out the steps to create a custom Search page and a custom Search Results page. All of this work can be done in the browser. Note that you can follow the same steps to create other types of search-related pages.

Creating a custom Search page is useful when you need a customized search query entry in the Search Center. Custom tabs can be created to make the custom Search pages available for the user. When you make use of the default page layout for the Search page, you'll get a Search Box Web Part on the page. The properties of this Web Part can be modified easily in the browser to meet the needs of users visiting the page. It is also possible to enrich the custom Search page with additional Web Parts to extend the out-of-the-box functionality.

You create a custom Search page in the browser by first navigating to the Search Center. In the Search Center, on the Site Actions menu, click Create Page. The page that will be rendered in the browser is displayed in Figure 3-4.

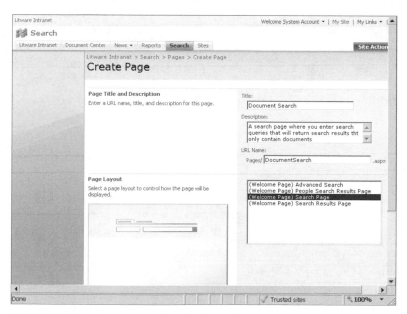

FIGURE 3-4 Creating a custom Search page

You enter a title and a description for the page. The value for the URL name is automatically generated based on the title that you have provided for the page. By default, the Search Center offers four available page layouts to choose from, as described earlier in this chapter. These page layouts are the only ones for the Search Center. More page layouts are available in the Master Pages And Page Layouts Gallery that is part of the infrastructure of the collaboration portal, but all of these layouts are hidden from administrators when they work in the Search Center; you'll learn about these additional layouts later in this chapter.

To create a custom Search page, select the (Welcome Page) Search Page item in the list, and then click the Create button to start the process of creation.

> **Note** The name of the page layout contains the name of the content type that is associated with the page layout. As mentioned earlier in this chapter, all of the out-of-the-box search-related page layouts are associated with the *Welcome Page* content type.

After a while, a new page is available in the browser. The page itself is a new item in the Pages document library that is part of the Search Center. This Pages document library is by default configured for versioning, enforced checkout, and content approval. This is why, as you can see in Figure 3-5, the page is checked out and at this moment available in draft mode.

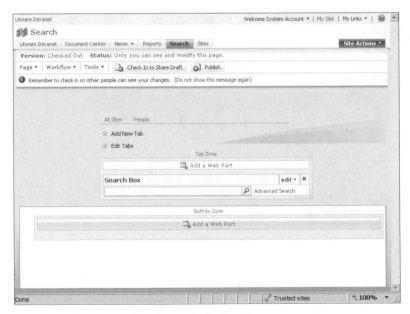

FIGURE 3-5 The custom Search page in draft mode

You change the status of the page to a published version by clicking the Publish button on the Page Editing toolbar. The page will be checked in, and the version number will be updated to a major version (for example, version 1.0). You'll check out and edit the custom Search page again later in this chapter, when we review the modifications you can make to the Search Box Web Part on the page.

A custom Search Results page often accompanies a custom Search page. A request by a business for a customized search query entry will probably lead to a similar request for the display of the search results. A custom Search Results page is created in much the same way as a custom Search page. Again in the Search Center, on the Site Actions menu, you click Create Page. The difference is the selection of the page layout—in this case, you select the (Welcome Page) Search Results Page item in the list, as shown in Figure 3-6.

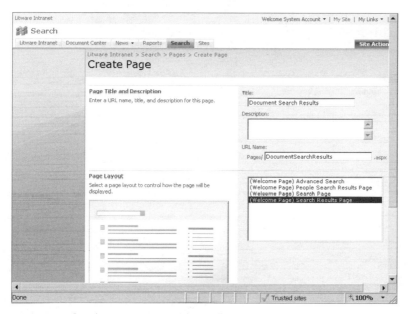

FIGURE 3-6 Creating a custom Search Results page

The created page, shown in Figure 3-7, holds many more search-related Web Parts by default. Again, for the time being, we are not yet going to worry about the configuration of each these Web Parts; that's something we'll deal with later. For now, you can simply publish the page so that it is checked in and published as a major version.

One final note before we continue with the next configuration task: Recall that all of the pages (apart from the administration pages) in a publishing site are stored as items in the Pages document library that is part of the infrastructure of the site. The two pages you created earlier are also stored in the Pages document library; you can verify this with a quick glance in that library. To do so, use the Site Actions menu to open the Pages document library that is part of the Search Center. On the View All Site Content menu, navigate to the page, where you can click Pages to open the document library. Figure 3-8 shows the items within this document library, including the custom Search page and the custom Search

Results page created earlier. Remember the name of the custom Search page; you'll need this name in the next section.

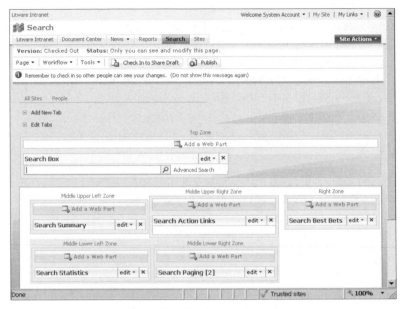

FIGURE 3-7 The custom Search Results page in edit mode

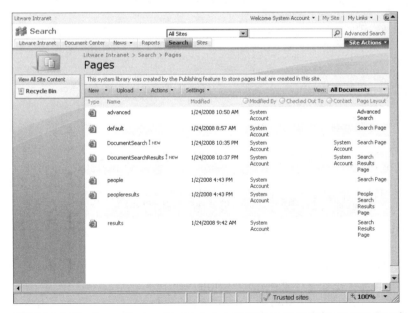

FIGURE 3-8 The Pages library with the custom Search page and the custom Search Results page

Creating Custom Tabs

Another recurring configuration task in the Search Center is the creation of a custom tab that will give access to a custom Search page. The custom tab is a regular item in a list. Actually, there are two lists, as you've seen. One list stores the tabs shown on Search pages, and one list stores the tabs shown on Search Results pages.

To create a custom tab, make sure that you are currently working in the Search Center. Next, on the Site Actions menu, select View All Site Content again. Links to the two lists are displayed in the View All Content page.

The first list is Tabs In Search Pages. Click New on the toolbar to create a new item in the list. Type **Documents** as the name for the tab. This is the name that will be displayed to the user in the Search page. Next, in the Page box, enter the name of the Search page that will be displayed in the browser when the user clicks the new tab. In this example, type **documentsearch.aspx**. The last item is the Tooltip box, where you enter a description to be displayed when the user pauses over the tab. Figure 3-9 shows the filled-in information for the new tab in the list. Click OK to confirm your work and have SharePoint create the new item in the list.

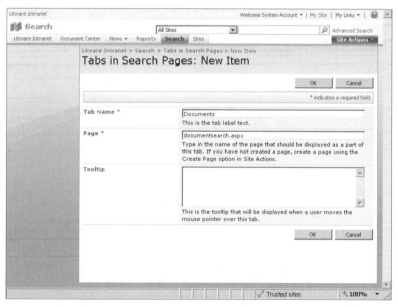

FIGURE 3-9 The definition of a new tab that is associated with a custom Search page

Our new tab is now visible whenever the user displays a Search page in the browser. But the tab is not yet visible when the user reviews the search results. The tabs for the Search Results pages are maintained in their own list, the Tabs In Search Results list. To open this list, follow the same steps as for the Tabs In Search Pages list. The item you create here is identical to the item you just created. The *Tab Name*, *Page*, and *Tooltip* values are the same as those shown in Figure 3-9.

You can verify your work by clicking the Search node in the top navigation bar of the portal. The home page of the Search Center now displays a tab list with your extra tab. Click the tab to navigate to your custom Search page. There is no real difference in the home page that is associated with the All Sites tab because you have not done any extra configuration for this page. But you'll notice in Figure 3-10 that the URL in the Address bar of the browser is set correctly to the custom Search page you created.

FIGURE 3-10 The custom tab connected to the custom Search page

Type a query, and then click the Go Search button. Notice that you are not yet redirected to your new custom Search Results page. This is because you still have to configure the Search Box Web Part on the custom Search page; we'll make this modification shortly. However, as you can see in Figure 3-11, the default Search Results page also shows the custom tab because you have created an entry for it in the corresponding tabs list.

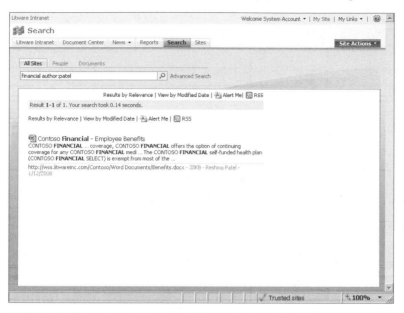

FIGURE 3-11 The custom tab is also visible on the Search Results pages.

Configuring Search Web Parts

A major task is the configuration of the various Search Web Parts found on the different Search pages that are part of the Search Center. This configuration is always done by modifying the properties exposed by each of the Web Parts. As with every SharePoint Web Part, the properties can be configured by editing the corresponding properties pages. For the Web Part you want to modify, on the Edit menu, you then click Modify Shared Web Part to display the tool pane in the browser. All of the properties that you can edit are displayed in the tool pane, organized in expandable sections.

> **Note** The Web Part properties can be modified for all visitors to the page, or they can be changed for only the user who applies the changes. The first option is also referred to as *modifying the shared Web Part instance*, while the second option is referred to as *modifying the personal version of the Web Part instance*. Here we'll assume that the changes will always be for all visitors—in other words, we will be working in shared mode.

The Search Box Web Part

The custom Search page connected to the Documents tab you created earlier contains a Search Box Web Part that must be configured. One reason you should do this is to redirect the Go Search button to the appropriate custom Search Results page in the Pages library. But as you'll learn, other configurations might be useful in certain scenarios.

The following is a list of typical configurations at the level of the Search Box Web Part:

- Configure the display of a Scope Picker.

- Change the look and feel of the Search box.

- Append additional query terms to the search query that the user inputs in the Search box.

- Configure the links to the Search Results page and the advanced Search page.

Let's cover the configuration of the Scope Picker first. By default, no Scope Picker is displayed in the Search Box Web Part. In the tool pane, in the Scopes Drop-Down section, you can specify a Scope Picker to be displayed. The result of the configuration is shown in Figure 3-12.

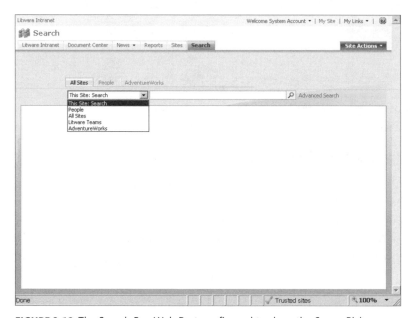

FIGURE 3-12 The Search Box Web Part configured to show the Scope Picker

The various drop-down mode options for the Scope Picker are summarized in Table 3-2.

TABLE 3-2 Drop-Down Mode Options for the Scope Picker

Drop-Down Mode	Description
Do Not Show Scopes Dropdown	This is the default. No Scope Picker is shown when this is the active mode.
Show Scopes Dropdown	The Scope Picker is populated with all of the search scopes (including the contextual scopes) that are part of the associated display group. (More on display groups later.)

Drop-Down Mode	Description
Show, And Default To 'S' URL Parameter	The previous chapter described the various parameters that can be part of the query string in the HTTP request that the search box is creating for the Search Results page. One of the parameters is the 's' parameter, which can contain the name of a search scope. Activating this dropdown mode will display the Scope Picker, and it will use the incoming value for the 's' parameter as the selected scope by default.
Show, And Default To Contextual Scope	A contextual scope is one that is not part of the display group that is associated with the Scope Picker. It is a scope that is created on the fly and dependent on the site where the Scope Picker is displayed. An example is *This Site: Search*.
Show, Do Not Include Contextual Scopes	Displays the Scope Picker, including all of the search scopes that are part of the associated display group. Does not show any of the contextual scopes.
Show, Do Not Include Contextual Scopes, And Default To 'S' URL Parameter	Displays the Scope Picker, displaying only the search scopes that are part of the associated display group and preselecting the scope that matches the value of the 's' parameter in the query string.

You can also specify the text of a label for the Scope Picker and a fixed width for the drop-down list in pixels, as shown in Figure 3-13.

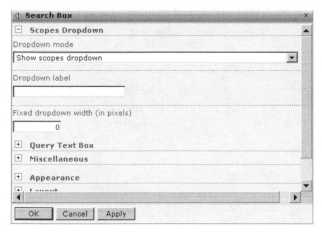

FIGURE 3-13 Configuring the Scope Picker for the Search Box Web Part

A number of properties can be configured to modify the look and feel of the text box that is used for expressing the search query, as shown in Figure 3-14.

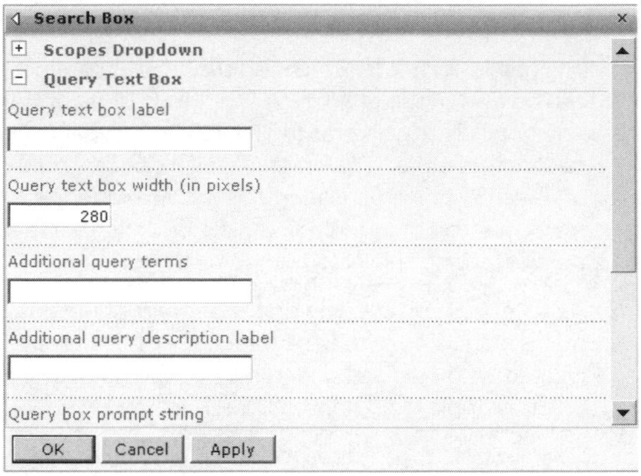

FIGURE 3-14 Configuring the Query text box that is part of the Search Box Web Part

First, you can specify the text for the label of the text box. The width of the Query text box is set by default to 280 pixels, but you can of course change this. An interesting property to set is *Additional Query Terms*. You enter here a single word, a collection of words, a phrase, or even property filters that will be appended to the search query that the user enters in the text box. This is useful for our custom Documents tab. The purpose of the Documents tab is to redirect users to a place where they formulate a search query and view only documents returned as the search results. Adding the *contenttype:document* as the additional query term immediately ensures this result. Notice in Figure 3-15 that the appended search query is displayed in the Search Box Web Part that is shown on the Search Results page.

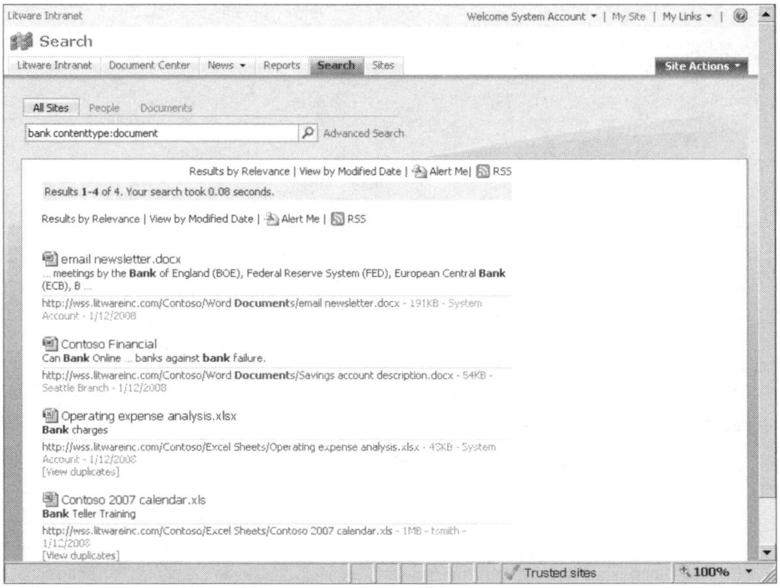

FIGURE 3-15 A property filter as an appended query term

A small label describing the additional query term can be displayed directly below the Query text box. This is useful to explain to the user what you as an administrator have configured at this level. Figure 3-16 shows this in the custom Search page.

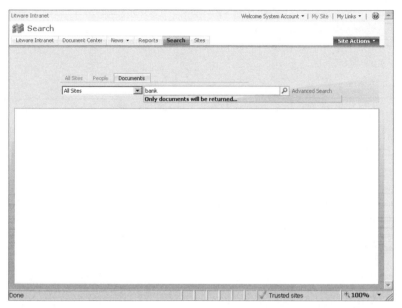

FIGURE 3-16 A description of the additional query term that will be appended to the end-user query

Another configuration at the level of the search text box is the definition of a query box prompt string. The name is a bit misleading, since no real prompt is shown. The value of the query box prompt string is displayed as the value of the text box when the text box does not have the focus. It is a small helpful string for users—for example, *<Enter your query here>*— that can be used to invite them to enter a query, as shown in Figure 3-17.

Go back for a second to Figure 3-15. It can be useful to define an additional query term that is appended to the one the user enters in the Query text box. But many times, you don't want the term to be displayed in the Search Text Box of the Search Results page, as is the case by default. One final configuration option you can set for the Search box is to clear the Append Additional Terms To Query check box so that the user will not see what you as administrator have configured at this level.

FIGURE 3-17 The search text box, inviting the user to enter a query

Figure 3-18 shows the Miscellaneous configuration options. You can, for example, replace the image for the Go Search button if you want. The position of the image can be configured—both left-to-right and right-to-left options are available. For both positions, there is the option to specify a URL to an image that will be displayed when the user pauses over the Go Search button.

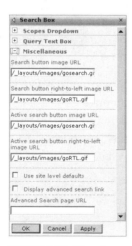

FIGURE 3-18 Miscellaneous configuration options for the Search Box Web Part

For the most part, the Search Center can operate on its own, making use of all of the pages it contains. You can, however, change this behavior and direct the Search Center to use the configurations that site collection administrators have made regarding redirection to the Search Results pages. In the Search Settings page at the level of the site collection, you can choose between delivering a search experience incorporating search scopes and using the osssearchresults.aspx page that is available as an application page in the 12\Template\ Layouts folder. Chapter 5 covers this administrative task. The property is a check box that is cleared by default. If you leave the default setting, you must enter a *relative URL* (a URL that starts from the current page), to the Search Results page. By default, this URL is the Search Results page that is provisioned by the Search Center. Because you have created a custom Search Results page, you can change the value of the target Search Results page to *documentsearchresults.aspx*.

Another configuration option is to hide or display the link to the Advanced Search page along with the specification of the URL itself. The default Advanced Search page can be replaced with the URL to your own custom advanced Search page if you have created one.

The last option is the name of the display group that is associated with the Scope Picker. By default, two display groups are available at the level of the site collection. Both groups function as a layer between the search scopes and the Scope Pickers. Each Scope Picker is connected to a display group that contains the search scopes that must be displayed. The creation and management of display groups is covered more in detail in Chapter 5.

The Search Core Results Web Part

The next Search Web Part to investigate from an administrator perspective is the Search Core Results Web Part. This Web Part is responsible for displaying the search results to the end user. Various configurations are available, and all are exposed within the tool pane for the Web Part, as shown in Figure 3-19.

FIGURE 3-19 Configuration options for the Search Core Results Web Part

We'll cover the following administration tasks now in more detail:

- Configuring the sorting and the paging of the search results

- Configuring the displayed details of the search results

- Working with fixed keyword queries

- Hiding or displaying the various links that are part of the user experience in this Web Part

The sorting of the search results is by default based on the score each result gets during relevance ranking. During the execution of the search, each search result gets a relevance score that is calculated based on many parameters, as will be explained in Chapter 5. A second option is sorting based on the date modified. The *Default Results View* property in the tool pane, shown in Figure 3-20, shows these two sort options. You'll likely get requests from businesses to allow for additional sorting options using other properties that are part of the search results. Responding to these requests is not easy, because extra sorting options are possible only by developing a custom search application using the query API. Chapter 8 covers a number of the techniques that can be useful here.

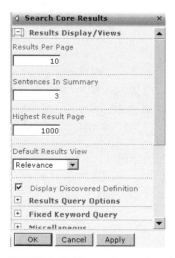

FIGURE 3-20 The sorting and paging configuration options for the Search Core Results Web Part

Paging is controlled at the level of the Search Core Results Web Part, but the paging options for the end user are actually displayed by the Search Paging Web Part, discussed later. As you can see in Figure 3-20, you control the number of results per page. This value is by default 10 results per page. You can also change the maximum number of pages that can be displayed to the end user. By default, the *Highest Result Page* property is set to 1000. This means that in total you can have 10,000 search results displayed on the Search Results page.

The *Sentences in Summary* property controls how many sentences are displayed for the description part of an individual search item. Three sentences are displayed by default, and you can increase that number to a maximum of 10.

A last configuration option in the Result Displays/Views section is the Display Discovered Definition check box. By default, this check box is selected, which means that the Search Core Results Web Part will communicate the results for the best bets and keywords to the Search Best Bets and Search High Confidence Web Parts on the page. These Web Parts are responsible for displaying these types of results. We'll have a look at how the communication between all the Search Web Parts on the Search Results page occurs in the section titled "Extending the End-User Search Experience Through Code" later in this chapter.

The second section in the tool pane is the Results Query Options section, shown in Figure 3-21. A first configuration here is the hiding or the display of the link for viewing duplicate results. The previous chapter explained duplicate search results from the perspective of the end user. Administrators can hide this link for users if needed. A side effect of hiding this link is that the search results now will include all the duplicate results that would otherwise have been hidden.

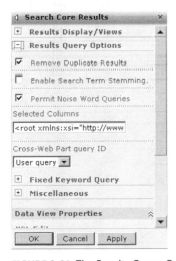

FIGURE 3-21 The Results Query Options configuration options for the Search Core Results Web Part

By default, search term stemming is not activated. *Search stemming* refers to the process of stripping off endings of words at query and index time so that different search terms will match and the search will retrieve documents containing related words. A keyword query like *transfer* will result by default only in search items that have an exact match for that word. There will be no matches included for related words like *transfer*, *transfers*, *transferring*, and so on. Activating search term stemming at the level of the Search Core Results Web Part will give you that result if it is needed. Figure 3-22 shows a sample query and the results when search stemming is activated.

Users can express a search query that consists completely of one or more noise words (such as *and* and *the*, also referred to as *stop words*); these types of queries are called noise word queries. An example of a noise word query is *and in.* The Permit Noise Words Queries check box can be cleared to prevent these types of queries; entering a noise word query will then return no results.

> **Note** The ability to create a query consisting of noise words is a new feature in Office SharePoint Server 2007. The noise word file in Microsoft SharePoint Portal Server 2003 did by default exclude all noise words from the index. The current version excludes only a few noise words to facilitate noise word searching.

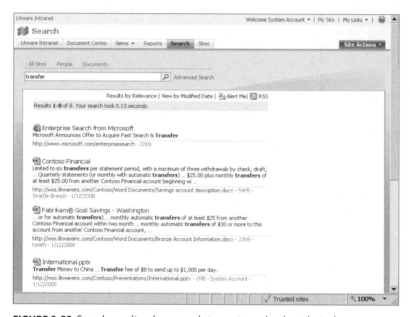

FIGURE 3-22 Search results when search term stemming is activated

The *Selected Columns* property is an important one. By default, the property contains the following XML string:

```
<root xmlns:xsi="http://www.w3.org/2001/XMLSchema-instance">
 <Columns>
  <Column Name="WorkId"/>
  <Column Name="Rank"/>
  <Column Name="Title"/>
  <Column Name="Author"/>
  <Column Name="Size"/>
  <Column Name="Path"/>
  <Column Name="Description"/>
  <Column Name="Write"/>
  <Column Name="SiteName"/>
  <Column Name="CollapsingStatus"/>
```

```
  <Column Name="HitHighlightedSummary"/>
  <Column Name="HitHighlightedProperties"/>
  <Column Name="ContentClass"/>
  <Column Name="IsDocument"/>
  <Column Name="PictureThumbnailURL"/>
 </Columns>
</root>
```

Search queries are sent to the query engine for execution. All of the search results are returned as an XML string to the Search Core Results Web Part. Each search result item will contain all of the metadata that is defined as *Column* elements in the *Selected Columns* property. All of these *Column* elements represent a managed property. Managed properties are created by administrators in the administration site of the SSP and are used to expose crawled metadata to the user. They map to one or more crawled properties. Chapter 5 explains the steps for accomplishing this task. When there is a need for more metadata to be included in the search results, you'll have to add an extra *Column* element for every managed property. This will often be requested when business data has been crawled. As you'll learn later in this chapter, most of the metadata for this type of data is not included in the search results without additional configuration of the *Columns* property. The following XML string can be used to include the date of creation as part of the information that is returned by the search engine. Remember from the previous chapter that by default, you'll get only the date of the last modification. You do not have to create a new managed property for this—there is already one available named *Created*. The only required action to include it in the *Columns* XML string is to create a new *Column* element like this and append it as a child element of the Columns element;

```
  <Column Name="Created"/>
```

Clearly, this will not be enough to display the new column in the search results. You also have to customize the XSL, basically including the statements that take the new column into consideration during the transformation of the XML into the HTML displayed as the body of the Search Core Results Web Part. We'll cover this in the section "A Closer Look at the XSL" later in this chapter. If you can't wait, you can click the XSL button in the tool pane and replace the XSL with the following code snippet. Before doing that, you might want to simply copy and paste the default XSL to a text file, since you'll need it again later on.

```
<xsl:stylesheet version="1.0" xmlns:xsl="http://www.w3.org/1999/XSL/Transform">
 <xsl:output method="xml" version="1.0" encoding="UTF-8" indent="yes"/>
  <xsl:template match="/">
   <xmp><xsl:copy-of select="*"/></xmp>
  </xsl:template>
</xsl:stylesheet>
```

The preceding XSL simply outputs all of the raw XML that is returned by the search engine. If you apply it, the Search Core Results Web Part will show you XML similar to the following. For brevity, only the first search result is listed. Notice that the results now also contain the data for the *Created* managed property.

```
<All_Results>
  <Result>
   <id>1</id>
   <workid>9492</workid>
   <rank>868</rank>
   <title>Marketing Strategies for Europe</title>
   <author>Administrator</author>
   <size>17080</size>
   <url>http://moss.litwareinc.com/MarketingManager/Presentations/Marketing Strategies
 for Europe.docx</url>
<urlEncoded>http%3A%2F%2Fmoss%2Elitwareinc%2Ecom%2FMarketingManager%2FPresentations%2FMarket
ing%20Strategies%20for%20Europe%2Edocx</urlEncoded>
   <description></description>
   <write>6/8/2007</write>
   <sitename>http://moss.litwareinc.com/marketingmanager</sitename>
   <collapsingstatus>0</collapsingstatus>
   <hithighlightedsummary>
    <c0>Marketing</c0> Strategies </hithighlightedsummary>
   <hithighlightedproperties>
    <HHTitle>
     <c0>Marketing</c0> Strategies for Europe</HHTitle>
<HHUrl>http://moss.litwareinc.com/<c0>Marketing</c0>Manager/Presentations/<c0>Marketing</c0>
 Strategies for Europe.docx</HHUrl>
   </hithighlightedproperties>
   <contentclass>STS_ListItem_DocumentLibrary</contentclass>
   <isdocument>1</isdocument>
   <picturethumbnailurl></picturethumbnailurl>
   <created>1/24/2007</created>
   <imageurl imageurldescription="Result of type:
document">/_layouts/images/icdocx.gif</imageurl>
  </Result>
</All_Results>
```

A last configuration available in the Results Query Options section is the *Cross-Web Part Query ID* property. It has been mentioned previously that all of the Web Parts that are available on the Search Results page are not connected to one another in the traditional SharePoint way. The *Cross-Web Part Query ID* property is used internally to connect the different Web Parts with one another.

> **Note** What exactly is meant by "the traditional SharePoint way"? If you go to a team site, for example, you are able to add Web Parts on the page that can communicate with one another. The communication is done through the SharePoint Web Part connections infrastructure. On the Edit menu of the Web Part in design mode, SharePoint lists all of the Web Parts that are available on the page and that are connectable. Web Parts can play the role of providers of data or consumers of data. Connecting Web Parts this way is useful if you need to deliver a master-detail representation of the data and the data is part of more than one Web Part on the page.

The following illustration summarizes what is going on behind the scenes:

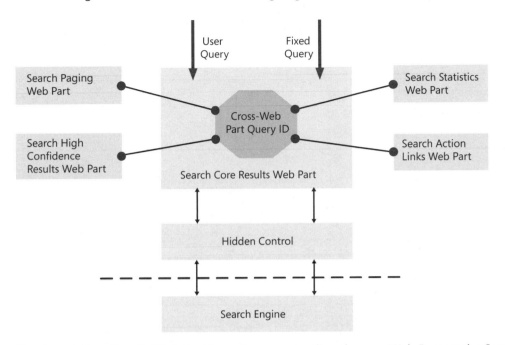

The Search Core Results Web Part is, as the name implies, the core Web Part on the Search Results page. This Web Part controls the execution of the search query that enters the page via the query string. It communicates internally with a hidden control that continues the processing of the search query by setting up a dialog with the search engine. Results coming from the search engine are translated into XML and passed back to the Search Core Results Web Part. The Web Part then uses the outcome of the search query itself for rendering the results using XSL transformation. The Web Part also plays a crucial role in the distribution of the search results to the other Web Parts that are available on the page. To accomplish this, the Search Core Results Web Part must be able to identify the other Web Parts. This identification is based on an internal connection that is established between the Search Core Results Web Part and the other Web Parts on the page that expose the *Cross-Web Part Query ID* property. All of the Web Parts with the same value for this property are internally linked with one another. This value is not really expressed as a number; it can be *User Query, Query 2, Query 3, Query 4,* or *Query 5*. The first value indicates that the Search Core Results Web Part is taking as input a query expressed by a user passed to it via the query string of the request. All of the other values can be used for scenarios where you do not work with user-related queries but where you are working with fixed keyword queries.

Configuring a fixed keyword query for the Search Core Results Web Part is an interesting technique if you plan to use the Search Web Parts outside a Search Center. Figure 3-23 shows the tool pane where you perform the configuration for a fixed keyword query. Let's go into a bit more detail.

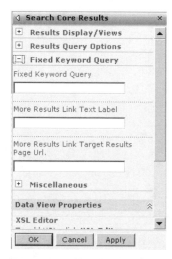

FIGURE 3-23 The Fixed Keyword Query configuration options for the Search Core Results Web Part

Assume that you receive a request from a business to display on the home page of a team site a list of the three most recent Microsoft Office Word 2007 documents containing the keyword *Contoso*. You could meet this request by building your own custom Web Part that internally executes a search query, but you can also accomplish the task fairly easily by adding and configuring a Search Core Results Web Part on the page. You can navigate to a home page of a team site to try it out.

First switch the home page of the team site to edit mode, and then add the Search Core Results Web Part on the page. The Web Part can be found in the Add Web Parts dialog box, as shown in Figure 3-24.

Note You must activate the Office SharePoint Server Search Web Parts Feature at the level of the site collection before the Search Web Parts are available in the Add Web Parts dialog box.

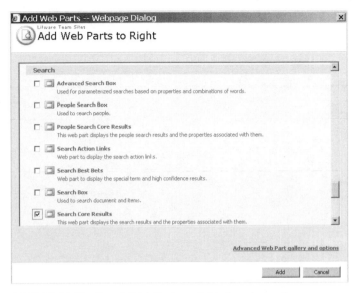

FIGURE 3-24 The Search Web Parts available for a team site

The Web Part will show nothing unless you configure it for a fixed query. You'll use the Edit menu for the Web Part to modify the properties in the tool pane. Here are the steps to create the display shown in Figure 3-25:

1. Expand the Fixed Keyword Query section, and type **contoso fileextension:docx** in the Fixed Keyword Query box.

2. Now expand the Results Query Options section. Here you must change the setting for the *Cross-Web Part Query ID* property.

3. Select *Query 2* to replace the default value.

4. Because this business requested to see only the five most recent documents, expand the Results Display/Views section, and change the Results Per Page setting to 3. Set the value for Highest Result Page to *1* and the Default Results View to Modified Date so that the results are sorted as requested.

You can configure two other properties in the Fixed Keyword Query section. A Search Core Results Web Part that is configured with a fixed keyword query can appear at the bottom of the results list a link for the user who is interested in getting more results. The text of this link can be set, as well as the URL. Imagine a scenario where you have a second SSP in the server farm and you allow the user to click the More Results link to have the same fixed query executed against the second search engine. This could also be a simple link back to the Search Center with the query in the '*k*' parameter enabling users to see more than three results.

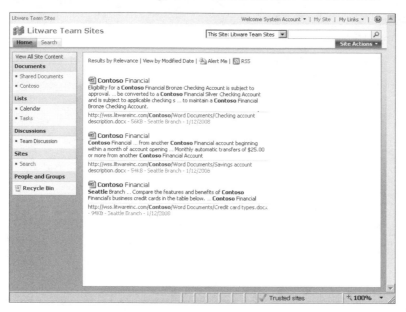

FIGURE 3-25 The Search Core Results Web Part configured with a fixed keyword query on the home page of a team site

The Miscellaneous section for the Search Core Results Web Part properties is shown in Figure 3-26. A first and interesting property is *Scope*. By default, this value is set to *All Sites*. If no Scope Picker is displayed in the Search Box Web Part, the search query will always default to what is specified as the value of the *Scope* property here. The People Search Results page uses this property to narrow results to people only. You might configure this property in scenarios where you create additional search tabs with a search scope that is fixed to a subset of content in the index. Chapter 5 briefly describes this use case for search scopes.

FIGURE 3-26 The Miscellaneous configuration options for the Search Core Results Web Part

Next you have a series of check boxes and options for hiding or displaying functionality in the Web Part. Note that most of these options are not directly useful in the Search Core Results Web Part in its current role on the Search Results page. As you'll learn in the section "Extending the End-User Experience Through Code" later in this chapter, the *Web Part* class (and now we are talking about the Microsoft .NET Framework class in the Search object model) that underlies the Search Core Results Web Part is also the *Web Part* class that is used for the display of the search action links on the Search Results page. Many of the configuration options described here are more appropriate in that context or in scenarios where the Search Core Results Web Part is configured to run with a fixed keyword query, as described earlier.

- **Show Messages**   Show or hide error messages in the Web Part.

- **Show Search Results**   If this check box is cleared, no results are displayed by the Web Part. If other Search Web Parts are connected to the Search Core Results Web Part (using the *Cross-Web Part Query ID* property, as seen earlier), they will still do what they are supposed to do.

- **Show Action Links**   This check box is cleared by default. Action links are by default displayed by a separate Web Part on the Search Results page.

- **Display "Relevance" View Option**   Specify whether to let users switch to the view where results are sorted based on the relevance ranking score.

- **Display "Modified Date" View Option**   Specify whether to let users switch to the view where results are sorted based on the modified date.

- **Display "Alert Me" Link**   Show or hide the Alert Me link.

- **Display "RSS" Link**   Show or hide the RSS link.

- **Sample Data**   Contains an XML string acting as a sample of the type of data returned by the search engine.

- **XSL Link**   Specify this setting if you decide not to embed the XSL within the Web Part instance. Later in this chapter, you'll see a scenario where this can be a useful property to work with.

- **Data View Caching Time-Out (Seconds)**   This property can be used to control the caching of the search results. You can set the duration for clearing the cache to the default setting 86400 seconds, or 24 hours.

- **Send First Row To Connected Web Parts When Page Loads**   The property is set by default to *true*, which means that the Search Core Results Web Part will send the first row to all the connected Web Parts when the page is loaded in the browser. This allows all of the connected Web Parts to get some initial state immediately, before getting the rest of the data from the Search Core Results Web Part.

At the end of this long list of configuration options for the Search Core Results Web Part, shown earlier in Figure 3-19, is one more option: the XSL Editor button. This is probably the most important configuration to be performed for this Web Part. As such, it warrants its own section, titled "A Closer Look at the XSL," later in this chapter. Feel free to jump to that section right now if you're impatient, but be sure to come back here to continue the overview of the configuration options for the other Search Web Parts.

The Search Action Links Web Part

Another Web Part available on the Search Results page is the Search Action Links Web Part. This Web Part supports the following actions:

- Sorting search results based on the relevance ranking.

- Sorting search results based on the modified date.

- Creating search-based alerts.

- Reviewing and possibly subscribing to the RSS feed generated for the search results.

Each of these operations can be turned on or off in the tool pane displaying the properties exposed by the Web Part, as shown in Figure 3-27.

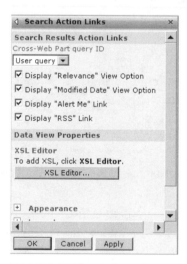

FIGURE 3-27 The configuration options for the Search Action Links Web Part

The Search Action Links Web Part is one of the Web Parts on the Search Results page that is connected internally to the Search Core Results Web Part via the *Cross-Web Part Query ID* property. By default, the value of this property is set to *User Query*. But remember the discussion regarding the use of a Search Core Results Web Part configured with a fixed keyword query on the home page of a team site. As shown earlier in Figure 3-25, all of the action links can be displayed as part of the Search Core Results Web Part content. However, you can also hide these links by opening the tool pane and clearing the Show Action Links check box. How do you then display the possible actions to the user? The answer is simple. The page can include a dedicated Search Action Links Web Part to display these links. To connect the Search Action Links Web Part to the Search Core Results Web Part, you'll have to change the value of the Cross-Web Part Query ID property to *Query 2*—exactly the same value as the Search Core Results Web Part. The user will then be able to perform an action in the Search Action Links Web Part that will have an immediate impact on the displayed search results, as shown in Figure 3-28.

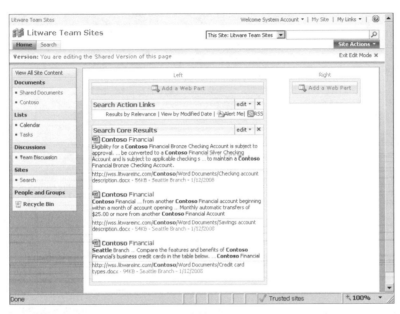

FIGURE 3-28 The Search Action Links Web Part connected to the Search Core Results Web Part

What could be the benefit of isolating the action links from the search results this way? The technique is useful when there is a need to add custom action links. The XSL that is part of the Search Core Results Web Part includes a section that is devoted to the proper display of the action links. You can add to that section the XSL for the additional actions, but it is cleaner to separate this from the XSL whose main responsibility is the rendering of the search results. You might also need to reuse the custom action XSL in many places. Using the Search Action Links Web Part with its own dedicated XSL for showing the actions is a good practice. The section "A Closer Look at the XSL" later in this chapter is devoted to describing the internals of the XSL and how you can add your own custom actions to it.

The Search Best Bets Web Part

The Search Best Bets Web Part, described in the previous chapter and shown on the right in Figure 3-29, is basically the same as the Search High Confidence Results Web Part, which is described in the next section.

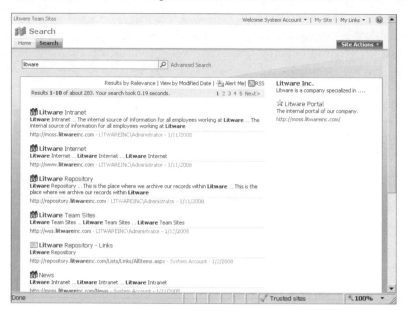

FIGURE 3-29 The Search Best Bets Web Part, on the right

The difference between the two Web Parts lies in the configuration of the properties that are exposed for each of them. The properties are classified in five sections in the tool pane. The following list summarizes what you can accomplish by configuring each property:

- **Results Display** This section, shown in Figure 3-30, contains a single, familiar, property: *Cross-Web Part Query ID*. This property defines the internal connection that is set up between this Web Part and the Search Core Results Web Part.

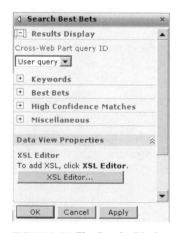

FIGURE 3-30 The Results Display configuration options for the Search Best Bets Web Part

■ **Keywords** This section, shown in Figure 3-31, contains two Boolean properties, and both are selected for the Search Best Bets Web Part. The first check box directs the Web Part to display the keyword name, and the second check box directs the Web Part to display the definition of the keyword. Chapter 5 shows how to create keywords and best bets as an administrator.

FIGURE 3-31 The Keywords configuration options for the Search Best Bets Web Part

■ **Best Bets** This section, shown in Figure 3-32, contains three Boolean properties, again all selected by default for this Web Part. The first check box controls the display of the titles of the best bets; these titles will be hyperlinked. The second check box can be configured to display or hide the description that the administrator associates with the best bet. The last check box controls the display of the URLs of the best bets. By default, a maximum of three best bets will displayed. You can change this value in the Best Bets Limit box if needed.

■ **High Confidence Matches** The properties in this section are blank for the Search Best Bets Web Part. The Search High Confidence Web Part, described in the next section, uses these settings to deliver its content; we'll review the properties there.

■ **Miscellaneous** The properties displayed in Figure 3-33 are similar in purpose to the ones discussed earlier for the Search Core Results Web Part. You can specify whether to hide or display error messages and provide sample data giving you an impression of the structure of the XML that you receive in the Web Part and an XSL link to an external file for replacing the XSL used for the transformation. You can also specify the caching options and select a check box to direct this Web Part to send its first best bet result to the other Web Parts that are connected to it internally through the query ID.

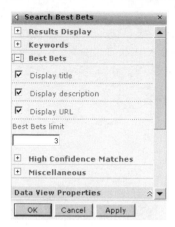

FIGURE 3-32 The Best Bets configuration options for the Search Best Bets Web Part

FIGURE 3-33 The Miscellaneous configuration options for the Search Best Bets Web Part

The Search High Confidence Results Web Part

To really appreciate this Web Part, enter the exact name of a user as your query string with the All Sites tab selected. You'll get a set of results similar to those shown in Figure 3-34 (provided that there exists a user exactly matching what you have entered). As you can see, the high confidence results are basically exact matches that are picked up and displayed by this Web Part. By default, only people-related metadata is configured for exact matches. In Chapter 5, you'll learn how to configure the high confidence results for other types of searches.

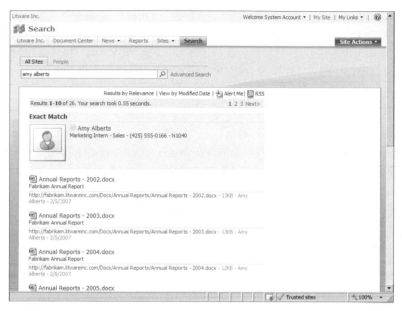

FIGURE 3-34 An exact match picked up and displayed by the Search High Confidence Results Web Part

As mentioned in the preceding section, this Web Part exposes the same configuration options as the Search Best Bets Web Part. The distinction here is that all of the properties in the Keywords and Best Bets sections are not set for the Search High Confidence Results Web Part. The other properties, shown in Figure 3-35, are the ones that get a value.

FIGURE 3-35 The High Confidence Matches configuration options for the Search High Confidence Results Web Part

First, you have the option to display or hide the titles of the matches. These will be displayed as links to the results. You also have the option to hide or display the image that is associated with the exact match. Clearing this check box would hide pictures in the results shown in Figure 3-34, which is of course a disappointment—people like to see faces. Other options let you show or hide the description of the exact match and the associated metadata or properties. By default, a maximum of one high confidence type match is displayed.

The Search Summary Web Part

This Web Part has a small set of configuration options, as shown in Figure 3-36. The first property specifies how the search query term is displayed to the user. The *Display Mode* property can be set to *Compact* or *Extended*. Error messages can be shown to or concealed from the user. The last property is the setting of the inner connection with the Search Core Results Web Part, again using the *Cross-Web Part Query ID* property.

FIGURE 3-36 The configuration options for the Search Summary Web Part

The Search Paging Web Part

The Search Paging Web Part is small but important. The properties available in the tool pane are shown in Figure 3-37.

FIGURE 3-37 The configuration options for the Search Paging Web Part

The Results Paging section contains properties for configuring the maximum number of links before and after the active page. Text labels or images can be displayed to enable the user to navigate from one page to the other. In the Miscellaneous section, you'll find the *Cross-Web Part Query ID* property again.

The Search Statistics Web Part

The configuration of this Web Part is straightforward. The properties available in the tool pane are shown in Figure 3-38.

FIGURE 3-38 The configuration options for the Search Statistics Web Part

The information can be rendered on one line or multiple lines. You can also specify what will be shown: number of results, total number of results, and search response time. The *Cross-Web Part Query ID* property is there to set up the internal connection with the Search Core Results Web Part.

The People Search Box Web Part

The People Search Box Web Part allows for relatively the same configuration options as the Search Box Web Part discussed earlier in this chapter. Two extra properties are available in the Miscellaneous section, as shown in Figure 3-39.

The Search Options pane, discussed at length in the previous chapter, enhances the end-user search experience by exposing managed properties that are part of the user profile in a simple and user-friendly way. You can decide to hide this feature if needed. More important, you can also extend the list of properties exposed in the Search Options pane.

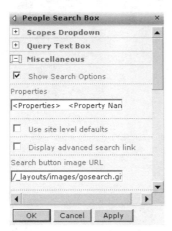

FIGURE 3-39 Two properties specific to the People Search Box Web Part

By default, the *Properties* property contains the following XML that stores the definition of the elements that make up the user experience in the Search Options pane:

```
<Properties>
<Property Name="FirstName" ManagedName="FirstName" ProfileURI="urn:schemas-microsoft-
com:sharepoint:portal:profile:FirstName"/>
<Property Name="LastName" ManagedName="LastName" ProfileURI="urn:schemas-microsoft-
com:sharepoint:portal:profile:LastName"/>
<Property Name="Department" ManagedName="Department" ProfileURI="urn:schemas-microsoft-
com:sharepoint:portal:profile:Department"/>
<Property Name="JobTitle" ManagedName="JobTitle" ProfileURI="urn:schemas-microsoft-
com:sharepoint:portal:profile:Title"/>
<Property Name="Responsibility" ManagedName="Responsibility" ProfileURI="urn:schemas-
microsoft-com:sharepoint:portal:profile:SPS-Responsibility"/>
<Property Name="Skills" ManagedName="Skills" ProfileURI="urn:schemas-microsoft-
com:sharepoint:portal:profile:SPS-Skills"/>
<Property Name="QuickLinks" ManagedName="QuickLinks" ProfileURI="urn:schemas-microsoft-
com:sharepoint:portal:profile:QuickLinks"/>
</Properties>
```

You can add another *Property* element containing information about the managed property. Assume, for example, that users want to easily find people matching certain interests. The user profile contains a property named Interests that is also by default exposed as a managed property. It is quite easy to expose this property in the Search Options pane, as shown in Figure 3-40.

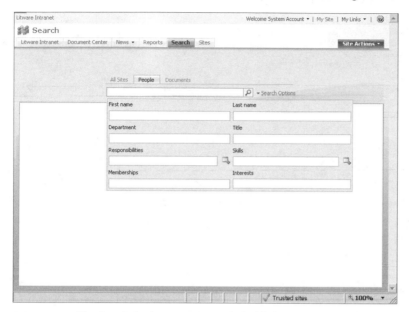

FIGURE 3-40 The Search Options pane extended with the *Interests* property

The following supplementary *Property* element will result in an extension to the Search Options pane:

```
<Property Name="Interests" ManagedName="Interests" ProfileURI="urn:schemas-microsoft-com:sharepoint:portal:profile:SPS-Interests"/>
```

The element contains the display name, the name of the managed property, and the value for *ProfileURI*. The value of *ProfileURI* is perhaps not obvious here. *ProfileURI* is a string that you can retrieve from the page showing the details of the crawled property. You navigate to the administration site of your SSP and the Search Settings page. Continue by clicking the Metadata Property Mappings link to search in the list of managed properties for the property named *Interests*. Figure 3-41 shows the page. Scroll down to find the managed property named Interests.

Don't click the managed property itself—click the *People:SPS-Interests* crawled property that is mapped to it. Figure 3-42 shows the page that displays the details of the crawled property. At the top of the page, you'll find the information you need to insert in the *Property* element described earlier.

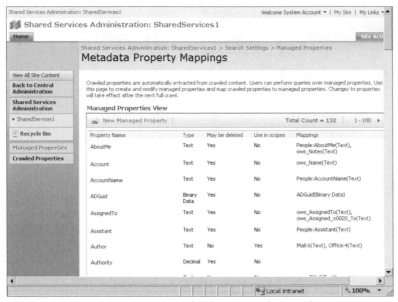

FIGURE 3-41 The administration page for the managed properties

FIGURE 3-42 The value of *ProfileURI* for the crawled property

The People Search Core Results Web Part

The search results of a people-related query are displayed primarily by the People Search Core Results Web Part on the People Search Results page. Refer to the section "The Search Core Results Web Part" earlier in this chapter, since most of the properties reviewed there are also available for the People Search Core Results Web Part.

There are, however, some differences. The first is the list of sorting options. Figure 3-43 shows the configurations that are available in the Results Display/Views section of the tool pane for the People Search Core Results Web Part.

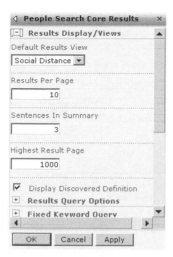

FIGURE 3-43 The Results Display/Views configuration options for the People Search Core Results Web Part

For the People Search Core Results Web Part, you do not have the option to sort on a modified date. This sorting option is replaced by the Social Distance sorting option, which was described in the previous chapter. The other available sorting option is sorting based on the relevance rank score.

All of the properties in the Results Query Options section are the same as for the Search Core Results Web Part. There is, however, a different XML string that is used for the *Selected Columns* property. The XML is now compiled from elements that expose the people-related metadata. The following is the default for that property:

```
<root xmlns:xsi="http://www.w3.org/2001/XMLSchema-instance">
 <Columns>
  <Column Name="AccountName"/>
  <Column Name="UserProfile_GUID"/>
  <Column Name="PreferredName"/>
  <Column Name="JobTitle"/>
  <Column Name="Department"/>
  <Column Name="WorkPhone"/>
  <Column Name="OfficeNumber"/>
  <Column Name="AboutMe"/>
  <Column Name="PictureURL"/>
  <Column Name="WorkEmail"/>
  <Column Name="WebSite"/>
  <Column Name="Path"/>
  <Column Name="HitHighlightedSummary"/>
  <Column Name="HitHighlightedProperties"/>
  <Column Name="Responsibility"/>
  <Column Name="Skills"/>
  <Column Name="SipAddress"/>
 </Columns>
</root>
```

You can easily add a new column here that points to one of the people-related managed properties.

The procedure to configure the People Search Core Results Web Part is the same as the one described earlier for the Search Core Results Web Part. Figure 3-44 shows an example of the People Search Core Web Part configured with a fixed query on the home page of a team site. All of the employees who have something to do with operations are listed—that is, all of them match the fixed query *operations*.

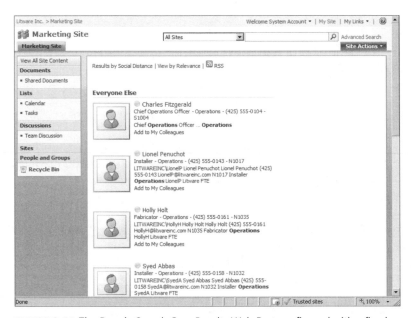

FIGURE 3-44 The People Search Core Results Web Part configured with a fixed query string

The rest of the properties grouped in the Miscellaneous section are identical to the ones you configure for the Search Core Results Web Part. The people-related search results are transformed in the same manner as the other search results by using an XSL that is accessible by clicking the XSL Editor button in the tool pane. The XSL used to render the people-related search results is discussed in the section titled "A Closer Look at the XSL" later in this chapter.

The Advanced Search Box Web Part

The last Web Part to review from an administrator angle is the Advanced Search Box Web Part. This Web Part is found on advanced Search pages, and it has plenty of configuration options for us to explore.

The Advanced Search box behaves differently from the Search box in the way it sends query parameters to the Search Results page. It employs an HTTP post request to send the query to the hidden search control on the results page. This control will in turn use the

FullTextSqlQuery class to execute the search instead of the *KeywordQuery* class. These classes are covered in detail in Chapter 8. The Advanced Search Box Web Part also hides the query in the Search box on the target results page.

The first set of properties is grouped in the Search Box section in the tool pane, as shown in Figure 3-45.

FIGURE 3-45 The Search Box configuration options for the Advanced Search Box Web Part

In Chapter 2, you learned about the three main areas of the Advanced Search box displayed to the user. All of the properties shown in Figure 3-45 can be used to configure the end-user search experience in what is known as the Search box area. The configuration is not a complex one—you simply specify which text box controls will be visible or hidden. You can also configure the label that is shown to the user for each of these controls.

The next section in the tool pane, Scopes, is shown in Figure 3-46. By default, no Scope Picker is displayed to the user in the Advanced Search Box Web Part. You can have the Web Part exhibit a Scope Picker by selecting the check box in the tool pane. In addition, you can set the label for the Scope Picker and also connect it to one of the display groups that is available at the level of the site collection. Two other pickers are visible by default: the Languages Picker and the Result Type Picker. Both can be hidden if needed, and you can set the text for their labels. The configuration of what they actually show is explained in a moment.

The third area in the Advanced Search Box Web Part is configured through the properties in the Properties section, shown in Figure 3-47.

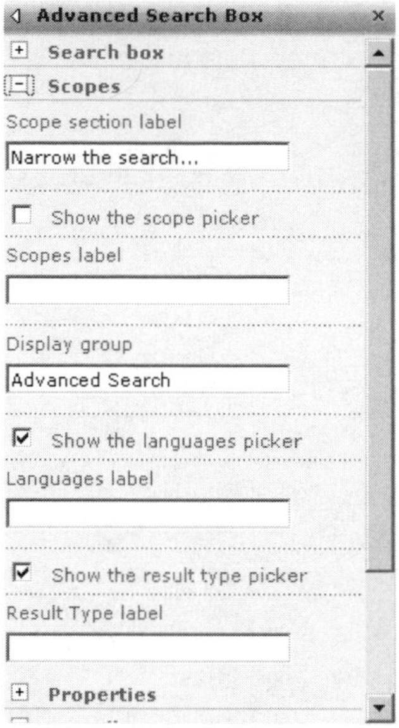

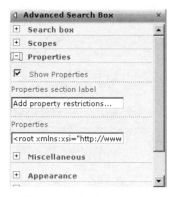

FIGURE 3-46 The Scopes section for the Advanced Search Box Web Part

FIGURE 3-47 The Properties configuration options for the Advanced Search Box Web Part

Users can use the Property Picker to create conditions including property filters for their queries. This functionality can be hidden if needed, but more interesting is that you can configure the content displayed in the property picker. The definition of that content is stored in the *Properties* property is an XML string similar to this:

```
<root xmlns:xsi="http://www.w3.org/2001/XMLSchema-instance">
 <LangDefs>
  <LangDef DisplayName="Arabic" LangID="1"/>
  <LangDef DisplayName="Bengali" LangID="69"/>
  <LangDef DisplayName="Bulgarian" LangID="2"/>
  <LangDef DisplayName="Catalan" LangID="3"/>
  <LangDef DisplayName="Chinese" LangID="4"/>
  <-- other elements removed for brevity -->
 </LangDefs>
```

```
<Languages>
 <Language LangRef="12"/>
 <Language LangRef="7"/>
 <Language LangRef="17"/>
 <Language LangRef="10"/>
</Languages>
<PropertyDefs>
 <PropertyDef Name="Path" DataType="text" DisplayName="URL"/>
 <PropertyDef Name="Size" DataType="integer" DisplayName="Size"/>
 <-- other elements removed for brevity -->
</PropertyDefs>
<ResultTypes>
 <ResultType DisplayName="All Results" Name="default">
  <Query/>
   <PropertyRef Name="Author" />
   <PropertyRef Name="Description" />
   <PropertyRef Name="FileName" />
   <-- other elements removed for brevity -->
  </ResultType>
  <ResultType DisplayName="Documents" Name="documents">
  <Query>IsDocument=1</Query>
  <PropertyRef Name="Author" />
  <PropertyRef Name="DocComments"/>
   <-- other elements removed for brevity -->
  </ResultType>
  <-- other elements removed for brevity -->
 </ResultTypes>
</root>
```

The first two child elements have to do with the language options displayed in the Advanced Search Web Part. The *LangDefs* element contains all of the potential languages for inclusion. The *Languages* element contains the actual list that is displayed to the user. Users can use this to filter results to include only documents written in the selected languages.

The *PropertyDefs* element lists all of the possible entries in the property picker. You must define for each of the entries the name of the managed property, the data type, and also the display name. The *PropertyDef* elements contain only the definition. The actual display of the properties is controlled by the *ResultTypes* element. For each *ResultType*, you define not only the *Query* but also the list of properties to be shown in the property picker.

Managed properties that are not yet part of this list or new managed properties created by the administrator in the SSP administration site must be registered first as a *PropertyDef* element. Assume, for example, that you have a managed property named *ProductCode*. The *PropertyDef* element to include in the XML can be the following:

```
<PropertyDef Name="ProductCode" DataType="string" DisplayName="Product Code"/>
```

To make it part of the user experience, you'll have to add a *PropertyRef* element as a child element for every *ResultType* element that you want the property to be associated with.

Here, for example, is the default *All Results* expanded with the new managed property *ProductCode*:

```
<ResultType DisplayName="All Results" Name="default">
  <Query/>
  <PropertyRef Name="Author" />
  <PropertyRef Name="Description" />
  <PropertyRef Name="FileName" />
  <-- other elements removed for brevity -->
  <PropertyRef Name="ProductCode" />
</ResultType>
```

You can create new entries in the Result Type picker to expose supplementary file extensions. The following XML snippet is a candidate child element of the *ResultTypes* element. Adding it to the XML will allow users to filter the results to include only Adobe .pdf file types.

> **Note** Users will benefit from this extra entry in the Result Type picker only if the file extension .pdf is included in the list of file types and if the proper *IFilter* is installed. The procedure to accomplish this is described in Chapter 5.

```
<ResultType DisplayName="All Results" Name="default">
  <Query FileExtension='pdf'/>
  <PropertyRef Name="Author" />
  <PropertyRef Name="Description" />
  <PropertyRef Name="FileName" />
  <-- other elements removed for brevity -->
  <PropertyRef Name="ProductCode" />
</ResultType>
```

A last property that we have to mention here is the single property that you'll find in the Miscellaneous section in the tool pane for the Advanced Search Box Web Part. This definition of the URL for a results page must be used for processing and displaying the search query.

A Closer Look at the XSL

There is often a thin line between the role of the administrator and the role of the developer in the world of SharePoint. Developers have to know their way around the various administration pages, while administrators often will come in contact with more developer-oriented technologies within their daily operations. To be effective, an administrator must, for example, have an understanding of the Collaborative Application Markup Language (CAML), configuration files such as web.config, and also, when it involves administration tasks related to search, a bit of knowledge about XSL. The topic of XSL is thus a good one to bridge the two parts within this chapter, allowing us to slowly but definitively move from the administrator angle to the developer angle.

We'll start with a review of the XSL of the search results, reviewing the out-of-the-box XSL that comes with the Search Core Results Web Part and continuing with some of its customization options. One popular customization is the extension of the XSL to include additional templates for rendering the extra columns that you get back from the search engine. A similar approach will be taken for the XSL that is used to render people-related search results. We'll conclude with a discussion of the XSL that is used for rendering the action links, including the technique to expose custom action links for end users in the Search Results pages.

Defining the Layout of the Search Results

The Search Core Results Web Part comes with a built-in XSL string that is used to transform the search results, which are returned to the Web Part as an XML string, into the view rendered as the body of the Web Part. You access this XSL in the tool pane for the Web Part using the XSL Editor button. It's not a bad idea to copy the complete string from the small text box that pops up if you click the button into a friendlier editing environment. The Microsoft Office SharePoint Designer is an option, and of course also Microsoft Visual Studio if you are developer-minded. Let's examine the flow of this XSL and review the steps that are needed to produce the results as they are displayed to the user.

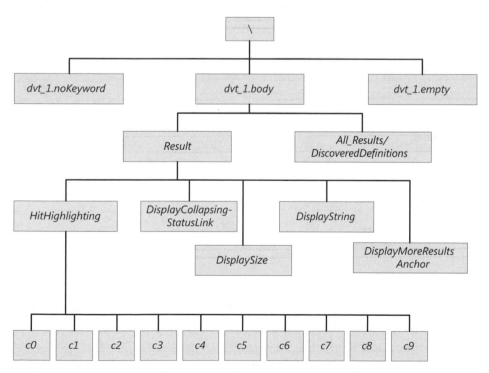

At the top of this XSL, you'll find the definition of various configuration parameters that are passed to the XSL at run time. A lot of these parameters are used to make decisions at some point during the transformation. All are values of properties that you can configure at the level of the Search Core Results Web Part in the tool pane, as described in the section "Configuring Search Web Parts" earlier in this chapter. Here is the full set:

```
<xsl:param name="ResultsBy" />
<xsl:param name="ViewByUrl" />
<xsl:param name="ViewByValue" />
<xsl:param name="IsNoKeyword" />
<xsl:param name="IsFixedQuery" />
<xsl:param name="ShowActionLinks" />
<xsl:param name="MoreResultsText" />
<xsl:param name="MoreResultsLink" />
<xsl:param name="CollapsingStatusLink" />
<xsl:param name="CollapseDuplicatesText" />
<xsl:param name="AlertMeLink" />
<xsl:param name="AlertMeText" />
<xsl:param name="SrchRSSText" />
<xsl:param name="SrchRSSLink" />
<xsl:param name="ShowMessage" />
<xsl:param name="IsThisListScope" />
<xsl:param name="DisplayDiscoveredDefinition" select="True" />
```

As you might know, XSL is read from the bottom to the top. The first pattern-matching rule is therefore to be found at the end of the string. It matches the root node of the XML to be transformed. This is the rule that initiates the whole process:

```
<!-- XSL transformation starts here -->
<xsl:template match="/">
 <xsl:if test="$AlertMeLink">
   <input type="hidden" name="P_Query" />
   <input type="hidden" name="P_LastNotificationTime" />
 </xsl:if>
 <xsl:choose>
   <xsl:when test="$IsNoKeyword = 'True'" >
     <xsl:call-template name="dvt_1.noKeyword" />
   </xsl:when>
   <xsl:when test="$ShowMessage = 'True'">
     <xsl:call-template name="dvt_1.empty" />
   </xsl:when>
   <xsl:otherwise>
     <xsl:call-template name="dvt_1.body"/>
   </xsl:otherwise>
 </xsl:choose>
</xsl:template>
```

All of the strings that start with a dollar sign ($) in the XSL are the values of the incoming parameters. Examples in the preceding snippet are *AlertMeLink*, *IsNoKeyword*, and *ShowMessage*. As mentioned, these are used to branch the XSL. The first test is a check box for showing the user the link to create alerts. If the option is available, two hidden fields are included in the output. Both are used to store information that is used by the alerting mechanism. If there is no keyword filled in by the user and the fixed query property is not set, the user will see a message indicating that something is wrong. The output is part of the template named *dvt_1.noKeyword* that is called in the body of the *xsl:choose* statement.

Here is the content of that template. It shows just the proper string for the proper context:

```
<!-- When there is no keyword to issue the search -->
<xsl:template name="dvt_1.noKeyword">
 <span class="srch-description">
   <xsl:choose>
    <xsl:when test="$IsFixedQuery">
      Please set the 'Fixed Query' property for the webpart.
    </xsl:when>
    <xsl:otherwise>
      Enter one or more words to search for in the search box.
    </xsl:otherwise>
    </xsl:choose>
 </span>
</xsl:template>
```

It is also possible that the user might enter a search query that results in zero items coming back from the search engine. If the administrator configured the Search Core Results Web Part to show an error message, the following template will be taken into consideration. The action links are displayed along with a message telling the user that nothing was found.

```
<!-- When empty result set is returned from search -->
<xsl:template name="dvt_1.empty">
 <div class="srch-sort">
   <xsl:if test="$AlertMeLink and $ShowActionLinks">
    <span class="srch-alertme" >
      <a href ="{$AlertMeLink}" id="CSR_AM1" title="{$AlertMeText}">
       <img style="vertical-align: middle;"
         src="/_layouts/images/bell.gif" alt="" border="0"/>
        <xsl:text disable-output-escaping="yes"> </xsl:text>
        <xsl:value-of select="$AlertMeText" />
      </a>
     </span>
   </xsl:if>
    <xsl:if test="string-length($SrchRSSLink) &gt; 0 and $ShowActionLinks">
     <xsl:if test="$AlertMeLink">
      |
     </xsl:if>
     <a type="application/rss+xml" href ="{$SrchRSSLink}"
      title="{$SrchRSSText}" id="SRCHRSSL">
       <img style="vertical-align: middle;" border="0"
         src="/_layouts/images/rss.gif" alt=""/>
        <xsl:text disable-output-escaping="yes"> </xsl:text>
        <xsl:value-of select="$SrchRSSText"/>
     </a>
    </xsl:if>
 </div>
 <br/><br/>
 <span class="srch-description" id="CSR_NO_RESULTS">
 No results matching your search were found.
```

```
<ol>
 <li>Check your spelling. Are the words in your query
   spelled correctly?</li>
 <li>Try using synonyms. Maybe what you're looking for uses
   slightly different words.</li>
 <li>Make your search more general. Try more general terms in
   place of specific ones.</li>
 <li>Try your search in a different scope. Different scopes can
   have different results.</li>
 </ol>
 </span>
</xsl:template>
```

The most interesting part here is the call to the *dvt_1.body* template. This is the template driving the rest of the transformation whenever the search query results in search result items returned by the search engine. A *DIV* element is inserted in the output. The following block is all about the rendering of the action links (if the option is turned on for the Web Part). Before the closing *DIV* element that is output, a call to find a matching template is performed. If we deal with a fixed keyword query configuration and the More Results link has been configured, it will be shown immediately after the closing *DIV* element.

```
<xsl:template name="dvt_1.body">
   <div class="srch-results">
  <xsl:if test="$ShowActionLinks">
  <div class="srch-sort"> <xsl:value-of select="$ResultsBy" />
   <xsl:if test="$ViewByUrl">
     |
   <a href ="{$ViewByUrl}" id="CSR_RV" title="{$ViewByValue}">
    <xsl:value-of select="$ViewByValue" />
   </a>
   </xsl:if>
   <xsl:if test="$AlertMeLink">
     |
    <span class="srch-alertme" > <a href ="{$AlertMeLink}" id="CSR_AM2"
title="{$AlertMeText}"><img style="vertical-align: middle;" src="/_layouts/images/bell.gif"
alt="" border="0"/><xsl:text disable-output-escaping="yes"> </xsl:text><xsl:value-
of select="$AlertMeText" /></a>
    </span>
   </xsl:if>
   <xsl:if test="string-length($SrchRSSLink) &gt; 0">
     |
    <a type="application/rss+xml" href ="{$SrchRSSLink}" title="{$SrchRSSText}"
id="SRCHRSSL"><img style="vertical-align: middle;" border="0" src="/_layouts/images/rss.gif"
alt=""/><xsl:text disable-output-escaping="yes"> </xsl:text><xsl:value-of
select="$SrchRSSText"/></a>
   </xsl:if>
  </div>
  <br /><br />
  </xsl:if>
  <xsl:apply-templates />
  </div>
  <xsl:call-template name="DisplayMoreResultsAnchor" />
</xsl:template>
```

So the fun really starts with the *<xsl:apply-templates />* call in the preceding XSL just above the *</DIV>* statement. Here we are really going to start processing the XML. Earlier in this chapter, when we examined the configuration of the Search Core Results Web Part, we looked briefly at the structure of the XML containing the search results. So that you don't have to turn back to that page, here again is the snippet of XML that the XSL is going to transform now:

```
<All_Results>
  <Result>
    <id></id>
    <workid></workid>
    <rank></rank>
    <title> </title>
    <author> </author>
    <size></size>
    <url></url>
    <urlEncoded></urlEncoded>
    <description></description>
    <write></write>
    <sitename> </sitename>
    <collapsingstatus></collapsingstatus>
    <hithighlightedsummary>
      <c0></c0>
    </hithighlightedsummary>
    <hithighlightedproperties>
      <HHTitle>
        <c0></c0>
      </HHTitle>
      <HHUrl></HHUrl>
    </hithighlightedproperties>
    <contentclass> </contentclass>
    <isdocument></isdocument>
    <picturethumbnailurl></picturethumbnailurl>
    <imageurl imageurldescription=""> </imageurl>
  </Result>
</All_Results>
```

There is a template that matches the *Result* node. One by one, the *Result* elements in the XML are transformed into *SPAN* and *DIV* elements. First, the icon is rendered. A couple of local variables retrieve the values of the attributes for the *ID* and the *URL*:

```
<!-- This template is called for each result -->
<xsl:template match="Result">
  <xsl:variable name="id" select="id"/>
  <xsl:variable name="url" select="url"/>
  <span class="srch-Icon">
    <a href="{$url}" id="{concat('CSR_IMG_',$id)}" title="{$url}">
      <img align="absmiddle" src="{imageurl}" border="0"
      alt="{imageurl/@imageurldescription}" />
    </a>
  </span>
```

Next is a block that transforms the title of the search result. The title is rendered as a hyperlink, and the text of the link is parsed for any keywords that are part of the search query. Up to 10 keywords can be highlighted.

```
<span class="srch-Title">
  <a href="{$url}" id="{concat('CSR_',$id)}" title="{$url}">
    <xsl:choose>
      <xsl:when test="hithighlightedproperties/HHTitle[. != '']">
        <xsl:call-template name="HitHighlighting">
          <xsl:with-param name="hh" select="hithighlightedproperties/HHTitle" />
        </xsl:call-template>
      </xsl:when>
      <xsl:otherwise>
        <xsl:value-of select="title"/>
      </xsl:otherwise>
    </xsl:choose>
  </a>
  <br/>
</span>
```

The highlighting itself is delegated to a couple of additional templates that abstract the whole process. Each keyword is identified with an element in the XML returned by the search engine. These are matched, and a bold element surrounding the value is returned for each of them.

```
<xsl:template name="HitHighlighting">
 <xsl:param name="hh" />
 <xsl:apply-templates select="$hh"/>
</xsl:template>

<xsl:template match="ddd">
  &#8230;
</xsl:template>
<xsl:template match="c0">
    <b><xsl:value-of select="."/></b>
</xsl:template>
<xsl:template match="c1">
    <b><xsl:value-of select="."/></b>
</xsl:template>
<xsl:template match="c2">
    <b><xsl:value-of select="."/></b>
</xsl:template>
<xsl:template match="c3">
    <b><xsl:value-of select="."/></b>
</xsl:template>
<xsl:template match="c4">
    <b><xsl:value-of select="."/></b>
</xsl:template>
<xsl:template match="c5">
    <b><xsl:value-of select="."/></b>
</xsl:template>
<xsl:template match="c6">
    <b><xsl:value-of select="."/></b>
</xsl:template>
```

```
<xsl:template match="c7">
    <b><xsl:value-of select="."/></b>
</xsl:template>
<xsl:template match="c8">
    <b><xsl:value-of select="."/></b>
</xsl:template>
<xsl:template match="c9">
    <b><xsl:value-of select="."/></b>
</xsl:template>
```

Let's continue with the XSL that takes care of the processing of the result. The next block is for the rendering of the description. Also in the description, you can have keywords that must be highlighted. The preceding templates are called again when needed.

```
<div class="srch-Description">
  <xsl:choose>
    <xsl:when test="hithighlightedsummary[. != '']">
      <xsl:call-template name="HitHighlighting">
        <xsl:with-param name="hh" select="hithighlightedsummary" />
      </xsl:call-template>
    </xsl:when>
    <xsl:when test="description[. != '']">
      <xsl:value-of select="description"/>
    </xsl:when>
  </xsl:choose>
</div >
```

The next part of the core template in the XSL deals with the processing of the *URL* value for the search result item. A hyperlink is constructed, and possible keywords are highlighted.

```
<p class="srch-Metadata">
  <span class="srch-URL">
    <a href="{$url}" id="{concat('CSR_U_',$id)}" title="{$url}" dir="ltr">
      <xsl:choose>
        <xsl:when test="hithighlightedproperties/HHUrl[. != '']">
          <xsl:call-template name="HitHighlighting">
            <xsl:with-param name="hh"
                select="hithighlightedproperties/HHUrl" />
          </xsl:call-template>
        </xsl:when>
        <xsl:otherwise>
          <xsl:value-of select="url"/>
        </xsl:otherwise>
      </xsl:choose>
    </a>
  </span>
```

Last is the processing for the other properties that are part of the search result item: the *size*, *author*, and *write* properties. Each has its own dedicated XSL template where the processing is defined.

```
<xsl:call-template name="DisplaySize">
   <xsl:with-param name="size" select="size" />
</xsl:call-template>
```

```
        <xsl:call-template name="DisplayString">
            <xsl:with-param name="str" select="author" />
        </xsl:call-template>
        <xsl:call-template name="DisplayString">
            <xsl:with-param name="str" select="write" />
        </xsl:call-template>
        <xsl:call-template name="DisplayCollapsingStatusLink">
            <xsl:with-param name="status" select="collapsingstatus"/>
            <xsl:with-param name="urlEncoded" select="urlEncoded"/>
            <xsl:with-param name="id" select="concat('CSR_CS_',$id)"/>
        </xsl:call-template>
    </p>
  </xsl:template>
```

The rendering of the information about the file size, the author of the item, and the last modification date is done in two generic templates:

```
<!-- The size attribute for each result is prepared here -->
<xsl:template name="DisplaySize">
  <xsl:param name="size" />
    <xsl:if test='string-length($size) &gt; 0'>
    <xsl:if test="number($size) &gt; 0">
     -
    <xsl:choose>
      <xsl:when test="round($size div 1024) &lt; 1">
          <xsl:value-of select="$size" /> Bytes
        </xsl:when>
        <xsl:when test="round($size div (1024 *1024)) &lt; 1">
            <xsl:value-of select="round($size div 1024)" />KB
        </xsl:when>
        <xsl:otherwise>
            <xsl:value-of select="round($size div (1024 * 1024))"/>MB
        </xsl:otherwise>
      </xsl:choose>
    </xsl:if>
  </xsl:if>
</xsl:template>
<!-- A generic template to display string with non 0 string length
    (used for author and lastmodified time -->
<xsl:template name="DisplayString">
  <xsl:param name="str" />
    <xsl:if test='string-length($str) &gt; 0'>
     -
    <xsl:value-of select="$str" />
    </xsl:if>
</xsl:template>
```

The link to view the possible duplicate items in the search results is processed by the XSL template named *DisplayCollapsingStatusLink*. Based on the value of the incoming *status* variable, a hyperlink is constructed with the proper text and URL.

```
<!-- document collapsing link setup -->
<xsl:template name="DisplayCollapsingStatusLink">
    <xsl:param name="status"/>
    <xsl:param name="urlEncoded"/>
```

```
    <xsl:param name="id"/>
    <xsl:if test="$CollapsingStatusLink">
      <xsl:choose>
          <xsl:when test="$status=1">
              <br/>
              <xsl:variable name="CollapsingStatusHref" select="concat(substring-
before($CollapsingStatusLink, '$$COLLAPSE_PARAM$$'), 'duplicates:&quot;', $urlEncoded,
'&quot;', substring-after($CollapsingStatusLink, '$$COLLAPSE_PARAM$$'))"/>
              <span class="srch-dup">
              [<a href="{$CollapsingStatusHref}" id="$id" title="{$CollapseDuplicatesText}">
              <xsl:value-of select="$CollapseDuplicatesText"/>
              </a>]
              </span>
          </xsl:when>
      </xsl:choose>
    </xsl:if>
</xsl:template>
```

Another block of XSL to look at is the one that takes care of the rendering of the More Results link at the bottom of the list of search results. The *DisplayMoreResultsAnchor* template is called within the core template named *dvt_1.body*, described earlier.

```
<xsl:template name="DisplayMoreResultsAnchor">
  <xsl:if test="$MoreResultsLink">
   <a href="{$MoreResultsLink}" id="CSR_MRL">
    <xsl:value-of select="$MoreResultsText"/>
   </a>
  </xsl:if>
</xsl:template>
```

All of the preceding XSL templates are applied on the *Result* node in the XML containing your search results. Possibly, you'll also see the discovered definitions in the results. These are rendered by the *All_Results/DiscoveredDefinitions* template:

```
<xsl:template match="All_Results/DiscoveredDefinitions">
  <xsl:variable name="FoundIn" select="DDFoundIn" />
  <xsl:variable name="DDSearchTerm" select="DDSearchTerm" />
  <xsl:if test="$DisplayDiscoveredDefinition = 'True' and
      string-length($DDSearchTerm) &gt; ">
    <script language="javascript">
      function ToggleDefinitionSelection()
      {
        var selection = document.getElementById("definitionSelection");
        if (selection.style.display == "none")
        {
          selection.style.display = "inline";
        }
        else
        {
          selection.style.display = "none";
        }
      }
    </script>
    <div>
```

```
    <a href="#" onclick="ToggleDefinitionSelection(); return false;">
      What people are saying about <b><xsl:value-of select="$DDSearchTerm"/></b></a>
    <div id="definitionSelection" class="srch-Description" style="display:none;">
      <xsl:for-each select="DDefinitions/DDefinition">
        <br/>
        <xsl:variable name="DDUrl" select="DDUrl" />
        <xsl:value-of select="DDStart"/>
        <b>
          <xsl:value-of select="DDBold"/>
        </b>
        <xsl:value-of select="DDEnd"/>
        <br/>
        <xsl:value-of select="$FoundIn"/>
        <a href="{$DDUrl}">
        <xsl:value-of select="DDTitle"/>
        </a>
      </xsl:for-each>
    </div>
  </div>
  </xsl:if>
</xsl:template>
```

Now that you have a good insight into the structure of the XSL that is initially delivered with the Search Core Results Web Part, it's time to cover some of the customization scenarios. Note that the customizations covered here are examples. You will no doubt have to come up with solutions to other requests made by users.

Customizing the Layout of the Search Results

We'll start with a small customization example. Assume that you've had a request to make a small change in the way the keywords are highlighted in the search results—instead of being displayed in bold, they should be highlighted in yellow.

To respond to this request, you navigate to the Search Center and enter a query that gives you a Search Results page filled with a sizable collection of search results. Switch the Search Results page to edit mode, and modify the shared properties of the Search Core Results Web Part. Click the XSL Editor button to open the dialog box with the initial XSL string. Because this is a small change, you can easily do the work in the dialog box itself. As mentioned earlier, up to 10 keywords can be highlighted in the details of a search result item display. For each of these, you have an XSL template. Changing one template should be enough to illustrate the idea. Find the template named *c0* in the XSL string, and change the contents as follows:

```
<span style='background-color:yellow'><xsl:value-of select="."/></span>
```

Save your work, and publish the page to see the search results, now with the yellow highlighting of the keyword, as shown in Figure 3-48.

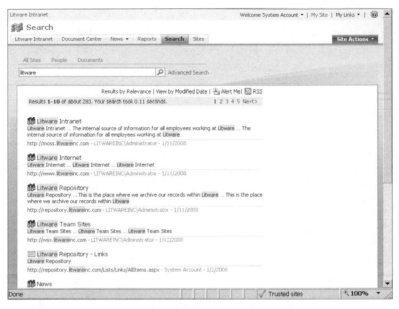

FIGURE 3-48 Customization of the highlighting in the search results

Another customization we'll work out is related to the work done earlier in this chapter. The Documents tab allows the user to enter a search query that returns only search results that have *Document* as the underlying content type. Figure 3-49 displays an example output with the default XSL.

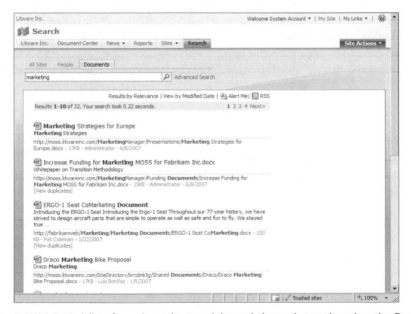

FIGURE 3-49 A list of search results containing only items that are based on the *Document* content type

What if users don't like the display in Figure 3-49? Look at another type of rendering, shown in Figure 3-50. What is the XSL customization needed to create this display? As you can see, the results are grouped by type of document. Every item is boxed, and the details are rendered in a different way from what you see in Figure 3-49. Also, a hyperlink is available that allows the user to open the library that contains the document displayed.

FIGURE 3-50 A more complex customization of the search results

Creating the XSL to render the results shown in Figure 3-50 is a bit more complicated than the alteration we did previously for highlighting. You'll probably need help from a tool that enables you to work out the XSL for this customization in a more WYSIWYG and automated way.

> **Note** Maybe you are very skilled in XSL and you are able to fire up Microsoft Notepad to crank out the XSL from scratch, but not a lot of people on this planet will be able to match you in this mission. It is a far better approach to employ an XSL editor to help you to construct the XSL needed. Many of these editors are available from third-party vendors.

Office SharePoint Designer 2007 is not exactly an XSL editor, but there is good support for the work you have to do here. First, there is an interesting Web Part, called the Data View Web Part. This is a Web Part that you can add only to Web Part pages in Office SharePoint Designer. Internally, it acts basically like the Search Core Results Web Part: data in the form of XML flows in as input, and using an XSL, the output results appear in the body of the Web Part as HTML. Office SharePoint Designer also uses IntelliSense when working with XSL, and most of the XSL can be visually edited. Let's explore the steps to create an XSL for the search results shown in Figure 3-50.

The requested grouping is based on the file extension of the document in the search results. This information is not directly available as one of the fields of the returned search details. A small change to the *Selected Columns* property of the Search Core Results Web Part will do the trick. In the Search Results page, switch the page to edit mode, and modify the shared properties of the Search Core Results Web Part. In the tool pane, expand the Results Query Options section to view the *Selected Columns* property. Open the XML in the dialog box, and add one more *Column* element to the initial list, as shown here:

```
<Column Name="FileExtension"/>
```

Perfect! You are now ready to concentrate on the XSL. The first step is to prepare sample data for the Data View Web Part to work with. The sample data in our case is the XML that is returned by the search engine. Earlier, you were introduced to the following small snippet of XSL that, when it is applied, returns the raw XML in the Search Core Results Web Part. Copy the default XSL that is part of the Search Core Results Web Part to a text file, since you'll need it later.

```
<xsl:stylesheet version="1.0" xmlns:xsl="http://www.w3.org/1999/XSL/Transform">
  <xsl:output method="xml" version="1.0" encoding="UTF-8" indent="yes"/>
    <xsl:template match="/">
      <xmp><xsl:copy-of select="*"/></xmp>
    </xsl:template>
</xsl:stylesheet>
```

Isolate the returned XML containing the search results in an XML file. You can do this by switching to the HTML source in the browser when the Search Results page is displayed and by copying the XML string that is part of the source. The XML string starts with a root node named *All_Results*. Notice that it also now includes the value for the *FileExtension* field for every result item.

Next open Office SharePoint Designer 2007. You are not going to make any modifications to a SharePoint site, but you still need to open one to be able to finish your work with the Data View Web Part. Once the site is opened in the designer, add a new .aspx page to the root of the site by clicking New on the File menu and then selecting ASPX. An empty Untitled1.aspx page is the result.

You'll import the XML file containing the sample data that will feed the Data View Web Part in a moment. On the Data View menu, click Manage Data Sources. The Data Source Library is displayed in one of the task panes, as shown in Figure 3-51.

You can add the XML file containing the search results with a click on the Add An Xml File link under the XML Files node. In the Data Source Properties dialog box, click the Browse button to navigate to the XML file, confirm the import, and finish by clicking the OK button in the next dialog box. The result is a subnode under the XML Files node in the Data Source Library. The subnode has the name of the imported XML file.

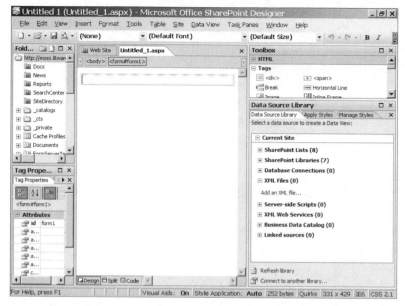

FIGURE 3-51 The Data Source Library in Office SharePoint Designer 2007

Figure 3-52 illustrates how you can now use the shortcut menu on the new node to select the Show Data option. The Data Source Details tab in the task pane is now activated, and it displays the sample data that is part of the XML file. Some of the data items are already selected and ready to be inserted in the page for the Data View Web Part. Select the *title*, *author*, *write*, *description*, and *hithighlightedsummary* fields, and then drag the fields onto the empty .aspx page.

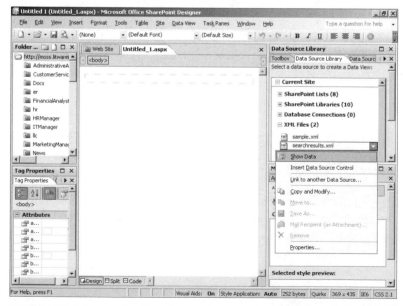

FIGURE 3-52 Selecting the Show Data option to review the contents of the XML file

An instance of the Data View Web Part is added to the page; it shows the search results already in a tabular format, as shown in Figure 3-53.

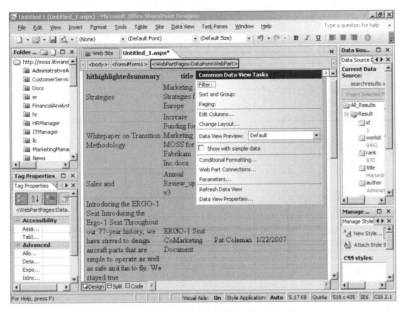

FIGURE 3-53 A first version of the Data View Web Part on the page

The display that we are trying to construct does not make use of the tabular layout. Figure 3-53 illustrates what happens if you expand the small smart tag that is associated with the Web Part. Figure 3-53 shows the small button that provides access to the smart tag menu in the upper-right corner of the page. The Common Data View Tasks dialog box contains many options, but for now, you'll make only one change: click Change Layout to display the Data View Properties dialog box, shown in Figure 3-54. Instead of the initial Basic Table view style, select the Repeating Form view style, and then click OK to close the dialog box.

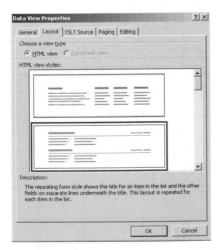

FIGURE 3-54 Changing the layout to the Repeating Form view style

The next step is the grouping of the items based on the type of document. Remember that you have included the extra field name *FileExtension* in the search results for this purpose. Open the Common Data View Tasks dialog box again by expanding the smart tag in the Data View Web Part, and select the Sort And Group option. In the Available Fields list, select the item name *fileextension*, and add it to the second list box. You want to use this field for the grouping, and therefore, you select the Show Group Header check box in the Group Properties area. Figure 3-55 shows the dialog box with the configuration for the grouping you want. Click OK to close the dialog box; the Data View Web Part regenerates its internal XSL to display the results nicely grouped by file extension.

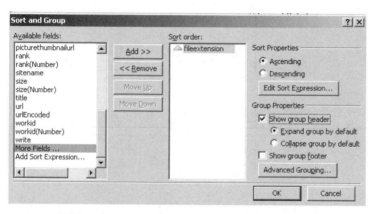

FIGURE 3-55 The configuration for the grouping of the search results

Now is a good time to switch the designer to split mode so that you can see the XSL that is used for the rendering of the results. One small change you might want to make is the removal of the actual label for the grouping line. Click in the Data View Web Part on the boldface text *fileextension*, and you'll notice that in the code editor, you immediately are positioned in the line that contains the XSL for the actual display. Remove the following lines, and when you've finished, click in the design view to check out the result of the change:

```
<xsl:text disable-output-escaping="yes" ddwrt:nbsp-preserve="yes"> </xsl:text>
<b><xsl:value-of select="$fieldtitle" /></b>
<xsl:if test="$fieldtitle">: </xsl:if>
```

Now you have nodes that have *DOCX*, *DOC*, or another file type as their text. Let's improve on this and change the XSL so that we have the name of the appropriate Microsoft Office system application. This will illustrate the rich support for writing XSL in the code editor. Position yourself again in the correct spot in the XSL by clicking in design view the text of the grouping node. The active line, which is part of an *<xsl:choose>* branching statement, should be

```
<xsl:value-of select="$fieldvalue" />
```

Remove the preceding line, and begin typing **<xsl:choose>**. Notice, as shown in Figure 3-56, that the IntelliSense support gives you all of the options that are available as you type the characters.

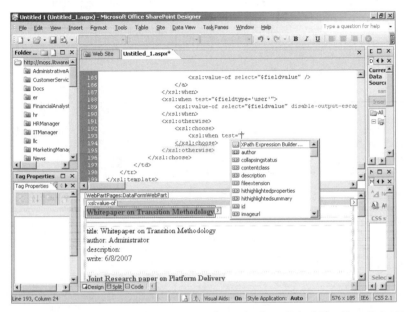

FIGURE 3-56 The rich IntelliSense support for authoring XSL in Office SharePoint Designer 2007

Complete the statements for the branching of the XSL by using the value of the *fileextension* field, as shown here:

```
<xsl:choose>
 <xsl:when test="fileextension='DOCX'">
  <b>Word 2007 Documents</b>
 </xsl:when>
 <xsl:when test="fileextension='DOC'">
  <b>Word Documents</b>
 </xsl:when>
 <xsl:when test="fileextension='XSLX'">
  <b>Excel 2007 Documents</b>
 </xsl:when>
 <xsl:when test="fileextension='XSL'">
  <b>Excel Documents</b>
 </xsl:when>
 <xsl:when test="fileextension='PPTX'">
  <b>PowerPoint 2007 Documents</b>
 </xsl:when>
 <xsl:when test="fileextension='PPT'">
  <b>PowerPoint Documents</b>
 </xsl:when>
 <xsl:otherwise>
  <b>Other Documents</b>
 </xsl:otherwise>
</xsl:choose>
```

The display of the title of the search result could be better. We'll place it above the horizontal rule, with the description just under it as the second line. The title should become a link containing the URL to the document in question. Click the title as it is currently displayed in design view. In code view, you are now positioned within the template named *dvt_1.rowview* containing the definition of the rendering of two rows: one containing the description and one containing the rest of the details of the search item. The following XSL can be used to replace this with a rendering that will bring you a step closer to what the user has in mind for the display:

```
<xsl:template name="dvt_1.rowview">
  <tr>
    <td width="100%">
        <xsl:value-of select="title" />
        <br/>
        <xsl:value-of select="description" />
    </td>
  </tr>
  <tr>
    <td width="100%">
        <xsl:value-of select="hithighlightedsummary/text()" />
        <br/>
        Document last modified on <xsl:value-of select="write" />
        by <xsl:value-of select="author" />.
        <br /><br />
    </td>
  </tr>
</xsl:template>
```

You can again use a smart tag to turn the title into a link. Click the small smart tag in the designer that is associated with one of your titles. Figure 3-57 provides a visual clue.

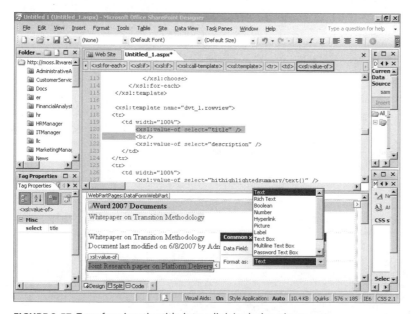

FIGURE 3-57 Transforming the title into a link in design view

Select *Hyperlink* as the value for the format. In the dialog box that appears as a result of your action, set the address to the value *{url}* and make sure that *{title}* is still the text that will be displayed to the user.

Now is probably a good time to verify the work already done within the Search Results page. Find the element named *XSL* in the code editor of Office SharePoint Designer 2007. Copy all of its inner text, and use this inner text to replace the XSL that is currently used by the Search Core Results Web Part. Save and apply the changes to see the transformation in action. If you have followed along, the rendering of the search results should be similar to what you see in Figure 3-58.

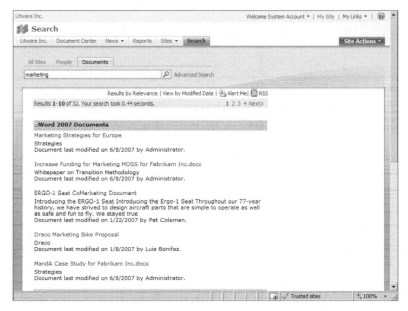

FIGURE 3-58 The search results transformed using the custom XSL so far

The values of the description and summary fields are tagged with elements identifying the keywords that must be highlighted. For now, you're not doing any of this. You should not have to spend much time on this, since in the default XSL that is part of the Search Core Results Web Part, the needed XSL templates are in place. Find the templates named *HitHighlighting*, *ddd*, and *c0* to *c9*. Copy the templates, and make them part of the XSL element in the code editor of Office SharePoint Designer 2007. Wherever you need the highlighting, you can make use of the new templates. A good candidate is the *HitHighlightingSummary* field. Find the line where the value is rendered (*<xsl:value-of select="hithighlightedsummary/text()" />*), and replace that line with the following:

```
<xsl:if test="hithighlightedsummary[. != '']">
 <xsl:call-template name="HitHighlighting">
  <xsl:with-param name="hh" select="hithighlightedsummary" />
 </xsl:call-template>
</xsl:if>
```

All of the keywords will now be rendered in bold, and we're coming closer to the end result. Spice it up now with some styles linked and used in the Search Center. The link displaying the title can be wrapped in a *SPAN* element connected to the CSS class *srch-Title*:

```
<span class="srch-Title"><a href="{url}" id="{concat('CSR_', $id)}">
<xsl:value-of select="title" /></a></span>
```

The *ID* attributes on search result links are crucial to the proper generating of reports storing information about how people are using search; this topic is covered in Chapter 4, "Search Usage Reports." If you do not include the attribute ID with the value *"{concat('CSR_', $id)}"* for the link, there will be no tracking of the clicked results. Chapter 4 documents this issue in more detail.

There is also a dedicated CSS class for the display of the description that is part of a search result item:

```
<span class="srch-Description"><xsl:value-of select="description" /></span>
```

And we can also immediately have the information regarding the author and the modification date displayed properly:

```
<span class="srch-Metadata">Document last modified on <xsl:value-of select="write" />
by <xsl:value-of select="author" />.</span>
```

One part of the original request is not addressed with the default XSL. Our users want to see a link associated with each search item that allows them to open the SharePoint library containing the document. This will be the final piece of our custom XSL, and it again is a nice demonstration of the powerful support for XSL in Office SharePoint Designer 2007. In the code editor, find the line rendering the author and the modification date again. Under it, add the following XSL:

```
<span class="srch-dup">[<a href="{substring-before(url,concat('/',title))}"
target="_blank">Open Containing Library</a>]</span><br /><br/>
```

Although this looks pretty complex, you'll get plenty of help from the XPath Expression Builder, which basically allows you to create the value for the *href* attribute of the link with a few simple clicks. The XPath Expression Builder is shown in Figure 3-59.

> **Note** Readers who are looking for ways to include the execution of some advanced scripting in the XSL via the *<msxsl:script>* tag might be disappointed—that tag is not supported in the Search Center by the Search Core Results Web Part. The Microsoft .NET XSL processor does support it, but only when explicitly enabled, and the Web Part does not do that.

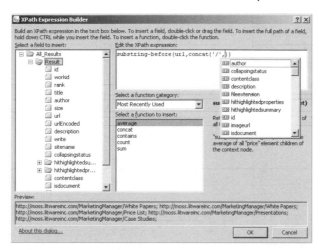

FIGURE 3-59 The XPath Expression Builder in Microsoft Office SharePoint Designer 2007

That's all we're going to cover here, but you can follow similar steps to apply many other enhancements to the XSL. You can again copy the XSL out of the code editor of Office SharePoint Designer 2007 and use it as the XSL for the Search Core Results Web Part. When you apply the new XSL, the rendering of the search results should look similar to the display shown earlier in Figure 3-50.

Displaying Custom Properties in the Search Results

The display of custom properties has already been covered to some extent in the preceding section, where the *fileextension* property was used for the grouping of the search results. Because this is one of the most requested customizations for the display of the search results, it deserves a bit more space here and another good example.

The index engine can be configured for the crawling of business data, as you'll see in Chapter 6, "Indexing and Searching Business Data," which is completely dedicated to this topic. The end-user search experience by default looks much like the one shown in Figure 3-60. Only the title and a small description are displayed. Often, there will be a request for the inclusion of more of the metadata in the rendering.

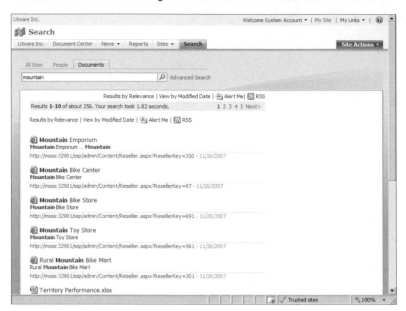

FIGURE 3-60 The default rendering of business data search results

Managed properties mapped to the metadata that you want to expose here have to be created by administrators in the search administration page at the level of the SSP. The steps to do this are covered in Chapter 5. For now, let's assume that the administrator has created the following managed properties representing metadata collected for a reseller: *ResellerName*, *ResellerAddress*, *ResellerZip*, *ResellerCity*, *ResellerCountry*, and *ResellerPhone*.

Your first task is to make sure that these fields are included in the XML returned by the search engine. Open the tool pane for the Search Core Results Web Part, and edit the *Selected Columns* property in the Results Query Options section. Insert the following list of *Column* elements:

```
<Column Name="ResellerName" />
<Column Name="ResellerAddress" />
<Column Name="ResellerZip" />
<Column Name="ResellerCity" />
<Column Name="ResellerCountry" />
<Column Name="ResellerPhone" />
```

The XSL can of course be customized in a number of ways. For simplicity, let's assume that we need a rather basic display of all of the extra details. We'll display them just above the URL of the search result item. In the tool pane of the Search Core Results Web Part, click the XSL Editor button. Locate the template that matches the *Result* node in the XSL. In that template, insert the following code snippet just above the rendering of the paragraph (the one associated with the *srch-Metadata* CSS class) for the URL:

```
<div class="srch-Description">
 <xsl:value-of select="reselleraddress" /> <br />
 <xsl:value-of select="resellerzip" /> -
 <xsl:value-of select="resellercity" />
 (<xsl:value-of select="resellercountry" />) <br />
 Phone: <xsl:value-of select="resellerphone" /> <br />
</div>
```

Apply the customized XSL, and review the results in the Search Core Results Web Part. Figure 3-61 shows the rendering of the resellers matching the entered search query string with the inclusion of the extra metadata.

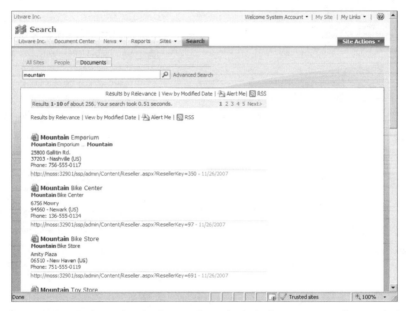

FIGURE 3-61 Business data in the search results, including extra metadata rendering included in the XSL

The *XSL Link* Property

In the preceding sections, we have already covered a number of customizations to the XSL used to render the search results. Expect a lot more of this type of work in the real world. We should pause here for a moment and ask ourselves whether there is a better approach for storing these XSL strings and whether there is a way to quickly make the custom XSL strings available in the locations where they are needed. Would it not be a good idea to introduce some level of reusability for the custom XSL strings?

These are definitely very good questions, and luckily, an immediate answer is available when you start using the *XSL Link* property that is exposed by Search Web Parts that use XSL for their rendering behavior. The *XSL Link* property is set to the URL for an XSL file, and when this is the case, the embedded XSL string is completely ignored. The location where you store the XSL files can be a document library that is part of the Search Center. But for that matter, it can be a place anywhere in the site collection or even outside it. As long as the user has the permission needed to navigate to it, it will be usable for the value of the *XSL Link* property in, for example, the Search Core Results Web Part.

You can test this quickly by creating a document library in the Search Center. On the Site Actions menu, click View All Site Content. On the toolbar, click the Create button, and then select the option to create a document library. Provide a title and possibly a description, and then continue with the provisioning of the instance. The files containing the XSL for the rendering of the search results can be nicely organized in a folder structure. For example, one folder for the basic customizations, one for the customizations at the level of the business data, one for customizations that are people-related, and so forth. This is a normal document library where you just store XSL files.

If you want to link, for example, the Search Core Results Web Part with one of the XSL files in the document library, you simply open the tool pane and set the URL of the XSL file you want to activate as the value of the *XSL Link* property. Apply the changes, and the XSL will override the embedded XSL string immediately.

Defining the Layout of the People Search Results

The Search Core Results Web Part is not the only Web Part working with an XSL for the rendering of the search results. If you have executed a People Query, your results will be rendered using an XSL that is embedded in the People Search Core Results Web Part.

The structure of the XML that will be transformed is a bit different compared with the XML discussed for the Search Core Results Web Part. It actually depends on the sorting option that you have selected. By default, the sorting is done based on the social distance, and you'll get the following raw XML:

```
<All_Results>
    <DummyResult>
      <Colleague />
    </DummyResult>
    <Result>
      <id>9</id>
      <accountname>LITWAREINC\PeterM</accountname>
      <userprofile_guid>59C5FEB9-26F0-48AA-95E3-E3CBB826E849</userprofile_guid>
      <preferredname>Peter Mullen</preferredname>
      <jobtitle>Product Compete Manager</jobtitle>
      <department></department>
      <workphone>(425) 555-0144</workphone>
      <officenumber>S1044</officenumber>
```

```
        <aboutme></aboutme>
        <pictureurl>http://moss:32901/personal/peterm/Shared Pictures/Profile
Pictures/PeterM.jpg</pictureurl>
        <workemail>PeterM@litwareinc.com</workemail>
        <website></website>
        <url>http://moss:32901/Person.aspx?guid=59C5FEB9-26F0-48AA-95E3-E3CBB826E849</url>
<urlEncoded>http%3A%2F%2Fmoss%3A32901%2FPerson%2Easpx%3Fguid%3D59C5FEB9%2D26F0%2D48AA%2D95E3
%2DE3CBB826E849</urlEncoded>
        <hithighlightedsummary>I assist our Product, Sales and <c0>Marketing</c0> teams by
providing actionable competitive insights.</hithighlightedsummary>
        <hithighlightedproperties>
          <HHTitle />
          <HHUrl>http://moss:32901/Person.aspx?guid=59C5FEB9-26F0-48AA-95E3-
3CBB826E849</HHUrl>
        </hithighlightedproperties>
        <responsibility>Competitive Research</responsibility>
        <skills>Orion;Neptune</skills>
        <sipaddress></sipaddress>
        <imageurl imageurldescription="File with extension:
spx">/_layouts/images/html16.gif</imageurl>
        <Colleague />
      </Result>
      <DummyResult>
        <ColleagueOfColleague />
      </DummyResult>
      <Result>
        <id>1</id>
        <accountname>LITWAREINC\DaveR</accountname>
        <userprofile_guid>DA38BB36-8F42-4E65-A534-ACD6A955F156</userprofile_guid>
        <preferredname>Dave Richards</preferredname>
        <!-- remaining part is left out for brevity-->
        <ColleagueOfColleague />
      </Result>
      <DummyResult>
        <Everyone />
      </DummyResult>
      <Result>
        <id>2</id>
        <accountname>LITWAREINC\SanjayJ</accountname>
        <userprofile_guid>19049F1B-B894-4671-BF8A-61C18FD9CABF</userprofile_guid>
        <preferredname>Sanjay Jacob</preferredname>
        <!-- remaining part is left out for brevity-->
        <EveryOne />
      </Result>
</All_Results>
```

You might be a bit surprised by the insertion of elements that are named *DummyResult*. Somebody in the product team might have an answer to why exactly this name was chosen, but basically, whenever you sort by social distance, you'll see these elements included in the XML. Sorting by social distance is, to be honest, not really a sorting, but more a grouping of the search results into different categories. The person in the search results can be you, your colleague, or even a colleague of a colleague; or when he or she is not a colleague, the person is categorized under the group *everyone*. Within each of the groups, relevance ranking is used to sort the items. If you sort the results by relevance, you have the following XML that is ready for transformation:

```
<All_Results>
    <Result>
      <id>1</id>
      <accountname>LITWAREINC\DaveR</accountname>
      <userprofile_guid>DA38BB36-8F42-4E65-A534-ACD6A955F156</userprofile_guid>
      <preferredname>Dave Richards</preferredname>
      <jobtitle>Director of Marketing</jobtitle>
      <department>Sales</department>
      <workphone>(425) 555-0108</workphone>
      <officenumber>S1008</officenumber>
      <aboutme></aboutme>
      <pictureurl></pictureurl>
      <workemail>DaveR@litwareinc.com</workemail>
      <website></website>
      <url>http://moss:32901/Person.aspx?guid=DA38BB36-8F42-4E65-A534-ACD6A955F156</url>
<urlEncoded>http%3A%2F%2Fmoss%3A32901%2FPerson%2Easpx%3Fguid%3DDA38BB36%2D8F42%2D4E65%2DA534
%2DACD6A955F156</urlEncoded>
      <hithighlightedsummary>Director of <c0>Marketing</c0>  <ddd /> Bike World joint
<c0>Marketing</c0>  <ddd /> Litware <c0>Marketing</c0> </hithighlightedsummary>
      <hithighlightedproperties>
        <HHTitle />
        <HHUrl>http://moss:32901/Person.aspx?guid=DA38BB36-8F42-4E65-A534-
ACD6A955F156</HHUrl>
      </hithighlightedproperties>
      <responsibility>Orion 2007 Project</responsibility>
      <skills></skills>
      <sipaddress></sipaddress>
      <imageurl imageurldescription="File with extension:
aspx">/_layouts/images/html16.gif</imageurl>
      <addtomycolleaguesurl>javascript:AddToColleagues('litwareinc\\daver')
</addtomycolleaguesurl>
    </Result>
</All_Results>
```

These two versions of the XML introduce a number of additional templates not included in the XSL for the Search Core Results Web Part. We'll cover these templates in the next section.

Let's first start with the rendering of the results when the results are sorted by relevance. The main part of the XML is again a list of *Result* elements, and each *Result* element contains child elements corresponding to managed properties. Some of these managed properties are part of the user profile maintained by the SSP for the person matching the query. Actually, the flow is similar to the flow described for the transformation occurring within the Search Core Results Web Part, as shown in the following illustration. In the XSL, the highlighting and the display of the size are done exactly as in the XSL for the Search Core Results Web Part.

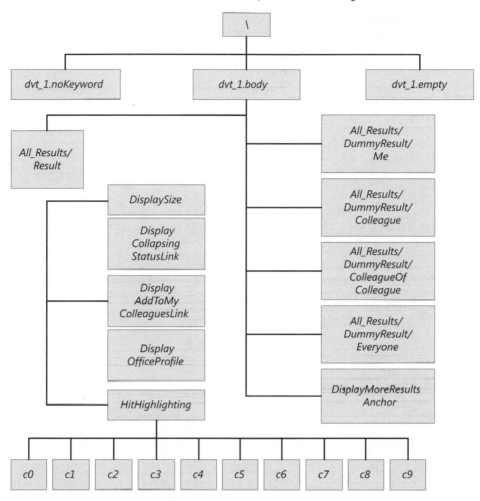

There are a couple of new templates that we have to look at in a bit more detail:

- **DisplayAddToMyColleaguesLink**   Office SharePoint Server 2007 is capable of maintaining a network of colleagues for the user. This information is part of that user's user profile. A link to add a person as a colleague is displayed in the search results. Clicking the link will execute a small JavaScript function that will take you to the page where you can complete the details for adding the person as a new colleague.

```
<xsl:template name="DisplayAddToMyColleaguesLink">
  <xsl:param name="url"/>
    <a href="{$url}">
     <xsl:value-of select="$AddToMyColleaguesText"/>
    </a><br/>
</xsl:template>
```

■ *DisplayOfficeProfile*   This template renders a number of properties that are part of the user profile. The job title, the department, the phone, and the office are by default part of the output. If you expose additional managed properties and you register these in the *Selected Columns* property of the People Search Core Results Web Part, you'll be able to extend this template to render those extra pieces of metadata.

```
<xsl:template name="DisplayOfficeProfile">
  <xsl:param name="title" />
  <xsl:param name="dep" />
  <xsl:param name="phone" />
  <xsl:param name="office" />
  <span class="psrch-Metadata">
  <xsl:if test='string-length($title) &gt; 0'>
   <xsl:value-of select="$title" />
   -
  </xsl:if>
  <xsl:if test='string-length($dep) &gt; 0'>
   <xsl:value-of select="$dep" />
   -
  </xsl:if>
  <xsl:if test='string-length($phone) &gt; 0'>
   <xsl:value-of select="$phone" />
   -
  </xsl:if>
  <xsl:if test='string-length($office) &gt; 0'>
   <xsl:value-of select="$office" />
  </xsl:if>
  </span>
  <br/>
</xsl:template>
```

The XSL statements in the template matching *All_Results/Result* contain statements similar to those in the XSL used by the Search Core Results Web Part. One interesting difference is the rendering of the presence information in the search result item. To start, you have the declaration of a number of variables at the top of the template:

```
<xsl:variable name="sip" select="sipaddress"/>
<xsl:variable name="prefix">IMNRC('</xsl:variable>
<xsl:variable name="suffix">')</xsl:variable>
```

Notice the value of the variable named *prefix*. This is the name of a JavaScript function that basically takes over the rendering of the small control that displays the presence information. Figure 3-62 illustrates the presence experience for the end user.

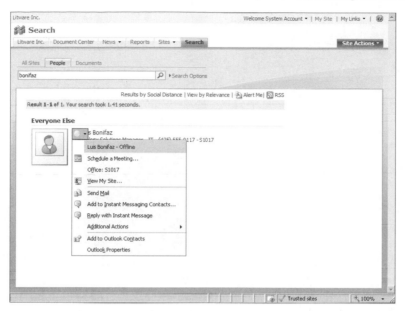

FIGURE 3-62 The presence information in the People Search Core Results Web Part

The call to the JavaScript function named *IMNRC* is included just in front of the title by the following code snippet—somewhere in the middle of the XSL for this template. It takes as input the Session Initiation Protocol (SIP) address or the e-mail address. The e-mail address will be used if no value for the *sipaddress* field is returned in the XML for the search results.

```
<span class="psrch-Title">
  <xsl:choose>
    <xsl:when test="sipaddress[. != '']">
      <img border="0" height="12" width="12" src="/_layouts/images/imnhdr.gif"
        onload="{concat($prefix, $sip, $suffix)}" ShowOfflinePawn="1"
        id="{concat('CSRP_',$id,',type=sip')}" />
    </xsl:when>
    <xsl:otherwise>
      <img border="0" height="12" width="12" src="/_layouts/images/imnhdr.gif"
        onload="{concat($prefix, $email, $suffix)}" ShowOfflinePawn="1"
        id="{concat('CSRP_',$id,',type=smtp')}" />
    </xsl:otherwise>
  </xsl:choose>
  <a href="{$url}" id="{concat('CSR_',$id)}">
    <xsl:value-of select="preferredname"/>
  </a>
</span>
```

Let's now have a look at this intriguing element named *DummyResult*. Each *DummyResult* element represents a category that is simply rendered as a header for a group of people, as shown in Figure 3-63.

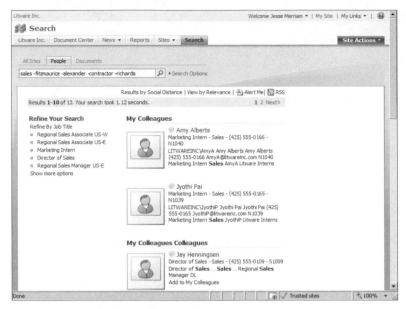

FIGURE 3-63 The *DummyResult* elements in action

In the XSL, you'll find a number of templates that match the nodes under the *DummyResult* element. They simply output the header text using the *srch-SocDistTitle* CSS class.

```
<xsl:template match="All_Results/DummyResult/Me">
    <span class="srch-SocDistTitle">
     <xsl:value-of select="$MeHeaderValue" />
    </span>
   </xsl:template>
<xsl:template match="All_Results/DummyResult/Colleague">
    <span class="srch-SocDistTitle">
      <xsl:value-of select="$CollHeaderValue" />
    </span>
</xsl:template>
<xsl:template match="All_Results/DummyResult/ColleagueOfColleague">
    <span class="srch-SocDistTitle">
      <xsl:value-of select="$CollOfCollHeaderValue" />
    </span>
</xsl:template>
<xsl:template match="All_Results/DummyResult/Everyone">
    <span class="srch-SocDistTitle">
      <xsl:value-of select="$EveryoneHeaderValue" />
    </span>
</xsl:template>
```

Defining the Layout for the Action Links

Action links can be rendered either as part of the Web Part displaying the search results or by the Search Action Links Web Part. The latter comes with a small XSL file that we'll look at in the next section.

To start, you have a couple of incoming parameters:

```
<xsl:param name="ResultsBy" />
<xsl:param name="ViewByUrl" />
<xsl:param name="ViewByValue" />
<xsl:param name="IsNoKeyword" />
<xsl:param name="ShowActionLinks" />
<xsl:param name="AlertMeLink" />
<xsl:param name="AlertMeText" />
<xsl:param name="SrchRSSText" />
<xsl:param name="SrchRSSLink" />
```

The core template is at the bottom of the XSL. Two small hidden fields are inserted to store data that is used by the alerting mechanism. These are rendered only when alerting is turned on at the level of the Web Part. At the end, the call is made for the *dvt_1.body* template:

```
<xsl:template match="/">
<xsl:variable name="Rows" select="/All_Results/Result" />
<xsl:variable name="RowCount" select="count($Rows)" />
<xsl:variable name="IsEmpty" select="$RowCount = 0" />
<xsl:if test="$AlertMeLink"><input type="hidden" name="P_Query" />
<input type="hidden" name="P_LastNotificationTime" />
</xsl:if>
<xsl:call-template name="dvt_1.body"/>
</xsl:template>
```

The actual rendering of the different actions is handled at the level of this *dvt_1.body* template. First is the rendering of the links for the sorting and then the rendering of the links for creating a search-based alert and the RSS feed.

```
<xsl:template name="dvt_1.body">
 <div>
  <xsl:if test="$ShowActionLinks">
   <div class="srch-sort-right">
     <xsl:value-of select="$ResultsBy" />
      <xsl:if test="$ViewByUrl"> | <a href ="{$ViewByUrl}" id="CSR_RV"
        title="{$ViewByValue}"><xsl:value-of select="$ViewByValue" /></a>
      </xsl:if>
     <xsl:if test="$AlertMeLink"> |
      <span class="srch-alertme" >
        <a href ="{$AlertMeLink}" id="CSR_AM2"
         title="{$AlertMeText}"><img style="vertical-align: middle;"
         src="/_layouts/images/bell.gif" border="0" alt=""/>
        <xsl:text disable-output-escaping="yes"> 
        </xsl:text><xsl:value-of select="$AlertMeText" /></a>
      </span>
```

```
        </xsl:if>
        <xsl:if test="$SrchRSSLink">| <a type="application/rss+xml"
          href ="{$SrchRSSLink}" title="{$SrchRSSText}" id="SRCHRSSL">
          <img style="vertical-align: middle;" border="0"
            src="/_layouts/images/rss.gif" alt=""/>
          <xsl:text disable-output-escaping="yes"> </xsl:text>
          <xsl:value-of select="$SrchRSSText"/></a>
        </xsl:if>
     </div>
    </xsl:if>
  </div>
</xsl:template>
```

Displaying Custom Actionable Links

You can extend the list of actionable links with your own custom actions. The example shown in Figure 3-64 is a link that allows the user to print the search results.

FIGURE 3-64 The custom action Print Results in the Search Action Links Web Part

The XSL for the custom action is inserted in the *dvt_1.body* template just before the closing *DIV* element:

```
| <a href="javascript:window.print()">Print Results</a>
```

Extending the End-User Search Experience Through Code

Next we'll have a look at the options for customizing and extending the search end-user experience from a developer angle. The goal is to give guidance on how you as a developer can create reusable extensions for the Search Center. The examples we'll cover include adding extra search-related page layouts and pages, adding tabs to the Search Center, dynamically adding and configuring the various Search Web Parts, and substituting the small Search box with a custom one.

Custom Search-Related Page Layouts

The role of a page layout is basically to provide a template for the actual pages that are created in the publishing site. The template defines what data will be captured, what the functionality is that will be delivered in the pages, and how the page is going to evolve from a draft version to a published version. Pages typically are not visible to everybody when they are in draft version. Publishing a page raises the version number from a minor one (0.1) to a major version number (1.0). Often this process is accomplished via a workflow.

More on Features

It is a best practice for SharePoint developers to make all solution components available by wrapping them in Features. A Feature is basically a collection of CAML files plus possibly .aspx pages and other types of helper files that are deployed to the front-end Web servers. The goal of a Feature is to make new functionality available within the server farm, all of the SharePoint sites hosted in an IIS Web Application, the site collection, or an individual site. Administrators can install a Feature and activate it when needed. For example, if there is a need for an extra tab connected to a custom search or Search Results page, you deliver this functionality as a Feature that administrators can activate in the Search Center. As a result, the new functionality becomes immediately available to the end user.

Features and all of the files making up the solution components (such as the accompanying .NET Framework assemblies) can also be packaged for automated distribution in a SharePoint server farm. This packaging is done through the creation of a SharePoint Solution. A SharePoint Solution is actually a Microsoft Cabinet file with the extension .wsp. SharePoint Solutions are added by administrators to the solution store that is part of the configuration database. The Solution Management page in the SharePoint 3.0 Central Administration gives administrators the option to deploy the solution to the front-end Web Servers and/or the application servers that are part of the server farm. In this chapter, we won't go that far—we'll concentrate here on building the solution components and delivering them using Features.

The four page layouts we looked at earlier in this chapter are not perfect examples of what page layouts are all about. They are not really used for capturing data, as for example, a page layout for a press release would be in a publishing portal. The page layouts for the Search Center are all about the arrangement and initial configuration of the various search-related Web Parts on the pages.

Until now, we have used the default page layouts that come with the Search Center. It is not difficult to provision new custom Search page layouts if you need them. Assume, for example, that a business requests a different type of Search page—they ask for a Search page where the Search Box Web Part is at the center of the page and immediately configured so that only specific business data can be searched for, as shown in Figure 3-65.

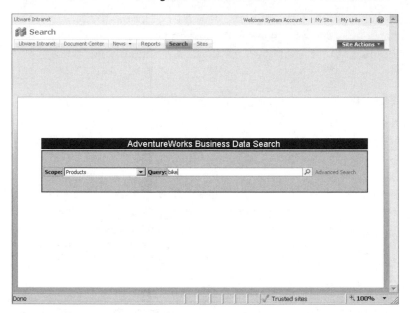

FIGURE 3-65 A custom Search page based on a custom page layout populated with a preconfigured Search Box Web Part

The same can be requested for the search results. The results can be displayed in the default Search Results page, but again there is the option to provision a custom page layout for the display. Search Results pages, like the one shown in Figure 3-66, can be created based on the custom page layout.

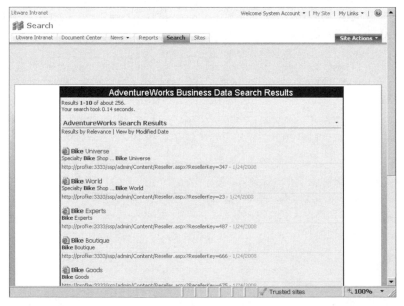

FIGURE 3-66 A custom Search Results page based on a custom page layout populated with a number of Search Web Parts

The custom pages we'll provide allow the user to play around only with data from the AdventureWorks SQL Server database. Only AdventureWorks business data is shown in the search results, and only the AdventureWorks-related search scopes are displayed by the Scope Pickers. The Search Web Parts are configured to include AdventureWorks-related metadata and will use custom XSL to render this as part of the search results end-user experience. Let's first walk through the steps for building a set of reusable search-related custom page layouts.

> **More Information**   The sample code in this chapter and throughout this book is available at the companion Web site. Note that, for brevity, not all of the code and the XML contained within the last solution is given in the chapter text, so it's a good idea to download the sample code—for this example, found in the CustomSearchCenterDemo folder—and open the Visual Studio project so that you can follow along.

The sample project contains a folder structure that matches the folder structure you'll find when you open Windows Explorer and navigate to the folder where Windows SharePoint Services 3.0 and Office SharePoint Server 2007 store the out-of-the-box Features. In Solution Explorer, open the Template\Features\AdventureWorks.Search folder, and review the contents. You'll see a number of XML files and also a subfolder named PageLayouts with some .aspx pages.

Open the Feature definition file, available as feature.xml, in the code editor of Visual Studio. The Feature is identified by a globally unique identifier (GUID), has its own title and description, and is scoped at the level of the site collection. Note that you can have all of the strings localized with the help of resource files.

```
<Feature Id="{3497A0E8-C80E-4271-9496-31D60C0A8A06}"
  Title="AdventureWorks Products Search Center Feature"
  Description="Custom Search Center components for the AdventureWorks products."
  Version="1.0.0.0"
  Scope="Site"
  Hidden="FALSE"
  ImageUrl="AdventureWorks/advlogo.jpg"
  xmlns="http://schemas.microsoft.com/sharepoint/">
  <ElementManifests>
   <ElementManifest Location="contenttype.xml"/>
   <ElementManifest Location="pagelayouts.xml"/>
  </ElementManifests>
</Feature>
```

The CAML in the Feature definition file contains one *ElementManifest* registration pointing to the definition of a content type and another *ElementManifest* registration for the provisioning of the three custom page layouts.

Let's have a closer look at the definition of the content type. Remember from previous discussions that each page layout in Office SharePoint Server 2007 is associated with a content type. The content type defines what the underlying metadata for the page layout is, along with the definition of the rules that have to be applied on that content. In the sample project, there is a custom content type named *AdventureWorks Search* that will be used instead of the *Welcome Page* content type. The latter is used for the default search-related page layouts. The new content type inherits from the *Page* content type, but there is no immediate need for new metadata since the custom search and Search Results pages you'll create are not really used for capturing data.

> **Note** It is still a good practice to create your own content type and not tie your custom page layouts directly to the Microsoft base content type. You might in the future need that additional custom metadata, and having your own content type already underlying your page layouts will make it easier to make that modification and push it to the pages that are created, even if these pages are in production.

Study for a moment the CAML definition for the content type contained in *contenttype.xml*. Open the file in the code editor of Visual Studio, or just have a look here:

```
<Elements xmlns="http://schemas.microsoft.com/sharepoint/">
  <ContentType ID="0x010100C568DB52D9D0A14D9B2FDCC96666E9F2007948130EC3DB064584E2199
54237AF3900AD75712D3AC24EABA74304EAE403CB4F"
    Name="AdventureWorks Search"
    Description="Content type used by the AdventureWorks Search page layouts"
    Group="AdventureWorks Publishing Content Types"
    Sealed="FALSE"
    Version="0">
    <FieldRefs></FieldRefs>
    <DocumentTemplate TargetName="/_layouts/CreatePage.aspx" />
  </ContentType>
</Elements>
```

The value for the *ID* attribute might look a bit strange, but it is actually fairly easy to construct. You first retrieve the *ID* of your parent content type. In our example, this is the *Page* content type. You append two zeros (*00*) to the *ID* of the parent. Next you create a new GUID, and you remove the curly braces and the dashes. This becomes the last part of the *ID* of your new content type.

> **More Information** The *Page* content type is defined by the PublishingResources Feature, which can be found in the 12\Features\PublishingResources folder. You can review all of the definitions for the publishing content types if you open the PublishingContentTypes.xml file in this folder. The element named *$Resources:cmscore,contenttype_page_name;* is the one used in the sample as the base content type.
>
> Additional content types that inherit from the *AdventureWorks Search* content type do not require a new GUID appended to the *ID*. Once you have uniquely forked your content types, you can create new IDs simply by adding *00* and increasing the number (*01*, *02*, and so on) with every new content type you want to make available.

The second *ElementManifest* element in the Feature definition file points to the pagelayouts. xml file. This CAML file contains the definition of the custom page layouts: one for Search pages, one for Search Results pages, and one for advanced Search pages. The following is the definition for the page layout that will be used to create the AdventureWorks dedicated Search pages. It does not yet contain the CAML for including the Search Box Web Part; this will be covered in a moment.

```
<Elements xmlns="http://schemas.microsoft.com/sharepoint/">
  <Module Name="PageLayouts" List="116" Path="PageLayouts" Url="_catalogs/masterpage">
    <File Url="AWsearch.aspx" Type="GhostableInLibrary" >
      <Property Name="Title" Value="AdventureWorks Search Page" />
      <Property Name="MasterPageDescription"
       Value="A dedicated page for searching in the AdventureWorks database" />
      <Property Name="ContentType"
       Value="$Resources:cmscore,contenttype_pagelayout_name;" />
      <Property Name="PublishingAssociatedContentType" Value=";#AdventureWorks
Search;;#0x010100C568DB52D9D0A14D9B2FDCC96666E9F2007948130EC3DB064584E219954237AF3900
AD75712D3AC24eabA74304EAE403CB4F;#" />
      <Property Name="PublishingPreviewImage"
        Value="~SiteCollection/_catalogs/masterpage/Preview Images/searchpage.gif,
~SiteCollection/_catalogs/masterpage/Preview Images/searchpage.gif" />
    </File>
  </Module>
</Elements>
```

The page layout files can be found in the Template\Features\AdventureWorks Search\ PageLayouts folder in Solution Explorer. The preceding CAML snippet provisions the AWsearch.aspx page. With the activation of the Feature built previously, this file will become an item in the Master Pages And Page Layouts Gallery. Every site collection that has the publishing infrastructure active contains one gallery of this type.

A *Module* element in combination with the *File* element does the trick of the provisioning. The *Module* element has a name, and it requires that you provide the details of the folder or the document library where the file has to be uploaded. The Master Pages And Page Layouts Gallery is identified with *ID 116*, which is the value for the *List* attribute of the *Module* element. The *Url* attribute is set to the relative path to the gallery in the virtual file system: *_catalogs/masterpage*. A final attribute for the *Module* element is the *Path* attribute. Its value is important, since this is the location where SharePoint will look for the .aspx file it needs to provision. In the sample project, this is the PageLayouts folder.

Every file that has to be provisioned to the location defined at the level of the *Module* element is represented by a *File* element. The first attribute of this element is *Url*; it contains the name of the .aspx file. The second attribute, named *Type*, has the value *GhostableInLibrary*, since the final destination of the .aspx file is a document library.

Note You use *Ghostable* as the value for the *Type* attribute if you intend to provision pages to internal folders within the virtual file system maintained by your SharePoint site instead of document libraries.

During the provisioning, a number of properties need to receive a value. You must see the provisioning really as creating an item in the Master Pages And Page Layouts Gallery. When you do this in the browser, you first select Page Layout on the New menu, and then you assign values to the different fields that are presented. The CAML definition basically does the same thing by means of *Property* elements that you create as part of the *File* element. The first two *Property* elements are for the title and the description of the new item in the gallery. The next *Property* element is used for the setting of the content type for the new item. Two content types are associated with the Master Pages And Page Layouts Gallery: one for master pages and one for page layouts. Setting the value of the *ContentType* property to *$Resources:cmscore,contenttype_pagelayout_name;* ensures that you'll have a page layout item in the gallery. The most important property is *PublishingAssociatedContentType*. The value is a ';#' delimited string: the first part of the string is the name of the content type that will be associated with the page layout, and the second part is the ID of the content type.

If you were to install and activate the Feature, including the pieces we have discussed so far, the result would be three entries in the Master Pages And Page Layouts Gallery, as shown in Figure 3-67.

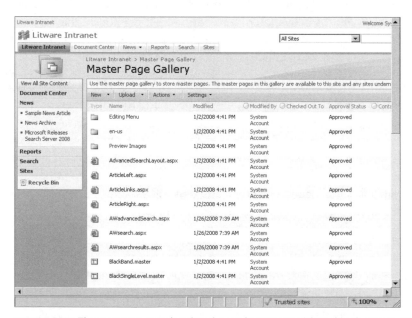

FIGURE 3-67 Three custom search-related page layouts provisioned in the Master Pages And Page Layouts Gallery

You can create pages based on the new page layouts when performing that operation in the top-level site of your portal. Figure 3-68 shows the Create Page page with the new page layouts displayed as part of the list.

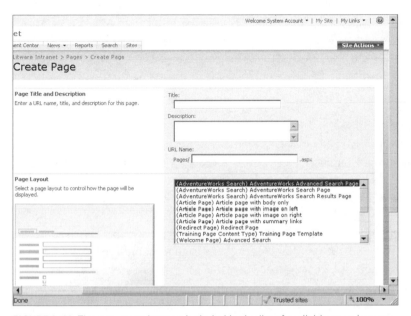

FIGURE 3-68 The new page layouts included in the list of available page layouts

There is, however, a tiny problem when you try to create pages based on the new page layouts from within the Search Center. The Search Center does not display the custom page layouts. It displays only the four default search-related page layouts. The reason for this is simple. In a site definition for a publishing site, you have the option to restrict the list of available page layouts. Earlier in this chapter, we reviewed the site definition for the Search Center With Tabs. If you quickly open the ONET.XML that is part of the *SRCHCEN* site definition (available in the 12\TEMPLATE\SiteTemplates\SRCHCEN folder) and you navigate to the *Configuration* element, you'll see the following activation of a Feature at the level of the site:

```
<Feature ID="22A9EF51-737B-4ff2-9346-694633FE4416">
  <Properties xmlns="http://schemas.microsoft.com/sharepoint/">
    <Property Key="WelcomePageUrl"
          Value="$Resources:cmscore,List_Pages_UrlName;/default.aspx" />
    <Property Key="AvailablePageLayouts"
Value="~SiteCollection/_catalogs/masterpage/searchmain.aspx:~SiteCollection/_catalogs/
masterpage/SearchResults.aspx:~SiteCollection/_catalogs/masterpage/PeopleSearchResults.
aspx:~SiteCollection/_catalogs/masterpage/AdvancedSearchLayout.aspx" />
    <Property Key="SimplePublishing" Value="true" />
  </Properties>
</Feature>
```

The Feature in question is displayed here. It contains a property named *AvailablePageLayouts*. This property is used to limit the list of page layouts. Changing the value here is not really an option. You'll have to programmatically fix this problem during the activation of your Feature. At that time, an event is fired, and you are able to connect some code using the rich Microsoft Office SharePoint Server Publishing API. You compile that code into a .NET Framework assembly that you deploy in the Global Assembly Cache (GAC). These types of assemblies are also referred to as *Feature Receivers*: the "Feature Receivers" sidebar provides more information if you are unfamiliar with this technique.

Feature Receivers

A *Feature Receiver* is a class in a .NET Framework assembly that is connected to the Feature within the Feature.xml file by means of two attributes: *ReceiverAssembly* and *ReceiverClass*. The first attribute has as a value the full strong name of the .NET Framework assembly, and the second attribute receives as a value the fully qualified name (that is, the namespace plus the name of the class). The class inherits from the *Microsoft.SharePoint.SPFeatureReceiver* class, which is an abstract class exposing four members that act as stubs for the four possible events that are triggered while administrators install, activate, deactivate, or uninstall the Feature. Here is the skeleton of a Feature Receiver:

```
using System;
using System.Collections.Generic;
using System.Text;
using Microsoft.SharePoint;

namespace AdventureWorks.Search
{
    public class AdvSearchFeatureReceiver : SPFeatureReceiver
    {
        public override void FeatureActivated
            (SPFeatureReceiverProperties properties)
        { }
        public override void FeatureDeactivating
            (SPFeatureReceiverProperties properties)
        { }
        public override void FeatureInstalled
            (SPFeatureReceiverProperties properties)
        { }
        public override void FeatureUninstalling
            (SPFeatureReceiverProperties properties)
        { }
    }
}
```

More in-depth coverage regarding Features and Feature Receivers can be found in *Inside Microsoft Windows SharePoint Services 3.0* (Microsoft Press, 2007), written by Ted Pattison and Daniel Larson.

The sample project contains a Feature Receiver class named *AWSearchFeatureReceiver*. This class demonstrates what can be done programmatically when the Feature is activated and deactivated. The part that we're interested in now is shown here:

```
public override void FeatureActivated(SPFeatureReceiverProperties properties)
{
    SPSite sitecol = (SPSite)properties.Feature.Parent;
    SPWeb searchsite = sitecol.OpenWeb("/SearchCenter");
    PublishingSite pubsite = new PublishingSite(sitecol);
    PublishingWeb pubweb = PublishingWeb.GetPublishingWeb(searchsite);
    int nrLayouts = pubweb.GetAvailablePageLayouts().GetLength(0);
    PageLayout[] pagelayouts = new PageLayout[ nrLayouts + 3];
    int i = 0;
    for (i = 0; i < nrLayouts; i++)
    {
        pagelayouts[i] = pubweb.GetAvailablePageLayouts()[i];
    }
    pagelayouts[i] = pubsite.PageLayouts["/_catalogs/masterpage/AWsearch.aspx"];
    pagelayouts[i+1] = pubsite.PageLayouts["/_catalogs/masterpage/AWsearchresults.aspx"];
    pagelayouts[i+2] = pubsite.PageLayouts["/_catalogs/masterpage/AWadvancedsearch.aspx"];
    pubweb.SetAvailablePageLayouts(pagelayouts, false);
    pubweb.Update();
    searchsite.Dispose();
}
```

Both the Microsoft.SharePoint.dll and the Microsoft.SharePoint.Publishing.dll are referenced within the project. The first two lines of code connect you to the site collection and then to the Search Center site. The Feature itself is scoped at the level of the site collection, and therefore, you can get a reference to the *SPSite* instance by casting the *Parent* property of the *SPFeature* object to the *SPSite* type. The *SPFeature* object is accessible itself via the incoming *SPFeatureReceiverProperties* parameter. A call to the *OpenWeb* method with the relative path (starting from the root) to the Search Center returns you the *SPWeb* instance. All types discussed here are part of the *Microsoft.SharePoint* namespace.

There are types in the *Microsoft.SharePoint.Publishing* namespace that map to the *SPSite* and *SPWeb* but expose additional functionality that is part of the publishing infrastructure. You can create a *PublishingSite* instance passing the *SPSite* instance to the constructor. A *PublishingWeb* instance is returned by calling the static method *GetPublishingWeb* of the *PublishingWeb* class. The input parameter is now the *SPWeb* instance.

The *GetAvailablePageLayouts* method of the *PublishingWeb* instance returns the four default Search page layouts described earlier as an array. This array must be extended with the new page layouts. The new page layouts are retrieved at the level of the site collection using the *PageLayouts* property exposed by the *PublishingSite* instance. A small loop does the trick to expand the array to include seven page layouts instead of four. Once the loop is finished, a call to the *SetAvailablePageLayouts* defined for the *PublishingWeb* type followed by a call to the *Update* method of the same type will push the changes to the content database.

Figure 3-69 shows the Search Center containing the three additional page layouts after the installation of the Feature.

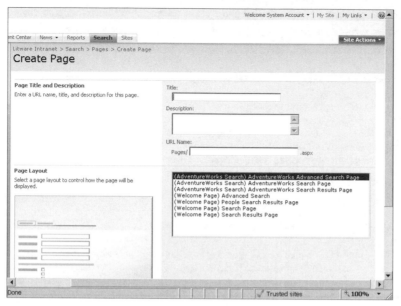

FIGURE 3-69 Custom Search Page Layouts in the Search Center

There are no pages yet created based on these new page layouts. The *AWSearchFeatureReceiver* class in the sample project contains a block of code that will make this happen during the activation of the Feature:

```
PageLayout AWsearchlayout =
    pubsite.PageLayouts["/_catalogs/masterpage/AWsearch.aspx"];
PageLayout AWresultslayout =
    pubsite.PageLayouts["/_catalogs/masterpage/AWsearchresults.aspx"];
PageLayout AWadvancedsearchlayout =
    pubsite.PageLayouts["/_catalogs/masterpage/AWadvancedsearch.aspx"];

PublishingPageCollection pages = pubweb.GetPublishingPages();

PublishingPage searchPage = pages.Add("AWsearch.aspx", AWsearchlayout);
searchPage.Title = "AdventureWorks Search Page";
searchPage.Update();

PublishingPage resultsPage = pages.Add("AWsearchresults.aspx", AWresultslayout);
resultsPage.Title = "AdventureWorks Search Results Page";
resultsPage.Update();

PublishingPage advancedSearchPage =
    pages.Add("AWadvancedsearch.aspx", AWadvancedsearchlayout);
advancedSearchPage.Title = "AdventureWorks Advanced Search Page";
advancedSearchPage.Update();

if (searchPage.ListItem.File.CheckOutStatus != SPFile.SPCheckOutStatus.None)
{
    searchPage.CheckIn(string.Empty);
    searchPage.ListItem.File.Publish(string.Empty);
}
```

```
if (resultsPage.ListItem.File.CheckOutStatus != SPFile.SPCheckOutStatus.None)
{
    resultsPage.CheckIn(string.Empty);
    resultsPage.ListItem.File.Publish(string.Empty);
}
if (advancedSearchPage.ListItem.File.CheckOutStatus != SPFile.SPCheckOutStatus.None)
{
    advancedSearchPage.CheckIn(string.Empty);
    advancedSearchPage.ListItem.File.Publish(string.Empty);
}
```

The *PublishingWeb* instance exposes the *GetPublishingPages* method that returns the collection containing objects of type *PublishingPage*. These are the pages available at that time in the *Pages* library. Creating a new page in the *Pages* library is not difficult. You call the *Add* method, giving it the name of the page you want to create and next the *PageLayout* instance you want to base the page on. You must call the *Update* method if you make changes to the properties of the new *PublishingPage* to push the changes to the content database.

A page created in the *Pages* library is initially checked out and therefore not published. A quick call to the *CheckIn* method at the level of the *PublishingPage* instance followed by a call to the *Publish* method at the level of the *SPFile* will do the job. The page is nothing more than a new file in the *Pages* document library, and as a result, all of the API operations at the level of *SPListItem* and *SPFile* are available to you.

To conclude the discussion of how you can provision custom page layouts and create pages based on those layouts programmatically, we'll have a look at the internals of the .aspx pages representing the page layouts. These pages are part of the Feature and are located in the PageLayouts folder. Opening one (AWSearch.aspx, for example) is sufficient to get an understanding of the structure of a page layout. The page inherits from the *PublishingLayoutPage* class defined in the *Microsoft.SharePoint.Publishing* namespace. The *meta:progid* attribute enables the customization of the page in Office SharePoint Designer 2007. The rest of the page follows the structure of a normal Web Part page containing one or more Web Part zones. These zones will be populated with one or more Search Web Parts in a moment.

A Developer View of the Search Web Parts

There are several search-related Web Parts, and all of them are advertised to the administrators via the Office SharePoint Server Search Web Parts Feature (physically represented as 12\TEMPLATE\FEATURES\SearchWebParts). This Feature can be activated in every type of site collection within your server farm, both for sites that have the publishing Features turned on and for sites that do not. As a result, you can also use these Web Parts on pages within a site collection consisting only of collaboration sites such as team sites, Wikis, blogs, and workspaces. If you open the Add A Web Part dialog box, you'll see the Web Parts listed under the Search group. In Search Center sites, they are also displayed as suggested Web Parts at the top of the list in the dialog box. Most of the Web Parts are delivered via Microsoft.Office.Server.Search.dll; the namespace to look for within this assembly is *Microsoft. Office.Server.Search.WebControls*.

> **Important** Before you continue reading, be aware that at the time of writing, Microsoft has sealed all of the Search Web Parts, and your options as a developer to configure them programmatically are not endless. A lot of restrictions are involved here, and as we look at the different Web Parts, we'll cover these to some extent.

Microsoft.Office.Server.Search.WebControls.AdvancedSearchBox

This is the only Web Part that is available by default on pages created based on the Advanced Search page layout. Table 3-3 lists all of the properties exposed by this Web Part; as you can see, most of these properties are self-explanatory.

TABLE 3-3 Microsoft.Office.Server.Search.WebControls.AdvancedSearchBox Properties

Property	Description
TextQuerySectionLabelText	Label for the search box section
AndQueryTextBoxLabelText	Label for the All Words search box
NotQueryTextBoxLabelText	Label for the None Of These Words search box
OrQueryTextBoxLabelText	Label for the Any Words search box
PhraseQueryTextBoxLabelText	Label for the Exact Phrase search box
ShowAndQueryTextBox	Check box to hide or display the All Words search box
ShowNotQueryTextBox	Check box to hide or display the None Of These Words search box
ShowOrQueryTextBox	Check box to hide or display the Any Words search box
ShowPhraseQueryTextBox	Check box to hide or display the Exact Phrase search box
ScopeSectionLabelText	Label for the Scopes section
ShowScopes	Check box to hide or display the Scope Picker control
ScopeLabelText	Label for the Scope Picker control
DisplayGroup	The display group that the Scope Picker control has to consult for the list of search scopes
ShowLanguageOptions	Check box to hide or display the language options
LanguagesLabelText	Label for the language options
ShowResultTypePicker	Check box to hide or display the Result Type Picker
ResultTypeLabelText	Label for the Result Type Picker
ShowPropertiesSection	Check box to hide or display the Properties section
PropertiesSectionLabelText	Label for the Properties section
Properties	XML defining what the content will be for the language options, the Result Type picker, and the Property Picker
SearchResultPageURL	URL of the page displaying the search results for the query executed via the advanced Search page

Let's return to the sample project. You have the option to add Web Parts to the pages you provision using the Feature by using either the declarative approach or the programmatic one. The declarative approach is an injection of the *AllUsersWebPart* CAML element in the elements.xml file—the file containing the provisioning definition of your page layouts. You'll see a sample of this approach in a moment. The Advanced Search Web Part instance can also be inserted in the page in a programmatic way during the activation of the Feature. Remember that the different search-related pages are also created at that time.

The following block of code shows how to get started:

```
SPFile advpage = searchsite.GetFile("Pages/AWadvancedsearch.aspx");
advpage.CheckOut();
SPLimitedWebPartManager wpmgr =
  advpage.GetLimitedWebPartManager(PersonalizationScope.Shared);
```

A call to the *GetFile* method of the *SPWeb* instance passing the relative *Url* of the page stored in the *Pages* library returns you the *SPFile* instance. Because you are working in a publishing site, a checkout is required before you can make modifications to the page. Every page in the *Pages* library is associated with a master page (for example, the default.master if you are working within a collaboration portal). One of the many controls that are made available within the master page is the *SPWebPartManager*. This is a hidden control that coordinates all of the Web Part infrastructure. You can grab the reference to this control by calling the *GetLimitedWebPartManager* method of the *SPFile* instance. The *PersonalizationScope* parameter allows you to get the instance controlling the shared view or the personal view of the page. Next you can create an instance of the *AdvancedSearchBox* class and configure the properties, as shown in the following snippet of code:

```
AdvancedSearchBox advWP = new AdvancedSearchBox();
advWP.Title = "AdventureWorks Advanced Search";
advWP.ShowAndQueryTextBox = true;
advWP.ShowNotQueryTextBox = true;
advWP.ShowOrQueryTextBox = true;
advWP.ShowPhraseQueryTextBox = true;
advWP.ShowLanguageOptions = false;
advWP.ShowScopes = true;
advWP.DisplayGroup = "AdventureWorks";
advWP.ShowPropertiesSection = true;
XmlDocument doc = new XmlDocument();
doc.LoadXml(GetResourceText("AdventureWorks.Search.AWSearchProperties.xml"));
advWP.Properties = doc.OuterXml;
advWP.SearchResultPageURL = "AWsearchresults.aspx";
```

The first set of properties is used to configure the display of the different controls that allow users to enter their queries. Our sample assumes that two shared search scopes, *AdventureWorks Products* and *AdventureWorks Employees*, have been created and are associated with a custom display group named *AdventureWorks* within the site collection. This is further explained in Chapter 5.

The interesting part is the setting of the property named *Properties*. It contains the XML that is used to populate the Languages Picker, the Result Type Picker, and the Property Picker. In the sample, a small XML file named AdvSearchProperties.xml is included as an embedded resource. This XML file contains the *PropertyDef* and *PropertyRef* elements. Both are used to expose three managed properties: *ProductNumber*, *ProductName*, and *ProductLine*. Those will be the only properties that users will be able to select in the Advanced Search page. Notice also the setting of the *SearchResultPageURL* property. The value is the custom Search Results page that is also part of the sample.

The final lines of code ensure that the Web Part instance is actually added to the page. The collection of Web Parts on the page is coordinated by the *SPWebPartManager*, and you use the *AddWebPart* method to place the new instance in one of the Web Part zones. Don't forget to check in and publish the page so that it becomes available to the users visiting the Search Center. Here is the code:

```
wpmgr.AddWebPart(advWP, "MidUpperRightZone", 1);
wpmgr.SaveChanges(advWP);
advpage.CheckIn(string.Empty);
advpage.Publish(string.Empty);
```

All of this will result in the Advanced Search page now containing the Advanced Search box configured with these properties, as shown in Figure 3-70.

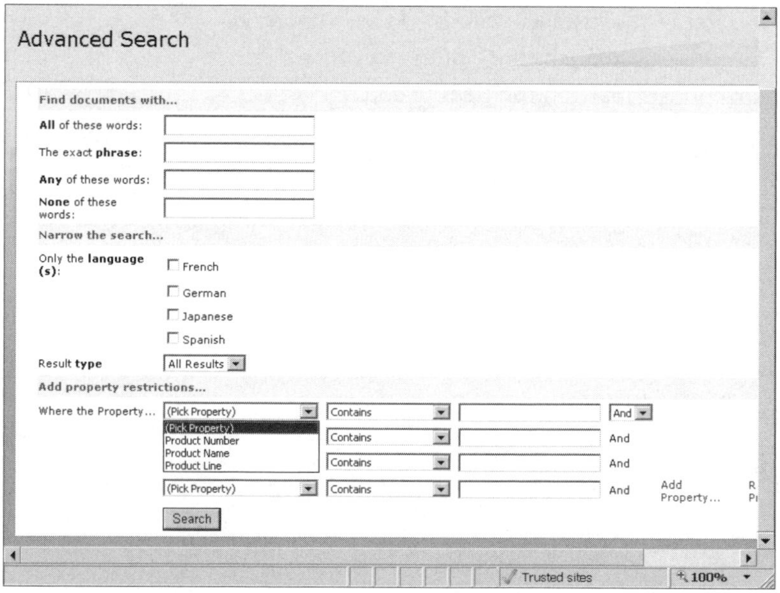

FIGURE 3-70 The customized Advanced Search Web Part

Microsoft.SharePoint.Portal.WebControls.SearchBoxEx

This Web Part captures the query entered by the user and is by default available on the pages based on the page layout for the Search pages. Table 3-4 lists all of the properties that are accessible in your code.

TABLE 3-4 Microsoft.SharePoint.Portal.WebControls.SearchBoxEx Properties

Property	Description
DropDownModeEx	This property is used to get or set the various modes listed in the Scope Picker. Six modes are defined by the *DropDownModesEx* enumeration: *HideScopeDD* for not showing the Scope Picker; *ShowDD* for showing the Scope Picker; *ShowDD_DefaultContextual* for showing the Scope Picker with the custom scopes and the contextual scopes, of which the last scope will be the default; *ShowDD_DefaultURL* for showing the Scope Picker with the custom scopes, of which the one passed via the 's' query string parameter will be the default; *ShowDD_NoContextual* for showing the Scope Picker excluding the contextual scopes; and *ShowDD_NoContextual_DefaultURL* for showing the Scope Picker excluding the contextual scopes and defaulting to the scope passed via the 's' query string parameter.
DropDownWidth	Width of the Scope Picker control in pixels.
TextBeforeDropDown	Text of the label for the Scope Picker.
TextBeforeTextBox	Text of the label for the Search text box.
TextBoxWidth	Width of the Search text box.
AppQueryTerms	Additional query terms that can be appended to the query entered by the user.
AppQueryTermsLabel	Label to be used for the additional query terms.
QueryPromptString	Text that can be displayed within the Search text box to invite the user to enter a query.
AppendToQuery	Check box to indicate whether the additional query terms have to be appended.
UseSiteDefaults	Check box to indicate whether to use the default Search Results page defined at the level of the site collection or the value provided for the *SearchResultPageURL*. If no value is provided, the results will be displayed by the default Search Results page: osssearchresults.aspx.
ShowAdvancedSearch	Check box to hide or display the Advanced Search link.
GoImageUrl	Link for the Go search button image.
GoImageUrlRTL	Link for the Go search button image right-to-left.
GoImageActiveUrl	Link for the active Go search button image.
GoImageActiveUrlRTL	Link for the active Go search button image right-to-left.

Property	Description
AdvancedSearchPageURL	URL for the Advanced Search page.
SearchResultPageURL	URL for the Search Results page.
DisplaySubmittedSearch	Check box to hide or display the submitted search in the Search Results page.
ScopeDisplayGroupName	Display group that defines the entries in the Scope Picker.

In the sample project, the Search Box Web Part is added to the AWsearch.aspx in a declarative way instead of the programmatic way that we used with the previous Web Part. Adding Web Parts declaratively can be done by adding an *AllUsersWebPart* element as a child element of the *File* element in the CAML file defining the page layout—in the sample, the pagelayouts.xml file. A first attribute for this element is the name of the Web Part Zone where you want to drop the Web Part, and the second is the order, in case there are multiple Web Parts. The following extract is from the pagelayouts.xml for AWsearch.aspx:

```
<AllUsersWebPart WebPartZoneID="MiddleLeftZone" WebPartOrder="1">
  <![CDATA[
   <WebPart xmlns:xsi="http://www.w3.org/2001/XMLSchema-instance"
    xmlns:xsd="http://www.w3.org/2001/XMLSchema"
    xmlns="http://schemas.microsoft.com/WebPart/v2">
  <Title>Search box</Title>
  <FrameType>None</FrameType>
  <Description>Used to search document and items.</Description>
  <IsIncluded>true</IsIncluded>
  <ZoneID>TopZone</ZoneID>
  <PartOrder>1</PartOrder>
  <FrameState>Normal</FrameState>
  <Width>420px</Width>
  <AllowRemove>true</AllowRemove>
  <AllowZoneChange>true</AllowZoneChange>
  <AllowMinimize>true</AllowMinimize>
  <AllowConnect>true</AllowConnect>
  <AllowEdit>true</AllowEdit>
  <AllowHide>true</AllowHide>
  <IsVisible>true</IsVisible>
  <Assembly>Microsoft.SharePoint.Portal, Version=12.0.0.0, Culture=neutral,
PublicKeyToken=71e9bce111e9429c</Assembly>
  <TypeName>Microsoft.SharePoint.Portal.WebControls.SearchBoxEx</TypeName>
  <DropDownModeEx
    xmlns="urn:schemas-microsoft-com:SearchBoxEx">ShowDD_NoContextual</DropDownModeEx>
  <TextBeforeDropDown
    xmlns="urn:schemas-microsoft-com:SearchBoxEx">Scope: </TextBeforeDropDown>
  <TextBeforeTextBox
    xmlns="urn:schemas-microsoft-com:SearchBoxEx">Query:</TextBeforeTextBox>
  <TextBoxWidth xmlns="urn:schemas-microsoft-com:SearchBoxEx">280</TextBoxWidth>
  <ShowAdvancedSearch
    xmlns="urn:schemas-microsoft-com:SearchBoxEx">true</ShowAdvancedSearch>
  <GoImageUrl
    xmlns="urn:schemas-microsoft-com:SearchBoxEx">/_layouts/images/gosearch.gif</GoImageUrl>
  <GoImageActiveUrl xmlns="urn:schemas-microsoft-com:SearchBoxEx">
    /_layouts/images/gosearch.gif</GoImageActiveUrl>
```

```
<GoImageUrlRTL xmlns="urn:schemas-microsoft-com:SearchBoxEx">
  /_layouts/images/goRTL.gif</GoImageUrlRTL>
<GoImageActiveUrlRTL xmlns="urn:schemas-microsoft-com:SearchBoxEx">
  /_layouts/images/goRTL.gif</GoImageActiveUrlRTL>
<AdvancedSearchPageURL xmlns="urn:schemas-microsoft-com:SearchBoxEx">
  AWadvancedSearch.aspx</AdvancedSearchPageURL>
<SearchResultPageURL xmlns="urn:schemas-microsoft-com:SearchBoxEx">
  AWsearchresults.aspx</SearchResultPageURL>
<ScopeDisplayGroupName xmlns="urn:schemas-microsoft-com:SearchBoxEx">
  AdventureWorks</ScopeDisplayGroupName>
<RegisterStyles xmlns="urn:schemas-microsoft-com:SearchBoxEx">true</RegisterStyles>
<ShouldTakeFocusIfEmpty xmlns="urn:schemas-microsoft-com:SearchBoxEx">
  true</ShouldTakeFocusIfEmpty>
</WebPart>
]]>
</AllUsersWebPart>
```

The *CDATA* portion can be easily generated by configuring a Search Web Part in the browser with the needed settings and consequently exporting it. The file you end up with has an extension *DWP* and is an XML file containing the portion you can copy to the *CDATA* section.

Microsoft.Office.Server.Search.WebControls.CoreResultsWebPart

An important Web Part to cover is the Search Core Results Web Part. This Web Part is responsible for the rendering of the results returned by the search engine to the user. Internally, the Search Core Results Web Part transforms the results (expressed in XML format) using a default XSL string. Earlier in this chapter, we covered the structure of this XSL extensively. The Web Part has a number of interesting properties that can be set programmatically; these properties are listed in Table 3-5.

TABLE 3-5 Microsoft.Office.Server.Search.WebControls.CoreResultsWebPart Properties

Property	Description
ResultsPerPage	Number of result items displayed on one page.
SentencesInSummary	Number of sentences that are displayed in the search result summary.
HighestResultPage	Maximum number of result pages displayed to the user.
DateView	Check box for hiding or displaying the link to sort the results by date modified.
RelevanceView	Check box for hiding or displaying the link to sort the results by relevance.
View	Value of type *ResultsView* setting the sorting either to date modified or to relevance ranking.
DisplayDiscoveredDefinition	Check box to hide or display the discovered definitions in the Web Part.
DuplicatesRemoved	Check box to indicate whether duplicate search results are removed from the list.

Property	Description
StemmingEnabled	Check box to make search term stemming active or inactive.
NoiseIgnored	Check box to allow or disallow noise words queries.
SelectColumns	XML string defining the list of columns or fields that have to be included in the XML returned by the search engine.
QueryNumber	Value for the *Cross-Web Part Query ID* property. Use this to connect multiple Web Parts on the page to execution of the query.
FixedQuery	Search query not entered by the user but hard-coded as part of the Core Results Web Part so that it can be used as a stand-alone Web Part on a page.
MoreResultsText	Text for the More Results link when displayed for a search result.
MoreResultsLink	Custom URL for the More Results link.
Scope	Name of the search scope to be used for filtering the search results.
ShowMessages	Check box to hide or show possible error messages displayed by the search service.
ShowSearchResults	Check box to hide or show the search results.
ShowActionLinks	Check box to hide or show the action links.
DisplayAlertMeLink	Check box to hide or show the Alert Me link.
DisplayRSSLink	Check box to hide or show the RSS link.
DateView	Check box to enable or disable Data View caching.

CoreResultsWebPart inherits from the *DataFormWebPart* defined in the *Microsoft.SharePoint.WebPartPages* namespace and exposes therefore a number of other members that are useful in a scenario where you want to programmatically alter the XSL that is used to render the search results. Table 3-6 summarizes the two important properties.

TABLE 3-6 *DataFormWebPart* **Properties Inherited by** *CoreResultsWebPart*

Property	Description
Xsl	String with the XSLT used to transform the XML containing the search results in the HTML making up the body of the Web Part.
XslLink	Link to a file containing the XSLT used to transform the XML containing the search results in the HTML making up the body of the Web Part.

In our sample, an instance of the *CoreResultsWebPart* is added programmatically to the AWSearchResults.aspx in the *AWFeatureReceiver* class. Here is the code:

```
SPFile respage = searchsite.GetFile("Pages/AWsearchresults.aspx");
respage.CheckOut();

SPLimitedWebPartManager reswpmgr =
    respage.GetLimitedWebPartManager(PersonalizationScope.Shared);
```

```
CoreResultsWebPart crWP = new CoreResultsWebPart();
crWP.Title = "AdventureWorks Search Results";
crWP.DisplayAlertMeLink = false;
crWP.DisplayRSSLink = false;
XmlDocument resdoc = new XmlDocument();
resdoc.LoadXml(GetResourceText
    ("AdventureWorks.Search.AWSearchResultsColumns.xml"));
crWP.SelectColumns = resdoc.OuterXml;
reswpmgr.AddWebPart(crWP, "ResultsZone", 1);
reswpmgr.SaveChanges(crWP);
respage.CheckIn(string.Empty);
respage.Publish(string.Empty);
```

The *SelectColumns* property is set to a custom XML string that is available in the project as an embedded resource in the assembly.

Microsoft.Office.Server.Search.WebControls.SearchStatsWebPart

This Web Part displays details about the execution of the search query. Table 3-7 lists the different properties that can be set programmatically.

TABLE 3-7 Microsoft.Office.Server.Search.WebControls.SearchStatsWebPart Properties

Property	Description
Mode	Value of type *StatsMode* with two possible options to display the statistics: on one line or on two lines
DisplayNumberOfPages	Check box to hide or display the number of pages of search results
DisplayTotalResults	Check box to hide or display the total number of results
DisplayResponseTime	Check box to hide or display the time for the search query to execute
QueryID	Property (exposed as the *Cross-Web Part Query ID* property in the tool pane) that ties the Web Part instance to the Search Core Results Web Part

Microsoft.Office.Server.Search.WebControls.SearchPagingWebPart

Another Web Part that can display information regarding the search results is the Search Paging Web Part. This Web Part gives the user the option to navigate through the various pages containing search results. The number of results per page is set via a number of properties discussed earlier for the Search Core Results Web Part. Table 3-8 lists all of the properties for the Search Paging Web Part.

TABLE 3-8 Microsoft.Office.Server.Search.WebControls.SearchPagingWebPart Properties

Property	Description
MaxAfterCurrent	Maximum number of links to pages shown before the link for the currently displayed page
MaxBeforeCurrent	Maximum number of links to pages shown before the link for the currently displayed page
NextLabel	Label for the Next Page link
NextLinkUrl	URL for the image displayed instead of the Next Page link
PreviousLabel	Label for the Previous Page link
PreviousLinkUrl	URL for the image displayed instead of the Previous Page link
QueryID	Property (exposed as the *Cross-Web Part Query ID* property in the tool pane) that ties the Web Part instance to the Search Core Results Web Part

Both the Search Statistics and the Search Paging Web Parts are added programmatically to the Search Results page in the sample project.

Microsoft.Office.Server.Search.WebControls.SearchSummaryWebPart

The Search Summary Web Part is a small Web Part that displays the summary for a search query in the Search Results page. It also offers the user the option to correct the query by displaying the Did You Mean... Feature. Table 3-9 lists the properties exposed by this Web Part.

TABLE 3-9 Microsoft.Office.Server.Search.WebControls.SearchSummaryWebPart Properties

Property	Description
Mode	Either a compact mode or an extended mode for the summary
ShowMessages	Check box to hide or display the text within the Web Part
QueryID	Property (exposed as the *Cross-Web Part Query ID* property in the tool pane) that ties the Web Part instance to the Search Core Results Web Part

Microsoft.Office.Server.Search.WebControls.HighConfidenceWebPart

A last Web Part that is available in the Microsoft.Office.Server.Search.dll is the Search High Confidence Web Part. This Web Part is used to display the results matching the keywords and the best bets as configured by the administrators at the level of the SSP or the local site collection. Table 3-10 summarizes the various properties that are programmatically accessible for this Web Part.

TABLE 3-10 Microsoft.Office.Server.Search.WebControls.HighConfidenceWebPart Properties

Property	Description
QueryID	Property (exposed as the *Cross-Web Part Query ID* property in the tool pane) that ties the Web Part instance to the Search Core Results Web Part.
BestBetsLimit	Maximum number of best bets to display for a single search.
DisplayBestBetTitle	Check box to hide or display the titles of best bets. Titles will be displayed as a link to the result.
DisplayDefinition	Check box to hide or display the definition for the keyword if available.
DisplayDescription	Check box to hide or display the descriptions given to best bets.
DisplayHCDescription	Check box to hide or display the descriptions given to high confidence results.
DisplayHCImage	Check box to hide or display the images associated with the high confidence results.
DisplayHCProps	Check box to hide or display other properties that are associated with a high confidence result.
DisplayHCTitle	Check box to hide or display the titles of high confidence results. Titles will be displayed as a link to the result.
DisplayTerm	Check box to hide or display the keyword.
DisplayUrl	Check box to hide or display the URL of the best bets.
ResultsPerTypeLimit	Maximum number of matches to display for each distinctive high confidence result.
Xsl	XSL string used to transform the results into the HTML displayed as the body of the Web Part.
XslLink	URL of the XSL file used to transform the results into the HTML displayed as the body of the Web Part.

Microsoft.SharePoint.Portal.WebControls.PeopleSearchBoxEx

PeopleSearchBoxEx is, like *SearchBoxEx*, a class from Microsoft.SharePoint.Portal.dll. Its base class is *SearchBoxEx*. Two extra properties, listed in Table 3-11, are used to configure the search box for entering a people-related query.

TABLE 3-11 Microsoft.SharePoint.Portal.WebControls.PeopleSearchBoxEx Properties

Property	Description
ShowSearchOptions	Check box to hide or display the extra search options that users can use for defining their search query
Properties	XML string containing all of the extra search options to be displayed

Creating Custom Search Tabs

Earlier in this chapter, you learned about the tabs that you can create for the Search Center. A tab gives access to a Search page. In the sample project, the tab for the Search pages and the tab for the Search Results pages are created during the activation of the Feature, as shown here:

```
SPListItem tab1 = searchsite.Lists["Tabs in Search Pages"].Items.Add();
tab1["TabName"] = "AdventureWorks";
tab1["Page"] = "AWSearch.aspx";
tab1["Comments"] = "Use this tab to search within the AdventureWorks database";
tab1.Update();

SPListItem tab2 = searchsite.Lists["Tabs in Search Results"].Items.Add();
tab2["TabName"] = "AdventureWorks";
tab2["Page"] = "AWSearch.aspx";
tab2["Comments"] = "Use this tab to search within the AdventureWorks database";
tab2.Update();
```

This code is nothing special. An *SPListItem* instance is created. Three fields for the new item are given a value. At the end, a call to the *Update* method is performed to push the changes to the content database. The result is shown in Figure 3-71.

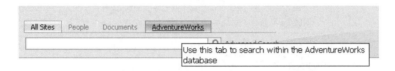

FIGURE 3-71 The AdventureWorks tab programmatically added to the Search Center

Creating a Custom Small Search Box

In Chapter 2, we looked at the small Search box that is part of the out-of-the-box end-user experience with both Windows SharePoint Services 3.0 and Office SharePoint Server 2007. Developers have the option to replace the small Search box with a custom version. This can be useful in scenarios where a business requires a predefined or an extended way of entering search queries. An obvious example is the ability for end users to make use of wildcards in search queries. Chapter 8 covers a sample that demonstrates how to enable wildcards for the user. You might also have a need for predefined search scopes or property filters.

Before we cover the process of creating a custom small Search box, we need to explore how the small Search box is rendered on pages. The small Search box comes in different flavors and is rendered by means of a very specific SharePoint ASP.NET server control named *DelegateControl*.

SharePoint delegate controls are useful types of controls that you'll encounter in many places in the master pages that are part of your SharePoint installation. A *DelegateControl* is an ASP.NET server control that is part of Microsoft.SharePoint.dll and is defined by the *Microsoft.SharePoint.WebControls* namespace. You can think of the control as the chameleon among the many SharePoint controls that are available in that namespace. Using the *DelegateControl*, SharePoint provides a level of flexibility for loading and displaying ASP.NET user controls or ASP.NET server controls to the user. Basically, this control defines a placeholder or region that is populated with content in a dynamic way. The syntax of the definition of a delegate control that is responsible for the rendering of the small Search box is shown here:

```
<SharePoint:DelegateControl runat="server" ControlId="SmallSearchInputBox" />
```

The value for the *ControlId* attribute is important. At the time of processing the page, the list of active Features is consulted, and any of the Features that contain a CAML element *Control* with that specific *ControlId* will be a candidate for the *DelegateControl*. There are two possible definitions within the *Control* element. You can deliver an ASP.NET Server control as follows:

```
<Control Id="" Sequence="" ControlClass="" ControlAssembly="">
 <Property Name=""></Property>
</Control>
```

The *Id* attribute here is the one that will be checked by the *DelegateControl*. The *Sequence* attribute is important in case the *DelegateControl* is forced to make a choice between two or more active Features that can deliver the functionality it needs to load and render. The *Control* element with the lowest sequence number is the one that will be chosen. In the case of an ASP.NET Server control, you must provide details for it via the *ControlClass* and the *ControlAssembly* attribute. The first attribute has the fully qualified name of the class as the value, and the second has the strong name of the assembly containing the class. *Property* elements can be used to preconfigure the instance that will be displayed by the *DelegateControl*. Every *Property* element matches a property of the ASP.NET Server control, and the value specified will be transferred to it.

You can also make available an ASP.NET user control (.ascx) with the *Control* element in the Feature. The syntax is as follows:

```
<Control Id="" Sequence="" ControlSrc="" />
```

Here again are the *Id* and the *Sequence* attributes. The *ControlSrc* attribute is set to the path of the .ascx file. A good place to store these ASP.NET user controls is in the 12\Template\ ControlTemplates folder.

Out-of-the-box, you'll find a Feature with a *Control* element that is installed with Windows SharePoint Services 3.0 and two more Features if you decide to deploy Microsoft Office SharePoint Server 2007. The Features are listed here:

■ *ContentLightup*   This Feature contains a bit more than the *Control* element—it is the Feature that is part of Windows SharePoint Services 3.0. It makes available the small Search box as an ASP.NET user control.

```
<Elements xmlns="http://schemas.microsoft.com/sharepoint/">
    <Control
        Id="SmallSearchInputBox"
        Sequence="100"
        ControlSrc="~/_controltemplates/searcharea.ascx">
    </Control>
    <!-- left out for brevity -->
</Elements>
```

This is the end-user experience for working with the small Search box when you work within a team site (or other type of site that is part of Windows SharePoint Services 3.0). We'll have a closer look at the .ascx in a moment.

■ *OSearchBasicFeature*   This Feature defines the small Search box as an ASP.NET Server control named *SearchBoxEx*. We examined this class earlier in this chapter. With the Feature, an instance is configured:

```
<Elements xmlns="http://schemas.microsoft.com/sharepoint/">
    <Control
        Id="SmallSearchInputBox"
        Sequence="50"
        ControlClass="Microsoft.SharePoint.Portal.WebControls.SearchBoxEx"
        ControlAssembly="Microsoft.SharePoint.Portal, Version=12.0.0.0,
Culture=neutral, PublicKeyToken=71e9bce111e9429c">
    <Property Name="GoImageUrl">/_layouts/images/gosearch.gif</Property>
    <Property Name="GoImageUrlRTL">/_layouts/images/goRTL.gif</Property>
    <Property Name="GoImageActiveUrl">/_layouts/images/gosearch.gif</Property>
    <Property Name="GoImageActiveUrlRTL">/_layouts/images/goRTL.gif</Property>
    <Property Name="DropDownMode">ShowDD</Property>
    <Property Name="SearchResultPageURL">/_layouts/osssearchresults.aspx
    </Property>
    <Property Name="ScopeDisplayGroupName"></Property>
    <Property Name="FrameType">None</Property>
    </Control>
</Elements>
```

The control is configured for the display of a Scope Picker.

■ *OSearchEnhancedFeature*   This Feature contains the same ASP.NET Server control as the preceding Feature. It is configured for a display without a Scope Picker but with a link to the Advanced Search page. This Feature is the one you'll see on the home page of the collaboration portal where a Search Center takes the role of displaying the search results.

```
<Elements xmlns="http://schemas.microsoft.com/sharepoint/">
    <Control
        Id="SmallSearchInputBox"
        Sequence="25"
        ControlClass="Microsoft.SharePoint.Portal.WebControls.SearchBoxEx"
        ControlAssembly="Microsoft.SharePoint.Portal, Version=12.0.0.0,
    Culture=neutral, PublicKeyToken=71e9bce111e9429c">
        <Property Name="GoImageUrl">/_layouts/images/gosearch.gif</Property>
        <Property Name="GoImageUrlRTL">/_layouts/images/goRTL.gif</Property>
        <Property Name="GoImageActiveUrl">/_layouts/images/gosearch.gif</Property>
        <Property Name="GoImageActiveUrlRTL">/_layouts/images/goRTL.gif</Property>
        <Property Name="UseSiteDefaults">true</Property>
        <Property Name="FrameType">None</Property>
        <Property Name="ShowAdvancedSearch">true</Property>
    </Control>
</Elements>
```

Chapter 8 goes into the details of how to build a custom small Search box as an ASP.NET Server control. For now, let's have a look at how you can deliver a custom ASP.NET user control that is slightly different from the default searcharea.ascx just to illustrate the principle of the *DelegateControl*.

Open the searcharea.ascx file from the 12\ControlTemplates folder, and review its contents. The code-behind for this user control can be found in the *SearchArea* class that is defined in the *Microsoft.SharePoint.WebControls* namespace and delivered with Microsoft.SharePoint. dll. Nothing spectacular is delivered with this class. The major part of the work is done directly in the user control. First is a block of server-side code, as shown here:

```
<%
string strScopeWeb = null;
string strScopeList = null;
string strWebSelected = null;
SPWeb web = SPControl.GetContextWeb(Context);
string strEncodedUrl= SPHttpUtility.EcmaScriptStringLiteralEncode
    (SPHttpUtility.UrlPathEncode(web.Url + "/_layouts/searchresults.aspx", false, false));
strEncodedUrl = "'" + strEncodedUrl + "'";
strScopeWeb = "'" + SPHttpUtility.HtmlEncode( web.Url ) + "'";
SPList list = SPContext.Current.List;
if ( list != null && ((list.BaseTemplate != SPListTemplateType.DocumentLibrary &&
    list.BaseTemplate != SPListTemplateType.WebPageLibrary) ||
    (SPContext.Current.ListItem == null) || (SPContext.Current.ListItem.ParentList == null)
    || (SPContext.Current.ListItem.ParentList != list)) )
{
    strScopeList = list.ID.ToString();
}
else
{
    strWebSelected = "SELECTED";
}
%>
```

Remember that this small Search box experience is the one that users see when working in Windows SharePoint Services 3.0 sites. It does not display any functionality that is configured at the level of the search settings in the SSP. The block of server code is only preparing the population of the Scope Picker. Only contextual scopes are displayed. The rest of the content within the .ascx has to do with the rendering of a drop-down list, a text box, and a button (displayed as an image) to submit the results. Here is the interesting piece of that code:

```
<a target='_self' href='javascript:'
onClick="javascript:SubmitSearchRedirect(<%=strEncodedUrl%>);javascript:return false;"
title=<%SPHttpUtility.AddQuote(SPHttpUtility.HtmlEncode(SearchImageToolTip),Response.Output)
;%> ID=onetIDGoSearch>
```

Assume now that we actually want to deliver a small Search box that on top of all of this also allows a user to submit the query to the results page that is part of the collaboration portal. For simplicity, we'll hard-code this URL assuming that we are in a controlled and fairly static environment where an administrator knows about this hard-code URL and can make the change to the .ascx in case the URL must be changed. In addition, all search results should be displayed in a newly opened browser window.

This is an easy one, so if you're up for it, open Microsoft Visual Studio and let's build this one from scratch. Create a new class library project. The name is not that important, since you'll use it only to create a Feature. There is no code involved with this project. Remove the class since you don't need it.

In Solution Explorer, create a folder structure as shown in Figure 3-72. This folder structure mimics the one where all of the files will be deployed.

FIGURE 3-72 The folder structure in the Visual Studio project for the custom small Search box

Next add a copy of the searcharea.ascx to the InsideSearch folder under the ControlTemplates folder. Open the file in the code editor. As mentioned earlier, we just want to allow the user to select a new option to have the query executed by the Search Center in the collaboration portal. Find the HTML and the server-side code that populates the Scope

Picker. Add your extra option at the end as a new *OPTION* element with a value and a text equal to *MOSS Search*, as shown here:

```
<SELECT id='idSearchScope' name='SearchScope' class='ms-searchbox' title=
<%SPHttpUtility.AddQuote(SPHttpUtility.HtmlEncode(SearchScopeToolTip),Response.Output)
;%>>
  <OPTION value=<%=strScopeWeb%> <%=strWebSelected%>> <SharePoint:EncodedLiteral
   runat="server" text="<%$Resources:wss,search_Scope_Site%>" EncodeMethod='HtmlEncode'
   Id='idSearchScopeSite'/>
  </OPTION>
<%
 if (strScopeList != null)
 {
%>
  <OPTION value=<%=strScopeList%> SELECTED> <SharePoint:EncodedLiteral runat="server"
   text="<%$Resources:wss,search_Scope_List%>" EncodeMethod='HtmlEncode'
   Id='idSearchScopeList'/> </OPTION>
<%
 }
%>
  <option value="MOSS">MOSS Search</option>
</SELECT>
```

> **Tip** Do not apply the formatting option of the content in the Visual Studio code editor. This will cause problems when rendering the user control.

Your next change is at the level of the button that is used to submit the query. Instead of relying on the *SubmitSearchRedirect* JavaScript function that is part of the Core.js, you'll take control of the redirecting yourself because you'd like to create a branch based on the selected value in the Scope Picker and you also need to display the results in a new browser window.

Add the following small JavaScript block at the bottom of the .ascx:

```
<script language="javascript">
  function SubmitRequest(option, wssurl)
  {
     var mossurl = "http://moss.litwareinc.com/searchcenter/Pages/Results.aspx?k=";
     var el = document.getElementById("idSearchString");

     if (el != null)
     {
       var qry = escapeProperly(el.value);
       if (option=="MOSS Search")
       {
        window.open(mossurl + qry);
       }
       else
       {
        var searchScope = document.getElementById("idSearchScope");
```

```
      if (searchScope !=null)
      {
        url = url + "?k=" + qry
        var searchScopeUrl=searchScope.value;
        if (searchScopeUrl)
        {
          url=url +"&u="+escapeProperly(searchScopeUrl);
        }
      }
      window.open(url);
    }
  }
}
</script>
```

Two input parameters are defined. The first is the text of the selected option, and the second is the URL that is prepared in the server-side code for the redirect to the Search Results page that is part of the site collection.

As mentioned, the URL for the Search Results page in the collaboration portal is hard-coded. The rest of the scripting code is the preparation of the proper URL with the required query string parameters and the call to the *open* method of the *window* object.

You are ready now to wrap this up in a Feature that will be scoped at the level of the site collection. Note that you can also use the other possible scopes: *Farm*, *WebApplication*, and *Web*. Create a Feature definition by adding a feature.xml file to the Template\Features\ InsideSearch.CustomSmallSearchBox folder in Solution Explorer. The content of the file is displayed here:

```
<Feature  Id="{DC22A115-4E9C-400b-8FDD-9ABD96C7C138}"
          Title="Inside Search Sample: Custom Small Search box"
          Description="Demonstrating how to deliver a new small search box experience"
          Version="1.0.0.0"
          Hidden="FALSE"
          Scope="Site"
          xmlns="http://schemas.microsoft.com/sharepoint/">
    <ElementManifests>
        <ElementManifest Location="elements.xml" />
    </ElementManifests>
</Feature>
```

The element manifest file is where you'll add the *Control* element. Create a file named elements.xml in the same folder as the feature.xml. Add the following content:

```
<Elements xmlns="http://schemas.microsoft.com/sharepoint/">
    <Control
        Id="SmallSearchInputBox"
        Sequence="5"
        ControlSrc="~/_controltemplates/InsideSearch/searcharea.ascx">
    </Control>
</Elements>
```

You of course use the same *Id* attribute value as the one that is defined as the value for the *ControlId* attribute at the level of the *DelegateControl*. To make sure that your custom small Search box will be picked up, you set the value of the *Sequence* attribute to *5*. The *ControlSrc* attribute points to the .ascx that you created previously.

The only thing to do now is to add an install.bat to your project so that all of this is copied to the 12 folder and the Feature is installed. Here is a possible batch file that executes these actions:

```
@SET TEMPLATEDIR="c:\program files\common files\microsoft shared\web server
extensions\12\Template"
@SET STSADM="c:\program files\common files\microsoft shared\web server
extensions\12\bin\stsadm"

Echo Copying files to TEMPLATE directory
xcopy /e /y TEMPLATE\* %TEMPLATEDIR%

Echo Installing feature
%STSADM% -o installfeature -name InsideSearch.CustomSmallSearchBox -force

cscript c:\windows\system32\iisapp.vbs /a "SharePointPool" /r

pause
```

An *xcopy* statement takes care of the copying of the Template folder within your project together with all of the subfolders and the files. The *STSADM* command-line utility does the job of installing the Feature. The second-to-last line is the recycling of the worker process. Make sure that you replace the name of the application pool with the one that is active on your side.

Once the Feature is installed, it can be activated. Navigate to the top-level site in your site collection, and open the Site Settings page from the Site Actions menu. Click Site Collection Features in the Site Collection Administration group. The Feature will be displayed in the middle of the list. Click the Activate button, and navigate back to the top-level site.

If everything worked out as it should have, you now can execute a search query in the small Search box against the index built for the site itself and the index that is under the control of the SSP. Figure 3-73 shows the custom small Search box with the additional entry in the Scope Picker.

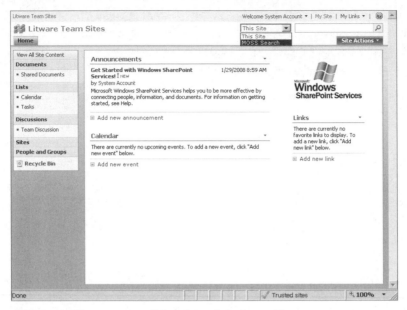

FIGURE 3-73 The custom small Search box in action

Summary

In this chapter, we've covered plenty of configuration options regarding the search end-user experience, both from an administrator perspective and from a developer one. The key message is that the Search Center is at the core of this experience. Administrators use the different properties exposed by the Search Web Parts to fine-tune the workings of the different search-related pages. Developers come in to extend this even further by delivering custom page layouts and pages—and possibly also custom Web Parts, as you'll discover in Chapter 8. Just don't forget that there's a thin line between an administrator and a developer when it comes to the customization of the search experience, as you saw in the section "Customizing the Layout of the Search Results" earlier in this chapter. An administrator frequently will have to configure the settings via modifications in XML or even XSL files. Developers must know the essentials of search administration before they can work with the classes exposed in the search APIs.

The next two chapters—Chapter 4, "Search Usage Reports," and Chapter 5, "Search Administration"—are very important for both the administrator and the developer. They detail important topics that need to be understood before real-world implementations can take place.

Chapter 4
Search Usage Reports

After completing this chapter, you will be able to

- Understand the technical architecture of search usage reporting.

- Enable search usage reporting for a Shared Services Provider (SSP).

- View and interpret search usage reports.

- Transform search usage metrics into actions, improving the search experience.

- Export search usage data to Microsoft Office Excel and Adobe Acrobat PDF.

Monitoring and analyzing search usage is an important aspect of optimizing the search experience for end users. Microsoft Office SharePoint Server 2007 facilitates two reports on multiple metrics, a Search Queries Report and a Search Results Report, that administrators can use to monitor the usage of the Search Centers in relevant site collections. The Search Centers basically log information about what users are searching for and what results they click. This chapter covers the details of both reports and how administrators access and interpret them. The first section provides a compact overview of each metric in both reports. The second section outlines the technical architecture of the search usage reporting feature. The next two sections show administrators how to enable query logging and access the reports. Last, we'll take a closer look at each report, and you'll learn how to export them into Microsoft Office Excel and Adobe Acrobat PDF. You'll find only limited coverage on customizing the reports or working with them through an application programming interface (API), as this capability is not supported by Microsoft. However, one hint is provided for reprogramming the Search Centers to log data to a custom reporting subsystem.

Overview of Search Usage Reporting

Search usage reporting, like searching itself, is a shared service that can be provided to multiple Internet Information Services (IIS) Web applications by a Shared Services Provider (SSP). (See Chapter 5, "Search Administration," for a detailed description of the concept of SSPs in relation to searching.) Each SSP collects search usage data from the Search Centers in multiple site collections hosted by different IIS Web applications. SSP administrators can in turn monitor the collective search usage from all of the connected Search Centers. It is additionally possible for site collection administrators to monitor the search usage of the Search Centers within their respective site collections.

Each SSP provides two search usage reports: the Search Queries Report and the Search Results Report. The details of each report and where to find them are covered in the section "Accessing the Reports" later in this chapter. The Search Queries Report contains the following information:

- **Number Of Queries**   Measures the number of queries over time. The report includes two graphs on this metric: one for the number of queries per day over the last 30 days and one for the number of queries per month over the last 12 months.

- **Query Origin Site Collections**   Tracks the URL of the site collections where queries originate from. This metric is available only to SSP administrators.

- **Number Of Queries Per Scope**   This metric measures how many queries go to each of the available search scopes. The report includes a section showing the distribution over the last 30 days.

- **Query Terms**   Tracks the actual keywords or phrases that users are searching for. The report includes a section with a list of the top queries over the last 30 days.

The Search Results Report contains data tables related to the search results of the various queries performed by the users. The metrics for search results are listed here:

- **Search Result Destination Pages**   Tracks the URL of the search results clicked by the users. The report includes a list of the top results clicked over the last 30 days.

- **Queries With Zero Results**   This metric tracks the queries that yield zero results. The report includes a list of such queries over the last 30 days.

- **Most Clicked Best Bets**   Tracks the titles of best bets clicked by users. This metric is presented as a list with the most-clicked best bets over the last 30 days.

- **Search Results With Zero Best Bets**   Tracks all the queries with no associated best bets. The report presents the data for this metric as a list of the search terms that did not yield any best bets during the last 30 days.

- **Queries With Low Clickthrough**   Tracks queries yielding results but where users do not tend to click any of them. This metric is also presented as a list of queries over 30 days in the report.

The preceding metrics are available to monitor the search usage of one or more Search Centers within a SharePoint farm. It is not possible to configure the tracking of additional metrics, nor is it possible to customize the two built-in reports or define custom reports. But the Search Queries Report and the Search Results Report are nonetheless helpful as is. You'll learn more about both reports and their metrics and how to interpret them to optimize the search experience later in this chapter. But let's first have a closer look at the architecture behind the search usage reporting component of SSPs.

Reporting Architecture

In this section, we'll take a peek under the hood of the search usage reporting component of SSPs. Feel free to skip this section if you need to know only about the end result of the actual reports and what they can do for you. However, the information about the architectural structure presented here might prove valuable to application developers customizing the Search Centers, in particular for customizing the look and feel of the search results using XSL. See Chapter 3, "Customizing the Search User Interface," for information about customizing the search results with XSL.

The technical concept behind the logging mechanism of search usage data differs significantly from the logging mechanism of site usage data. The latter is a feature available at the level of Microsoft Windows SharePoint Services 3.0 in the technology stack. Site usage data is logged to binary files on exposed Web front-end servers in the farm, whereas search usage data from all Web front-end servers is logged to the associated SSP database. A further discussion on site usage data is beyond the scope of this book.

The schematic drawing shown on the next page outlines the general architecture of the search usage reporting component.

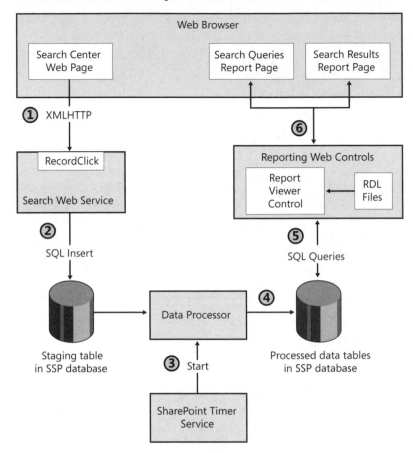

1	A Search Center employs JavaScript code in the Web browser to dynamically send an XML package to the Search Web service of Office SharePoint Server 2007. The XML package contains information about the current query and about the result clicked. The package is also sent if the user leaves the results page without clicking a result. The JavaScript code issues an XMLHTTP request to dynamically call the *RecordClick* method exposed by the Search Web service.
2	The Search Web service dissects the XML package and inserts a new row of data into a staging table in the SSP database. The name of this table is *MSSQLLogUnprocessed*.
3	A timer job named Office SharePoint Usage Analytics Processing is launched every 15 minutes by the SharePoint timer service to run the data processor.
4	The data processor picks up and processes all new data that landed in the staging table. It then stores the results in a set of live data tables in the SSP database.
5	The appropriate tables in the SSP database are queried, and the data is fed to the Report Viewer control, which in turn builds a graph or a table with the data for one metric. The concrete report is governed by a Report Definition Language (RDL) file, which is an XML file defining the layout of the report.
6	The Search Queries Report page and the Search Result Query page contain five Report Web controls each. These pages load quickly without data in the graphs or tables. They instead load asynchronously in the browser.

It is essential to realize that search usage data is logged only as a result of user actions in the Search Centers. By clicking any link on a Search Center page, users will trigger a JavaScript method, sending usage data to the Search Web service. Queries sent through the official Microsoft .NET Framework query API by custom applications or custom Web Parts are *not* logged. Data is logged only via the *RecordClick* method on the Search Web service. Custom search applications are, however, not able to call this method, as the Search Web service ignores usage data from all clients other than the standard Search Center.

The Search Center sends information about the current search session as an XML string to the Search Web service. At first glance, it might not make sense to document the XML format here, since SharePoint ignores data from third-party clients. But with a little JavaScript trick, it's actually possible to reprogram the Search Centers to send usage data to a custom Web service instead. But first, let's examine the format of the XML string. The trick will then be revealed in the section "Sending Usage Data to a Custom Web Service" later in this chapter.

XML Format of the *RecordClick* Parameter

The *RecordClick* method of the Search Web service accepts a single parameter named *clickInfoXml* of type *string*. The Search Center sends an XML package of the following format as the parameter value:

```xml
<i xmlns:xsi="http://www.w3.org/2001/XMLSchema-instance"
   xmlns:xsd="http://www.w3.org/2001/XMLSchema"
    a="false"
    d="false"
    g="b3fed6c9-503d-4a8a-887c-bf7168a78b4d"
    h="0"
    m="0x06DE4F9CA8CB5370C8C6883CF1E05C76CE4D7748,3436713409"
    n="245"
    p="MOSS"
    q="hr"
    t="2007-11-27T10:36:49.6421392-08:00"
    u="http://moss.litwareinc.com/searchcenter/Pages/results.aspx"
    v="0"
    x="1"
    xmlns="urn:Microsoft.Search">
 <f>false</f>
 <r>7</r>
 <s>All Sites</s>
 <c>http://intranet.litwareinc.com/Docs</c>
 <z>http://intranet.litwareinc.com/myhr</z>
 <z>http://intranet.litwareinc.com/News</z>
 <z>http://intranet.litwareinc.com/myhr/Lists/Announcements/AllItems.aspx</z>
 <z>http://intranet.litwareinc.com/orionwiki</z>
 <z>http://intranet.litwareinc.com/SiteDirectory</z>
</i>
```

The element values shown here are an example from a single search session. Table 4-1 lists the definitions for each attribute and element in the XML package. The package can be generated programmatically by using the .NET Framework class *System.Xml.Serialization.XmlSerializer* to serialize the *Microsoft.Office.Server.Search.Query.QueryInfo* class to an XML string.

TABLE 4-1 Description of Attribute Nodes and Element Nodes in the XML Package

Node	Description
a	Advanced Search. Evaluates to *true* if the user searched from the Advanced Search page; otherwise, evaluates to *false*.
c	Clicked URL. Specifies the URL of the search result clicked by the user.
d	Did You Mean... Evaluates to *true* if the search yielded a spelling suggestion; otherwise, *false*.
f	Continued Session. Can be *true* or *false*.
g	Site GUID. Specifies the globally unique identifier (GUID) of the site collection where the Search Center resides.
h	Number of high confidence results.
m	Digest. Basically a checksum to verify the authenticity of the XML package.
n	Total number of results.
p	Query Server. The server name of the query server/Web front-end server.
q	Query String. The search terms entered by the user.
r	Clicked URL Rank. The index of the search result clicked by the user.
s	Search Scope. The name of the search scope being searched. This XML element can appear more than once when multiple scopes are searched.
t	Search Time. A timestamp indicating the time when the query was executed.
u	Results URL. The URL of the search results page.
v	Results view.
x	Number of best bets.
z	Nonclicked URL. The URL of a higher-ranking result that was *not* clicked. This XML element is present when the user does not click the top search result. The XML package will, for instance, contain four <z> elements if the user clicks the fifth search result.

The *m* attribute is the reason the *RecordClick* method ignores logging requests from third-party clients. The value of this attribute contains a digest—that is, a checksum of the entire XML package. Providing an incorrect value here will invalidate the entire XML package, and the *RecordClick* method will simply throw it away instead of inserting a new row into the staging database. The problem for third-party clients is that they technically cannot compute a valid digest value; only the Microsoft Web Parts are able to do so.

Sending Usage Data to a Custom Web Service

Now that we've examined the XML format of the usage data, it's time to reveal a little trick you can use to direct the Search Centers to send data to a custom Web service instead. This is useful if you want to format and send search usage data to another reporting system. Start by developing and installing a new custom Web service for SharePoint—for example, one with the request URL *http://server/_vti_bin/mysearch.asmx*. Add one method named *RecordClick* that accepts one parameter named *clickInfoXml* of type *string*. The method should not specify any return value.

Next, find and open the file named Search.js on all Web front-end servers in the farm. For a typical installation, this file is located in the directory C:\Program Files\Common Files\ Microsoft Shared\web server extensions\12\TEMPLATE\LAYOUTS\1033. Locate the method named *SendSoap* in the file, and insert the following line of JavaScript code after the first curly brace:

```
postUrl = postUrl.replace('search.asmx', 'mysearch.asmx');
```

The Search Centers will from this point on log usage data via your custom *RecordClick* method instead of via the *RecordClick* method of the standard Search Web service.

> **Important** Modifications to the Search.js file might be reverted when you apply a Microsoft SharePoint service pack.

Report Definition Language (RDL) Files

Each chart and table in the usage reports is generated by the Report Viewer control, which takes a Report Definition Language (RDL) file as input. This is basically an XML file defining the data to present and how to present it. The RDL file format is defined by Microsoft SQL Server Reporting Services; consult the documentation of this product for more detailed in-formation about RDL files. The RDL files defining the charts and tables of the Search Queries Report and the Search Results Report are loaded from disk on the Web front-end servers. For a typical installation, these files are located in the directory C:\Program Files\Microsoft Office Servers\12.0\Bin\Analytics.

It is possible to do some basic customization of the reports. You can change the size and colors of the graphs and tables. But you cannot change the time span or the scope of the data shown in the reports.

Dependencies on the Search Results XSL

Recall that the Search Center is responsible for logging usage data via the *RecordClick* method on the Search Web service. Let's have a look at how exactly this works. Awareness of the technique employed by the Search Center to collect and log search usage data is of great importance when customizing the search results. XSL developers working on custom XSL for the Search Core Results Web Part must be very careful not to break the tracking of clicked search results. See the section "A Closer Look at the XSL" in Chapter 3 for in-depth information about customizing the search results using XSL.

The tracking of clicked search results can be broken easily, because the Search Center employs a clever piece of JavaScript code to track search usage. But this piece of code has some dependencies on the XSL string of the Search Core Results Web Part and the People Core Results Web Part, which are important not to break. These dependencies will be revealed in a moment. First it is necessary to answer the obvious questions: Why use JavaScript at all? Why not let the search engine itself track search usage to avoid this loose coupling between search and search usage reporting?

There are of course very good reasons for the product team to have chosen the JavaScript approach. The main reason is the ability to track the search results that users are clicking and correlating this with their queries. This makes it possible to track queries where users decide not to click any search result. See the section "Queries With Low Clickthrough" later in this chapter for an example of this metric. The technical concept behind the JavaScript approach is, on page load, to automatically wire up all search result links to also call a JavaScript method when clicked. The method in turn registers the URL of the clicked result with the *c* parameter in the XML package described earlier. The package is then shipped to the reporting subsystem via the Search Web service. The JavaScript also wires up the *window.unload* event in the browser to track when users are leaving the Search Center or starting a new search instead of clicking a search result.

The JavaScript responsible for wiring up search result links and the *window.unload* event is shown here. It is emitted in the HTML response by the Search Core Results Web Part and the People Core Results Web Part.

```
<script type='text/javascript'>
  var QLC=0;
  function AddHandler(e, f){
    var o=eval(e);
    eval(e+'=o?function(){o();f();}:f;');
  }
  function WireLinks(url, action, env, start){
    var links=document.body.getElementsByTagName('a');
    for (var i=0;i<links.length;i++)
      if(/^(CSR|BBR|SRP)_/.exec(links[i].id))
        links[i].onclick = function(){SendClick(url,action,env,start,this); QLC=1;};
    AddHandler('window.onunload',function(){if(!QLC)SendSoap(url,action,env);});
  }
```

```
AddHandler('window.onload',function(){
  WireLinks('http://moss.litwareinc.com/SearchCenter/_vti_bin/search.asmx',
   'urn:Microsoft.Search/RecordClick','<soap:Envelope xmlns:soap="http://schemas.xmlsoap.
org/soap/envelope/"><soap:Body><RecordClick xmlns="urn:Microsoft.Search"><clickInfoXml><
![CDATA[<i xmlns:xsi="http://www.w3.org/2001/XMLSchema-instance" xmlns:xsd="http://www.
w3.org/2001/XMLSchema" a="false" d="false" g="b3fed6c9-503d-4a8a-887c-bf7168a78b4d" h="0" m=
"0xE0D0D18210C346E13253F2F67FA2E62906781223,3436720486" n="280" p="MOSS" q="energy" t="2007-
11-27T21:34:46.5282016\u002b01:00" u="http://moss.litwareinc.com/searchcenter/Pages/Results.
aspx" v="0" x="0" xmlns="urn:Microsoft.Search"><f>false</f><r>0</r><s>All Sites</s> </
i>]]></clickInfoXml></RecordClick></soap:Body></soap:Envelope>',0);});
</script>
```

Take a look at the *WireLinks* method. It enumerates over all anchor elements on the search results page. Links having an *id* attribute where the value starts with *CSR_*, *BBR_*, or *SRP_* are wired up to call the *SendClick* method. Table 4-2 describes these *id* prefixes.

TABLE 4-2 Link *id* Prefixes

Prefix	Description
*CSR_*	Core Search Result link
*BBR_*	Best Bets Result link
*SRP_*	Search Result Paging link

Removing or changing these *id* prefixes in the XSL will simply break the *WireLinks* method and thereby also the tracking of clicked results. The default XSL of the Search Core Results Web Part does, for instance, render the title as follows:

```
<span class="srch-Title">
  <a href="{$url}" id="{concat('CSR_',$id)}" title="{$url}">...</a>
</span>
```

Notice that the value of the *id* attribute is assembled using the *concat* method. The title link of the first result will get the *id CSR_1*, the next result will be *CSR_2*, and so on. So the key message of this section is this: Do not change this *id*. Keep it when customizing the XSL.

Enabling or Disabling Search Usage Reporting

SSP administrators can enable and disable logging, as shown in Figure 4-1. The Search Centers connected to the SSP will, when Search Query Logging is enabled, automatically log search usage data. The JavaScript for wiring up links shown in the preceding section is not emitted in the HTML when Search Query Logging is disabled.

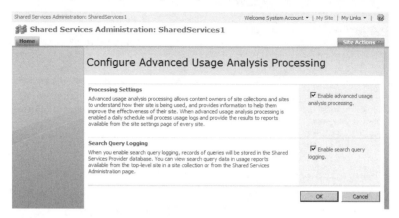

FIGURE 4-1 Enabling or disabling Search Query Logging

The following steps explain how to navigate to the page shown in Figure 4-1 and change the Search Query Logging setting:

1. Open SharePoint 3.0 Central Administration.

2. Navigate to the administration site of the SSP for which you want to enable or disable Search Query Logging.

3. In the group Office SharePoint Usage Reporting, click the Usage Reporting link.

4. Select or clear the Enable Search Query Logging check box.

5. Click OK to save the configuration change.

The Enable Advanced Usage Analysis Processing option is related to site usage analysis, which is beyond the scope of this book.

Accessing the Reports

The search usage reports are available at two levels: at the level of the SSP and at the site collection level. The reports at the level of the SSP can be accessed by SSP administrators to monitor the collective search usage of all the Search Centers served by the SSP. Site collection administrators can access similar reports for each site collection containing an active Search Center. The reports at this level track search usage from all the Search Centers inside the site collection. In addition to the scope, there is only one small difference between the reports at the two levels. The Search Queries Report at the level of the SSP contains the additional metric Query Origin Site Collections, as mentioned in the section "Overview of Search Usage Reporting" earlier in this chapter.

The reports at the SSP level are available from the associated Shared Services Administration site, as shown in Figure 4-2.

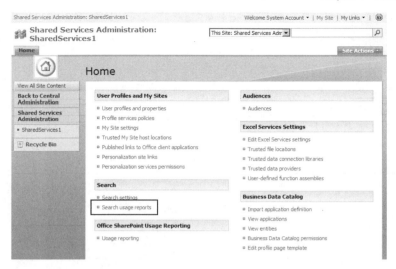

FIGURE 4-2 Accessing search usage reports at the level of an SSP

In the Search group, click the Search Usage Reports link to access the Search Queries Report and the Search Results Report. These reports are described in detail in the next two sections.

Site collection administrators can access their reports from the Site Settings menu of the top-level site in the site collection. Figure 4-3 illustrates the Site Settings menu of a site collection named Litware Inc. available at the URL *http://moss.litwareinc.com*. The entry point for the reports is the Site Collection Usage Reports link in the Site Collection Administration group.

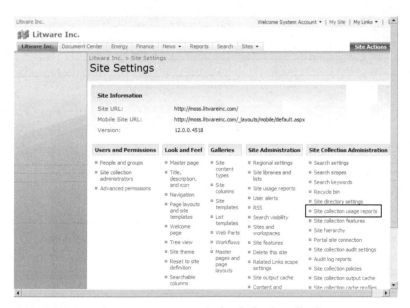

FIGURE 4-3 Accessing usage reports at the level of a site collection

Clicking this link will not bring you directly to the Search Queries Report, as the equivalent entry link at the SSP level does. It will instead bring you to the Site Collection Usage Summary page, shown in Figure 4-4.

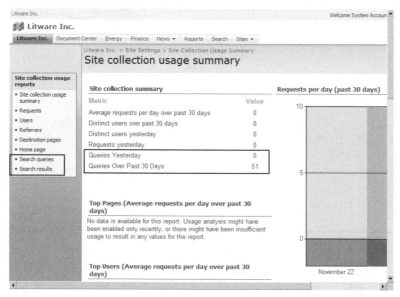

FIGURE 4-4 Search usage reporting at the level of a site collection

This page is mainly focused on general site collection usage, which is a topic beyond the scope of this book. However, the page is still shown here because it includes two useful search-related metrics summarizing the number of queries executed in the site collection yesterday and over the past 30 days.

The search usage reports from this summary page can be accessed from the navigation pane on the left, as shown in Figure 4-4.

Search Queries Report

The Search Queries Report contains four metrics summarizing what users are searching for and how often. Figure 4-5 shows an excerpt of the report at the level of an SSP.

The following subsections describe each metric used by this report. All data on the page is generated from a rolling data window of 30 days or 12 months. These time periods are fixed, and therefore it is not possible to specify alternative time periods, such as last month, month to date, last 60 days, quarter 1, and so on.

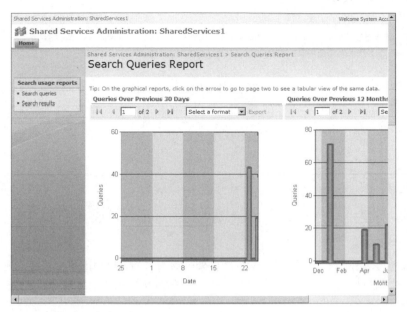

FIGURE 4-5 Search Queries Report

Queries Over Previous 30 Days and Queries Over Previous 12 Months

The first two subreports show the trend in the number of queries over time. The Queries Over Previous 30 Days subreport shows the total number of queries per day inside a 30-day rolling window. The Queries Over Previous 12 Months subreport shows the total number of queries per month inside a 12-month rolling window. Both subreports have two available views: a cylinder bar chart and a table. The default view is the chart shown in Figure 4-6.

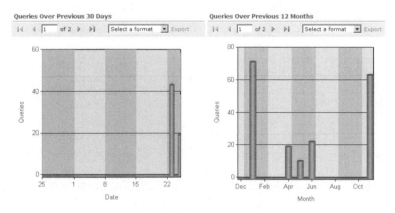

FIGURE 4-6 Graphical representation of the Number Of Queries metric

The tabular view of each subreport is available by clicking the small blue right arrow on the gray toolbar at the top of each subreport. This will switch the subreports to page 2, which is the tabular view, as shown in Figure 4-7.

Queries Over Previous 30 Days		Queries Over Previous 12 Months	
Date	Queries	Month	Queries
November 25	20	November, 2007	64
November 23	44	June, 2007	23
		May, 2007	11
		April, 2007	20
		January, 2007	72

FIGURE 4-7 Tabular representation of the Number Of Queries metric

The tabular view is useful and easier to interpret when you need to know the exact number of queries on a specific date or in a specific month.

The metric described here is generally useful to monitor the trend in the number of queries over time. It can answer questions such as these: Are any users searching at all? Is the trend in the number of queries climbing or falling? On what days during a week is search used the most? How much is search actually being used on weekends and holidays?

Top Query Origin Site Collections Over Previous 30 Days

The Top Query Origin Site Collections Over Previous 30 Days subreport enumerates all the site collections that users have been searching from. This metric is, as previously mentioned, available only at the SSP level. It clearly does not make sense at the level of the site collection. This subreport is also equipped with two views: a pie chart and a table. Figure 4-8 shows an example of both views.

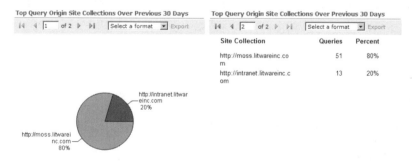

FIGURE 4-8 Graphical and tabular representations of Top Query Origin Site Collections Over Previous 30 Days

Only top site collections with at least one originating query over the last 30 days are included in the subreport. Each site collection is represented by its URL. The pie chart shows the activity distribution expressed in percentages among the site collections. The table view additionally shows the exact number of queries originating from each site collection.

The purpose of this metric is to help you determine which Search Centers (assuming one for each site collection) are in fact being used and how much.

Queries Per Scope Over Previous 30 Days

The usage of search scopes can also be tracked. (See Chapter 5 for a detailed review of search scopes.) The Queries Per Scope Over Previous 30 Days subreport lists the names of all search scopes used in queries over the last 30 days. It supports all scopes, whether they are defined at the SSP level or at the level of the site collection. Like the previous subreports, this one also includes two views: a pie chart and a table. Figure 4-9 shows an example of both views.

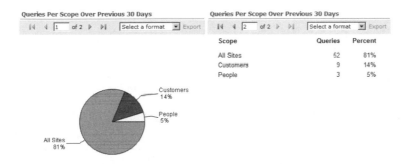

FIGURE 4-9 Graphical and tabular representation of Queries Per Scope Over Previous 30 Days

The pie chart shows the activity distribution expressed in percentages among the search scopes. The table view additionally shows the exact number of queries in which the search scope was used.

This metric can help you find the search scopes that are useful to end users. You might have created and exposed one or more search scopes that were expected to be useful during the gathering of requirements for the search experience. But if these search scopes are rarely used, it might be worthwhile to consider removing them again. Less clutter in the search experience is usually good news to end users and their productivity.

Top Queries Over Previous 30 Days

The Top Queries Over Previous 30 Days subreport lists the top queries—that is, search terms—that users have been searching for over the last 30 days. The list is presented in a table view, as shown in Figure 4-10.

Each row in the table represents a unique query string followed by the name of the search scope used and the number of occurrences. A small Search box on the toolbar at the top of the page provides simple searching within the visible list. This metric is designed primarily to help you get an overview of the most popular search terms in the business.

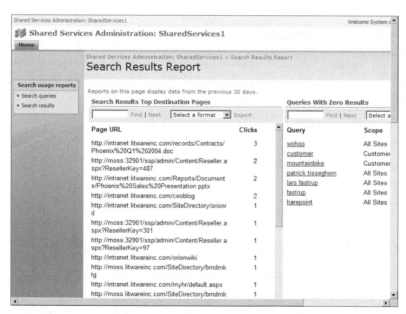

FIGURE 4-10 Tabular representation of Top Queries Over Previous 30 Days

Search Results Report

The Search Results report contains five metrics summarizing information about search results. Figure 4-11 shows an excerpt of the report at the level of an SSP.

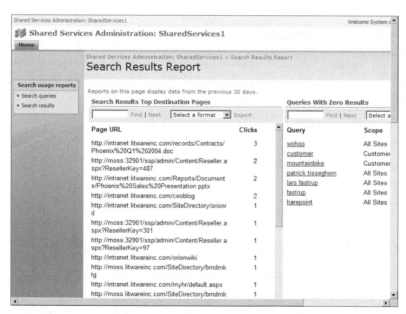

FIGURE 4-11 Search Results Report

The following subsections describe each metric in the report. All data on the page is generated from a rolling window of 30 days. The time span of this window is also hard-coded in the same way it is for the Search Queries Report reviewed in the preceding section.

All metrics in this report are presented in only a table view. There are no bar charts or pie charts in the report.

Search Results Top Destination Pages

The Search Results Top Destination Pages subreport tracks the URL of search results clicked by users. The table view shown in Figure 4-12 lists the top search results over the previous 30 days.

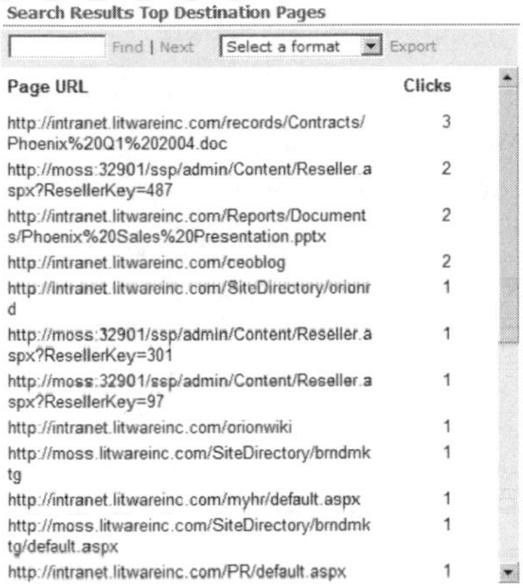

Page URL	Clicks
http://intranet.litwareinc.com/records/Contracts/Phoenix%20Q1%202004.doc	3
http://moss:32901/ssp/admin/Content/Reseller.aspx?ResellerKey=487	2
http://intranet.litwareinc.com/Reports/Documents/Phoenix%20Sales%20Presentation.pptx	2
http://intranet.litwareinc.com/ceoblog	2
http://intranet.litwareinc.com/SiteDirectory/orionrd	1
http://moss:32901/ssp/admin/Content/Reseller.aspx?ResellerKey=301	1
http://moss:32901/ssp/admin/Content/Reseller.aspx?ResellerKey=97	1
http://intranet.litwareinc.com/orionwiki	1
http://moss.litwareinc.com/SiteDirectory/brndmktg	1
http://intranet.litwareinc.com/myhr/default.aspx	1
http://moss.litwareinc.com/SiteDirectory/brndmktg/default.aspx	1
http://intranet.litwareinc.com/PR/default.aspx	1

FIGURE 4-12 Search Results Top Destination Pages

Each row in the table shows the URL of a search result along with the number of times it was clicked in a Search Center. You'll find this part of the Search Results Report useful for learning about the most popular pieces of information in the business.

Queries With Zero Results

Users will sometimes hit keywords yielding zero results. There are basically two scenarios where this event is likely to occur: First, the user might have been searching for information that is not available in the business or that has not yet been indexed by SharePoint. Second, the user might simply have misspelled one or more keywords in the query. This type of event is fortunately also tracked, and the table in Figure 4-13 shows an example of seven queries that yielded zero results.

Each query is accompanied by the name of the search scope and the number of times that users experienced zero results for the query. The table will list only the top 25 queries with zero results. Clicking the linked query will open the Search Center, where the query is executed again.

Queries With Zero Results

| Find | Next | Select a format ▼ | Export |

Query	Scope	Occurrences
wohoo	All Sites	1
customer	Customers	1
mountainbike	Customers	1
patrick tisseghem	All Sites	1
lars fastrup	All Sites	1
fastrup	All Sites	1
harepoint	All Sites	1

FIGURE 4-13 Queries With Zero Results

You should pay special attention to this metric when there is a significant trend among users to search for certain keywords where they obviously expect some results. A great way to improve the search experience and provide guidance for users on these types of queries is to create a best bet for the keyword or keyword phrase. The best bet can in turn help direct users to the information they expect, or it can simply explain why they did not find any results. See Figure 2-15 in Chapter 2, "The End-User Search Experience," for an example of a best bet, and see Chapter 5 for more information about creating a best bet and associating it with keywords.

Most Clicked Best Bets

Best bets are editorial results associated with one or more keywords or keyword phrases. They are useful for advertising links to important information in the business. It might also be useful to know whether these best bets have any effect on the end users—that is, whether the best bets are frequently clicked. The Search Results Report therefore includes a metric tracking the number of times each best bet has been clicked over the previous 30 days. Figure 4-14 shows an example of four best bets, each clicked one time.

Most Clicked Best Bets

| Find | Next | Select a format ▼ | Export |

Best Bet	Clicks
Brand Marketing	1
Marketing	1
My HR	1
PR	1

FIGURE 4-14 Most Clicked Best Bets

The best bets are ranked in descending order by the number of clicks. However, only the top 25 entries are included in the list.

Queries With Zero Best Bets

The Search Results Report includes two metrics on best bets. The first metric was described in the preceding section. The second metric, Queries With Zero Best Bets, tracks queries not associated with one or more best bets. You can correlate this metric with the Queries With Zero Results metric to identify new best bet candidates. The subreport in Figure 4-15 shows an example of multiple queries with zero best bets.

FIGURE 4-15 Queries With Zero Best Bets

The top 25 queries are ranked in descending order by the number of occurrences.

Queries With Low Clickthrough

This last subreport on the Search Results Report page, Queries With Low Clickthrough, is generated from metric tracking queries where users do not tend to click any results. It can, in other words, tell you how often users are searching in vain. For example, a possible trend could be that users are often searching for the keyword *HR* but that *HR* is always spelled out *Human Resources* in all relevant content. Hence, users will not find and click any relevant information when searching for this abbreviation.

Let's assume that the users in this case expect to find the home page of the HR department. You can alleviate this problem in several ways. One option is to create a replacement synonym in the search engine thesaurus, replacing *hr* with *human resources* at query time. (See Chapter 5 for complete coverage of the thesaurus.) This option will work fine if the results ranking algorithm includes the home page at the top of the results. If it does not, you might consider creating a best bet instead.

Figure 4-16 shows an example of the Queries With Low Clickthrough subreport. Queries are listed in ascending order by their clickthrough rate percentage. This percentage is calculated from the number of times the query was executed by users and the number of times they in turn clicked a result. A query executed 100 times and with only one clickthrough will yield a one percent clickthrough rate. Queries with a zero percent clickthrough rate are included only when the Show 0% Queries check box is selected.

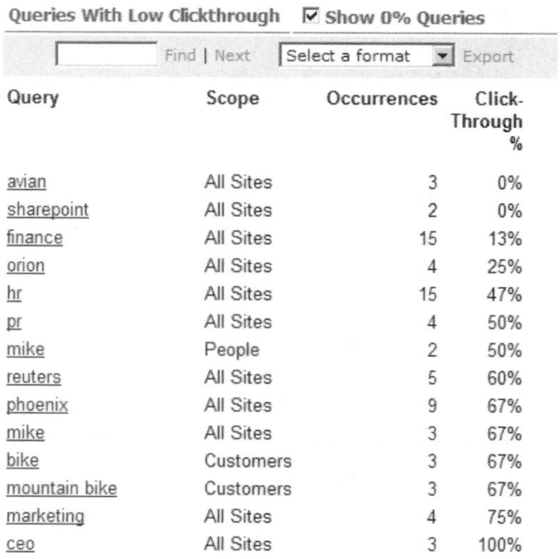

Queries With Low Clickthrough	☑ Show 0% Queries		
[____] Find | Next Select a format ▼ Export			
Query	**Scope**	**Occurrences**	**Click-Through %**
avian	All Sites	3	0%
sharepoint	All Sites	2	0%
finance	All Sites	15	13%
orion	All Sites	4	25%
hr	All Sites	15	47%
pr	All Sites	4	50%
mike	People	2	50%
reuters	All Sites	5	60%
phoenix	All Sites	9	67%
mike	All Sites	3	67%
bike	Customers	3	67%
mountain bike	Customers	3	67%
marketing	All Sites	4	75%
ceo	All Sites	3	100%

FIGURE 4-16 Queries With Low Clickthrough

Exporting Search Usage Data

The look and feel of the Search Queries Report and the Search Results Report presented in the preceding two sections is not customizable. Nor can you view data beyond the 30-day data window. Historical data also is not stored for later recall. Instead, every subreport can be exported to Microsoft Office Excel or to an Adobe Acrobat PDF file.

Exporting a single subreport is simply a matter of selecting the export format from the drop-down list on the toolbar and then clicking the Export link, as shown in Figure 4-17.

FIGURE 4-17 Export usage data

Exporting Data to Microsoft Office Excel

Exporting subreports to Microsoft Office Excel is useful if you need to

- Create reports with a new look and feel but using the same data.
- Save data before it slides out of the 30-day window.

Selecting Excel in the drop-down list and clicking the Export link shown earlier in Figure 4-17 will create a new Excel document, which you are in turn prompted to save on disk or to open directly in Excel. Figures 4-18 and 4-19 show an example of exporting the Queries Over Previous 12 Months subreport. This subreport yields two sheets in the Excel document, the bar chart on Sheet1 and the underlying data on Sheet2. Subreports without a graph view will yield just a single sheet containing the data.

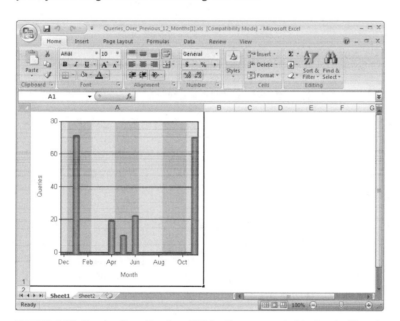

FIGURE 4-18 Queries Over Previous 12 Months as exported to Excel—Sheet1

Having the raw data at your disposal in Excel gives you a virtually endless range of possibilities to create and print custom reports.

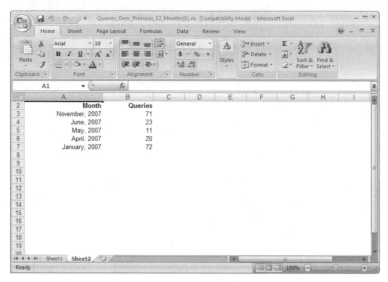

FIGURE 4-19 Queries Over Previous 12 Months as exported to Excel—Sheet2

Exporting Data to Adobe Acrobat PDF

Each subreport can also be exported to an Adobe Acrobat PDF document, which is a very useful feature when you need to

- Print the report.

- Save the report as is for later recall.

Selecting Acrobat (PDF) File in the drop-down list and clicking the Export link shown earlier in Figure 4-17 will create a new PDF document, which you are in turn prompted to save on disk or to open in the Adobe Acrobat application if installed. Figures 4-20 and 4-21 show an example of exporting the Queries Over Previous 12 Months subreport. This subreport yields two pages in the PDF document: the bar chart on page 1 and the data table on page 2. Subreports without a graph view will yield just a single page containing the data table.

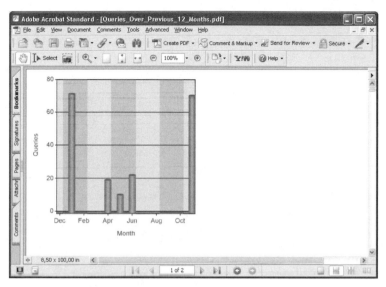

FIGURE 4-20 Queries Over Previous 12 Months as exported to PDF—page 1

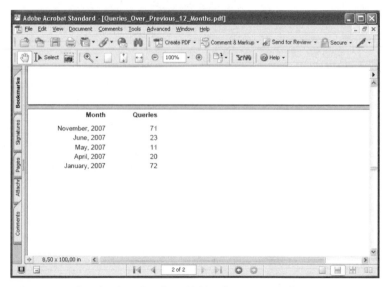

FIGURE 4-21 Queries Over Previous 12 Months as exported to PDF—page 2

Summary

In this chapter, you've learned virtually everything there is to know about the search usage reports and the technical architecture that drives them. You've also learned how to transform some of the metrics in the reports into concrete actions, improving the search experience for end users. In the next chapter, you'll learn how to work with SSPs to provide the search usage reporting infrastructure and more.

Chapter 5
Search Administration

After completing this chapter, you will be able to

- Understand the relationship between Shared Services Providers (SSPs) and Search.

- Administer search settings at the farm level, at the level of SSPs, and at the site collection level.

- Configure the search engine to index content from different sources.

- Configure the search engine to index other file types such as Adobe Acrobat PDF and Microsoft Office OneNote 2007.

- Influence crawls by creating crawl rules.

- Manage search scopes.

- Manage metadata in the search index.

- Optimize search result ranking.

- Manage the Search service.

- Control the crawler using crawler impact rules.

- Work with the thesaurus.

- Automate administration tasks using Microsoft Windows PowerShell.

This chapter covers all the knobs and dials available to you as an administrator of the Enterprise Search engine that ships with Microsoft Office SharePoint Server 2007. The first section introduces the important relationship between Search and SSPs. The second section offers a compact overview of all the administrative settings and the level at which they are managed. Next is a section covering the administrative aspects of getting the search engine up and running in a new farm. After the search engine is ready for use, you'll learn about the administrative search settings available at different administration and security levels in the farm. Last, the chapter concludes with a section on automating selected administrative tasks by using Microsoft Windows PowerShell version 1.0.

In this chapter, the discussion of working with the administrative settings is combined with best practices, stories linking to real-world scenarios, and detailed descriptions of important concepts. The detailed descriptions will help you gain more in-depth knowledge about the nature of full crawls and incremental crawls. The concept behind the authentication mechanism implemented by the crawler is also discussed in detail.

Search Is a Shared Service

Microsoft Office SharePoint Server 2007 includes a new concept known as *Shared Services Providers* (SSPs). An SSP is a collection of components that can provide common services to multiple Internet Information Services (IIS) Web applications in a SharePoint server farm. You will at a minimum need to create one instance of an SSP in your farm before the IIS Web applications can start consuming the available services. But you can create more than one instance of an SSP, or you can share SSPs across multiple farms. Creating a new SSP is discussed in the section "Creating a New SSP" later in this chapter. To gain a better understanding of common search deployment scenarios and search topologies, reviewing when it makes sense to create multiple instances of an SSP, see Chapter 7, "Search Deployment Considerations."

Enterprise Search is one of the services offered by SSPs. Here is the complete list of services that you get out-of-the-box with Office SharePoint Server 2007:

- User Profile Application (People Management)
- Office SharePoint Server Search
- Usage Analytics
- Session State

These services are included in the standard edition of the product. The enterprise edition adds a few more services:

- Excel Services
- Forms Services
- Business Data Catalog (BDC)

The Usage Analytics service includes search-related usage reports, which are covered in Chapter 4, "Search Usage Reports." The present chapter will not go into any more details on the other services, as they are outside the scope of this book. See *Inside Microsoft Office SharePoint Server 2007*, by Patrick Tisseghem (Microsoft Press, 2007), for more in-depth information about these services.

One SSP is responsible for one physical content index. It is not possible to create additional physical indexes inside an SSP. The main reason for the product team to choose this option was to provide better relevancy of search results. In most cases, you actually do not need more than one physical index, as one SSP supports at least 50 million documents. This is not a physical limit but the number of documents Microsoft has tested for.

Overview of Search Administration Settings

The settings of the different search-related features available in the search engine of Office SharePoint Server 2007 are managed at three different levels. The first and topmost level is the farm level, with settings that apply across all instances of SSPs. The second level is that of a single SSP instance, which allows you to manage settings separately for each instance. The third level is at the site collection. The available settings for each level are listed here.

- **Farm level**   SharePoint farm administrators can
  - ❑ Start and configure the Search service on index and query servers in the farm.
  - ❑ Create and configure new SSPs.
  - ❑ Configure proxy settings to have some or all content crawled through a proxy server.
  - ❑ Configure crawler timeout settings.
  - ❑ Define crawler impact rules to control the crawler and make it less aggressive on selected sites.

- **SSP level**   Administrators of SSPs can
  - ❑ Create content sources for crawling content from one or more sources.
  - ❑ Define crawl rules to influence the behavior of the crawler.
  - ❑ Define crawl schedules to schedule full crawls and incremental crawls of each content source.
  - ❑ Remove unwanted items in the content index with immediate effect in the search results.
  - ❑ Specify the user name and password for the default content access account used by the crawler to authenticate with sites. The crawler needs these credentials to download content from sites that might otherwise deny the crawler to access the content.
  - ❑ Inspect crawl logs to troubleshoot crawls.
  - ❑ Define server name mappings to alter the host name of crawled Uniform Resource Locators (URLs) in search results.
  - ❑ Install *IFilters* and protocol handlers to support file types and content sources that are not available by default.
  - ❑ Add or remove file types that are picked up by the crawler.
  - ❑ Create shared search scopes to group content in the index.
  - ❑ Map crawled properties to managed properties.

- ❑ Specify authoritative pages to tune relevancy by click distance, which is the minimal number of mouse clicks it will take a user to navigate from the result page to the authoritative page.

- ❑ Enable or disable search-based alerts.

- ❑ Specify a target Search Center for the small Search box on personal sites.

- ❑ Create a custom thesaurus for one or more languages.

- ❑ Specify noise words that should be prevented from entering the index.

- ❑ Enable or disable diacritic-sensitive search. This concept is discussed in the section "Diacritic-Sensitive Search" later in this chapter.

- ■ **Site collection level**   Administrators of the site collection can

  - ❑ Specify a target Search Center for the small Search box on pages within the site collection.

  - ❑ Create local search scopes to group content in the index.

  - ❑ Create search scope display groups.

  - ❑ Create editorial search results using keywords and best bets.

  - ❑ Exclude one or more sites from a crawl.

  - ❑ Exclude one or more site columns from being picked up as properties by the crawler.

  - ❑ Exclude lists from a crawl.

The details of the preceding settings will be explored in the remainder of this chapter, starting with the farm-level administration of SSPs.

Administration of Shared Services Providers

This section covers all aspects of preparing and configuring the appropriate search services in a new SharePoint farm. Administrators must master the topics described here when deploying SharePoint using any topology other than a single-server deployment. The installation program for Office SharePoint Server 2007 offers an option to install a ready-to-use farm with one preconfigured SSP, allowing you to get started fast. But you should still study this section, even if you're using only single-server deployments, to learn about the Search service and how to create a new SSP instance.

Configuring and Starting the Search Service

Before you create a new SSP instance, you first need to know a little about the underlying Microsoft Windows service that hosts the search engine services. Be careful not to confuse the Windows service with a shared service, as these are conceptually very different. There is only one instance of the Office SharePoint Search service in Windows on each search server and index server in a farm. But there can be several SSP instances, and they all connect to the same instance of the Windows Search service, as shown here:

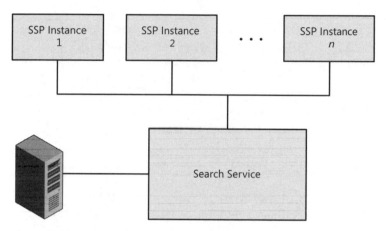

The Office SharePoint Search service in Windows can play the following two roles on a server:

- Crawling content and building index files (one content index per SSP)
- Serving search requests from users

The first role is known as the *index server role* and can be split out to a separate server for improved performance. The second role is the *search server role*, which typically runs on the same physical servers as the Web front-end servers. The index server will, if you make this split, automatically propagate all index changes across the network to these Web front-end servers.

Hence the Search service must be started on all Web front-end servers and index servers in the farm. Figure 5-1 shows where to start the service on one of the physical servers in the farm.

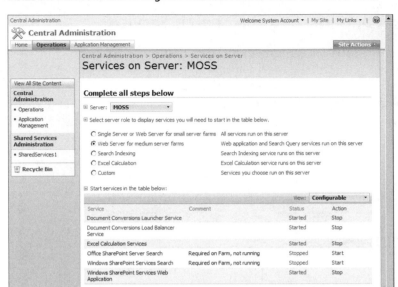

FIGURE 5-1 Starting the Search service

Clicking the Start link will not start the service right away; you must first configure it. You will therefore first need to fill in the configuration form, as shown in Figure 5-2.

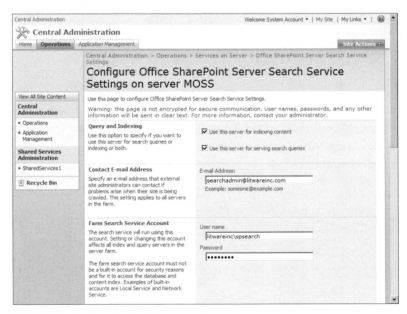

FIGURE 5-2 Configuring the Search service

The settings to be specified here depend largely on the farm topology. The following list describes the groups of settings:

- **Query And Indexing**   This group contains check boxes for the index server role and the search server role. Select both check boxes if you plan to use only a single server for all SharePoint roles. If your farm topology plan includes one or more dedicated index servers, select the first check box on the index servers and the second check box on the Web front-end servers. Please note that an SSP can be serviced by only one index server at a time, so it doesn't make sense to install more than one index server if you plan for only one SSP.

- **Contact E-Mail Address**   The e-mail address specified here is included in all HTTP Web requests that the crawler issues to external sites. This gives the administrators of these sites a chance to contact you if the crawler causes any problems for them.

- **Farm Search Service Account**   This is the account that the search process will run as; it must be a Windows domain account if you have more than one server in your farm. For security reasons, it is also recommended that you specify a least-privileged account—that is, an account with just enough privileges to run. Avoid specifying an administrator account here, especially in a production system. It is easy to set up a least-privileged account. Just add a normal user account to your Active Directory security group—for example, with the login name *spsearch*. SharePoint will automatically grant the required privileges to this account on the appropriate servers, including the database server.

- **Index Server Default File Location**   This setting, shown in Figure 5-3, denotes the default file location where the index server should store its index. Note that this location cannot be changed here if needed but you can specify a different path when creating an SSP. The indexing process generates a significant amount of disk activity, and you might therefore consider dedicating a high-speed disk drive to host the index files. This consideration is especially important for production systems with large amounts of content to be indexed.

FIGURE 5-3 Index Server Default File Location

- **Indexer Performance**   This setting, shown in Figure 5-4, controls how much load the indexing process can place on the index server and the search database. You should consider a lower setting than Maximum if you do not have a dedicated index server and dedicated search database server. The result might otherwise be a degraded user experience as the response time of the Web front-end server increases.

FIGURE 5-4 Indexer Performance

- **Web Front End And Crawling** The indexer normally hits the same Web front-end servers as the users to index the content stored within the SharePoint sites. To improve the user experience and improve indexing performance, you might consider using this option to dedicate an entire Web front-end server to the indexer. It is recommended that you install the dedicated Web front-end server on the same physical server as the indexer. This approach will reduce network traffic and speed indexing. Figure 5-5 shows this option, which appears farther down on the page shown earlier in Figure 5-2.

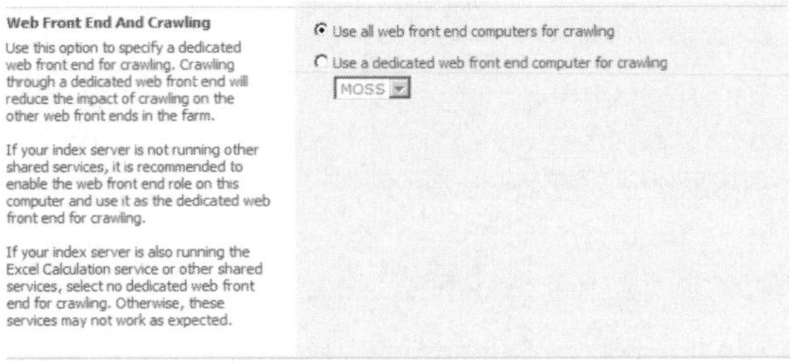

FIGURE 5-5 Web Front End And Crawling

- **Query Server Index File Location** This settings group, shown in Figure 5-6, is displayed on the page only when you are configuring the Search service to use the query server role—in other words, when you have selected the second check box in the Query And Indexing group. The file location specified here determines where the indexes, propagated from the index server to the query servers, are stored.

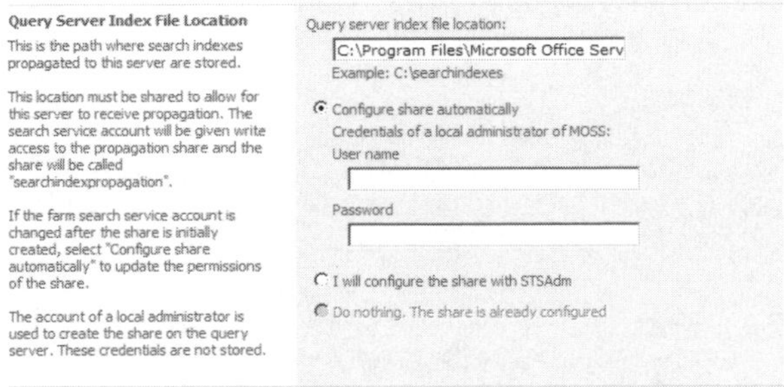

FIGURE 5-6 Query Server Index File Location

Click OK at the bottom of the page to apply the settings and start the Search service. You can now verify that the Windows service was installed and started successfully, as shown in Figure 5-7. Check that the Status column reads *Started* and that the Log On As column gives the account you specified during the configuration.

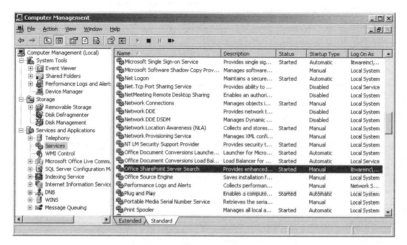

FIGURE 5-7 Verifying that the Search service is running

Tip The internal name of the Search service is *OSearch*. It can be stopped and started from the Windows command line using the following two commands:

```
net stop osearch

net start osearch
```

Creating a New SSP

With the Search service started, we are now ready to create an SSP, which in turn gives us a new physical content index. Open SharePoint 3.0 Central Administration, select Application Management in the top navigation bar, and then click the Create Or Configure This Farm's Shared Services link to view the page shown in Figure 5-8.

FIGURE 5-8 Creating a new SSP

Click the New SSP option on the toolbar to begin creation of a new SSP. This will in turn open the configuration form, shown in Figure 5-9.

FIGURE 5-9 Configuring the new SSP

Use the settings in the SSP Name group to specify a name for the SSP—for example, SharedServices2—and to select an IIS Web application for the SSP administration site. The page contains six additional groups of settings, of which only the following two are directly related to searching:

- **Search Database**   Each SSP requires two databases: a *core database* shared by all the services in the SSP plus a *search database* storing frequently changing data. The search database contains the metadata store. In most cases, you will simply create the databases on the same SQL server that hosts the SharePoint content databases. But on larger systems, the indexing process can create a large amount of disk activity on the disk drive where the search database is stored. A relevant performance consideration is to place the database files on a dedicated high-speed disk drive. You can additionally decide to dedicate another SQL server to the SSPs. Figure 5-10 shows the options for creating the search database.

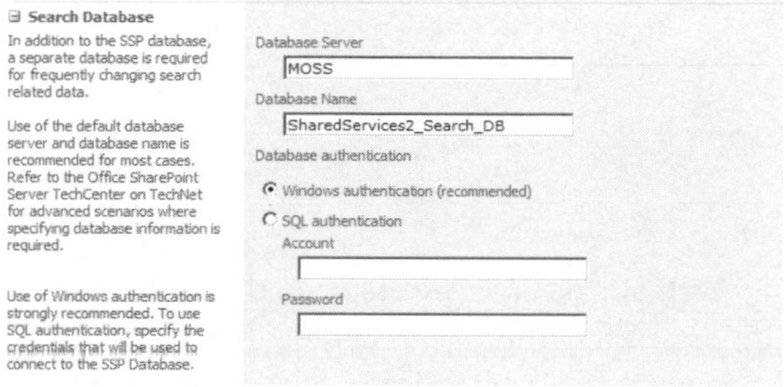

FIGURE 5-10 Search Database

■ **Index Server**   This settings group, shown in Figure 5-11, enables you to select the index server that should serve the new SSP. The Index Server drop-down list includes all of the servers in the farm configured to use the index server role, as described earlier. The Index Server setting implies that an SSP can be served by only one index server, but an index server can serve multiple SSPs.

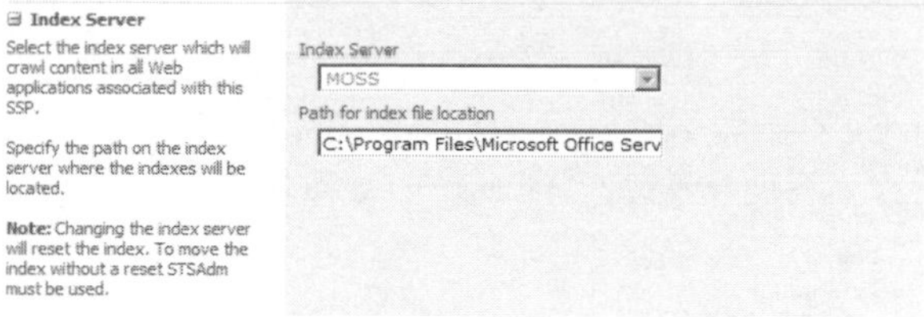

FIGURE 5-11 Index Server

Click OK to apply the settings and start the SSP creation process.

Associating an SSP with IIS Web Applications

The vast majority of installations will need only one SSP. In a few special cases, described in Chapter 7, you will need more than one SSP.

But let's for a moment assume that you have two SSPs, as shown in Figure 5-12.

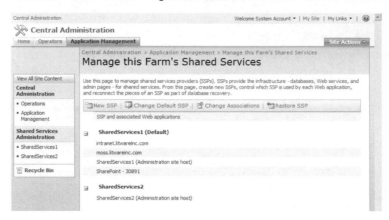

FIGURE 5-12 Managing two SSPs

As you can see, all content IIS Web applications are associated with the default SSP (SharedServices1). This in turn means that the Search Centers hosted by these IIS Web applications will execute queries against the content index of this SSP. It is not possible to configure the Search Centers to search against an SSP other than the one that the content IIS Web application is associated with.

New IIS Web applications are automatically associated with the default SSP—SharedServices1 in the present discussion. But you can always change the association if required by clicking the Change Associations link shown earlier in Figure 5-12. This will display the form shown in Figure 5-13.

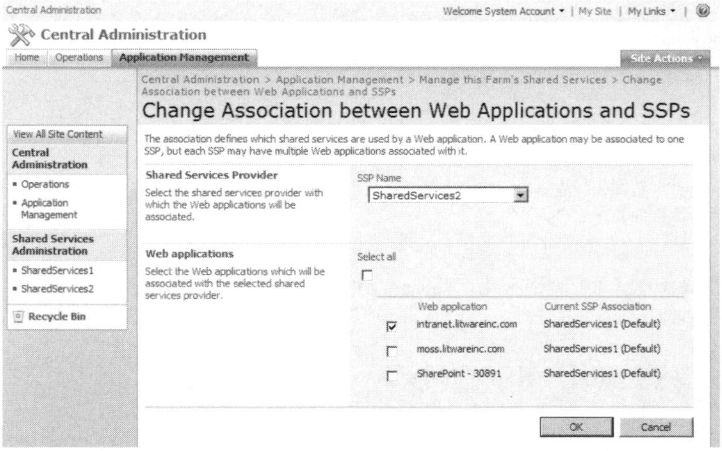

FIGURE 5-13 Associating Web applications with another SSP

First select the SSP that you want to associate existing IIS Web applications with. Then select the IIS Web applications that you want to associate, and click OK to apply the changes.

From then on, the Search Centers in the checked IIS Web applications will search against the content index of the specified SSP.

Managing the Search Settings of an SSP

Having started the Search service and created a new SSP instance, we are now ready to start indexing some content. This section describes the various search-related options available to each SSP instance. You can access search settings at the level of the SSP by navigating to the appropriate SSP administration site and clicking the Search Settings link, as shown in Figure 5-14.

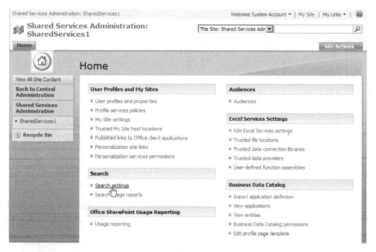

FIGURE 5-14 Accessing the search settings from an SSP administration site

Clicking the Search Settings link brings you to the top-level configuration page of the SSP-level search settings, as shown in Figure 5-15.

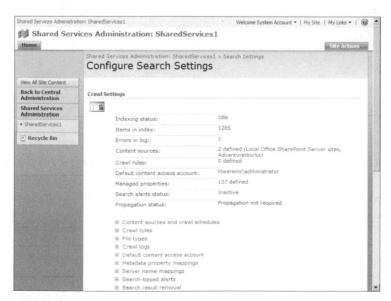

FIGURE 5-15 Top-level page of search settings at the SSP level

Managing Content Sources

One of the most important tasks for search administrators is to properly configure the SSP with the different content sources to index. Office SharePoint Server Search 2007 is very flexible here, allowing you to index content from virtually any source. You can by default index content from the following types of sources:

- Windows SharePoint Services 3.0 sites
- Windows SharePoint Services 2.0 sites
- Non-SharePoint Web sites
- User profiles
- Windows file shares
- Microsoft Exchange Server public folders

And with some extra installation and configuration steps, you can also index these content sources:

- **Business data**   This could include, for instance, business data from SAP or Siebel systems, but can also be business data from proprietary systems inside your organization. See Chapter 6, "Indexing and Searching Business Data," for complete coverage of this topic.

- **Lotus Notes databases**   The SharePoint administrator must run a post-installation setup wizard on the index server to enable this feature.

If that's not enough, you can also look for and install third-party add-ons (protocol handlers) to index content from other back-end systems such as:

- Exchange Mailboxes
- EMC Documentum
- FileNet
- Hummingbird

A *protocol handler* is the component responsible for communicating with the content source being indexed. It contains the logic to connect to and enumerate the content of the content source. The SharePoint indexer has a pluggable framework that allows you to install additional protocol handlers next to the ones you get out-of-the-box. Later in this chapter, you'll learn about another component, called an *IFilter*, which is the component responsible for breaking a specific document format into plain chunks of text.

> **Note** There are many third-party protocol handlers and *IFilters* available to support different systems and file formats. Later in this chapter, we'll install a third-party *IFilter* from Adobe to enable support for indexing PDF files.

Last is the option to develop a custom protocol handler with the necessary business logic to access specialized or proprietary systems. This is not a trivial task, however, and should not be underestimated. This topic is covered in detail in Chapter 9, "Advanced Search Engine Topics."

Indexing SharePoint Sites

New SSPs are by default configured to index the content of all the IIS Web applications that they are associated with. This is handled via a single content source definition named Local Office SharePoint Server Sites, as shown in Figure 5-16.

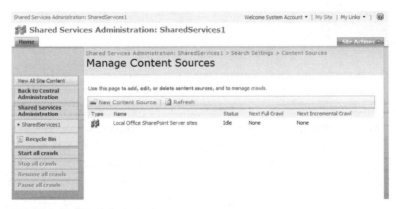

FIGURE 5-16 The default content source

Clicking the linked name of the content source will display its settings, as shown in Figure 5-17. An interesting group of settings is the Start Addresses group. This group simply lists the root URL of all the Web applications to index. New IIS Web applications associated with the SSP are automatically added to this list. The other settings in this page are described in the section "Configuring Crawl Schedules" later in this chapter.

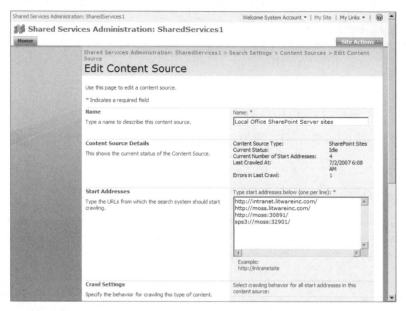

FIGURE 5-17 Details of the default content source

Let's look at how to index additional SharePoint sites. In many organizations, a common scenario is to have two SharePoint farms: one Microsoft Office SharePoint Server 2007 farm for the company's structured intranet and a Windows SharePoint Services farm for the large number of team collaboration sites that are typically created. The download version of the Windows SharePoint Services farm does not include Enterprise Search capabilities. Each Windows SharePoint Services site allows users to search only within the site. However, often there is request for search capability across multiple sites. This can be achieved by pointing an SSP in the Office SharePoint Server farm to all the content IIS Web applications of the Windows SharePoint Services farm.

You could simply add the addresses to the list of start addresses in the default content source mentioned earlier. But it might be a better idea to create a new content source for the external SharePoint sites. Doing so will make it easier to isolate the content in a search scope and will also make it possible to specify a different crawl schedule for the content. The concept of crawl schedules is discussed in the section "Configuring Crawl Schedules" later in this chapter. Let's create a new content source named External SharePoint Sites. Start by clicking the New Content Source button shown earlier in Figure 5-16, and then configure the new content source as shown in Figure 5-18.

Enter the URLs of the SharePoint Web applications or site collections you need to index. You can enter up to 500 start addresses for each content source. Click OK at the bottom of the page to save the new content source. You will now have two SharePoint content sources, as shown in Figure 5-19.

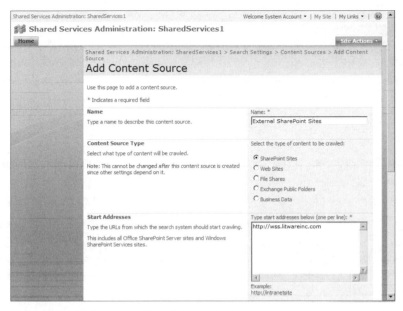

FIGURE 5-18 Adding a new SharePoint content source

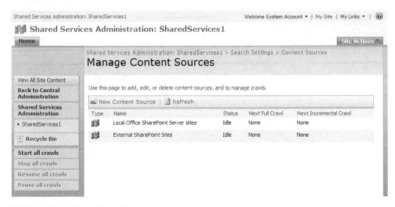

FIGURE 5-19 Two SharePoint content sources

Indexing Web Sites

You've now seen how SharePoint can be configured to index itself by creating a content source for SharePoint sites. But you can also use the search engine in Office SharePoint Server 2007 to index non-SharePoint Web sites—that is, any type of HTML Web site. This is known as *standard Web crawling*, and it can be useful if you want to index your legacy intranet or other Web applications developed on a different technology platform than Windows SharePoint Services.

The most significant differences from indexing SharePoint sites as described in the preceding section are as follows:

- New pages and sites are indexed by following the links displayed on each page. A SharePoint content source simply asks SharePoint for the complete list of content to index.

- Incremental crawls for Web sites are much slower than incremental crawls for SharePoint sites.

- There is no security trimming of Web pages. In contrast to the Web sites crawler, the SharePoint sites crawler stores item-level access control information in the index to ensure that users will find only content that they are authorized to view.

Important The Web sites crawler is designed primarily for the indexing of Web sites of decent structural quality. Sites using all JavaScript menus and no standard hyperlinks will quickly bring the crawler to a dead end. Content created using Microsoft Silverlight, Adobe Flash, and similar technologies is also not indexed.

With this in mind, let's now create a new content source for indexing some SharePoint-related blogs on the Internet. Start by clicking the New Content Source link shown earlier in Figure 5-16, and then configure the new content source for indexing these blogs, as shown in Figure 5-20.

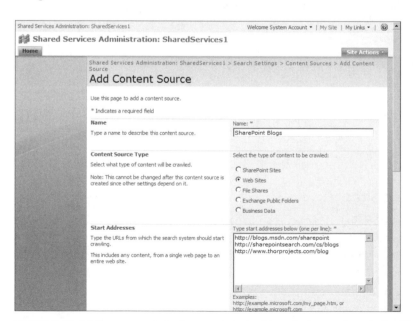

FIGURE 5-20 Adding a new content source to index blogs that are not created as SharePoint sites

Specify a name for the new content source—in this example, **SharePoint Blogs**. Then select the Web Sites option, and type one or more start addresses of the blogs to index.

> **Note** The capability to specify multiple start addresses is an improvement over the Web sites crawler in Microsoft SharePoint Portal Server 2003, which let you enter only one start address per content source.

The Crawl Settings group, shown in Figure 5-21, lets you control the behavior of the crawl.

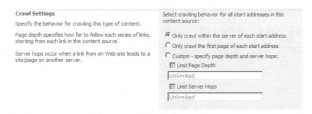

FIGURE 5-21 Crawl settings for Web sites

The effects of the possible crawl settings shown in Figure 5-21 are as follows:

- **Only Crawl Within The Server Of Each Start Address**   This option will crawl all discoverable pages on the specified server. The phrase *within the server* is literally everything on the server regardless of whether you specify a deep URL as the starting address. Specifying a deep URL for a subsite deep in the site hierarchy will not limit the crawler to that branch of this site. It will also crawl all parent and sibling sites. For example, when you specify the start address *http://blogs.msdn.com/sharepoint*, the crawler will also index sibling sites like *http://blogs.msdn.com/joelo*.

- **Only Crawl The First Page Of Each Start Address**   This simply disables the link-following mechanism of the crawler.

- **Custom**   Use this option to limit the page depth and the number of allowed server hops—that is, the following of links to other servers.

The last group of settings in the Add Content Source page shown earlier in Figure 5-20 is the Crawl Schedules group, which will be covered shortly. The concept of scheduled crawls is essentially the same for all types of content sources. Crawl rules can also affect the behavior of the Web sites crawler. This topic is covered in more detail in the section "Configuring Crawl Rules" later in this chapter.

Indexing File Shares

An important consideration when SharePoint is introduced as the new collaboration tool in an organization is what to do with existing documents residing on various file shares. How can you migrate your existing file shares to SharePoint? It can easily be a daunting or even an undesirable task to migrate existing documents to SharePoint document libraries.

You might instead simply decide to draw a line in the sand and tell your users that from tomorrow they should stop sharing new documents on file shares and start using SharePoint document libraries instead. You might in the same context also tell them to move their still relevant documents to the appropriate document libraries as they go. You will as an administrator assist them by making all existing file shares searchable from within the Search Center available with Office SharePoint Server 2007.

The approach you choose for migrating file shares to SharePoint of course depends on your organization. But the suggestion given here is easy and could work well for many. It's a bit like moving into a new house. You're probably surprised to discover the large quantities of useless stuff that you managed to collect in the attic or in the garage. You then decide to use the event of moving as a good opportunity to get rid of all the rubbish you'll never need again. Getting rid of unwanted stuff will also save you some effort moving it to the new place and organizing it there.

The files share crawler that is part of the Office SharePoint Server 2007 indexer has the following features and characteristics:

- Indexes files and folder names.

- Stores access control lists (ACLs) from NTFS file shares in the index to allow for proper security trimming of results.

- Indexes only known file types. See the section "File Types" later in this chapter for more information about registering new file types.

To illustrate all of the preceding list items, let's take a look at how to configure the indexer of Office SharePoint Server 2007 to index file shares. Start the creation of a new content source by clicking the New Content Source link shown earlier in Figure 5-16, and then configure the content source as shown in Figure 5-22.

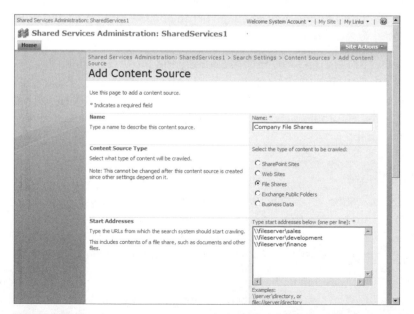

FIGURE 5-22 Creating a new content source for indexing Windows file shares

File Shares vs. SharePoint Document Libraries

One of the ideas behind SharePoint is to eliminate or at least reduce the need for file shares when it comes to sharing documents. How often have you heard about the large chaotic file shares that rule in many organizations? These file shares have a tendency to just keep growing wild in terms of size and folder structure.

The file share concept is of course not dead. There are still plenty of useful scenarios where a file share makes perfect sense. But SharePoint is superior when it comes to sharing documents for any size group of people. SharePoint lets you create *document libraries*, which are containers where users can create and upload documents in SharePoint. The major benefits of document libraries over file shares are as follows:

- **Clear context**   Documents will exist in the context of a SharePoint Web site, with a title, an owner, other team members, and so on. So here you have a chance to make a tighter coupling between documents and specific projects or topics.

- **Version control**   Keep track of older versions of the same document. File shares are often littered with copies of the same document as a kind of pseudo version control—for example files like Mydocument1.doc, Mydocument2.doc, and Mydocument_Final.doc.

- **Two-stage recycle bin**   No risk of losing any documents by accidental deletion. This can help to stop users from creating renamed copies of their documents such as Mydocument_old.doc.

- **Excellent metadata support**   Easily define and associate metadata with documents.

- **Workflows**   Create workflows for documents that need to follow a specific business process.

- **Content types**   These are definitions for the different document types you want to store in SharePoint.

- **Alerts**   Get e-mail notifications on document changes.

- **Event handlers**   Register custom event handlers to execute custom actions whenever documents are created, updated, or deleted.

Type a name for the new Content Source—in this example, **Company File Shares**. Then select File Shares and type the UNC of the file shares to index.

The page shown in Figure 5-22 also contains a group of settings labeled Crawl Settings, allowing you to control the behavior of the crawl. Figure 5-23 shows the two available options in this group.

FIGURE 5-23 Crawl settings for file shares

The first option, The Folder And All Subfolders Of Each Start Address, instructs the crawler to traverse the entire folder structure from the starting addresses. The second option will limit the crawl to files in the root folder of the specified start addresses. Crawl schedules and crawl rules are also relevant to the crawling of file shares. These topics are covered in the sections "Configuring Crawl Schedules" and "Configuring Crawl Rules" later in this chapter.

Indexing Business Data

The Business Data Catalog (BDC) is a large topic in itself, deserving of its own chapter; see Chapter 6 for complete coverage of this topic.

It will suffice for now just to nail down the procedure for creating a new content source for indexing business data. Navigate to the administration site of the appropriate SSP, and start the creation of a new content source by clicking the New Content Source link shown earlier in Figure 5-16. When the page shown in Figure 5-24 appears, select Business Data to configure the new content source for indexing BDC applications that represent models of your business data stored in the BDC metadata store.

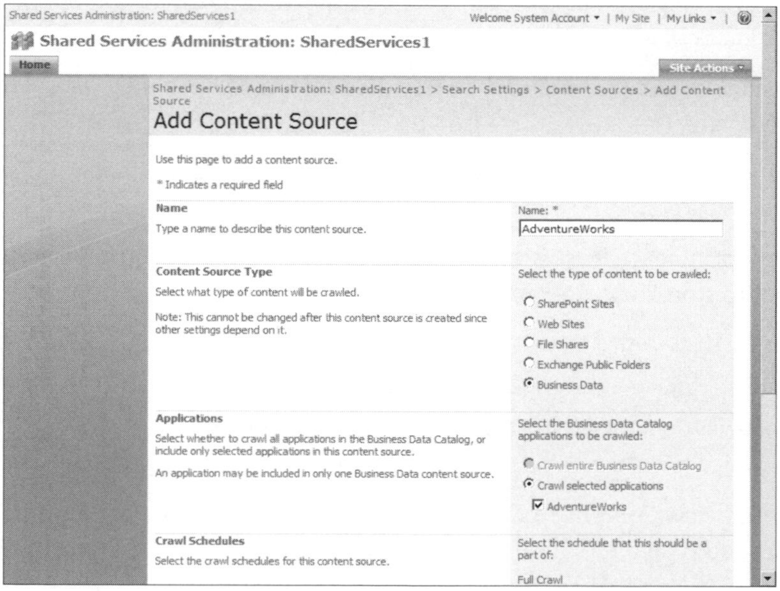

FIGURE 5-24 Adding a new content source for indexing business data

Specify a name for the new content source—in this example, **AdventureWorks**. This example creates a new business data content source for indexing the sample SQL database named AdventureWorks from Microsoft.

Indexing Lotus Notes Databases

Office SharePoint Server 2007 also includes support for indexing IBM Lotus Notes databases. You'll need to complete a few additional installation steps before you can create new Lotus Notes content sources and index Lotus Notes databases.

> **Note** This section also applies to SharePoint Portal Server 2003, as the mechanism for indexing Lotus Notes Databases has not changed in the 2007 version.

1. **Install the Lotus Notes client**. SharePoint requires the Lotus Notes client to be installed on the index server to perform the crawls of the Notes databases. Depending on the existing Lotus Notes setup in your organization, you can choose to install either an R5 or an R6 version of the Lotus Notes client. Upon successful installation, you should check that the client can successfully connect to the Lotus Domino server of the business.

2. **Download and install the Lotus C++ API Toolkit for Notes/Domino 3.0**. SharePoint also requires a library file named lcppn30.dll. This file is not distributed with SharePoint and must first be downloaded from the IBM Web site. The file is packaged as part of the Lotus C++ API Toolkit. After you have downloaded and extracted the file, copy it to the C:\Program Files\Microsoft Office Servers\12.0\Bin directory.

3. **Run the Lotus Notes Index Setup Wizard**. By default, you cannot create a new Lotus Notes content source in the same way you can create a new content source for indexing Web sites or file shares as described earlier. After installing the Lotus Notes client and the lcppn30.dll file, you will also need to run a special Lotus Notes Setup Wizard on the SharePoint index server. The wizard will perform the required post-installation steps of the SharePoint indexer to include support for crawling Lotus Notes databases.

   The Lotus Notes Index Setup Wizard is included as an .exe file in the Office SharePoint Server 2007 installation. The file is named NotesSetup.exe and can be found in the folder C:\Program Files\Microsoft Office Servers\12.0\Bin. Start the wizard, and click Next to proceed to the wizard page shown in Figure 5-25.

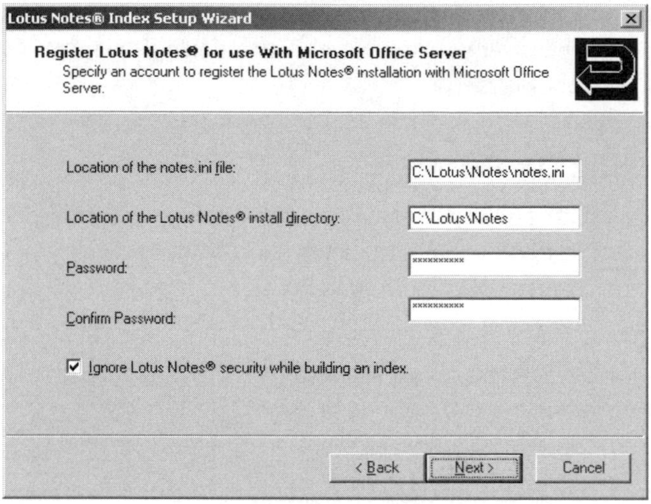

FIGURE 5-25 The Lotus Notes Index Setup Wizard

Type the location of the notes.ini file in the top text box. This file is usually located in the Lotus Notes installation directory. In the second text box, type the path where you installed the Lotus Notes client in step 1. Then type the password of the account used to connect to the Lotus Notes directory. This must be the password of the account that you specified in the Lotus Notes client when establishing a connection to the Lotus Domino server.

Note   In this example, we'll choose to ignore Lotus Notes security, as this is a fairly complicated topic that is beyond the scope of this book. Briefly, it is possible to direct SharePoint to map Lotus Notes identification numbers to Windows domain accounts to honor Notes security and perform appropriate security trimming of search results. Microsoft Knowledge Base article 288816 explains the mapping of accounts; it can be found at *http://support.microsoft.com/kb/288816*.

Clicking the Next button will start the configuration process and will, when finished, tell you whether the configuration succeeded or failed. The configuration will fail if, for example, it cannot find the lcppn30.dll library.

4. **Create Lotus Notes content sources**. After the Lotus Notes Setup Wizard completes successfully, you can create a new Lotus Notes content source, as shown in Figure 5-26.

   Selecting Lotus Notes in the Content Source Type group will display the Lotus Notes Server, Database, And Properties settings group. Use this group to specify the server and the database you want to index.

Note You cannot specify multiple databases here as you can for Web sites and file shares. You must create a new content source for each Lotus Notes database to be indexed.

FIGURE 5-26 Creating a new Lotus Notes content source

The Nature of Full and Incremental Crawls

The SharePoint indexer can perform two types of crawls to fetch and index content: full crawls and incremental crawls. Be aware that you cannot run an incremental crawl on a new content source before first having completed at least one full crawl.

Note The crawler does not change the files on the host servers in any way. Instead, the files on the host servers are simply accessed and read, and the text and metadata for those files are sent to the index server to be indexed. However, because the crawler reads the content on the host server, some servers that host certain sources of content might update the last-accessed date on files that have been crawled.

Incremental crawls generally complete much faster than full crawls, as they access only content that has been updated since the last crawl. The efficiency of incremental crawls does, however, depend on the type of the content source being crawled. This is because the different content sources each employ a different strategy for finding updated content, as outlined in Table 5-1.

TABLE 5-1 Incremental Crawl Strategies

Content Source Type	Speed	Incremental Crawl Strategy
SharePoint sites	Fastest	The crawler relies on the change log in Windows SharePoint Services for enumerating the list of all changes since the last incremental crawl. This strategy is extremely efficient, as the crawler knows exactly what has changed.
Web sites	Slow	Incremental crawls of Web sites are fairly slow because the crawler will need to make an HTTP request to each known page to detect whether it has been updated since the last incremental crawl.
File shares	Fast	The crawler will reindex only files where the last modified timestamp is newer than the timestamp of the last incremental crawl. Please note that the crawler does not and cannot react to Windows file system events—that is, notification-based crawling is not supported.
Exchange Server public folders	Fast	The crawler will reindex only items where the last modified timestamp is newer than the timestamp of the last incremental crawl.
Business data	Fast	Fast if support for incremental crawls has been implemented properly for the BDC application in question.

A full crawl will always enumerate and index all existing content encompassed by the content source definition, making it significantly slower than an incremental crawl. It is therefore recommended that you choose incremental crawls over full crawls whenever possible. The following list outlines the different scenarios where a full crawl is required to keep the index in sync with the content:

- When a new managed property has been defined and mapped to one or more crawled properties.

- When the mapping of crawled properties for an existing managed property is changed.

- When one or more .aspx pages have been updated. (The crawler is not able to detect when .aspx pages have been modified.)

- When one or more crawl rules have been added, modified, or deleted.

- When a new file type is registered or when an existing file type is removed.

- When a service pack is installed on servers in the farm.

- When the index is corrupted for unexplained reasons.

Incremental crawls are automatically turned into full crawls when one of the following conditions occurs:

- A full crawl of the content source has never been performed.

- The previous crawl was stopped by the SSP administrator.

- A content database was restored.

Another important issue related to the nature of full and incremental crawls is a concept known as *continuous propagation*. This is a new feature in Office SharePoint Server 2007, and it basically means that the indexer will continuously propagate index changes to the query servers during a crawl. This in turn reduces the time from when content is added, updated, or deleted until the change is reflected in the search results.

> **Note** The indexer of SharePoint Portal Server 2003 does not feature continuous propagation. It will not propagate the updated index to the query servers before the crawl is completed. But crawls can potentially take hours or even days to complete in large enterprises with large amounts of content. SharePoint users could therefore experience a significant time lag from the point where they changed some content until that change is reflected in the search results.

SSP administrators can manually trigger crawls from the content source menu, as shown in Figure 5-27.

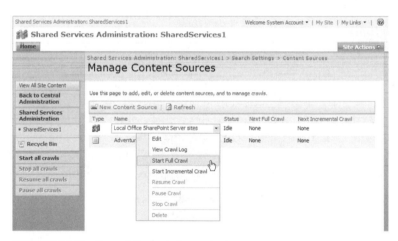

FIGURE 5-27 Starting a full crawl of a content source

In the next section, you'll learn how to configure crawl schedules to trigger the crawls automatically on a scheduled basis.

Configuring Crawl Schedules

SSP administrators must configure appropriate crawl schedules for each content source to automatically keep the index up to date with the content it represents. Crawl schedules can be specified for all types of content sources. Each content source accepts one schedule for full crawls and another for incremental crawls.

> **Important** No crawl schedule is specified for the default content source named Local Office SharePoint Server Sites, shown earlier in Figure 5-16. The SSP administrator should therefore plan a crawl schedule for this content source during the initial configuration of the SSP. Users will otherwise not experience up-to-date search results when searching for content on the SharePoint sites.

For large volumes of content, it is important to consider the frequency of each crawl schedule. The most important factors to consider when deciding on the frequency of the crawl schedules for the different content sources are as follows:

- Content that is updated frequently should also be crawled more frequently than content that is updated less frequently. This implies that you must also split these different types of content into different content sources to specify multiple schedules.

- Content that is hosted on slower servers should be crawled separately from content hosted on faster servers.

- Periods of peak usage.

Crawl schedules should be planned according to the availability, performance, and bandwidth of the SharePoint index server and the servers hosting the crawled content. It is highly recommended to consider the following best practices when planning content sources and their crawl schedules:

- Create different content sources for servers with different availability.

- Schedule incremental crawls to occur during times when there is low demand on the servers hosting the content to be crawled. This consideration becomes less significant if the appropriate steps have been taken to minimize the performance penalty that the indexer puts on the system. This includes steps like having a dedicated index server, a dedicated Web front-end for the crawler, and a responsive SQL database cluster.

- Avoid having too many overlapping crawl schedules. Try to divide the crawls into different time periods to distribute the load over time.

- Schedule full crawls only for the reasons listed in the preceding section.

The configuration pages for all types of content sources include the option to specify a schedule for a full crawl and a schedule for an incremental crawl, as shown in Figure 5-28.

Clicking one of the two Create Schedule links will display a dialog box in which you can specify the frequency of the schedule. Here it is possible to specify a daily, weekly, or monthly schedule, plus a minute-based repetition interval within the day.

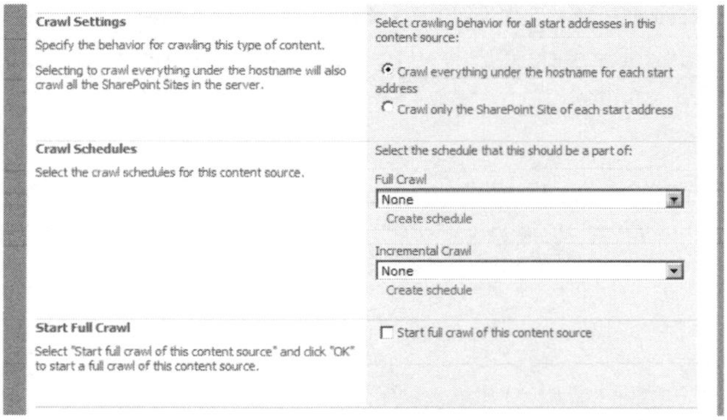

FIGURE 5-28 Crawl schedules for a content source

Configuring Crawl Rules

Crawl rules are a mechanism for influencing the behavior of the crawler when it crawls specific sites. A single crawl rule is created basically by specifying a URL wildcard pattern matching sites plus a set of options for setting the desired behavior of the crawler for these sites. Crawl rules are useful for influencing the crawler in the following ways:

- **Exclude content from being crawled.** This option is useful for excluding irrelevant subsections of one or more sites that elsewhere contain relevant information. You would otherwise not crawl these sites—that is, specify the start address in a content source.

- **Follow links on the URL without crawling the URL itself.** This type of rule will prevent the crawler from adding the URL of matching pages to the index and continue the crawl by following the links on that page. Such rules are useful when crawling pages that do not contain relevant content but only links to relevant content.

- **Crawl complex URLs.** This rule will instruct the crawler to include pages containing query parameters in the URL—that is, URLs that contain a question mark after the file name, as in *http://www.hostname.com/default.aspx?ID=10*. The crawler will by default ignore pages with query parameters in the URL—that is, complex URLs. There is a very good reason for this. The problem with complex URLs is that they can easily make the crawler enter an infinite loop—for example, when a page links to itself with slightly different parameters in the URL on each request.

- **Crawl SharePoint content as HTTP pages.** This rule is necessary when crawling SharePoint servers sitting behind a firewall as seen from the index servers.

- **Crawl sites with a different content access account.** The crawler will by default rely on the default content access account specified for the SSP to access the content on the servers being crawled. But if the default account does not have read access to all the content encompassed by the content sources, you have the option to specify different credentials for different sites by creating appropriate crawl rules with this option.

- **Crawl sites with a client certificate.**   Crawling Secure Sockets Layer (SSL) encrypted sites—that is, sites that can be accessed only with the HTTPS protocol—require a crawl rule to facilitate a client certificate.

> **Important** Crawl rules will apply across all content sources defined within the same SSP. Additionally, crawl rules should never be used as a way of defining content sources but only to guide the crawler in handling content crawled from the start addresses of the content sources defined for the SSP.

The following steps will create a new crawl rule:

1. Open SharePoint 3.0 Central Administration.

2. Navigate to the administration site of the SSP for which you want to specify a new crawl rule.

3. Click the Search Settings link.

4. In the Search Settings page, click the Crawl Rules link.

5. Start the creation of a new crawl rule by clicking the New Crawl Rule option on the toolbar. This will display the Add Crawl Rule page, shown in Figure 5-29.

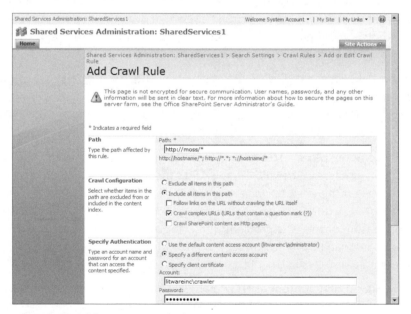

FIGURE 5-29 Adding a new crawl rule

6. Type a specific path or wildcard pattern in the Path box.

7. Specify the crawl configuration options you want to apply to matching content items.

8. Specify the authentication method that the crawler should use to access matching items.

9. Click OK to create the new crawl rule.

The example shown in Figure 5-29 represents a crawl rule that instructs the compiler to crawl complex URLs on all sites hosted by the *moss* server.

The example also illustrates how to specify different credentials for accessing the content. Let's explore a few more URL wildcard patterns and how the crawler interprets them. Table 5-2 lists some common crawl rule patterns and their effect on the crawler.

TABLE 5-2 Examples of Wildcard Patterns in Crawl Rules

Path	Effect
http:///**	Matches all host servers and all items on these servers.
*http://www.litwareinc.com/**	Matches all content on the host server *www.litwareinc.com*.
http://www.litwareinc.com/.aspx*	Matches all Web pages with the .aspx file extension on the host server *www.litwareinc.com*.
*http://www.litwareinc.com/folder**	Matches all documents and Web pages where the URL starts with *http://www.litwareinc.com/folder*.
http://.litwareinc.com/**	Matches all items on all subdomains of the litwareinc.com domain. URLs like *http://moss.litwareinc.com* and *http://intranet.litwareinc.com* will match this rule.
://.litwareinc.com/**	Matches all protocols, subdomains, and items on the litwareinc.com domain.
://.aspx*	Matches every document with the file extension .aspx.

At times, you might doubt whether the content will actually match your crawl rules. The only way to test this in SharePoint Portal Server 2003 was to start a crawl and inspect the crawl logs to determine whether the crawler included and excluded content as expected. But this was a painfully slow and annoying way to figure out whether you made an error in the crawl rules.

To help you be more productive, Microsoft has introduced a much welcomed and nifty little improvement in Office SharePoint Server 2007. You can now test a specific URL against the crawl rules to determine whether the rules will include or exclude the URL during a crawl. Figure 5-30 shows the Manage Crawl Rules page of all defined crawl rules and lets you test a specific URL against them.

FIGURE 5-30 Testing crawl rules

The order of the crawl rules is very important, and you also have the option to rearrange them by clicking the drop-down arrows in the Order column on the right in Figure 5-30. The crawler will exclude an item from the crawl if the first rule matching the URL of that item is an exclusion rule. On the other hand, the same item will be included in the crawl if the first matching rule is an inclusion rule. The item will naturally also be included in the crawl in the case of no matching rules.

Instant Removal of Search Results

Consider a scenario where a manager accidentally uploads a confidential document to a public SharePoint document library. The crawler then manages to index the document before the manager discovers the mistake and removes it. He subsequently learns that the document is still appearing in the search results, which is puzzling, because he expected that deleting the document would also remove it from the search results right away.

The manager then decides to give you a call to ask why the document is still appearing in the search results. You're in luck, as Office SharePoint Server 2007 includes a new search result removal feature to help out in scenarios like this. This feature enables you to type the URL of one or more results that should immediately be removed from the index. They are removed without the need to wait for the crawler to pick up the change and update the index.

A more common scenario is the need to eliminate single irrelevant search results—for example, a link to a Search Center site. Removing a search result also creates a new crawl rule to prevent that result from entering the index again on the next full crawl. You can find the search result removal feature by navigating to the SSP Search Settings page and clicking the Search Result Removal link. This will display the Remove URLs From Search Results page, shown in Figure 5-31.

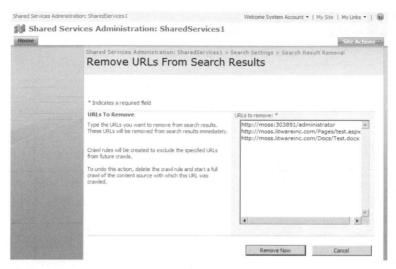

FIGURE 5-31 Instant removal of search results

Figure 5-31 shows an example of removing three search results by typing the individual URLs of the results. Clicking Remove Now will immediately remove these items from the index. SharePoint will additionally set up a new exclusion crawl rule for each URL to exclude them in future crawls.

> **Note**   You cannot use wildcard patterns here as you can when manually creating new crawl rules, as explained in the preceding section. When you need to exclude a whole range of related search results, it might be easier to simply create a new exclusion crawl rule and begin a full crawl.

Crawler Authentication Schemes

To index protected content, the crawler is also equipped with an authentication mechanism to gain access to that content as an authorized user would. This is a critical feature of the crawler, as SharePoint sites and Windows file shares are usually configured with access restrictions. External non-SharePoint Web sites might sometimes also host protected content that you need to index. Indexing public Web sites is of course no issue.

The crawler will by default try to authenticate itself with the default content access account using the NTLM authentication protocol. Different authentication methods and access accounts can optionally be configured via crawl rules. But the crawler supports only three authentication methods. The crawler will fail to authenticate, and hence also fail to index any content, if the content source being crawled is configured with an unsupported authentication method. Table 5-3 lists the authentication methods supported by the crawler.

TABLE 5-3 Supported and Unsupported Authentication Methods

Authentication Method	Supported by Crawler
Basic	Yes
Certificates (HTTPS)	Yes, via crawl rules
NTLM (Integrated Windows)	Yes
Digest	No
Kerberos (Integrated Windows)	No
ASP.NET Forms	No
Web Single Sign-On (SSO)	No

The limited set of supported authentication methods has some implications when it comes to the crawling of SharePoint Web applications. The crawler will essentially fail to index content on IIS Web applications that are configured only for forms-based authentication, Kerberos-based authentication, or any other authentication method not supported by the crawler. But there is of course a nice solution to this problem. The solution is to extend the Web applications to multiple IIS Web sites.

SharePoint farm administrators can extend each Web application to a maximum of five different IIS Web sites. Each site will serve the same content but can be configured to use different authentication methods. Each of the five sites is in turn mapped to a URL zone in the farm. The five possible zones are referred to by the names *Default, Intranet, Internet, Custom,* and *Extranet*. The authentication method used by the crawler must match the authentication method of at least one zone of the Web application being crawled.

It is, however, not irrelevant which authentication method the different zones are configured for. This is because the crawler will always poll the zones in a specific order until it finds one configured with the same authentication method as the crawler. The crawler will fail if it meets a zone configured for Kerberos or Digest authentication before it meets a zone configured for one of the supported authentication methods. The following flow chart illustrates the polling order of the zones and the decision logic for detecting the appropriate authentication method.

It is recommended to configure the *Default* zone to use one of the authentication methods supported by the crawler—that is, Basic, Certificates, or NTLM. Use one or more of the other zones when you need to employ forms-based authentication or one of the other authentication methods not supported by the crawler.

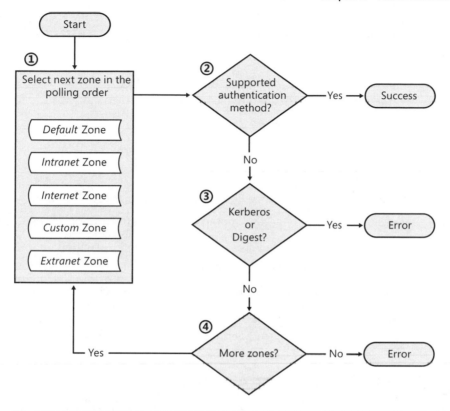

1	The crawler identifies all the available zones of the IIS Web application being crawled. It then starts to poll the authentication method of the zones, starting with the *Default* zone.
2	If the authentication method of the zone is the same as the authentication method configured for the crawler, the crawler will select this method and proceed to the authorization phase.
3	Authentication fails if the zone is configured for Kerberos or Digest authentication. The crawler will in turn abort the authorization process and fail to index any content.
4	Authentication fails if there are no more zones in the polling order. The crawler will in turn abort the authorization process and fail to index any content from the IIS Web application.

These restrictions to the authentication mechanism in the crawler might of course lead to scenarios where the *Default* zone is used only by the crawler. You might not want to allow any users to access the Web application via this zone. You can prevent this simply by not publishing the URL of the *Default* zone. A more secure way to prevent anyone but the crawler from accessing the zone is to configure the IIS Web site of the zone to block all incoming requests except those from the crawler. The following procedure shows how to achieve this with the IIS Manager:

1. Open the IIS Manager on the SharePoint server by clicking Start, clicking Administrative Tools, and then clicking Internet Information Services (IIS) Manager.

2. Find the Web site that represents the *Default* zone.

3. Right-click the Web Site node, and select Properties on the shortcut menu.

4. Select the Directory Security tab.

5. In the IP Address And Domain Name Restrictions group, click Edit.

6. Select Denied Access.

7. Add the IP address of the SharePoint server running the index component that is responsible for crawling the Web application in question.

8. Repeat steps 1 through 7 on all remaining Web front-end servers in the farm.

Last, it is also crucial to ensure that the default content access account and the content access accounts defined via crawl rules have read permission for the content being crawled.

The Default Content Access Account

The default content access account is the account that the crawler will use by default to authenticate itself against a content source. Each SSP can use a different account if necessary. The account applies across all content sources defined for the same SSP. Use crawl rules to override the default account for the content sources or Web site areas that require the crawler to authenticate with different credentials.

Important Do not specify an account that is an administrator on the target server. The crawler will otherwise index unpublished versions of documents in the document libraries where versioning is enabled. It is also a potential security risk to specify an administrator account.

Tip Create a dedicated user account for the crawler in your Active Directory—for example, **domain\spcrawler**. You do not need to assign any special privileges to this account.

You can configure the account by clicking the Default Content Access Account link in the Search Settings page at the SSP level. This will display the Default Content Access Account page, shown in Figure 5-32.

FIGURE 5-32 Configuring Default Content Access Account

The account is automatically configured for read access to new site collections on the IIS Web applications associated with the SSP. This was not the case in SharePoint Portal Server 2003.

Inspecting the Crawl Logs

The crawler logs useful information about each item being indexed to the database of the SSP. The crawl log is a useful tool for troubleshooting the crawler when it is not crawling the content as expected. Only SSP administrators are able to inspect the crawl log.

The crawl log will generally contain the following three types of events:

- **Success**   A success event is added to the crawl log for every item that is successfully added to the index by the crawler.
- **Warning**   The crawler can access the content but not index it for some reason or another. Common reasons include:
  - The file type (file extension) is not included in the file types list of the SSP.
  - The item was excluded by a crawl rule.
  - The item was excluded by the Robots.txt file or by a *NOINDEX* attribute.
  - The item was deleted since the last crawl.
  - The crawler could not load the *IFilter* component that is needed to break down the document into smaller text chunks. This problem will arise only if you rely on a third-party *IFilter* for certain special file types.
- **Error**   The crawler cannot connect to the content source and access the content. Common reasons include:
  - The content server does not respond.
  - The content access account with which the crawler tries to authenticate itself does not have read permission for the content.

Each SSP has one crawl log that is categorized by content source. SSP administrators therefore have the option to inspect log entries across all content sources at the same time or zoom in on a particular one. A summary view of all entries in the crawl log is available from the Search Settings page on the SSP administration site. Click the Crawl Logs link to navigate to the Crawl Log page, shown in Figure 5-33.

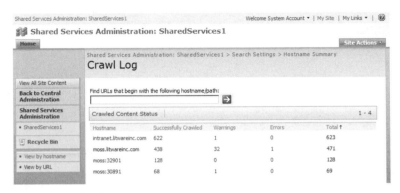

FIGURE 5-33 Crawl Log page

Click one of the Hostname links or the View By URL link to start inspecting individual entries in the crawl log. This will bring you to the page shown in Figure 5-34.

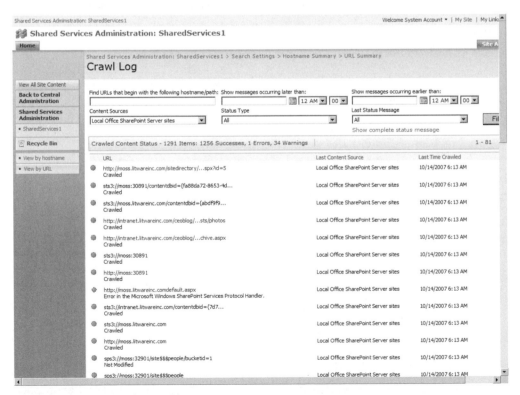

FIGURE 5-34 Inspecting the crawl log

The URL view of the crawl log shown in Figure 5-34 can be used to inspect single entries. The log usually contains many entries—it can in fact easily contain millions of entries in larger production systems. Some filtering options are therefore available to narrow the scope to a smaller and more focused number of entries relevant to the issue you seek to resolve. The log can be filtered by the following properties:

- URL
- Content Source
- Date
- Status Type (Success, Warning, or Error)
- Last Status Message

The Last Status Message option lets you choose to show only log entries with a specific status message encountered by the crawler.

Server Name Mappings

Some crawl scenarios call for a mechanism to map the address of the crawled content to another address. Server name mappings are designed to do just that.

Consider a scenario where you have a Web site hosting a large number of static HTML files. There is no guarantee that a Web crawl would discover all pages, and for efficiency reasons, it would also be a better solution to crawl the files directly off the disk via a file share. But the URL of search results should direct users to the Web server hosting the files and not to the file share, which they will not have access to anyway. Creating a server name mapping can fix this and map the file share addresses to the corresponding Web addresses. For instance, it could map the file share URL *file://moss/wwwroot/index.htm to http://moss/index.htm*.

Server name mappings should not be confused with alternate access mappings. You should avoid any overlap here, as the two mappings will otherwise create a conflict. Use alternate access mappings to map the addresses of the crawled Web applications in the farm to the different URL zones from which users can access the same content. Use server name mappings to map addresses of content that the alternate access mappings do not apply to—that is, content stored outside the farm.

You can manage server name mappings by clicking the Server Name Mappings link in the Search Settings page at the SSP level. This action will bring you to the Server Name Mappings page, shown in Figure 5-35.

FIGURE 5-35 Server Name Mappings

Clicking the New Mapping link will add a new server name mapping to the list. Specify the address at which the content will be crawled and the address that will be displayed in search results. The mapping is applied at crawl time, and a full crawl is required to update the crawled URL of existing content in the index.

File Types

The crawler will index content only from files with a file extension explicitly registered with the SSP. Each file type must additionally be associated with an *IFilter* that is installed on the index server. *IFilters* are the components responsible for breaking documents into chunks of plain text for the index.

Supported File Types

Office SharePoint Server 2007 ships with a few *IFilters* and a default file type inclusions list to handle some common file formats out-of-the-box. Table 5-5 lists these *IFilters* and the file extensions associated with each filter. The file extensions in bold are included by default in the file type inclusions list. The nonbold file extensions are supported by the *IFilter* but must be added manually to the file type inclusions list before the crawler will also include content from these file types in the index.

TABLE 5-5 *IFilters* **and Included File Types Provided Out-of-the-Box**

IFilter	Associated File Extensions
Microsoft Office Filter (handles all legacy Microsoft Office formats)	**.doc**, **.dot**, .pot, .pps, **.ppt**, .xlb, .xlc, **.xls**, .xlt
Office Open XML Format Word Filter	**.docx**, **.docm**
Office Open XML Format PowerPoint Filter	**.pptx**, **.pptm**
Office Open XML Format Excel Filter	**.xlsx**, **.xlsm**
HTML Filter	**.ascx**, **.asp**, **.aspx**, **.htm**, **.html**, .htw, .htx, .odc, **.pub**, .stm

IFilter	Associated File Extensions
Plain Text Filter	.asx, .bat, .c, .cmd, .cpp, .dic, .h, .hxx, .ibq, .inf, .ini, .inx, .js, .log, .m3u, .pl, .reg, .rtf, **.txt**, .vbs, .vtx
E-Mail Filter	**.eml**, **.mht**, **.mhtml**, **.msg**, .nws
XML Filter	**.xml**
(No Filter)	**.exch**, **.jhtml**, **.jsp**, **.mspx**, **.nsf**, .one, **.php**, **.tif**, **.tiff**, **.url**, **.vdx**, **.vsd**, **.vss**, **.vst**, **.vsx**, **.vtx**

The default file type inclusions list includes a number of file extensions not associated with an *IFilter*, as indicated by the last row in Table 5-5. When no *IFilter* is registered for a given file extension, the crawler will still add the file to the index, but it will index only the basic file properties, such as name, extension, last modified date, and other file properties. The file content is simply ignored, and the file will thus be searchable only by the basic file properties.

Configuring the Indexer to Support Additional File Types

The file types supported out-of-the-box are not sufficient for most organizations. One other common file type that almost everybody needs is the Portable Document Format (PDF) from Adobe. Adobe offers a PDF *IFilter* that will work with SharePoint; it can be downloaded for free from *http://www.adobe.com*. Other common file formats for which you will need to manually install a supporting *IFilter* are Microsoft Office Visio, Microsoft Office OneNote, and archive files like .zip and .cab.

You can find many more third-party *IFilters* by doing a simple search for the keyword *ifilter* on one of the common Internet search engines. *IFilters* are available for special file formats like Autodesk Design Web Format (DWF), Microsoft Office Project, OpenOffice, PostScript, Windows help file, WordPerfect, and more. Some are available for free; others are not.

> **Note**   Most of today's third-party *IFilters* were developed for the x86 Windows platform and might not support the Windows x64 platform. For instance, as of this writing, the Adobe PDF *IFilter* does not support the x64 platform.

The following steps show how to add one or more new file extensions to the file types inclusion list:

1. Open the SSP administration site for the SSP that you need to configure.

2. In the Shared Services Administration page, click the Search Settings link in the Search section.

3. In the Configure Search Settings page, click the File Types link.

4. In the Manage File Types page, click the New File Type option on the toolbar.

5. Specify the file extension (without the preceding period [.]) that you want to add to the file type inclusions list, as shown in Figure 5-36. Then click OK to save the change.

FIGURE 5-36 Adding a new file extension

6. Repeat steps 4 and 5 for every file extension you want to add.

7. Start a full crawl of the content sources containing files with the specified file extensions if an appropriate *IFilter* is already registered.

The crawler will hereafter recognize all files with the specified file extensions. The content of the new file types is, however, indexed only if the appropriate *IFilters* have also been registered in the Windows registry on the index server. Updating the Windows registry is usually handled by the installation program of the *IFilter*. You might, however, still encounter situations where a third-party *IFilter* has been registered only for the Windows indexing service and maybe also for SharePoint Portal Server 2003, but not for Office SharePoint Server 2007. *IFilters* must be registered separately for the search engine of Office SharePoint Server 2007.

The following steps outline the procedure for manually registering a new *IFilter* in the Windows registry.

1. Log in as a local administrator on the index server.

2. Open the Windows Registry editor. This can be done by clicking Start, clicking Run, and then typing **regedit**.

3. Locate the globally unique identifier (GUID) of the *IFilter* unless you already have this at hand. You'll need to search the registry for the file name of the *IFilter* DLL file until you find the registry key *HKEY_CLASSES_ROOT\CLSID\{<GUID>}\InprocServer32* containing a reference to the DLL file. Copy the GUID to the clipboard.

4. Open Notepad, and type or copy the following code into it:

```
Windows Registry Editor Version 5.00
[HKEY_LOCAL_MACHINE\SOFTWARE\Microsoft\Office Server\12.0\Search\Setup\Filters\.<ext>]
"Extension"="<ext>"
"FileTypeBucket"=dword:00000001
"MimeTypes"="<MIME Type>"
```

```
[HKEY_LOCAL_MACHINE\SOFTWARE\Microsoft\Office Server\12.0\Search\Setup\
ContentIndexCommon\Filters\Extension\.<ext>]
@="{<GUID>}"
```

Replace *<ext>* with the appropriate file extension and *<GUID>* with the *IFilter* GUID from step 3.

5. Save the file in Notepad to a file named install.reg or any other file name with the .reg file extension.

6. In Windows Explorer, double-click the install.reg file created in step 5. This will merge the registry settings listed for the file into the Windows registry.

7. If the Open File—Security Warning dialog box appears, click Run.

8. Restart the Search service from a Windows command line using the following commands:

   ```
   net stop osearch
   ```

   ```
   net start osearch
   ```

9. Start a full crawl of the content sources containing files of the types supported by the *IFilter*.

Adding new file extensions to the file type inclusions list and registering new *IFilters* always requires you to initiate a full crawl of all the appropriate content sources before the changes are reflected in the search results.

Configuring the Indexer to Support PDF Documents

Let's have a specific look at installing and configuring the free PDF *IFilter* from Adobe.

 Note As of this writing, you can install this *IFilter* only on index servers running on a 32-bit Windows server. If you are running a 64-bit system, you need to look for alternative PDF *IFilters* available from vendors other than Adobe. We also recommend that you visit *http://www.adobe. com* to check whether Adobe has released a 64-bit *IFilter* since this book went into print.

The procedure for adding support for PDF files is quite simple, as the Adobe installation program does all the dirty work of registering the *IFilter* in the Windows registry. Proceed as follows:

1. Log in as a local administrator on the index server where you want to install the PDF *IFilter*.

2. Open a Web browser, and navigate to *http://www.adobe.com*.

3. Search for the keywords *PDF IFilter*, and click the search result for the latest version of the *IFilter*.

4. Download the *IFilter* to the index server.

5. Run the *IFilter* installation program, and follow the on-screen instructions.

6. Add the *pdf* file extension to the file types inclusion list of all SSPs, as described in the preceding section.

7. Restart the Search service as described in the section "Configuring and Starting the Search Service" earlier in this chapter.

8. Start a full crawl of all content sources containing PDF files to include them in the content index.

All existing PDF documents will be searchable once the full crawl completes. But you will soon discover a small imperfection. A PDF icon is missing for PDF documents in search results as well as in document libraries. The Adobe installation program unfortunately does not register an icon with SharePoint, and you will therefore need to do this manually, as follows:

1. Log in as a local administrator on all the Web front-end servers in the farm.

2. Use the image search feature of an Internet search engine to find and download a 16-by-16-pixel PDF icon.

3. Copy the PDF icon to the folder C:\Program Files\Common Files\Microsoft Shared\Web server extensions\12\TEMPLATE\IMAGES.

4. Open the DOCICON.XML file in the folder C:\Program Files\Common Files\Microsoft Shared\Web server extensions\12\TEMPLATE\XML with Notepad or preferably a dedicated XML editor.

5. Add the entry **<Mapping Key="pdf" Value="pdf16.gif" />** as an inner element of the *<ByExtension>* element.

6. Reset the Internet Information Services (IIS) server to apply the change to the SharePoint sites.

Your SharePoint farm is now properly configured to handle PDF documents.

Configuring the Indexer to Support Microsoft OneNote Documents

Let's also take a look at the procedure for installing and configuring the Microsoft OneNote *IFilter*, as this differs somewhat from the PDF *IFilter*. The procedure for the OneNote *IFilter* is as follows:

1. Log in as a local administrator on the index server where you want to install the *IFilter*.

2. Install Microsoft Office OneNote 2007 on the index server.

> Note The Office OneNote 2007 *IFilter* can crawl both OneNote 2003 and Office OneNote 2007 files. The Office OneNote 2003 *IFilter* can crawl OneNote 2003 files only.

3. Add the .one file extension to the file types inclusion list of all SSPs, as described in the section "Configuring the Indexer to Support Additional File Types" earlier in this chapter.

4. Save the following Windows registry settings to a file named install.reg:

```
Windows Registry Editor Version 5.00
[HKEY_LOCAL_MACHINE\SOFTWARE\Microsoft\Office Server\12.0\Search\Setup\Filters\.one]
"Extension"="one"
"FileTypeBucket"=dword:00000001
"MimeTypes"="application/msonenote"

[HKEY_LOCAL_MACHINE\SOFTWARE\Microsoft\Office Server\12.0\Search\Setup\ContentIndexCommon\
Filters\Extension\.one]
@="{B8D12492-CE0F-40AD-83EA-099A03D493F1}"
```

5. Double-click the file to merge the settings with the Windows registry.

6. Restart the Search service as described in the section "Configuring and Starting the Search Service" earlier in this chapter.

7. Start a full crawl of all content sources containing OneNote files to include them in the content index.

Your SharePoint farm is now properly configured to handle OneNote documents.

Search Scopes

The search engine of Office SharePoint Server 2007 has one, and only one, physical index for each SSP in a farm. This implies that the content from all the content sources defined for the SSP is crawled into the same index. Users can in turn search across all the content using one query, which is indeed a nice thing. But many search application scenarios also call for a mechanism to automatically narrow user queries to a logical group of content within the physical index. This mechanism is facilitated in the form of *search scopes*.

Search scopes can be created at the SSP level and at the site collection level by shared services administrators and site collection administrators, respectively. Search scopes at the SSP level are referred to as *shared scopes* because they are available to search applications in all the site collections consuming the services of the SSP. Scopes defined at the site collection are known as *local scopes* because they are not visible or available to any other site collections in the farm.

Common use cases for search scopes include:

- **Scoping of search tabs**   The tabbed search experience of the Search Centers sometimes relies on search scopes to isolate the relevant content in the index for each search tab. Consider a scenario where it has been decided to provide a Search Center with three search tabs: All Sites, People, and Customers. The search experience of each tab has been optimized for the type of content being searched—that is, the layout of the search results has been customized to present the results in the most optimal and user-friendly way on each tab. To successfully implement this scenario, you will also need to create a supporting search scope for each tab and configure the respective search results Web Parts for the respective scopes. See Chapter 3, "Customizing the Search User Interface," for more information about creating search tabs and Search Centers.

- **Top-level categories**   The search tabs scenario does not display the search scopes directly to the end users—it displays them only indirectly via the search tabs. But it is also possible to display them for direct selection in the Search Centers. Scopes can be displayed as a drop-down list for single selection or as check boxes for multiple selections. You can also use scopes as a type of category that users can apply to their searches. Consider a scenario where you have indexed a large product database with the BDC. The products are tagged with different categories that users want to be able to search independently. But they also want to have the option to search across all product categories. You could meet these requirements simply by creating a search scope named *All Products* plus a specific search scope for each category.

> **Note**   This approach might not be suitable if you are working with a fine-grained hierarchical taxonomy defining hundreds or thousands of categories.

- **Custom search applications**   Search application developers can also specify search scopes programmatically when querying the content index. See Chapter 8, "Search APIs," for more information about this topic.

Search scopes in SharePoint Portal Server 2003 were based on content sources and were tied to crawling. A consequence of this design was that search scopes could not have overlapping content. Creating a new search scope also required a full crawl of the content before the scope became searchable. These inconveniences have all been addressed in Office SharePoint Server 2007 by introducing a new rules-based search scope engine. It has an orthogonal design separating the scopes completely from the crawling process. An *orthogonal design* in this context means that scopes are applied to the content without any ties to the way the content was crawled.

Each scope can employ one or more inclusion/exclusion rules of different kinds to form its boundaries. A single rule can scope content by the crawled URL, by content source, or by a managed property (metadata). It is also perfectly legal to apply similar rules to different search scopes, meaning that they can now have overlapping content.

Evaluating the rules at query time would be a dead end performance-wise for the query servers. Search scopes are therefore automatically compiled against the content index by the search scope engine to tag all matching content as being a member of the scope. It will thus suffice for the query servers to test for these simple tags in the index when a scope is specified in a search. The performance penalty for using scopes is therefore minimal or nonexistent at best.

Now that we've covered the theory of search scopes, let's get our hands dirty and create some scopes.

Creating a New Shared Search Scope

Creating a new search scope is a multiple-step process. The first step is to create an empty scope and then provide a name and optionally also a description for it. The next step is to define the rules that must be fulfilled by content to be included in the scope. The last step is to wait for the search scope compilation process to start and complete.

Let's create a new shared search scope named *Products*. Start by logging in as an SSP administrator and navigating to the administration site of the SSP—in this case, SharedServices1—that should host the new scope. Click the Search Settings link in the Search group. In the Configure Search Settings page, click the View Scopes link in the Scopes group. The View Scopes page will be displayed, as shown in Figure 5-37.

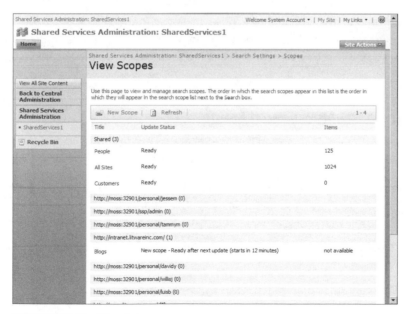

FIGURE 5-37 The View Scopes page

The View Scopes page provides an overview of all shared scopes as well as all local scopes. The Update Status column indicates whether the search scope has been compiled and is ready to search. The Items column indicates how many items in the content index match the rules of the scope. Click the New Scope link on the toolbar to create the new *Products* search scope, as shown in Figure 5-38.

FIGURE 5-38 Creating a new, empty, scope

Specify a title and optionally also a description for the new scope. The Target Results Page option can be ignored unless you plan to expose the scope in the Search drop-down list of the small Search box. Click OK to confirm your input and create a new, empty, search scope. The new scope will in turn appear in the *Shared* search scopes group shown earlier in Figure 5-37.

Adding Rules to the New Search Scope

You must add at least one rule to a search scope before it can be compiled and used in queries. It is possible to add the following four types of rules:

- **Web Address**   Rules that match items by URL. Use rules of this type to include content from Web sites, file shares, Exchange Server public folders, or any other content that has a URL in the search index.

- **Property Query**   Rules that match items having a specific value for the specified managed property.

- **Content Source**   Rules that match items by the content source that the item was crawled from. Please note that content source rules are available only for shared search scopes. They cannot be applied to local search scopes.

- **All Content**   This rule simply includes all content in the index.

A behavior must also be specified for each rule. The behavior indicates how the rule should be applied to the overall scope. A scope-wide filter is used when combining the items matching all rules to determine what content the scope contains. The possible behavior options are listed here:

- **Include**   Any item that matches the rule will be included unless the item is excluded by another rule.

- **Require**   Every item in the scope must match the rule.

- **Exclude**   Items matching the rule will be excluded from the scope.

Let's add a Web Address rule to our *Products* scope. Locate the scope in the View Scopes page shown earlier in Figure 5-37, and then click it to display its drop-down menu. Select the Edit Properties And Rules option to open the Scope Properties And Rules page, shown in Figure 5-39.

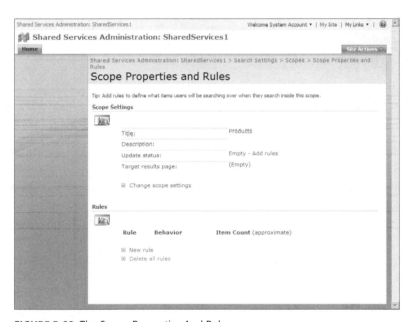

FIGURE 5-39 The Scope Properties And Rules page

This page provides an overview of the scope settings as well as the rules defined for the scope. Click the New Rule link, and then select Web Address, as shown in Figure 5-40.

Selecting this option displays the Web Address group, where you can scope content by Folder, Hostname, or Domain Or Subdomain. In this example, we specify *http://intranet. litwareinc.com/records* to include all content from the records site and possible subsites. Select Require in the Behavior group to exclude all content where the crawled URL does not start with *http://intranet.litwareinc.com/records*.

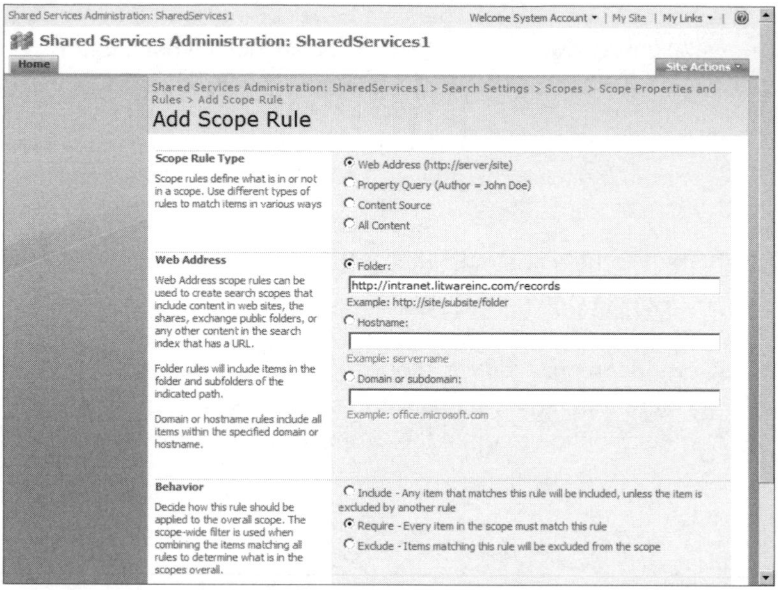

FIGURE 5-40 Adding a Web Address rule

Let's also add a Property Query rule. In the Scope Properties And Rules page shown earlier in Figure 5-39, click the New Rule link, and then select Property Query, as shown in Figure 5-41.

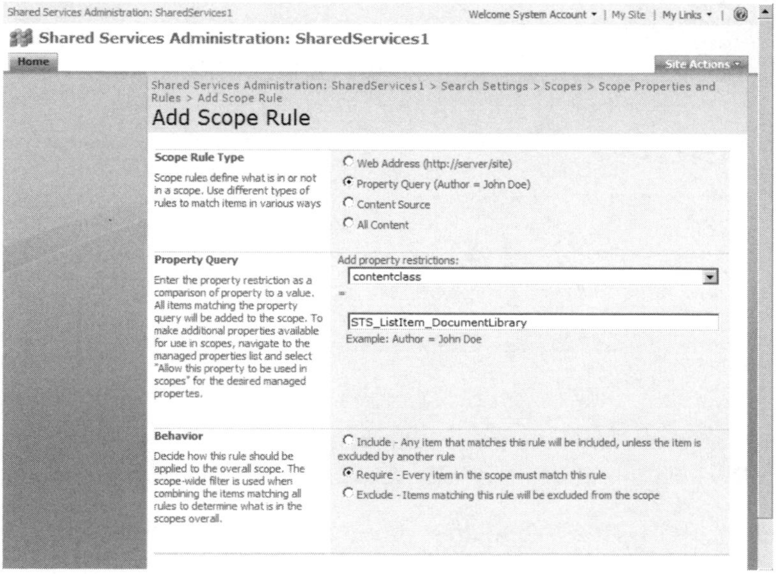

FIGURE 5-41 Adding a Property Query rule

Selecting this option displays the Property Query group, where you can select a managed property and define a specific value that it must equal. The rule will match only items having the exact value you typed. It is not possible to match partial values by using wildcards or regular expressions. The Add Property Restrictions drop-down list by default allows you to select among only the following four managed properties:

- **Author** The full profile name of the last person who modified the item.
- **ContentClass** This property applies to content crawled from SharePoint or Exchange content sources. Here are a few examples of values that this property can assume:
  - **STS_List_DocumentLibrary** Indicates that the indexed item is a document library.
  - **STS_ListItem_DocumentLibrary** Indicates a list item in a document library.
  - **STS_ListItem_Announcement** Indicates a list item in a list created from the Announcement list template.
  - **STS_ListItem_738** List item from a custom list with the template ID *738*.
  - **STS_Site** Indicates that the indexed item is a SharePoint Web site.
  - **urn:content-class:SPSPeople** Indicates a person from the profile store.
- **Site** This property will match items where the URL starts with the specified value. It essentially achieves the same effect as the Folder option of the Web Address rule.
- **SiteName** This property will match items where the site URL equals the specified value.

Additional managed properties can be added to this list by selecting the Allow This Property To Be Used In Scopes check box in the settings page for each managed property. See the section "Managed Properties" later in this chapter for more details on working with managed properties.

As the second rule for our Products scope, let's add a rule that excludes all content but documents from SharePoint document libraries. All documents in SharePoint document libraries created from the default document library template will have the value *STS_ListItem_DocumentLibrary* assigned to the *contentclass* property. Hence you should create the rule as shown earlier in Figure 5-41. Select the Require option to exclude all content but documents from standard SharePoint document libraries.

After we've added these two new rules to the Products scope, the Scope Properties And Rules page for this search scope will now look as shown in Figure 5-42.

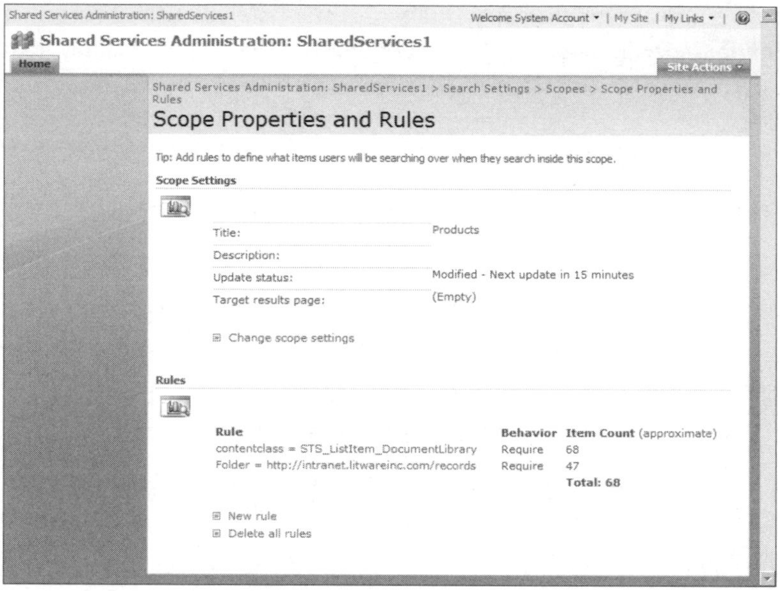

FIGURE 5-42 Search scope with two required rules

All rules and their behaviors are listed in the Rules section, including the number of items matching each rule. The total count is the approximate number of items in the index matching all rules—that is, the approximate number of items in the scope.

Configuring the Search Scope Compiler

After you have created a new search scope, it might take up to 15 minutes before the search scope is compiled for the first time—that is, before it becomes searchable. The reason for this behavior is that the search scope compiler is by default configured to run an update of all search scopes every 15 minutes. You can see when the next update is due in the Scopes group in the Configure Search Settings page, as shown in Figure 5-43.

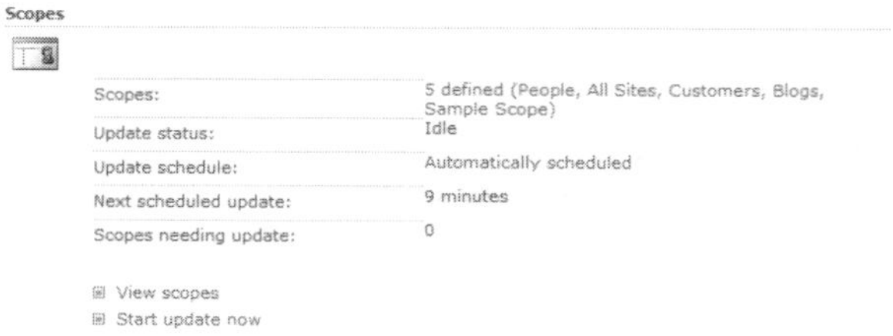

FIGURE 5-43 Search scopes overview

In this example, the next update is due in 9 minutes. If you can't wait for this to happen, simply click the Start Update Now link to start the compiler and update all existing scopes.

Site administrators creating local scopes can't do this, however—they will always need to wait for the next automatic update.

The automatically scheduled updates can also be turned off from the Specify Update Schedule page, shown in Figure 5-44. (Click the Automatically Scheduled link shown in Figure 5-43 to navigate to this page.)

FIGURE 5-44 Specifying a manual or an automatic update schedule

Select On Demand Updates Only, and then click OK to turn off automatic updates of search scopes. From that point on, search scopes will be updated only when the shared services administrator clicks the Start Update Now link shown earlier in Figure 5-43.

The Default Scopes on a New SSP

New SSPs are always created with two shared search scopes: a shared scope named All Sites, which returns all content in the index except people from the user profile store of the same SSP, and a shared scope named People, which isolates people from the user profile store in the index. The People Search tab in the Search Center gives access to a dedicated Search and Search Results pages when working with the People scope.

The rules of these two search scopes are shown in Figures 5-45 and 5-46.

Rules

Rule	Behavior	Item Count (approximate)
All Content	Include	(all items)
contentclass = urn:content-class:SPSPeople	Exclude	125
		Total: 1024

FIGURE 5-45 The default scoping rules of the All Sites scope

Rules

Rule	Behavior	Item Count (approximate)
contentclass = urn:content-class:SPSPeople	Include	125
		Total: 125

FIGURE 5-46 The default scoping rule of the People scope

You can keep these scopes as is, delete them altogether in favor of new scopes, or just modify their rules. It all depends on the search requirements of your business.

Metadata Property Mappings

The search engine of Office SharePoint Server 2007 can index unstructured information as well as structured information. *Unstructured information* refers to the usually large amounts of unstructured text found in such places as word processor documents, e-mail messages, and Web pages. *Structured information* is data that will fit into rows and columns—for instance, metadata like document title, author, creation date, last modified date, and file size. The search engine has excellent support for indexing metadata, providing a great infrastructure for implementing the metadata strategy in your organization.

The search engine stores metadata separately from the free text index, which is designed for unstructured information. Metadata is stored in a few tables in the SQL database of the SSP, known as the *metadata store*. We'll explore the metadata store in more detail later in this chapter. At this point, suffice it to say that the metadata store basically returns metadata for display in the search results as well as providing a means to filter results.

In the SharePoint world, a single piece of metadata is known as a *property*, which is also a term that Microsoft generally uses for metadata throughout all of its products. SharePoint operates with two kinds of properties: *crawled properties* and *managed properties*. Crawled properties are automatically added to the metadata store as they are discovered by the crawler. The complete list of crawled properties can therefore quickly add up to a considerable length, but this will usually be only a small subset of the crawled properties that are actually needed for searching and for displaying in the search results. Moreover, crawled properties can also have lengthy names that would make them hard to reference when customizing the search experience. This was a problem in SharePoint Portal Server 2003, which operated only with crawled properties. Managed properties are a new concept introduced in Office SharePoint Server 2007. They are created by SSP administrators and provide an easier and more consistent experience for managing and using the subset of crawled properties that matters to the business.

The ability of the crawler to autodiscover metadata makes it fairly easy to determine the kind of metadata that already exists on documents in the business. Simply point the crawler to the documents and start indexing them, and you will soon have a complete list of all the metadata in use. The crawler can discover metadata from the following sources:

- **File properties**   Always include the standard file properties like file name, file extension, file date, and file size. Additional file properties, such as the ones shown in Figure 5-47, are also indexed for all types of Microsoft Office system documents but not for other file formats, including PDF documents. The latter have their own embedded document properties, which are propagated to the index by the Adobe *IFilter*.

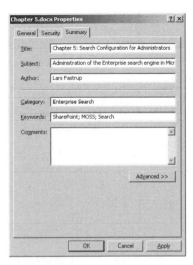

FIGURE 5-47 File properties

- **SharePoint list columns**   All columns in SharePoint lists and libraries are also indexed as crawled properties.

- **Meta tags of HTML documents**   Meta tags like *<meta name="Author" content="Lars Fastrup" />* listed in the *<head>* element of the document.

- **Business Data Catalog applications**   The data columns of entities defined in the BDC application definition files.

- **E-mail messages**   The standard e-mail message *IFilter* propagates the Subject field and the To field as properties to the index.

- **User profile store**   Includes all user profile properties defined in the user profile store of an SSP.

- **Lotus Notes**   Data columns from Lotus Notes databases.

- **Other**   Third-party *IFilter*s and protocol handlers can also push new crawled properties into the metadata store.

The whole concept of metadata property mappings is simply to allow SSP administrators to map crawled properties to managed properties, which can in turn be used in the search experience. The administration interface for mapping properties can be reached from the Search Settings page on the SSP administration site. Let's first examine the nature of crawled properties.

Crawled Properties

Each SSP maintains a list of crawled properties in the metadata store. Properties are automatically added here as the index service component discovers them when crawling content. The list is shared across all content sources defined for the SSP.

To view the list of crawled properties, click the Metadata Property Mappings link in the Configure Search Settings page shown earlier in Figure 5-15. Then select the Crawled Properties view in the left pane, as shown in Figure 5-48.

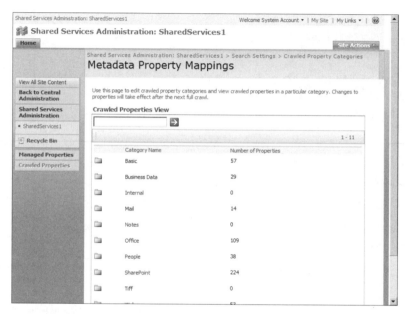

FIGURE 5-48 Crawled properties

The crawled properties are grouped by category, based on the protocol handler or *IFilter* used. Third-party protocol handlers and *IFilters* can add categories in addition to the ones shown in Figure 5-48. Because the crawler picks up all properties, the list of crawled properties can grow very long. A Search box has been provided to quickly locate specific properties.

> **Note** The Search box for crawled properties is a new addition in Office SharePoint Server 2007. In SharePoint Portal Server 2003, you could browse only the list of crawled properties.

You do not need to know the fully qualified name of a crawled property to search for it; you can simply enter any part of the name. Let's try a search for *Keywords*, as shown in Figure 5-49.

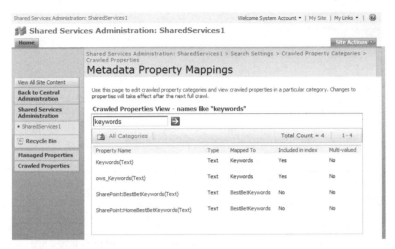

FIGURE 5-49 Searching crawled properties

In this case, the query yields four keyword-related properties. The Type column reveals the data type of the property. The list of supported data types is shown here:

- *Binary*
- *Date And Time*
- *Decimal*
- *Integer*
- *Text*
- *Yes/No*

The Mapped To column lists the names of the managed properties that the crawled property is optionally mapped to. This column will be empty if the crawled property has not been mapped to any managed properties. The Included In Index column indicates whether property values are also included in the index—that is, if the property is searchable. Text-type properties are by default included in the index, but properties of any other type are not. The Multi-Valued column indicates whether one or more items in the index contain multiple values for the property.

Properties where the item values are not included in the index can, however, be reconfigured to include the values. Simply click the property name in the Property Name column, and then select the Include Values For This Property In The Search Index check box, as shown in Figure 5-50.

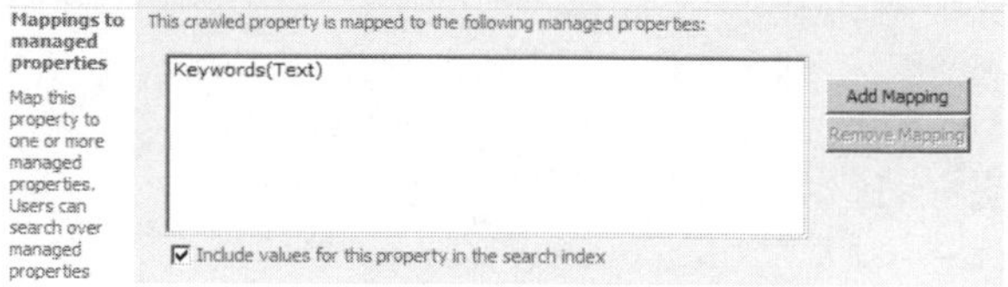

FIGURE 5-50 Including property values in the index

A full crawl of all affected content sources is required before the values are included in the index.

Managed Properties

Metadata—that is, crawled properties that you plan to make part of the search user experience—must first be mapped to appropriate managed properties. Use cases for managed properties include the following:

- **Expose for advanced search**   Managed properties can be exposed to end users in the Advanced Search page of a Search Center. They can in turn use the managed property to apply a property value filter to the search results. See Chapter 3 for more information about customizing the advanced search experience. Managed properties are, however, always searchable for power users via the new search query syntax. (*Power users* are users who are knowledgeable about the full search query syntax.) They can, for instance, simply type **author:luisa** to find documents authored by persons named Luisa.

- **Display in search results**   Search results always display item metadata—usually title, description, URL, author, date, and size. But you can essentially customize the search results to display any available metadata. The only requirement is that the metadata be available as a managed property in the index.

- **Use in search scope rules**   Managed properties can also be configured for use in search scope rules.

- **Custom relevancy ranking**   Increase or decrease the amount by which your custom properties influence the ranking score. No administration interface is available for adjusting weights, however—this can be done only through the Microsoft .NET Framework administration application programming interface (API). See Chapter 8 for more information about how to do this.

Another great feature of managed properties is that you can map several crawled properties to the same managed property. This makes it possible to join different crawled properties that are semantically the same to a single managed property. Consider the scenario where different groups of people inside your organization have used different names for the same semantic piece of metadata, say, for tagging documents with a project name. One group dubbed its property *Project Name* with a space, while the other group used *ProjectName* without a space. As the SSP administrator, you can decide to create a single managed property named *Project* and map it to both crawled properties.

> **Important** Creating a new managed property and mapping it to one or more crawled properties requires a full crawl of all appropriate content sources. The property will otherwise not be searchable, nor will it display any values in search results.

The list of managed properties can be viewed by selecting the Managed Properties link shown earlier in Figure 5-48. This Managed Properties view is also the default view when you click the Metadata Property Mappings link in the Configure Search Settings page. The Managed Properties view is shown in Figure 5-51.

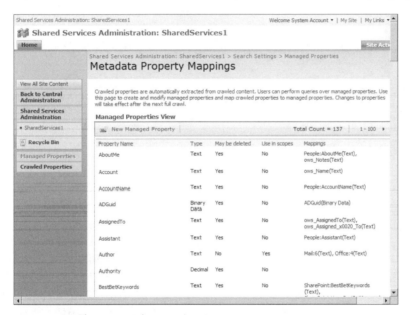

FIGURE 5-51 The Managed Properties view

Unlike crawled properties, managed properties are neither grouped nor searchable. These features are simply not necessary here, as the list of managed properties is usually quite short compared with the list of crawled properties. The Managed Properties view is instead divided into pages, each showing a maximum of 100 managed properties. Use the small left and right arrows in the upper-right corner to switch between the available pages.

New SSPs are created with about 140 managed properties, and it is recommended not to delete any of these. If you do, you risk unexpected behavior in the search experience.

Creating a New Managed Property

SSP administrators can add new managed properties as needed by clicking the New Managed Property link shown earlier in Figure 5-51. Recall the earlier project name scenario, where two groups of users have caused the crawler to discover two crawled properties that are semantically the same. Let's create a new managed property named *ProjectName* that maps to the crawled properties from both groups, as shown in Figure 5-52.

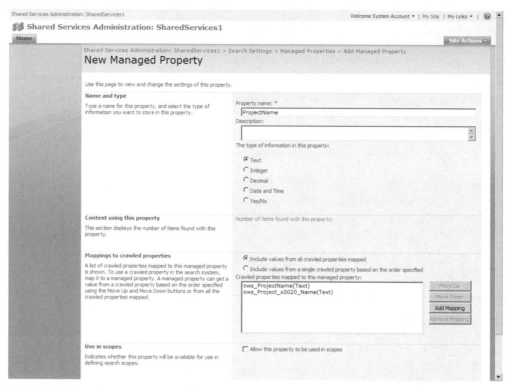

FIGURE 5-52 Creating a new managed property

Type the name of the new managed property in the required field Property Name. Space characters and special characters like *&!#"@* are not accepted. Then specify the data type by selecting Text, as the crawled properties in this example are of this type. Managed properties support the same data types as crawled properties. Binary data types, however, are only for internal use, and it is therefore not possible to create managed properties of this type.

The next step is to specify the mappings to the crawled properties. In this example, we will assume that these properties originate from columns in a document library. The first group created a column labeled Project Name with a space, and the second group used ProjectName without a space. The crawler picks up these columns as crawled properties with the names *ows_ProjectName* and *ows_Project_x0020_Name,* respectively. Click Add Mapping to find the crawled properties and add them to the list, as shown in Figure 5-52. Use the options in the Mappings To Crawled Properties group to control how the crawler should assign values to the managed property. There are two options with the following characteristics:

- **Include Values From All Crawled Properties Mapped**   This option will instruct the crawler to assign the values of all crawled properties to the managed property. Multiple values are separated by the characters *;#*.

- **Include Values From A Single Crawled Property Based On The Order Specified**   This option will instruct the crawler to assign the value from the first crawled property having a nonempty value.

Attention should be paid to these options only when documents might have values for more than one of the crawled properties. There is no such risk in our project name example, as the properties *ows_ProjectName* and *ows_Project_x0020_Name* are mutually exclusive. The last option to consider is the Allow This Property To Be Used In Scopes check box. Select this option when there is also a need to use the managed property in search scope rules.

Last, click OK to create the managed property. It will in turn appear in the list of managed properties shown earlier in Figure 5-51. The property will not be fully operational in the search experience, however, until another full crawl has completed.

Making a List Column Searchable

This procedure outlines the necessary steps for creating a new list column, including it as a property in the index, and making it searchable in the search experience. Skip to step 3 if the column already exists in one or more lists.

1. Navigate to the settings page of the list that will receive the new column.

2. In the Column group, click the Create Column link to define and add a new column to the list. Alternatively, click the Add From Existing Site Columns link to use a predefined column definition.

3. Assign a value to at least one item in the list. Click the list item, and then select Edit Properties on the drop-down menu to edit the column value. Click OK to save the change.

4. From the Search Settings section on the SSP administration site, start an incremental crawl of the content source named *Local Office SharePoint Server Sites*.

5. Wait for the crawl to complete.

6. Staying at the SSP administration site, go to the Metadata Property Mappings page, and add a new managed property with a name of your choice. The managed property should be created with a data type compatible with the data type of the list column. The *Text* data type is the default and also the most commonly used.

7. Map the new managed property to the crawled property representing the list column. The crawled property should have been discovered automatically during the incremental crawl in steps 4 and 5.

8. Repeat step 3 to update the timestamp of the list item.

9. Repeat steps 4 and 5 to include column values in the metadata store. Launch a full crawl instead if the column already exists with values for other list items.

10. After the second crawl completes, navigate to a Search Center on a Web application associated with the SSP.

11. In the Search box, type a property query using the name of the managed property created in step 6, followed by a colon and the column value to search for—for example, *Flavor:Chocolate* if you created a managed property named *Flavor*.

12. Verify that you receive the correct results for the list items having the specified value assigned to the list column.

The managed property can also be displayed in the Advanced Search page in the Search Center. See Chapter 3 for detailed information.

Auto-Creating Managed Properties

It is also possible to configure the crawler to automatically create and map a new managed property for each new crawled property it discovers. This is a very convenient feature if you want to allow site collection administrators to work with managed properties without the intervention of SSP administrators. This feature can be enabled at the level of each crawled property group. In the Metadata Property Mappings page shown earlier in Figure 5-48, click the appropriate group, and then select the Edit Category item on the drop-down menu. This opens the Edit Category page, shown in Figure 5-53.

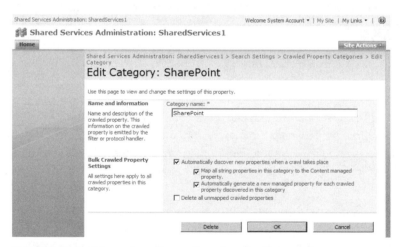

FIGURE 5-53 Enabling automatic creation of managed properties

Select the Automatically Generate A New Managed Property For Each Crawled Property Discovered In This Category check box, and then click OK to save the change.

High Confidence Result Properties

The Search Results pages in Search Centers can include a Web Part for showing high confidence results before the regular results. High confidence results are results that the search engine believes are an exact match for the user query. The only type of high confidence results available without further configuration is people results. The behavior of high confidence results is controlled by a fixed set of managed properties that are mapped to crawled properties of the user profile store. The only way to change the behavior of high confidence results is to change these crawled property mappings. Table 5-6 lists the set of managed properties related to high confidence results and the default mappings to crawled properties.

TABLE 5-6 High Confidence Results Properties

Managed Property	Crawled Property Mapping
HighConfidenceDisplayProperty1	People:Title
HighConfidenceDisplayProperty2	People:WorkPhone
HighConfidenceDisplayProperty3	People:Department
HighConfidenceDisplayProperty4	People:Office
HighConfidenceDisplayProperty5	People:PreferredName
HighConfidenceDisplayProperty6	People:Title
HighConfidenceDisplayProperty7	People:Office
HighConfidenceDisplayProperty8	People:AboutMe
HighConfidenceDisplayProperty9	People:SPS-Responsibility
HighConfidenceDisplayProperty10	People:SPS-Skills
HighConfidenceDisplayProperty11	People:WorkEmail
HighConfidenceDisplayProperty12	Not mapped
HighConfidenceDisplayProperty13	Not mapped
HighConfidenceDisplayProperty14	Not mapped
HighConfidenceDisplayProperty15	Not mapped
HighConfidenceImageURL	ows_PictureURL People:PictureURL
HighConfidenceMatching	People:PreferredName People:WorkEmail People:UserName
HighConfidenceResultType	DAV:contentclass

When a client application asks the search engine to return high confidence results, the search engine will return a fixed set of metadata for each matching high confidence result. It will return available values for the numbered properties 1 through 15 plus any available value for the *HighConfidenceImageURL* property.

The crawled property mappings of the *HighConfidenceMatching* property determine how the search engine produces high confidence results. The default configuration yields a high confidence result when the search query matches the exact name, the work e-mail, or the user name of a person in the user profile store.

The Metadata Store

Crawled property definitions, managed property definitions, and crawled property values are all stored in a set of Microsoft SQL Server tables known as the metadata store. The definitions of crawled properties and managed properties are stored in the SSP database—that is, the core database of the SSP. But the property values of all crawled documents are stored in a separate database dedicated to frequently changing search-related data. The database name and the database server of both are specified during the creation process of the SSP, as described in the section "Creating a New SSP" earlier in this chapter.

> **Note** Using Microsoft SQL Server as a repository for metadata is a new innovation in Office SharePoint Server 2007. The metadata store of SharePoint Portal Server 2003 was file based. It simply stored all metadata in a single large file named sps.edb and with a closed file format.

In a typical setup, the names of the SSP core database and the SSP search database are *SharedServices1_DB* and *SharedServices1_Search_DB*, respectively. Each of the two SSP databases contains several search-related tables. Only a few of the tables are related to the metadata store, however. Table 5-7 lists the tables that make up the metadata store.

TABLE 5-7 Key Database Tables in the Metadata Store

Database	Table Name	Description
SSP Core	*MSSCrawledPropCategory*	Stores the definitions of the categories for crawled properties.
	MSSCrawledProperties	Stores the definitions for all crawled properties discovered by the crawler.
	MSSManagedPropAliases	Stores the aliases for key properties.
	MSSManagedProperties	Stores the definitions of all managed properties.
SSP Search	*MSSDocProps*	Stores the managed property values for all crawled documents. Each document occupies one row for each managed property for which it has value. Hence, this table easily grows to millions of rows.

There's usually no need to know about these database tables. They are considered to be internal elements of the SharePoint product platform. But they are nonetheless still open for a peek, which can be useful in situations where the SharePoint administration interface and the SharePoint API fall short. One such situation is when you want to determine the full range of distinct values for a managed property. This range can be found only by executing SQL queries directly against the metadata store.

> **Important** Do not directly apply any modifications to the SharePoint databases, as this is not supported by Microsoft.

Consider the situation where you have a managed property named *ProjectName* for which you want to find a distinct list of project names. You can find out using almost any tool that can connect to the SSP databases, execute SQL queries, and then show the results. But the most obvious tool is of course the Microsoft SQL Server Management Studio application included in Microsoft SQL Server 2005. To execute queries against the database using this tool, log in to a machine where it is installed and start it. Finding the distinct list of property values requires two SQL queries. The purpose of the first query is to identify the property ID (PID) of the managed property. This is achieved by querying the *MSSManagedProperties* table by the name of the managed property. The SQL syntax for the query in this situation is shown here:

```
SELECT PID FROM MSSManagedProperties WHERE FriendlyName='ProjectName'
```

This will yield an integer number above 400—for example, 414, as shown in Figure 5-54.

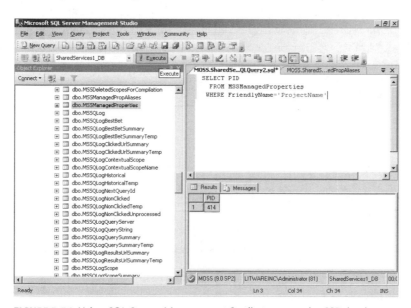

FIGURE 5-54 Using SQL Server Management Studio to query the SSP databases

The PID is needed as a parameter in the second query that is executed against the *MSSDocsProps* table using the following SQL statement:

```
SELECT DISTINCT strVal FROM MSSDocProps WHERE PID=414
```

This will yield the complete list of distinct project names across all crawled documents. The query will work for all managed properties having the data type *Text*. Replace *strVal* with *llVal* for *Integer* data types.

Authoritative Pages

A paramount feature of any Enterprise Search engine is to first show the most relevant results with respect to what the user wants to find. The product team has worked together with Microsoft Research to deliver a significantly improved ranking engine for the search component of Office SharePoint Server 2007. The new ranking engine considers a range of different parameters to compute the final ranking score (a number between 0 and 1000) of each item matching the specified search query. The parameters can be divided into *dynamic ranking parameters* and *static ranking parameters*. The dynamic parts of the overall ranking score are calculated at query time, as they depend on the content or property values for a content item.

Static parameters are computed at crawl time, because they are not dependent on the content or the property values for a content item. One of the static parameters considered in the overall ranking score is *authoritative pages*, which provide SSP administrators with a way to fine-tune relevancy by click distance. The concept of authoritative pages is based on assigning selected pages or sites to one of the following four authoritative page levels:

- Most authoritative
- Second-level authoritative
- Third-level authoritative
- Sites to demote

The relevance of Web pages will in turn increase with shorter click distances to the first three authoritative page levels, each having a different relevance multiplier. The fourth authoritative pages level will typically cause associated results to appear near the end of the search results. Top-level pages for new Web applications are automatically added as most authoritative.

When planning authoritative page settings, consider the purpose of each site, and review its subsites. Group authoritative sites into the three levels by importance, and group the sites that are not likely to be relevant as sites to demote. Good practices to use when planning authoritative page settings include:

- SharePoint sites central to high-priority business processes will typically be most authoritative.

- Sites that encourage collaboration or action are likely to be more authoritative than sites that are merely informative.

- Sites that are informative but not central to high-priority business processes or used for collaboration are likely to be in the second or third level of authoritative sites.

- External sites will typically be less authoritative, because your organization cannot control the content on those sites.

You don't need to assign an authoritative page setting to every site. It is a good idea to select relevance for a small number of sites that you know are most authoritative or less relevant and then adjust the authoritative page settings during normal operations based on feedback from users and information in the query logs and crawl logs.

The list of authoritative pages is available from the Configure Search Settings page shown earlier in Figure 5-15. In that page, in the Authoritative Web Pages group, select the Specify Authoritative Pages link to add or remove authoritative pages, as shown in Figure 5-55.

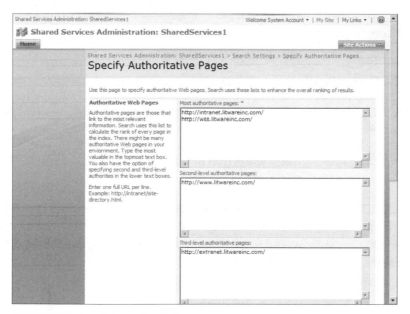

FIGURE 5-55 Specifying authoritative pages

Nonauthoritative pages must be specified in the Sites To Demote list, shown in Figure 5-56.

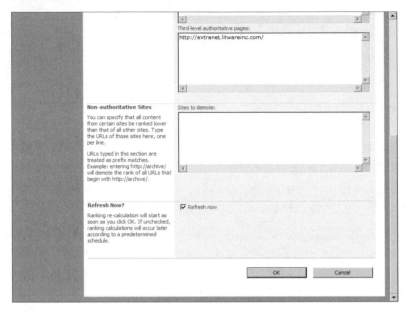

FIGURE 5-56 Specifying nonauthoritative sites

Changes to the list of authoritative pages or the list of nonauthoritative pages does not require a full crawl. The search engine will automatically recalculate the static ranking values according to a predetermined schedule. Select the Refresh Now check box to force the recalculation as soon as you click OK to save the settings.

Search-Based Alerts

A search-based alert allows a user to subscribe to changes in the search results for a particular search query. Upon creating a search alert from a Search Center, users can choose to be alerted to all changes in the search results, or just when new items appear, or when existing items are modified. The search engine will in turn monitor the search query and alert the user by e-mail when changes to the search results are detected.

Technically, the search engine maintains a list of all search-based alerts for each SSP. The list includes information about the search query and the last time a notification was sent to the user. A timer job will start processing the list when a full crawl or an incremental crawl has propagated changes to the content index. The timer job will basically loop over all the alerts, execute the stored search query, and examine the results. A notification is generated for results where the last modified timestamp is newer than the timestamp of the last notification sent to the user.

The search alert subsystem does not support immediate alerts as you know them from SharePoint list alerts; it supports only a daily or a weekly summary frequency. Immediate search alerts would pose a risk of overloading the query servers and the e-mail server. But please note that search alerts can still put a significant load on the query servers when many users start using this feature.

SSP administrators therefore have an option to deactivate search-based alerts as follows:

1. Open SharePoint 3.0 Central Administration.

2. Navigate to the administration site of the SSP for which you want to disable search-based alerts—in this example, SharedServices1.

3. Click the Search Settings link.

4. Click the Search-Based Alerts link to open the page shown in Figure 5-57.

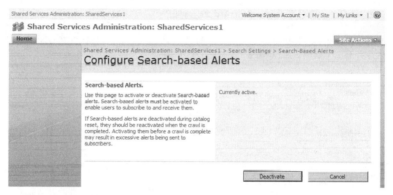

FIGURE 5-57 Deactivating or activating search-based alerts

5. Click Deactivate to deactivate search-based alerts for the SSP.

There is one situation where it is always advisable to deactivate search alerts: when the content index is reset and all content is crawled all over again. Search alerts should not be activated again until the first full crawl completes. Users may otherwise receive notifications that they have received before.

Resetting the Index

SSP administrators can quickly reset the content index if necessary. This action will reset the file-based free text index on all query servers as well as the managed property values in the metadata store. The crawled property definitions and the managed property definitions are, however, not deleted. Users will obviously start receiving empty search results on all search queries immediately after such a reset.

Resetting the index is a fairly drastic move and should be considered carefully, especially in production environments. Common reasons for resetting the index include the following:

- You know or suspect that the index contains a lot of old data.

- You know or suspect that the index contains corrupted data.

- You have changed several settings (for example, crawl rules), and you want to perform a full crawl to reflect these changes.

- You realize a problem with security where users are able to view search results that should have been trimmed. Resetting the index removes this security leak immediately.

The procedure for resetting the index is as follows:

1. Open SharePoint 3.0 Central Administration.

2. Navigate to the administration site of the SSP for which you want to reset the index—in this example, SharedServices1.

3. Click the Search Settings link.

4. Click the Reset All Crawled Content link to open the page shown in Figure 5-58.

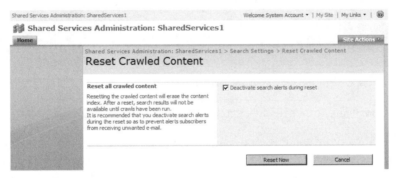

FIGURE 5-58 Resetting the content index

5. Verify that the Deactivate Search Alerts During Reset check box is selected. Users might otherwise receive notifications for search results that they have received before.

6. Click Reset Now to reset the content index of the SSP.

Search-based alerts must be activated again manually by the SSP administrator after the index has been completely rebuilt.

Managing the Search Service

Most crawl-related search settings are managed separately at the SSP level and at the Web site level. A few exceptions to this rule are proxy server settings and crawler impact rules, which are managed at the farm level across all SSP instances. SharePoint administrators can manage these settings from the Manage Search Service page, shown in Figure 5-59. To navigate to this page, open SharePoint 3.0 Central Administration, and then select Application Management on the top navigation bar. Locate the Search group, and then click the Manage Search Service link.

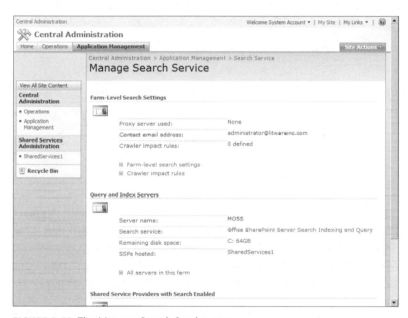

FIGURE 5-59 The Manage Search Service page

The first section in this page, Farm-Level Search Settings, provides a status for the proxy server in use and the number of crawler impact rules. The Query And Index Servers section lists all query servers and index servers in the farm, along with some status information for each. The last section, Shared Service Providers With Search Enabled, lists all SSPs providing searching. SSPs that are configured to provide only one or a few selected services other than Search are not listed. For instance, this could be an SSP that is configured to provide only Microsoft Office Excel services or Forms services.

Farm-Level Search Settings

The proxy server and the contact e-mail address listed in the Farm-Level Search Settings section can be configured from the subconfiguration page Manage Farm-Level Search

Settings, shown in Figure 5-60. Click the Farm-Level Search Settings shown earlier in Figure 5-59 to navigate to this page.

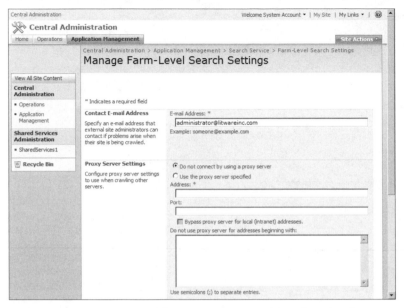

FIGURE 5-60 Upper sections of the Manage Farm-Level Search Settings page

The first configuration section allows you to specify the contact e-mail address for the search administrator. The crawler will in turn provide this contact information in requests to the content sources being crawled. In other words, the crawler will leave its fingerprint in the log files of the servers being crawled. When crawling external sites, you will be a good citizen by specifying a monitored e-mail address here. This will give external site administrators a fair chance to contact you if problems arise when their site is being crawled.

The second configuration section presents the proxy server settings. Select Do Not Connect By Using A Proxy Server to instruct the crawler to connect directly to all sites. This is, by the way, also the default setting. But some scenarios call for the crawler to connect to sites via a proxy server, including the following:

- **Restricted Internet access** Many organizations do not allow any machines on their internal network to connect directly to the Internet. They require machines to connect to external servers via a central gateway like the Microsoft Internet Security and Acceleration (ISA) Server, and the SharePoint crawler will thus also not be able to connect directly to any external sites. The solution is to configure the gateway server as the proxy server, as shown earlier in Figure 5-60.

- **Caching of crawled content** A proxy server can also be used to cache all crawled content, which can be useful when dealing with external content of unknown availability.

- **Advanced content modification**   This is admittedly a rare case, but you can theoretically develop a custom proxy server that modifies or removes content before it reaches the SharePoint index. This could be useful for instance for advanced Web site crawling, where you need to prevent all non-content-related text from being included in the index—for example, the text from navigation menus.

Select the Use The Proxy Server Specified option to instruct the crawler to connect to sites via a proxy. Next, enter the address and the port of the proxy server to use. The Address box accepts the NETBIOS name or the IP address of the proxy server. Select the Bypass Proxy Server For Local (Intranet) Addresses check box to instruct the crawler to bypass the proxy server when crawling local content. Specify the start addresses of all local content in the large text box below the check box.

The third configuration section, shown in Figure 5-61, allows you to configure the timeout settings of the crawler. The default settings of 60 seconds are usually fine, but crawling very slow systems might call for an increase in the time the crawler should be allowed to wait for a response.

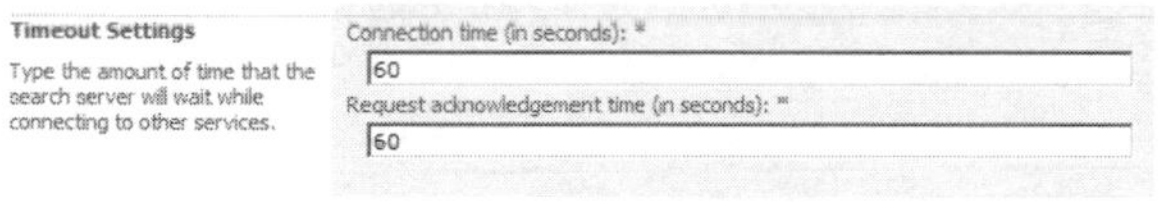

FIGURE 5-61 Timeout Settings

The Connection Time box specifies the number of seconds the crawler should be allowed to wait while connecting to other services. The Request Acknowledgment Time box specifies the number of seconds the crawler should be allowed to wait for another service to acknowledge a request to connect to that service.

The fourth and last configuration section, shown in Figure 5-62, allows you to configure the crawler to ignore SSL certificate name warnings.

FIGURE 5-62 Ignore SSL Certificate Name Warnings

Select this option if you are using the HTTPS protocol to crawl content and you know that the SSL certificate name does not exactly match the expected name. It is recommended, however, to select this option only if you trust all crawled sites to be legitimate.

Crawler Impact Rules

The crawler will by default run at full speed, requesting multiple content items at the same time. This behavior can potentially place a significant load on the servers serving the requests from the crawler. Your own internal servers might easily be able to accommodate the load. But you should pay special attention to the impact that the crawler has on external servers. Placing a huge load on foreign servers might trigger the administrators of those servers to block traffic from your crawler or, worse, block all traffic from your gateway IP address.

Crawler impact rules are a mechanism to control the crawler and differentiate how aggressively it will crawl different servers. SharePoint administrators can create prioritized crawler impact rules to control how many simultaneous requests the crawler is allowed to send to servers within a specific range of addresses. In the Manage Search Service page shown earlier in Figure 5-59, click the Crawler Impact Rules link to manage the list of rules. This list is by default empty, but Figure 5-63 shows an example with five rules.

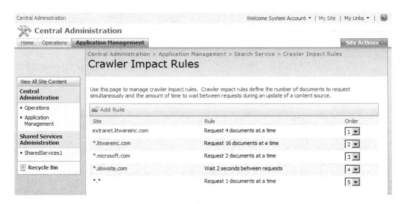

FIGURE 5-63 Example of five crawler impact rules

The first rule allows the crawler to send four simultaneous requests to servers on the address *extranet.litwareinc.com*, and the second rule allows sixteen simultaneous requests to all other servers on the litwareinc.com domain. The third rule allows two simultaneous requests to servers on the *microsoft.com* domain, and the fourth rule allows one request every two seconds to servers on the *slowsite.com* domain. The last rule limits the crawler to one request at a time for all other sites in the known universe. Click the Add Rule link to add a new crawler impact rule to the list. This will take you to the Add Crawler Impact Rule page, shown in Figure 5-64.

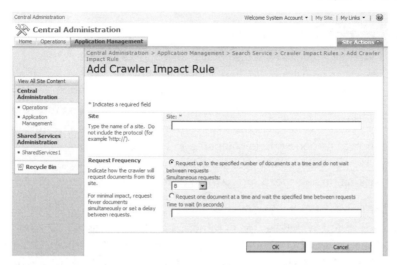

FIGURE 5-64 Adding a new crawler impact rule

Each crawler impact rule requires you to specify the address for which the rule applies and the maximum allowed request frequency. In the Site field, you can specify the address of a specific site such as *http:// www.litwareinc.com* or a wildcard pattern to apply the rule to a range of sites. Table 5-8 describes how the wildcard characters * and *?* can be used to apply a single crawler impact rule to a range of different sites.

TABLE 5-8 Examples of Wildcard Site Patterns

Site	Description
*	Applies the rule to all sites.
.	Applies the rule to all sites with dots in the name.
*.litwareinc.com	Applies the rule to all sites in the *litwareinc.com* domain.
*.com	Applies the rule to all sites that end with the top-level domain name *.com*.
www?.litwareinc.com	Applies the rule to the sites *www1.litwareinc.com, www2.litwareinc.com, www3.litwareinc.com*, and so on. The rule accepts any character in place of the question mark character.

The Request Frequency setting specifies the maximum number of simultaneous pending requests that the crawler can have for sites matching the rule. The Simultaneous Requests drop-down list offers a selection of values 1, 2, 4, 8, 16, 32, and 64.

Advanced Control of the Crawler

The crawler will internally launch multiple parallel execution threads to send simultaneous requests to the sites being crawled. Each thread will handle one request at a time. This approach is significantly faster than crawling all content serially inside one thread. The reason for this is that a pending I/O request will block the execution thread until the remote server responds, and the time it takes even the fastest server with a good network connection to respond is long compared to the execution speed of a modern microprocessor. Increasing the number of requesting threads is therefore crucial to increase the CPU utilization and speed the crawling process.

Based on the hardware configuration, the crawler will automatically calculate the number of threads to use, with 64 as the maximum. If for some reason you want the crawler to use a specific number of threads, you can modify the *RobotThreadsNumber* value under the Windows registry key HKLM\SOFTWARE\Microsoft\Office Server\12.0\Search\Gathering Manager. By default, this value is set to *"0"*, which implies that the crawler will automatically calculate the number of threads to use. Specifying another nonnegative number will instruct the crawler to explicitly use that number of threads.

Increasing the number of threads will increase the indexing performance up to the point where the crawler reaches 100 percent CPU utilization. Any increase in the number of threads beyond this point will not improve performance.

Crawler impact rules are also directly related to the Indexer Performance setting in the Office SharePoint Search service settings page shown earlier in Figure 5-4. This setting applies to the crawling of all sites not matching any crawler impact rules. The Indexer Performance setting is overruled for sites with a matching crawler impact rule.

Best practice when crawling external sites outside your control is to initially set the crawler impact rules to make as small an impact as possible. Use the crawl logs to determine the time it takes the crawler to index the sites, and compare this with the accepted level of freshness of the crawled content. Experiment with different request frequencies to find an acceptable impact level and an acceptable level of content freshness.

Configuring the Preferred Search Center for Personal Sites

A *personal site* is its own site collection and does not warrant its own Search Center, as other site collections sometimes do. For personal sites, it is more desirable to create a Search Center that is shared across all personal sites. This could be the same Search Center as the one created for the typical intranet portal. It could also be a dedicated Search Center created on the same Web application hosting the personal sites. You will in any case need to tell SharePoint where the Search Center is. The small Search box on personal sites needs this piece of information to determine which URL to redirect the user query to. See Chapter 2, "The End-User Search Experience," for more information about creating a new Search Center.

At the level of the site collection, it is indeed possible to configure the target Search Center for the small Search box. But it is not really feasible to specify the Search Center at this level, as you would then have to do it for each user having a personal site. Office SharePoint Server 2007 therefore includes a special setting to configure the preferred Search Center for personal sites at the level of the SSP. The setting will apply across all personal sites provided by the SSP.

SSP administrators can configure the preferred Search Center as follows:

1. Open SharePoint 3.0 Central Administration.

2. Navigate to the administration site of the SSP for which you want to configure the preferred Search Center—in this example, SharedServices1.

3. In the User Profiles And My Sites group, click the My Site Settings link.

4. Specify the absolute URL of the preferred Search Center, as in the example shown in Figure 5-65. A URL is said to be *absolute* when the host name is included in the URL string.

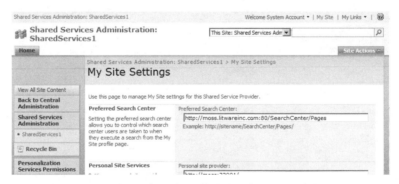

FIGURE 5-65 Setting the preferred Search Center for personal sites

5. Click OK at the bottom of the page to apply the new setting.

The URL of the preferred Search Center should end with the URL name of the Pages document library if the Search Center was created from a publishing-enabled site template. The Search Center With Tabs template is one such template.

Managing Site-Level Search Settings

So far in this chapter, we've covered all the search administration settings at the level of the SSPs and at the farm level. These settings are managed by SharePoint administrators and SSP administrators, respectively. This section covers another group of search administration settings that are available to site collection administrators, and to some extent also site owners, at the following three levels:

- **SharePoint site collection**   Settings at this level include local search scopes, the Search Center URL for the small Search box, and keywords associated with best bets.

- **SharePoint Web site**   Excludes selected columns from being crawled or excludes the entire site and its content from being crawled.

- **SharePoint list**   Excludes the list and its content from being crawled.

Settings at the level of the site collection and at the level of the Web site can be accessed from the Site Settings page, shown in Figure 5-66. All links to search-related administration pages have been emphasized with a frame. The Searchable Columns link and the Search Visibility link are available in the Site Settings page of all Web sites, whereas the links in the Site Collection Administration group are available only in the Site Settings page of the top-level Web site in a site collection.

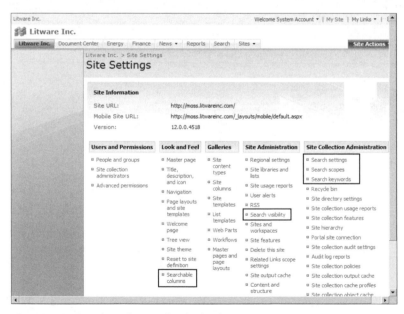

FIGURE 5-66 Search settings at the site level

Settings at the level of a SharePoint list are accessible only from the settings menu of the list itself, as you'll see shortly.

Binding the Search Box to a Search Center

Most pages within your SharePoint portals and individual sites include a small Search box in the upper-right corner, as shown in Figure 5-67. The small Search box basically allows users to initiate a search session directly from these pages, and it will in turn redirect them to a Search Center site containing the search Web Parts executing the search query and displaying the results. See Chapter 2 for a complete description of the small Search box and for a guide to creating a Search Center.

FIGURE 5-67 The small Search box

The small Search box can be tied to any Search Center you want. It can send the search query and the user to a Search Center within the same site collection, or it can go to a Search Center in a different site collection. Just make sure that users have access to the site collection. Site collection administrators can configure the target URL of the Search Center to use in the Search Settings page, shown in Figure 5-68. (To display this page, click the Search Settings link in the Site Settings page shown earlier in Figure 5-66.)

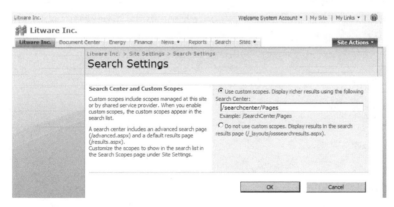

FIGURE 5-68 Settings for the small Search box

Selecting the Use Custom Scopes option will instruct the small Search box to target the Search Center specified in the text input field immediately below. The Scope Picker of the small Search box will in turn include custom scopes as well as contextual scopes. Custom scopes include shared scopes as well as local scopes. However, only custom scopes listed in the display group Search Dropdown are included in the Scope Picker. The concept of display groups is covered in the next section.

The Scope Picker will always include a contextual scope named This Site, narrowing the search to the site level. But it also sends user queries to the Search page included in Windows SharePoint Services 3.0, and it cannot be configured to redirect to a Search Center. Selecting the Do Not Use Custom Scopes option will instruct the small Search box to ignore custom scopes. The Scope Picker will include only contextual scopes and will always send user queries to the Search page of Windows SharePoint Services 3.0.

Managing Local Search Scopes

The section "Search Scopes" earlier in this chapter describes the concept of search scopes in detail and how to manage shared scopes at the SSP level. Local scopes are managed at the level of the site collection by site collection administrators. Managing local scopes is almost identical to managing shared scopes. The only differences are listed here:

- Local scopes introduce a new option known as display groups, which will be covered in detail in this section.

- Local scopes cannot include rules of type Content Source.

- Site collection administrators cannot kick-start the search scope compiler at will. They are required to wait for the next scheduled update, when their scopes will be compiled to include items matching the rules defined for the scope.

This section will focus on explaining the details that are specific to local scopes. The details for adding rules to a search scope are not covered here. In the Site Settings page shown earlier in Figure 5-66, click the Search Scopes link to view the list of available scopes in the View Scopes page, shown in Figure 5-69.

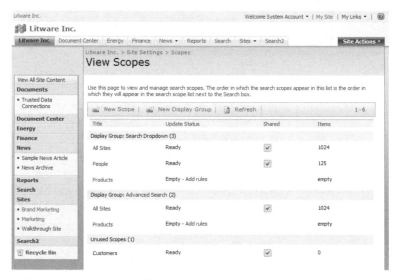

FIGURE 5-69 Managing local scopes

This list of scopes includes all the shared scopes of the SSP associated with the IIS Web application that hosts the site collection. Shared scopes are indicated by a yellow check mark in the Shared column, but they cannot be managed from here. All local scopes show no icon in the Shared column. The process of creating a new local scope can be initiated by clicking the New Scope link on the toolbar, which will display the form shown in Figure 5-70.

FIGURE 5-70 Creating a local scope

Compared with the equivalent page for creating a shared scope, this page does include an extra option for specifying the display groups that the new scope should be a member of. *Display groups* are a concept that maps search scopes to the end-user search experience. Search scopes that are not a member of a display group will also not be visible to end users. Office SharePoint Server 2007 defines two display groups out-of-the-box: Search Dropdown, which tells the small Search box and the Search Box Web Part which custom scopes to include in the Scope Picker; and Advanced Search, which tells the Advanced Search Web Part which custom scopes to display to the end user. See Chapter 3 for detailed information about using display groups in the end-user search experience.

Shared scopes can also be included in one or more display groups, but only from the Edit Scope Display Group page, shown in Figure 5-71. This page is accessed by clicking the linked name of the display group in the View Scopes page shown earlier in Figure 5-69.

In the Scopes group, check all scopes that should be members of the display group. Use the drop-down lists in the Position From Top column to specify the display order of the scopes inside the display group. The drop-down list in the Default Scope group specifies which scope will be selected by default in the Scope Picker of the small Search box and the Search Box Web Part.

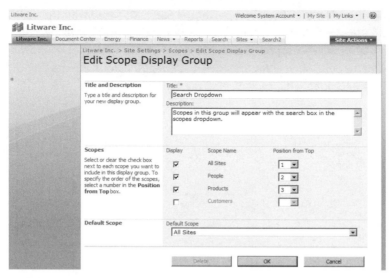

FIGURE 5-71 Configuring the Search Dropdown display group

New display groups can also be created and mapped to the appropriate Web Parts. The Scope Picker of the small Search box is, however, permanently mapped to the Search Dropdown display group.

Managing Keywords

Keywords are words or phrases that are specific to your business. They can be associated with one or more best bets, which are essentially editorial results that appear in a prominent place on the first results page. The concept is somewhat similar to keyword-sensitive ads or sponsored links on the major Internet search engines. The purpose is different in the Enterprise domain, however, where keywords are usually employed to help users find and become aware of important information. For instance, it could be a requirement that employees should easily be able to find a Web page listing all the commonly used abbreviations and acronyms in the company. The requirement dictates that they should find a link to the page when searching for any of the terms *abbreviation, abbreviations, acronym, acronyms,* or *glossary*.

A good way to identify new, relevant keywords is to use the new Usage Reporting feature in Office SharePoint Server 2007. The reports titled "Queries with Zero Results" and "Queries with Zero Best Bets" might provide one or more candidate keywords. See Chapter 4 for a complete review of all of the available usage reports.

Site collection administrators can manage keywords and the associated best bets at the level of the site collection. In the Site Settings page shown earlier in Figure 5-66, click the Search Keywords link to start managing keywords, as shown in Figure 5-72.

FIGURE 5-72 The Manage Keywords page, for viewing and searching existing keywords

This page lists all the keywords defined for the current site collection. It also includes a search function for eased navigation in situations where the list of keywords has grown long. The best bets associated with the different keywords are presented in a Search Center by the Best Bets Web Part, which is included by default in a Search Center. See Chapter 3 for a detailed discussion of the Bests Bets Web Part and how it can be customized.

Add a new keyword by clicking the Add Keyword link on the toolbar. This will display the form shown in Figure 5-73.

FIGURE 5-73 Adding a new keyword with an associated best bet

In the Keyword Information group, specify the primary keyword or phrase that should trigger all associated best bets to be displayed in the Search Results page. Use the Synonyms field to optionally specify additional keywords or phrases separated by a semicolon.

In the Bests Bets group, add one or more best bets that should be displayed when users enter a matching keyword or phrase in the Search box. New best bets are added by clicking the Add Best Bet link to display the form shown in Figure 5-74.

FIGURE 5-74 Adding a best bet

This is where you enter the information to display in the search results, which includes the URL of a document or a Web page, a title, and an optional description. Click OK to save the new best bet to the parent page shown earlier in Figure 5-73. Use the options in the Publishing group and the Contact group on that page to specify a publishing schedule and the name of the person to contact when the keyword requires review.

Excluding Web Sites from a Crawl

It is sometimes desirable to exclude the content within a SharePoint Web site from crawls. A good example is a Search Center site, which does not really contain any useful information to end users. SSP administrators could indeed create a crawl rule that excluded the site from all crawls. But site collection administrators can also exclude the site without having to contact an SSP administrator. In the Site Settings page, click the Search Visibility link to go to the Search Visibility page, shown in Figure 5-75.

In the Indexing Site Content group, select the No option to exclude all content within the site. The crawler will in turn simply skip the site and not include any of its content in the index. Use the options in the second configuration group, Indexing ASPX Page Content, to specify whether the crawler should index content on .aspx pages within the site. The setting does not, however, have any effect when No is selected in the first options group.

> **Tip** SharePoint page designers can add the following HTML element manually to all pages that they do not want the index server to crawl:
>
> `<META NAME="ROBOTS" CONTENT="NOHTMLINDEX"/>`
>
> The element should be added to the HTML *<HEAD>* section of a page.

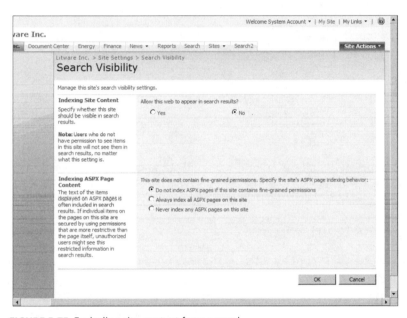

FIGURE 5-75 Excluding site content from a crawl

Excluding Columns from a Crawl

By default, the crawler picks up columns in any type of SharePoint list as a new crawled property. But columns that are based on a site column definition can optionally be excluded from crawls and prevented from entering the index. In the Site Settings page, click the Searchable Columns link to navigate to the Search Settings For Fields page, shown in Figure 5-76.

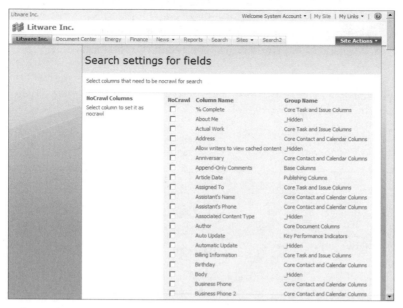

FIGURE 5-76 Excluding columns from a crawl

This page will enumerate all the site columns defined at the current site level. Select the NoCrawl check box for all the site columns that you want to exclude from future crawls.

Excluding Lists from a Crawl

The last option for excluding content exists at the level of the SharePoint list settings. It enables site collection administrators, site owners, and list owners to exclude the list and all the content within it from crawls. In the settings page of the list, click the Advanced Settings link to display the page where the settings group shown in Figure 5-77 is found.

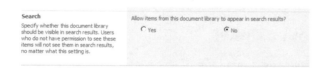

FIGURE 5-77 Excluding a list from a crawl

Selecting the No option tells the crawler to exclude the specific list from a crawl.

Thesaurus

The thesaurus is an XML file for defining related search terms with respect to the content in the index. This is very useful when the index contains documents using different terms for semantically equal topics. Users will, without appropriate configuration of the thesaurus, find only the documents containing the term they entered in the Search box and not the documents using synonym terms.

This problem would quickly become apparent, for instance, on a whisky portal with multiple content authors. Some would type **whisky**, while others would be more comfortable using **scotch**. But it is not acceptable to require portal visitors searching for whisky-related content to know about this difference. They must find all documents, regardless of whether they search using the term *whisky* or the term *scotch*. This can be fixed by specifying both terms as synonyms in the thesaurus. And *whisky* can also be spelled as *whiskey*. But because of the built-in stemmer in the search engine, there is no need to also specify this as a synonym in the thesaurus. The stemmer will automatically reduce *whiskey* to *whisky*.

Each natural language is associated with its own thesaurus XML file. Table 5-9 lists the file name of the associated XML file for some of the supported languages.

TABLE 5-9 Excerpt of Supported Languages

Language	File Name
Chinese-Simplified	tschs.xml
Chinese-Traditional	tscht.xml
Czech	tscsv.xml
Dutch	tsnld.xml
English-International	tseng.xml
English-US	tsenu.xml
French	tsfra.xml
German	tsdeu.xml
Hungarian	tshun.xml
Italian	tsita.xml
Japanese	tsjpn.xml
Korean	tskor.xml
Polish	tsplk.xml
Portuguese (Brazil)	tsptb.xml
Russian	tsrus.xml
Spanish	tsesn.xml
Swedish	tssve.xml
Thai	tstha.xml
Turkish	tstrk.xml

The thesaurus used depends on the language specified by client applications sending query requests to the search engine. Application developers using the Microsoft .NET Framework

Query API should therefore remember to set the *Culture* property on the *Query* class. See Chapter 8 for a complete description of working with the query API. The search engine will use the language-neutral thesaurus tsneu.xml if no language is specified. The search Web Parts included in Office SharePoint Server 2007 specify the preferred language of the current user. This information is provided in the HTTP request header by Web browsers, which in turn relies on users or IT administrators to configure it.

Every instance of an SSP has its own set of thesaurus XML files. They reside in the directory *drive:\Program Files\Microsoft Office Servers\12.0\Data\Office Server\Applications\<Search Application Name>* on the server. *Search Application Name* is a GUID identifying the search application of an SSP. It can therefore be tricky to locate the correct directory if there are multiple search application directories. The name is also not easy to find; it is in fact not directly available anywhere from the administration interface. But it can found using a simple PowerShell script, as described in the section "Detecting the Search Application Name for an SSP" later in this chapter.

The thesaurus is applied at query time, and therefore modifying it does not require a full crawl. This implies that it is also necessary to apply changes to the thesaurus files on all query servers in the farm. Another important fact about the query servers is that they cache the thesaurus in memory and must therefore be restarted before changes will take effect. It is enough to just restart the Search service, as described in the section "Configuring and Starting the Search Service" earlier in this chapter.

Here are the contents of the thesaurus XML file in its default form:

```
<XML ID="Microsoft Search Thesaurus">
  <thesaurus xmlns="x-schema:tsSchema.xml">
  <diacritics_sensitive>0</diacritics_sensitive>
    <expansion>
      <sub>Internet Explorer</sub>
      <sub>IE</sub>
      <sub>IE5</sub>
    </expansion>
    <replacement>
      <pat>NT5</pat>
      <pat>W2K</pat>
      <sub>Windows 2000</sub>
    </replacement>
    <expansion>
      <sub>run</sub>
      <sub>jog</sub>
    </expansion>
  </thesaurus>
</XML>
```

The XML file supports specifying related search terms as an expansion set and as a replacement set. Both types are described separately in the following two sections. The *<diacritics_ sensitive>* tag indicates whether the terms specified in the expansion and replacement sets are accent-insensitive or accent-sensitive. Specify the values *0* and *1*, respectively. The nature of diacritic-sensitive searching is also explained later in this chapter.

Expansion Sets

You can use *expansion sets* to specify two or more terms that are synonyms of one another. At query time, the search engine will expand matching user queries to include all the terms, no matter which one the user typed. For instance, our earlier whisky example can be implemented with an expansion set as follows:

```
<XML ID="Microsoft Search Thesaurus">
  <thesaurus xmlns="x-schema:tsSchema.xml">
  <diacritics_sensitive>0</diacritics_sensitive>
    <expansion>
      <sub>whisky</sub>
      <sub>scotch</sub>
    </expansion>
  </thesaurus>
</XML>
```

Adding a third synonym for *whisky* and another expansion set for *brandy* would look like this:

```
<XML ID="Microsoft Search Thesaurus">
  <thesaurus xmlns="x-schema:tsSchema.xml">
  <diacritics_sensitive>0</diacritics_sensitive>
    <expansion>
      <sub>whisky</sub>
      <sub>scotch</sub>
      <sub>bourbon</sub>
    </expansion>
    <expansion>
      <sub>brandy</sub>
      <sub>cognac</sub>
    </expansion>
  </thesaurus>
</XML>
```

Each expansion set is its own set of synonyms and does not influence other sets. You can define as many expansion sets as you need.

> **Note** The thesaurus in SharePoint Portal Server 2003 included an option to specify weight factors on expansion terms. This feature has been discontinued in Office SharePoint Server 2007.

Replacement Sets

The second related-terms mechanism in the thesaurus is *replacement sets*, which can be employed to enable users to find results with search terms that do not exist in the index. A single replacement set defines one or more patterns and one substitution term. At query time, the search engine will replace matching patterns with the substitution term. Continuing the whisky example, let's define a replacement set to enable a search for whisky by the terms *good stuff* and *strong stuff.* This would look as follows in the XML file:

```
<XML ID="Microsoft Search Thesaurus">
  <thesaurus xmlns="x-schema:tsSchema.xml">
    <diacritics_sensitive>0</diacritics_sensitive>
    <replacement>
      <pat>good stuff</pat>
      <pat>strong stuff</pat>
      <sub>whisky</sub>
    </replacement>
  </thesaurus>
</XML>
```

Again, you can define as many replacement sets as you need. Replacement sets can also be used to ignore typical misspellings of words that users are known to misspell. The new Did You Mean ... feature in Office SharePoint Server 2007 should, however, minimize the need to use the thesaurus for this purpose.

Noise Words

Noise words are words that should be prevented from entering the index during a crawl. They are sometimes also referred to as *stop words.* The primary purpose is to prevent the index from becoming bloated with frequently occurring words. In English, such words include *and, is, in, it, of, the,* and *to.* Other types of noise words are ones that are considered politically incorrect or offensive. Further examples include your company name and words like *copyright* that appear frequently in documents and Web pages.

> **Note** Most noise words that were present in the noise word files of SharePoint Portal Server 2003 have been removed in Office SharePoint Server 2007. Only a few words have survived, as the new version of the search engine now scales to accommodate common words that were previously excluded from the index.

Noise words are listed in the language-specific plain-text files in the same directory as the thesaurus XML files. For U.S. English, the file name is noiseenu.txt. The last three letters in the file name denote the language in the same way they do for the thesaurus files.

Diacritic-Sensitive Search

A *diacritic,* also known as an *accent,* is a small sign or symbol added to a letter to alter pronunciation or to distinguish similar words. A diacritical mark can appear above or below a letter, or in some other position. The nature of diacritical marks varies from language to language, and only a few languages do not use them. English is actually one of these few languages! But French, Spanish, Danish, and Swedish are a few examples of the majority of languages with letters containing diacritics. The French language, for instance, uses the following combinations of letters and diacritical marks:

à â ç é è ê ë î ï ô û ù ü ÿ

Diacritic-sensitive search is turned off by default in the search engine, meaning that diacritical marks are simply ignored at crawl time as well as at query time. Consider a document containing the French word *économie*, which contains a diacritical mark above the first letter. With diacritic-sensitive search turned off, searching for *economie* or *économie* will yield the same results. But you can turn on this feature, if you have a preference for diacritic sensitivity. Turning it on will instruct the search engine to include diacritical marks when it determines whether two words are equal. In other words, search results will yield only results containing keywords with the same diacritical marks as the user included in the search query keywords.

Only SharePoint server administrators can enable or disable diacritic-sensitive search using the SharePoint command-line tool STSADM.EXE. The command-line syntax is shown here:

```
stsadm
  -o osearchdiacriticsensitive
  -ssp <ssp name>
  [-setstatus <True|False>]
  [-noreset]
  [-force]
```

Here *ssp name* is the name of the SSP to change or view the setting for. Changing this setting with the *setstatus* option requires you to reset the index and perform a full crawl of all existing content. Use the *noreset* option to defer this to a later time. Use the *force* option to suppress the interactive confirmation of resetting the content index. The following example shows how to enable diacritic-sensitive searching for the SSP named SharedServices1:

```
stsadm -o osearchdiacriticsensitive -ssp sharedservices1 -setstatus True -force
```

The equivalent command for a Windows SharePoint Services 3.0 deployment is shown here:

```
stsadm -o spsearchdiacriticsensitive -setstatus True -force
```

Using PowerShell to Automate Administrative Tasks

Although Windows SharePoint Services 3.0 and Office SharePoint Server 2007 are not directly integrated with Microsoft Windows PowerShell, it is still possible to use PowerShell to automate administrative tasks in both products. This is possible because of the tight integration in PowerShell with .NET Framework objects, allowing you to load .NET Framework assemblies, instantiate objects, and call methods on these objects. SharePoint administrators can therefore employ PowerShell to write scripts that automate various tasks via the

SharePoint .NET Framework object model. Software developers can also develop and install new PowerShell commands in their favorite .NET Framework language, for a more tight integration with SharePoint. In this section, we'll review the basics for creating and running PowerShell scripts against the .NET Framework object model of Microsoft Office SharePoint Server Search. This will require basic .NET Framework skills and a basic knowledge of the SharePoint object model.

According to the Microsoft Windows PowerShell Web site, the PowerShell "command line and scripting language helps professionals achieve greater control and productivity." PowerShell is not included in Windows Server 2003 and must therefore first be installed on your SharePoint server. It can be downloaded for free from the Microsoft Web site. After you complete the installation, from a PowerShell command line, execute the following command:

```
set-executionpolicy RemoteSigned
```

This command is necessary to enable support for the execution of unsigned scripts. They will otherwise need to be signed with a certificate, which is a topic that is outside the scope of this book. The next step is to load the appropriate .NET Framework assemblies to access the SharePoint object model. You can automate this process by creating a PowerShell script file named LoadAssemblies.ps1. Use Notepad or any other text editor to create this file and to add the following lines:

```
## LoadAssemblies.ps1
[System.Reflection.Assembly]::Load("Microsoft.SharePoint, Version=12.0.0.0, Culture=neutral,
PublicKeyToken=71e9bce111e9429c")
[System.Reflection.Assembly]::Load("Microsoft.SharePoint.Portal, Version=12.0.0.0,
Culture=neutral, PublicKeyToken=71e9bce111e9429c")
[System.Reflection.Assembly]::Load("Microsoft.Office.Server, Version=12.0.0.0,
Culture=neutral, PublicKeyToken=71e9bce111e9429c")
[System.Reflection.Assembly]::Load("Microsoft.Office.Server.Search, Version=12.0.0.0,
Culture=neutral, PublicKeyToken=71e9bce111e9429c")
```

Execute the script from the PowerShell command line using the command *./LoadAssemblies. ps1*, as shown in Figure 5-78.

FIGURE 5-78 Loading SharePoint .NET Framework assemblies in PowerShell

Having loaded the appropriate SharePoint .NET Framework assemblies, we are now ready to start working with the SharePoint object model. A simple beginner's task is to view the properties of the *SPFarm* object that represents your SharePoint server farm. Type the command

[Microsoft.SharePoint.Administration.SPFarm]::Local to list all the properties of the global instance of this object, as shown in Figure 5-79.

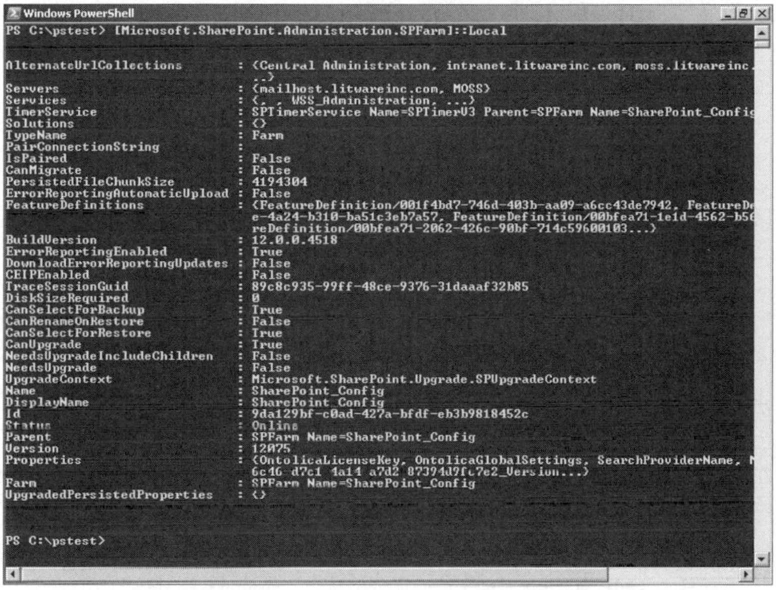

FIGURE 5-79 Viewing the properties of the global *SPFarm* object

A description of all the properties is not relevant here, but you can for instance tell by the *Status* property that the farm is *Online*.

Detecting the Search Application Name for an SSP

When working with the thesaurus, you need to know the search application name of the SSP to locate the thesaurus file associated with the SSP instance. See the section "Thesaurus" earlier in this chapter for details on this topic. Here it will suffice to present a PowerShell script that will show the search application name of the SSP named SharedServices1. The script can be implemented with three lines of code, as follows:

```
## GetSSPSearchAppName.ps1
$serverCtx=[Microsoft.Office.Server.ServerContext]::GetContext("SharedServices1")
$searchCtx=[Microsoft.Office.Server.Search.Administration.SearchContext]::GetContext($serverCtx)
$searchCtx.Name
```

The name displayed by the script turns out to be a GUID—for example, 829dd501-3ad7-4e27-88a6-67721fab8d4a.

Scripting a New Content Source

It can sometimes be convenient to script the creation of the content sources for an SSP, especially if you have many or you have a staged environment. The first solution that often springs to mind is to use the STSADM command-line tool in Office SharePoint Server 2007 to script the creation of content sources. But STSADM does not support this operation. However, the object model for administering Office SharePoint Server 2007 includes full support for all administrative operations, including the creation of new content sources. See Chapter 8 for complete coverage of working with the administration object model. Because content sources are exposed in the object model, you can also create a PowerShell script that automates the creation of new content sources.

The following PowerShell script creates a new Web content source named *Blogs* with the start addresses of three SharePoint blogs. The script actually creates a Web content source identical to the one created in the section "Indexing Web Sites" earlier in this chapter.

```
## CreateCS.ps1
01:$serverCtx=[Microsoft.Office.Server.ServerContext]::GetContext("SharedServices1")
02:$searchCtx=[Microsoft.Office.Server.Search.Administration.SearchContext]::GetContext($se
rverCtx)
03:$content=[Microsoft.Office.Server.Search.Administration.Content]($searchCtx)
04:$sspContentSources=$content.ContentSources
05:$contentSource=$sspContentSources.Create([Microsoft.Office.Server.Search.Administration.
WebContentSource], "Blogs")
06:$contentSource.MaxPageEnumerationDepth = 5
07:$contentSource.MaxSiteEnumerationDepth = 1
08:$startAddresses=$contentSource.StartAddresses
09:$startAddresses.Add([System.Uri]("http://blogs.msdn.com/sharepoint"))
10:$startAddresses.Add([System.Uri]("http://sharepointsearch.com/cs/blogs"))
11:$startAddresses.Add([System.Uri]("http://www.thorprojects.com/blog"))
12:$contentSource.Update()
```

 Note The line numbers are added only for convenient reference here. They must be omitted for the script to execute.

Digesting the script line by line yields the following:

- **Line 1**   Obtain a server context to the SSP named SharedServices1.

- **Line 2**   Use the server context to obtain a context to the search service of the SSP instance.

- **Lines 3 and 4**   Obtain an object reference to the collection of content sources for the SSP.

- **Line 5**   Create a new Web content source named *Blogs*, and add it to the collection of content sources. Replace *WebContentSource* with *SharePointContentSource* to create a SharePoint content source instead of a Web content source. Doing so requires you to delete lines 6 and 7, as the *MaxPageEnumerationDepth* property and the *MaxSiteEnumerationDepth* property are specific to the Web content source.

- **Lines 6 and 7**   Limit the page depth to 5 and the server hops to 1.

- **Lines 8 through 11**   Add three start addresses to the content source.

- **Line 12**   Save the changes to the SSP database.

You are now better equipped to start creating your own scripts that automate the creation of content sources for your own SSPs. You can of course also extend the script to modify or delete existing content sources.

Scripting a Crawl

Now that we've created the new Web content source named *Blogs* in the preceding section, the time has come to kick off the first full crawl of it. This can of course be achieved from the administration site of the SSP as usual. But it can also be scripted in PowerShell as follows:

```
## StartCrawl.ps1
$serverCtx=[Microsoft.Office.Server.ServerContext]::GetContext("SharedServices1")
$searchCtx=[Microsoft.Office.Server.Search.Administration.SearchContext]::GetContext($serve
rCtx)
$content=[Microsoft.Office.Server.Search.Administration.Content]($searchCtx)
$sspContentSources=$content.ContentSources
$contentSource=$sspContentSources["Blogs"]
$contentSource.StartFullCrawl()
```

The first four lines are identical to the *CreateCS.ps1* script. The last two lines pick the content source named *Blogs* from the collection of content sources and call the *StartFullCrawl* method on it. Starting an incremental crawl can also be done by changing the last line to this:

```
$contentSource.StartIncrementalCrawl()
```

Scripting a New Search Scope

For the same reasons why scripting content sources can be convenient, scripting the creation of search scopes can also be convenient at times. The following PowerShell script creates a new shared search scope named Documents In Records Repository for the SSP named SharedServices1. Having created the scope, the script then adds two rules to it.

```
## CreateScope.ps1
01:$ClassServerCtx = [Microsoft.Office.Server.ServerContext]
02:$ClassSearchCtx = [Microsoft.Office.Server.Search.Administration.SearchContext]
03:$SCT = [Microsoft.Office.Server.Search.Administration.ScopeCompilationType]
```

```
04:$SRFB = [Microsoft.Office.Server.Search.Administration.ScopeRuleFilterBehavior]
05:$USRT = [Microsoft.Office.Server.Search.Administration.UrlScopeRuleType]

## Get Context
06:$serverCtx=$ClassServerCtx::GetContext("SharedServices1")
07:$searchCtx=$ClassSearchCtx::GetContext($serverCtx)

## Find Managed Property named contentclass
08:$schema=[Microsoft.Office.Server.Search.Administration.Schema]($searchCtx)
09:$contentClassProp=$schema.AllManagedProperties["contentclass"]

## Create Scope
10:$scopes=[Microsoft.Office.Server.Search.Administration.Scopes]($searchCtx)
11:$scope=$scopes.AllScopes.Create("Documents in Records Repository","Scope description",$nu
ll,$true,"results.aspx",$SCT::AlwaysCompile)

## Add URL scope rule
12:$urlRule=$scope.Rules.CreateUrlRule($SRFB::Require, $USRT::Folder, "http://intranet.
litwareinc.com/records")

## Add Property scope rule
13:$contentClassRule=$scope.Rules.CreatePropertyQueryRule($SRFB::Require, $contentClassProp,
"STS_ListItem_DocumentLibrary")

## Update scope with the changes
14:$scope.Update()
```

 Note The line numbers are added only for convenient reference here. They must be omitted for the script to execute.

Digesting the script line by line yields the following:

- **Lines 1 through 5**   Create convenient aliases for classes and enumerations used farther down.

- **Line 6**   Obtain a server context to the SSP named SharedServices1.

- **Line 7**   In turn, use the server context to obtain a context to the Search service of the SSP instance.

- **Lines 8 and 9**   Obtain an object reference to a managed property named *contentclass*.

- **Lines 10 and 11**   Create the search scope, and obtain a reference to the new object that represents it.

- **Line 12**   Add a URL rule that requires content to start with the URL *http://intranet.litwareinc.com/records*.

- **Line 13**   Add a property rule that requires content to be a list item in a document library.

- **Line 14**   Save the changes to the SSP database.

This concludes the coverage of automating a few administrative search tasks with PowerShell. There are of course many other interesting tasks to automate, which is actually fairly easy to do if you understand object-oriented programming, the .NET Framework, and the C# programming language. Just study the .NET Framework object models of Windows SharePoint Services 3.0 and Office SharePoint Server 2007. Whatever these object models enable you to achieve can be scripted with PowerShell.

Summary

In this chapter, you learned about all aspects of the administration of the Enterprise Search engine in Office SharePoint Server 2007. You should now be fully prepared to install, configure, and operate the search engine. The next chapter covers indexing content using the Business Data Catalog, a topic that was introduced in this chapter.

Chapter 6
Indexing and Searching Business Data

After completing this chapter, you will be able to

- Understand the challenges addressed by the Business Data Catalog (BDC).

- Create an application definition file containing the declarative syntax to make the business data indexable and searchable.

- Understand the various steps involved in the administration, configuration, and customization of the indexing and searching of business data.

- Get a jump-start in the runtime object model of the BDC, and learn how to search and find business data directly in a Web Part.

The preceding chapters gave you a brief introduction to the indexing and searching of business data. This chapter goes a bit further, giving you more details on how to configure the indexing of business data along with some techniques for customizing the end-user experience when it comes to searching and reviewing search results that contain business data. To start, there is a review of what the BDC is all about, the challenges it addresses, and the benefits of using it within your organization. It is important to acquire a good understanding of the different components that make up the BDC architecture before you start configuring the index engine for crawling the business data. You'll learn about the creation of application definition files, but do keep in mind that this is a book on indexing and searching. Therefore, the focus will be on the elements that are needed for indexing and searching the business data. Application definition files contain the model of the business data that you want to work with. Once this model is imported, some administrative tasks have to be done to let the crawler start indexing the business data. The end-user experience is similar to the one we looked at in Chapter 2, "The End-User Search Experience." A couple of additional topics regarding customization will be explored in this chapter, along with some of the programming techniques for communicating with the runtime object model that is exposed at the level of the BDC.

Introducing the Business Data Catalog

Unlocking business data stored in traditional databases and line-of-business (LOB) systems is one of the main priorities within agile organizations these days. Being *agile* as an organization implies that you are trying to respond in the quickest and most flexible way to new market conditions and changing environment variables, both internal and external ones. Adopting a proactive approach when doing business is an excellent way to address these challenges. One helpful factor in this is ensuring that everybody within the company is able to access the right information for his or her job at the right time. This constant focus on finding ways to improve how information workers within their daily operations get access to and act upon data is extremely important but not easy, especially if you understand that this often involves accessing enterprise-critical data that is likely to be kept in highly structured, very dedicated, and secured data stores. Access to this data is not always optimal. Information workers are often confronted with an end-user experience that is completely different from the one they are familiar with.

Consider, for example, a salesperson named Joe. Microsoft Office Outlook is Joe's comfort zone. This is the application that he immediately opens when entering the office after his first cup of coffee. For most of the day, all the work he does is within this environment. Joe receives e-mail messages with requests from customers regarding the products he is responsible for. His job is to respond swiftly and accurately to these requests. To get access to the data needed to respond to these inquiries, however, he must switch quite frequently to an arcane user interface that is used to access, for example, a mainframe system where the data is stored. Other information that is more related to the customer is again found in another external system. This is not an optimal way of working for Joe, and he has already submitted a request to the IT department asking for a software solution that would enable him to access the data directly from within the Outlook environment and also in the Microsoft Office SharePoint Server 2007 sites he frequently visits during the day. Being able to integrate the external data in these environments will make Joe more productive in his daily job.

But taking a proactive approach is about more than the end-user experience. In fact, enterprise LOB systems are frequently shielded from end users because of security concerns. This is of course a good thing, since the systems store enterprise data that is of great importance to the organization. A granular access control to the systems is seldom an option, for many reasons. One major reason in a lot of companies is that the security level needed for the information workers is often based on contextual information. Take Joe again as an example. As a salesperson, he is responsible for the customer relationships within a certain sales region. The information regarding his responsibilities is nicely recorded as part of his user profile, which is stored and maintained by Office SharePoint Server 2007. However, it is a tough task for the IT department to use this information for fine-tuning the access control at the level of the mainframe.

It is clear that we are talking here about two separate worlds: the dynamic and ever-changing world of the information workers and the static, highly structured world of the LOB back-end systems. The gap between these two worlds is called the *results gap*. The major goal of the BDC is to be a facilitator for IT departments when they are looking for solutions that can bridge the two worlds.

Business Data Catalog Architecture

The BDC is a new shared service that is available in your SharePoint server farm after the deployment of Office SharePoint Server 2007 and the creation of a Shared Services Provider (SSP). Chapter 5, "Search Administration," introduced the concept of the SSP and explained the role of the index and search engine that is part of the SSP services. The BDC should be seen as middle-layer software whose purpose is to bridge the results gap described earlier. Compare the BDC to the Open Database Connectivity (ODBC) layer that has been around for many years. Before ODBC, developers had to learn the native application programming interfaces (APIs) for the many database applications they had to access. Point-to-point applications were common in those days. A *point-to-point application* is an application component where one end, the environment of the information worker, for example, connects directly with the other end, the store where the data is available. This often resulted in a number of maintenance problems because of the tight coupling between the two sides and because the developer had to learn the native API of the data store. ODBC brought a lot of relief to the developer community because now they had to learn only one API: the ODBC API. ODBC sits between the two sides that have to be connected and enables developers to work with a more loosely coupled architecture. Once the required ODBC drivers have been installed and configured, the access to the data stores is abstracted for the developers, who simply connect their front-end applications using the ODBC runtime API. Note that ODBC has evolved into newer technologies such as OLEDB and ADO.NET—technologies that are familiar to the Microsoft .NET Framework developer of today.

As mentioned, the BDC acts in much the same manner as ODBC. It is more universal, however, in the sense that it connects not only to the traditional data stores but also to LOB systems that can run on completely different platforms than the ones that are used by the information workers.

We are able to connect in two ways to back-end systems by using the BDC:

- **Using ADO.NET**   This group of back-end systems encompasses the traditional data stores such as Microsoft SQL Server and Oracle databases. But it goes further than this. Any database that is accessible through the ADO.NET, OLEDB, and ODBC layers is part of this group. The BDC has logic built in to formulate requests for data as an ADO.NET request, and it can consequently execute the request against the data store in question.

- **Using Web service proxies**   Back-end systems that have no means of exposing their data using Microsoft-related database access technologies (as described in the preceding list item) have to expose the business data through a layer of Web services that the BDC is able to connect to. The BDC is capable of generating a *Web service proxy*, which is basically a wrapper class that hides the complexity of communicating with the Web service. This wrapper class will be instantiated when the BDC has to respond to queries from the front-end layer.

The BDC architecture is shown in the following illustration:

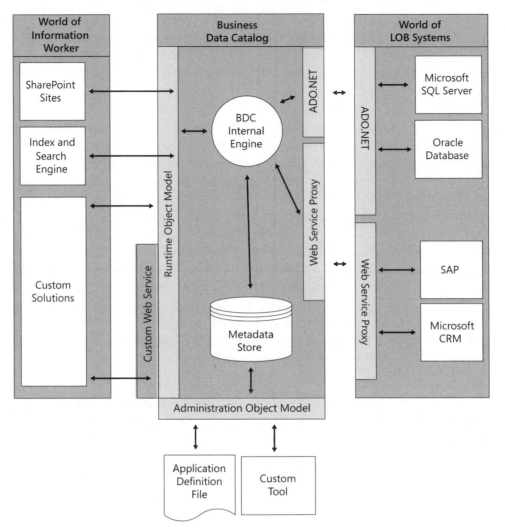

One of the core components in the BDC architecture shown here is a database that stores the metadata information regarding the business data that must be accessed. In addition, all of the configuration data that is associated with the metadata is also stored in this database. An administration object model is available to populate and access this metadata, as you'll learn in the next section. There is a second object model: the runtime object model. Its goal is to enable the communication of the requests to the internal engine that is part of the BDC. The engine translates the request based on the information it finds in the metadatabase into the properly formatted request, which is submitted to the back-end systems. The resulting data is communicated again using the runtime object model to the world of the information workers. As you'll see in the section "Managing the Permissions" later in this chapter, administrators have the means to configure the access control at various levels of the business data. All of that configuration is applied when the request is processed. A powerful caching mechanism is also in place. Caching is important in order to minimize the direct communication with the back-end systems and to provide the end user with good performance.

After the loading of the metadata in the database is complete and administrators have configured the access control, power users and developers are ready to start using or building front-end solution components that work with the business data. At the time of this writing, the BDC is very much SharePoint-focused. You'll notice that Office SharePoint Server 2007 comes with a number of Business Data Web Parts that you can immediately drop onto Web Part pages within SharePoint sites. After a small configuration, you can connect those Web Parts with the different pieces that are part of the business data. The out-of-the-box experience goes even further. User profile properties can be mapped to business data, and it is also possible to create metadata at the level of the lists and document libraries. This metadata is bound to the data exposed by the BDC.

The power of the BDC lies in its runtime object model, however. Mastering this object model means that you can build custom SharePoint solution components that deliver the business data to the user in any way you want. By default, this runtime object model is accessible in a direct way only with your application running within the context of SharePoint or running on the machine on which Office SharePoint Server 2007 is installed. You can remotely access the runtime object model of the BDC if you build a layer of custom Web services that are deployed and running in the context of SharePoint. These Web services can translate the remote requests into the object model calls that are understood by the BDC.

In short, the BDC provides a rich and powerful infrastructure that we can use to bridge the gap between Joe's world and the world of the structured data that he is required to use within his daily operations. Let's now have a step-by-step look at how you can create a model of the business data and how you can perform the required configurations in order for the index engine to crawl the data.

Modeling the Business Data

An important step in this whole story is the creation of a model of the business data that you want to get access to. Behind the scenes, the model that you create is stored in a number of tables that are part of the SSP database. We refer to this collection of tables as the *metadata store* of the BDC.

Seasoned SharePoint developers know very well that it is *not* a good practice to perform work directly in the databases that are used by SharePoint when, for example, they are accessing content that is stored in the various lists and document libraries that are part of the

SharePoint sites. The object models are there to abstract that data layer. The same is true for the BDC.

There are basically two ways of constructing a business data model, and each follows its own procedure for dropping the model in the metadata store:

- **Declarative approach**   Most people construct the model of the business data in a declarative way. Working declaratively means that you do not really code the model but that you define it in an XML file. This file is known as the *application definition file*. The XML you write must be valid against a *schema* (which we'll look at in a moment). Once the work has been done, you or the administrator will have to import the application definition file into the metadata store via a page that is part of the administration site of the SSP.

- **Programmatic approach**   The BDC comes with two object models. The first is the runtime object model, which we'll look at briefly at the end of this chapter. This API can be used by developers to access all of the artifacts that are part of the model, including entitities, properties, methods, actions, and possibly associations between the entities. Caching is turned on by default to deliver a good user experience when retrieving the business data. The second object model is the administration object model. This object model does not include the use of the caching infrastructure and is aimed at supporting administrative operations within the BDC, such as the importing of the application definition files and the security configuration, and also the creation of the model in the metadata store. Using this administration object model, you can create custom applications or designers that skip the creation and importing of an application definition file and immediately do all of the work using the metadata store.

This second approach is beyond the scope of this book, but you can read about it in *Inside Microsoft Office SharePoint Server 2007*, by Patrick Tisseghem (Microsoft Press, 2007). That book also contains the details of the various XML elements that you can use in the application definition file if you decide to use the declarative approach. For this book, we'll give our full attention to only those elements that are related to the searching and indexing of the business data. Since the declarative approach is the most common approach, we'll use that one here.

> **Note**   Before you start defining the XML, you should perform a detailed analysis of your business data. Many modeling techniques and tools are available, and we'll assume that you have done that preparation work already.

Creating an Application Definition File

An application definition file contains the model of the business data as a collection of XML elements. There are basically two roads that you can take to create your application definition files. First is the difficult way of creating the XML: You open an editor, create the XML file, and start writing your XML elements. The editor is preferably Microsoft Visual Studio 2005 or Microsoft Visual Studio 2008, since you can activate IntelliSense support for the XML you are writing. IntelliSense support is enabled when you associate the bdcmetadata.xsd schema (located in the [Program Files]\ Microsoft Office Servers\12.0\Bin folder) with your XML file. This is done by configuring the Schemas property in the Properties dialog box when the XML file is opened in the editor. Figure 6-1 shows you what you have to do.

Note The XML displayed in Figure 6-1 is part of small number of sample application definition files that are contained in the Office SharePoint Server 2007 Software Developer Kit (SDK). There are more helpful samples and tools included in the SDK that are related to the BDC. One of them, the BDC Definition Editor, is discussed in just a moment.

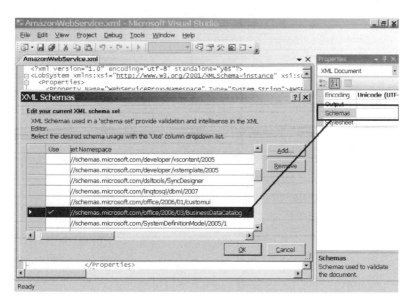

FIGURE 6-1 Activating IntelliSense support for application definition files in Visual Studio

You can avoid typing all of the XML by using one of the available designer tools. At the time of this writing, two well-known BDC design tools are available. The first is a commercial product called the BDC Meta Man, available at *http://www.bdcmetaman.com*. This tool is highly recommended if the creation of application definition files is a common task within your daily job as a SharePoint developer. The other designer tool is free and is called the BDC Definition Editor. It is part of the Office SharePoint Server 2007 SDK 1.02. We'll use the BDC Definition Editor in this chapter. You still have to perform plenty of manual steps within the BDC Definition Editor, as you'll see, but it's not a bad idea to go through the process to learn more about the XML elements that are involved in an application definition file.

Again, we'll use a practical example to illustrate the steps for creating an application definition file. Remember Joe, the sales guy? He, like many of the employees in his company, works a lot with Microsoft Dynamics Customer Relationship Management (CRM) 4.0. In this LOB system, he finds all the information regarding his customers, opportunities, contacts, activities, and so forth. Let's see how you can use the BDC Definition Editor to create an application definition file that models some of the data that is part of the Dynamics CRM 4.0 database. That data is what Joe wants to see more integrated into his daily work environment—his SharePoint sites and Office Outlook 2007.

> **Note** You can of course connect to other data stores or LOB systems. Both design tools mentioned earlier can be used to connect to Microsoft SQL Server databases, Oracle databases, and other databases through OLEDB and ODBC. If no access is possible through these data layer services, there is also the option to connect the tools to the business data via one or more Web services.

Dynamics CRM 4.0 comes with a collection of Web services that expose an API that can be used to remotely connect to and act on the CRM data. There is also a set of table views in the SQL Server CRM database in addition to the Web services. We can connect to these views directly, and therefore, we'll use them in the steps to create our application definition file.

Figure 6-2 shows the BDC Definition Editor the first time the tool is opened.

Click the Add LOB System option to add an LOB System to the designer. The Add LOB System dialog box shown in Figure 6-3 appears.

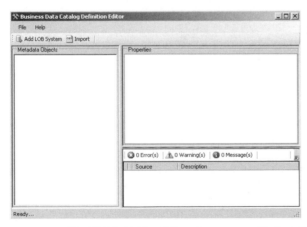

FIGURE 6-2 The BDC Definition Editor that comes with the Office SharePoint Server 2007 SDK

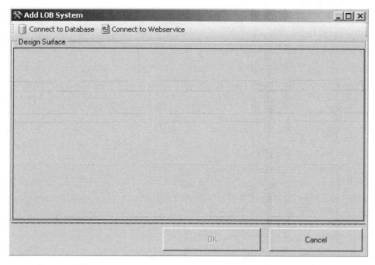

FIGURE 6-3 Adding an LOB System

An LOB System is basically the model that is about to be created. It is represented in the application definition file as the *LobSystem* element:

```
<LobSystem xmlns:xsi="http://www.w3.org/2001/XMLSchema-instance"
xsi:schemaLocation="http://schemas.microsoft.com/office/2006/03/BusinessDataCatalog
BDCMetadata.xsd" Type="Database" Version="1.0.0.0" Name="CRM_Accounts"
xmlns="http://schemas.microsoft.com/office/2006/03/BusinessDataCatalog"> </LobSystem>
```

Two types are possible: *Database* and *WebService*. These options are also presented in the BDC Definition Editor. The connection string is required in case the *Database* option is selected. An example of such a connection string is shown in Figure 6-4.

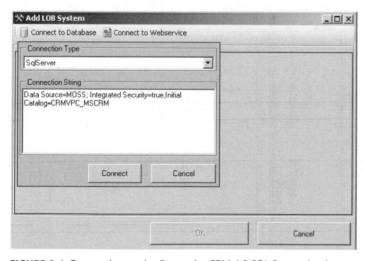

FIGURE 6-4 Connecting to the Dynamics CRM 4.0 SQL Server database

The URL for the .asmx file is required input when the connection to the business data is made through a Web service. In both cases, an *LobSystemInstance* is added to the application definition file as a child element of the *LobSystem* root. *LobSystemInstance* elements store the connection and authentication details used by the BDC when executing the queries against the database or when executing the Web methods at the level of the Web service.

```
<LobSystemInstances>
    <LobSystemInstance Name="CRM_Accounts_Instance">
      <Properties>
        <Property Name="rdbconnection Data Source"
                  Type="System.String">localhost</Property>
        <Property Name="rdbconnection Initial Catalog"
                  Type="System.String">CRMVPC_MSCRM</Property>
        <Property Name="rdbconnection Integrated Security"
                  Type="System.String">True</Property>
        <Property Name="DatabaseAccessProvider" Type=
  "Microsoft.Office.Server.ApplicationRegistry.SystemSpecific.Db.DbAccessProvider">
  SqlServer</Property>
        <Property Name="AuthenticationMode" Type=
  "Microsoft.Office.Server.ApplicationRegistry.SystemSpecific.Db.DbAuthenticationMode">
  PassThrough</Property>
      </Properties>
    </LobSystemInstance>
  </LobSystemInstances>
</LobSystemInstances>
```

There are four possible values for the *AuthenticationMode* attribute when connecting to databases:

- *PassThrough*   This is the default. When this option is used, the BDC will use the account of the impersonated user to connect to the SQL Server database.

- *RevertToSelf*   This option is used when the BDC is required to take the account that is defined as the application pool identity.

- *RdbCredentials*   This option and *WindowsCredentials* (defined next) work in conjunction with the Single Sign-On (SSO) service. SSO allows for the storage of mappings between accounts in a secure credential store. These mappings can be picked up by applications such as the BDC. In *RdbCredentials* mode, the BDC authenticates the user initiating the request for data by using database credentials from its default SSO service. The database credentials are added to the connection string and transmitted to the database server.

- *WindowsCredentials*   Similar to *RdbCredentials*. The BDC will authenticate the user initiating the request for data by using Microsoft Windows credentials from its default SSO service.

Once the BDC Definition Editor is able to connect to the database, both tables and views can be dropped onto the design surface. Figure 6-5 displays the design surface populated with the *FilteredAccount* view. All of the views within the CRM database that start with the prefix *Filtered* are candidates for becoming entities in the application definition file.

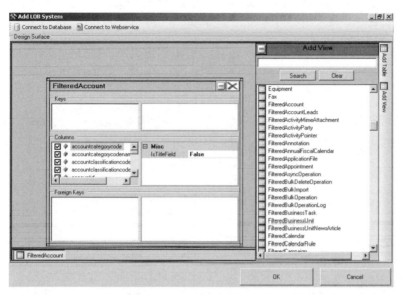

FIGURE 6-5 The design surface of the BDC Definition Editor, with one view ready to be configured

Before we have a closer look at the entities, we have to make one additional configuration of a property at the level of the LOB System. When saving the work done in the designer, we end up again in the main editor. Figure 6-6 displays what has been created so far.

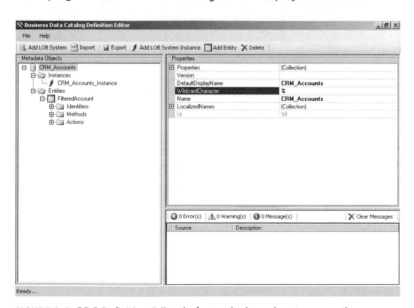

FIGURE 6-6 BDC Definition Editor before assigning values to properties

We have to assign a value to one property at the level of the *LobSystem* element. The property is *WildcardCharacter*, and as a result of our working with a SQL Server database, its value is set to %. This character will be used by the BDC to support wildcard searches—something you'll learn about in a moment. The result of this setting is a new *Property* element in the application definition file:

```
<Properties>
   <Property Name="WildcardCharacter" Type="System.String">%</Property>
</Properties>
```

Every view or table added to the design surface shown earlier in Figure 6-5 maps to an *Entity* element in the application definition file. The *FilteredAccount* view is represented in the XML as follows:

```
<Entities>
  <Entity EstimatedInstanceCount="10000" Name="FilteredAccount" />
</Entities>
```

However, the definition of the entity is at this moment fairly incomplete and therefore not really useful. The required additional work can be completed in the editor itself. The panel on the left summarizes all of the XML elements that are currently available. Clicking an element updates the panel on the right, which displays the various properties for the selected element.

Figure 6-7 shows the *Account* element and its properties.

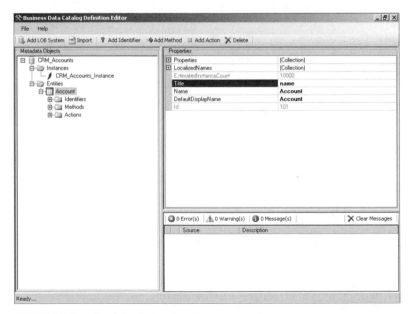

FIGURE 6-7 Details of the *Account* entity

At first, the *Title* attribute is empty, but it is a good idea to give it a value since it will be used by the Business Data Picker and also when displaying the results when executing a search query. The value is stored as part of a *Property* element in the XML:

```
<Properties>
   <Property Name="Title" Type="System.String">name</Property>
</Properties>
```

The values for the *Name* and *DefaultDisplayName* attribute are changed from *FilteredAccount* to *Account*. This is simply because *Account* is easier to work with than *FilteredAccount*. Nothing else needs to be done at the level of the *Entity* element itself.

The goal of the BDC is to retrieve one or more instances for this entity. Before the BDC can do this, you need to add the definition of a couple of methods. Various types of methods can be executed by the BDC. The three methods that are important in the context of this book are listed here:

- *Finder* **method**   The execution of an instance of this method returns multiple entity instances. This is typically a method accepting one or more filters. (We'll look at filters in a moment.)

- *FindSpecific* **method**   This type of method returns one entity instance. The retrieval is done based on a field that acts as an identifier.

- *IDEnumerator* **method**   This method is an important one if you want to have the crawler index all of the details of the entity. Basically, the method returns all of the primary keys for the entity. (More on the *IDEnumerator* method at the end of this section.)

The last two types of methods require the definition of a field that is used to identify the entity. In the CRM database, an account is identified by a primary key named *accountid*. Identifiers are typically primary keys in the database. An identifier is added to the BDC Definition Editor by selecting first the *Identifiers* node in the left panel and then clicking Add Identifier on the toolbar.

Figure 6-8 shows the details of the identifier in the editor.

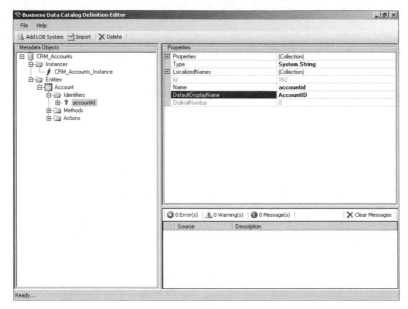

FIGURE 6-8 The identifier for the *Account* entity

In the XML, the identifier is defined as an *Identifier* element that is part of the *Identifiers* element, as shown here. The *Identifiers* element itself is a child element of the *Entity* element.

```
<Identifiers>
 <Identifier TypeName="System.String" Name="accountid" DefaultDisplayName="AccountID" />
</Identifiers>
```

We'll add a total of three methods to the definition of the entity: *GetAccount*, *GetAccounts*, and *GetAccountIDs*. The *GetAccount* method will return exactly one entity instance. This method is easily added by selecting the *Methods* node in the left panel and then clicking Add Method on the toolbar. A couple of properties need values. The *Name* and *DefaultDisplayName* properties can both be set to *GetAccount*. The value of the *RdbCommandText* property is the SQL statement that the BDC must execute to get the entity instance in question. There is no direct support for constructing the SQL query other than a multiple-line text box. This is good for simple queries, although for more complicated queries, a query builder is useful. The Microsoft SQL Server 2005 Management Studio can help to a certain degree. For the sample we are working on, the value for the *RdbCommandText* is the following:

```
SELECT [accountid]
      , [name]
      , [address1_line1]
      , [address1_city]
      , [address1_country]
      , [address1_postalcode]
FROM [CRMVPC_MSCRM].[dbo].[FilteredAccount]
WHERE [accountid] = @accountid
```

The value for the *RdbCommandType* property remains *Text* because we are executing a raw SQL statement. The *StoredProcedure* option is chosen if the method will execute a stored procedure that is part of the SQL Server database. Figure 6-9 displays the new method.

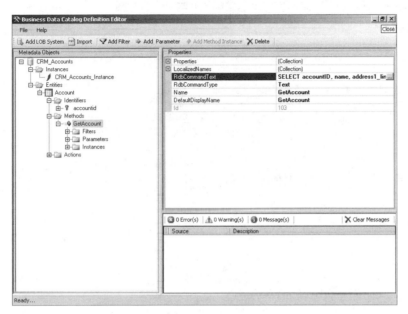

FIGURE 6-9 The *GetAccount* method definition

The definition of the *GetAccount* method in the application definition file is part of the child nodes under the *Methods* element (which is itself a child node of the *Entity* element):

```
<Methods>
  <Method Name="GetAccount">
    <Properties>
        <Property Name="RdbCommandType" Type="System.Data.CommandType, System.Data,
Version=2.0.0.0, Culture=neutral, PublicKeyToken=b77a5c561934e089">Text</Property>
        <Property Name="RdbCommandText" Type="System.String">
            SELECT [accountid],[name], [address1_line1],
            [address1_city],[address1_country],[address1_postalcode]
            FROM [CRMVPC_MSCRM].[dbo].[FilteredAccount]
            WHERE [accountid] = @accountid</Property>
    </Properties>
  </Method>
</Methods>
```

Notice that there is one parameter named *@accountid*. The application definition file must contain the definition for this parameter. In the BDC Definition Editor, a *Parameters* node is available in the left panel under the *GetAccount* node. A *Parameter* node can be added directly below it by clicking Add Parameter on the toolbar. In the dialog box that appears, the type of the parameter must be set. There are four types of parameters: *In*, *InOut*, *Out*, and *Return*. The *@accountid* is of type *In*. The name of the *Parameter* element is typically set to the same string as is used within the SQL statement.

The *Parameter* element must have a *TypeDescriptor* element associated with it. The *TypeDescriptor* element contains type information for the parameter, along with information about the filters and identifiers that might be associated with it. In the BDC Definition Editor, a *TypeDescriptor* for the parameter is created by selecting the parameter in the left panel and then clicking Create Root TypeDescriptor on the toolbar. Figure 6-10 shows the model, including the *Parameter* and the *TypeDescriptor*. The value of the *Name* and *DefaultDisplayName* attributes can be set to any meaningful string if needed.

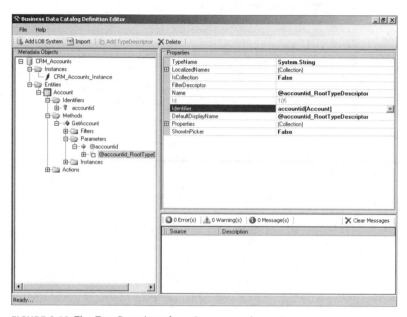

FIGURE 6-10 The *TypeDescriptor* for a *Parameter* element

The *TypeName* attribute is set to *System.String* and not to *System.Guid*, even though the field is defined as such in the CRM database. At the time of this writing, the BDC does not handle globally unique identifier (GUID) types very well. The parameter is to be associated with the *Identifier* element created earlier. This is done by setting the *Identifier* attribute to the name of the *Identifier* element.

The XML in the application definition file that corresponds to what you have configured in the BDC Definition Editor is shown here:

```
<Parameters>
  <Parameter Direction="In" Name="@accountid" DefaultDisplayName="AccountID">
    <TypeDescriptor TypeName="System.String" IdentifierName="accountid"
    Name="@accountid_RootTypeDescriptor" />
  </Parameter>
</Parameters>
```

One parameter definition is not enough. Remember that the execution of the SQL query returns one entity instance with a number of fields. The BDC needs to know how it will receive this data and the type information for each of the fields. The definition of this new *Parameter* element can again be done in the BDC Definition Editor by selecting the *Parameters* node in the left panel and then clicking Add Parameter on the toolbar. The type of the parameter is now set to *Return*. A proper value for the attributes *Name* and *DefaultDisplayName* can be set.

There are three *TypeDescriptor* elements for this *Parameter* element. The first is created by selecting the *Parameter* node previously created in the left panel and then clicking Create Root TypeDescriptor on the toolbar. Notice that the value of the *TypeName* attribute is already set to *System.Data.IDataReader, System.Data, Version=2.0.0.0, Culture=neutral, Pub licKeyToken=b77a5c561934e089*. You cannot change this value; the value indicates to the BDC that it will get an instance implementing the *IDataReader* interface. Don't worry about the details—the BDC knows what it has to do with this instance. Next is the information regarding the type of each element that will be part of the incoming stream of data. The *TypeDescriptor* element is a child element of the one that we just created in the left panel. The value of the *TypeName* attribute is now set to *System.Data.IDataRecord, System.Data, Version=2.0.0.0, Culture=neutral, PublicKeyToken=b77a5c561934e089*. If you want, you can change the name and the default display name of the *TypeDescriptor* element.

More *TypeDescriptor* elements are needed to complete this *Parameter* element definition. Every one of the return fields that are included in the *SELECT* part of the SQL query must be detailed with a *TypeDescriptor* element that is a child element of the one that was just added. All of them are of type *System.String*, and they have a name that is equal to the name of the field itself. The first element is *accountid*; it must also be associated with the one and only *Identifier* element we have for the entity. The next elements are *name, address1_line1, address1_city, address1_postalcode*, and *address1_country*. All of these can be configured with a user-friendly display name, but the name itself must correspond to the name of the field in the *SELECT* statement. Figure 6-11 shows the complete set of *TypeDescriptor* elements for the *Return* parameter.

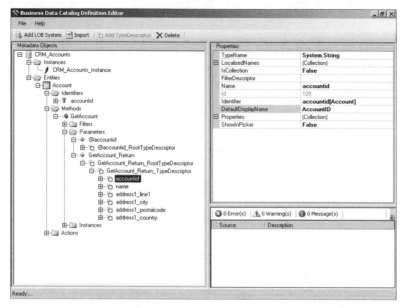

FIGURE 6-11 All of the *TypeDescriptor* elements for the *Return* parameter

In the application definition file, all of this is represented as follows:

```
<Parameter Direction="Return" Name="GetAccount_Return">
  <TypeDescriptor TypeName="System.Data.IDataReader, System.Data, Version=2.0.0.0, Cul
ture=neutral, PublicKeyToken=b77a5c561934e089" IsCollection="true"
Name="GetAccount_Return_RootTypeDescriptor">
    <TypeDescriptors>
      <TypeDescriptor TypeName="System.Data.IDataRecord, System.Data, Version=2.0.0.0,
Culture=neutral, PublicKeyToken=b77a5c561934e089"
Name="GetAccount_Return_TypeDescriptor">
        <TypeDescriptors>
          <TypeDescriptor TypeName="System.String" IdentifierName="accountid"
Name="accountid" DefaultDisplayName="AccountID" />
          <TypeDescriptor TypeName="System.String" Name="name"
           DefaultDisplayName="Company" />
          <TypeDescriptor TypeName="System.String" Name="address1_line1"
           DefaultDisplayName="Address" />
          <TypeDescriptor TypeName="System.String" Name="address1_city"
           DefaultDisplayName="City" />
          <TypeDescriptor TypeName="System.String" Name="address1_postalcode"
           DefaultDisplayName="Postal Code" />
          <TypeDescriptor TypeName="System.String" Name="address1_country"
           DefaultDisplayName="Country" />
        </TypeDescriptors>
      </TypeDescriptor>
    </TypeDescriptors>
  </TypeDescriptor>
</Parameter>
```

A final child element to create for the *GetAccount* method is the *MethodInstance* element. This element identifies the method for the BDC as one of a specific type. The type is set at the level of a *MethodInstance* element. Creating a *MethodInstance* element is done by first selecting the Instances node in the left panel and then clicking Add Method Instance on the toolbar. The Create Method Instance dialog box, shown in Figure 6-12, displays the options that are available.

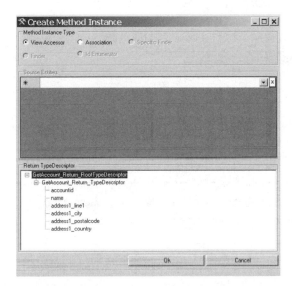

FIGURE 6-12 Creating a *MethodInstance* element of type *Specific Finder*

The *GetAccount* method is of type *SpecificFinder*, and the return type is the root *TypeDescriptor* element. You might want to change the name and the display name for the new *MethodInstance* element to, for example, *GetAccountInstance*.

The *MethodInstance* element is represented in the application definition file as follows:

```
<MethodInstances>
  <MethodInstance Type="SpecificFinder" ReturnParameterName="GetAccount_Return"
    ReturnTypeDescriptorName="GetAccount_Return_RootTypeDescriptor"
    ReturnTypeDescriptorLevel="0" Name="GetAccountInstance" />
</MethodInstances>
```

That's all the required elements for the first method. The completed work can be verified by executing the *MethodInstance* element, just as the BDC would do at run time. Right-click the new *MethodInstance* element in the left panel, and then select the *Execute* option. In the dialog box that appears, shown in Figure 6-13, you can enter the ID for an account and execute the query.

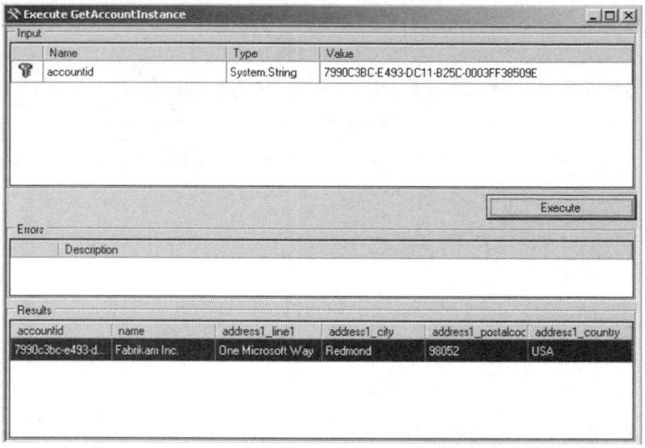

FIGURE 6-13 Executing a *MethodInstance* element

The second method that will be part of the model for the CRM data that salesperson Joe has to access is named *GetAccounts*. It is created in a similar way to the first method, except that this method is of type *Finder* and thus is destined to return multiple entity instances. The SQL statement for *RdbCommandText* is the following (assuming that you allow a wildcard filter on the *name* field and that a limited set of fields is returned):

```
SELECT
  [accountid], [name]
FROM
  [CRMVPC_MSCRM].[dbo].[FilteredAccount]
WHERE
  [name] LIKE @name
```

This method works with a filter, and because of this, a *FilterDescriptor* element has to be part of the model for the *GetAccounts* method. The controls delivering the end-user experience will typically pick up this information and display it so that the user can enter a query that returns, for example, all of the accounts containing the string *'works'*. To create a *FilterDescriptor* element, select the *Filters* node in the left panel, and then click Add Filter on the toolbar. An important attribute to set here is *FilterType*. Notice that many options are available in the drop-down list. The names of the types of filters give you a good idea of what they are used for. The most popular filter type is the default: *WildcardFilter*. Figure 6-14 displays the definition of the *FilterDescriptor* element.

FIGURE 6-14 Definition of the *FilterDescriptor* element

The representation in the application definition file of the new method and the filter is as follows:

```
<Method Name="GetAccounts">
  <Properties>
    <Property Name="RdbCommandText" Type="System.String">
      SELECT [accountid], [name] FROM [CRMVPC_MSCRM].[dbo].[FilteredAccount]
      WHERE [name] LIKE @name
    </Property>
    <Property Name="RdbCommandType" Type="System.Data.CommandType, System.Data, Ver
sion=2.0.0.0, Culture=neutral, PublicKeyToken=b77a5c561934e089">Text</Property>
  </Properties>
  <FilterDescriptors>
    <FilterDescriptor Type="Wildcard" Name="name" />
  </FilterDescriptors>
</Method>
```

The *GetAccounts* method is completed by creating the input and return parameters along with all of the *TypeDescriptor* elements, as was done for the *GetAccount* method. Just one little remark concerning the *TypeDescriptor* element for the first parameter definition (the one of type *In*): the *FilterDescriptor* attribute for that parameter is set to the *FilterDescriptor* element that was created previously. This is necessary because this field is the one that is going to be used for a filtering operation. Figure 6-15 shows the work completed for the *GetAccounts* method in the BDC Definition Editor.

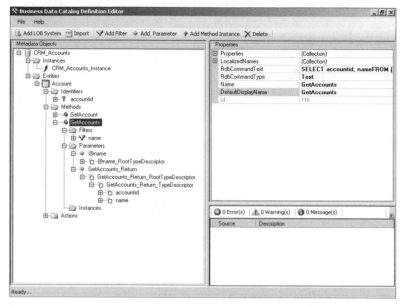

FIGURE 6-15 Parameters for the *GetAccounts* method

The output in the application definition file looks like this:

```
<Parameters>
  <Parameter Direction="In" Name="@name">
    <TypeDescriptor TypeName="System.String" AssociatedFilter="AccountName"
     Name="@name_TypeDescriptor" />
  </Parameter>
  <Parameter Direction="Return" Name="GetAccounts_Return">
    <TypeDescriptor TypeName="System.Data.IDataReader, System.Data, Version=2.0.0.0,
Culture=neutral, PublicKeyToken=b77a5c561934e089" IsCollection="true"
Name="GetAccounts_Return_RootTypeDescriptor">
      <TypeDescriptors>
        <TypeDescriptor TypeName="System.Data.IDataRecord, System.Data, Version=2.0.0.0,
Culture=neutral, PublicKeyToken=b77a5c561934e089"
Name="GetAccounts_Return_TypeDescriptor">
          <TypeDescriptors>
            <TypeDescriptor TypeName="System.String" Name="name"
             DefaultDisplayName="Company" />
            <TypeDescriptor TypeName="System.String" IdentifierName="accountid"
             Name="accountid" DefaultDisplayName="AccountID" />
          </TypeDescriptors>
        </TypeDescriptor>
      </TypeDescriptors>
    </TypeDescriptor>
  </Parameter>
</Parameters>
```

A final piece in the definition of the *GetAccounts* method is the *MethodInstance* element. For this element, we'll use the *Finder* type, as shown in Figure 6-16.

FIGURE 6-16 The *MethodInstance* for the *GetAccounts* method

Again, executing the *MethodInstance* element is useful to verify whether the completed work is configured correctly for the BDC. Figure 6-17 displays the results of the execution with a filter on the name *Contoso*.

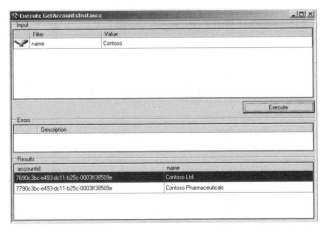

FIGURE 6-17 Execution of the *GetAccountsInstance MethodInstance* element, which returns two entity instances when the filter is set to 'Contoso'

One last method is important in the context of this book. This method is of type *IdEnumerator* and is added in the same manner as the two previously discussed methods. The method is named *GetAccountIDs*, and the value of the *RdbCommandText* is a simple SQL query like this one:

```
SELECT [accountid] FROM [CRMVPC_MSCRM].[dbo].[FilteredAccount]
```

There is no WHERE condition in the SQL statement, which means only one definition of a parameter is needed—the *return* parameter. Here is the XML in the application definition file for the *GetAccountIDs* method and its parameter:

```
<Method Name="GetAccountIDs">
  <Properties>
    <Property Name="RdbCommandText" Type="System.String">
        SELECT [accountid] FROM [CRMVPC_MSCRM].[dbo].[FilteredAccount]
    </Property>
    <Property Name="RdbCommandType" Type="System.Data.CommandType, System.Data,
Version=2.0.0.0, Culture=neutral, PublicKeyToken=b77a5c561934e089">Text</Property>
  </Properties>
  <Parameters>
    <Parameter Direction="Return" Name="GetAccountIDs_Return">
      <TypeDescriptor TypeName="System.Data.IDataReader, System.Data, Version=2.0.0.0,
Culture=neutral, PublicKeyToken=b77a5c561934e089" IsCollection="true"
Name="GetAccountIDs_Return_RootTypeDescriptor">
        <TypeDescriptors>
          <TypeDescriptor TypeName="System.Data.IDataRecord, System.Data,
Version=2.0.0.0, Culture=neutral, PublicKeyToken=b77a5c561934e089"
Name="GetAccountIDs_Return_TypeDescriptor">
            <TypeDescriptors>
              <TypeDescriptor TypeName="System.String" IdentifierName="accountid"
                Name="accountid" DefaultDisplayName="AccountID" />
            </TypeDescriptors>
          </TypeDescriptor>
        </TypeDescriptors>
      </TypeDescriptor>
    </Parameter>
  </Parameters>
</Method>
```

The *MethodInstance* element to be associated with the *GetAccountIDs* method is of type *IdEnumerator,* as shown in Figure 6-18.

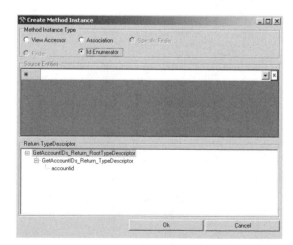

FIGURE 6-18 A *MethodInstance* of type *IdEnumerator*

In the application definition file, the *MethodInstance* element is defined as:

```
<MethodInstances>
  <MethodInstance Type="IdEnumerator" ReturnParameterName="GetAccountIDs_Return"
    ReturnTypeDescriptorLevel="0" Name="GetAccountIDsInstance" />
</MethodInstances>
```

Executing this method returns all of the identifiers for the accounts available in the CRM database.

The same steps can be repeated for other entities that you want to include in the model in order to come up with a more complete application definition file. For the scope of this book, the model we have is good enough. Let's now cover the steps to configure the crawler so that it will index our business data.

Importing the Application Definition File

Application definition files contain the model that is imported into the BDC metadata store. Importing the application definition file is a straightforward process. It is done by administrators who have access to the administration site of the SSP. This site gives access to many of the administration tasks that have to be done for the half dozen shared services that are under the control of an SSP. The BDC is one of these.

You first navigate to the SharePoint 3.0 Central Administration site; from here, you can link to the administration site of the SSP. Note that within the server farm, more than one SSP can be running. On the home page of the SSP administration site, you'll find a set of links related to the BDC, as shown in Figure 6-19.

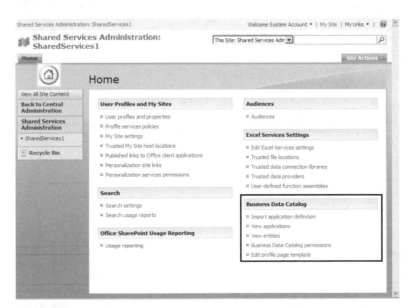

FIGURE 6-19 The administration of the BDC at the level of the SSP

The first link is named Import Application Definition and is self-evident. It redirects you to a page where you can upload one of your application definition files. Note that during the importing, the XML that is contained within the application definition file is validated against the same XML schema that you might have used while creating the XML in Visual Studio to get IntelliSense support. Figure 6-20 displays the page in question.

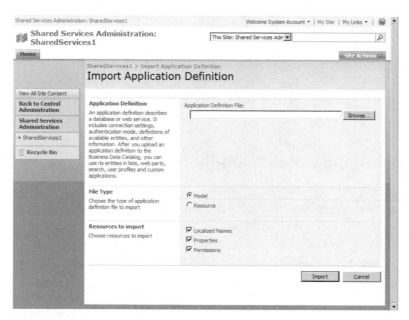

FIGURE 6-20 Administration page for importing an application definition file

Notice that two types of imports are available. The first option, importing the model, is the option you'll use most often. The model is the one we built in the preceding section. It is also possible to import only the resource definitions that are part of an application definition. Resources can be strings you have localized, properties, and access control lists that are associated at various levels within the application definition.

The import procedure takes just a couple of seconds or sometimes a couple of minutes, depending on the size of the application definition. If no errors are reported, you'll see the page shown in Figure 6-21.

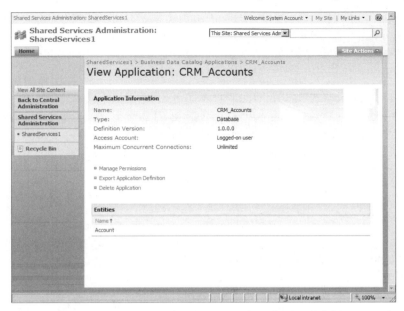

FIGURE 6-21 Configuration page for the imported application definition

Managing the Permissions

Administrators can set permissions at various levels. To start with, you have permissions at the level of the BDC itself. The configuration of the BDC is done by navigating back to the home page of the administration site of the SSP. From there, the Business Data Catalog Permissions link will take you to a page where you can manage the permissions at this global level. Here you can add users and groups and assign the following permissions:

- **Edit**   Update and delete objects and create child objects. Users with this permission on the BDC itself can import application definitions. Applies to all objects.

- **Execute**   Execute a method instance. Users with this permission can view instances of an entity that has finder methods. Applies to method instances, which are descendants of entities.

- **Select In Clients**   Select an entity when configuring Business Data Web Parts, columns, or other clients. Applies to entities.

- **Set Permissions**   Set permissions for all levels in the BDC: the level of the BDC, the applications, and the entities. Applies to all objects.

Changes to the permissions at this level are not automatically applied to the imported application definitions. You have to explicitly copy all permissions to descendants. This is done on the Manage Permissions page, which you can access from a link on the home page of the administration site of the SSP.

The permissions can be configured individually per imported application definition, and they can even be refined at the level of the entity itself. On the home page of the administration site for the SSP, the View Applications link redirects you to a page where you can review each of the application definitions. The Business Data Catalog Applications page is shown in Figure 6-22.

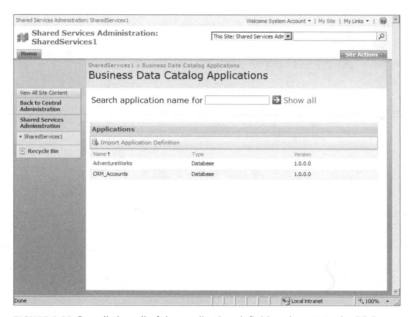

FIGURE 6-22 Page listing all of the application definitions known to the BDC

When you click one of the applications, you'll see a page that lists all of the entities that are part of the model for that application, as shown in Figure 6-23. At the top of that page is the Manage Permissions link, which takes you to a page where you can see the permissions defined at the global level. You can disable the inheritance and adjust the permission levels according to the real-world scenario you are addressing.

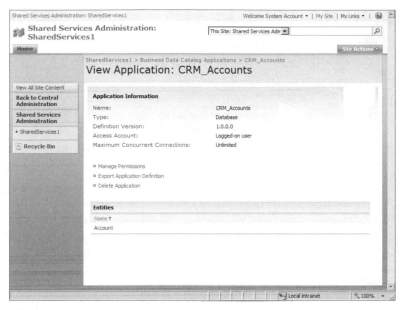

FIGURE 6-23 The list of entities for a BDC application

The same fine-tuning of the permissions can also done at the level of the entity. When you click an entity, as shown in Figure 6-23, you'll see a page displaying the details of that entity. Figure 6-24 shows an example. Here too you'll find a Manage Permissions link that you can click to disable the inheritance of the permissions and adjust accordingly.

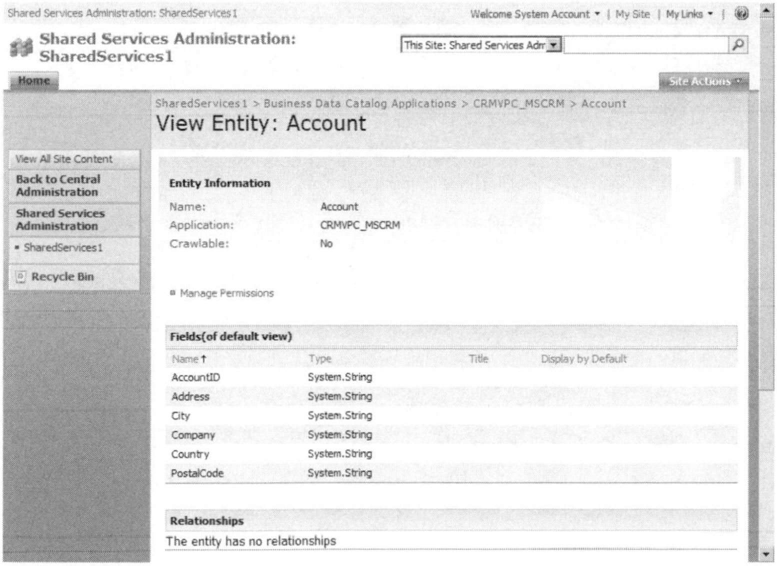

FIGURE 6-24 The details of an entity

Using the Business Data Web Parts

Office SharePoint Server 2007 comes with a number of Business Data Web Parts that power users can use to connect to the BDC. Let's use these to quickly test the work done on the application definition file instead of executing *MethodInstance* elements in the BDC Definition Editor as we did before.

The Business Data Web Parts can be used within any of your SharePoint sites where at the level of the site collection you have the Office SharePoint Server Enterprise Site Collection Features active. You can verify this by navigating to the Site Collection Features page via the Site Settings page. To display this page, on the Site Actions menu, click Site Settings. Figure 6-25 shows the Site Collection Features page with the Feature activated.

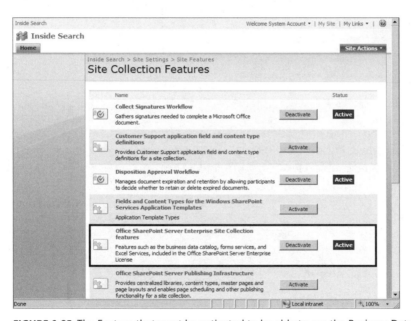

FIGURE 6-25 The Feature that must be activated to be able to use the Business Data Web Parts

The Web Parts can be added to any of your Web Part pages—for example, the home page of a site. Switch the page to edit mode from the Site Actions menu. Figure 6-26 displays the Add Web Parts dialog box, which contains a group named Business Data.

This group makes available the five types of Business Data Web Parts. The uses of each of these Web Parts are summarized in Table 6-1.

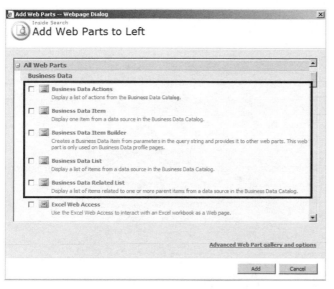

FIGURE 6-26 The Business Data group in the Add Web Parts dialog box

TABLE 6-1 The Five Business Data Web Parts and Their Uses

Web Part	Description
Business Data Actions	This Web Part can show, for a specific entity instance, all of the actions that the user can perform for a specific entity instance. You typically connect the Business Data Actions Web Part with one of the other Business Data Web Parts.
Business Data Item	The details of an individual entity instance—for example, an account—can be delivered via the Business Data Item Web Part.
Business Data Item Builder	You can use this Web Part on the so-called profile pages. These are basically normal SharePoint pages that you navigate to, attaching identifier information in the query string regarding a specific entity instance so that the Business Data Item Builder Web Part can pick it up and display the details of the entity in question.
Business Data List	The Business Data List Web Part is probably the one that will be used most often on SharePoint pages. It can display a list of instances of one of the entities registered in the BDC.
Business Data Related List	This Web Part is useful if you have created associations between entities in the BDC. The Business Data Related List Web Part is not one that can exist on its own. You can add it to a page only where you have already placed another Web Part, such as the Business Data List Web Part.

The Business Data List Web Part is used to connect to the *Account* entity that we modeled earlier. After it is added to the home page of a SharePoint site, it is configured like any other Web Part by using the tool pane, as shown in Figure 6-27.

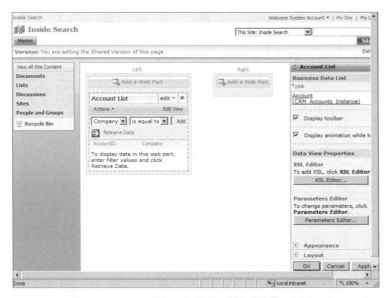

FIGURE 6-27 Configuring the Business Data List Web Part

The Business Data Type Picker lists only the entities that the current user has access to. When the *Account* entity is selected and the changes are applied to the Web Part, all of the information that is stored as part of the model in the metadata store is retrieved by the Web Part. The Business Data List Web Part can execute method instances of type *Finder*. Figure 6-28 shows how the Web Part displays the filter named *Company* defined as part of the metadata. Executing a search for all of the entity instances that contain '*on*' in the name of the company returns results like the ones shown in Figure 6-28.

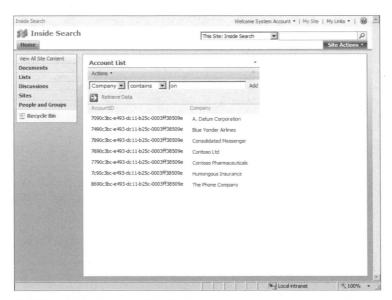

FIGURE 6-28 The Business Data List Web Part, showing some accounts from Dynamics CRM 4.0

On the same page, an instance of the Business Data Item Web Part can be added and can be configured much like the Business Data List Web Part. The Business Data Type Picker can also be used to select the *Account* entity. When the configuration is applied, a connection can be established between the Business Data List Web Part and the Business Data Item Web Part. The latter can show the details of the selected account in the first Web Part. Connectible Web Parts are powerful within the Web Part infrastructure delivered with Microsoft Windows SharePoint Services 3.0, and they are useful here on the page to display a master-detail view of the information retrieved from the Dynamics CRM 4.0 system via the BDC. Figure 6-29 illustrates this nicely.

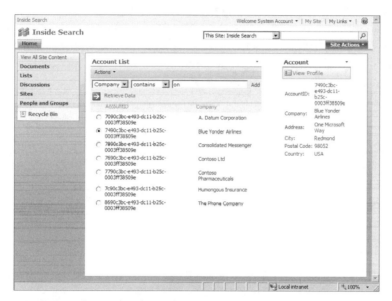

FIGURE 6-29 Connecting the Business Data List Web Part with the Business Data Item Web Part to provide a master-detail view of the CRM data

In short, by using the Business Data Web Parts, we can ensure that information workers are able to retrieve the business data that we have modeled in the metadata store. But there is more to explore. The business data can also be indexed, and searching for business data can become an integrated part within the overall end-user search experience.

Administration and Configuration

There is a good reason for including a chapter on the BDC in this book on indexing and searching. The index engine that is part of Office SharePoint 2007 is capable of crawling the CRM data that we have unlocked with the creation and importing of the application definition file. The model that was declaratively constructed within that XML file contains an entity exposing a method of type *IDEnumerator*. That is basically the core piece within the model that is required when you want to have the business data crawled. A number of administration tasks must be completed to notify the index engine of the new business data, however. We'll briefly review these tasks, and along the way, we'll also review some of the configuration and customization procedures you can use to enhance the end-user search experience for this type of data. Remember that Chapter 2, "The End-User Search Experience," and Chapter 5, "Search Administration," provide a lot more detail on each of these tasks. You might want to go back to these chapters to review and then apply what you have learned.

Creating a Content Source

If you want your business data to be indexed, your first task is to create a new content source. Open the administration site of the SSP that is responsible for the index file that you want to work with, and navigate to the Configure Search Settings page. This page includes a Content Sources And Crawl Schedules link that takes you to the page where the new content source can be created. You provide a name for the new content source on the Add Content Source page and select the Business Data content source type, as shown in Figure 6-30.

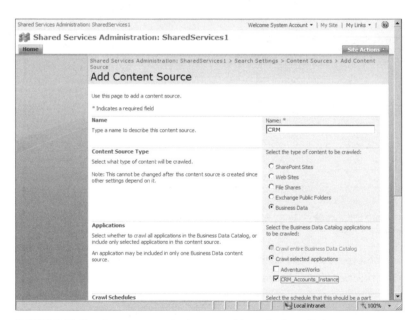

FIGURE 6-30 Creating a new content source of type *Business Data*

The selection of the Business Data content source type refreshes the page, and you'll get to see all of the available BDC applications. In Figure 6-30, two applications are part of the metadata store. The first, AdventureWorks, allows access to the data that is part of the Microsoft SQL Server AdventureWorks sample database, and the second, CRM_Accounts_ Instance, is the application that we looked at in the section "Modeling the Business Data" earlier in this chapter. The last part of the configuration of the new content source is the specification of the crawl schedule that you want to apply. There are two options: Full Crawl and Incremental Crawl. A full crawl must be started for the new content source.

Crawling business data will take a while because of the numerous things that are done behind the scenes. To start, the crawler will contact the BDC with the default content access account. You can override this default account with a more dedicated account by creating a new crawl rule, as discussed in Chapter 5. The account used is quite important because that will be the one that will be used to authenticate with the Microsoft CRM database. Remember from the preceding sections in this chapter that within your application definition file, you are defining how the authentication will be done. For the CRM database, we specified the *PassThrough* authentication mode, which means that the BDC will use the default content access account to access the database.

Once authenticated, the crawler can start doing its work. It will first ask the BDC to execute an instance of a method of type *IDEnumerator*. There is one in the application definition named *GetAccountIDsInstance*. The instance returns all of the primary keys for the accounts back to the crawler. One by one, the crawler will call the BDC again, but now asking for the execution of a method of type *SpecificFinder* and providing it with the primary key of the account in question. The execution of this method instance will result in the return of all of the details of the account. That information will be used to create a profile page, which is the default action at the level of the entity. The content on the profile page is included in the index file by the crawler. That is the information that will become searchable.

As mentioned, a full crawl is needed at the start. And while the indexer is busy crawling, it updates a log, which is a good thing to consult to verify the work of the crawler. You can view the crawl log by navigating to the Manage Content Sources page and, in the Edit Control Block (ECB) for the CRM content source, selecting View Crawl Log. Figure 6-31 displays the crawl log that was created after a full crawl of the CRM content source.

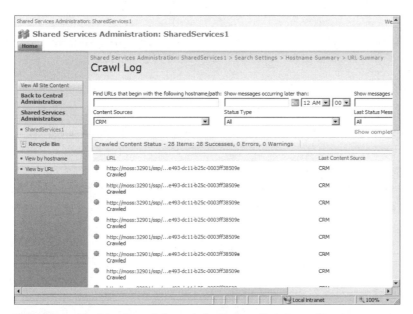

FIGURE 6-31 The log after a full crawl of a *Business Data* type of content source

Searching for Business Data

Crawling the business data is enough to allow the users to start querying for that data. The end-user search experience is not that great here, since not a lot of the metadata is actually displayed in the search results. Figure 6-32 displays the results of a query executed by a user in a Search Center Lite.

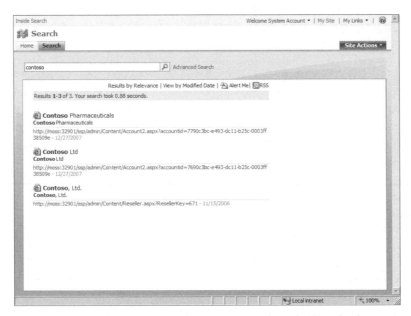

FIGURE 6-32 Search results containing two accounts from the CRM database

Chapter 3 already covered the customization of this end-user search experience in depth. We'll quickly review some of the steps for enhancing the experience in the next few sections.

Creating Managed Properties

The Search Core Results Web Part shown earlier in Figure 6-32 does not display a lot of details regarding the account found in the CRM database. We see only the name of the company and a link to navigate to the profile page, which shows all of the details of the account. This can be enhanced with some customizations at the level of the XSL that is used by the Web Part to render the search results. Before this is possible, however, you'll have to expose the metadata to be displayed in the search results using managed properties.

To start, you should check out the list of crawled properties. Figure 6-33 displays the Metadata Property Mappings page in the administration site of the SSP. This page gives you access to the lists of managed and crawled properties. On the left, in the Quick Launch bar, you'll see two links that let you switch between the lists.

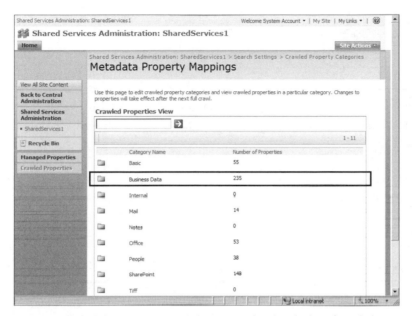

FIGURE 6-33 Metadata Property Mappings page, showing the list of crawled properties

All of the properties that were collected during the crawling of the CRM business application are part of the Business Data category. This category includes all of the fields that are returned by the *GetAccounts* method. These are the fields you'll want to map to managed properties if your intent is to include the fields in the display of the search results. Start by switching to the list of managed properties and then clicking New Managed Property on the toolbar. The property has a name and a possible description. All of the properties that are about to be created for our example here are of type *Text*, and each is mapped to its corresponding crawled property. Note that no spaces or special characters are allowed in the name of a managed property. Figure 6-34 shows an example.

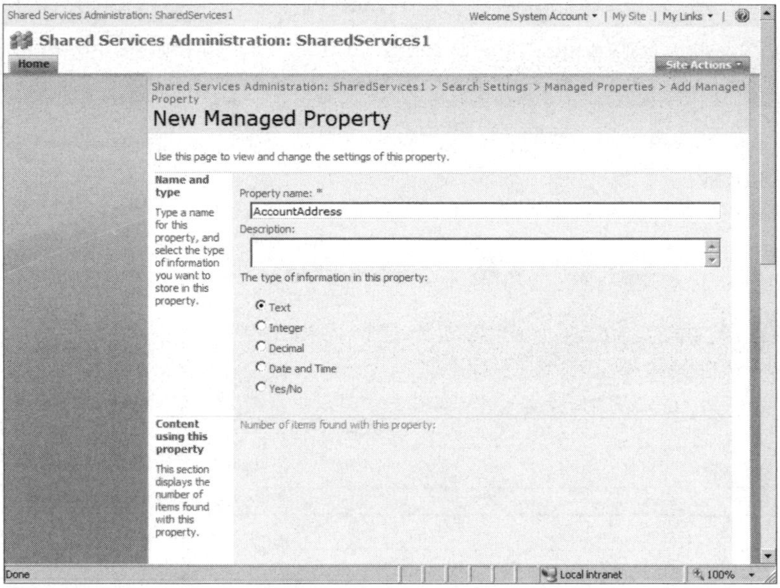

FIGURE 6-34 Creation of a new managed property named *AccountAddress*

The mapping is done by clicking Add Mapping on the page. In the dialog box that appears, you'll find the crawled property again under the Business Data category. Figure 6-35 shows the bottom part of the New Managed Property page, with the mapped property.

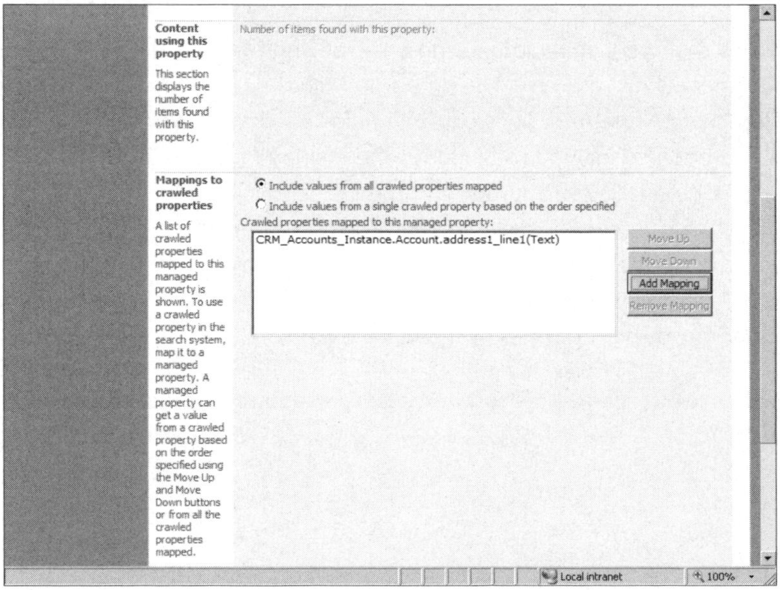

FIGURE 6-35 The mapping of a crawled property

One by one, you can expose the metadata for the CRM data as the following managed properties: *AccountCompany*, *AccountAddress*, *AccountCity*, *AccountPostalCode*, and *AccountCountry*.

There is one more managed property to create. It will be used as a criterion for the creation of a new search scope later and also for some of decisions to make in the XSL for the search results. The managed property is named *BDCEntityName*, and it is mapped to the *__BdcEntityName* crawled property. Don't forget to select the check box at the very bottom of the page to make this property available when creating search scope rules.

An incremental crawl of the BDC-related content sources must be done before you can proceed with the customization of the end-user search experience.

Creating a Search Scope

Going back to Figure 6-32, you'll notice that it shows search results that also contain items from other content sources. Very often, it is a good idea to create a dedicated search scope for a specific category of business data. We can create, for example, a search scope that is an additional option for the user to limit the results to only those that are coming from the CRM database and only those that are associated with the *Account* entity that has been modeled. Chapter 5 discussed in detail the administration tasks involved with search scopes. The focus in that chapter was primarily on the creation of shared search scopes—that is, the search scopes that are created at the level of the SSP. Let's see what we can do at the level of the site collection by creating a local search scope. This search scope will be usable only within that site collection.

A local search scope can be easily created if you are a site collection administrator within a site collection where you have users searching for business data. Using the Site Actions menu within the top-level site, you can open the Site Settings page and then click the Search Scopes link, which redirects you to a page where you can review not only the display groups that are currently active but also the search scopes created at the level of the SSP. Click New Scope on the toolbar to create a local search scope named *CRM Accounts*. As you'll notice on the page displayed in Figure 6-36, there is also an option to immediately include the new scope in one or more of the available display groups. Remember that the display groups actually define what the Scope Pickers display as possible options to the user working in the Search Centers.

Search scopes are driven by rules. After you click OK on the Create Scope page, you'll return to the View Scopes page, where you'll see the newly created scope and a link to start adding the rules. The goal is to filter the search results so that they contain only items that are related to the *Account* entity.

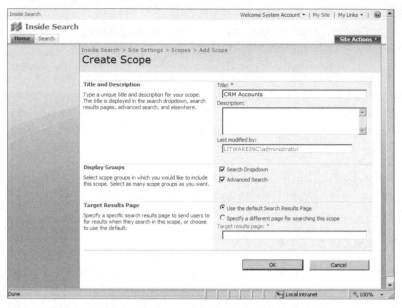

FIGURE 6-36 Creating a local search scope for the CRM business data

The Add Scope Rule page invites you to select a type of scope rule. Notice that when you create a local search scope, you are not able to use the content source as a criterion in the rule. But remember that we covered the creation of a couple of managed properties in the preceding section. The *BDCEntityName* property is the one that's going to be useful here. As shown in Figure 6-37, you can create a scope rule of type *Property Query* and use the expression *BDCEntityName = Account* as the condition for the rule.

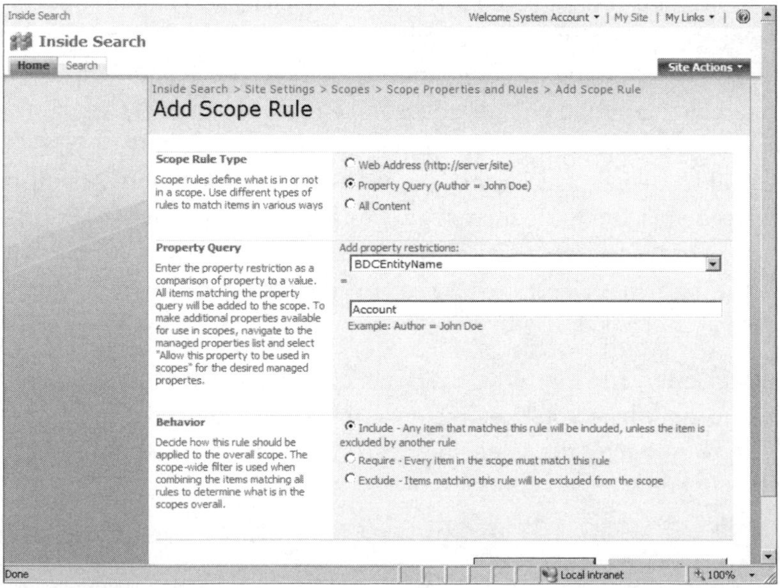

FIGURE 6-37 Adding a scope rule to the local search scope

The new search scope is ready to be used from the moment the index file has been updated. This can take a while. If you don't want to wait, you can always navigate to the Search Settings in the administration site of the SSP and start the update for the search scopes manually. Figure 6-38 shows the View Scopes page at the level of the site collection. Notice that for our example, 26 items in the index file have been flagged as belonging to the local search scope, also an indication that the search scope is ready to be used.

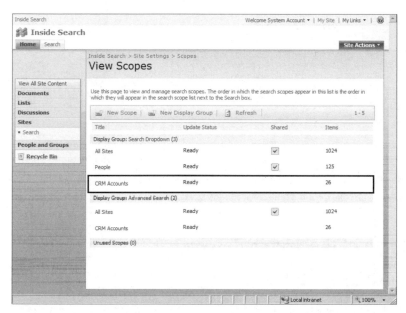

FIGURE 6-38 The local search scope now updated and ready to be used

Search scopes are displayed to users in small controls called Scope Pickers. If you work within a Search Center, you'll have to make the Scope Picker visible on the search page and possible to be seen also on the search results page if needed. By default, the Search Box Web Parts on these pages do not show Scope Pickers. However, a Scope Picker is easy to activate by switching the pages to edit mode. Next, open the tool pane for modifying the properties of the Search Box Web Part on this page. The Dropdown Mode property can be set to Show Scopes Dropdown to make the Scope Picker visible. Figure 6-39 shows a possible outcome of this configuration.

FIGURE 6-39 Search results filtered using the local search scope

Configuration of the Search Results XSL

Figure 6-39 demonstrates again the lack of details shown when the search results represent business data items. This type of display in the real world is often not sufficient for the information workers. As you saw in Chapter 3, the results are displayed by the Search Core Results Web Part after an XSL transformation that occurs on the XML that is returned by the hidden object on the page. That hidden object executes the search query by doing the internal communication with the search engine. Since we have already exposed the crawled metadata as managed properties, we are able to display that extra data by quickly making small modifications to the XSL.

To start, make sure that you have a search results page open in the browser. You switch this page to edit mode, and then you modify the shared properties of the most important Web Part on this page: the Search Core Results Web Part. One customization you must do before you can start with the customization of the XSL is to add the new managed properties in the XML that is set as the value for the Columns property of the Web Part. The Columns property is part of the Results Query Options group. Expand that group and open the XML string in the small dialog box so that you can make the changes. You add one *Column* element for each of the custom managed properties. The following is the full value for the *Columns* element after that change:

```
<root xmlns:xsi="http://www.w3.org/2001/XMLSchema-instance">
   Columns>
      <Column Name="WorkId"/>
      <Column Name="Rank"/>
```

```
        <Column Name="Title"/>
        <Column Name="Author"/>
        <Column Name="Size"/>
        <Column Name="Path"/>
        <Column Name="Description"/>
        <Column Name="Write"/>
        <Column Name="SiteName"/>
        <Column Name="CollapsingStatus"/>
        <Column Name="HitHighlightedSummary"/>
        <Column Name="HitHighlightedProperties"/>
        <Column Name="ContentClass"/>
        <Column Name="IsDocument"/>
        <Column Name="PictureThumbnailURL"/>
        <Column Name="BDCEntityName"/>
        <Column Name="AccountCompany"/>
        <Column Name="AccountAddress"/>
        <Column Name="AccountCity"/>
        <Column Name="AccountPostalCode"/>
        <Column Name="AccountCountry"/>
    </Columns>
</root>
```

Notice that the *BDCEntityName* managed property is also included. This will allow you to branch your rendering logic in the XSL in a moment. The XSL is used not only for rendering results that are part of the CRM business data but also for rendering other types of results. Therefore, branching the XSL may be required to achieve the desired outcome.

There are of course numerous customizations you can make at the level of the rendering of the search results. Remember from Chapter 3 that you can use Microsoft Office SharePoint Designer 2007 or any other tool that can provide you with a visual design experience for working with the XSL. In this chapter, we'll limit ourselves to just making sure that the extra pieces of information are displayed to the user.

Back in the tool pane that displays the properties of the Search Core Results Web Part, click XSL Editor to open a dialog box containing the XSL that is included by default. You might want to copy this XSL into a editor such as Visual Studio to give you a better editing experience.

The change is done at the level of the XSL template with the *match* attribute set to the value *Result*. This is the main block of the rendering logic. The name of the company is already nicely displayed as the title of the search result. Remember that in the application definition file, we included a *Title* property for the *Account* entity. This value is picked up here as the text value for the link to the profile page that is associated with the account. Notice also that the *Identifier* element in the application definition file is used to construct the query string that is part of the URL for that link. If you are missing any of this in your configuration, you'll have to go back to the application definition file and verify that all of that modeling information is actually part of the definition. If you have to make a change to the application definition file, you'll have to reimport the entire file along with a new full crawl of the content source that was created for crawling the data.

The customization of the search results should happen only for information related to the CRM account data. Therefore, the entire customization is dependent on the value of *BDCEntityName*. If that value is equal to *Account*, the values of the custom managed properties need to be displayed. Figure 6-40 shows the results, including both items that have a customized display and one item that does not.

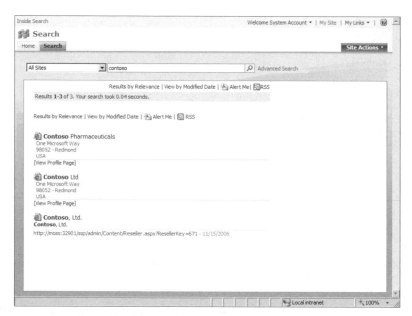

FIGURE 6-40 Customized display of search results for the *Account* entity

The following XSL snippet is responsible for customizing the display of the managed properties:

```
<xsl:choose>
  <xsl:when test="bdcentityname[. = 'Account']">
    <div class="src-Description">
      <span style="padding-left:5px">
        <xsl:value-of select="accountaddress"/>
      </span>
      <br></br>
      <span style="padding-left:5px">
        <xsl:if test="accountpostalcode[. != '']">
          <xsl:value-of select="accountpostalcode"/> -
        </xsl:if>
        <xsl:value-of select="accountcity"/>
      </span>
      <br></br>
      <span style="padding-left:5px">
        <xsl:value-of select="accountcountry"/>
      </span>
    </div>
```

```xml
        <p class="srch-Metadata">
          <a href="{$url}" id="{concat('CSR_U_',$id)}" title="{$url}" dir="ltr">
            [View Profile Page]
          </a>
        </p>
      </xsl:when>
      <xsl:otherwise>
        <div class="srch-Description">
          <xsl:choose>
            <xsl:when test="hithighlightedsummary[. != '']">
              <xsl:call-template name="HitHighlighting">
                <xsl:with-param name="hh" select="hithighlightedsummary" />
              </xsl:call-template>
            </xsl:when>
            <xsl:when test="description[. != '']">
              <xsl:value-of select="description"/>
            </xsl:when>
          </xsl:choose>
        </div >
        <p class="srch-Metadata">
          <span class="srch-URL">
            <a href="{$url}" id="{concat('CSR_U_',$id)}" title="{$url}" dir="ltr">
              <xsl:choose>
                <xsl:when test="hithighlightedproperties/HHUrl[. != '']">
                  <xsl:call-template name="HitHighlighting">
                    <xsl:with-param name="hh" select="hithighlightedproperties/HHUrl" />
                  </xsl:call-template>
                </xsl:when>
                <xsl:otherwise>
                  <xsl:value-of select="url"/>
                </xsl:otherwise>
              </xsl:choose>
            </a>
          </span>
          <xsl:call-template name="DisplaySize">
            <xsl:with-param name="size" select="size" />
          </xsl:call-template>
          <xsl:call-template name="DisplayString">
            <xsl:with-param name="str" select="author" />
          </xsl:call-template>
          <xsl:call-template name="DisplayString">
            <xsl:with-param name="str" select="write" />
          </xsl:call-template>
          <xsl:call-template name="DisplayCollapsingStatusLink">
            <xsl:with-param name="status" select="collapsingstatus"/>
            <xsl:with-param name="urlEncoded" select="urlEncoded"/>
            <xsl:with-param name="id" select="concat('CSR_CS_',$id)"/>
          </xsl:call-template>
        </p>
      </xsl:otherwise>
</xsl:choose>
```

Notice that there is no highlighting of possible keywords from the search query here. You might want to include that also in the XSL if needed. And one more item to remember: the names of the elements in the incoming XML containing the search results are always lowercase.

Working with the Business Data Catalog Runtime Object Model

In this last section, we'll cover some of the techniques for building custom Web Parts that communicate under the hood directly with the runtime object model of the BDC. The runtime object model is not directly related to the index and search engine that is part of Office SharePoint Server 2007, but it is useful in the real world since it shows how to programmatically launch a search query for the data that is made available through the BDC. Figure 6-41 shows the custom BDC Account Info Web Part on the home page of a SharePoint site. You enter a query similar to the one you enter when using the Business Data List Web Part and then click Execute to display the results in the *GridView* control.

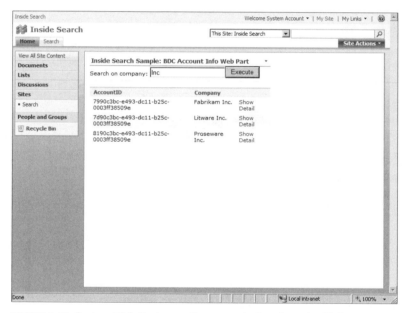

FIGURE 6-41 Custom Web Part executing a search directly to the BDC

The grid displays the results, including a link that allows the user to jump to the profile page containing the details of the account, as shown in Figure 6-42.

More Information The sample project reviewed here is part of the downloadable package containing the samples and files that are used in this book. The name of the project is InsideSearch.BDCWebPart; you might want to open it in Microsoft Visual Studio 2008. The project delivers the Web Part as a Feature. Before you execute the install.bat file that accompanies the project, you must register the Web Part as a *SafeControl* in the web.config file of the Internet Information Services (IIS) Web application hosting the SharePoint site that you are going to work with. Additionally, you have to copy the dynamic-link library (DLL) in the BIN folder of the IIS Web application folder.

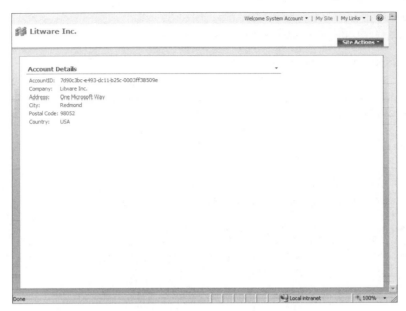

FIGURE 6-42 The profile page for the selected account entity

At the start of this chapter, we looked at the architecture of the BDC and the two object models exposed by the BDC: the administration object model and the runtime object model. The sample project uses both of them. However, the purpose of the custom Web Part is to get to the business data in a direct way and not to perform administration tasks. Consequently, the majority of the classes we'll communicate with are part of the latter object model. The runtime object model also makes sure that we leverage all of the caching infrastructure that is part of the BDC infrastructure.

The assembly that contains the two object models is *Microsoft.SharePoint.Portal.dll*. Every Microsoft .NET Framework project that will do work with the BDC will have to include a reference to this assembly. In most projects, you'll add other references to SharePoint-related assemblies like *Microsoft.SharePoint.dll*. This is the case in the sample project because the *SPGridView* control is used to display the results of the simple query to the users.

If you open the AccountInfoWebPart.cs file in the editor, you'll notice the different namespaces that are listed at the top. Two are related to the work that will be done with the BDC:

```
using Microsoft.Office.Server.ApplicationRegistry.MetadataModel;
using Microsoft.Office.Server.ApplicationRegistry.Runtime;
```

The first namespace groups all of the classes that are part of the administration object model. A couple of these classes are used in the code to retrieve the required information regarding the model that is available in the BDC metadata store. The second *using* statement is for the namespace in which all of the classes are defined that are part of the runtime object model.

That's the one that is used to get to the business data. The other namespaces you'll find in the file are needed for the proper working of the Web Part.

The Web Part class contains the required code to render the various user interface controls as the body of the Web Part. That is not of great importance for us here. The procedure that might require more explanation is the *SearchAccount* procedure, which is called when the user clicks the Execute button:

```
private void SearchAccount()
{
    NamedLobSystemInstanceDictionary instances =
        ApplicationRegistry.GetLobSystemInstances();
    LobSystemInstance instance = instances["CRM_Accounts_Instance"];
    Entity entity = instance.GetEntities()["Account"];
    Method method = entity.GetMethods()["GetAccounts"];
    MethodInstance methodinstance = method.GetMethodInstances()["GetAccountsInstance"];
    FilterCollection filters = methodinstance.GetFilters();
    WildcardFilter filter = (WildcardFilter)filters[0];
    filter.Value = string.Format("%{0}%", this.textBoxQuery.Text);
    IEntityInstanceEnumerator entities =
        (IEntityInstanceEnumerator)entity.FindFiltered(filters, instance);
    DataTable tbl = null;
    while (entities.MoveNext())
    {
        if (tbl == null)
            tbl = entities.Current.EntityAsDataTable;
        else
            entities.Current.EntityAsDataRow(tbl);
    }
    this.gridViewResults.DataSource = tbl;
    this.gridViewResults.DataBind();
}
```

The start of the procedure is a call to the *GetLobSystemInstances* method, which is exposed as a static method of the *ApplicationRegistry* class. It returns a collection of all of the *LobSystemInstance* objects that are stored in the BDC metadata store. One is named *CRM_Accounts_Instance*, and this is the object that gives us access to the CRM data.

The list of entities is retrieved by calling the *GetEntities* method at the level of the *LobSystemInstance* object. Out of that list, one object named *Account* is isolated, and a reference is stored in a variable of type *Entity*. In our model, not a lot of methods are defined for the entity. But it is of course possible that there are dozens of methods and that each of them can have its own dedicated filters that are part of the model. By first getting a reference to the *MethodInstance* object representing the *GetAccountsInstance* method, you are able to get to the collection of *Filter* objects. One filter is available in the model. It is a filter of type *wildcard*, and in the object model, you have a type that can be used to cast the generic *Filter* object into the more specific *WildcardFilter* type. The value of this filter is set to whatever the user has entered in the text box. The value is enclosed within the wildcard characters.

The execution of the method is done by calling a method named *FindFiltered* at the level of the *Entity* object. It is also possible to execute the *MethodInstance* itself, but because there is only one *Finder* type of method defined in the model for our entity, we can use the *FindFiltered* method. The result of the execution is an enumerator of type *IEntityInstanceEnumerator*.

The final part of the procedure is the processing of the results. An ADO.NET *DataTable* is constructed out of the stream of entity instances and is bound to the *SPGridView* instance that is part of the control tree of the Web Part. The result is what you can see in Figure 6-41.

There is one last interesting block of code that must be explained. It is the code that is executed when the user requests to see the details of one of the search results. The code is part of an event handler for the *SelectedIndexChanged* event of *SPGridView*:

```
void gridViewResults_SelectedIndexChanged(object sender, EventArgs e)
{
    GridViewRow row = this.gridViewResults.SelectedRow;
    NamedLobSystemInstanceDictionary instances =
        ApplicationRegistry.GetLobSystemInstances();
    LobSystemInstance instance = instances["CRM_Accounts_Instance"];
    Entity entity = instance.GetEntities()["Account"];
    IEntityInstance entityinstance = entity.FindSpecific(row.Cells[0].Text,instance);
    if (entityinstance != null)
    {
        string accountid = entityinstance.GetFormatted("accountid").ToString();
        Action action = entity.GetDefaultAction();
        SPUtility.Redirect(string.Format(action.Url, accountid),
            SPRedirectFlags.Static, HttpContext.Current);
    }
}
```

The first part of the code is basically the same as in the *SearchAccounts* procedure described earlier. The goal, however, is to find one specific entity. That is why you'll notice in the code the call to the *FindSpecific* method exposed by the *Entity* class. The value of the *accountid* field is retrieved by a call to the *GetFormatted* method that is exposed by the object of type *IEntityInstance*—the one that is returned by the *FindSpecific* method.

A profile page is created for every entity that you import from your application definition file. The link to the profile page containing the details of the entity is the default action of an entity. Assuming that you have not changed this behavior, you can use the *GetDefaultAction* method at the level of the *Entity* class to get a reference to an *Action* object. The *Action* object exposes several properties. After the insertion of the *accountid* into the value of the *Url* property, a redirect is executed so that the user sees the proper profile page rendered in his or her browser.

Many other operations can be performed within SharePoint solutions components like the custom Web Part in the sample project. But you should now have a good idea of the options and how to proceed further.

Summary

Every organization that searches for ways of bridging the gap between the world of the information workers and the structured world of the LOB systems should consider the BDC as a possible solution. In this chapter, we have not reviewed all of the options that are possible with the BDC. The main focus was on indexing and searching and how those topics are related to the business data that is made available through the BDC. Unlocking business data for the information workers in SharePoint sites means that you have to model the data first, and you've learned that creating application definition files is the way to do this. Don't forget that designers are available that can help you in this task. The models of your business data have to be imported and converted to records that are stored in the metadata store of the BDC. Once the metadata is in place, the fun starts, and you'll provide your users with the option to work with some of the out-of-the-box Web Parts such as the Business Data Web Parts. The data can be crawled if the required artifacts are present in the model. After a crawl of that data, it is again a question of configuration and customization to make the end-user search experience match the required needs of the business within your organization.

Chapter 7
Search Deployment Considerations

After completing this chapter, you will be able to

- Determine factors affecting performance, scalability, availability, and security when deploying an Enterprise Search solution with Microsoft Office SharePoint Server 2007.

- Understand server farm topology.

- See the advantages of dedicating a Web front-end server to the crawler.

- Provide free Enterprise Search capabilities to Microsoft Windows SharePoint Services 3.0 using Microsoft Search Server 2008 Express.

- Choose the appropriate server hardware.

- Calculate the required amount of server disk space.

- Optimize the performance of index servers, query servers, and search database servers.

The Enterprise Search engine included in Microsoft Office SharePoint Server 2007 is a very scalable piece of technology. It scales from the smallest business with few users and a limited amount of content to large enterprises with thousands of users and huge amounts of content. The simplest possible deployment model is the *single-server model*, where all components, including the database, are installed on a single physical server. But as business requirements for performance, scalability, availability, and security grow, it quickly becomes necessary to move, or scale out, different components of SharePoint to different physical servers. The scale-out architecture of the search engine is powerful and is key to the success of the search engine in the Enterprise Search space.

But scaling out also comes at the cost of increased installation and setup time and increased hardware costs, software license costs, and maintenance costs. It also increases complexity, requiring more skills and training of system planners and administrators. Consequently, it is important to carefully review and understand the requirements of the business to select the optimal deployment topology. Inadequate deployments can lead to frustrating query response times for users and slow indexing of new or changed content. On the other hand, oversized deployments will simply generate unnecessary costs.

The primary focus of this chapter is to help you choose the deployment topology that is just right for your business. The first section introduces the key factors you should consider when making this decision. The second section outlines a range of common deployment topologies and the situations for which they are appropriate. Next is a review of software boundaries and the recommended hardware infrastructure (vendor independent). Following that, you'll find a section on calculating the required disk space for search servers and database servers and a section on performance optimization. The chapter concludes with an example of a server farm deployment and how it performs with respect to search. This chapter provides only limited guidance on configuring the search engine. Please consult Chapter 5, "Search Administration," for more detailed information.

Key Factors to Consider When Deploying Search

Planning a deployment strategy is important, especially for larger enterprises with significant requirements for the search components as well as the other components of SharePoint. Many factors should be taken into consideration when planning an optimal, successful deployment of your SharePoint environments. These factors can generally be divided into the following four categories:

- **Performance**   Factors in this category are related to planning for an appropriate level of responsiveness, or throughput, for each component in a SharePoint farm. This includes software components as well as hardware components. Performance considerations are analyzing a baseline to determine historical run rates and business requirements and, most important, sticking to budget.

- **Availability**   Server hardware and software configurations can fail, with the risk of rendering a SharePoint farm completely or partly inaccessible to users. Availability is about reducing this risk by installing redundant hardware and redundant software services. But again, availability considerations often also require a tradeoff between requirements and costs.

- **Scalability**   Scalability factors are related to the capability of a SharePoint farm to increase total throughput under an increased load by adding more hardware and software resources.

- **Security**   Protecting confidential content from unauthorized access and protecting servers from hostile attacks are paramount factors in any SharePoint production environment.

The following subsections will examine each category in more detail and highlight the key factors to consider with respect to deploying search in a production environment.

Performance Factors

Achieving an acceptable or an excellent level of search performance basically requires a focus on minimizing query response time and increasing the speed of the indexer, also known as the crawler. The performance-related factors include the following:

- **Query response time**   End users will naturally expect a fast response time for search results when searching content. Therefore, it is important to understand the factors that lead to an increase in the amount of time it takes the search engine to search the content index and display the results to the user. The primary factors that increase response time are listed here:

  - Insufficient hardware configuration of the servers where the query server component is installed. The division of server roles is described in the section "Search Components and Their Roles" later in this chapter.

  - On average, an excessive number of concurrent queries compared with the number of requests the server farm can handle per second.

  - Long and CPU-intensive processes running on the query server. The most obvious case occurs when the index server is installed on the same physical server as the query server. However, these could also be other processes such as third-party applications.

- **Indexing speed**   This factor concerns the time it takes the indexer to include new and changed content in the index—that is, the time lag from when a user adds or modifies content until that content is reflected in the search results. Large amounts of dynamic content together with requirements for minimal time lag call for special attention to this factor. Methods for optimizing the performance of the indexer are described in the section "Optimizing Index Server Performance" later in this chapter.

- **Database performance**   Most SharePoint components rely heavily on Microsoft SQL Server databases, and the search components are no exception. Methods for optimizing the performance of the search database are also examined in the section "Optimizing Database Server Performance" later in this chapter.

- **Software boundaries**   Microsoft has tested and published the software-related performance and capacity limits of Office SharePoint Server 2007. Exceeding these limits might result in reduced performance. The software boundaries specifically related to searching are listed in the section "Software Boundaries" later in this chapter.

- **Hardware configuration**   Depending on factors such as the number of concurrent users, the volume of content to be indexed, and the nature of installed services and applications, SharePoint can place significant requirements on the server hardware configuration. This topic is also examined in more detail in the section "Hardware Recommendations" later in this chapter.

- **Network latency and bandwidth**   The different components and services required in a full deployment of SharePoint can be scaled out to multiple physical servers connected by a network. A dedicated database server is the first and most important step to consider for improved scalability and performance. But database transactions from all SharePoint components will in turn need to travel across the network.

 Note Network latency is the time in milliseconds it physically takes to send data packets across a network to a receiver and get back a response.

It is important to consider appropriate measures toward minimizing the latency and maximizing the bandwidth of the network connecting the servers. The worst possible outcome is a network saturated with traffic. This would be a very serious performance bottleneck, and adding more server hardware will just make it worse. Recommendations for avoiding this situation are also outlined in the section "Hardware Recommendations."

Developing and deploying an effective solution on the SharePoint platform should include careful planning for optimal performance. The time spent here is an excellent investment in the long term. It will help minimize user frustration and support calls. It will also help minimize the risk of fostering a highly stressed situation in which unexpected performance problems need to be fixed after Enterprise Search goes live.

 More Information For more information about estimating performance and capacity requirements for SharePoint search deployments, visit *http://technet2.microsoft.com/Office/ en-us/library/5465aa2b-aec3-4b87-bce0-8601ff20615e1033.mspx*. Alternatively, search for the words *plan sharepoint performance* using one of the major Internet search engines.

Availability Factors

The concept of *availability* for any software system refers to the ability of the system to respond predictably to requests. The time when the system does not respond predictably is known as *downtime*. A common measure of availability is the *number of nines*, as outlined in Table 7-1.

TABLE 7-1 Correlation Between Downtime Percentages and Calendar Time

Acceptable Uptime Percentage	Downtime per Day	Downtime per Month	Downtime per Year
95	72.00 minutes	36 hours	18.26 days
99	14.40 minutes	7 hours	3.65 days
99.9	86.40 seconds	43 minutes	8.77 hours
99.99	8.64 seconds	4 minutes	52.60 minutes
99.999	0.86 seconds	26 seconds	5.26 minutes

A system with a guaranteed uptime of 99.999 percent is also referred to as a system with "five nines of availability." Each nine of availability requires additional and possibly very expensive measures to guarantee. The minimum level of acceptable availability should always be carefully weighed against increased implementation time, increased complexity, and increased hardware, software, and maintenance costs.

Factors for improving the availability of the search components in a SharePoint server farm include:

- **Enterprise hardware** Stick with enterprise hardware vendors with a proven track record for delivering high-quality equipment and support. It is also critical to buy only servers with Enterprise focus.

- **Redundant hardware** Critical servers representing a single point of failure will need to be equipped with redundant hardware such as redundant array of independent disks (RAID), dual network connections, and redundant power supplies. For databases, a mirrored or clustered failover server is also an option to consider.

- **Uninterruptible power supply (UPS)** Consider installing UPS hardware backup to protect against a power failure. This will prevent servers from crashing in the event of short power failures and will ensure graceful shutdowns during longer power outages. Most computer hardware does not tolerate even a single missing period on the power grid—that is, 1/60 Hz or 1/50 Hz, depending on your country. Installing a UPS will smooth out such glitches from the power grid. Mission-critical systems might additionally need a diesel engine connected to a power generator to provide cover for lengthy power outages.

- **Clustered database server** The SQL Server hosting the SharePoint databases represents a single point of failure. The best way to improve the availability of this component is to cluster or mirror it.

- **Redundant query servers** The search query component of Office SharePoint Server 2007 is redundant, and increased availability is achieved simply by installing two or more servers running the query service. Redundant hardware considerations for the query servers are thus less important here. The consequence of downtime is manifested in an error in the Search Centers when users attempt to search the content.

- **Index servers with redundant hardware**   Unlike the search query component, the search index component of Office SharePoint Server 2007 is not redundant. Increased availability is achieved only through redundant hardware. Indexer downtime does not cut off users from searching content, however, as long as the search query component is running. The only consequence of downtime for the indexer might be an outdated index, meaning that users might not be able to find recent documents.

Redundant Array of Independent Disks (RAID)

RAID is a technology that allows multiple hard disks to be combined into a single logical unit using special hardware. The hardware presents itself as a single hard disk to the Windows operating system, and applications like SharePoint will be unaware of its presence. Disks can be combined in different configurations for improved performance and scalability through aggregation or for improved availability through redundancy. Different RAID configurations are denoted by a RAID level, and the most commonly used levels are RAID 0 through RAID 6. A RAID 0 level configuration is designed for improved performance and scalability but not for improved availability—that is, fault tolerance. A RAID 0 array requires at least two disks and provides improved performance by parallel read/write of data across all disks in the array. It is also scalable, as demand for additional storage is simply a question of adding more disks. The availability of a RAID 0 array is, however, quite poor. A single disk failure destroys the array, which becomes more likely with more disks in the array.

If high availability is important, a RAID 1 level configuration should be considered, as it is designed to mirror all data to separate disks. The array requires at least two disks and will continue to work as long as at least one drive is functioning. As a bonus, a RAID 1 array also offers increased read performance, as the same data can be read from all disks in parallel. The downsides are reduced write performance and reduced capacity. Another strategy for achieving a high level of availability and improved read performance is to install disks in a RAID 5 array. This does not mirror all data as a RAID 1 array does. Instead, it uses the space of one disk to store the parity of data on the other disks in the array. This enables the array to mathematically reconstruct data in the event of a disk failure. It can tolerate only a single disk failure at one time, however. The array is destroyed if two or more disks fail at the same time. The advantage of a RAID 5 array over a RAID 1 array is increased capacity with the same number of identical disks. They share the downside of reduced write performance.

Different RAID levels can also be mixed to get the best of both worlds. For example, RAID 10 (RAID 1+0) conceptually consists of multiple level 1 arrays with a level 0 array on top. It requires an even number of disks, with four as a minimum, and provides fault tolerance and improved performance. The downside is increased complexity. RAID is a large subject in itself, and it is beyond the scope of this book to examine the other possible levels not referenced in this chapter.

To review, the guaranteed level of availability is basically a combination of installing an appropriate level of redundant hardware and selecting an appropriate farm topology. Different topologies with different levels of availability are discussed in the section "Common Topology Models" later in this chapter.

More Information For more information about SharePoint availability, visit *http://technet2. microsoft.com/Office/en-us/library/9ccfb27f-ecba-4b7d-b9a0-88fac71478a31033.mspx*. Alternatively, search for the words *plan sharepoint availability* using one of the popular Internet search engines.

It is important to consider availability during the early planning phases of a SharePoint production environment. Together with performance, availability is key to identifying the appropriate hardware configuration and server topology of the farm.

Database Mirroring and Clustering

High availability of databases can be implemented by arranging the database servers in a mirror or in a cluster. A *database mirror* is a standby server that supports rapid failover with no loss of data. Two Microsoft SQL Servers configured in a mirror present themselves as a single logical database server on the network. Data change transactions committed to the logical database are always written to both physical database servers. A *database cluster* also provides a failover database server. It differs from a database mirror in the sense that data is not copied to the failover server. Data is instead stored on a shared high-availability disk resource on the network. Each database server in a cluster is referred to as a *node*. Each node can be configured to fail over to any other node in the cluster during a hardware failure, an operating system failure, or a planned upgrade.

Scalability Factors

In software engineering, *scalability* refers to the ability of a given system to handle growing amounts of work. Typically, this refers to the capability of increasing the total throughput of the system under an increased load by adding extra hardware. With respect to SharePoint search, scalability refers to the following:

- **Future growth** The ability to scale the indexer to handle a growing volume of content and the ability to scale the query servers to handle larger peaks of concurrent queries.

- **Software boundaries** Although the search engine of Office SharePoint Server 2007 is highly scalable, it does not scale indefinitely. Through testing, Microsoft has identified a number of software boundaries that should not be exceeded in any farm. Exceeding these limits will gradually result in reduced performance, even if extra hardware is added. The detailed software boundaries are listed in the section "Software Boundaries" later in this chapter.

The primary methods for scaling the search components are listed here:

- **Install additional query servers.**   Query servers are redundant, and scaling them is simply a question of adding one or more additional servers.

- **Install a dedicated index server.**   Document crawling and indexing is a resource-intensive process, and dedicating a physical server to the indexer is highly recommended. You will in fact be forced to do this if you settle on a farm topology with more than one query server. The reason for this is revealed in the section "Search Topologies" later in this chapter.

- **Configure a dedicated Web front-end server for crawling.**   The crawler normally scans all the Web front-end servers when indexing SharePoint sites. This implies that it shares the Web front-end servers with all users and that it needs to request content across the network. Installing a Web front-end server on the index server itself and dedicating it to the crawler can boost the speed of content crawling.

- **Add more processors and memory.**   When possible, adding more processors and memory to query servers and index servers helps them scale to a bigger workload. This approach is especially important when scaling index servers, because unlike query servers, these are not redundant. Query servers typically have one or two processors, while it is more common for index servers to have four processors.

- **Install faster disks.**   Preferably use disks with at least 7200 rpm and 8 ms seek time or less. This is also an important factor for scaling the throughput of index servers as well as query servers.

- **Use disk arrays.**   In addition to increasing performance and availability, employing RAID in certain configurations also delivers improved scalability. The total disk space of disks arranged in a RAID 10 configuration is simply scaled up by adding more disks in pairs of two.

The scalability of an example deployment is discussed in the section "Measuring the Performance of an Example Deployment" later in this chapter.

Security Factors

Every organization employing a SharePoint solution must also pay careful attention to ensure a solid security apparatus to prevent unauthorized access, data theft, and data loss. Fortunately, Office SharePoint Server 2007 provides a high level of security, and it has a good array of security features that organizations can use to build a highly secure solution. It is important for SharePoint administrators to be familiar with these security features as well as with the standard security features of the Windows operating system and the Active Directory directory service. Knowledge about firewalls and other factors for improving external security is also a must.

> **More Information**   For more information about securing Office SharePoint Server 2007, visit *http://technet2.microsoft.com/Office/en-us/library/3df68222-235b-45de-82fa-b89166c5c6bd1033.mspx*. Alternatively, search for the words *plan sharepoint security* using one of the popular Internet search engines.

The primary security factors related to deploying an Enterprise Search solution with SharePoint are as follows:

- **Search service account**   The query component and the indexer component of the search engine execute inside the process of the Search service, which must be started on all query servers and index servers. The important issue to discuss at this point is the Windows domain account, which administrators must provide when installing SharePoint on servers in the farm. Avoid specifying an administrator account for the service process. Instead, it is highly recommended to provide a least-privileged account—for example, a normal user account named *DOMAIN*\spsearch. SharePoint will automatically grant the account all required permissions on the local server. Consult the section "Configuring and Starting the Search Service" in Chapter 5 for more detailed information about configuring and starting the Search service.

- **Crawler account**   The crawler of the indexer component will naturally need permission to access and download all content, and it is highly recommended to specify a least-privileged account here as well—for example, *DOMAIN*\spcrawler. Make sure that the password does not expire on this account, and avoid specifying an administrator-level account. This will be a security weakness, but it will also make the crawler index unpublished documents in document libraries where versioning is enabled. A default content access account must be specified for each Shared Services Provider (SSP) instance. Differentiated access accounts inside each SSP can be realized through crawl rules.

- **Security trimming of search results**   A paramount feature of Enterprise Search engines is the ability to trim search results with respect to the credentials of each user. In other words, the search engine should hide all results for content the user is not authorized to view. Security trimming is an inherent feature of SharePoint search and does not require any special configuration. It simply respects the permission settings on all content indexed from SharePoint sites. Equally, it also respects all permission settings on content indexed from Windows file shares and Microsoft Exchange Server public folders. But security trimming of content indexed from other sources is not inherent. For example, content indexed via the Business Data Catalog (BDC) is by default not subject to security trimming. Security trimming can, however, be implemented by developing and installing a custom security trimmer. See Chapter 9, "Advanced Search Engine Topics," for complete coverage of this topic.

Note The lack of proper security trimming is often the decisive reason popular Internet search engines fail in the enterprise.

■ **Data isolation**   The data security requirements for a business sometimes specify total and unquestionable isolation of data between different groups of users. This is often the case in hosted environments where the same server hardware might serve different customers. For searching, this implies that there must be a guarantee that one customer cannot accidentally or viciously retrieve search results of content from other customers. Managing appropriate permissions on access accounts is of course a priority, but not enough for a total separation of data. Building a waterproof solution should be implemented by providing a separate content index for each customer—that is, a separate SSP instance. See the section "Search Is a Shared Service" in Chapter 5 for more information about SSPs. Deploying a separate content index for isolated groups of users is also highly recommended to avoid excessive security trimming of search results.

It is additionally very common in production environments to block all outbound traffic initiated by servers and to restrict inbound traffic by IP address to application servers and database servers. Client computers need to be able to access only the Web front-end servers. Even they can be restricted to accept traffic only from a network load balancer (NLB), which in turn becomes the only gateway to the farm from the outside. A detailed discussion of this type of security consideration is clearly beyond the scope of this book, but we encourage you to seek more detailed information about this topic.

Search Topologies

A *topology* in the context of SharePoint search refers to a specific way of arranging and connecting the various search-related software components across physical servers in a farm. This section provides an overview of the different types of search topologies you can deploy with Office SharePoint Server 2007. We will also review a topology in which Microsoft Search Server 2008 Express is used to provide cross-site search capabilities to a Windows SharePoint Services 3.0 farm.

More Information Parts of the topology-related information in this section are of a general nature and are not specific to searching. It is beyond the scope of this book to provide full coverage of planning a full farm topology. Please consult other books such as the *Microsoft Office SharePoint Server 2007 Administrator's Companion*, by Bill English (Microsoft Press, 2007), for full coverage on that topic.

The product architecture supports topologies that are scalable, flexible, maintainable, reliable, and secure. Designing a topology for small businesses with few requirements is fairly straightforward, as two servers will usually do the job. But designing an optimal topology for businesses with more requirements is more complex. It calls for careful considerations and decisions regarding the required capacity, performance, availability, scalability, and security measures outlined in the section "Key Factors to Consider When Deploying Search" earlier in this chapter.

The search engine in Office SharePoint Server 2007 is composed of three logical building blocks—that is, software components from which it is possible to deploy search topologies of different scale. Each component is encapsulated in its own software service representing a specific role in the topology. Deploying a specific topology is basically a question of planning for the number of physical servers in the farm and their role assignments. Assigning roles is actually not a matter of installing different software on each server. Every server has the same SharePoint files, and role assignment is achieved simply by starting the appropriate services on each server. SharePoint administrators can do that from the Services On Server page in the Central Administration site.

Figure 7-1 shows the Services On Server page, listing all the available services on the server named MOSS. All services are started in this example. The index server role and the query server role are selected when starting the service named Office SharePoint Server Search. See the section "Configuring and Starting the Search Service" in Chapter 5 for detailed information about starting this service.

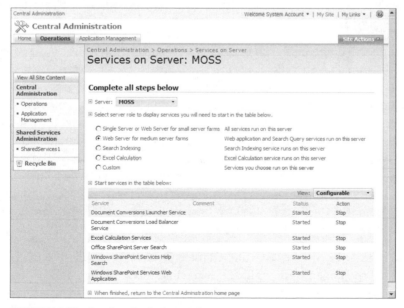

FIGURE 7-1 The Services On Server page

Before diving into specific topologies, let's first review the responsibilities of each search component.

Search Components and Their Roles

The software components of the search engine specifically encompass an index server, a query server, and a Web front-end server. Each component additionally requires a connection to a SQL database server in the farm. The role of the database is quite important to search and is therefore described in this section as well.

Role of the Index Server

The index server is responsible for crawling content and building one content index per SSP. One index server can serve multiple SSPs—that is, it can crawl all the content sources defined for each associated SSP and update its content index. But on the other hand, an SSP cannot be served by more than one index server at a time, indicating that the role of the index server is not redundant.

Deploying multiple index servers is a perfectly sound way to improve capacity. Just be aware that you also need at least the same number of SSPs in the farm to use them. It is equally important to realize that it is not possible for users to search across multiple SSPs. Consequently, a topology with multiple index servers is applicable only for farms having at least the same number of isolated content Web applications as index servers. Recall that a Web application is associated with an SSP, which is in turn associated with a specific index server.

The crawler component of the index server is capable of crawling content from a wide range of content sources, including SharePoint sites, external Web sites, file shares, Microsoft Exchange Server public folders, BDC applications, and Lotus Notes databases. The index server has a "pluggable" architecture, allowing you to install third-party protocol handlers to crawl types of content sources other than those supported out-of-the-box. Technically, the crawler launches multiple processes and threads to operate with many simultaneous network requests to the content sources. This approach maximizes CPU utilization on the index server, but it can also place a significant load on the content sources being crawled. Fortunately, it is possible to control the crawler using crawler impact rules. See the sections "Managing Content Sources" and "Crawler Impact Rules" in Chapter 5 for more information about content sources and crawler impact rules, respectively.

Next, the text in crawled documents is extracted using an *IFilter* and added to the content index. An *IFilter* is a component responsible for extracting text from one or more specific file formats. The pluggable architecture of the index server also allows you to install third-party *IFilters* such as the Adobe PDF *IFilter*. Third-party or custom protocol handlers and *IFilters* will need to be installed only on servers with the index server role. See the sections "Protocol Handlers" and "*IFilters*" in Chapter 9 for full coverage of protocol handlers and *IFilters*.

The discovery and indexing of document metadata is also handled by the index server. And last, the index server is responsible for copying the content index to all query servers in the farm. It does so through a concept known as *continuous propagation*, meaning that it will continuously update the index on the query servers as the crawl progresses. Metadata is not propagated to the query servers, however, but is instead stored in the database of the SSP.

Role of the Web Front-End Server

The primary responsibility of Web front-end servers in a farm is to display content to users. But they also play an important role with respect to searching, as the crawler visits these servers when downloading content from SharePoint sites. *External content*—that is, content stored outside the farm—is accessed directly by the index server, without the help of a Web front-end server.

> **Note** A Web front-end server is any server in your farm where the Windows SharePoint Services Web Application service is running.

The index server will by default use all front-end Web servers to crawl content from SharePoint sites in the farm. But it is also possible to configure a dedicated Web front-end server for crawling and exclude it from the network load balanced rotation of incoming user requests to Web front-end servers in the farm. A major benefit of this approach is that it relieves the normal Web front-end servers of the load from the crawler, which can be considerable. For best performance, it is recommended to configure the index server itself as the dedicated Web front-end server. This will eliminate the need for the index server to send requests across the network. The Web front-end server will, however, still need to request its content across the network from the database server.

Role of the Query Server

The query server is responsible for executing user search queries against the content index of an SSP and returning matching results sorted by relevancy or date. Standard free-text queries are executed against the local copy of the index on the query server. Metadata queries are routed to the database server hosting the SSP search database. Regardless of the query, search results are always constructed from the document metadata stored in the SSP database. This includes all metadata such as title, author, URL, file size, and last modified date as well as any custom metadata.

Unlike the index server role, the query server role is redundant. Multiple query servers can be employed to serve queries against the same content index. Scaling to an increasing number of queries is accomplished simply by adding query servers. The recommended topology for query servers is to deploy them across the same physical servers hosting the Web front-end role. But it is also possible to deploy dedicated query servers, which can sometimes be an advantage or a requirement in large environments.

> **Note** If the query role is installed on the same server computer as the index role, content indexes are no longer propagated to external query servers. Therefore, you need separate servers for the index role and the query role if you plan to deploy more than one query server. You can alternatively opt to install the index role on the database server in smaller deployments.

A last note also worth mentioning is that the content of queries served by a query server is cached for subsequent requests to improve performance of repeated queries.

Role of the Database Server

Almost all data in SharePoint is stored in a number of SQL database instances. The only exception is the content index of each SSP, which is stored in the file system on index servers and query servers. But the search metadata store of each SSP is also held in an SQL database. Each SSP is associated with two SQL database instances, holding the following data for the search engine:

- Metadata—that is, crawled properties and managed properties
- Crawl logs
- All settings like content sources, crawl rules, search scopes, and so on
- Other internal stuff

The database server role is the most critical role of all from the perspective of availability. Ultimately, index servers, query servers, and Web front-end servers all depend on the availability of the database server. Deploying the database server role with availability in mind is therefore an important consideration.

Consequences of Downtime for Each Server Role

Now that we've reviewed the four server roles required for searching, Table 7-2 describes the consequences of downtime for each server role. These consequences assume that all other roles are still fully operational.

TABLE 7-2 Consequences of Downtime by Role

Role	Consequence of Downtime
Index server	Content is not crawled, and the indexes of associated SSPs might be outdated. Users will still be able to search, but the search results will not include new or updated content.
Web front-end server (crawling only)	Local SharePoint content sources are not crawled, and the indexes of associated SSPs might be outdated. All other content sources are still crawled by the indexer.
Query server	Users will not be able to search for any content. The indexer will still keep content indexes up-to-date, and it will propagate all changes to the query server after it comes online again.
Database server	Downtime on the database server hosting the farm configuration database will render the entire farm inaccessible.
	Downtime on database servers dedicated to SharePoint content databases will render associated SharePoint sites inaccessible.
	Downtime on database servers dedicated to SSP search databases will bring query servers and index servers to a halt. Users will still be able to navigate SharePoint sites, but they will not be able to search for any content.

Understanding the potential consequences of downtime for each role will help you prioritize the allocation of servers in your farm.

Common Topology Models

By definition and according to the architecture, there are no real topology restrictions in Office SharePoint Server 2007. You are free to deploy farms of any size with any available services enabled on each server. It is even possible to deploy an entire farm with only one role! However, there are some guidelines and best practices presented in this chapter that you should pay attention to. The only real caveat, also noted by Microsoft in the open topology model, is the limitation whereby the index server role must be deployed to a separate server if the topology includes more than one query server.

> **Note** Microsoft SharePoint Portal Server 2003 came with topology restrictions. It supported only a few named topologies, including single server, small farm, medium farm, and large farm.

This section outlines a number of common topology models for deploying Office SharePoint Server 2007. Each model will naturally focus on searching and less on other aspects of SharePoint. The presence of an Active Directory is assumed in all models except for the single-server deployment, where it is optional but recommended.

Single-Server Deployment

In a single-server deployment scenario, all services are, as the name implies, deployed to a single physical server or a single virtual server image, as shown in the following illustration:

 User Requests

 Web Front-End Server
Query Server
Index Server
Application Server
Database Server

The application server role shown in the topology illustration refers to all non-search-related application roles like Microsoft Office Excel Calculation Services and Forms Services.

Query performance and scalability are limited beyond a few concurrent users, and index-ing will negatively affect overall performance for larger document libraries where users are frequently adding and modifying content. The level of guaranteed availability is also low, but it can be improved to some degree by following the applicable hardware availability recom-mendations presented in the section "Hardware Recommendations" later in this chapter. The main advantages of this topology are quick and easy deployment, low hardware costs, and low software license costs. It is, however, recommended only for evaluation purposes and development environments. Production environments should plan for at least a two-server farm topology.

The installation program in Office SharePoint Server 2007 includes a special option for easy installation and deployment of a stand-alone server. Select the Basic option during installa-tion, as shown in Figure 7-2, to install the software and automatically configure and start all services on a single server.

The installation program will also install Microsoft SQL Server 2005 Express on the same server when you choose the basic installation. The Express edition of SQL Server 2005 is limit-ed to one CPU and 1 gigabyte (GB) of memory. The collective size of databases is additionally limited to 4 GB. Installing any other topology or hitting any of the limits in SQL Server 2005 Express requires you to choose the Advanced installation option and then manually start and configure services.

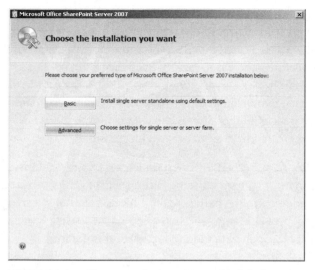

FIGURE 7-2 Installing a stand-alone server with default settings

Two-Server Farm

A two-server farm is the minimal recommended topology for production environments. It is a two-tiered environment where the first server is running all roles in the SharePoint farm and the second server is dedicated to the database server role, as shown in the following illustration:

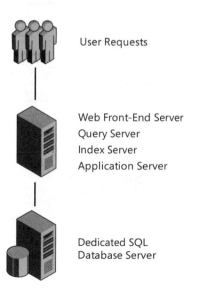

User Requests

Web Front-End Server
Query Server
Index Server
Application Server

Dedicated SQL
Database Server

Performance capabilities and availability are still very limited, but scalability is significantly improved by moving the SQL Server to a dedicated server. The farm can easily be scaled to handle increasing loads by adding a dedicated index server and more Web front-end servers. Similarly, rising requirements for an increased level of availability can also be achieved by adding more redundant Web front-end servers together with clustering of the database server. The level of availability built into this topology is statistically worse compared with the single-server topology because it includes more hardware that can potentially fail. A critical failure on any of the two servers will render the entire farm inaccessible.

Although it is technically possible to install SQL Server 2005 Express on the database server, it is highly recommended and in most scenarios also required to install at least the standard edition of SQL Server 2005. In addition to the hardware limitations mentioned earlier, the Express edition also does not support clustering and mirroring of databases. Therefore, it is impossible to increase availability through data redundancy with this edition.

Three-Server Farm

Adding a third server to a farm can yield improved performance or a higher level of availability, but not both. For improved performance, use it to run the index server role as well as the other application server roles, as shown in the following illustration. The query server role is best kept on the Web front-end server. For improved availability, use the third server for a second SQL Server to form a database cluster. A three-server farm is, however, below the recommended size for a high-availability deployment, which requires at least four servers to reach.

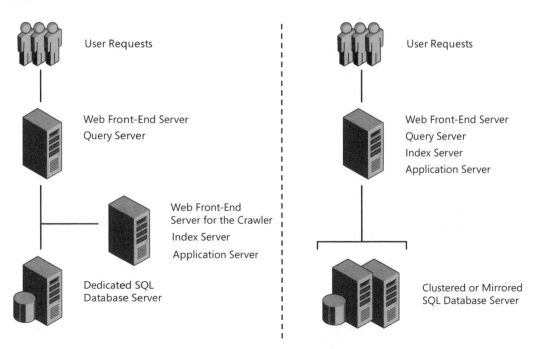

User Requests

Web Front-End Server
Query Server

Web Front-End
Server for the Crawler
Index Server
Application Server

Dedicated SQL
Database Server

User Requests

Web Front-End Server
Query Server
Index Server
Application Server

Clustered or Mirrored
SQL Database Server

Performance can be further improved in the first scenario by enabling a dedicated Web front-end server for crawling on the index server. This will speed crawling of SharePoint sites and remove the impact of the crawler from the Web front-end server accessed by users. Other application server roles can also run on the index server.

Four-Server Farm

Deploying a high-availability solution requires a least four servers, as shown in the following illustration. (Using five servers is highly recommended, as you'll see in the next section, "Five-Server Farm.")

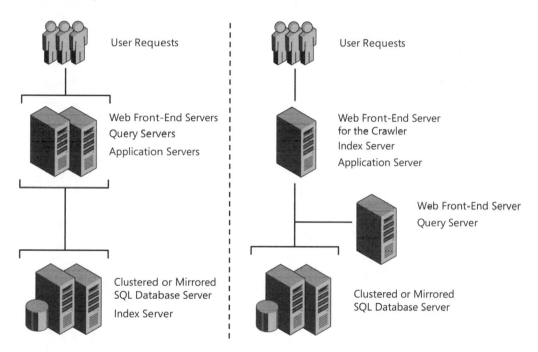

With four servers, servers one and two must host both the Web front-end server role and the query role. Additional application server roles, such as Excel Calculation Services, can be installed on one or both servers. Servers three and four must form a clustered or mirrored database server. A caveat with this farm size is that the index server will need to be deployed to one of the database servers, as it cannot be deployed to any of the query servers. Doing so would stop the index server from propagating the index to the second query server.

If it is not desirable to deploy the index server to any database server and availability is not a critical requirement, a slightly different topology might be applicable—one in which the second Web front-end server/query server is dropped in favor of an index server with a dedicated Web front-end server for crawling. Other application server roles can also be deployed to the index server in this topology.

Five-Server Farm

A five-server farm, as shown in the following illustration, is the best and most common baseline topology to start from when performance, availability, and scalability are all critical factors to the business. With five servers, it is possible to achieve a high level of availability as well as great performance capabilities.

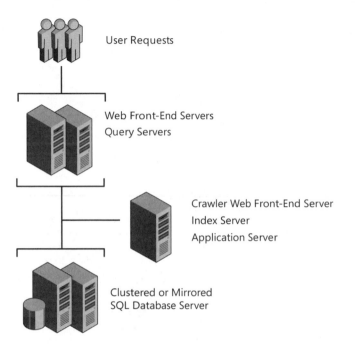

Servers one and two host both the Web front-end server role and the query role, servers three and four form a clustered or mirrored database server, and server five hosts the index server role along with a dedicated Web front-end server for crawling. The decision where to put other redundant application server roles like Excel Calculation Services and Microsoft Office Project Server 2007 depends on whether the farm should be optimized for performance or availability. For best performance, deploy these roles to the index server, and for best availability, deploy them to the Web front-end server/query servers.

Six-Server Farm

Add a second application server to the five-server farm topology, as shown in the following illustration, to optimize the farm for both performance and availability with respect to the deployment of application server roles beyond search. This topology provides maximum redundancy with a minimum number of servers.

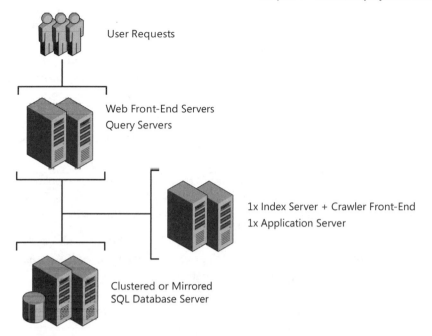

User Requests

Web Front-End Servers
Query Servers

1x Index Server + Crawler Front-End
1x Application Server

Clustered or Mirrored
SQL Database Server

Having two application servers, however, does not imply that both should host the index server role. Like most other application server roles, the index server role is not redundant. In most cases, only one of the application servers will need to host the index server role. Two index servers are applicable only in scenarios where you have multiple SSPs that could be served with advantage by different index servers. The advantage is better performance, as each SSP is served by its own index server instead of sharing one index server with the other SSPs.

N-Server Farm

Let's not continue with a seven-server farm topology. Instead, recall that there are no topology restrictions for deploying Office SharePoint Server 2007. Therefore, within a single farm, you can deploy as many Web front-end servers, query servers, index servers, application servers, and database servers as you need.

For large enterprises and hosting environments with thousands of active users and huge amounts of content and where performance, availability, scalability, and data isolation are critical, a multitiered deployment with many servers is an obvious choice. Such environments can employ a complete tier for each server role as described here and shown in the following illustration:

- **Presentation tier**   Represented by two or more redundant and load-balanced Web front-end servers. Increased capacity to deliver acceptable performance under increasing load is achieved simply by adding more servers. However, you should not expect capacity to increase significantly beyond five Web servers per database server. This is roughly the limit where the database server becomes saturated with requests from the Web servers.

- **Query tier**   Contains two or more redundant query servers. Each query server receives a local copy of indexes from the index servers. Two query servers will support searching a maximum of 200 content databases. An additional query server is needed for every 100 content databases in the farm.

- **Index tier**   Includes one or more index servers. The maximum possible number is one index server for each SSP.

- **Application tier**   Includes two or more servers for other redundant application server roles like Excel Calculation Services and Office Project Server 2007. When needed, this tier can additionally be split into a dedicated tier for each of these roles.

- **Data tier**   Employs one or more database clusters. Distributing content databases across multiple database clusters is the recommended way to scale the database tier to handle more traffic from the Web front-end servers. A dedicated cluster for SSP databases is also worth considering. It will relieve the content database clusters of traffic from query servers, index servers, and other application servers.

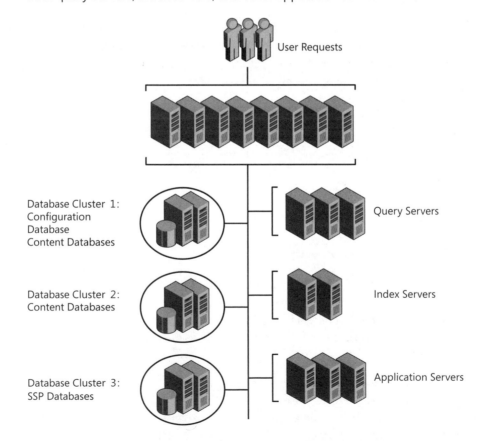

Not only do extreme environments like this call for a high-bandwidth network connecting all the servers, but they also call for intelligent routing of the network traffic between the different tiers.

Windows SharePoint Services Farm with Microsoft Search Server 2008

The search engine included in Windows SharePoint Services 3.0 has limited functionality compared with the Enterprise Search engine included in Office SharePoint Server 2007. These limitations include:

- No cross-site searching. Windows SharePoint Services 3.0 enables users to search only within one site collection at a time.
- Cannot index external content from Web sites, file shares, and so on.
- No concept of search scopes.
- Cannot index, search, and display custom metadata.

The same limitations also apply to Windows SharePoint Services 2.0 compared with SharePoint Portal Server 2003. Some or all of these limitations have been an issue for years for most Windows SharePoint Services consumers not wanting to upgrade to the paid version of SharePoint. For SharePoint Portal Server 2003, there was additionally a problem of a missing licensing model for the search engine in a stand-alone configuration.

The release of Microsoft Search Server 2008 Express was seen as very good news by most or all of these consumers. With this product, all of the preceding limitations are fairly easy to overcome. Just deploy a stand-alone server with this product and point its crawler to the Web front-end servers of the Windows SharePoint Services farm, as shown in the following illustration:

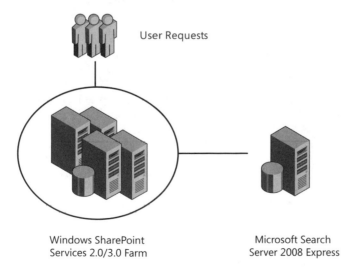

User Requests

Windows SharePoint
Services 2.0/3.0 Farm

Microsoft Search
Server 2008 Express

However, to search, users will need redirection to the Search Center hosted on the search server, as it does not integrate with the small Search Box on most Web pages. A little software development or a third-party product is required to implement a nice integration. Consider the following options when choosing the search experience you want to deliver to end users:

- **Do nothing.**   Educate users to navigate to the Search Center of the search server when they need to search for something. This is the cheapest solution but also the least user-friendly one.

- **Deploy a new Search box.**   Develop a new Search box that will automatically direct the user and his or her query to the new Search Center. Deploy this Search box to all sites in the farm.

- **Use the Search Web service.**   Develop a new Search Web Part that connects to the search engine through the Search Web service. Deploy the Search Web Part along with a new Search box to all sites in the farm. See the section "The Query Web Service" in Chapter 8, "Search APIs," for complete coverage of working with the Search Web service.

> **Note** Search Server 2008 Express is a downloadable product but is limited to a single-server deployment. If you need to scale it for high performance and availability, you'll need to purchase Microsoft Search Server 2008 when released.

Choosing a Baseline Topology

The server farm topologies reviewed earlier in this chapter can all be considered as a starting point for your deployment. Because the topology management of Office SharePoint Server 2007 is flexible, you can always scale the server farm with additional servers at a later time. But you can save time and avoid stress and frustration when you publish your solution by carefully evaluating the requirements important to selecting the appropriate baseline topology.

The following flowchart will help you choose the baseline topology that best meets the requirements of your deployment.

| 1 | Answer **yes** if you plan to deploy SharePoint for evaluation purposes only, or if you plan to use it for development purposes. For development, it is a big advantage to install all components, including the database, on a single machine. Having everything local makes it easier to deploy and debug code—in other words, you don't need to worry about remote debugging.

Answer **no** if you plan for a production environment or a preproduction stage environment. |

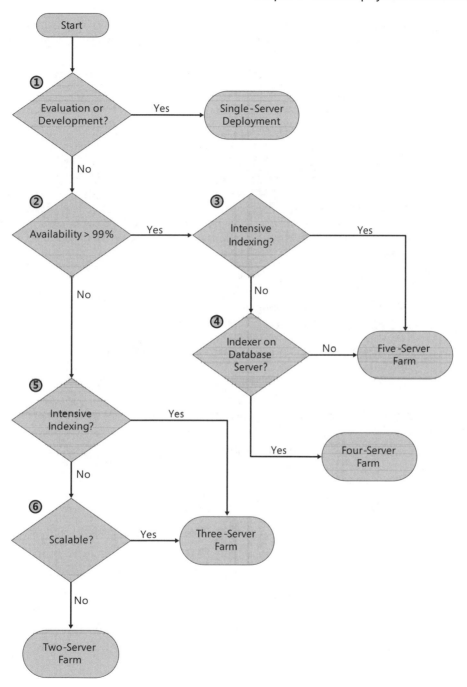

2	Answer **yes** if you require a guaranteed level of availability that is 99 percent or greater. In other words, answer **yes** here if you can answer **yes** to any of the following questions: ❑ Is the availability of data critical to the business? ❑ Will users have trouble performing their jobs when the farm is down? ❑ Is a downtime period of more than one day unacceptable? Answer **no** if availability is not a critical requirement and downtime periods of more than one day are acceptable.
3	Answer **yes** if the farm is going to contain a lot of dynamic content, resulting in intensive use of resources by the indexer. This is a typical scenario when deploying a collaboration solution with SharePoint in a large enterprise. The content is typically very dynamic here, as users frequently create and modify content. Answer **no** if the farm is largely going to contain static content that is not updated on a frequent basis. This could, for example, be a corporate Web site deployment where content is updated only once a day and where most users have only read access to the content.
4	Answer **yes** if it is an acceptable solution to install the index server role on the same server as the database server. Answer **no** if this solution is not acceptable.
5	Same as 3.
6	Answer **yes** if at a later time you plan to scale with additional Web front-end servers and query servers. Answer **no** if you do not expect to add more Web front-end servers and query servers.

The exact configurations of the resulting server farm topologies are the same as those outlined earlier. For topologies where this chapter suggests two possible configurations, the flowchart selects the configuration on the left.

Software Boundaries

With software, it is possible to implement the same functionality in many different ways. Given the same hardware, some implementations will perform by an order of magnitude better than other implementations. It all depends on the algorithms used at the different hot spots in the application. Therefore, performance capabilities and scalability are also affected by the internal software architecture and specific implementation of SharePoint. Fortunately, SharePoint is a well-thought-out product designed with performance and scalability in mind.

However, it is not always feasible to choose a design that scales indefinitely. Such designs often come at the price of increased time and costs for development and testing, as well as increased complexity to deploy the product. Ultimately, design is a trade-off between a prioritized list of feature requests, simplicity vs. complexity, development costs, and time to market. For example, the search engine in Office SharePoint Server 2007 currently scales to about 50 million documents per index, while most Internet search engines and a few Enterprise Search engines scale to billions of documents. But scaling a search engine this much also requires a highly distributed architecture with distributed indexes.

We can't rule out the possibility that the product team will one day decide to invest in and follow this path. If they do, it will be to support SharePoint in the largest enterprises with extreme requirements for searching. For the vast majority of SharePoint customers, a 50-million-document limitation is not an issue.

During exhaustive testing of Office SharePoint Server 2007, Microsoft has identified a number of logical limits that it is not recommended to exceed. Crossing them might gradually reduce performance even if extra hardware is added. Table 7-3 lists the logical limits that are related to searching.

TABLE 7-3 Logical Limits (Source: Microsoft)

Entity	Limit	Notes
Search indexes	One per SSP Maximum of 20 per farm	Office SharePoint Server 2007 supports one content index per SSP. It is not recommended to have more than 20 SSPs per farm.
Indexed documents	50,000,000 per SSP	This is not a hard limit, but exceeding it might gradually reduce performance faster than you can add more hardware. Split content across multiple SSPs to get around this limit.
Content sources	500 per SSP	This is a hard limit enforced by the system.
Start addresses	500 per content source	This is a hard limit enforced by the system.
Alerts	1,000,000 per SSP	This is the limit that Microsoft has tested for.
Scopes	200 per site	This is the recommended limit per site, and it is additionally not recommended to have more than 100 scope rules per scope.
Display groups	25 per site	These are used for a grouped display of scopes through the user interface.
Crawl rules	10,000 per SSP	This is a soft limit that it is not recommended to exceed.
Keywords	15,000 per site	It is recommended not to specify more than 10 best bets and five synonyms per keyword.
Crawled properties	500,000 per SSP	The properties (metadata) discovered during a crawl.
Managed properties	100,000 per SSP	The properties used by the search system in queries. It is not recommended to specify more than 100 crawled property mappings per managed property.

Entity	Limit	Notes
Authoritative pages	200 per relevance level	The recommended maximum number of sites in each of the four relevance levels.
Results removal	100	The maximum recommended number of URLs that should be removed from the system in one operation.
Crawl logs	50,000,000	Number of entries in the crawl log.

More Information All of the software boundaries identified by Microsoft, including the non-search-related ones, have been published on Microsoft TechNet, at *http://technet2. microsoft.com/ Office/en-us/library/6a13cd9f-4b44-40d6-85aa-c70a8e5c34fe1033.mspx*. Alternatively, search for the keywords *office sharepoint software boundaries* on one of the major Internet search engines. The Knowledge Base article should be listed as the first search result.

Hardware Recommendations

In addition to the topology selected and the software boundaries, performance capabilities and availability are also governed by hardware limitations and redundancy, respectively. This section makes a number of general recommendations to help you choose the right hardware for your server farm. The following recommendations are primarily concerned with choosing hardware for optimal performance:

- **Buy 64-bit hardware.**   Although SharePoint can be deployed to 32-bit servers, it is highly recommended that you opt for 64-bit hardware along with a Windows Server 64-bit operating system. Not only does this boost performance, but it is also a more future-proof choice, as future versions of SharePoint will support only 64-bit servers. In other words, your 32-bit hardware will be obsolete the day you decide to upgrade to the next version of SharePoint. Choosing 64-bit hardware will additionally make it possible to add more than 4 GB of memory to the server. The only caveat when choosing 64-bit hardware is related to the availability of 64-bit compilations of some third-party *IFilter*s. A 32-bit *IFilter* will not work on a 64-bit index server. If you depend on one or more 32-bit *IFilter*s that are not yet available for 64-bit, consider deploying a dedicated 32-bit index server.

- **Use multiple-core processors.**   SharePoint is a highly multithreaded application. Web front-end servers process user requests in separate threads, and each application pool in Internet Information Services (IIS) maps to a separate process. Index servers employ multiple processes and threads to crawl and index content. Query servers and databases also employ a multithreaded architecture to serve concurrent requests. Therefore, you should avoid single-core processors—opt for dual-core or quad-core processors or more when possible.

- **Install multiple processors.**   Consider multiple-processor motherboards for servers hosting roles that are not redundant. This allows you to scale index servers and database servers to the maximum. Multiple processors are of course also relevant for redundant server roles like Web front-end servers and query servers if you prefer to have a minimum number of servers in the farm.

- **Use large amounts of memory.**   It is very important to install enough memory in all servers. Inadequate amounts of memory will trigger a lot of slow disk swapping activity. It is a good practice to start with 4 GB of RAM.

- **Use fast memory.**   Make sure to buy memory with the fastest bus speed supported by the processors.

- **Use fast disks.**   Deploy the fastest storage you can afford to host I/O-intensive data files. For best performance and reliability, choose small computer system interface (SCSI) drives or serial advanced technology attachment (SATA) II drives, which are generally less costly than SCSI drives.

- **Use disk arrays.**   Arrange multiple disks in a RAID 10 array to boost performance and increase availability at the same time. Use RAID 5 where disk write performance is less critical but availability is not. Consider a RAID 10 array for data that is frequently modified and RAID 5 for data that is rarely updated. For example, use RAID 5 for the operating system files and RAID 10 for the SharePoint content Index files.

- **Install a gigabit network.**   For low latency and high bandwidth, connect servers in a farm with a gigabit (1 GB) backbone network at the minimum.

Another important factor for boosting performance and capacity is to isolate I/O-intensive data files onto their own disk spindles. One disk spindle equals one magnetic read/write head of a disk. Disks are the slowest component of any system, and performance bottlenecks can quickly arise if different applications are forced to compete for spindle time. The following list helps you understand where it is worthwhile investing in dedicated disk arrays:

- **Database servers**   Isolate databases onto separate spindles in this order: temporary database, transaction logs, SSP databases, content databases, and the SharePoint configuration database.

- **Search servers**   Query servers and index servers are major consumers of disk I/O. Therefore, it makes a big difference to isolate the content index onto separate spindles.

Table 7-4 lists the minimum and recommended requirements for processor, memory, and hard disks for a single-server deployment.

TABLE 7-4 Minimum and Recommended Hardware Configuration for Single-Server Deployments

Component	Minimum	Recommended
Processor	32-bit, single-core, 2.5 gigahertz (GHz)	64-bit, dual-core or quad-core processor at 2.5 GHz or faster.
Memory	1 GB	2 GB for evaluation; 4 GB for development.
Disk space	3 GB of free space	This should not be an issue with modern disks. Opt for a 120-GB disk or larger.
Disk configuration	Any	Install separate disks for the operating system, Web server, database, and search.

Deploying a server farm to host your production environment typically requires more hardware. Table 7-5 lists the minimum and recommended requirements for processor, memory, hard disks, and network for Web front-end servers, query servers, index servers, and database servers in a server farm topology. These requirements are based on one role per server, and installing more than one role on any one server might therefore require more memory and processor power.

TABLE 7-5 Minimum and Recommended Hardware Configuration for Servers in a Farm

Component	Minimum	Recommended
Processor	32-bit, single-core, 2.5 GHz	64-bit, dual-core or quad core processor at 2.5 GHz or faster. Two or four physical 64-bit multiple-core processors are recommended for index servers and database servers.
Memory	2 GB	4 GB for SharePoint servers. 8 GB for database servers.
Disk space	3 GB of free space	See the next section, "Calculating Required Disk Space."
Disk configuration	Any	SCSI disks in RAID 5 for files with little or moderate I/O consumption. High-speed SCSI disks with 2 millisecond (ms) access time and at least 150 MB/s transfer rate in a RAID 10 configuration for I/O-intensive files.
Network	100 megabits per second (Mbps) between servers	1 gigabit per second (Gbps).

Installing hardware of the recommended caliber is of course not the cheapest solution. Choosing the appropriate hardware might therefore be a tradeoff between the requirements of the business and what it can afford. If you end up planning for many servers with many dedicated SCSI disk arrays, from a price and maintenance perspective, it might also be a good idea to consider deploying a storage area network (SAN) solution instead. A *SAN solution* is a physically separate server on the network that provides shared storage for other servers. Each server with a need for plenty of fast storage is allotted some of the shared storage, and software represents it as a local drive on the server. A huge benefit with SAN solutions is centralized management of the physical drives.

Calculating Required Disk Space

This section describes how to calculate disk space requirements for the content indexes and search databases in a farm server topology. The calculated disk space requirement for a content index applies to index servers as well as query servers. However, if both roles are hosted on the same server, you do not need to calculate double the amount of space.

Calculating the Size of the Content Index

The size of a content index lies in the range 5 percent to 12 percent of the size of the crawled content. For example, consider crawling 1,000,000 documents with a total file size of 500 GB. This would yield a content index in the range 25 GB to 60 GB (worst case). But because a full crawl builds a new copy of the index and the old index is not deleted until the crawl is complete, you need to calculate the required index size twice. To have a safe margin, it is generally recommended to calculate the amount of required disk space by multiplying the estimated size of the index by a factor of 2.5. Multiplying 0.12 by 2.5 yields the following formula for calculating the required amount of disk space for the content index:

Required disk space = 0.3 x Size of crawled content

The required disk space for the preceding example is then 0.3 x 500 GB, which equals 150 GB. The size of the operating system files, SharePoint system files, and other files is included in addition to this amount. But these files are ideally also stored on another physical disk, as recommended earlier in this chapter.

Calculating the Size of the Search Database

Each SSP creates two databases, and one is dedicated to search. The search database primarily holds the metadata of all crawled documents, and it generally requires more disk space than the content index. This is especially true when crawling many SharePoint sites that are rich in metadata. Use the following formula to calculate the required amount of disk space for the search database:

Required disk space = 0.5 x Size of crawled content

For our example in the content index section, this formula yields a required disk size of 250 GB for the search database.

Performance Optimization

For your convenience, this section recaps all of the performance-related recommendations found in this chapter. Performance recommendations are given for index servers, query servers, and database servers.

Optimizing Query Server Performance

If users often experience long query execution times in the Search Centers, check your query server deployment against the following recommendations:

- Use a baseline topology that allows you to scale the farm with additional query servers.
- Use 64-bit multiple-core processors.
- Install at least 4 GB of memory.
- Isolate the content index files on separate high-speed SCSI disks in a RAID 10 configuration. Add more spindles to the disk array to increase total I/O throughput.
- Omit any antivirus scanning of the index files.

Optimizing Index Server Performance

If you experience unacceptable performance of the crawler, check your deployment against the following recommendations:

- Use a dedicated server for the index server role.
- Configure the index server itself as a dedicated Web front-end server for the crawler. This eliminates double network hops. *Double hops* occur when both the crawler and the Web front-end server need to work across the network.
- Use two or four 64-bit multiple-core processors.
- Install at least 4 GB of memory.
- Isolate the content index files on separate high-speed SCSI disks in a RAID 10 configuration. Add more spindles to the disk array to increase total I/O throughput.
- Omit any antivirus scanning of the index files.
- Increase the number of crawl threads via the Windows registry, as described in the section "Crawler Impact Rules" in Chapter 5.
- Reduce the amount of full crawls. Stick with incremental crawls, and make sure they run on schedule so that each crawl can be completed before the next is due.

Optimizing Database Server Performance

The database is the most critical component in any server farm topology, as all the other components depend on it. Optimizing the other components for performance doesn't make sense if in reality the bottleneck is found on the database server. Use the following recommendations to improve performance:

- If possible, split the SSP databases onto a separate database server.

- Use two or four 64-bit multiple-core processors.

- Install at least 8 GB of memory.

- Isolate configuration database and content databases into separate SCSI disks in a RAID 5 configuration.

- Isolate search databases, temporary databases, and temporary database logs onto separate high-speed SCSI disks in a RAID 10 configuration. Add more spindles to the disk array to increase total I/O throughput.

- Create a temporary data file for every processor core on your server.

- Defragment databases and drives on a regular basis.

- Omit any antivirus scanning of database files.

Measuring the Performance of an Example Deployment

Up to now, this chapter has presented numerous recommendations for improving performance. But wouldn't it also be nice to get a general feeling of how search is likely to perform in a specific server farm topology with some specific hardware? This section is dedicated to answering this question. It will provide you with a general idea of what it takes to reach a certain level of performance.

It is, however, a very time consuming and expensive task to install a serious server farm, fill it with lots of sample content, and measure the performance. Fortunately, Microsoft has already done this for us, and their test environment and test results are summarized here.

Test Environment

The server farm topology of the test environment includes one to eight separate query servers, one index server, one SSP, and one dedicated database server. The query servers and the index server were all running the default configuration of Office SharePoint Server 2007 Enterprise Edition on the Microsoft Windows Server 2003 64-bit operating system with Service Pack 1 (SP1). The database server was running Microsoft SQL Server 2005. Table 7-6 specifies the hardware configuration used for each type of server.

TABLE 7-6 Hardware Configuration Used for Each Type of Server

Server Role	Hardware
Query servers	Four dual-core Intel Xeon 2.66-GHz processors, 32-GB RAM
	40-GB RAID 5 disk array for the operating system files
	956-GB RAID 10 disk array for the content index and the operating system paging file
Index server	Four dual-core Intel Xeon 2.66-GHz processors, 32-GB RAM
	40-GB RAID 5 disk array for the operating system files
	956-GB RAID 10 disk array for the content index and the operating system paging file
Database server	Four dual-core Intel Xeon 2.66-GHz processors, 32-GB RAM
	40-GB RAID 5 disk array for the operating system files
	956-GB SCSI RAID 10 disk array for the *SharedServices_Search_DB* database (dedicated SCSI controller)
	273-GB SCSI RAID 10 disk array for the *SharedServices_DB* database (shared SCSI controller)
	273-GB SCSI RAID 10 disk array for the *TempDb* database (shared SCSI controller)
	273-GB SCSI RAID 10 disk array for log files (shared SCSI controller)
	136-GB SCSI RAID 10 disk array for the *SharePoint_Config* database (shared SCSI controller)

All servers were connected with a gigabit (1 billion bits/second) network. Approximately 50 million items were crawled for testing, including 10 million items from SharePoint sites, 15 million documents from file shares, 15 million Web pages from external Web servers, and 2.5 million people profiles, plus 7.5 million other items. The crawled items were 10 KB to 100 KB in size. The size of the resulting content index grew to 100 GB, and the size of the search database grew to 600 GB.

Testing Query Server Performance

The maximum number of queries per second was measured for eight different farm configurations ranging from one query server to eight. The number of index servers and database servers remained constant at one of each. Table 7-7 presents the results of the query server load testing.

TABLE 7-7 Query Server Performance in Different Farm Configurations

Query Servers	Queries per Second	Query Server CPU Load	Database Server CPU Load
1	24	99 percent	7 percent
2	48	97 percent	13 percent
3	71	95 percent	21 percent

Query Servers	Queries per Second	Query Server CPU Load	Database Server CPU Load
4	93	92 percent	29 percent
5	115	91 percent	39 percent
6	133	87 percent	53 percent
7	148	80 percent	64 percent
8	146	66 percent	60 percent

Notice that adding query servers boosts capacity for up to seven query servers. But adding query server number eight does not help; instead, it actually reduces the capacity a little.

Testing Index Server Performance

The time to perform a full crawl was measured as 35 days. This translates to about 1.4 million documents a day and 15 documents a second. Incremental crawls will of course complete faster, depending on the rate of change in the document library. A document library where users frequently add and update content will take longer for incremental crawls to process as the rate of change goes up. For example, if one percent of the content changed since the last crawl, an incremental crawl will take roughly 9 hours to complete.

Please note that these test results are highly dependent on the content sources being crawled and their responsiveness. The turnaround time for full crawls as well as incremental crawls is likely to be shorter in environments with greater bandwidth and greater responsiveness of the content sources. Moreover, the incremental crawl strategy of external Web servers is not very efficient compared with the incremental crawl strategy of SharePoint sites. See the section "The Nature of Full and Incremental Crawls" in Chapter 5 for more information about the incremental crawl strategy for the different types of content sources.

Summary

This chapter has provided numerous recommendations for deploying a high-performance, scalable, highly available, and secure Enterprise Search solution using Office SharePoint Server 2007. Appropriate planning of a SharePoint production environment is a key ingredient to its success among end users, who basically want to find relevant information fast. Over the years, using Internet search engines, they have learned to expect nothing less than that. The next chapter moves on to a new topic, the application programming interfaces (APIs) of the search engine.

Chapter 8
Search APIs

After completing this chapter, you will be able to

- Understand your options as a developer when working with the Enterprise Search features that are part of Microsoft Office SharePoint Server 2007.

- Support administrators with additional tools and utililities in their work using the new search administration object model.

- Construct search queries in your code using both the keyword syntax and the SQL syntax.

- Programmatically execute a search query and process the results in your custom SharePoint solutions or custom applications.

- Remotely submit a search query to the Search Web service and process the returned results in smart client applications.

This chapter is fully dedicated to the different search application programming interfaces (APIs), or object models, that are part of Microsoft Office SharePoint Server 2007. We start with an overview of the Microsoft .NET Framework assemblies that contain the many classes that can be used by developers to build custom solutions that support both administrators configuring and managing the index and search engine and end users executing queries and reviewing the results in the browser or a smart client application. Next we'll look at the brand-new search administration object model. The major classes are discussed using a sample application that is part of the download package for this book. Using this practical approach, you'll learn how to help administrators to be more productive in their work.

Often, you'll need to execute a search query programmatically. Your first action will be to formulate the query. This chapter covers the two possible ways of doing this and continues with the classes in the query object model that are used to execute the query. The execution can be started in the context of a SharePoint site—for example, a custom Web Part that you make available on a page. Another option is an application that is running on the desktop of the end user and that communicates remotely with the Enterprise Search features of Office SharePoint Server 2007. The Search Web service that enables these types of scenarios is discussed at the end of this chapter.

Introducing the Search Application Programming Interfaces

Both Microsoft Windows SharePoint Services 3.0 and Office SharePoint Server 2007 provide numerous options for developers to communicate with the search features. Chapter 10, "Searching with Windows SharePoint Services 3.0," covers the different techniques you can use to access the Search service programmatically in Windows SharePoint Services 3.0. For the rest of this chapter, we'll cover object models that are included in Office SharePoint Server 2007. As you'll learn, many classes and techniques will be similar, because both layers of SharePoint are now based on a common implementation of Microsoft Search. This is of course good news for developers and also for the administrators.

The two object models are described in brief here:

- **Search administration object model**   As mentioned, this is a brand-new object model that delivers a rich collection of classes that developers can use to programmatically complete the operations that administrators perform in the Search Administration site of the Shared Services Provider (SSP). And as you'll learn in the next section, there are even configurations and optimizations of the index and search engine that can be done only in a programmatic way.

- **Query object model**   Readers who have experience with the earlier version of Microsoft SharePoint Portal Server 2003 might have worked with the *QueryProvider* class to execute search queries in, for example, custom Web Parts. The support for this class is still available, but the class is considered obsolete. A new, revamped query object model is available, and it makes the programming model a lot easier and more transparent than was the case in the past. The section "The Query Object Model" later in this chapter covers the major classes that deliver this new way of executing search queries and processing the results. Note that there are also important changes in the way you formulate the query; these will be covered as well.

The Search Administration Object Model

The new search administration object model consists of a great number of classes that are bundled together in the *Microsoft.Office.Server.Search.dll* and defined in the *Microsoft.Office. Server.Search.Administration* namespace. This object model can be used to develop custom applications such as console applications, Microsoft PowerShell commandlets, and Windows-based applications. The classes can also be used in custom solution components that can be integrated into SharePoint 3.0 Central Administration or other SharePoint sites to help administrators do a better job in managing the index and search infrastructure.

The following diagram illustrates the available options in the search administration object model:

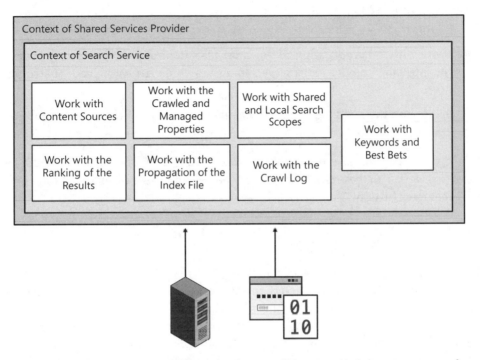

The related classes are accessible only after you have acquired the necessary references to the context of the SSP and the Search Web service that it hosts. We'll have a look at this preparation work in just a few moments. Once all is in place, the fun starts, and within your applications and solution components, you'll be able to perform the following tasks:

- **Work with content sources**   Create and manage the locations that have to be crawled. Configure the crawl schedules and the rules that might have to be applied during the crawling.

- **Work with crawled and managed properties**   Review all of the data collected during the crawl and dropped in the property store in the search database. Use this information to create managed properties that you expose to enrich the end-user search experience in various ways.

- **Work with shared and local search scopes**   Create and manage the search scopes at the two available levels: the level of the SSP and the level of the local site collection. Create the rules, and compile the search scopes. Visualize the scopes in the Scope Picker control in the small Search box that is displayed on the home page of, for example, your collaboration portal or in the Scope Picker controls on the Advanced Search pages.

- **Work with keywords and best bets**   Create and manage the search results that you want to highlight as important results to the user on the Search Results pages.

- **Work with the ranking of the results**   Configure to a certain degree the various factors that have an impact on the relevance ranking of the search results.

- **Work with the propagation of the index file**   Control the copying or propagation of the index file from the index servers to the search servers within your SharePoint server farm.

- **Work with the crawl log**   Review in a different way the information logged by the crawler.

All of the classes involved in these tasks are described in the following sections. But before the actual work with these classes is covered, we need to take a closer look at the preparation work that must be done.

The *ServerContext* Class

It is important to review the *ServerContext* class before we look at the other classes that are part of the search APIs. The *ServerContext* class is defined in the *Microsoft.Office.Server* namespace and is part of the *Microsoft.Office.Server.dll*. You use this class to retrieve a reference to the context of the SSP that you want to work with. The class provides the run-time methods for the Shared Services that are under the control of an SSP. Remember that all of the indexing and search capabilities included in Office SharePoint Server 2007 are part of these Shared Services.

> **More Information**   To work with the *ServerContext* class and with the *SearchContext* class discussed in the next section, you need to add references to the following .NET Framework assemblies to your Microsoft Visual Studio project: *Microsoft.SharePoint.dll*, *Microsoft.Office.Server.dll*, *Microsoft.Office.Server.Search.dll*, and *System.Web.dll*.

The reference to the context of the SSP can be retrieved in a number of ways by using the *ServerContext* class. The first technique uses the *Current* property to get the context while your code is already running in a SharePoint context, as shown here. This is the case when your code is executed in a custom SharePoint Web Part on a custom SharePoint page that is used to extend the infrastructure.

```
ServerContext context = ServerContext.Current;
```

A second technique uses the *Default* property, which gives us the default instance for the local server farm. Server farms can operate with multiple SSPs configured. One SSP is always flagged as the default SSP. New Internet Information Services (IIS) Web applications that are extended in order to host SharePoint portals or sites are automatically associated with the default SSP. This can be modified by administrators in SharePoint 3.0 Central Administration if needed.

```
ServerContext context = ServerContext.Default;
```

A last technique uses the *GetContext* method, which is used when your code runs outside the context of SharePoint. Examples of these types of applications are command console applications, Windows-based applications, and the Microsoft Management Console (MMC). The download package includes a Windows-based application named InsideSearchAdminSample that we'll use in this chapter to illustrate the many options you have when working with the search administration object model. The four possible ways of calling the *GetContext* method all differ in the way you deliver the parameter that is required for the retrieval of the context of the SSP: you can provide the method with an *HttpContext* reference, a reference to an *SPSite*, a reference to an *SPWebApplication*, or just the name of the SSP as a string.

> **More Information** *SPSite* and *SPWebApplication* are two classes that are part of *Microsoft. SharePoint.dll*. An object of type *SPSite* represents a site collection. An object of type *SPWebApplication* represents an IIS Web application. (In the old days, this was called the *virtual server.*)

The following code is executed to connect to the context of the SSP:

```
ServerContext serverContext = null;
serverContext = ServerContext.GetContext(textBoxSSP.Text);
```

The value of the variable in the preceding snippet will be *null* if the name entered by the user does not match one of the SSPs that are available in the local server farm.

The *SearchContext* Class

Once you have the reference to the SSP, you have access to the services that it hosts. One of these is the Search Web service, and a reference to it must be retrieved before you can continue the work with the different administration classes in the object model.

The reference that is needed is one of type *SearchContext*. The class is made available by *Microsoft.Office.Server.Search.dll* and is part of the *Microsoft.Office.Server.Search. Administration* namespace. This is your entry object within the search administration object model, and it exposes nearly the same interface as the *ServerContext* class described in the preceding section.

Again, two static members are important: the *Current* property and the *GetContext* method. The former can be used only when your code runs in the context of SharePoint; the latter is the one to use outside the context. The *GetContext* method accepts three possible arguments: the name of the search application (only if running in the context of one of the portals), a reference to the *ServerContext* object, and a reference to an *SPSite* object. By using the reference to the site collection, you avoid having to include the details of the SSP in your application. Enough information is encapsulated in the *SPSite* instance that can be used internally to retrieve the reference to the context of the SSP with which the IIS Web application hosting the site collection is associated.

Here is a typical call to retrieve the *SearchContext* reference, with the parameter context being the reference to the *ServerContext* object covered in the preceding section:

```
SearchContext searchContext = null;
searchContext = SearchContext.GetContext(serverContext);
```

Important If you use the *SPSite* instance as the parameter for getting the context, it is recommended that you take care of the disposal of the *SPSite* instance in your code. Disposing of the instance will free up the internal resources that it holds immediately, thus minimizing the effect on the memory load. A good approach to accomplish this without too much trouble is the use of the *using* statement that is part of the C# language. At the end of the *using* code block, the instance will be disposed of implicitly. Here is an example:

```
SearchContext context = null;
using (SPSite site = new SPSite("http://moss.litwareinc.com"))
{
    context = SearchContext.GetContext(site);
}
```

The *SearchContext* class exposes a couple of interesting members. One of these is the *Reset* method. Call this method with utmost care because it will clean up the entire index and all of the metadata that has been collected and stored in the search database. However, the search administration configuration, such as the list of the already defined content sources, will be preserved.

The configuration of diacritic sensitivity for the Search Web service can be done with the *UpdateDiacriticSensitive* method. This method sets the *DiacriticSensitive* property, a setting that is used for configuring the search engine so that it accounts for accents, such as those found in the French language.

The format of the e-mail messages that are sent to visitors who create alerts for the search results can be configured via the *UpdateAlertNotificationFormat* method. The use of this method will update the *AlertNotificationFormat* property.

A last method is the *UpdateQueryLoggingEnabled* method. This method turns the query logging on or off. The status information is exposed by using the *QueryLoggingEnabled* property. Don't forget that logging each of the queries performed by the users can be an expensive operation.

Working with Content Sources

The sample project contains a Windows-based form that illustrates all of the work you can do with content sources in your managed code. It's a good idea to open the form in code view and then review and test the code as you work through this section. Figure 8-1 shows the form, with all of the possible actions that can be performed using content sources and the related crawl rules.

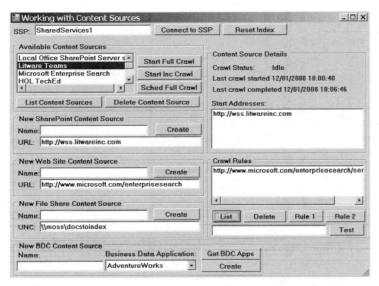

FIGURE 8-1 The form in the sample application, exposing the different actions on content sources and crawl rules that can be performed programmatically

The *Content* class is the starter class when you intend to manage content source. It enables access to the different classes at the lower level that represent each of the possible types of content sources. The *Content* class is also the class to start with for the other types of configurations you want to perform, such as the search scopes, crawl rules, and crawl settings.

You create an instance of the *Content* class by providing it with the reference to the *SearchContext* object. The following snippet does the job:

```
Content content = null;
content = new Content(searchContext);
```

Listing Content Sources

A first possible administration task that you can support is the display of all of the currently available content sources, their details, and the status of the crawling. The list of content sources is retrieved via the *ContentSources* property of the *Content* class. The *ContentSources* property gives you access to all of the defined content sources with, of course, all of the methods in place to manipulate this collection. A content source is represented by the *ContentSource* class in the object model. A simple loop over the *ContentSourceCollection* can populate, for example, a small list box control:

```
listBoxContentSources.Items.Clear();
listBoxContentSources.DisplayMember = "Name";
foreach (ContentSource contentsource in content.ContentSources)
{
    listBoxContentSources.Items.Add(contentsource);
}
```

The details and the status of an individual content source are available via the many properties that are exposed by the *ContentSource* class. One of these properties, *StartAddresses*, returns the start addresses for the content source:

```
ContentSource selContentSource = (ContentSource)listBoxContentSources.SelectedItem;
listBoxStartAddresses.Items.Clear();
foreach (object startaddress in selContentSource.StartAddresses)
{
    listBoxStartAddresses.Items.Add(startaddress);
}
```

Information about the status of the crawling of the content source is available through the *CrawlStatus*, *CrawlCompleted*, and *CrawlStarted* properties. The values for the *CrawlStatus* property are summarized in Table 8-1. The other two properties contain a date and time value.

TABLE 8-1 *CrawlStatus* **Property Values**

Value	Description
CrawlingFull	Busy executing a full crawl.
CrawlingIncremental	Busy executing an incremental crawl.
CrawlPausing	Busy pausing a crawl.
CrawlStopping	Busy stopping a crawl.
Idle	No crawling action at this moment.
Paused	Crawl is paused.
ProcessingNotifications	Busy processing notifications.
Recovering	Busy recovering from a crawl.
ShuttingDown	Busy shutting down the crawl.

The *ContentSource* class is actually a base class for all types of content sources that can be created using the search administration object model. The class hierarchy for the content sources is shown here:

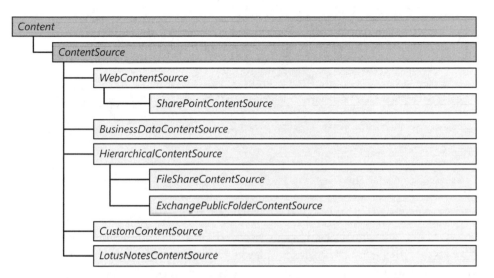

The specific content source classes are important when you start adding new content sources. Every type of content source has its specific members that must be configured in your application. Let's have a look at a number of the common types of content sources and how they can be created programmatically.

Creating a Content Source for SharePoint Sites

The first type of content source that is covered in the sample application is one for crawling content that is available in a Windows SharePoint Services 3.0 site. This type of content source is represented in the object model as a *SharePointContentSource* class.

> **Note** The SharePoint site that you have in mind for the new content source cannot yet be part of the start addresses of an already existing content source. This is probably the case if you follow along and intend to create a new content source for one of the sites you currently have running on your machine. The URL for that site is probably part of the start addresses of the *Local Office SharePoint Server Sites* content source. To proceed and create a separate content source for the SharePoint site, you'll have to remove the URL from that list of start addresses.

A new *ContentSource* object is created when you call the *Create* method exposed by the *ContentSourcesCollection*. This collection is available through the *ContentSources* property at the level of the *Content* object. Two parameters are required: the type of content source you're about to create and the name of the new content source as it will be registered for the SSP. The value for the first parameter is the type *SharePointContentSource*.

Based on this information, the *Create* method returns an object that can be cast to the *SharePointContentSource* type:

```
try
{
  ContentSource newContentSource =
      this.content.ContentSources.Create(typeof(SharePointContentSource),
                                  textBoxSPContentSourceName.Text);
  SharePointContentSource newSPContentSource =
      (SharePointContentSource)newContentSource;
  newSPContentSource.SharePointCrawlBehavior = SharePointCrawlBehavior.CrawlSites;
  newSPContentSource.StartAddresses.Add(new Uri(textBoxSPUrl.Text));
  newSPContentSource.Update();
  MessageBox.Show("New content source added!");
}
catch (Exception ex)
{
  MessageBox.Show(ex.ToString());
}
```

The *SharePointContentSource* object inherits all of the members described earlier for the *Content* class. Additional members are exposed. One, the *SharePointCrawlBehavior* property, can be set to the value *CrawlSites* or the value *CrawlVirtualServers*. This option specifies that the crawler should crawl only the particular site collection. If you opt for the second value, the crawler will crawl the entire server and everything within it.

The URL for the site collection is added as a string to the *StartAddresses* property of the new *SharePointContentSource* object. You call the *Update* method to start the creation of the new content source and update its properties. The result is an additional entry in the list of content sources, with details as shown in Figure 8-2. No crawling has been configured for the content source yet; we'll cover this in a moment.

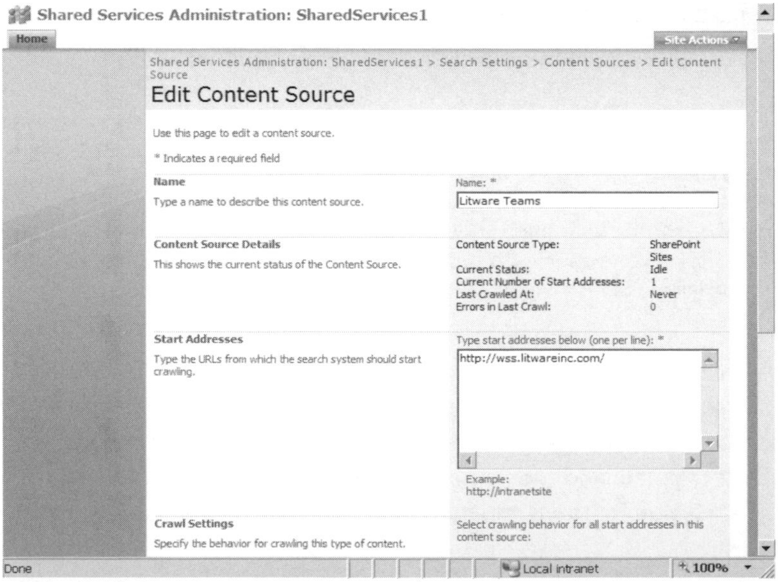

FIGURE 8-2 A new content source of type *SharePoint Sites*

Creating a Content Source for Web Sites

The creation of a new content source that stores the details for the crawling of a Web site is similar to the technique described in the preceding section. Here is the code that creates a content source of type *WebContentSource*. The external site *http://www.microsoft.com/ enterprisesearch* is added as a start address.

```
try
{
  ContentSource newContentSource =
      this.content.ContentSources.Create(typeof(WebContentSource),
                                    textBoxWebContentSourceName.Text);
  WebContentSource newWebContentSource = (WebContentSource)newContentSource;
  newWebContentSource.StartAddresses.Add(new Uri(textBoxWebURL.Text));
  newWebContentSource.MaxSiteEnumerationDepth = 1;
  newWebContentSource.MaxPageEnumerationDepth = 2;
  newWebContentSource.Update();
  MessageBox.Show("New content source added!");
}
catch (Exception ex)
{
  MessageBox.Show(ex.ToString());
}
```

Notice that two properties are set: *MaxSiteEnumerationDepth* and *MaxPageEnumerationDepth*. Setting these properties is important because they are used to control the number of site hops and page hops that the crawler can take from the start address of the content source.

Creating a Content Source for File Shares

Creating a content source for crawling a file share is again similar to what you've done earlier. You can use the property named *FollowDirectories* in the *FileShareContentSource* class to restrict the crawl to only the root folder and none of the subfolders under it:

```
try
{
  ContentSource newContentSource =
    this.content.ContentSources.Create(typeof(FileShareContentSource),
                                  textBoxFSContentSourceName.Text);
  FileShareContentSource newFSContentSource = (FileShareContentSource)newContentSource;
  newFSContentSource.StartAddresses.Add(new Uri(textBoxFSUNC.Text));
  newFSContentSource.FollowDirectories = false;
  newFSContentSource.Update();
  MessageBox.Show("New content source added!");
}
catch (Exception ex)
{
  MessageBox.Show(ex.ToString());
}
```

Creating a Content Source for Business Data Catalog Applications

The last example of the creation of a new content source with the search administration object model is one that will store the details for crawling business data that is made accessible via the Business Data Catalog (BDC). Chapter 6, "Indexing and Searching Business Data," covers the procedure for configuring the BDC with application definitions that can be used as start addresses of a *BusinessDataContentSource* object.

To programmatically retrieve the business applications that are available in the metadata store of the BDC, you have to first add a reference to the *Microsoft.SharePoint.Portal.dll* in your project. Two namespaces, *Microsoft.Office.Server.ApplicationRegistry.Infrastructure* and *Microsoft.Office.Server.ApplicationRegistry.MetadataModel*, contain the classes that you'll need to populate, for example, a drop-down list with the names of the *LobSystemInstances*:

```
SqlSessionProvider.Instance().SetSharedResourceProviderToUse(textBoxSSP.Text);
NamedLobSystemInstanceDictionary instances =
      ApplicationRegistry.GetLobSystemInstances();
foreach (LobSystemInstance app in instances.Values)
{
  comboBoxBDCApps.Items.Add(app.Name);
}
```

In the preceding code, the first line connects the *ApplicationRegistry* class to the SSP. An instance of the *SqlSessionProvider* class is initialized with this value. This instance is used internally for the subsequent operations with the BDC. The drop-down list is simply populated with the names of all of the available *LobSystemInstance* objects that are returned by calling the *GetLobSystemInstances* method that is exposed by the main class in the runtime object model of the BDC: the *ApplicationRegistry* class.

The code to create the content source is shown here:

```
try
{
   ContentSource newContentSource =
        content.ContentSources.Create(typeof(BusinessDataContentSource),
                                 textBoxBDCContentSourceName.Text);
   BusinessDataContentSource BDCContentSource =
        (BusinessDataContentSource)newContentSource;
   Uri bdcuri = BusinessDataContentSource.ConstructStartAddress
               (searchContext.Name, comboBoxBDCApps.SelectedItem.ToString());
   BDCContentSource.StartAddresses.Add(bdcuri);
   BDCContentSource.Update();
   MessageBox.Show("Content source created!");
}
catch (Exception ex)
{
   MessageBox.Show(ex.ToString());
}
```

A BDC application definition does not have a URL associated with it. Therefore, you'll notice that in the preceding code, an object of type *Uri* is created using the *ConstructStartAddress* method of the *BusinessDataContentSource* object. The arguments that are required for this method are the name of the Search Web service and the name of the *LobSystemInstance* that you want to crawl. The result of this method is a *Uri* in the following format:

```
bdc://324e7ad5-f5b0-4711-a8cd-a678a200cca2/__bk800084002500
```

Configuring the Crawling of a Content Source

The base class, *ContentSource*, exposes methods to start, pause, resume, and stop the crawling of the content source. To start a full crawl, you call the *StartFullCrawl* method like this:

```
ContentSource selContentSource = (ContentSource)listBoxContentSources.SelectedItem;
if (selContentSource.CrawlStatus == CrawlStatus.Idle)
   selContentSource.StartFullCrawl();
else
   MessageBox.Show("Content source is not idle. Full crawl cannot be started!");
```

An incremental crawl is started in a similar way, with a call to the *StartIncrementalCrawl* method. You stop a full or an incremental crawl prematurely with a call to the *StopCrawl* method. The *PauseCrawl* method and the *ResumeCrawl* method are the two methods that you use to control the crawling itself.

Both the full and the incremental crawl can be scheduled by setting the *FullCrawlSchedule* property or the *IncrementalCrawlSchedule* property to an instance of one of the following classes, all of which have the *Microsoft.Office.Server.Search.Administration.Schedule* class as their base class:

- **DailySchedule**   Use this class to specify the number of days between crawls.

- **WeeklySchedule**   Use this class to specify the number of weeks between crawls.

- **MonthlyDateSchedule**   Use this class to specify the days of the month and months of the year when the crawl should occur.

- **MonthlyDayOfWeekSchedule**   Use this class to specify the days of the month, the weeks of the month, and the months of the year when the crawl should occur.

The following code demonstrates how to configure one of the content sources to start a full crawl every two weeks, on Monday of each week:

```
ContentSource selContentSource = (ContentSource)listBoxContentSources.SelectedItem;
WeeklySchedule sched = new WeeklySchedule(this.searchContext);
sched.WeeksInterval = 2;
sched.DaysOfWeek = DaysOfWeek.Monday;
selContentSource.FullCrawlSchedule = sched;
selContentSource.Update();
```

Deleting a Content Source

Content sources can be programmatically deleted by first retrieving the reference of the *ContentSource* object and next calling the *Delete* method, as shown in the following code:

```
ContentSource selContentSource = (ContentSource)listBoxContentSources.SelectedItem;
selContentSource.Delete();
MessageBox.Show("Content source has been deleted!");
```

Creating and Configuring Crawl Rules

You use crawl rules for a number of purposes. At times, you might want to prevent the crawling of the content in a specific path that is part of the content source definition. Consider, for example, the content source for crawling the Microsoft site that we have created earlier. Maybe you also need to prevent the crawler from accessing a specific part of that site. A crawl rule can also be used to configure the opposite scenario. Maybe the subsite is already defined as excluded because the parent site is excluded, but you want to crawl the subsite anyway. A last possible scenario where crawl rules are important is the configuration of specific authentication credentials for a content type. There is a default content access account, but you might need another one for a particular content source.

A crawl rule is represented by the *CrawlRule* class in the *Microsoft.Office.Server.Search. Administration* namespace. A crawl rule is not directly associated with a content source. The list of defined crawl rules is exposed with the *CrawlRules* property of the entry class in the search namespace, the *Content* class:

```
listBoxRules.Items.Clear();
listBoxRules.DisplayMember = "Path";
foreach (CrawlRule rule in this.content.CrawlRules)
{
    listBoxRules.Items.Add(rule);
 }
```

You create a crawl rule with a call to the *Create* method of the *CrawlRuleCollection* that is exposed with the *CrawlRules* property in the preceding code. The sample application contains an example of the creation of two crawl rules: one that explicitly includes the path of a Web site in the crawling and one that sets new credentials for the crawling of the file share that previously was configured with a content source. The following is the code you execute to create the first type of rule:

```
CrawlRule rule = this.content.CrawlRules.Create
    (CrawlRuleType.InclusionRule,
     "http://www.microsoft.com/enterprisesearch/serverproducts/*");
rule.CrawlAsHttp = true;
rule.FollowComplexUrls = false;
rule.Update();
```

The first parameter of the *Create* method is of type *CrawlRuleType*. This small enumeration lets you pick two values: *InclusionRule* or *ExclusionRule*. The rule you are creating can explicitly include a path or exclude that path. The path is provided as the value of the second parameter. The *CrawlAsHttp* property is set to *true* to indicate that the crawler should crawl the content found by following the path as HTTP content. The *FollowComplexUrls* property is set to *false* to have the crawler ignore content with URLs that contain the question mark (*?*) character. The last line in the code is important. A call to the *Update* method of the *CrawlRule* object will update the search database with your changes.

Another use of a crawl rule is the configuration of a specific account for the crawling of a certain path. This code illustrates a possible approach:

```
CrawlRule rule = this.content.CrawlRules.Create
        (CrawlRuleType.InclusionRule, @"\\moss\docstoindex");
string pwdstring = "pass@word1";
System.Security.SecureString pwd = new System.Security.SecureString();
foreach (char c in pwdstring)
    pwd.AppendChar(c);
rule.SetCredentials(CrawlRuleAuthenticationType.BasicAccountRuleAccess,
                @"litwareinc\administrator", pwd);
rule.CrawlAsHttp = false;
rule.Update();
```

The type of this crawl rule is *CrawlRuleType.InclusionRule*. The *CrawlRule* class exposes a method named *SetCredentials* that is overloaded in a number of ways. The code sample illustrates how to configure the path with an account and a password. The first parameter is of type *CrawlRuleAuthenticationType*, and we use the *BasicAccountRuleAccess* for this one. Other options are available: *CertificateRuleAccess*, *DefaultRuleAccess*, and *NTLMAccountRuleAccess*. The first and last options are probably obvious. The *DefaultRuleAccess* option directs the crawler to use the default content access account credentials for accessing the path defined by the crawl rule. Notice that the password that is given as the value of the third parameter of the *SetCredentials* method is delivered as an instance of the *System.Security.SecureString* class. This .NET Framework class provides a level of protection for the string storing the password.

Figure 8-3 displays the result of the two crawl rules created with the sample application in the Search Administration site of the SSP.

Crawl rules can be tested to verify whether they are doing their work correctly. The *CrawlRule* class exposes a *Test* method that you can call with a string containing the URL for a path you'd like to verify with the rule, as shown here. The method returns *True* or *False*.

```
CrawlRule rule = (CrawlRule)listBoxRules.SelectedItem;
if (rule.Test(textBoxPathToTest.Text))
    MessageBox.Show("Rule seems to work!");
else
MessageBox.Show("Bad luck! Rule does not work for this path!");
```

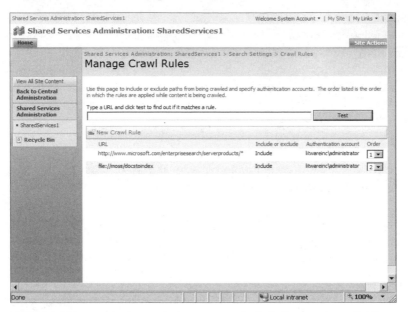

FIGURE 8-3 Two crawl rules created programmatically in the sample application

Working with Search Scopes

A second important concept when discussing the search administration object model is the whole notion of *search scopes*. From an administrator's perspective, a search scope is a sub-division of the index built up by the crawler. The items in the index will be matched again to one or more rules created by the administrator. From a user's perspective, a search scope is a means to limit the amount of search results returned after a search query to only those that match the rules contained within the search scope. Examples might be: get me only the search results for one specific content source, or get me only the documents authored by Brian Cox.

Again, there is rich support to programmatically perform all of the actions that are traditionally done by the administrator in the browser. The sample application, displayed in Figure 8-4, illustrates the common actions that you can perform using search scopes.

This time, the entry object to start with is the *Scopes* object. This type and all of the other types used in this section are defined in the *Microsoft.Office.Server.Search.Administration* namespace contained in *Microsoft.Office.Server.Search.dll*. The *Scopes* class is the top-level class in the search scope object model and contains the *Scope* class to work with an individ-ual search scope, the *ScopeRule* class and its specific subclasses, and the *ScopeDisplayGroup* class. All are reviewed in a moment.

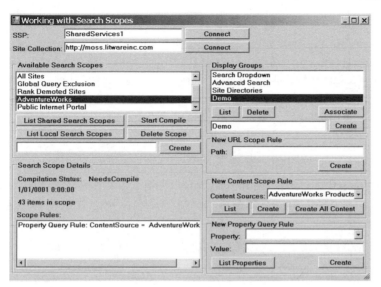

FIGURE 8-4 The sample application, illustrating the common actions to support administrative tasks when working with search scopes

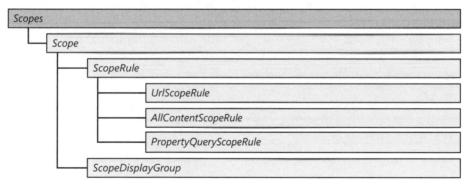

Just like the *Content* object described earlier, the *Scopes* constructor needs an instance of the *SearchContext* class as a parameter:

```
Scopes scopes = new Scopes(searchContext);
```

As you've learned earlier in this book, search scopes can be created at two levels: as a shared search sope at the level of the SSP and as a local search scope at the level of a site collection. The connection to the site collection is done by creating an instance of the *SPSite* class.

```
SPSite sitecollection = new SPSite(textBoxSiteCollectionURL.Text);
```

Don't forget to dispose of the *SPSite* instance when the work is done in your application:

```
if (this.sitecollection != null)
    sitecollection.Dispose();
```

Listing Search Scopes

A number of members are exposed in the *Scopes* class that you can use to retrieve one specific search scope or a list of scopes. The *GetScope* method returns one local scope if you supply it with the URL of the site collection and the name of the scope. The following line of code returns an instance of the *Scope* class that represents one of the search scopes available within the *moss.litwareinc.com* site collection:

```
Scope scope = this.scopes.GetScope(
        new Uri("http://moss.litwareinc.com"), "AdventureWorks Products");
```

One specific shared search scope can be retrieved by calling the *GetSharedScope* method. You just have to provide it with the name of the scope, and the method will return you the instance of the *Scope* class:

```
Scope scope = this.scopes.GetSharedScope("People");
```

To retrieve all of the search scopes, including the local, the shared, and the internal search scopes, you work with the *AllScopes* property of the *Scopes* instance. But maybe you want to be more specific. The *Scopes* instance exposes two methods to get a subset of all of the search scopes: *GetScopesForSite* and *GetSharedScopes*. The latter does not have any parameters; the former must be called with the URL of a site collection. Note that both methods do not return a *ScopeCollection* but instead return an *IEnumerable* that you use to list the *Scope* instances in, for example, a list box. The list of returned scopes does not include contextual scopes. Here is how you retrieve the list of shared search scopes:

```
listBoxSearchScopes.Items.Clear();
listBoxSearchScopes.DisplayMember = "Name";
foreach (Scope scope in this.scopes.GetSharedScopes())
{
  listBoxSearchScopes.Items.Add(scope);
}
```

And here is how you retrieve the list of the search scopes defined in a site collection:

```
listBoxSearchScopes.Items.Clear();
listBoxSearchScopes.DisplayMember = "Name";
foreach (Scope scope in
        this.scopes.GetScopesForSite(new Uri(textBoxSiteCollectionURL.Text)))
{
  listBoxSearchScopes.Items.Add(scope);
}
```

A final method that you can use to retrieve a list of search scopes is the *GetUnusedScopesForSite* method. We'll cover this method in the section "Listing Display Groups" later in this chapter, when we discuss how to work with the display groups in a site collection.

The *Scope* class has different members, each exposing some details for the search scope. One important property is *CompilationState*. It shows you the status of the compilation of the search scope. Possible values are *Compiled, Empty, Invalid, NeedsCompile, NeedsRecompile,* and *QueryExpanded.* Another interesting property is *Count,* which returns all of the items in the content index that are part of the search scope. The following code displays all of this, including the last compilation time in the sample application:

```
Scope scope = (Scope)listBoxSearchScopes.SelectedItem;
labelCompilationStatus.Text = scope.CompilationState.ToString();
labelLastCompilationTime.Text = scope.LastCompilationTime.ToString();
if (scope.CompilationState == ScopeCompilationState.Compiled)
    labelCount.Text = scope.Count.ToString() + " items in scope";
```

A search scope will not be useful without one or more rules that are associated with it. The *Scope* instance exposes a property named *Rules* that returns an instance of the *ScopeRuleCollection* that you can use to populate a user interface control. The *ScopeRule* class is the base class for three more specific classes: *PropertyQueryScopeRule, AllContentScopeRule,* and *UrlScopeRule.* A scope rule that uses a managed property for the definition of the condition is one of type *PropertyQueryScopeRule.* The *AllContentScopeRule* is, as its name implies, the one that flags all of the items in the content index matching the defined search scopes. An individual content source, a URL to an individual site or the location of a network share that has been crawled, is defined via a rule of type *UrlScopeRule.* The following code populates a list box with all of the rules that are associated with a selected search scope in the sample application:

```
listBoxScopeRules.Items.Clear();
foreach (ScopeRule rule in scope.Rules)
{
    switch (rule.RuleType)
    {
        case ScopeRuleType.AllContent:
            AllContentScopeRule arule = (AllContentScopeRule)rule;
            listBoxScopeRules.Items.Add("All Content Rule");
            break;
        case ScopeRuleType.PropertyQuery:
            PropertyQueryScopeRule prule = (PropertyQueryScopeRule)rule;
            listBoxScopeRules.Items.Add("Property Query Rule: " +
                    prule.Property.Name + " = " + prule.Value);
            break;
        case ScopeRuleType.Url:
            UrlScopeRule urule = (UrlScopeRule)rule;
            listBoxScopeRules.Items.Add("URL Rule: " + urule.MatchingString);
            break;
        default:
            break;
    }
}
```

The different types of rules will be covered in just a moment. The *ScopeRule* base class exposes the *RuleType* property, which is useful as a criterion to branch your code. The criterion for a rule of type *PropertyQueryScopeRule* is stored as values for the properties *Property* and *Value.*

Compiling Search Scopes

The compilation of the search scopes can be started explicitly in your code by calling the *StartCompilation* method that is part of the list of members exposed by the *Scopes* class. It is not a bad idea to first verify whether there are actually search scopes that need compilation. The *ScopesNeedingCompilation* property returns the number of scopes that require an update:

```
if (scopes.ScopesNeedingCompilation > 0)
{
    scopes.StartCompilation();
    MessageBox.Show("Compilation is started!");
}
else
{
    MessageBox.Show("No search scopes need to be updated");
}
```

Two properties of the *Scopes* class, *AverageCompilationDuration* and *CompilationPercentComplete*, can give you information about the duration of the compilation and the percentage of the compilation that is completed.

Deleting Search Scopes

Both a local and a shared search scope can be deleted by calling the *Delete* method at the level of the individual *Scope* instance:

```
Scope scope = (Scope)listBoxSearchScopes.SelectedItem;
scope.Delete();
```

Creating Search Scopes

New search scopes are created with a call to the *Create* method, which is exposed by the *ScopeCollection*. This collection itself is exposed with the *AllScopes* property of the *Scopes* class. The *Create* method requires values for six parameters. The first parameter is the name of the new search scope. The second parameter can be used for a description. The third parameter is used to differentiate between a local and a shared search scope. If you provide *null* as the value for the URL of the owning site, you'll create a shared search scope. A local search scope is created when you set the URL of an existing site collection as the value for this parameter. The fourth parameter is a flag for the display of the search scope in the administration user interface. Set this flag to *false* if you want to create a hidden search scope. The fifth parameter is the alternate results page URL. The sixth parameter is the type of compilation that you want to associate with the search scope. Two options are possible here: *AlwaysCompile* and *ConditionalCompile*. The first option configures the search scope to have it always compiled no matter how many scope rules you have attached to it. The

ConditionalCompile option configures the scope for a compilation only if more than 24 scope rules are defined for it. The following code creates a new shared search scope:

```
Scope newSharedScope = scopes.AllScopes.Create
        (textBoxScopeName.Text, string.Empty, null, true,
          "results.aspx", ScopeCompilationType.AlwaysCompile);
```

The next snippet of code creates a local search scope for one of the existing site collections:

```
Scope newLocalScope = scopes.AllScopes.Create
        (textBoxScopeName.Text, string.Empty,new Uri("http://moss.litwareinc.com")
        , true,"results.aspx", ScopeCompilationType.AlwaysCompile);
```

Creating Scope Rules

Search scopes that have no defined scope rules are useless. As mentioned earlier, different types of rules are possible. To start, let's review the code needed to create a rule that specifies that content from a specific URL is to be included in the search scope:

```
Scope scope = (Scope)listBoxSearchScopes.SelectedItem;
if (scope != null)
{
    UrlScopeRule rule = scope.Rules.CreateUrlRule
        (ScopeRuleFilterBehavior.Include, UrlScopeRuleType.HostName,
          textBoxRulePath.Text);
    scope.Update();
    MessageBox.Show("URL Rule Created!");
}
```

Rules are created with one of the methods exposed with the *ScopeRuleCollection* type. The collection is returned with the *Rules* property of the *Scope* instance. *CreateUrlRule* creates a scope rule based on the display URL of the content item. A number of parameters are defined for it. The first parameter is the *filterBehavior* parameter, which must be set to *Exclude*, *Include*, or *Require*. All three are made available through the *ScopeRuleFilterBehavior* enumeration. The second parameter is the type of the path that is given as a value for the third parameter. Again, three values are possible here, all defined within the *UrlScopeRuleType* enumeration: *Domain*, *Folder*, or *HostName*. The latter is used in the sample because we are targeting content that is located in a Web site. Use the *Folder* type if you are targeting a network path, and use *Domain* for the name of, for example, a server.

The following code creates a rule that associates the search scope with one of the available content sources. The type of this rule is *PropertyQueryScope*. The rule stores a criterion specifying that a managed property named *ContentSource* is matched with the name of a content source. The code to work with managed properties is reviewed in full in the next section. In short, managed properties are accessed through the *Schema* object that is also part of the *Microsoft.Office.Server.Search.Administration* namespace. In the sample application, you select first a search scope and then a content source and then execute this code:

```
Scope scope = (Scope)listBoxSearchScopes.SelectedItem;
ContentSource contentsource = (ContentSource)comboBoxContentSources.SelectedItem;
if ((scope != null) && (contentsource != null))
{
    Schema schema = new Schema(searchContext);
    PropertyQueryScopeRule rule = scope.Rules.CreatePropertyQueryRule
     (ScopeRuleFilterBehavior.Include, schema.AllManagedProperties["ContentSource"] ,
      contentsource.Name);
    scope.Update();
}
```

The *PropertyQueryScopeRule* instance is returned when executing the *CreatePropertyQueryRule* method defined for the *ScopeRuleCollection* type. After you provide a value for the filter behavior, you provide the method with an instance of the class *ManagedProperty*. That instance is the one with the name *ContentSource*, retrieved from the list of managed properties with the *AllManagedProperties* property exposed by the *Schema* class. The last parameter receives the name of the content source. Figure 8-5 displays an example of these types of rules defined for one of the search scopes in the SSP administration site.

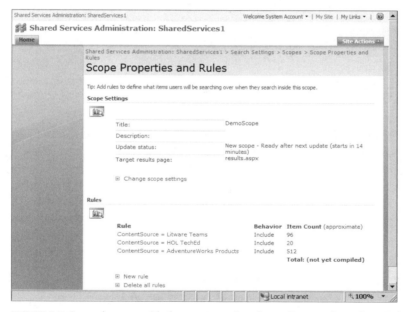

FIGURE 8-5 A search scope with three scope rules of type *PropertyQueryScopeRule*, each used to connect an existing content source as a filtering criterion

A rule that will include the content crawled by all of the available content sources is the easiest one to create. The instance of the *AllContentScopeRule* class is created by calling the *CreateAllContentRule* method exposed by the *ScopeRuleCollection* class, as shown here. No parameter values are required.

```
Scope scope = (Scope)listBoxSearchScopes.SelectedItem;
if (scope != null)
{
    AllContentScopeRule rule = scope.Rules.CreateAllContentRule();
    scope.Update();
}
```

The last block of sample code that is related to scope rules illustrates how to associate a rule of type *PropertyQueryScopeRule*. Managed properties that can be used to enable scoping are retrieved again using the *Schema* class (discussed in more detail in the section "Working with Managed Properties" later in this chapter). Notice the check on the value of the *EnabledForScoping* property. Only a few managed properties out of the complete list are candidates for use in a scope rule.

```
Schema schema = new Schema(searchContext);
comboBoxProps.Items.Clear();
comboBoxProps.DisplayMember = "Name";
foreach (ManagedProperty prop in schema.AllManagedProperties)
{
    if (prop.EnabledForScoping)
        comboBoxProps.Items.Add(prop);
}
```

The *ManagedProperty* instance, along with the value you want to match it with, are the values for parameters for the *CreatePropertyQueryRule* method:

```
Scope scope = (Scope)listBoxSearchScopes.SelectedItem;
ManagedProperty prop = (ManagedProperty)comboBoxProps.SelectedItem;
if ((scope != null) && (prop != null))
{
    PropertyQueryScopeRule rule = scope.Rules.CreatePropertyQueryRule
        (ScopeRuleFilterBehavior.Include, prop, textBoxPropValue.Text);
    scope.Update();
}
```

Listing Display Groups

Search scopes are not immediately visualized in the end-user search experience. The Scope Picker controls are connected to a display group that lists all of the local and shared search groups that can be shown in the drop-down list that they render in the browser. A display group is represented by the *ScopeDisplayGroup* class, also available in the *Microsoft.Office. Server.Search.Administration* namespace. Display groups can be created within the Search Administration site of the SSP or locally for one of the site collections that are hosted on IIS Web applications that are bound to the SSP. All of these display groups can be retrieved with the *AllDisplayGroups* property that is exposed for the *Scopes* class:

```
listDisplayGroups.Items.Clear();
listDisplayGroups.DisplayMember = "Name";
foreach (ScopeDisplayGroup displaygroup in scopes.AllDisplayGroups)
{
```

```
        listDisplayGroups.Items.Add(displaygroup);
}
```

You can be more specific by making use of the *GetDisplayGroupsForSite* method or the *GetDisplayGroup* method. Both methods are also exposed by the *Scopes* class. Give the first method the URL for the site collection, and it will return an *IEnumerable* that you can use to show only the display groups that are locally defined for that site collection. The second method returns one instance of the class *ScopeDisplayGroup*. In addition to the URL of the site collection, you also need to provide the method with the name of the display group. Here is the code to loop over all of the display groups for the *moss.litwareinc.com* site collection:

```
listDisplayGroups.Items.Clear();
listDisplayGroups.DisplayMember = "Name";
foreach (ScopeDisplayGroup displaygroup in
        scopes.GetDisplayGroupsForSite(new Uri(textBoxSiteCollectionURL.Text)))
{
    listDisplayGroups.Items.Add(displaygroup);
}
```

Managing Display Groups

A new display group is created by calling the *Create* method of the *ScopeDisplayGroupCollection* type. The collection is exposed via the *AllDisplayGroups* property at the level of the *Scopes* class. You pass the name of the new display group and the description as the values for the first two parameters. The third parameter is the URL of the site collection. Use a Boolean as the value of the last parameter to indicate whether you want to have the display group visualized in the administration user interface:

```
ScopeDisplayGroup newgroup = scopes.AllDisplayGroups.Create
        (textBoxDisplayGroupName.Text, string.Empty,
         new Uri(textBoxSiteCollectionURL.Text), true);
```

A display group is deleted with a simple call to the *Delete* method of the *ScopeDisplayGroup* instance:

```
ScopeDisplayGroup group = (ScopeDisplayGroup)listDisplayGroups.SelectedItem;
if (group != null)
{
    group.Delete();
}
```

It is simple to make one of the available search scopes a member of a display group. You call the *Add* method exposed for the *ScopeDisplayGroup* instance and pass it a reference to the instance of the *Scope* class that represents the search scope, as shown here:

```
Scope scope = (Scope)listBoxSearchScopes.SelectedItem;
ScopeDisplayGroup group = (ScopeDisplayGroup)listDisplayGroups.SelectedItem;
if ((scope != null) && (group != null))
```

```
{
    group.Add(scope);
    group.Update();
}
```

Working with Managed Properties

During the crawl of a SharePoint content source or a BDC content source, values for properties are collected that can be exposed by the administrator as managed properties. These operations can be performed programmatically. Your entry point this time is the *Schema* object that is created with a *SearchContext* instance as the parameter:

```
Schema schema = new Schema(searchContext);
```

The *Schema* object exposes members and gives us access to other classes related to the management of metadata, as shown here:

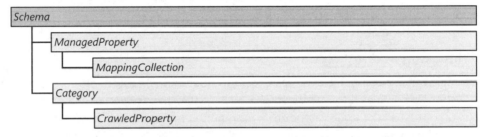

The metadata collected by the crawler can be mapped to managed properties, which can become part of the conditions in the scope rules for custom search scopes. Chapter 3, "Customizing the Search User Interface," covered the use of managed properties as additional search criteria in the Advanced Search Web Part. They can also be displayed in the search results if the XSL that is used to transform the search results in the HTML rendered by the browser is modified. We'll take a closer look at how you can list the many properties that the crawler collects in the property store in the search database and then go through the steps of creating and exposing managed properties programmatically.

Figure 8-6 shows the Windows-based form in the sample application that will be used to illustrate the work that can be done with managed properties.

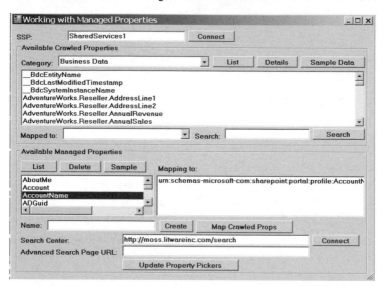

FIGURE 8-6 Working with managed properties in the sample application

Listing Crawled Properties

In a real-world scenario, the crawler will collect thousands of custom properties that are part of the indexed content. To make all of this manageable, the properties are grouped together in categories. Each of these categories is represented in the *Microsoft.Office.Server.Search. Administration* namespace as an instance of the *Category* class. The *Schema* class exposes the *AllCategories* property, which returns a *CategoryCollection* instance that can be used to populate one of the controls in the user interface of your application:

```
if (schema != null)
{
    comboBoxCategories.Items.Clear();
    comboBoxCategories.DisplayMember = "Name";
    foreach (Category cat in schema.AllCategories)
    {
        comboBoxCategories.Items.Add(cat);
    }
}
```

The members of a category can be retrieved with the *GetAllCrawledProperties* method that is exposed by a *Category* instance, as shown here. This method returns an *IEnumerable* so that you can loop over all of the individual *CrawledProperty* instances and display them in the user interface.

```
Category cat = (Category)comboBoxCategories.SelectedItem;
if ((schema != null) && (cat != null))
{
    listBoxCrawledProps.Items.Clear();
    listBoxCrawledProps.DisplayMember = "Name";
```

```
foreach (CrawledProperty prop in cat.GetAllCrawledProperties())
{
    listBoxCrawledProps.Items.Add(prop);
}
}
```

The *Category* class also exposes other interesting members. The *GetCrawledProperty* method can be used to retrieve a single *CrawledProperty* instance. Crawled properties are identified by a globally unique identifier (GUID), and you must provide this GUID as the value for the first parameter of the method. You do not retrieve an individual crawled property based on the name. In addition to the GUID value, you also provide the name of the category and the value for the *variantType* parameter. All of this information can be extracted from the individual *CrawledProperty* instance using the following code:

```
CrawledProperty prop = (CrawledProperty)listBoxCrawledProps.SelectedItem;
StringBuilder sb = new StringBuilder();
sb.AppendLine("CRAWLED PROPERTY DETAILS");
sb.AppendLine("Name: " + prop.Name);
sb.AppendLine("GUID: " + prop.Propset.ToString());
sb.AppendLine("Variant Type: " + prop.VariantType.ToString());
MessageBox.Show(sb.ToString());
```

Another way to retrieve crawled properties with the *Category* instance is the call to the *GetUnmappedCrawledProperties* method. This method again returns an enumerator, but this time making only the category's unmapped crawled properties available. The *CrawledProperty* instance stores information about whether it is mapped in the *IsMappedToContents* property.

And because there can be thousands of crawled properties, a method named *QueryCrawledProperties* will be quite useful in your applications. The following code shows how to work with this method:

```
Category cat = (Category)comboBoxCategories.SelectedItem;
CrawledProperty prop = (CrawledProperty)listBoxCrawledProps.Items[0];
if ((schema != null) && (cat != null) && (prop != null))
{
    listBoxCrawledProps.Items.Clear();
    listBoxCrawledProps.DisplayMember = "Name";
    foreach (CrawledProperty cprop in cat.QueryCrawledProperties
                    (textBoxQuery.Text, 100, prop.Propset, prop.Name, true))
    {
        listBoxCrawledProps.Items.Add(cprop);
    }
}
```

The text for the query does not have to contain any wildcards. These will be added automatically as a prefix and a suffix to the text when you execute the method. The second parameter is used to limit the number of results that should be returned. The method also needs the GUID and the name of a crawled property in the list. It will search either forward or backward starting from that property.

The *CrawledProperty* class exposes a method named *GetMappedManagedProperties* that is useful if you want to verify which managed properties are already mapped to it:

```
CrawledProperty prop = (CrawledProperty)listBoxCrawledProps.SelectedItem;
if (prop != null)
{
    comboBoxCrawlManProps.Items.Clear();
    comboBoxCrawlManProps.DisplayMember = Name";
    if (prop.IsMappedToContents)
    {
        foreach (ManagedProperty mprop in prop.GetMappedManagedProperties())
        {
            comboBoxCrawlManProps.Items.Add(mprop);
        }
    }
    else
    {
        MessageBox.Show("Property is not mapped!");
    }
}
```

And to conclude, there is also a method named *GetSamples* that is exposed by the *CrawledProperty* instance. You pass a number of samples to return, and you'll get an indication of what the actual data is that has been crawled by the indexer. The following code builds a string with 10 lines, each containing a value of a specific crawled property:

```
CrawledProperty prop = (CrawledProperty)listBoxCrawledProps.SelectedItem;
if (prop != null)
{
    StringBuilder sb = new StringBuilder();
    foreach (string sample in prop.GetSamples(10))
    {
        sb.AppendLine(sample);
    }
    MessageBox.Show(sb.ToString());
}
```

Listing Managed Properties

The creation and the configuration of an SSP results in the creation of a large number of managed properties that are directly available to enhance the end-user search experience. The collection of *ManagedProperty* objects can be retrieved via the *AllManagedProperties* property that is exposed by the *Schema* class:

```
if (schema != null)
{
    listBoxManagedProps.Items.Clear();
    listBoxManagedProps.DisplayMember = "Name";
    foreach (ManagedProperty prop in schema.AllManagedProperties)
    {
        listBoxManagedProps.Items.Add(prop);
    }
}
```

Part of the details of a managed property is the list of crawled properties that are mapped to it. The list is returned when you call the *GetMappedCrawledProperties* method. There is one parameter that receives the number of *CrawledProperty* objects to return:

```
ManagedProperty prop = (ManagedProperty)listBoxManagedProps.SelectedItem;
if (prop != null)
{
    listBoxManToCrawl.Items.Clear();
    listBoxManToCrawl.DisplayMember = "Name";
    foreach (CrawledProperty cprop in prop.GetMappedCrawledProperties(10))
    {
        listBoxManToCrawl.Items.Add(cprop);
    }
}
```

Similar to the *CrawledProperty* class, the *ManagedProperty* class exposes a method named *GetSamples* that returns a collection of sample values for the managed property. There is also a *GetDocumentsFound* method that can be useful if there is a need for retrieving the number of documents that will be found when the managed property is used.

The *ManagedProperty* class exposes a number of important properties that control how and where the managed property can be used. First is the *EnabledForScoping* property, which contains a Boolean indicating whether the property can be used in search scopes. A second property is *FullTextQueriable*, which is used to control whether the property can be used in Enterprise Search SQL queries. In the section "Building Search Queries" later in this chapter, you'll learn about the syntax that is used for constructing this type of query. One other property that is worth mentioning is the *Weight* property. This is used to configure the weight setting for the managed property, and its value plays an important role in the algorithm that is used to calculate the relevance ranking. In a moment, we'll cover some of these configurations in more detail.

Managing a Managed Property

You call the *Create* method exposed by the *ManagedPropertyCollection* class to add a new managed property. The collection is returned with the *AllManagedProperties* property of the *Schema* class. The first parameter receives the name of the managed property. No spaces are allowed in the name of the property. The second parameter is a value of the *ManagedDataType* enumeration and specifies the data type for the managed property. The following code creates a managed property of type *ManagedDataType.Text*:

```
try
{
    schema.AllManagedProperties.Create
        (textBoxManagedPropName.Text, ManagedDataType.Text);
    MessageBox.Show("New managed property created!");
}
catch (Exception ex)
{
    MessageBox.Show(ex.ToString());
}
```

The *ManagedProperty* class has a *Delete* method in case you have to remove a managed property from the collection.

An important operation that is supported at the level of the *ManagedProperty* class is the mapping of one or more crawled properties. The mapping is accomplished by adding a new *Mapping* object containing the details of an individual crawled property to the *MappingCollection* instance that is internally stored within the *ManagedProperty* instance. The *MappingCollection* instance is retrieved via the *GetMappings* method of the *ManagedProperty* instance. This method returns *null* if no mappings are stored yet. If this is the case, you'll need to create an instance of the *MappingCollection* class.

The constructor of the *Mapping* class requires you to pass the details of the crawled property. You pass the GUID, the name, the variant type, and the ID of the managed property itself. Once you have a new or an updated *MappingCollection* instance, you'll pass it to the *ManagedProperty* instance by calling the *SetMappings* method:

```
ManagedProperty prop = (ManagedProperty)listBoxManagedProps.SelectedItem;
if (prop != null)
{
    try
    {
        MappingCollection mappings = null;
        if (prop.GetMappings() != null)
            mappings = prop.GetMappings();
        else
            mappings = new MappingCollection();
        foreach (CrawledProperty cprop in listBoxCrawledProps.SelectedItems)
        {
            mappings.Add(
                new Mapping(cprop.Propset, cprop.Name, cprop.VariantType, prop.PID));
        }
        prop.SetMappings(mappings);
        MessageBox.Show("Selected crawled properties are mapped to managed property!");
    }
    catch (Exception ex)
    {
        MessageBox.Show(ex.ToString());
    }
}
```

Now that you have learned how to create managed properties and map them to one or more crawled properties, it's time to have a look at how you can expose these properties in the Property Picker that is part of the Advanced Search Box Web Part available on the Advanced Search page in the Search Center. To start, you have to get a reference to the page itself. The classes used in the following code are all part of *Microsoft.SharePoint.dll*. *SPSite* represents the site collection, *SPWeb* represents one site, and *SPFile* represents a page. You get a reference to the Advanced Search page by passing the URL of the page to the *GetFile* method that is exposed by the *SPWeb* instance.

```
SPSite sitecollection = new SPSite(textBoxSiteCollectionURL.Text);
SPWeb searchcenter = sitecollection.OpenWeb();
SPFile advsearchpage = searchcenter.GetFile(textBoxAdvSearchPageURL.Text);
```

There is by default one Web Part on the page. A reference to this Web Part of type *Microsoft.Office.Server.Search.WebControls.AdvancedSearchBox* can be retrieved by using *Microsoft.SharePoint.WebPartPages.SPLimitedWebPartManager*. The *SPFile* instance has a method named *GetLimitedWebPartManager* that you call to get a reference of *SPLimitedWebPartManager*:

```
SPLimitedWebPartManager wpmgr =
        advsearchpage.GetLimitedWebPartManager(PersonalizationScope.Shared);
AdvancedSearchBox wp = (AdvancedSearchBox)wpmgr.WebParts[0];
```

Chapter 3 covered all of the properties of each of the different Search Web Parts that are available in the Search Center to deliver the end-user search experience. The Advanced Search Box Web Part exposes a property named *Properties* that contains an XML string defining all of the data that is displayed by the Language Picker, the Results Type Picker, and the Property Picker, as shown here. This XML can be loaded in a *System.Xml.XMLDocument* instance in order to modify it easily.

```
XmlDocument doc = new XmlDocument();
doc.LoadXml(wp.Properties);
```

The following code creates the needed XML elements to make the managed property available in the Property Pickers. First a new *PropertyDef* element is created with the required attributes. In the second part of the code, a new *PropertyRef* element is added for each of the *ResultType* nodes. This will make the managed property available no matter which result type option is selected on the Advanced Search page.

```
XmlNode propdefNode = doc.SelectSingleNode("/root/PropertyDefs");
XmlElement newPropDefEl = doc.CreateElement("PropertyDef");
XmlAttribute att1 = doc.CreateAttribute("Name");
att1.Value = prop.Name;
newPropDefEl.Attributes.Append(att1);
XmlAttribute att2 = doc.CreateAttribute("DataType");
att2.Value = prop.ManagedType.ToString();
newPropDefEl.Attributes.Append(att2);
XmlAttribute att3 = doc.CreateAttribute("DisplayName");
att3.Value = prop.Name;
newPropDefEl.Attributes.Append(att3);
propdefNode.AppendChild(newPropDefEl);
XmlNodeList resultTypeNodes = doc.SelectNodes("//ResultType");
foreach (XmlNode node in resultTypeNodes)
{
    XmlElement newPropRefEl = doc.CreateElement("PropertyRef");
    XmlAttribute att = doc.CreateAttribute("Name");
    att.Value = prop.Name;
    newPropRefEl.Attributes.Append(att);
    node.AppendChild(newPropRefEl);
}
```

The final lines update the value of the *Properties* property for the Web Part and save the changes using the *SaveChanges* method of the *SPLimitedWebPartManager* instance:

```
wp.Properties = doc.OuterXml;
wpmgr.SaveChanges(wp);
```

Improving Relevance

Search results are by default ranked by relevance by a complex algorithm. Many parameters play a role in the final outcome of the calculation of the ranking of the search results. The search administration object model includes a number of classes that can be used by developers to modify some of these relevance parameters.

The base class to work with is the *Ranking* class that is part of the *Microsoft.Office.Server. Search.Administration* namespace. You create an instance of the entry class in a similar way as for the previous entry classes:

```
Ranking ranking = new Ranking(searchContext);
```

Figure 8-7 shows the Windows-based form that is part of the sample application illustrating some of the developer options for influencing the relevance ranking.

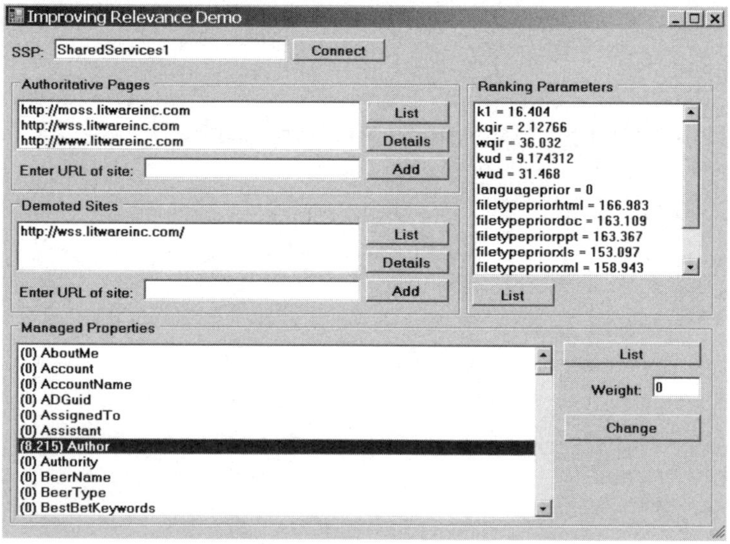

FIGURE 8-7 Programmatically configuring the ranking parameters

Adding Authoritative Pages

Authoritative pages have a lot of weight in the relevance ranking calculation. They are typically identified by the administrators on the search administration pages. Chapter 5,

"Search Administration," covers all the details on this subject. The *Ranking* class exposes the *AuthorityPages* property, which returns an *AuthorityPageCollection* instance. Each page is represented by an *AuthorityPage* object in that collection:

```
if (ranking != null)
{
    listBoxPages.Items.Clear();
    listBoxPages.DisplayMember = "Url";
    foreach (AuthorityPage page in ranking.AuthorityPages)
    {
        listBoxPages.Items.Add(page);
    }
}
```

An *AuthorityPage* instance has three properties that store the important data for the page: *Url*, *Status*, and *Level*. The value of the *Status* property is an *AuthorityPageStatus* enumeration with the following options: *CrawledSuccesfully*, *CrawledWithErrors*, *NotCrawled*, and *StatusNotInitialized*. The value of the *Level* property stores the authority level number for the page, as shown here. The most-authoritative pages have a level set to 0.

```
AuthorityPage page = (AuthorityPage)listBoxPages.SelectedItem;
StringBuilder sb = new StringBuilder();
if (page != null)
{
    sb.AppendLine("Status: " + page.Status);
    sb.AppendLine("Level: " + page.Level);
}
MessageBox.Show(sb.ToString());
```

You can add a new entry for *AuthorityPages* quite easily with a call to the *Create* method of the *AuthorityPageCollection*. The URL of the page and the value for the initial authority level are passed as arguments to the method:

```
AuthorityPage newpage = ranking.AuthorityPages.Create(new Uri(textBoxSiteURL.Text), 1);
```

Adding Demoted Sites

Another parameter for the relevance ranking algorithm that is exposed in the search administration object model is the list of demoted sites. Demoted sites contain content that is less relevant than other content for any query. The list of demoted sites is returned by the *DemotedSites* property of the *Ranking* class as a *DemotedSiteCollection*:

```
if (ranking != null)
{
    listBoxDemotedSites.Items.Clear();
    listBoxDemotedSites.DisplayMember = "Url";
    foreach (DemotedSite demotedSite in ranking.DemotedSites)
    {
        listBoxDemotedSites.Items.Add(demotedSite);
    }
}
```

The *DemotedSite* class is a simple class exposing only a *Url* property and a *CrawledDocumentCount* property. The latter returns the number of crawled documents for the site. A site is marked as a demoted site by calling the *Create* method of the *DemotedSiteCollection* and passing it the URL of the site:

```
DemotedSite demotedSite =
    ranking.DemotedSites.Create(new Uri(textBoxURLDemotedSite.Text));
```

Ranking Parameters

The collection of all of the ranking parameters is returned by the *RankingParameters* property of the *Ranking* class. The *RankParamCollection* contains a *RankParameter* instance for each of the parameters. A *RankParameter* instance has two properties: *Name* and *Value*. The parameters are listed in Table 8-2.

TABLE 8-2 Ranking Parameters

Parameter	Description
k1	Saturation constant for term frequency
Kqir	Saturation constant for click distance
wqir	Weight of click distance for calculating relevance
Kud	Saturation constant for URL depth
wud	Weight of URL depth for calculating relevance
languageprior	Weight for ranking applied to content in a language that does not match the language of the user
filetypepriorhtml	Weight of HTML content type for calculating relevance
filetypepriordoc	Weight of Microsoft Office Word content type for calculating relevance
filetypepriorppt	Weight of Microsoft Office PowerPoint content type for calculating relevance
filetypepriorxls	Weight of Microsoft Office Excel content type for calculating relevance
filetypepriorxml	Weight of XML content type for calculating relevance
filetypepriortxt	Weight of plain-text content type for calculating relevance
filetypepriorlistitems	Weight of list item content type for calculating relevance
filetypepriormessage	Weight of Microsoft Office Outlook e-mail message content type for calculating relevance

The following lines of code list all of the parameters and their values:

```
if (ranking != null)
{
    listBoxRankingParameters.Items.Clear();
```

```
    foreach (RankingParameter par in ranking.RankingParameters)
    {
        listBoxRankingParameters.Items.Add(par.Name + " = " + par.Value);
    }
}
```

You can update the value of a parameter if needed. It is not possible, however, to add, delete, or rename parameters.

Changing the Property Weight

Managed properties also play a role within the ranking of the results. Each managed property has a weight that can be changed programmatically to influence the relevance ranking.

> **Important** Be careful when you decide to make changes to the property weights because these weights can have an adverse effect on the overall relevance of the system.

The *ManagedProperty* class exposes the *Weight* property. In the list of managed properties that are available by default, only the *Author* managed property has a weight of more than 0.

Working with Keywords, Definitions, and Best Bets

Chapter 5 covered the administration tasks that are involved with the keywords, definitions, and best bets. The search administration object model also provides support for these operations. Figure 8-8 shows the Windows-based form from the sample application that illustrates some of the operations that can be done using keywords, definitions, and best bets.

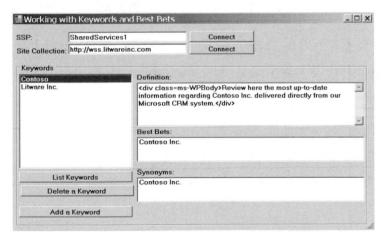

FIGURE 8-8 Working with keywords and best bets

Your entry class for working with the keywords, definitions, and best bets is the *Keywords* class. An instance is created by providing this class with the reference to the *SearchContext* instance and the URL of the site collection that you want to work with.

```
Keywords keywords = new Keywords(searchContext, new Uri(textBoxSiteCollectionURL.Text));
```

All of the keywords defined at the level of the site collection can be retrieved using the *AllKeywords* property of the *Keywords* class. The property returns a *KeywordCollection* with each of the keywords represented with an instance of the *Keyword* class:

```
listBoxKeywords.Items.Clear();
listBoxKeywords.DisplayMember = "Term";
foreach (Keyword keyword in keywords.AllKeywords)
{
    listBoxKeywords.Items.Add(keyword);
}
```

The *Keywords* class also exposes the *GetFilteredKeywords* method, which returns all keywords that match the specified filter and value for the site. Two other methods, *GetAllBestBets* and *GetFilterBestBets*, return *BestBetCollection* instances.

A *Keyword* instance has a property *Term* that stores the name of the keyword. Synonyms are stored in the *SynonymCollection*, available through the *Synonyms* property of the *Keyword* instance. The best bets that are associated with the keyword are stored in the *BestBetCollection* that is available through the *BestBets* property of the *Keyword* class. Other properties of interest for the *Keyword* class are *Definition*, *StartDate*, *EndDate*, and *ReviewDate*. Here is the code that renders some of the details of a selected keyword in the sample application:

```
Keyword keyword = (Keyword)listBoxKeywords.SelectedItem;
if (keyword != null)
{
    textBoxDefinition.Text = keyword.Definition;
    listBoxBestBets.Items.Clear();
    listBoxBestBets.DisplayMember = "Title";
    foreach (BestBet bestbet in keyword.BestBets)
    {
        listBoxBestBets.Items.Add(bestbet);
    }
    listBoxSynonyms.Items.Clear();
    listBoxSynonyms.DisplayMember = "Term";
    foreach (Synonym synonym in keyword.Synonyms)
    {
        listBoxSynonyms.Items.Add(synonym);
    }
}
```

You add a new keyword to the site collection by calling the *Create* method of the *KeywordCollection* class, as shown in the following code. The string for the term and the value for the publishing start date are delivered as parameters in the constructor. All of the other details, such as the string for the definition, the inclusion of synonyms, and the association with best bets, are performed afterwards, with the created *Keyword* instance. Don't forget to call the *Update* method of the *Keyword* instance to push all of your work to the content database.

```
Keywords keywords = new Keywords(searchContext, new Uri(textBoxSiteCollectionURL.Text));
Keyword keyword = keywords.AllKeywords.Create("Litware Inc.", DateTime.Today);
keyword.Definition = "Litware is a company specialized in ....";
BestBet bestbet = keyword.BestBets.Create("Litware Portal",
    "The internal portal of our company.", new Uri("http://moss.litwareinc.com"));
Synonym syn = keyword.Synonyms.Create("Litware");
keyword.Update();
MessageBox.Show("New Litware Keyword and Best Bet Created!");
```

More Information   We've now covered a large part, but not all, of the search administration object model. The Office SharePoint Server Software Development Kit (SDK) is the best place to complement this part of the chapter if more information is needed for your development work.

Building Search Queries

A search query can be expressed by building a simple string consisting of keywords or by making use of the powerful but more complex Enterprise Search SQL query language that extends the standard SQL-92 and SQL-99 database query syntax and is tuned for compiling full-text search queries.

Keyword Syntax

The keyword syntax is a new query syntax introduced in Office SharePoint Server 2007 that greatly reduces the complexity of formulating a search query. Of course, reducing complexity in the syntax also has as a catch: search queries using the keyword syntax do not fully leverage the power of the search engine. They are passed directly to the Enterprise Search service for execution. However, as this is often not required, keyword syntax is quickly becoming a popular query language that targets not only the end user but also the developer building custom search experiences for the end user. It is also a query language that is consistently used for executing Microsoft Office system, Windows, and Microsoft Live searches.

The core of this query syntax is, of course, the keywords. In addition to keywords, there is also the option to include property filters in the query. There are three possible options when using keywords:

- **A word**   The query consists of the keyword expressed as a word, including one or more characters without spaces or punctuation.

- **A phrase**   Multiple keywords can be combined into a phrase separated by spaces, but the words must be enclosed in quotation marks.

- **A prefix**   The query consists of a prefix, or a part of a word taken from the beginning of the word.

There is support for required and excluded terms. To include a required term, you simply use a plus sign (+) in front of the keyword. To exclude a term, you use a minus sign (-) in front of the keyword. Here is an example of a query trying to find everything that contains the keyword *business* but excluding the results where *business* is used in the phrase *Business Data Catalog*:

```
business -"Business Data Catalog"
```

Property filters can be included in the search query to narrow the focus of the keyword search based on the inclusion or exclusion of managed properties, scopes, and collapsed results. *Collapsed results* are used to display or hide the duplicates in the search results. Here is an example of how to search for all of the documents created by Mike Fitzmaurice that contain the keyword *business*:

```
business +author:fitzmaurice +isDocument:1
```

Enterprise Search SQL Query Syntax

The Enterprise Search SQL query syntax allows for more complex search queries and is therefore also used in more advanced search solutions. A query formulated in the SQL syntax is a string that must adhere to the following structure:

```
SELECT <columns>
FROM <content source>
WHERE <conditions>
ORDER BY <columns>
```

A sample project named SQLSearchQueriesSample is available in the download package. Figure 8-9 displays the simple Windows-based application, where you can enter a query or select one of the predefined samples and then review the matching search results. In the section "The Query Object Model" later in this chapter, we'll have a detailed look at the code that makes it all possible.

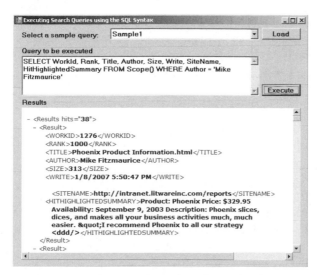

FIGURE 8-9 Executing search queries written using the SQL syntax

For now, let's concentrate on the possible constructions and some of the best practices that you should be aware of.

The *SELECT* Statement

Within the *SELECT* part, you specify the columns that you want to include in the search results. The *SELECT* clause syntax is as follows:

```
<column> [ {, <column>} … ]
```

You must include at least one column of information to retrieve. Multiple columns are separated with commas.

> **Warning** The use of the SQL asterisk (*) is not permitted, nor is the use of column aliasing and limiting of the column length. Readers familiar with the traditional SQL syntax are warned that important restrictions are applied to the use of the SQL syntax for search queries executed by Office SharePoint Server 2007. The following page in the SDK contains the full set of restrictions: *http://msdn2.microsoft.com/en-us/library/ms494614.aspx*.

The *FROM* Clause

The *FROM* part can contain only the *SCOPE* statement in Office SharePoint Server 2007. This is a major change from Office SharePoint Portal Server 2003, where you specified the scope name in the *FROM* class. Remember that from now on, you specify the scope name in the *WHERE* clause, as follows:

```
SELECT title, author, rank FROM scope() WHERE "scope"='All Sites'
```

The scope name is case sensitive, and you must include double quotation marks around the scope, as demonstrated in the preceding sample. You are allowed to combine more than one scope in the query. The following construction, for example, is allowed and returns results from both the *All Sites* scope and the *AdventureWorks* scope:

```
SELECT title, author, rank
FROM scope()
WHERE "scope"='All Sites' AND "scope"='AdventureWorks'
```

The *WHERE* Clause

Using the scope as a possible condition in the *WHERE* part is not the only option. The *WHERE* part is also the place where you include the columns and the possible conditions that the columns have to match to. All types of predicates can be used, from the traditional and familiar ones ("=","!=","<",">") to specific ones such as *LIKE, DATEADD, NULL*, and the full-text predicates *FREETEXT* and *CONTAINS*.

Column Names

Columns can be used with their exact name or through column group aliases that are inserted using *WITH...AS* predicates. Aliases can be helpful to increase the readability of the query by, for example, shortening the names of the columns. Here is the syntax you need to follow to work with column aliasing:

```
… WHERE [ WITH(<columns>) AS #<alias_name>] [,WITH(<columns>) AS #<alias_name>]
```

An alias can represent one or more columns, and when they are referred to in a *WHERE* clause predicate, the condition is applied to each of the columns in the group. The logical values resulting from matching each column are combined using the *OR* logical operator.

Column aliases can be used only within the *WHERE* clause, and only the *FREETEXT* predicate supports their use. The *CONTAINS* predicate does not support column grouping and aliasing.

Two groups of predicates are available: non-full-text predicates and full-text predicates. Let's have a closer look at the elements that you can use in the query syntax for each of these.

Non-Full-Text Predicates

This group of predicates is useful if the query contains conditions that try to match values of columns without the need for special linguistic processing during the execution of the query. An example of this additional processing is the search for synonyms in a thesaurus file. There are five non-full-text search predicates.

The *LIKE* Predicate   The common *LIKE* predicate is used to perform a pattern-matching comparison on the specified column. You are probably familiar with the traditional SQL syntax for formulating queries that are executed against relational databases such as SQL Server 2005. The *LIKE* predicate can be used in a similar way in SharePoint search queries. The following query returns all of the Microsoft Office PowerPoint presentations (documents with file extension equal to *pptx*) that Pat Coleman has created, for the *All Sites* search scope:

```
SELECT WorkId, Rank, Title, Author, Size, Write, SiteName, HitHighlightedSummary
FROM Scope()
WHERE "scope"='All Sites' AND fileextension='pptx' AND Author LIKE 'Pat Coleman'
```

The pattern matching done using the *LIKE* predicate is supported only for columns that contain a single value, as in the *Author* column used in the example. Multivalued columns, like the *Skills* and *Responsibilities* columns that contain information stored in the user profiles, cannot be used.

Wildcards, however, are allowed for the *LIKE* predicate. The most common representation of the wildcard is the percent sign (%). You can use this wildcard to extend the string with zero or more of any characters, as in the following sample. Every author whose name includes the sequence of characters *ole*, no matter what precedes or follows the sequence, will be included in the search results.

```
SELECT WorkId, Rank, Title, Author, Size, Write, SiteName, HitHighlightedSummary
FROM Scope()
WHERE "scope"='All Sites' AND fileextension='pptx' AND Author LIKE '%ole%'
```

Another option for defining a wildcard is the underscore (_). Use it to match any single character. Perhaps you're not sure whether Coleman is spelled with a *C* or a *K*. The following query returns both spellings:

```
SELECT WorkId, Rank, Title, Author, Size, Write, SiteName, HitHighlightedSummary
FROM Scope()
WHERE "scope"='All Sites' AND fileextension='pptx' AND Author LIKE 'Pat _oleman'
```

You can be more restrictive regarding the range or set of characters that is used for the matching by using square brackets ([ ]) as the wildcard literal instead of the underscore. The characters that can be used during the matching operation shown here are restricted to *C, c, K,* or *k*:

```
SELECT WorkId, Rank, Title, Author, Size, Write, SiteName, HitHighlightedSummary
FROM Scope()
WHERE "scope"='All Sites' AND fileextension='pptx' AND Author LIKE 'Pat [CcKk]oleman'
```

One last wildcard produces opposite results. A caret (^) preceding the set of characters in square brackets restricts the matching to any single character that is not within the specified range or set. The following example gives us results that will not contain entries authored by Pat Koleman:

```
SELECT WorkId, Rank, Title, Author, Size, Write, SiteName, HitHighlightedSummary
FROM Scope()
WHERE "scope"='All Sites' AND fileextension='pptx' AND Author LIKE 'Pat [^K]oleman'
```

The Literal Value Comparison   You are probably familiar with the standard comparison operators for the matching of a single-value column to a literal value. Table 8-3 summarizes the supported operators.

TABLE 8-3 Comparison Operators

Operator	Description
=	Equal to
!= or <>	Not equal to
>	Greater than
>=	Greater than or equal to
<	Less than
<=	Less than or equal to

The DATEADD **Function**   This function is used when there is a need to perform time and date calculation during the execution of the query. The function is allowed only when the matching properties store the date and time in the *date* type. The following sample query returns all PowerPoint presentations with a creation date less than a year ago:

```
SELECT WorkId, Rank, Title, Author, Size, Write, SiteName, HitHighlightedSummary
FROM Scope()
WHERE "scope"='All Sites' AND fileextension='pptx'
    AND Write >= DATEADD (YEAR, -1, GETGMTDATE())
```

Three parameters are allowed when you call this function in the query. The first specifies what the unit is that will be used during the calculation. Options are *YEAR, QUARTER, MONTH, WEEK, DAY, HOUR, MINUTE,* and *SECOND*. Note that the values are not case sensitive and do not require any quotation marks enclosing them. The second parameter must be supplied with the offset value (the number of days, months, or years). Only negative values are allowed here. The third parameter is the timestamp from which to calculate the offset. No hard-coded literals are allowed here. Instead, you must use either the *GETGMTDATE* function, which returns you the current date and time in Greenwich Mean Time (GMT), or the result of another *DATEADD* function.

Multivalued (*ARRAY*) Comparisons   The predicates described earlier can be applied only on columns that store a single value. What about multivalued columns? The *ARRAY* predicate can be used if there is a need to include matching operations for these types of columns. The syntax to use is shown here:

```
ARRAY [<literal>,<literal>]
```

You compare an array of literal values against the values that are made available with the column. All literal values must be enclosed in square brackets, as illustrated in the following example, which, when executed, returns all persons who have at least one of the listed responsibilities:

```
SELECT WorkId, Rank, Title, Author, Size, Write, SiteName, HitHighlightedSummary,skills
FROM Scope()
WHERE "scope"='People' AND Responsibilities = SOME ARRAY['Sales', 'Procurement']
```

Figure 8-10 shows the result when this query is executed within the sample application. Mike Fitzmaurice is a match because one of his responsibilities is *Sales*.

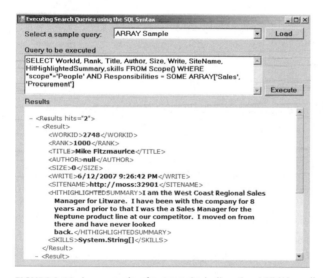

FIGURE 8-10 An example of a query including the *ARRAY* predicate matching a list of responsibilities against the multivalued Responsibilities column

The optional quantifier plays an important role in the final outcome of the query. If no quantifier is used, every element that is part of the value of the *Responsibilities* column is compared with the element in the same position in the literals contained in the *ARRAY* predicate. The comparison begins with the first element and progresses through the last element. If all elements on the left side are equivalent to the corresponding elements on the right side, you have a match.

If the query is formulated as follows using the *ALL* quantifier, every person must have all of the responsibilities listed within the square brackets:

```
SELECT WorkId, Rank, Title, Author, Size, Write, SiteName, HitHighlightedSummary,skills
FROM Scope()
WHERE "scope"='People' AND Responsibilities = ALL ARRAY['Sales', 'Procurement']
```

The *SOME* or *ANY* quantifier is the least restrictive. If a person has one of the responsibilities that are enclosed in square brackets, a match occurs.

The *NULL* Predicate   The last non-full-text predicate is the *NULL* predicate. You can use this predicate to test whether a column has a value. The following query returns all persons that do not have any responsibility registered as part of their user profile:

```
SELECT WorkId, Rank, Title, Author, Size, Write, SiteName, HitHighlightedSummary,skills
FROM Scope()
WHERE "scope"='People' AND Responsibilities IS NULL
```

Full-Text Predicates

Two predicates support full-text searching on columns that contain text: *CONTAINS* and *FREETEXT*. The first predicate is used to perform a matching on single words or phrases, with some options to include linguistic processing. The second predicate is more useful in queries where the matching involves extra linguistic processing.

The *FREETEXT* Predicate   This predicate supports searching for words and phrases in documents containing combinations of the search words spread throughout the document. It uses the following syntax:

```
FREETEXT ([<full-text_column>,]'<freetext_condition>'[,<LCID>])
```

The full-text column is optional and can be the name of a column, an asterisk (*), or the value *DEFAULTPROPERTIES*. In most cases, you will not use an explicit definition of a column since your goal with the *FREETEXT* predicate is to have the matching done on the entire index. The following query illustrates how to find all documents that contain the word *SharePoint*:

```
SELECT WorkId, Rank, Title, Author, Size, Write, SiteName, HitHighlightedSummary
FROM Scope()
WHERE "scope"='All Sites' AND contenttype='Document'
     AND FREETEXT(defaultproperties,'SharePoint')
```

Items are returned if they meet the comparisons and logical combinations defined in the *WHERE* clause of the query. If the result of the search condition is *TRUE*, the item will be included. It is very important when you start using the *FREETEXT* predicate that the items be assigned rank values according to how well they match the search conditions. Refer to the sidebar "Best Practices for Proper Relevance Ranking" for more information about best practices that are documented in the SDK and that will have a positive effect on the ranking of the matching search results.

Best Practices for Proper Relevance Ranking

It is important to follow a number of basic guidelines when constructing SQL queries. The structure of your query has important consequences for the relevance ranking of the search results. Take a look, for example, at the following two keyword searches using the *FREETEXT* predicate. (The rest of the SQL string is omitted for simplicity.)

```
FREETEXT(defaultproperties, '+sharepoint +search')

FREETEXT(defaultproperties, 'sharepoint') AND FREETEXT(defaultproperties, 'search')
```

Both queries are valid and yield the same results, but with a different ranking. Do you know which one yields the best results ranking? The first one! It is recommended that you only use one *FREETEXT* predicate in a search query. Each *FREETEXT* clause represents a separate query, and therefore, the ranking is calculated separately. *FREETEXT* classes are not combined, and consequently, the results ranking will not be optimal.

Another important guideline is to specify *DefaultProperties* as *Column* for the *FREETEXT* predicate for optimal ranking of results. *DefaultProperties* references the default set of properties to include in the ranking algorithm and results in all of the indexed text properties that have nonzero weight being searched. You can alternatively use the *WITH* predicate to define your own set of properties if you are not happy with the default one. This is helpful if you need to promote results containing the keywords on your own custom properties.

The *FREETEXT* predicate can also be configured for implicit *AND* searching or implicit *OR* searching. Take a look at these two queries:

```
SELECT WorkId,Path,Title,Write,Author
FROM Scope()
FREETEXT(defaultproperties, 'sharepoint "Mike Fitzmaurice" ')

SELECT WorkId,Path,Title,Write,Author
FROM Scope()
FREETEXT(defaultproperties, 'sharepoint ') AND Author='Mike Fitzmaurice'
```

The Boolean restriction in the query will greatly reduce the number of possible matches to the query, without affecting the ranking values that are calculated based on the *FREETEXT* clause in the query. This is because the ranking value for the Boolean restriction portion of the query is always 1000. That number is the maximum possible ranking value. The rank result is the rank calculated for the value of the *FREETEXT* clause, because this value is lower than 1000.

Here are other samples of queries that use the *FREETEXT* predicate illustrating some of the more common scenarios:

- Executing this query returns search results containing at least one of the keywords *SharePoint* and *Search*:

```
SELECT WorkId,Path,Title,Write,Author
FROM Scope()
WHERE FREETEXT(defaultproperties, 'SharePoint Search')
ORDER BY Rank Desc
```

- Executing this query returns search results containing both the *SharePoint* and *Search* keywords:

```
SELECT WorkId,Path,Title,Write,Author
FROM Scope()
WHERE FREETEXT(defaultproperties, '+SharePoint +Search')
ORDER BY Rank Desc
```

- Executing this query returns search results containing the exact phrase *SharePoint Search*:

```
SELECT WorkId,Path,Title,Write,Author
FROM Scope()
WHERE FREETEXT(defaultproperties, ' "SharePoint Search" ')
ORDER BY Rank Desc
```

- Executing this query returns search results containing both the *SharePoint* and *Search* keywords but not the keyword *WSS*:

```
SELECT WorkId,Path,Title,Write,Author
FROM Scope()
WHERE FREETEXT(defaultproperties, '+SharePoint +Search -WSS')
ORDER BY Rank Desc
```

- Executing this query returns search results containing the keyword *SharePoint* and results that are authored by a person named *John*:

```
SELECT WorkId,Path,Title,Write,Author
FROM Scope()
WHERE FREETEXT(defaultproperties, 'SharePoint')
      AND CONTAINS(Author,' "John" ')
ORDER BY Rank Desc
```

- Executing this query returns search results containing the keyword *SharePoint* and that were modified within the last 30 days:

```
SELECT WorkId,Path,Title,Write,Author
FROM Scope()
WHERE FREETEXT(defaultproperties, 'SharePoint')
      AND Write<=DATEADD(DAY,30,GETGMTDATE())
ORDER BY Rank Desc
```

The CONTAINS Predicate   The *CONTAINS* predicate performs comparisons on columns that contain text similar to the *FREETEXT* predicate, but it can go a step further because it supports additional features in addition to matching the words that are part of the predicate. If you use the *CONTAINS* predicate, it is also possible to match inflectional forms of the words, search using wildcards, and search using proximity.

> **Note** Wildcards are not an option when using the *FREETEXT* predicate.

The syntax to follow for this predicate is shown here:

```
…CONTAINS([<full-text_column>,]'<contains_condition>'[,<LCID>])
```

Again, the reference to the full-text column is optional. The value can be the name of the column, the asterisk (*), or the *ALL* word. The last two options define the same configuration: force the search to be performed for all indexed text properties. Similar to the *FREETEXT* predicate, there is the option to specify a local search. When provided, the appropriate word breaker, noise word list, inflectional forms, and sort order are taken into account when the search query is executed.

The content that makes up the condition must be enclosed in single quotation marks, and again a number of combinations and options are available. Here is a simple example of the use of the *CONTAINS* predicate with a query returning all of the documents that contain the word *marketing*:

```
SELECT WorkId, Rank, Title, Author, Size, Write, SiteName, HitHighlightedSummary
FROM Scope()
WHERE "scope"='All Sites' AND contenttype='Document' AND CONTAINS('Marketing')
```

When searching for a phrase or multiple words, you use the same syntax. Unlike the *FREETEXT* predicate, the *CONTAINS* predicate allows for inclusion of the asterisk (*) as the wildcard character. The next query, for example, returns all documents that have the possible extensions for the word *market*, such as *marketing* or *marketer*:

```
SELECT WorkId, Rank, Title, Author, Size, Write, SiteName, HitHighlightedSummary
FROM Scope()
WHERE "scope"='All Sites' AND contenttype='Document' AND CONTAINS('Market*')
```

Words, phrases, and wildcard strings can be combined using the AND, OR, or NOT statement. An example is the next query, which returns all documents containing the word *marketing* but not the word *financial* or any of its extensions:

```
SELECT WorkId, Rank, Title, Author, Size, Write, SiteName, HitHighlightedSummary
FROM Scope()
WHERE "scope"='All Sites' AND contenttype='Document'
    AND CONTAINS('"marketing" AND NOT "financial*"')
```

Options that are supported only with the *CONTAINS* predicate are the use of the *NEAR* term and the *FORMSOF* term. You use the *NEAR* term to specify that the two content search terms that you include in the predicate must be located relatively close to one another in order for them to be recognized as matching.

> **Note** The NEAR term can be replaced by the tilde (~).

An example of a query using the *NEAR* term is shown here:

```
SELECT Rank, Title, Url, Author
FROM Scope()
WHERE "scope"='All Sites' AND CONTAINS('"Litware" NEAR "Fitzmaurice"')
```

The *FORMSOF* term is used to add extra linguistic processing of the words that are included in the predicate. The syntax is like this:

```
FORMSOF (<generation_type>,<match_words>)
```

There are two possible values for the type of linguistic processing that needs to take place. If you use the value *INFLECTIONAL*, you indicate to the Search service that it must match alternative inflection forms of the words included in the predicate. Consider, for example, the following query. It will certainly result in matches that contain the word *buy*, but within the results, you'll also find matches with possible alternative forms of the word, such as *bought*, *buys*, *buying*, and others.

```
SELECT Rank, Title, Url, Author, HitHighlightedSummary FROM Scope() WHERE "scope"='All
Sites' AND CONTAINS('FORMSOF(INFLECTIONAL,"buy")'
```

The second-generation type value for the *FORMSOF* term is *THESAURUS*. You use this option if you want to see matches with words that have the same meaning as the given word. Alternative meanings are retrieved from the thesaurus files that are part of the Office SharePoint Server 2007 infrastructure. The following query will also result in matches for the word *jog*, since that is defined as a synonym for the word *run*:

```
SELECT Rank, Title, Url, Author, HitHighlightedSummary
FROM Scope()
WHERE "scope"='All Sites' AND CONTAINS('FORMSOF(THESAURUS,"run")'
```

The *ORDER BY* Clause

The last part of the SQL statement is the *ORDER BY* clause, which gives you the option to sort the query results based on the value of one or more columns specified. You actually use the

ORDER BY clause in a similar way in traditional SQL queries. Here again is the query from the preceding section, but now the results are ordered by the Title column:

```
SELECT Rank, Title, Url, Author, HitHighlightedSummary
FROM Scope()
WHERE "scope"='All Sites' AND CONTAINS('FORMSOF(THESAURUS,"run")'
ORDER BY Title ASC
```

The Query Object Model

The new managed API to support the execution of an Enterprise Search query is encapsulated within the *Microsoft.Office.Server.Search.dll* and defined within the *Microsoft.Office.Server.Search.Query* namespace. The assemblies contain a completely new set of classes in Office SharePoint Server 2007. The earlier version of SharePoint—SharePoint Portal Server 2003—contained the *QueryProvider* class, which has become obsolete in the query object model. The class is still defined and available for compatiblllty reasons, but Microsoft deemphasizes the use of this class in your code.

Two classes are important here. Both inherit from the *Query* class, an abstract class that is not intended to be used directly in code. The *Query* class encapsulates the base implementation for the *KeywordQuery* and *FullTextSqlQuery* classes, as shown in the following illustration. The first class is used to execute queries that are formulated using the keyword syntax. The second class is used when the query is constructed using the SQL syntax. By now, you should be convinced of the rich options and the flexibility that are possible when creating queries using the SQL syntax. This syntax is a bit more difficult to use, however, as compared with the simple keyword syntax.

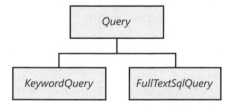

It is important to note that both the *KeywordQuery* and *FullTextSqlQuery* classes use the same flow for the execution of the query. They both expose properties to assign possible configurations of options and the query that has to be executed. The *Execute* method that is exposed for both classes executes the query and returns the search results in the same manner as a set of *IDataReader* objects. All these common members are defined at the level of the *Query* class.

The *Query* Class

The *Query* class defines the common properties and methods that are inherited by the *KeywordQuery* and *FullTextSqlQuery* classes. The following list describes the properties of interest for the *Query* class:

- **AuthenticationType**   The value of this property is of type *QueryAuthenticationType* enumeration with two options: *NtAuthenticatedQuery* and *PluggableAuthenticatedQuery*. The first option specifies that the query uses Windows-based authentication, while the second option directs the query to use the pluggable authentication that is based on cookies—also referred to as *forms-based authentication*. The choice is almost always not yours to make. The value depends typically on the authentication mode that has been set at the level of the IIS and the configuration of the IIS Web application hosting the SharePoint site that runs that query. In your code, use the value of the static property *AuthenticationMode* of the *SPSecurity* class to branch the code and set the proper value for the *AuthenticationType* property. *SPSecurity* is a class that is part of *Microsoft.SharePoint.dll*, defined in the *Microsoft.SharePoint* namespace and with static security management members exposed.

  ```
  if (SPSecurity.AuthenticationMode != AuthenticationMode.Windows)
      query.AuthenticationType = QueryAuthenticationType.PluggableAuthenticatedQuery;
  else
      query.AuthenticationType = QueryAuthenticationType.NtAuthenticatedQuery;
  ```

- **Culture**   This property stores the information regarding the locale to be used for the query and the culture, or language, information to use for things such as stemming, noise words, thesaurus, and more. The value can be the culture that is currently active. The *CultureInfo* class that is part of the *System.Globalization* namespace has a static property *CurrentCulture* that you can easily reuse for your query.

  ```
  query.Culture = CultureInfo.CurrentCulture;
  ```

- **EnableStemming**   Use this property to turn the stemming on or off. Note that if the property is used with the *FullTextSqlQuery* class, the stemming will occur only for the search terms that are specified in the *FREETEXT* predicate that is part of the query.

  ```
  query.EnableStemming = true;
  ```

- **HighlightedSentenceCount**   Search results can contain a number of sentences representing the summary of the query per item. With this property, you can define how many sentences there will be for the hit-highlighted summary.

  ```
  query.HighlightedSentenceCount = 3;
  ```

- **IgnoreAllNoiseQuery**   You use this property to allow or not allow a query consisting only of noise words. By default, the property has the value *true*.

  ```
  Query.IgnoreAllNoiseQuery = false;
  ```

- *KeywordInclusion*   This is an important property that you use to specify whether the query results contain all or any of the specified search terms. The value is of type *KeywordInclusion* enumeration with two options: *AllKeywords* and *AnyKeywords*. The first option indicates that the query returns only the search results containing all of the keywords, while the second option is less strict, with the query returning search results that contain any of the query terms. When the property is set using the *FullTextSqlQuery* class, it is applied only to the search terms specified in the *FREETEXT* predicate.

```
query.KeywordInclusion = KeywordInclusion.AnyKeyword;
```

- *QueryText*   This is probably the most important property, since it is the one used to assign the query string to be executed. The syntax you use to express the query restricts the choice of the class to instantiate. When the *QueryText* is a simple string following the keyword syntax, you must instantiate the *KeywordQuery* class. If you opt for a full SQL syntax, you have no other choice than to instantiate the *FullTextSqlQuery* class. Here is an example of the latter scenario:

```
query.QueryText = "SELECT ... FROM Scope() WHERE ... ORDER BY ...";
```

- *ResultTypes*   Many types of items can be included in the search results. Use the *Result Types* property to define which types you want to include. The value is of type *ResultType* enumeration with the following options: *DefinitionResults* for the inclusion of the definitions of the keywords matching the search query, *HighConfidenceResults* for the high confidence results matching the search query, *None* if you are not specifying a result type, *RelevantResults* for the inclusion of the main search results from the content index matching the search query, and finally *SpecialTermResults* for the best bets matching the search query. If you do not specify a value for the property, all of the various types of results will be included.

```
Query.ResultTypes = ResultType.RelevantResults;
```

- *RowLimit*   Use this property to specify the maximum number of rows returned in the search results.

```
query.RowLimit = 10;
```

- *StartRow*   Use this property to specify the first row to be included in the search results.

```
query.StartRow = 0;
```

- *Timeout*   Often you'll want to avoid long-running queries. Use the *Timeout* property to set the number of milliseconds that elapse before the query request times out.

```
Query.Timeout = 360;
```

- *TrimDuplicates*   Set this property to *true* when you want to avoid duplicates in the search results.

```
query.TrimDuplicates = true;
```

Notice that the *Query* class implements the *IDisposable* interface. It is good practice to call the *Dispose* method if you have finished with the query or if you perform all of the calls within the code block of a *using* statement. In the next two sections, when we look at the *KeywordQuery* and the *FullSqlQuery* classes, we'll come back to this.

The *Execute* method is used to execute the query assigned to the *QueryText* property. The results of the query are returned as an object of type *ResultTableCollection*.

As mentioned, you will not code directly against the *Query* class. Instead, you'll create instances of one of the two classes that derive from it. Let's take a closer look at these two classes.

The *KeywordQuery* Class

A sample application named SearchKeywords is part of the downloadable package of demos. This application illustrates the different options that you have as a developer when you need to execute a search query constructed with the keyword syntax. It is a good idea to open the project in Visual Studio .NET and follow along as you read about this new class. Figure 8-11 shows the user interface that is part of this application.

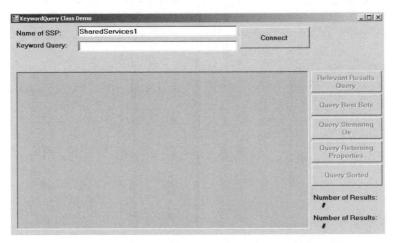

FIGURE 8-11 The SearchKeywords sample application used to demonstrate how to program using the *KeywordQuery* class

Both the *KeywordQuery* class and the *FullTextSqlQuery* class, described in the next section, are instantiated in the same manner. Because the objects execute a query against the Search Web service and the Search Web service is part of the Shared Services, it is necessary to provide information about the SSP that you want to connect to. The *Microsoft.Office.Server. ServerContext* class is again helpful here, both when your code is executed in the context of SharePoint and when it is executed outside SharePoint. The sample application is a Windows-based application, and therefore it can obtain the reference to the context of the SSP only through the static *GetContext* method of the *ServerContext* class. Here is the code that is executed when you click the Connect button:

```
ServerContext serverContext = ServerContext.GetContext(textBoxSSP.Text);
if (serverContext == null)
    MessageBox.Show("Could not connect to SSP!");
else
{
    //-- enabling of the buttons
}
```

To create the actual instance of the *KeywordQuery* class, you pass an instance of the *ServerContext* object, an instance of an *SPSite* object, or the string of the search application name as the parameter for the contructor. The following code illustrates how to start with the *KeywordQuery* class:

```
KeywordQuery keywordQry = new KeywordQuery(serverContext);
```

Don't forget that the base class of the *KeywordQuery* class implements the *IDisposable* interface and thus can be freed of any of its resources when the instance is no longer needed in the application. That is why you'll also find at the end of the block of code that creates the instance of the *KeywordQuery* class the following line calling the *Dispose* method of the instance:

```
keywordQry.Dispose();
```

After all of this, it is a matter of assigning the values for one or more properties that prepare the query and that the classes inherit from the *Query* class. Each of the buttons that you can click in the sample application illustrates one of the supported use cases when executing a query like this.

The first button, named Relevant Results Query, prepares the *KeywordQuery* instance to search for the relevant results. The choice of the type of result you are interested in is defined using the *ResultTypes* property. Next, the *QueryText* property is set with the query string entered in the text box, and the query is executed with a call to the *Execute* method:

```
KeywordQuery keywordQry = new KeywordQuery(serverContext);
keywordQry.ResultTypes = ResultType.RelevantResults;
keywordQry.QueryText = textBoxKeyword.Text;
ResultTableCollection results = keywordQry.Execute();
```

The result of the execution is an object of type *ResultTableCollection*. You can always use the *Exists* method exposed by this class to verify whether the collection actually contains the *ResultTable* instance you had in mind. Also check the verification of the value of the *SpellingSuggestion* property. Users see in the Search Center a label with the Did You Mean? information suggesting that they correct their query. You can display the same type of help to the users of your application, as shown in Figure 8-12, with a suggested correction of *marketing* for the entered keyword *marketin*. If a suggestion is generated, the *SpellingSuggestion* stores an XML string consisting of one element.

```
if (results.Exists(ResultType.RelevantResults))
{
  if (results.SpellingSuggestion != string.Empty)
  {
      XmlDocument doc = new XmlDocument();
      doc.LoadXml(results.SpellingSuggestion);
      labelDidYouMean.Text = "Did you mean? " + doc.DocumentElement.InnerText;
  }
}
```

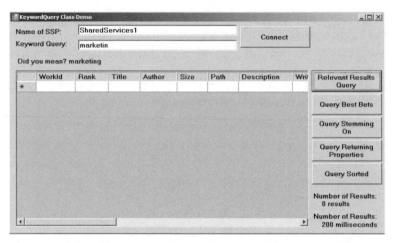

FIGURE 8-12 The Did You Mean? feature, displaying the suggestion that came back from the Search Web service

To process the results, you obtain a reference to the *ResultTable* that is part of *ResultTableCollection*. Most of the time, converting the *ResultTable* to a normal ADO.NET *DataTable* is advised, since you can then hook up the *DataTable* very easily with user controls in your Windows-based application or in your ASP.NET Web application.

> **Note** Conversion to an ADO.NET *DataTable* is of course not your only option. The Office SharePoint Server 2007 SDK contains the full description of the large set of methods that are supported by the *ResultTable* class. Most of the methods are prefixed with *GET* and specialize in getting a value out of the *ResultTable* instance, converting it immediately to the proper data type. Examples are *GetDateTime*, *GetChar*, *GetDouble*, *GetInt32*, *GetString*, and so forth.

Two properties are exposed by the *ResultTableCollection* instance that contain information about the time it took to execute the query: *DatabaseTime* and *ElapsedTime*. The *ResultTable* instance itself has two properties that make available the number of items that match the query: *RowCount* and *IsTotalRowsExact*. When the number of matched items is too large, you'll get an approximate number of records.

```
ResultTable resultTable = results[ResultType.RelevantResults];
DataTable tbl = new DataTable();
tbl.Load(resultTable, LoadOption.OverwriteChanges);
dataGridView1.DataSource = tbl;
labelDatabaseTime.Text = results.DatabaseTime.ToString() + " milliseconds";
labelNumberResults.Text = resultTable.RowCount.ToString() + " results";
```

A last interesting block of code that is included in the code-behind for the Relevant Results Query button is shown here. In the construction of the query, you can include noise words that are typically ignored. The list of ignored noise words can be retrieved through the *IgnoredNoiseWords* property exposed by the *KeywordQuery* class.

```
string[] nw = results.IgnoredNoiseWords;
StringBuilder sb = new StringBuilder();
sb.AppendLine("IGNORED NOISE WORDS\n\n");
foreach (string s in nw)
{
    sb.AppendLine(s);
}
MessageBox.Show(sb.ToString());
```

Figure 8-13 shows the results when executing a query with the Relevant Results Query button.

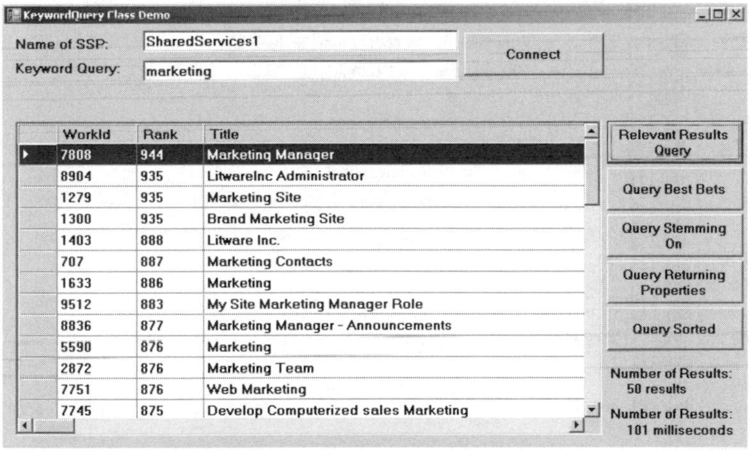

FIGURE 8-13 Relevant results in the sample application

The Query Best Bets button executes the query in a similar way but now retrieves only the best bets. Chapter 5 covered most of the details of the administration of the best bets, and you'll probably remember that best bets are created not at the level of the SSP but at the local level of a site collection, as shown in Figure 8-14.

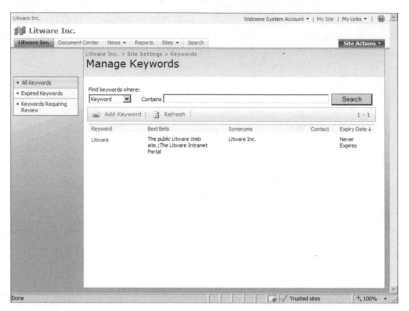

FIGURE 8-14 Best bets created in the *http://moss.litwareinc.com* site collection

Your code must therefore include some context information regarding this site collection. Here is the full block of code that is executed when you click the Query Best Bets button in the sample application:

```
KeywordQuery keywordQry = new KeywordQuery(serverContext);
keywordQry.SiteContext = new Uri("http://moss.litwareinc.com");
keywordQry.ResultTypes = ResultType.SpecialTermResults;
keywordQry.QueryText = textBoxKeyword.Text;
ResultTableCollection results = keywordQry.Execute();
if (results.Exists(ResultType.SpecialTermResults))
{
    ResultTable resultTable = results[ResultType.SpecialTermResults];
    DataTable tbl = new DataTable();
    tbl.Load(resultTable, LoadOption.OverwriteChanges);
    dataGridView1.DataSource = tbl;
    labelDatabaseTime.Text = results.DatabaseTime.ToString() + " milliseconds";
    labelNumberResults.Text = resultTable.RowCount.ToString() + " results";
}
else
{
    MessageBox.Show("No Special Terms Results Table Returned!");
}
keywordQry.Dispose();
```

The *KeywordQuery* class exposes the *SiteContext* property that you can use to provide the URL of the site collection that can add context to the execution of the search query. The *ResultTypes* property is set to the *ResultType.SpecialTermResults* that will return us the list of best bets, as shown in Figure 8-15.

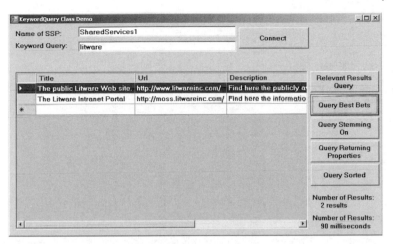

FIGURE 8-15 Using the *KeywordQuery* class to have only the best bets returned with the execution of a query

The Query Stemming On button in the sample application activates stemming for the words in the keyword query. This is done by setting the *EnableStemming* property of the *KeywordQuery* instance to *true* before executing the query. Test this using, for example, *'buy'* or *'run'*, and you'll notice that clicking the Query Stemming On button will result in more items displayed in the grid compared with the same query executed using the first two buttons.

The result of a query executed with the Query Returning Properties button is displayed in Figure 8-16. By default, the execution of a query with the *KeywordQuery* class does not give you a lot of control over the columns that you want to see returned unless you configure the *PropertyInformation* array that can be part of the internals of the *KeywordQuery* instance.

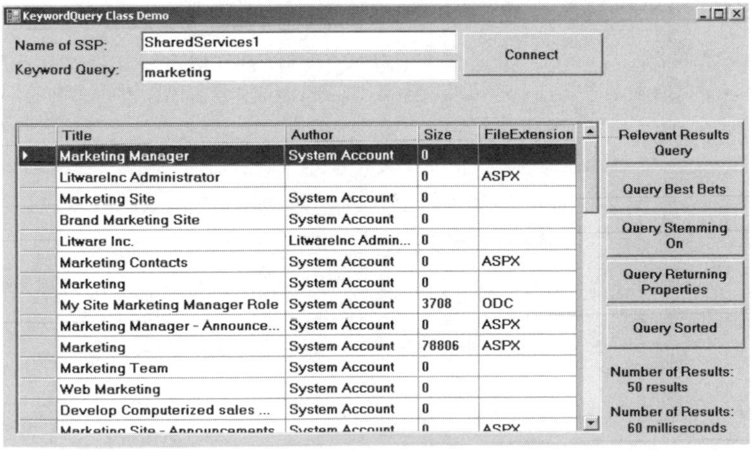

FIGURE 8-16 Controlling the properties that are returned for the search results

The *KeywordQuery* class exposes two properties that give access to the value of this *PropertyInformation* array, as shown in the following. The first is *GetProperties*, which returns the array. The more interesting property is *SelectProperties*, which is used to add strings representing managed properties to the array. The Search Web service will count the custom set of fields that you want it to return to you, as shown earlier in Figure 8-16.

```
KeywordQuery keywordQry = new KeywordQuery(serverContext);
keywordQry.ResultTypes = ResultType.RelevantResults;
keywordQry.SelectProperties.Add("Title");
keywordQry.SelectProperties.Add("Author");
keywordQry.SelectProperties.Add("Size");
keywordQry.SelectProperties.Add("FileExtension");
keywordQry.QueryText = textBoxKeyword.Text;
ResultTableCollection results = keywordQry.Execute();
```

The Query Sorted button adds an extra option to this by performing a sort operation on the search results. The sorting is accomplished by setting the value of the *SortList*. Add the names of the properties you want to perform the sorting on and the direction of the sorting using a value of the *SortDirection* enumeration, as shown here:

```
KeywordQuery keywordQry = new KeywordQuery(serverContext);
keywordQry.ResultTypes = ResultType.RelevantResults;
keywordQry.SelectProperties.Add("Title");
keywordQry.SelectProperties.Add("Author");
keywordQry.SelectProperties.Add("Size");
keywordQry.SelectProperties.Add("FileExtension");
keywordQry.SortList.Add("Size", SortDirection.Descending);
keywordQry.QueryText = textBoxKeyword.Text;
ResultTableCollection results = keywordQry.Execute();
```

The *FullSqlQuery* Class

You instantiate from the *FullSqlQuery* class to support the execution of a query constructed with the SQL syntax. This enables you to execute more complex queries. If you browse through the members of the class, you'll notice, however, that the class interface itself does not expose as many specific members as the *KeywordQuery* class discussed in the preceding section. Actually, only the constructors and the *Execute* method are overridden, or in other words, specialized, within the *FullSqlQuery* class.

In the *SQLSearchQueriesSample* that we used earlier to demonstrate the various options that are supported within the SQL syntax, you'll find the following block of code that executes the query:

```
using (FullTextSqlQuery qry =
    new FullTextSqlQuery(ServerContext.GetContext("SharedServices1")))
{
    ResultTableCollection results = null;
    ResultTable relevantResults = null;
```

```
        qry.StartRow = 0;
        qry.RowLimit = 100;
        qry.HighlightedSentenceCount = 3;
        qry.EnableStemming = true;
        qry.TrimDuplicates = true;
        qry.ResultTypes = ResultType.RelevantResults;
        qry.QueryText = textBoxQuery.Text;
        try
        {
           results = qry.Execute();
           if (results.Count > 0)
           {
             relevantResults = results[ResultType.RelevantResults];
             StringBuilder buffer = new StringBuilder(10240);
             using (XmlTextWriter writer = new XmlTextWriter(new StringWriter(buffer)))
             {
                 writer.Formatting = Formatting.Indented;
                 writer.WriteStartElement("Results");
                 writer.WriteAttributeString("hits", relevantResults.TotalRows.ToString());
                 while (relevantResults.Read())
                 {
                    writer.WriteStartElement("Result");
                    for (int i = 0; i < relevantResults.FieldCount; i++)
                    {
                        writer.WriteStartElement(relevantResults.GetName(i));
                        object val = relevantResults.GetValue(i);
                        if (val != null)
                            writer.WriteString(val.ToString());
                        else
                            writer.WriteString("null");
                        writer.WriteEndElement();
                    }
                    writer.WriteEndElement();
                 } writer.WriteEndElement();
                 string xml = buffer.ToString();
                 StreamWriter sw = new StreamWriter(@"C:\temp\results.xml", false);
                 sw.Write(xml);
                 sw.Close();
                 webBrowserResults.Navigate(@"C:\temp\results.xml");
             }
           }
           else
           {
             MessageBox.Show("No results found!");
           }
        }
        catch (Exception ex)
        {
           MessageBox.Show(ex.ToString());
        }
    }
}
```

The instance of the class is created in this sample with the *using* statement. The *using* statement in C# encapsulates all of the actions that have to be performed on the object, and before leaving the code block, it will call the *Dispose* method for the created object. This is another approach for disposing of the object in addition to the one described earlier, where we explicitly called the *Dispose* method of the instance.

Just as before, once the instance is created, you'll prepare the execution of the query by setting values for the properties that you inherit from the base *Query* class. Note that no properties other than the inherited properties are exposed by the *FullSqlQuery* class. The query itself is of course a bit more complicated because it is expressed with the SQL syntax. That syntax has been discussed in full earlier in this chapter.

The execution of the query is started with a call to the *Execute* method, which gives us again an instance of the *ResultTableCollection*. You extract the *ResultTable* instance from this collection for further processing. The processing in this sample is different from the processing done in the sample discussed for the *KeywordQuery* class. Here, we are not loading the results in an ADO.NET *DataTable*. The results are processed one by one, and an XML file is created that is, when completed, loaded in a Web browser control in the Windows-based application. Notice in particular the block that contains a loop over all of the fields that are returned to create the XML elements. This information is retrievable at the level of the *ResultTable* instance. The *FieldCount* returns the number of columns that are part of a search result item. The name of the column is retrieved with a call to the *GetName* method, passing it the index of the column. The actual value is retrieved with a call to the *GetValue* method, again passing it the index of the column.

Building, Packaging, and Deploying a Custom Document Searcher Web Part

Let's now go through a real-world sample from scratch. Step by step, you'll apply some of the techniques covered earlier in this chapter, including also some useful hands-on experience for developing, packaging, and deploying custom search functionality in SharePoint sites. The sample consists of a custom-developed Web Part that will allow users within a SharePoint site to search in the content index for Microsoft Office system documents. The query that is entered is translated into SQL syntax in code and executed using an instance of the *FullSqlQuery* class. The results are displayed in a customized way using an *SPGridView* control, one of the ASP.NET 2.0 server controls that comes with Windows SharePoint Services 3.0. Figure 8-17 displays the end result of this work.

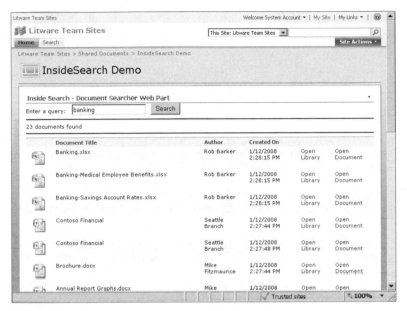

FIGURE 8-17 The Document Searcher Web Part in action

The process does not end with the coding, however. You'll also perform the steps to communicate your work to Windows SharePoint Services 3.0 through a new Feature that you'll build following the best practices that are fully documented in the book *Inside Windows SharePoint Services 3.0*, written by Ted Pattison and Daniel Larson (Microsoft Press, 2007). Last, the Feature and Solution components are packaged in a SharePoint solution and deployed in the SharePoint server farm.

Note The development environment used for the creation of this sample is Microsoft Visual Studio 2005. There is of course no problem in using Microsoft Visual Studio 2008 for your development. The classes we'll work with can be used in both environments.

Here is a summary of the steps that you'll follow:

- **Developing the user interface of the Web Part**   In this step, the focus is on the development of the class that represents the Web Part and the user interface delivered with it. No real functionality or logic is provided in this stage for the Web Part.

- **Making the Web Part available as a Feature**   You'll add all of the files that make up the Feature within your Visual Studio project. The Feature helps you to advertise the Web Part in SharePoint. Users will see the Web Part in the list of available Web Parts and will be able to add the Web Part to one of the pages in collaboration sites such as a team site or a workspace and in portals such as collaboration portals or publishing portals.

■ **Developing the query execution and processing the results**   In this step, you'll return to the Visual Studio project and extend the class with the code to prepare a search, execute it, and process the results.

■ **Exposing the Web Part properties**   The final piece of code that is added to the Web Part project exposes a number of properties that can be configured by the user through the Web Part tool pane. This way, the user can personalize the Web Part.

■ **Packaging the Web Part in a SharePoint solution**   Once tested and debugged, the Web Part assembly and the Feature files are prepared for distribution and deployment in the entire server farm. Windows SharePoint Services 3.0 allows for the packaging of all of the solution components in a file with the extension .wsp, also called a SharePoint solution file. This file is handed over to the administrators, who can continue the deployment of the solution within the SharePoint server farm. You'll also learn how to make sure that the Web Part receives the required security permissions to execute the embedded code during its deployment in the farm, following the best practices and guidelines for the deployment of custom Web Parts.

Developing the User Interface of the Web Part

The development of the Web Part can be done in multiple ways. One approach is to use the Visual Studio Extensions for Windows SharePoint Services 3.0.

> **More Information**   At the time of this writing, the Visual Studio Extensions for Windows SharePoint Services 3.0 are available as a download from the Microsoft Download Center (*http://www.microsoft.com/downloads/details.aspx?FamilyId=3E1DCCCD-1CCA-433A-BB4D-97B96BF7AB63&displaylang=en*). The latest version is version 1.1.

Once installed, the Visual Studio Extensions extend your Visual Studio development environment with project templates, item templates, and additional features. All of these will help you in the development of SharePoint-specific types of solutions in Visual Studio. Although useful in some scenarios, at the time of this writing, the Visual Studio Extensions for Windows SharePoint Services 3.0 do not offer you the required full control to support the development cycle of such an application in all of its phases. That is the major reason why we won't use them for the custom Web Part sample.

The approach we will take is a widely accepted one and fully documented in *Inside Windows SharePoint Services 3.0* (Microsoft Press, 2007). The SharePoint project will be created like a normal .NET Framework development project, mainly from scratch, resulting in some additional plumbing work that will have to be done, but with the benefit of full control over the work, testing, debugging, possible source control, and deployment steps.

As shown in Figure 8-18, you begin by starting Visual Studio. Here you create a new project of type *Class Library*. The name of the project is *DocumentSearcherWebPart*.

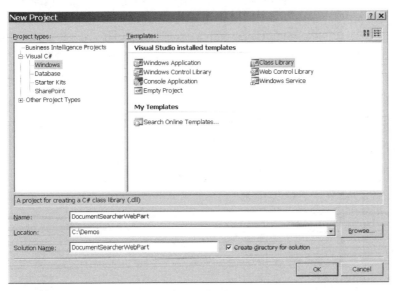

FIGURE 8-18 Starting the development with the creation of a project of type *Class Library* in Visual Studio

Windows SharePoint Services 3.0 uses the same Web Part infrastructure as the one included in ASP.NET 2.0. This is a big change compared with the earlier version, where Windows SharePoint Services came with its own dedicated Web Part infrastructure. The result of using the ASP.NET 2.0 Web Part infrastructure is that developers are now advised to build SharePoint Web Parts as ASP.NET 2.0 Web Parts. Translated into development language, this means that the base class you must use for your Web Part class is a base class that is part of *System.Web.dll*, an ASP.NET 2.0 assembly, instead of *Microsoft.SharePoint.dll*, a SharePoint-specific assembly.

Note Readers who have questions regarding compatibility with the earlier generation of Web Parts should not worry. Windows SharePoint Services 3.0 comes with a small compatibility layer that runs on top of the new ASP.NET 2.0 Web Part infrastructure. This guarantees that version 2.0 Web Parts will run without problems on the version 3.0 infrastructure. However, it is a best practice to create new Web Part projects using the ASP.NET 2.0 development approach for Web Parts.

You must add a reference to *System.Web.dll* in your class library project. Right-click the project, and then select Add Reference on the shortcut menu to open the Add Reference dialog box. In the list of available components, find the System.Web component, and add this reference by clicking OK.

Proceed with a change to the namespace for the class that is part of the project. Change the namespace to *InsideSearch.WebParts*, and also modify the name of the class itself to *DocumentSearcher*. For the class to become an ASP.NET 2.0 Web Part class, it has to inherit from the *System.Web.UI.WebControls.WebParts.WebPart* class. Add the *System.Web.UI.WebControls.WebParts* namespace, along with a couple of additional namespaces that you'll need for the rest of the code, to the list of *using* statements at the top of the class. Here is what you should have right now:

```
using System;
using System.Collections;
using System.Collections.Generic;
using System.Text;
using System.Data;
using System.Web;
using System.IO;
using System.Web.UI.WebControls.WebParts;
using System.Web.UI.WebControls;
using System.Web.UI;

namespace InsideSearch.WebParts
{
    public class DocumentSearcher: WebPart
    {
    }
}
```

The goal of a Web Part is to render functionality on a Web Part page. Web Part pages are .aspx pages that contain the required Web Part infrastructure, such as the *SPWebPartManager* control and one or more *SPWebPartZone* controls. The *SPWebPartManager* is contained within the master page, while the Web Part zones are automatically available if you create a Web Part page in the SharePoint sites or if you plan to use the Web Part on existing site pages such as the home page of the site. For the custom Web Part that we are about to create, the user interface consists of a couple of server-side ASP.NET controls and one of the Web controls that are part of *Microsoft.SharePoint.dll*. To use the SharePoint Web controls, you must add the reference to this assembly in your project. Proceed in a similar way as with the *System.Web.dll*, but now add the component named Windows SharePoint Services. You'll find this component at the bottom of the list in the Add Reference dialog box. To facilitate the work, add the *using* statement for the *Microsoft.SharePoint.WebControls* namespace and two extra *using* statements for later use, as shown here:

```
using Microsoft.SharePoint.WebControls;
using Microsoft.SharePoint.Utilities;
using Microsoft.SharePoint;
```

The creation and the configuration of the instances for the required user interface controls are done in a number of steps. First, add the following class-level variable declarations, which will store the references to the different ASP.NET controls you'll create in a moment:

```
private Label labelQuery = null;
private TextBox textBoxQuery = null;
private Button buttonQuery = null;
private SPGridView gridResults = null;
private Label labelResults = null;
```

The *SPGridView* control enhances the classic ASP.NET *GridView* control with additional SharePoint functionality. One of these new functions is the automatic adaptation of the control to the look and feel that is defined by the SharePoint theme that is currently active for the site.

The *WebPart* class, our base class for our own custom Web Part, exposes the *CreateChildControls* method that you can override. Within this method, you place the code to create the instances of the different controls that will become part of the collection of child controls of the Web Part:

```
protected override void CreateChildControls()
{
    labelQuery = new Label();
    textBoxQuery = new TextBox();
    buttonQuery = new Button();
    gridResults = new SPGridView();
    labelResults = new Label();

    labelQuery.Text = "Enter a query: ";
    buttonQuery.Text = "Search";
    labelResults.Text = "No results displayed...";

    gridResults.AutoGenerateColumns = false;
    BoundField fld1 = new BoundField();
    fld1.DataField = "FileExtension";
    gridResults.Columns.Add(fld1);
    BoundField fld2 = new BoundField();
    fld2.HeaderText = "Document Title";
    fld2.DataField = "Title";
    gridResults.Columns.Add(fld2);
    BoundField fld3 = new BoundField();
    fld3.HeaderText = "Author";
    fld3.DataField = "Author";
    gridResults.Columns.Add(fld3);
    BoundField fld4 = new BoundField();
    fld4.HeaderText = "Created On";
    fld4.DataField = "Write";
    gridResults.Columns.Add(fld4);
    CommandField fld5 = new CommandField();
    fld5.SelectText = "Action1";
    fld5.ShowSelectButton = true;
    gridResults.Columns.Add(fld5);
```

```
            CommandField fld6 = new CommandField();
            fld6.SelectText = "Action2";
            fld6.ShowSelectButton = true;
            gridResults.Columns.Add(fld6);

            Controls.Add(labelQuery);
            Controls.Add(textBoxQuery);
            Controls.Add(buttonQuery);
            Controls.Add(gridResults);
            Controls.Add(labelResults);
        }
```

Review the code for a moment. The *SPGridView* instance gets six columns. Five of them are of type *BoundField* and are each mapped to the corresponding field, as it will be returned by the Search Web service when the query is executed. There are two fields of type *CommandField*. These fields are not bound to a data field but are added to enable a couple of actions that the user can perform on the search result item. Later, we'll make sure that these fields have the proper URL assigned to them to complete the user action.

The base *WebPart* class also defines a *RenderContents* method that you override to detail the rendering of the user interface. Look at the Web Part as one building block in the overall user interface of the page in the browser; one of the most important tasks of the Web Part is the rendering of one part of the HTML that goes back to the client. The following code creates a layout and calls the *RenderControl* method for each of the child controls. The rendering of the HTML is done with an instance of the *HtmlTextWriter* class that is provided as an incoming parameter for the *RenderContents* method. This instance has members that you can use to output HTML in a direct way, such as a call to the *Write* method, or in a more concealed way, such as the calls to the *RenderBeginTag* and the *RenderEndTag* method.

```
protected override void RenderContents(HtmlTextWriter writer)
{
    writer.RenderBeginTag(HtmlTextWriterTag.Div);
    labelQuery.RenderControl(writer);
    writer.Write("  ");
    textBoxQuery.RenderControl(writer);
    writer.Write("  ");
    buttonQuery.RenderControl(writer);
    writer.RenderEndTag();
    writer.RenderBeginTag(HtmlTextWriterTag.Hr);
    writer.RenderEndTag();
    labelResults.RenderControl(writer);
    writer.RenderBeginTag(HtmlTextWriterTag.Hr);
    writer.RenderEndTag();
    writer.RenderBeginTag(HtmlTextWriterTag.Div);
    gridResults.RenderControl(writer);
    writer.RenderEndTag();
}
```

Note The creation of the user interface of the Web Part might seem like a very tedious operation, and it definitely is. No What You See Is What You Get (WYSIWYG) experience is available for the creation and configuration of the various controls that make up the user interface. Have a look at the SmartPart community project to see an alternative approach for building Web Parts. (The SmartPart has been developed by Jan Tielens and is available from CodePlex at the following URL: *http://www.codeplex.com/smartpart*.) The SmartPart is a generic Web Part that is designed to load ASP.NET 2.0 user controls and to render these as Web Parts on the SharePoint pages. The user controls, ASP.NET 2.0 files with the extension .ascx, are created in a Web site or Web application project in Visual Studio. You benefit from the rich design experience that is part of the development environment. Instead of creating controls in code, you drag them from the toolbox onto the design surface, where you also have a lot additional features for helping you in the customization and configuration of the controls. Working this way of course gives you a boost in productivity when the user interface is to be composed of a rich and a complex set of user interface controls.

There is one last thing to add to the Web Part project before we can continue with the next step. The Web Part assembly is going to be deployed as a private assembly for the IIS Web application that hosts the site collection where the Feature will be activated. Deploying a Web Part assembly as a private assembly is a best practice but requires the assembly to be annotated with the following attribute:

```
[assembly: System.Security.AllowPartiallyTrustedCallers]
```

You add this attribute in the assemblyinfo.cs file, which can be found in the Properties folder that is part of your project in Solution Explorer. Once this is done, you can build your project. In case you have compilation errors, you need to resolve these and build again. If the build succeeds, you are ready to proceed.

Making the Web Part Available as a Feature

Features make solution components available in the world of SharePoint. For our custom Web Part, we'll use a Feature to include the Web Part in the list of advertised Web Parts. The Web Part Gallery, a document library at the level of the site collection, contains all of the Web Parts that users will see in the Add Web Parts dialog box. To advertise your Web Part, you'll need a small XML file that describes the Web Part, and you'll have to upload that file in the Web Part Gallery. The XML file typically has the extension .webpart, and it is included in the collection of files that make up the Feature. Administrators install Features using the STSADM command-line utility. Once installed, Features are activated when there is the need to make the functionality—for example, the Web Part—available within the SharePoint environment.

More Information   Chapter 3 introduced the notion of Features. A Feature is basically a collection of files. Most of these files are XML files following the Collaborative Application Markup Language (CAML). CAML allows for the declarative definition of the metadata identifying the Feature and its configuration settings. You continue with this declarative approach by creating additional XML files that further detail the Feature functionality. Features can make many solution components available: enhancements to the user interface of SharePoint, custom workflow templates, new list templates, new field types and content types, and so forth. For each of these categories, you'll employ different CAML elements within the definition.

All of the Feature files are collected in a folder that must be copied to the 12\TEMPLATE\ FEATURES folder. To facilitate the copying within your development environment, you mimic the same folder structure in Solution Explorer in Visual Studio. Depending on what exactly needs to be copied, you start from the 12 folder or from the TEMPLATE folder. The files that we have to copy will all go under the TEMPLATE folder, so that is our start folder, as shown in Figure 8-19. Under this start folder, you create a FEATURES folder and an IMAGES folder.The FEATURES folder has one more subfolder, InsideSearch.DocumentSearcher, where you'll put the CAML files that make up your Feature.

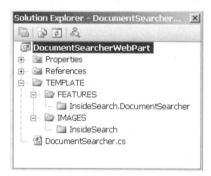

FIGURE 8-19   Folder structure for the Visual Studio Web Part project

The first file that you add to the InsideSearch.DocumentSearcher folder is a new XML file. Right-click the folder, select Add, and then select New Item to open a dialog box displaying all of the possible item templates to choose from. Find and select the XML file. Name the XML file **feature.xml**, and then open the file in the XML editor that is part of Visual Studio. You can remove the version declaration line.

Note   It is common to use feature.xml as the name of this file, but this name is not required. Using another name will, however, limit some of the options you have when you use the STSADM command-line utility to install the Feature. We'll come back to this in a moment.

The feature.xml file is called the Feature definition file, and it is used to store the metadata regarding the Feature itself. As mentioned earlier, the content is expressed in XML language that adheres to the schema definitions that are commonly referred to as CAML. While authoring CAML, it is a good idea to activate IntelliSense within the Visual Studio XML editor. With the feature.xml file open in the editor, set the value of the Schema property, available in the Properties box that is part of Visual Studio, to the path of the wss.xsd file. This schema file can be found in the 12\TEMPLATE\XML folder. Use the XSD Schemas dialog box, shown in Figure 8-20, to browse to this XML Schema file. The dialog box is opened by clicking the Browse button associated with the Schema property in the Properties box.

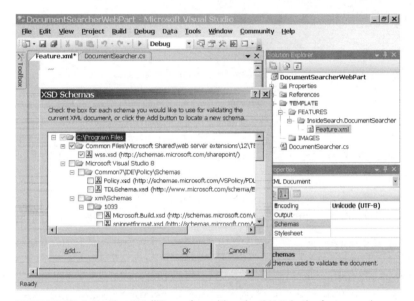

FIGURE 8-20 Activating IntelliSense for writing the CAML in the feature.xml

Now you can start writing the XML. The root element is the *Feature* element. You'll notice immediately when you start to type in the XML editor that IntelliSense is a great help. The *Feature* element has a number of attributes that must or can get a value, as follows:

- *ID*   A Feature is identified by a globally unique identifier (GUID). Visual Studio lets you create a new GUID by selecting the Create GUID option on the Tools menu. This activates a small tool that can be used to create a new GUID in one of several formats. The GUID that is used in CAML must follow the registry format, as shown in Figure 8-21. Click the Copy button, close the tool, and paste the new GUID as the value for the *ID* attribute of the *Feature* element.

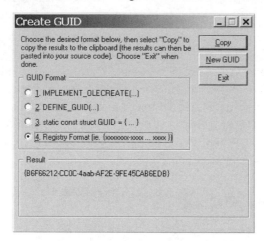

FIGURE 8-21 Creating a new GUID that will become the *ID* of the Feature

- **Title**   The Feature gets a title, which is a string that can be localized instead of hard-coded. Localization is done by including .NET Framework resource files, represented as .resx files, in your project. For each locale that you want to support, you'll store the strings as key-value pairs. For our work here, we'll assign a hard-coded string to the *Title* attribute.

- **Description**   This is an optional string that you can use to store additional text that will appear on the Feature administration page. This page will be discussed in a moment.

- **ImageUrl**   This is again an optional attribute that can be set to the name of an image file that is available in the 12\TEMPLATE\IMAGES folder or a subfolder under it. We have an IMAGES folder with a subfolder within the project folder structure. You can add a small image to the subfolder that can be connected to your Feature using the *ImageUrl* attribute. A relative URL is sufficient.

- **Scope**   This is a very important attribute that you must set to either *Farm*, *WebApplication*, *Site*, or *Web*. Web Part Features are typically scoped at the level of the site collection, and therefore the value of the attribute in our example must be set to *Site*. Other Features might have to be scoped more widely. If that is the case, you assign the value *Farm* or *WebApplication*. A good example of a farm-level Feature is spelling checking. This functionality within SharePoint is activated once for the complete SharePoint server farm. There is no need to go to the individual site collections or sites and activate it there. A custom list template, on the other hand, or some customization for the user interface of SharePoint is typically scoped at the level of the individual site. The value you must set for site-level scoping is *Web*.

- **Hidden**   By default, the Feature will be visible on the administration page. Set the value of this attribute to *TRUE* if you don't want this to happen. Note that many alternatives for entering *TRUE* are offered with IntelliSense, but only the fully capitalized notation will work. If the Feature is hidden, you'll limit the options to activate the Feature for administrators. They can activate the Feature only by using the STSADM command-line utility included in Windows SharePoint Services 3.0 or by activating other Features that have an activation dependency defined for the hidden Feature within their own Feature definition file. Activation dependencies are out of scope for this book but are fully covered in *Inside Windows SharePoint Services 3.0* (Microsoft Press, 2007).

Other attributes are useful, but these are not required for our sample. Here is the definition of the *Feature* element in the XML file at this moment:

```
<Feature xmlns="http://schemas.microsoft.com/sharepoint/"
    Id = "{94B80DE7-3738-4ca1-99DA-28EF9B38A74C}"
    Title="Inside Search: Document Searcher Web Part Feature"
    Description="A sample Feature from the Inside Search book."
    ImageUrl="InsideSearch/Logo.jpg"
    Scope="Site"
    Hidden="FALSE">
</Feature>
```

The preceding *Feature* definition is a valid one, but it will not make anything available when it is activated. You must point to another CAML file that contains the definition of the actual functionality that will be delivered when the Feature is activated. No information is included within our Feature regarding the Web Part that we want to advertise in SharePoint site collections. The XML file that contains this type of information is referred to as the *element manifest file*. You refer to it in the feature.xml file by creating a child element of the *Feature* element named *ElementManifests*. In our project, one *ElementManifest* element suffices. It has just one attribute, named *Location*, which must be set to the relative location of the XML file containing the details of the Web Part.

Recall the Web Part Gallery that we looked at earlier in this section. The goal with the Feature is to add a small XML file with the extension .webpart to this document library when administrators activate the Feature we are building here. This extra XML file will be included in the collection of Feature files and is referenced here in the feature.xml file through an *ElementFile* element that is also a child element of the *ElementManifests* element. Again, you provide the relative location of the .webpart file. It will be copied along with the other CAML files to the 12\TEMPLATE\FEATURES folder.

Here is the final content of the feature.xml file:

```
<Feature xmlns="http://schemas.microsoft.com/sharepoint/"
    Id = "{94B80DE7-3738-4ca1-99DA-28EF9B38A74C}"
    Title="Inside Search: Document Searcher Web Part Feature"
    Description="A sample Feature from the Inside Search book."
    ImageUrl="InsideSearch/Logo.jpg"
    Scope="Site"
    Hidden="FALSE">
    <ElementManifests>
        <ElementManifest Location="elements.xml"/>
        <ElementFile Location="documentsearcher.webpart"/>
    </ElementManifests>
</Feature>
```

Now create a new XML file named elements.xml in the InsideSearch.DocumentSearcher folder, and again activate IntelliSense by using the *Schema* property. An element manifest file is opened, with the *Elements* element as the root element. Depending on the type of functionality you are going to activate, the child elements will be different. For the Web Part, the goal is to add a new item to the Web Part Gallery. A *Module* element and a *File* element will accomplish this for us. The *Module* element contains the details of the location in the virtual file system that is maintained for a site collection. A folder named _catalogs/wp in this file system is exposed as the Web Part Gallery in the administration user interface. The path to this folder is the value for the *Url* attribute, and the *List* attribute gets the template ID of this gallery, which is 113. The *File* element defines what to upload. With the value of the *Url* attribute, you point to the documentsearcher.webpart file that you'll create in a moment. This file goes into the Web Part Gallery when the Feature is activated. Since the final destination is a document library and not an internal folder, you have to set the value of the *Type* attribute to *GhostableInLibrary*:

```
<Elements  xmlns="http://schemas.microsoft.com/sharepoint/">
  <Module
      Name="WebParts"
      List="113"
      Url="_catalogs/wp" >
      <File
          Url="documentsearcher.webpart"
          Type="GhostableInLibrary" />
  </Module>
</Elements>
```

The last XML file to add to the InsideSearch.DocumentSearcher folder is named documentsearcher.webpart. You do not have any IntelliSense support here, since the XML that you'll embed is not defined by the *wss.xsd* schema. The XML starts with the *webParts* root element and continues with a *webPart* element as the only child element. Two parts define the metadata for the Web Part. The first part is contained within the *metaData* element. In it, you'll find the *type* element with the *name* attribute that stores the full type name for the Web Part. A *full type name* is a comma-delimited string with the fully qualified name of the class (that is, namespace plus class name) as the first piece of the value and the name of the assembly as the second piece. If you have signed your assembly, you'll have to insert here the full strong name of the assembly.

More Information Signing the assembly can be done by first creating a public/private keyword pair in Visual Studio. The support for this operation is provided in the Properties dialog box for the project, on the Signing tab. You can direct Visual Studio to create a new .snk file that will be included in the project or load an existing keyword pair. The information in the keyword pair is used when you build the project. The result of the build is a strong-named assembly that can be deployed in the Global Assembly Cache (GAC) if needed. In our sample, we'll deploy the Web Part assembly as a private assembly. Therefore, the signing of the assembly is not really needed here.

The second element under the *metaData* element is used for the error message when the addition of the Web Part to a page fails.

The other part of information contained within the *webPart* element is optional. The *data* element can contain individual *property* elements for the setting of the metadata for the Web Part item, as it will be uploaded to the Web Part Gallery. In the following XML, you can see the setting for the title and the description of the Web Part:

```
<webParts>
  <webPart xmlns="http://schemas.microsoft.com/WebPart/v3">
    <metaData>
      <type name="InsideSearch.WebParts.DocumentSearcher, DocumentSearcherWebPart,
Version=1.0.0.0, Culture=neutral, PublicKeyToken=null" />
        <importErrorMessage>
          Cannot import Document Searcher Web Part.</importErrorMessage>
    </metaData>
    <data>
      <properties>
        <property name="Title" type="string">
         Inside Search - Document Searcher Web Part</property>
        <property name="Description" type="string">
         Sample Web Part illustrating how to programmatically execute a
         search query.</property>
      </properties>
    </data>
  </webPart>
</webParts>
```

This concludes all of the work for the XML files that make up our Feature. It is time now to test the Feature and the user interface of the Web Part. A number of actions need to be performed, and they are best grouped together in a small batch file that becomes part of the root folder of your Web Part project. This batch file can be named install.bat.

To start, all of the Feature files and also the helper files such as the image that is associated with the Feature have to be copied to the 12\TEMPLATE folder. Because the folder structure in your project follows the same folder structure as the destination folder, the copying is done easily with the following entry in the batch file:

```
REM -- Copying the Feature Files
@SET TEMPLATEDIR=
  "c:\program files\common files\microsoft shared\web server extensions\12\Template"
xcopy /e /y TEMPLATE\* %TEMPLATEDIR%
```

Next is the copying of the assembly to the BIN folder that is part of the physical folder associated with the IIS Web application hosting the site collection that you want to use for the testing of your Web Part. Create this folder if necessary. The following code shows the entry in the batch file that does the job. Note that the actual location can be different on your SharePoint machine.

```
REM -- Copying the assembly
@SET DESTDIR="C:\Inetpub\wwwroot\wss\VirtualDirectories\wss.litwareinc.com80\bin"
copy BIN\DEBUG\DocumentSearcherWebPart.dll DocumentSearcherWebPart.dll
```

Features must be installed before they can be activated. The next lines in the batch file make sure that first any previous activations are undone and that the Feature is uninstalled. After that, a clean installation and activation can be performed. The value of the *url* parameter is dependent on your SharePoint environment and the site collection you are targeting.

```
REM -- Cleaning up
@SET STSADM=
 "c:\program files\common files\microsoft shared\web server extensions\12\bin\stsadm"

%STSADM% -o deactivatefeature -name  InsideSearch.DocumentSearcher
        -url "http://wss.litwareinc.com"
%STSADM% -o uninstallfeature -name  InsideSearch.DocumentSearcher -force

REM -- Install and activate
%STSADM% -o installfeature -name  InsideSearch.DocumentSearcher
%STSADM% -o activatefeature -name  InsideSearch.DocumentSearcher
        -url "http://wss.litwareinc.com"
```

The final action in the batch file can be the recycling of the worker process that is running your SharePoint site collection. This action is not strictly needed here, since the assembly is not deployed to the GAC. However, on your development machine, for testing and debugging purposes, you'll want to make sure that you always work with the correct version of the assembly. Therefore, add the last action as the final lines in the batch file:

```
REM - Recycling
cscript c:\windows\system32\iisapp.vbs /a "SharePointPool" /r
```

More Information The worker process can also be destroyed with the execution of an *IISRESET* command. This operation, however, removes all worker processes (the ones that are started with w3wp.exe) from memory. With a call to the iisapp.vbs script, providing it the name of the application pool that is associated with the IIS Web application, you'll be more granular and destroy only selected worker processes.

Save all of your work in the install.bat file, and then execute it. It is best to verify that all of the copying and the operations with the Feature were successful. Note that the first time you execute the batch file, the deactivation of the Feature will result in an error. That error can be ignored. None of the others can.

To verify whether all went well, you can do the following:

- Check the BIN folder of the IIS Web application folder for the existence of the *DocumentSearcherWebPart.dll*.

- Check the 12\TEMPLATE\FEATURES folder for the existence of a subfolder InsideSearch. DocumentSearcher containing three XML files.

- Check the 12\TEMPLATE\IMAGES\InsideSearch folder for the existence of the small image that is associated with the Feature.

- Open the root site of the site collection that runs on the IIS Web application you have targeted with your Feature. Navigate through the Site Actions and Site Settings menus to the Site Settings page. Under the Site Collection Administration header, find the Site Collection Features link, which will redirect you to the administration page for all of the Features that are scoped at the level of the site collection. Figure 8-22 shows the page displaying the list of Features. Some of them, like the Document Searcher Web Part Feature, are activated already; others can be activated on this page.

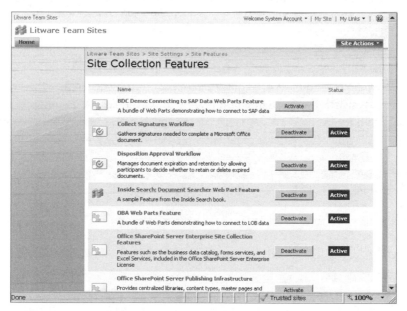

FIGURE 8-22 The Document Searcher Web Part Feature displayed as an activated Feature on the Site Collection Features page

- Verify the existence of the .webpart file in the Web Part Gallery. Navigate again to the top-level site in the site collection and on the Site Settings page. Under the Galleries header, click the Web Parts link to open the page displaying the Web Part Gallery. In the list of existing items, you should find documentsearcher.webpart.

One more task must be accomplished. The copying of the files and the installation and activation of the Feature must be complemented with the registration of the Web Part as a safe control in the web.config file that is part of the IIS Web application folder. Open the web.config in Visual Studio, and add the following entry as the last element in the *SafeControls* element:

```
<SafeControl
  Assembly=
    "DocumentSearcherWebPart, Version=1.0.0.0, Culture=neutral, PublicKeyToken=null"
  Namespace="InsideSearch.WebParts"
  TypeName="*"
  Safe="True" />
```

More Information The value of the *Assembly* attribute is the name of the assembly. If the assembly is signed, you must set a string with the first eight bytes of the public key as the value for the *PublicKeyToken* attribute. The *Namespace* attribute stores the namespace that defines the Web Part class. You can assign the name of the class to the *TypeName* attribute. The asterisk (*) is often used here to specify that all classes in the namespace are to be registered as safe Web Parts. The *Safe* attribute obviously must be assigned the value *True* for the Web Part to be registered as such.

Navigate now to the home page of one of the sites in the site collection, or create a new Web Part page that expands the list of pages that are part of the site. To add the Web Part on the page, you must switch the page to edit mode by using the Edit Page menu in the Site Actions section on the page. The Add A Web Part button displays the Add Web Parts dialog box, with your new Web Part in the Miscellaneous section, as shown in Figure 8-23.

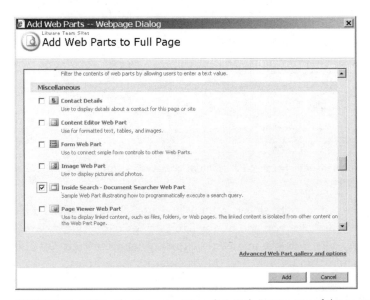

FIGURE 8-23 Adding the Document Searcher Web Part to one of the pages

Figure 8-24 displays the first version of the Web Part. Nothing really exciting is happening. At this moment, the page simply displays the initialized controls that make up the user interface.

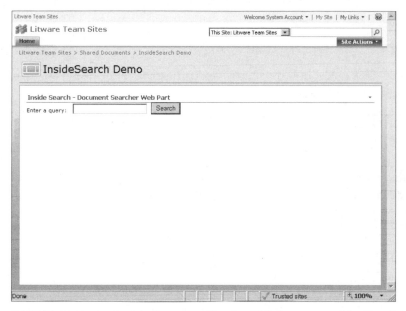

FIGURE 8-24 Version 1 of the Document Searcher Web Part on one of the SharePoint pages

Developing the Query Execution and Processing the Results

Now that you have the Web Part up and running in one of your sites, you can return to the Visual Studio development environment and complete the logic for executing the search query and processing the search results.

The coding requires access to classes that are part of *Microsoft.Office.Server.dll*, *Microsoft. SharePoint.dll*, and *Microsoft.Office.Server.Search.dll*. References to all of these assemblies are added as was done earlier.

> **Tip** Many SharePoint-related components are listed in the Add Reference dialog box, and often it is difficult for beginning SharePoint developers to find the component needed just by looking at its name. Sort the list on the Path column to find the assemblies more quickly. All of the assemblies that are in the 12\ISAPI folder are SharePoint assemblies.

Additional *using* statements for namespaces that will be used in the class must be added at the top of the editor with the contents of the DocumentSearcher.cs file, as shown here:

```
using Microsoft.SharePoint.WebControls;
using Microsoft.Office.Server;
using Microsoft.Office.Server.Search.Query;
using Microsoft.SharePoint.Utilities;
using Microsoft.SharePoint;
```

A first block of code is executed when the user clicks the button in the Web Part. An *event handler* is a method that will contain that code. You create an event handler in the *CreateChildControls* method, immediately after the line of code that sets the *Text* property of the button:

```
buttonQuery.Click += new EventHandler(buttonQuery_Click);
```

The *buttonQuery_Click* procedure contains by default one line for throwing an exception, as shown in the following code. Remove this line.

```
void buttonQuery_Click(object sender, EventArgs e)
{
}
```

The construction of the query is done using the SQL syntax and is prepared by creating and assigning the following variable as the first line in the event handler:

```
string qryText =
    "SELECT FileExtension, Title, Author, Write, SiteName, Path " +
    "FROM Scope() " +
    "WHERE \"scope\"='All Sites' AND " +
    "       IsDocument=1 AND " +
    "       CONTAINS('{0}')";
```

The instance of the *FullTextSqlQuery* class is best created within a *using* statement so that it is disposed of immediately when the work is completed on the object:

```
using (FullTextSqlQuery qry =
    new FullTextSqlQuery(ServerContext.GetContext("SharedServices1")))
{
}
```

Within the *using* statement, there is first the block of code that prepares the execution of the query, as shown here. The details have been discussed earlier in this chapter.

```
ResultTableCollection results = null;
ResultTable relevantResults = null;
qry.StartRow = 0;
qry.RowLimit = 200;
qry.TrimDuplicates = true;
qry.ResultTypes = ResultType.RelevantResults;
qry.QueryText = string.Format(qryText, textBoxQuery.Text);
```

The query is executed, and the results are loaded in an ADO.NET *DataTable*, since that makes it easy to transfer the data to the instance of the *SPGridView* control in the Web Part:

```
try
{
    results = qry.Execute();
    if (results.Count > 0)
    {
```

```
relevantResults = results[ResultType.RelevantResults];
DataTable tbl = new DataTable();
tbl.Load(relevantResults, LoadOption.OverwriteChanges);
gridResults.DataSource = tbl;
gridResults.DataBind();
```

The remaining code deals with the display of the data in the *SPGridView* control. The first column is populated with the images representing each of the file extensions. The images can be linked from anywhere, but you can add them to the IMAGES\InsideSearch folder in Solution Explorer so that they become part of the SharePoint solution you are building here. Notice that when the file extension is not matched with an image, the row is hidden. Only Microsoft Office system documents are shown.

```
foreach (GridViewRow r in gridResults.Rows)
{
    string extension = tbl.Rows[r.RowIndex]["FileExtension"].ToString();
    string imageURL = "<img src='/_layouts/images/InsideSearch/{0}.GIF'" +
                      "width='40' height='40'>";
    switch (extension.ToUpper())
    {
        case "DOCX":
            imageURL = string.Format(imageURL, "WORD2007");
            break;
        case "DOC":
            imageURL = string.Format(imageURL, "WORD");
            break;
        case "XLSX":
            imageURL = string.Format(imageURL, "EXCEL2007");
            break;
        case "XLS":
            imageURL = string.Format(imageURL, "EXCEL");
            break;
        case "PPTX":
            imageURL = string.Format(imageURL, "POWERPOINT2007");
            break;
        case "PPT":
            imageURL = string.Format(imageURL, "POWERPOINT");
            break;
        default:
            r.Visible = false;
            break;
    }
    r.Cells[0].Text = imageURL;
```

The last two columns also have to be updated. Each must make available a link for either opening the document directly or for redirecting to the document library where the document is stored:

```
    string path = tbl.Rows[r.RowIndex]["Path"].ToString();
    string containingFolder = path.Substring(0, path.LastIndexOf('/'));
    r.Cells[4].Text = "<a href='" + containingFolder + "'>Open Library</a>";
    r.Cells[5].Text = "<a href='" + path + "'>Open Document</a>";
}
```

The final block in this procedure is the display of the number of items found and the closing of the *if* statement and the *try-catch* statement:

```
        labelResults.Text = relevantResults.RowCount.ToString()
    }
    else
    {
        labelResults.Text = "No results found... try again!";
    }
}
catch (Exception ex)
{
}
```

It is again a good time to build the project, to execute the install.bat, and to refresh the page in the SharePoint site containing the Web Part. Actually, the execution of the install. bat is not required here. Copying the new version of the assembly to the BIN folder of the IIS Web application is enough. Figure 8-25 shows how the search results are displayed by the *SPGridView* control.

FIGURE 8-25 Searching for all Contoso-related Microsoft Office system documents

Exposing the Web Part Properties

We'll add a small enhancement to the Web Part as it is now. Currently, execution of the search query returns all types of Microsoft Office system documents. Users would like to decide which Office system file types the query should return, and they want to have this configuration stored somewhere so that when they return to the page, the Web Part remembers these settings.

Web Parts running in SharePoint have a number of properties associated with them by default. These properties can be edited for every user, when working in shared mode, or individually per user, when working in personal mode. On top of these common properties, you can expose your own custom properties in the class that represents the Web Part—in our project, the *DocumentSearcher* class.

The property to expose to the user must store a list of Booleans. Each is used within the Web Part to include or exclude a specific file type in the results view for the user. The following is the declaration of such a variable and property:

```
private bool[] fileTypes = new bool[6] {true,true,true,true,true,true} ;
[Personalizable(PersonalizationScope.Shared), WebBrowsable(false)]
public bool[] FileTypes
{
    get { return fileTypes; }
    set { fileTypes = value; }
}
```

The two attributes, *Personalizable* and *WebBrowsable*, are applied to the property to tell SharePoint that you want to make this property configurable for the user. The *Personalizable* attribute can have two values: *PersonalizationScope.Shared* or *PersonalizationScope.User*. We'll support the first mode for our configuration. The property must not be included in the list of common properties. The attribute *WebBrowsable* with the parameter value *false* will take care of this.

Because you are not including the property in the list of common properties, you'll have to expose it using your own tool pane, also called the *editor part*. This part is represented in the code as a new public class named *DocumentSearcherEditorPart*. Add it to the project, and update the list of *using* statements for the namespaces so that it matches the following:

```
using System;
using System.Collections;
using System.Collections.Generic;
using System.Text;
using System.Web;
using System.Web.UI;
using System.Web.UI.WebControls;
using System.Web.UI.WebControls.WebParts;
```

Your class must inherit from the *EditorPart* class defined in the *System.Web.UI.WebControls.WebParts* namespace:

```
namespace InsideSearch.WebParts
{
    public class DocumentSearcherEditorPart: EditorPart
    {
    }
}
```

The base class delivers two methods that must be implemented: *SyncChanges* and *ApplyChanges*. In a moment, you'll add the code to each of them. Just implement them for now, and remove the lines that throw the exception.

You first have to write the code to build the user interface of the custom editor part. For each of the file types, a check box control is rendered. Variables declared within the class are set to references to objects that are created, as was the case in your Web Part class, by overriding the *CreateChildControls* method of the parent class:

```
private CheckBox checkBoxDocx = null;
private CheckBox checkBoxDoc = null;
private CheckBox checkBoxXlsx = null;
private CheckBox checkBoxXls = null;
private CheckBox checkBoxPptx = null;
private CheckBox checkBoxPpt = null;

protected override void CreateChildControls()
{
    this.Controls.Add(new LiteralControl("Select types to display:<br />"));
    this.checkBoxDocx = new CheckBox();
    this.checkBoxDocx.Text = "Word 2007 Documents";
    this.Controls.Add(this.checkBoxDocx);
    this.Controls.Add(new LiteralControl("<br />"));
    this.checkBoxDoc = new CheckBox();
    this.checkBoxDoc.Text = "Word 97-2007 Documents";
    this.Controls.Add(this.checkBoxDoc);
    this.Controls.Add(new LiteralControl("<br />"));
    this.checkBoxXlsx = new CheckBox();
    this.checkBoxXlsx.Text = "Excel 2007 Workbooks";
    this.Controls.Add(this.checkBoxXlsx);
    this.Controls.Add(new LiteralControl("<br />"));
    this.checkBoxXls = new CheckBox();
    this.checkBoxXls.Text = "Excel 97-2007 Workbooks";
    this.Controls.Add(this.checkBoxXls);
    this.Controls.Add(new LiteralControl("<br />"));
    this.checkBoxPptx = new CheckBox();
    this.checkBoxPptx.Text = "PowerPoint 2007 Presentations";
    this.Controls.Add(this.checkBoxPptx);
    this.Controls.Add(new LiteralControl("<br />"));
    this.checkBoxPpt = new CheckBox();
    this.checkBoxPpt.Text = "PowerPoint 97-2003 Presentations";
    this.Controls.Add(this.checkBoxPpt);
}
```

The *SyncChanges* method is called the moment your custom editor part is displayed to the user. Its main function is to retrieve the current values from the custom properties exposed in the Web Part. This is why the first line is a call to the *EnsureChildControls* method of the base class. A check is done to determine whether the child controls are available, and if that is not the case, a call to the *CreateChildControls* method will ensure that they are indeed created and ready to be populated with the values from the *FileTypes* property exposed in the custom Web Part. The reference to the Web Part instances is available through the *WebPartToEdit* property that is inherited from the base class. A proper cast to the *DocumentSearcher* type is necessary so that you can easily access the *FileTypes* property.

```
public override void SyncChanges()
{
    this.EnsureChildControls();
    DocumentSearcher targetPart = (DocumentSearcher)this.WebPartToEdit;
    this.checkBoxDocx.Checked = targetPart.FileTypes[0];
    this.checkBoxDoc.Checked = targetPart.FileTypes[1];
    this.checkBoxXlsx.Checked = targetPart.FileTypes[2];
    this.checkBoxXls.Checked = targetPart.FileTypes[3];
    this.checkBoxPptx.Checked = targetPart.FileTypes[4];
    this.checkBoxPpt.Checked = targetPart.FileTypes[5];
}
```

The second method that does some work with the *FileTypes* property and the child controls is the *ApplyChanges* method. This method is executed when the user clicks OK or Apply in the tool pane. The values of the check box controls are now used to update the *FileTypes* array.

```
public override bool ApplyChanges()
{
    this.EnsureChildControls();
    DocumentSearcher targetPart = (DocumentSearcher)this.WebPartToEdit;
    targetPart.FileTypes[0] = this.checkBoxDocx.Checked;
    targetPart.FileTypes[1] = this.checkBoxDoc.Checked;
    targetPart.FileTypes[2] = this.checkBoxXlsx.Checked;
    targetPart.FileTypes[3] = this.checkBoxXls.Checked;
    targetPart.FileTypes[4] = this.checkBoxPptx.Checked;
    targetPart.FileTypes[5] = this.checkBoxPpt.Checked;
    return true;
}
```

The custom editor part is probably also more identifiable if it has a title that is displayed to the user. The setting of the *Title* property can be done in the constructor for the class, like this:

```
public DocumentSearcherEditorPart()
{
    this.Title = "Document Searcher Properties";
}
```

All of the work in the *DocumentSearcherEditorPart* is completed now. Before you can test it, however, you'll have to add a bit more code in the Web Part class. You'll update two variables: one that stores the number of documents that are shown and one for the number of documents that aren't shown because of the property settings. The result is displayed in the label at the end. In the *case* statements, documents of a specific file type are either displayed or not, depending on the Boolean value that is stored in the *FileTypes* property. Most of the code is already there—you just add the lines shown in bold to it:

```
int nrVisibleDocs = 0;
int nrInvisibleDocs = 0;
foreach (GridViewRow r in gridResults.Rows)
{
    string extension = tbl.Rows[r.RowIndex]["FileExtension"].ToString();
    string imageURL =
      "<img src='/_layouts/images/InsideSearch/{0}.GIF' width='40' height='40'>";
    switch (extension)
    {
        case "DOCX":
            imageURL = string.Format(imageURL, "WORD2007");
            r.Visible = fileTypes[0];
            if (r.Visible) nrVisibleDocs++; else nrInvisibleDocs++;
            break;
        case "DOC":
            imageURL = string.Format(imageURL, "WORD");
            r.Visible = fileTypes[1];
            if (r.Visible) nrVisibleDocs++; else nrInvisibleDocs++;
            break;
        case "XLSX":
            imageURL = string.Format(imageURL, "EXCEL2007");
            r.Visible = fileTypes[2];
            if (r.Visible) nrVisibleDocs++; else nrInvisibleDocs++;
            break;
        case "XLS":
            imageURL = string.Format(imageURL, "EXCEL");
            r.Visible = fileTypes[3];
            if (r.Visible) nrVisibleDocs++; else nrInvisibleDocs++;
            break;
        case "PPTX":
            imageURL = string.Format(imageURL, "POWERPOINT2007");
            r.Visible = fileTypes[4];
            if (r.Visible) nrVisibleDocs++; else nrInvisibleDocs++;
            break;
        case "PPT":
            imageURL = string.Format(imageURL, "POWERPOINT");
            r.Visible = fileTypes[5];
            if (r.Visible) nrVisibleDocs++; else nrInvisibleDocs++;
            break;
        default:
            r.Visible = false;
            break;
    }
    r.Cells[0].Text = imageURL;
    string path = tbl.Rows[r.RowIndex]["Path"].ToString();
    string containingFolder = path.Substring(0, path.LastIndexOf('/'));
    r.Cells[4].Text = "<a href='" + containingFolder + "'>Open Library</a>";
    r.Cells[5].Text = "<a href='" + path + "'>Open Document</a>";
}
labelResults.Text = relevantResults.RowCount.ToString() + " documents found " +
    "(" + nrVisibleDocs.ToString() + " Office documents in view / "
    + nrInvisibleDocs.ToString() + " not in view)";
```

The fact that the Web Part comes with its own custom editor part must also be communicated to SharePoint. This is done with an override of the *CreateEditorParts* method. The method returns the collection of *EditorPart* instances, both the default and the custom ones. The custom *EditorPart* instance is added to it with the following code. Don't forget to assign a unique identifier to the *EditorPart* to avoid conflicts.

```
public override EditorPartCollection CreateEditorParts()
{
    List<EditorPart> editorParts = new List<EditorPart>(1);
    EditorPart part = new DocumentSearcherEditorPart();
    part.ID = this.ID + "_DocSearch";
    editorParts.Add(part);
    EditorPartCollection baseParts = base.CreateEditorParts();
    return new EditorPartCollection(baseParts, editorParts);
}
```

When the build of the project succeeds, you can verify the work again in the browser. Figure 8-26 shows the Web Part in edit mode with the custom editor part displayed to the user.

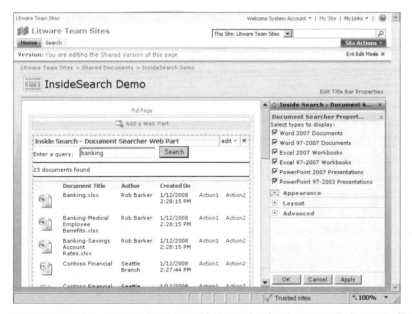

FIGURE 8-26 The custom editor part with the option for the user to hide certain file types from the display

Packaging the Web Part in a SharePoint Solution

The final steps in this walk-through illustrate how you can create a SharePoint solution containing the work you have done. Solution files can be handed over to the administrators, who will add the solution to the solution store and deploy it from there to the various front-end Web servers that are part of the server farm.

The SharePoint solution is basically a Microsoft Cabinet file, but with a .wsp extension instead of a .cab extension.

 Note A number of community tools are available from the CodePlex site (*http://www.codeplex. com*). You should have a look at the SharePoint Solution Package creation tool for Windows SharePoint Services 3.0 and Office SharePoint Server 2007, abbreviated as WSPBuilder, and the STSDEV tool. The STSDEV tool is a more general SharePoint developer tool that supports more than just the building of your SharePoint solution package. Both of these tools will give you a boost in productivity since they take over many of the manual steps that you normally have to undergo for the creation of the SharePoint solution. In this section, we'll go through these steps so that you have a basic understanding of the required procedure.

A SharePoint solution package contains, in addition to the .NET Framework assemblies and the Feature files, a manifest.xml file. This file can be considered as the installation script, and the content is again formulated using CAML. Let's create this file first. Create a new folder named Solution under the root of your project in Solution Explorer. In this folder, add a new blank XML file with the name manifest.xml. Activate IntelliSense for writing the CAML by assigning the path to the wss.xsd as the *Schema* property of the file.

The root element of the XML is the *Solution* element. It has one important attribute: *SolutionId*. You create a new GUID, using the Create GUID tool in Visual Studio, and assign it as the value:

```
<Solution xmlns="http://schemas.microsoft.com/sharepoint/"
  SolutionId="{20328AF1-8FB9-4956-B07F-EC351D6CBD81}">
</Solution>
```

The project contains one Feature that makes the custom Web Part available in SharePoint sites. You indicate to SharePoint where it will find the Feature files by first adding the *FeatureManifests* element and next one child element named *FeatureManifest*. This child element stores the location in the solution file for the feature.xml file. SharePoint has enough information with this to have all of the files copied to their proper location on the front-end Web servers, and it will also install the Feature for you.

```
<FeatureManifests>
  <FeatureManifest Location="InsideSearch.DocumentSearcher\feature.xml"/>
</FeatureManifests>
```

The assembly with the code of the two classes that make up the project will be added directly to the root of the SharePoint solution package. Using an *Assembly* element, a child element of the *Assemblies* element that you add directly under the *Solution* element, you communicate this to SharePoint, and you also indicate with the *DeploymentTarget* attribute where the assembly must be copied to. The value *WebApplication* will direct SharePoint to copy the DLL in the private application folder (the BIN folder) of the IIS Web application folder. The value *GlobalAssemblyCache* tells SharePoint to drop the assembly in the GAC. The latter location is a trusted place, and the code in the assembly is automatically fully trusted. A best practice is to select the first option and have the Web Part follow the trust level set by the administrator in the web.config file for the IIS Web application.

```
<Assemblies>
  <Assembly Location="DocumentSearcherWebPart.dll" DeploymentTarget="WebApplication">
  </Assembly>
</Assemblies>
```

Web Parts must be registered as safe controls in the web.config file. You can include this action along with the required information with a *SafeControl* element, as shown here. The *SafeControl* element is a child element of the *SafeControls* element, by itself a child element of the *Assembly* element.

```
<SafeControls>
  <SafeControl
    Assembly=
    "DocumentSearcherWebPart, Version=1.0.0.0, Culture=neutral, PublicKeyToken=null"
    Namespace="InsideSearch.WebParts"
    TypeName="*"
    Safe="True"/>
</SafeControls>
```

The *SafeControl* has four attributes that need a value: *Assembly*, *Namespace*, *TypeName*, and *Safe*. All of these attributes were discussed in the section "Making the Web Part Available as a Feature" earlier in this chapter. You can also easily copy this information from the documentsearcher.webpart file that is part of the Feature folder in your Visual Studio project.

This is the required minimum set of CAML elements that is needed to make the Web Part available. Don't forget, however, that the assembly is deployed as a private assembly and as a result depends on the trust it gets from the administrator in the web.config file. If the trust level is set to the default level, *WSS_Minimal*, your Web Part will not be able to execute its code that communicates with the Windows SharePoint Services 3.0 and Office SharePoint Server 2007 object models. *WSS_Minimal* provides only the needed trust to have the Web Part hosted in ASP.NET and to execute the rendering of the HTML basically without communicating with any assemblies other than *System.Web.dll*. As a result, users will see the page returning an error, as shown in Figure 8-27.

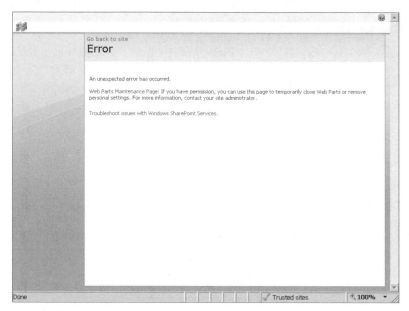

FIGURE 8-27 The error returned to the user when the Web Part does not get the required permission to execute its code

The error message can be displayed in more detail when you make two modifications in the web.config file. The first modification is assigning the value *true* to the *CallStack* attribute of the *SafeMode* element:

```
<SafeMode MaxControls="200" CallStack="true" DirectFileDependencies="10"
    TotalFileDependencies="50" AllowPageLevelTrace="false">
</SafeMode>
```

The second modification is to the *mode* attribute of the *customErrors* element. The value is by default set to *On*. Setting it to the value *Off*, as shown here, will result in the display of the raw ASP.NET error on the SharePoint page, as shown in Figure 8-28.

```
<customErrors mode="Off" />
```

Notice in Figure 8-28 that the exception is thrown because the request for the permission of type *Microsoft.SharePoint.Security.SharePointPermission* failed. What should you do about this? One way to solve the problem is to deploy the Web Part assembly in the GAC. Another way is to include the permissions you need for the proper working of the Web Part in the manifest file of the SharePoint solution. During the deployment, administrators can decide to grant these permissions to your assembly.

FIGURE 8-28 The raw ASP.NET error indicating a security problem with the Web Part

The request for the required permissions is to be included in the manifest.xml with the *CodeAccessSecurity* element, a child element of the *Solution* element:

```
<CodeAccessSecurity>
  <PolicyItem>
    <PermissionSet class="NamedPermissionSet" version="1"
      Description="Document Searcher Permission Set">
        <IPermission class="AspNetHostingPermission" version="1" Level="Minimal"/>
        <IPermission class="SecurityPermission" version="1" Flags="Execution" />
        <IPermission class="System.Security.Permissions.FileIOPermission, mscorlib,
Version=2.0.0.0, Culture=neutral, PublicKeyToken=b77a5c561934e089"   version="1"
Read="C:\Program Files\Common Files\Microsoft Shared\Web Server Extensions\12;$AppDir$"
Write="$AppDir$" Append="$AppDir$" PathDiscovery="$AppDir$"/>
        <IPermission version="1" Unrestricted="True"
         class="Microsoft.SharePoint.Security.SharePointPermission,
Microsoft.SharePoint.Security, Version=12.0.0.0, Culture=neutral,
PublicKeyToken=71e9bce111e9429c" />
    </PermissionSet>
    <Assemblies>
        <Assembly Name="DocumentSearcherWebPart" />
    </Assemblies>
  </PolicyItem>
</CodeAccessSecurity>
```

Two elements are included as child elements of the *CodeAccessSecurity* element: *PolicyItem* and *Assemblies*. The first contains a *PermissionSet* element with all of the *IPermission* elements, each representing a specific permission that you'd like to see granted for your assembly. The second element stores information about the assembly itself using the *Assembly* element.

IPermission elements are associated with a class of which the details—that is, the type information—is either set directly as the value of the *Class* attribute or defined at a higher level in the code-access security file that is associated with the trust level in the web.config file. If you review the contents of the web.config file, you'll encounter the association of the *WSS_Minimal* and *WSS_Medium* trust levels with their respective code-access security configuration files:

```
<securityPolicy>
  <trustLevel name="WSS_Medium" policyFile="C:\Program Files\Common Files\Microsoft
Shared\Web Server Extensions\12\config\wss_mediumtrust.config" />
  <trustLevel name="WSS_Minimal" policyFile="C:\Program Files\Common Files\Microsoft
Shared\Web Server Extensions\12\config\wss_minimaltrust.config" />
</securityPolicy>
```

After the deployment of the SharePoint solution with custom permissions, a copy of the active configuration file will be taken, and the custom permissions will be appended to the content. That new configuration file then becomes the active trust level in the web.config file of the IIS Web application where the SharePoint solution is deployed. If you open one of these configuration files, you'll notice that the first block is a listing of types that are referred to in the individual *IPermission* elements at the end:

```
<configuration>
  <mscorlib>
    <security>
      <policy>
        <PolicyLevel version="1">
          <SecurityClasses>
            <SecurityClass Name="AllMembershipCondition"
Description="System.Security.Policy.AllMembershipCondition, mscorlib, Version=2.0.0.0,
Culture=neutral, PublicKeyToken=b77a5c561934e089" />
            <SecurityClass Name="AspNetHostingPermission"
Description="System.Web.AspNetHostingPermission, System, Version=2.0.0.0,
Culture=neutral, PublicKeyToken=b77a5c561934e089" />
            <SecurityClass Name="FirstMatchCodeGroup"
 Description="System.Security.Policy.FirstMatchCodeGroup, mscorlib, Version=2.0.0.0,
Culture=neutral, PublicKeyToken=b77a5c561934e089" />
...
```

Going back to the manifest file in the project, the value of the *Class* attribute of the *IPermission* element can be assigned to a name of one of these *SecurityClass* elements.

Each type of permission you ask for has some specific attributes that are mapped to the properties that are exposed in the security class. A closer look at, for example, the *SharePointPermission* class reveals your options, but let's not worry about this and instead ask for support for all of the options by setting the *Unrestricted* attribute to *True*.

> **Note** The request for the *FileIOPermission* might seem a bit odd, but we have to include it in the list of permissions because of how *SPGridView* works internally with a JavaScript file that must be accessed at run time.

The identification of the assembly can be done in two ways, depending on the status of the assembly. If the assembly is a strong-named assembly, it has been signed using an .snk file, and you have the option to include the full details of the assembly in the *Assembly* element. This includes the full public key information. There is also the option to simply provide the physical name of the assembly, as is done for our sample here because that is the only option.

More Information The Office SharePoint Server 2007 SDK contains a two-part article about requesting permissions in the SharePoint solution manifest file: "Development Tools and Techniques for Working with Code in Windows SharePoint Services 3.0 (Parts 1 and 2)," by Patrick Tisseghem. The article is also available online in the Windows SharePoint Services Developer Center (*http://msdn2.microsoft.com/en-us/library/bb530302.aspx*).

All of the content of the SharePoint solution package is now ready. The creation of the package itself is done using the command-line utility named makecab.exe. This utility is available as part of the SDK if you install Visual Studio, or as a separate download included in the Microsoft Cabinet SDK. The input is a text file with the extension .ddf that defines the structure of the cabinet file. You can include this as a new file in the Solution folder of your project. You are free to choose the name of the file.

The diamond-directive file (.ddf) is a small text file that consists of two sections. Important in the header block is the name of the file that is created as well as information about the destination of it:

```
.OPTION EXPLICIT
.Set CabinetNameTemplate=DocumentSearcherWebPart.wsp
.set DiskDirectoryTemplate=CDROM ; All cabinets go in a single directory
.Set CompressionType=MSZIP ;** All files are compressed in cabinet files
.Set UniqueFiles="OFF"
.Set Cabinet=on
.Set DiskDirectory1=.
```

The second block is the definition of the list of files that will be included in the cabinet file. One by one, they are retrieved from their source location and dropped either in the root of the cabinet file like the first two or in a folder that is set using the *DestinationDir* parameter.

```
Solution\manifest.xml
bin\Debug\DocumentSearcherWebPart.dll

.Set DestinationDir=InsideSearch.DocumentSearcher
TEMPLATE\FEATURES\InsideSearch.DocumentSearcher\feature.xml
TEMPLATE\FEATURES\InsideSearch.DocumentSearcher\elements.xml
TEMPLATE\FEATURES\InsideSearch.DocumentSearcher\documentsearcher.webpart

.Set DestinationDir=IMAGES\InsideSearch
TEMPLATE\IMAGES\InsideSearch\EXCEL.GIF
TEMPLATE\IMAGES\InsideSearch\EXCEL2007.GIF
```

```
TEMPLATE\IMAGES\InsideSearch\Logo.GIF
TEMPLATE\IMAGES\InsideSearch\POWERPOINT.GIF
TEMPLATE\IMAGES\InsideSearch\POWERPOINT2007.GIF
TEMPLATE\IMAGES\InsideSearch\WORD.GIF
TEMPLATE\IMAGES\InsideSearch\WORD2007.GIF
```

If all of this is done, you can call the MakeCab.exe tool as follows:

```
"c:\Program Files\Microsoft Visual Studio 8\SmartDevices\SDK\SDKTools\makecab.exe" /f
solution\package.ddf
```

The result is the SharePoint solution package. You might quickly change the extension from .wsp to .cab to verify the contents of the compressed file. A double-click on the file opens it in Windows Explorer, and if all is there and in its correct folder, you are ready to hand over the SharePoint solution package to the administrators. Figure 8-29 displays the folder with the contents of the compressed file.

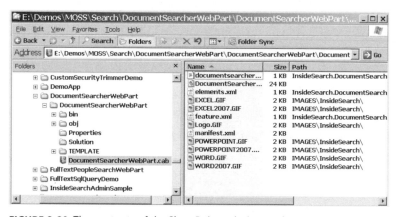

FIGURE 8-29 The contents of the SharePoint solution package

SharePoint solution packages must first be registered in the configuration database of the farm. Adding the solution to this database, in what we commonly refer to as the solution store, is done with the STSADM command-line utility, as follows:

```
set STSADM=%CommonProgramFiles%\Microsoft Shared\web server extensions\12\BIN\stsadm.exe
"%STSADM%" -o addsolution -filename DocumentSearcherWebPart.wsp
```

All of this can be done directly in the command prompt window, but it is best to create again batch files that you can easily reuse. The option that is used is *addsolution*, and it requires you to pass the name of the SharePoint solution file using the *filename* parameter.

In SharePoint 3.0 Central Administration, on the Operations tab, under the heading Global Configuration, you'll find a Solution Management link that redirects you to the page listing all of the solutions that are part of the solution store. If all went well during the call of the STSADM utility, you'll find your solution included in this list, with a status of Not Deployed, as shown in Figure 8-30.

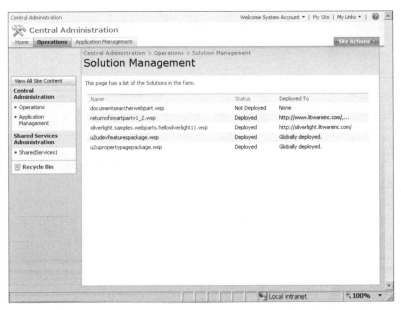

FIGURE 8-30 The Solution Management page, displaying the contents of the solution store

Click the name of the solution to navigate to the properties page, shown in Figure 8-31. As you'll notice, this page mentions the code access security policy request.

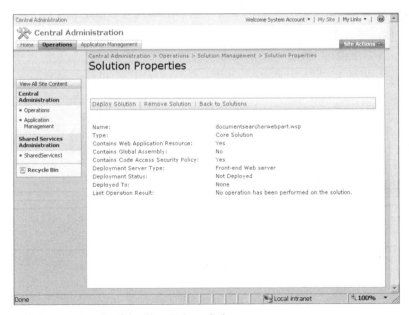

FIGURE 8-31 Details of the SharePoint solution

Now click the Deploy Solution link on the toolbar. The Deploy Solution page, shown in Figure 8-32, is used to configure when the deployment actually will take place and where the solution will be deployed. Notice the remark at the bottom that warns the administrator of the additional permissions that are requested in the manifest file of the solution.

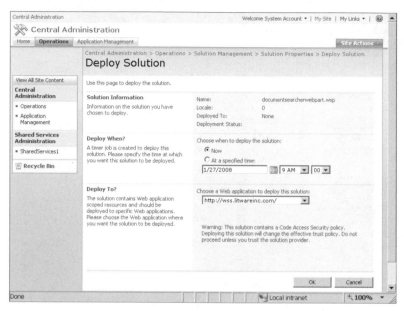

FIGURE 8-32 The overview page of what is deployed, how it is deployed, and some remarks for the administrator

You can now proceed with the deployment and verify your work in the site collection where you have deployed the Web Part. The Feature that is part of the solution has been installed but not yet activated. That will be the first thing to do, and as we have seen, this action makes the Web Part available to the user. Add the Web Part to the page. Even under minimal trust, the Web Part is allowed to communicate with the SharePoint object models and deliver the search support that was requested by the users.

More Information Simply handing over the SharePoint solution package to the administrators might not be enough for you. You might need more deployment-friendly support, delivering, for example, a Microsoft Installer (.msi) file that can be used to automate the last few steps in this walk-through. Lars Fastrup has released a small, handy tool called the SharePoint Installer on CodePlex that you can use to deliver the SharePoint solution to the administrators. This tool walks the administrators through a small wizard and, based on their selections, adds the solution to the solution store and deploys it to the selected IIS Web applications.

Building a Custom Small Search Box

The dedicated document search functionality can also be delivered with a custom small Search box instead of a Web Part, or maybe a combination of the two, as is demonstrated by the accompanying sample named SmallDocumentSearcher in the download package. Chapter 3 covered the workings of the small Search box in detail, so we can be brief here.

The small Search box is picked up on the master pages that are active in the different sites via the SharePoint *DelegateControl* control. This control will load either an ASP.NET user control or an ASP.NET server control for display. The choice depends on the Features that are active at that time and that contain a *Control* element with an ID that is known by the *DelegateControl*. If there is one match, the details of the *Control* element will be used to deliver the user interface. If more than one match is found, the Feature that contains a *Control* element with the smallest sequence number will be the one that delivers the control to be displayed.

The SmallDocumentSearcher sample project includes a Feature with the following code in the element manifest file:

```
<Elements xmlns="http://schemas.microsoft.com/sharepoint/">
    <Control
        Id="SmallSearchInputBox"
        Sequence="10"
        ControlClass="InsideSearch.Controls.SmallDocumentSearcherBox"
        ControlAssembly="SmallDocumentSearcherBox, Version=1.0.0.0, Culture=neutral, Pub
licKeyToken=69e44574501227b0">
        <Property Name="SearchResultPageURL">
            /_layouts/InsideSearch/docresults.aspx</Property>
    </Control>
</Elements>
```

The Feature points to a small ASP.NET server control inside the assembly that, once loaded, displays a small text box and button to the user, as shown in Figure 8-33.

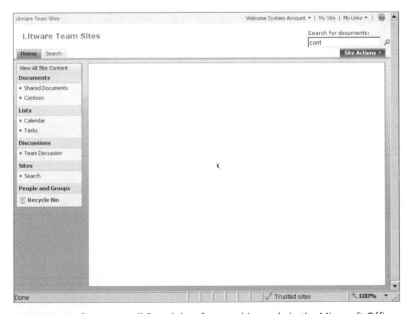

FIGURE 8-33 Custom small Search box for searching only in the Microsoft Office system documents

The search is not executed within the control but done on a custom application page. The passing of the query happens through the query string. The URL for this page is defined with the property *SearchResultPageURL* in the Feature file. The code executed on the application page is exactly the same as the code executed by the custom Web Part in the section "Building, Packaging, and Deploying a Custom Document Searcher Web Part" earlier in this chapter. The results are displayed again using an *SPGridView* on the application page, as shown in Figure 8-34.

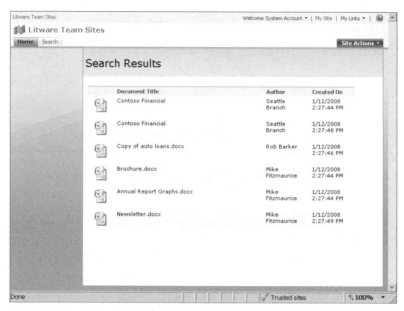

FIGURE 8-34 The custom application page, displaying the search results

The Query Web Service

All of the coding samples we have looked at up to now in this chapter require access to the context of SharePoint. In other words, the code must be executed on the machine that has a SharePoint installation. Applications that are deployed to the users' desktops are not able to retrieve all of this context information, and as a result, within these types of applications, you cannot use code that directly calls classes and members that are exposed by the different object models you've seen. Executing the code remotely entails that you use Web services.

There are many Web services that are part of the infrastructure of a SharePoint installation. Most of them are located in the 12\ISAPI folder. Remote execution of search queries is possible with the Office SharePoint Server 2007 Query Web service, represented by the search. asmx file. The endpoint URL, the URL you use to connect to the Web service, is shown here:

```
http://Server_Name/[sites/][Site_Name/]_vti_bin/search.asmx
```

Figure 8-35 displays the page that is generated if you make that call with the different Web methods that you can execute programmatically.

FIGURE 8-35 Methods exposed by the Query Web service

The following list provides an overview of the use of each of these Web methods. We'll then proceed with a practical example of how you can deliver support for users in Microsoft Office Word 2007 to execute a query and process the results in their documents.

- ■ *GetPortalSearchInfo*   This method is marked obsolete and therefore should not be called anymore. It returns a string containing the names of all of the local and shared search scopes that can be used in the scope of the site collection.

- ■ *GetSearchMetaData*   This method returns an ADO.NET *DataSet* that contains two tables: a table with the list of managed properties and a table for the list of local and shared search scopes that can be used in the site collection. You should use this method in place of the previous *GetPortalSearchInfo* method to get access to the search scopes.

- ■ *Query*   Use this method to execute a search query. The query can be formulated using the keyword syntax or the SQL syntax. The results are returned in an XML string. The input that is required for the Web method is an XML string that uses the *Microsoft. Search.Query* schema for Enterprise Search. More on this in a moment.

- ■ *QueryEx*   This method accepts an XML string with the query parameters similar to the *Query* Web method, but this time, the return value is an ADO.NET *DataSet*. The benefit of this method is that the results can be easily bound to the ASP.NET or Windows-based user interface controls that display the results to the user.

- **Registration**   The *Query* Web method can be registered as a Microsoft Office Research service in the Microsoft Office system clients. The Research pane allows the users in the Microsoft Office system applications to quickly submit queries to the registered Web services and get the results delivered in their familiar Office system environment. At the end of this section, you'll find an explanation of how this works.

- **Status**   This method can be called to quickly determine the current status of the search service.

The *QueryPacket* Element

You have to encapsulate the query that must be executed in an XML string that adheres to the *Microsoft.Search.Query* schema. Both the *Query* and the *QueryEx* Web methods expect the query in the following format:

```
<QueryPacket>
    <Query>
        <QueryId />
        <SupportedFormats>
            <Format />
         </SupportedFormats>
        <Context>
            <QueryText />
            <OriginatorContext />
        </Context>
        <Range>
            <StartAt />
            <Count />
        </Range>
        <Properties>
            <Property />
        </Properties>
        <SortByProperties>
            <SortByProperty />
        </SortByProperties>
        <EnableStemming />
        <TrimDuplicates />
        <IncludeSpecialTermResults />
        <IgnoreAllNoiseQuery />
        <IncludeRelevantResults />
        <IncludeHighConfidenceResults />
    </Query>
</QueryPacket>
```

Here is an example of a simple instance of such a *QueryPacket* that results in the execution of a query using the keyword syntax and returning results containing the term *Contoso*:

```
<QueryPacket xmlns='urn:Microsoft.Search.Query'>
  <Query>
    <SupportedFormats>
      <Format>urn:Microsoft.Search.Response.Document.Document</Format>
```

```
    </SupportedFormats>
    <Context>
      <QueryText language='en-US' type='STRING'>Contoso</QueryText>
    </Context>
  </Query>
</QueryPacket>
```

The root element is the *QueryPacket* element with the *xmlns* attribute storing the schema that is used to validate the XML. The value is always the same in Enterprise Search. The parameters for the query are all delivered as child elements of the *Query* element. The one-and-only response format that is supported by the clients in the context of Enterprise Search is *urn:Microsoft.Search.Response.Document.Document*. You define this information using the *SupportedFormats* element and the *Format* element.

The core of the *QueryPacket* element is the *Context* element. The *QueryText* child element stores the actual search query that will be issued to the Web service. There are two important attributes: *type* and *language*. The value of *type* is used to indicate whether the query is formulated with the keyword syntax or the SQL syntax. If the keyword syntax is used, the query must have the value *STRING*. If the SQL syntax is used, the query must be set to *MSSQLFT*. The *language* attribute is also important and identifies the language of the keyword search. Value *type* is *xml:lang*, and if specified, this is interpreted by Enterprise Search as the query locale. If no value is given, the default value is the language of the site.

Other elements can be included in *QueryPacket* that allow you to control the execution of the query. Here is an overview:

- **Range**   Use this element to pass information about the range of the query. Two child elements can be used: the *StartAt* element, for specifying the result to return as the initial result, and the *Count* element, for specifying the maximum number of results that you want to see returned.

- **Properties**   You can pass the names of the managed properties you want to see included in the search results. Each managed property is included using a *Property* child element, and the name attribute of this element is set to the name of the managed property.

- **SortByProperties**   Use this element to pass the required sorting order individually represented by the *SortByProperty* element, as follows:

  ```
  <SortByProperty name=managedProperty Direction={Ascending|Descending} Order=Integer>
  ```

- **EnableStemming**   Enables stemming, if needed.

- **TrimDuplicates**   Specifies whether duplicate results collapsing is enabled.

- **IncludeSpecialTermsResults**   Use this element if you want to have results other than the relevant results included in the response. This can be, for example, the best bet results.

- **IgnoreAllNoiseQuery**   Specifies whether the Search Web service should ignore noise words in the search query.

- **IncludeRelevantResults**   By default, turned on, but this element can be turned off if you don't want the relevant results returned in the response.

- **ImplicitAndBehavior**   Used when you want to specify whether there is a default *AND* between keyword terms.

- **IncludeHighConfidenceResults**   Specifies whether high confidence results should be included in the response returned by the Query Web service.

The *ResponsePacket* Element

The response that is returned depends on the method you are using to execute the query and also the type of syntax that is used for the query.

Response for the *Query* Method

If you are calling the *Query* method using the keyword syntax or the SQL syntax, the following typical response is returned:

```
<ResponsePacket xmlns="urn:Microsoft.Search.Response">
  <Response domain="QDomain">
    <Range>
      <StartAt>1</StartAt>
      <Count>10</Count>
      <TotalAvailable>88</TotalAvailable>
      <Results>
        <Document xmlns="urn:Microsoft.Search.Response.Document">
          <Action>
            <LinkUrl>http://www.litwareinc.com</LinkUrl>
          </Action>
          <Properties xmlns="urn:Microsoft.Search.Response.Document.Document">
            <Property>
              <Name>TITLE</Name>
              <Type>String</Type>
              <Value>Litware Internet</Value>
            </Property>
            <Property>
              <Name>PATH</Name>
              <Type>String</Type>
              <Value>http://www.litwareinc.com</Value>
            </Property>
            <Property>
              <Name>DESCRIPTION</Name>
              <Type>String</Type>
              <Value>The public face of the Litware Company</Value>
            </Property>
            <Property>
              <Name>WRITE</Name>
```

```
                <Type>DateTime</Type>
                <Value>2008-01-11T14:50:30+01:00</Value>
            </Property>
            <Property>
                <Name>RANK</Name>
                <Type>Int64</Type>
                <Value>903</Value>
            </Property>
            <Property>
                <Name>SIZE</Name>
                <Type>Int64</Type>
                <Value>0</Value>
            </Property>
        </Properties>
    </Document>
[omitted for brevity]
        </Results>
    </Range>
    <Status>SUCCESS</Status>
  </Response>
</ResponsePacket>
```

The XML delivered within the *ResponsePacket* root element is valid against the *Microsoft. Search.Registration.Response* schema. The *Response* element has a number of child elements—*StartAt*, *Count*, and *TotalAvailable*—that deliver general information about the executed search query. Every search result item is delivered within a *Document* element. The *Action* element contains the URL and possibly the file type information for the search result. For the keyword query delivered with the *Query* method, a default set of properties is returned, each delivering one piece of the search result item details. *Property* elements contain a *Name* element for the name of the property and a *Type* element with the type information; the actual value is part of the *Value* element. By default, the *ResponsePacket* for the *Query* method delivers the values, if not *null*, for the following properties:

- *Title*
- *Path*
- *Description*
- *Write*
- *Rank*
- *Size*

You can also explicitly control which properties or columns are returned. In case of a keyword syntax query, this is controlled through the *Properties* property in the *RequestPacket* that you send to the Web service. You must include all of the preceding default properties if you choose this option—they are required properties.

Here is an example of a request that executes the same query as the preceding example, but now with the inclusion of the *Author* column:

```
<QueryPacket xmlns="urn:Microsoft.Search.Query">
  <Query domain="QDomain">
    <SupportedFormats>
      <Format>urn:Microsoft.Search.Response.Document.Document</Format>
    </SupportedFormats>
    <Context>
      <QueryText language="en-US" type="STRING">Contoso</QueryText>
    </Context>
    <Properties>
      <Property name='Title'></Property>
      <Property name='Path'></Property>
      <Property name='Description'></Property>
      <Property name='Write'></Property>
      <Property name='Rank'></Property>
      <Property name='Size'></Property>
      <Property name='Author'></Property>
    </Properties>
  </Query>
</QueryPacket>
```

If the query is formulated using the SQL syntax, it is easier to create, because the list of returned columns is defined in the *SELECT* clause. Here is an example of how the author information can be included in the search results:

```
<QueryPacket xmlns="urn:Microsoft.Search.Query">
  <Query domain="QDomain">
    <SupportedFormats>
      <Format>urn:Microsoft.Search.Response.Document.Document</Format>
    </SupportedFormats>
    <Context>
      <QueryText language="en-US" type="MSSQLFT">
          SELECT title, path, description, write, rank, size, author
          FROM SCOPE() WHERE FREETEXT('office')
      </QueryText>
    </Context>
  </Query>
</QueryPacket>
```

One final note about the response format of the *Query* method is that the response can include only relevant results. Other result types can be retrieved only by using the *QueryEx* method, described next.

Response for the *QueryEx* Method

Executing the same keyword query using the *QueryEx* method returns the results in the following format:

```
<Results>
  <RelevantResults>
    <WorkId>1482</WorkId>
    <Rank>872</Rank>
    <Title>Contoso</Title>
    <Author>System Account</Author>
    <Size>0</Size>
    <Path>http://wss.litwareinc.com/Contoso/Forms/AllItems.aspx</Path>
    <Write>2008-01-12T14:28:48+01:00</Write>
    <SiteName>http://wss.litwareinc.com</SiteName>
    <CollapsingStatus>0</CollapsingStatus>
    <HitHighlightedSummary>Turn on more accessible mode Skip to main content Turn off
      more accessible mode Litware Team Sites Welcome  My Site My Links
      Litware Team Sites      Home Site Actions Litware Team Sites  &amp;gt;
      &lt;c0&gt;Contoso&lt;/c0&gt; &lt;ddd/&gt; </HitHighlightedSummary>
    <HitHighlightedProperties>&lt;HHTitle&gt;&lt;c0&gt;Contoso&lt;/c0&gt;&lt;/HHTitle
      &gt;&lt;HHUrl&gt;http://wss.litwareinc.com/&lt;c0&gt;Contoso&lt;/c0&gt;
      /Forms/AllItems.aspx&lt;/HHUrl&gt;</HitHighlightedProperties>
    <ContentClass>STS_List_DocumentLibrary</ContentClass>
    <IsDocument>0</IsDocument>
  </RelevantResults>
  <RelevantResults>
    <WorkId>1626</WorkId>
    <Rank>857</Rank>
    <Title>Contoso, Ltd.</Title>
    <Size>0</Size>
    <Path>http://profke:3333/ssp/admin/Content/Reseller.aspx?ResellerKey=671</Path>
    <Write>2008-01-24T23:33:24.296875+01:00</Write>
    <SiteName>324e7ad5-f5b0-4711-a8cd-a678a200cca2</SiteName>
    <CollapsingStatus>0</CollapsingStatus>
    <HitHighlightedSummary>&lt;c0&gt;Contoso&lt;/c0&gt;, Ltd.</HitHighlightedSummary>
    <HitHighlightedProperties>&lt;HHTitle&gt;&lt;c0&gt;Contoso&lt;/c0&gt;,
      Ltd.&lt;/HHTitle&gt;&lt;HHUrl&gt;http://profke:3333/ssp/admin/Content
      /Reseller.aspx?ResellerKey=671&lt;/HHUrl&gt;</HitHighlightedProperties>
    <IsDocument>0</IsDocument>
  </RelevantResults>
</Results>
```

The *QueryEx* method returns the search results in a *System.Data.DataSet* object with a default set of properties included per search result. Only properties that have an actual value are inserted in the response. The default properties are listed here:

- *WorkId*

- *Rank*

- *Title*

- *Author*

- *Size*

- *Path*

- *Description*

- *Write*

- *SiteName*

- *CollapsingStatus*

- *HitHighlightedSummary*

- *HitHighlightedProperties*

- *ContentClass*

- *IsDocument*

- *PictureThumbnailURL*

The *DataSet* object contains a *System.DataSet.DataTable* object for each result type that is returned. The different result types that can be returned are as follows:

- *Relevant*, in a table named *RelevantResults*

- *High Confidence*, in a table named *HighConfidenceResults*

- *Special Terms*, in a table named *SpecialTermsResults*

Again, the list of properties that you want to include in the response is adaptable. In a keyword syntax query, you again define them using the *Properties* property. For a SQL syntax query, you work at the level of the *SELECT* clause in the query itself.

Custom Business Data Search Task Pane in Microsoft Office Word 2007

Now that you've seen the possible formats and options for the request and the response while communicating with the Query Web service, let's see this Web service in action within a small sample application. This sample is available for download and filed under the name BusinessDataSearchPane in the sample package.

The sample application involves an add-in for Microsoft Office Word 2007 that extends the application with a custom Ribbon and a custom task pane. The task pane is displayed by clicking the one button that makes up the custom Ribbon. In the task pane, the user can enter a query and have this query executed remotely by calling the Query Web service. The results are displayed immediately in the task pane itself, and the user has the option to populate content controls with one of the search result items. An impression of the sample is shown in Figure 8-36.

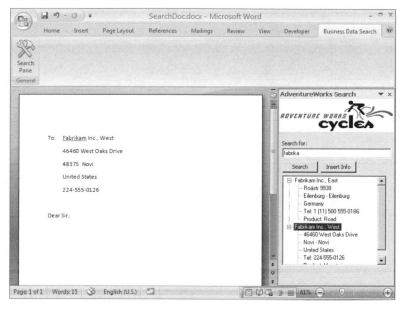

FIGURE 8-36 Searching business data remotely in Office Word 2007

The integration displayed in Figure 8-36 is delivered in the Office system application with an add-in that has been created with the Visual Tools for Office (VSTO), an extension of the Visual Studio 2005 or 2008 development environment for building Microsoft Office 2003 and 2007 Office system solutions. It is best to do the work in Visual Studio 2008—the development experience is better because of the additional templates, designers, and wizards for creating these types of solutions. Figure 8-37 shows the different types of project templates for 2007 Office system that you can start with.

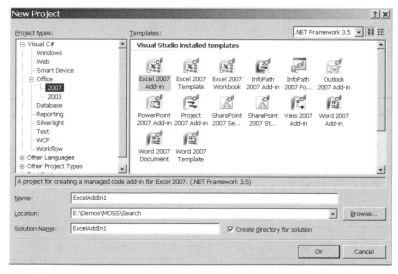

FIGURE 8-37 Project templates for building 2007 Office system solutions in Visual Studio 2008

There is support for the construction of a custom Ribbon by using a designer, as shown in Figure 8-38. Tabs, groups, buttons, and other Ribbon controls can be quickly added from the toolbox. After the properties are set for each of the controls that you are using, you can work on the code-behind in a way similar to the development experience you have when working on, for example, a Windows-based application.

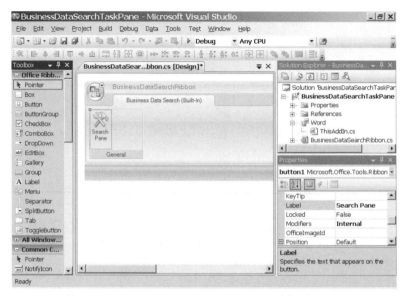

FIGURE 8-38 The design experience for creating custom Ribbons

The task pane is a normal Windows-based user control that is populated with the controls that are needed to deliver the user interface. The pane is displayed by clicking the button on the Ribbon. The code in the event handler is straightforward:

```
private void buttonPane_Click(object sender, RibbonControlEventArgs e)
{
    Microsoft.Office.Tools.CustomTaskPane customTaskPane =
        Globals.ThisAddIn.CustomTaskPanes.Add
        (new AdventureWorksPane(), "AdventureWorks Search");
    customTaskPane.Visible = true;
    customTaskPane.Width = 400;
}
```

An instance of the *CustomTaskPane* class is added to the collection of task panes that are internally maintained by the add-in. Custom task panes are by default not visible; you make them visible by setting the *Visible* property to *true*.

The code-behind class for the user control contains a call to the Query Web service. To facilitate the communication with the Web service, you let Visual Studio generate a proxy class. Proxy classes shield you from the complicated HTTP and SOAP calls when sending requests and accepting responses. A proxy class for the Web service is created in Visual Studio by adding a Web reference to the project. In the dialog box that is displayed, you enter the end-point URL to the Web service and then just add the reference to your project.

Once the proxy class is there, the first lines of code will create an instance of it and next set the credentials that will be passed to the Web service:

```
QueryService searchService = new QueryService();
searchService.Credentials = System.Net.CredentialCache.DefaultCredentials;
```

In the preceding code, the credentials of the current user are passed. You can also create a new instance of the *System.Net.NetworkCredential* class and then define the user name, domain, and password and use that for the authentication.

The sample uses a query constructed with the SQL syntax and works only if you have done some preparation work. The sample assumes that the *AdventureWorks* database, and especially the information about the resellers, is crawled and part of the content index. Next, you must have a search scope named *AdventureWorks* that limits the search results to only the *AdventureWorks* content source. And last, there are some managed properties that are used in the SQL query. All of this has already been covered in earlier chapters in this book, so we won't go into details here.

The query itself is built with these two variables that will get the keyword entered by the user in the task pane:

```
private string sqlQueryTemplate =
    "SELECT ResellerCompany, ResellerAddress, ResellerPostalCode, " +
    "        ResellerCity, ResellerCountry, ResellerPhone, ResellerProductLine " +
    "FROM SCOPE() " +
    " WHERE \"Scope\" = 'AdventureWorks' AND CONTAINS('\"*{0}*\"')";

private string queryPacketTemplate = "<?xml version=\"1.0\" encoding=\"utf-8\" ?>"
    + "<QueryPacket xmlns=\"urn:Microsoft.Search.Query\">"
    + "<Query domain=\"QDomain\"><SupportedFormats>"
    + "<Format>urn:Microsoft.Search.Response.Document.Document</Format>"
    + "</SupportedFormats>"
    + "<Range><StartAt>1</StartAt><Count>100</Count></Range> "
    + "<Context><QueryText language=\"en-US\" type=\"MSSQLFT\">"
    + "{0}</QueryText></Context>"
    + "</Query></QueryPacket>";
```

The execution is done with a call to the *QueryEx* method. Remember that this method returns you an ADO.NET *DataSet*, always a good thing to have, due to the ease of processing the rows storing the results.

```
string sqlQuery = string.Format(sqlQueryTemplate, textBoxQuery.Text);
string queryXml = string.Format(queryPacketTemplate, sqlQuery);
DataSet ds = searchService.QueryEx(queryXml);
```

The results are displayed in a tree view control, as shown here, but of course you can use your own creativity to process and display the results differently. Notice the managed properties that expose the details of the business data that has been crawled.

```
DataTable tbl = ds.Tables["RelevantResults"];
ResultTreeview.Nodes.Clear();
if (tbl.Rows.Count > 0)
{
    foreach (DataRow r in tbl.Rows)
    {
        TreeNode resNode = new TreeNode(r["ResellerCompany"].ToString());
        ResultTreeview.Nodes.Add(resNode);
        resNode.Tag = r;
        TreeNode det1Node = new TreeNode(r["ResellerAddress"].ToString());
        resNode.Nodes.Add(det1Node);
        TreeNode det2Node = new TreeNode(r["ResellerCity"].ToString() + " - "
            + ["ResellerCity"].ToString());
        resNode.Nodes.Add(det2Node);
        TreeNode det3Node = new TreeNode(r["ResellerCountry"].ToString());
        resNode.Nodes.Add(det3Node);
        TreeNode det4Node = new TreeNode("Tel: " + r["ResellerPhone"].ToString());
        resNode.Nodes.Add(det4Node);
        TreeNode det5Node = new TreeNode("Product: " +
            r["ResellerProductLine"].ToString());
        resNode.Nodes.Add(det5Node);
    }
}
else
{
    MessageBox.Show("No results!");
}
```

A last piece of the sample that is interesting to review is the inserting of the selected customer details in the Office Word 2007 document. The document can contain content controls that are populated either by binding them to XML data that is stored in the document itself or by using the following code, which transfers the customer details one by one to the available content controls. This code assumes that you have a *using* statement for the *Microsoft. Office.Interop.Word* aliased as *Word*.

```
private void buttonInsert_Click(object sender, EventArgs e)
{
    Word.Application app = (Word.Application)Globals.ThisAddIn.Application;
    try
    {
        TreeNode selNode = ResultTreeview.SelectedNode;
        if (selNode.Tag != null)
        {
            DataRow r = (DataRow)selNode.Tag;
            if (app.ActiveDocument.ContentControls.Count > 0)
            {
```

```
            object ctr = null;
            ctr = 1;
            app.ActiveDocument.ContentControls.get_Item(ref ctr).Range.Text =
                ["ResellerCompany"].ToString();
            ctr = 2;
            app.ActiveDocument.ContentControls.get_Item(ref ctr).Range.Text =
                r["ResellerAddress"].ToString();
            ctr = 3;
            app.ActiveDocument.ContentControls.get_Item(ref ctr).Range.Text =
                r["ResellerPostalCode"].ToString();
            ctr = 4;
            app.ActiveDocument.ContentControls.get_Item(ref ctr).Range.Text =
                r["ResellerCity"].ToString();
            ctr = 5;
            app.ActiveDocument.ContentControls.get_Item(ref ctr).Range.Text =
                r["ResellerCountry"].ToString();
            ctr = 6;
            app.ActiveDocument.ContentControls.get_Item(ref ctr).Range.Text =
                r["ResellerPhone"].ToString();
        }
        else
        {
            Word.Range rng = app.ActiveDocument.Content;
            rng.InsertAfter("Company: " + r["ResellerCompany"].ToString());
            rng.InsertAfter("Address: " + r["ResellerAddress"].ToString() + ", " +
                r["ResellerPostalCode"].ToString() + " - " +
                r["ResellerCity"].ToString());
            rng.InsertAfter("Country: " + r["ResellerCountry"].ToString());
        }
    }
    else
    {
        MessageBox.Show("Select a customer first!");
    }
    }
    catch (Exception ex)
    {
    }
}
```

The sample illustrates only a small selection of the options that you have as a developer to remotely program with the Query Web service. You no doubt will have many other possible business cases within your organization.

Registering the Query Web Service as a Research Service

As mentioned earlier, the Query Web service is equipped with the required support to be registered as a Research service in the Microsoft Office system products.

In 2007 Office system, the Research pane can be opened from the Review Ribbon. In the Proofing group is a Research button that displays a pane similar to the sample reviewed in the preceding section. Figure 8-39 shows the Research pane in Microsoft Office Excel 2007.

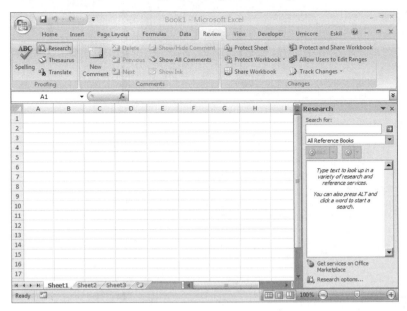

FIGURE 8-39 The Research pane in Microsoft Office Excel 2007

The Research Options link at the bottom of the Research pane lets you maintain the Research options. Click this link to display the Research Options dialog box, shown in Figure 8-40.

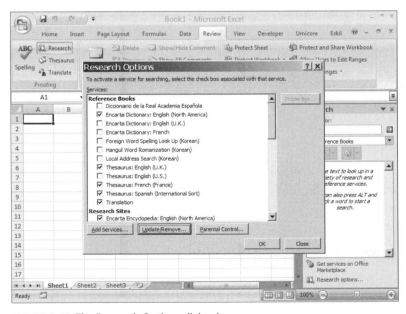

FIGURE 8-40 The Research Options dialog box

To add the Query Web service, you click the Add Services button. The Add Services dialog box, shown in Figure 8-41, is used to enter the endpoint URL to the Web service. Note that the addition of the service is basically a creation of a key in the Windows registry.

Administrators can push this change to all of the desktops in the company using, for example, Active Directory policies.

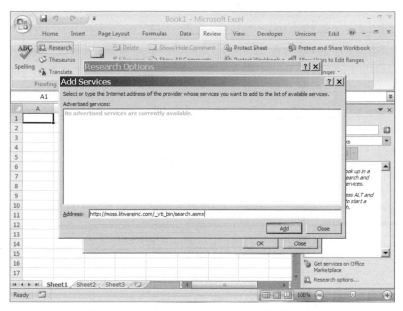

FIGURE 8-41 Adding the endpoint URL to the Query Web service

By clicking the Add button, you are basically calling the *Registration* method that is exposed by the Query Web service. The method returns the required information for the communication with the Web service, as shown in Figure 8-42.

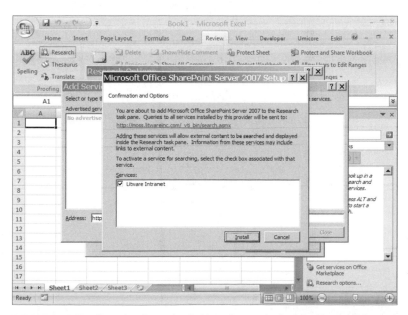

FIGURE 8-42 Confirmation from the *Registration* method of the Query Web service

You are now ready to enter queries in the small Search box and have these sent to the Web service for execution. The results are displayed instantly in the Research pane, as shown in Figure 8-43.

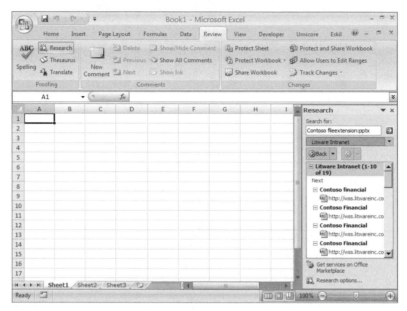

FIGURE 8-43 An Enterprise Search executed in the Research pane

Summary

Plenty of code was covered in this chapter demonstrating the two search APIs that are included in *Microsoft.Office.Server.Search.dll*. The first part of this chapter covered the new search administration object model, and the second part reviewed the improved query object model. The various topics we covered illustrate the rich support that you have as a developer for building custom search front-end solution components that extend or possibly replace the out-of-the-box administration and end-user search experience. The next chapter goes even further and introduces you to a number of advanced programming topics, such as the creation of custom protocol handlers, *IFilters*, and custom security trimmers. Mastering the techniques covered in this and the subsequent chapter will give you all of the tools you need as a developer to operate within the Microsoft Enterprise Search space.

Chapter 9
Advanced Search Engine Topics

After completing this chapter, you will be able to

- Understand the detailed architecture of the search engine.

- Develop and install custom *IFilters*.

- Develop and install custom protocol handlers.

- Develop and register custom security trimmers.

- Understand and use Faceted Search.

The topics we've looked at up to now in this book are actually peripheral to the core of the Enterprise Search engine. They all rely on and build on top of the basic indexing and searching features provided out-of-the-box. But the search engine itself also comes with a pluggable architecture that allows you to extend it to index other types of content sources as well as other file formats. The content crawler of the search engine connects to content sources via a broker known as a *protocol handler*, and the crawler needs exactly one protocol handler for each type of content it is asked to index. Documents pulled from any content source are in turn processed by a second type of component known as an *IFilter*, which extracts all text and metadata from the documents. Each filter can support one or more file formats.

This chapter starts with a deep dive into the detailed architecture and inner workings of the search engine, giving you a good understanding of the pluggable architecture. Next, you are initiated in the art of developing and installing your own *IFilters* and protocol handlers. However, not many Microsoft Office SharePoint Server 2007 developers will ever need to worry about this. Third-party filters and protocol handlers are readily available in the marketplace at low cost and in some cases even for free. The Business Data Catalog (BDC) discussed in Chapter 6, "Indexing and Searching Business Data," is essentially a configurable protocol handler that enables you to index data from virtually any source as long as it can be arranged in rows and columns. You will need to consider developing your own protocol handlers and filters only if you need to index highly specialized content sources and file formats. But the efforts and knowledge required should not be underestimated. You will need to be proficient at developing multithreaded safe Component Object Model (COM) components in C/C++. COM is an interface standard for the development of software components and was introduced by Microsoft in 1993. A multithreaded safe COM component must be implemented in such a way that multiple instances of the same component can run in parallel without corruption of data. It is also essential to master pointer arithmetic and memory management in the C/C++ programming language.

The search engine can also be extended with a custom security trimmer that you can employ to suppress selected search results from being displayed to the user. However, you should consider custom security trimmers only when security trimming is needed against content sources where user permissions do not map to Microsoft Windows domain users and groups. The built-in security trimmer automatically trims all results for which an access control list (ACL) is available. When you need a custom security trimmer, fortunately, it is rather simple to develop one, as it runs in managed code. The biggest issue is to devise an algorithm that performs well—that is, one that does not result in long query response times.

The chapter concludes with a discussion of Faceted Search and how it can be implemented on top of the search engine. *Faceted Search* is a technique providing users with intelligent suggestions (*facets*) for narrowing the scope of the search. Faceted Search has become a popular and useful feature in the Enterprise Search space, as it has proved itself to be more intuitive for users to understand and use than an advanced search form.

Detailed Search Engine Architecture

The search engine consists of two major components: an index engine and a query engine. These components can run on the same server, or they can be distributed to dedicated index servers and query servers, respectively. Chapter 7, "Search Deployment Considerations," provides detailed coverage of common deployment scenarios. The following subsections delve into the detailed architecture of the content index, the index engine, and the query engine. For a high-level overview of the search architecture, see Chapter 1, "Introducing Enterprise Search in SharePoint 2007."

 More Information See the article "Enterprise Search Architecture" on the Microsoft Development Network (MSDN) at *http://msdn2.microsoft.com/en-us/library/ms570748.aspx*.

Shared Services Provider Content Index

Each Shared Services Provider (SSP) configured to provide searching has its own separate content index, as shown in the following illustration. Every instance of a content index is composed of a full inverted index stored on the file system and a property store that resides in the SSP Search database.

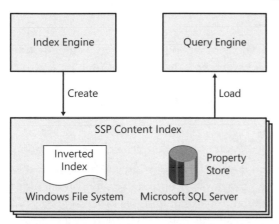

The role of the inverted index is to support fast free-text searching with good relevancy ranking of the matching results. The property store plays two important roles. First, it stores metadata (properties) and access control information for each item that is indexed. Second, it allows queries to filter results by property values on documents.

In general terms, the inverted index contains a list of all unique keywords encountered during crawls, noise words excluded. For each keyword, it again contains a list with references to all documents in which the keyword appears. Last, each document entry in this list also contains a list of all the positions of the keyword within the document. The keyword positions are needed for phrase searching as well as near searching. The near search method finds results where keywords are within 50 words of each other in a document.

More Information For book references and a computer-scientific explanation of a full inverted index, search one of the major Internet search engines for the keywords *full inverted index*.

The files that make up the inverted index of each SSP are stored in the default folder C:\Program Files\Microsoft Office Servers\12.0\Data\Office Server\Applications\<SSP GUID> on the index server as well as on the query servers. See the section "Detecting the Search Application Name for an SSP" in Chapter 5, "Search Administration," to learn how the index folder for an SSP can be identified by its globally unique identifier (GUID). The internal format of the index files is closed—that is, not published and documented by Microsoft. The files can be modified only indirectly from protocol handlers and *IFilters* by sending text and property values through the Indexing Pipeline. See the next section for a detailed description of the Indexing Pipeline.

The property store, also known as the metadata store, is stored in regular database tables on a SQL Server in the farm. See the section "The Metadata Store" in Chapter 5 for a list of the related tables.

Index Engine

The index engine is responsible for crawling content and building up a content index for each SSP that is served by it. A physical server where the index engine is running is also referred to as an index server. A SharePoint server farm can include multiple index servers, but each SSP can be served by only one index server at a time. On the other hand, one index server can serve multiple SSPs.

The architecture of the index engine, shown in the following illustration, was designed for speedy indexing of content, which is an important aspect when you have large volumes of content. Acceptable speed is achieved by crawling content in many parallel processes and threads, thus optimizing CPU utilization. The use of multiple processes is a key factor in implementing scalability on servers with multiple core CPUs and multiple physical CPUs. Crawling content one document at a time would be extremely slow, as the CPU would spend most of its time waiting for content servers to respond and for the content to travel across the network.

The key components of the index engine include the following:

- **Search Service Process**   The core of the index engine runs in the process of the Search service on each index server. This is the same process in which the query engine runs if enabled to run on the same server. For the index engine, the Search Service Process runs the Gather Manager and Indexing Pipeline components (described in a moment). The name of the process as displayed in the Windows Task Manager is mssearch.exe.

- **Gather Manager**   This component manages the crawls of content sources for all the associated SSPs. It also manages a crawl queue for each content source from which it retrieves the URLs to crawl. Each URL is simply passed on for further processing to the appropriate protocol handler in a separate process known as the Filter Daemon. Crawls will start from the start addresses specified for each content source. Protocol handlers will in turn try to discover additional URLs and feed them back to the crawl queue via the gatherer. The gatherer will again delegate the new URLs to the appropriate protocol handlers while respecting crawl rules and crawler impact rules. The crawl will continue until the crawl queue is emptied or the crawl is manually aborted by an administrator.

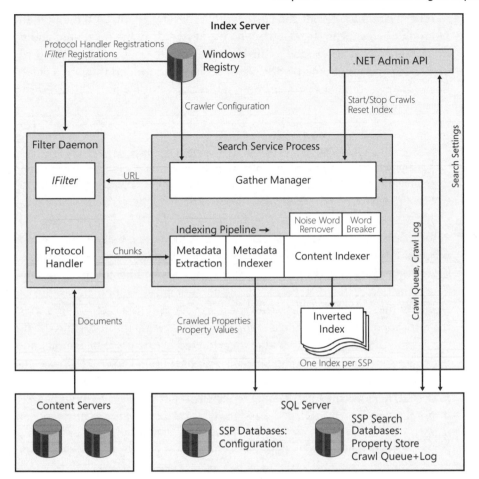

- **Indexing Pipeline**   Content downloaded by protocol handlers and parsed by *IFilter*s is fed to the Indexing Pipeline, which processes the new content and adds it to the index. A series of internal plug-ins with different responsibilities constitutes the pipeline. First, the Metadata Extraction plug-in is responsible for extracting additional metadata from documents when possible. For Microsoft Office system documents, the Metadata Extraction plug-in is able, for instance, to guess the title from the document content if the title property for the document is empty. Furthermore, it also tries to detect the natural language of the document content. A successful language detection results in a language code value for the managed property named *DetectedLanguage*. Next, the property store is updated by the Metadata Indexer plug-in with all the metadata properties of the document, including the URL, title, modified date, and author, as well as other system properties and custom properties if present. Last, the Content Indexer plug-in updates the inverted index with the keywords in the document and their positions. Metadata is also added to the inverted index to enable simple keyword searching on property values. In this plug-in, keywords are also looped through a language-dependent word breaker to split composite words. Noise words are also recognized and discarded here.

> **Note** Although the Indexing Pipeline has a modular plug-in architecture, it is not possible to write your own plug-ins. Microsoft has deliberately not published the application programming interface (API) for these kinds of plug-ins, as poorly written and improper plug-ins carry a risk of destroying the Search Service Process.

- **Filter Daemon**   The Gather Manager launches multiple parallel Filter Daemon processes dedicated to the execution of protocol handlers and *IFilters*. With help from protocol handlers and *Ifilters*, a Filter Daemon is responsible for downloading content and extracting text and metadata for the content index. During crawls, the Gather Manager decides which URL to crawl next and sends it to a Filter Daemon, which loads the appropriate protocol handler and *IFilter* based on the protocol and the file extension of the URL. The text and metadata extracted by the protocol handler and the *IFilter* are sent into the Indexing Pipeline in smaller units known as *chunks*. The advantage of moving protocol handlers and *IFilters* outside the Search Service Process is twofold. First, it allows the index engine to scale content crawling to multiple CPUs. Second, it protects the Search Service Process from fatal errors in custom protocol handlers and *IFilters*. The Gather Manager constantly monitors all live Filter Daemons and simply destroys those that for some reason stop responding. The name of the Filter Daemon process as displayed in the Windows Task Manager is mssdmn.exe.

- **Protocol Handler**   A protocol handler is responsible for connecting and authenticating with a specific type of content repository and downloading content items from it. URLs are received via the Filter Daemon from the Gather Manager, and content items that are successfully downloaded are passed on to an appropriate *IFilter* for parsing. The search engine includes several protocol handlers, but you can also install third-party protocol handlers as well as building your own. Protocol handlers are covered in more detail later in this chapter.

- ***IFilter***   An *IFilter* is responsible for extracting textual content and metadata from files stored in a specific format. The search engine includes a set of *IFilters* for common file formats, but you can again also install third-party ones as well as build your own. *IFilters* are also covered in greater detail later in this chapter.

In addition to the property store, the two databases of each SSP contain a whole range of other tables used internally by the index engine. For example, the index engine uses the databases as persistent storage for its crawl queues and crawl logs. The Windows registry contains all crawl settings for the indexer—specifically, the content sources, file extensions, crawl rules, crawler impact rules, and server name mappings configured by SSP administrators through the administration user interface covered in Chapter 5. Alternatively, settings can also be configured from custom applications using the Microsoft .NET Framewok API, as described in Chapter 8, "Search APIs."

> **Note** The SSP crawl settings stored in the Windows registry are located under the key named HKEY_LOCAL_MACHINE\SOFTWARE\Microsoft\Office Server\12.0\Search\Applications\ <SSP GUID>\Gather.

The Windows registry database on the index server is also the place where all *IFilter*s and protocol handlers are registered as plug-ins to the index engine. Registration of custom protocol handlers and *IFilter*s is described in the sections "Installing a Protocol Handler on Index Servers" and "Installing an *IFilter* on Index Servers" later in this chapter.

Query Engine

The query engine is responsible for processing queries from the Search Centers and any other applications sending queries through the Public .NET Query API or the Query Web service. It facilitates a multithreaded architecture, allowing multiple queries to be processed in parallel. A query is always executed against the content index of a specific SSP. The query engine is not capable of querying the content indexes of multiple SSPs in one request.

Keyword queries are executed against the inverted index on the local file system to find matching and relevant results. Metadata queries are executed against the SSP Search database to find matching results. A metadata query is basically a filter query and does not compute a rank score for each result, as is the case when the inverted index is queried. Combined keyword and metadata queries are also accepted, and the final result set is simply the union of the keyword query results and the metadata query results.

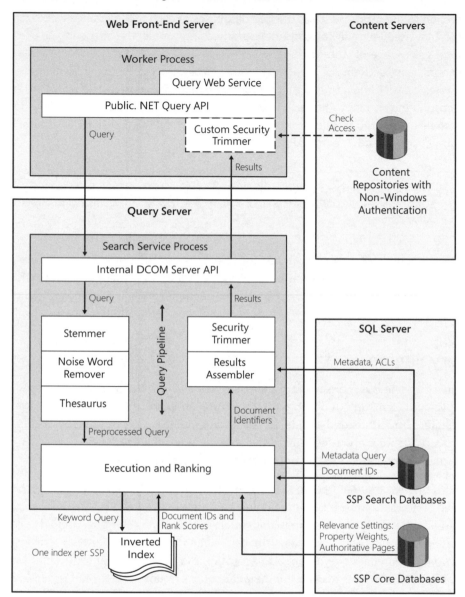

The key components of the query engine include the following:

- **Search Service Process**   The query engine executes inside this process on each query server. This is the same process in which the index engine runs if enabled on the same server. The name of the process as displayed in the Windows Task Manager is mssearch.exe.

- **Internal DCOM Server API**   The query engine is implemented in C/C++ as a Distributed Component Object Module (DCOM), allowing remote servers to communicate with it. This architecture is what allows you to scale out the query engine onto dedicated query servers. The Public .NET Query API essentially translates requests into DCOM requests and sends them to the query engine.

- **Stemmer**   Reduces query keywords to their stem form to make sure that the search results also include documents using inflected forms of the word. For example, consider three documents, each containing one instance of the same word but in different forms. Document one contains the word *computer*, while documents two and three contain the words *computers* and *computing*, respectively. A search for the keyword *computing* without stemming would yield only document three. With stemming enabled, the search yields all three documents. Stemming is different for each language and is supported for all major languages in the world. For each query, client applications must specifically tell the query engine which language it should assume for stemming.

- **Noise Word Remover**   Noise words are detected and removed during indexing and are therefore not present in the index. But users often use noise words in their queries. Consequently, it is also necessary for the query engine to detect these noise words and remove them from the queries, as they would otherwise yield zero results. See the section "Noise Words" in Chapter 5 for more information about the nature of noise words.

- **Thesaurus**   Isolates all terms in the query and performs a lookup of each term. If an expansion set is matched, the query term is expanded to include all the synonyms defined for the expansion set. This helps users find all relevant documents when different synonyms are used across the document corpus. If a replacement set is matched, the query term is replaced with the term defined in the Thesaurus. Replacement sets allows users to search for terms that do not exist in the index. See the section "Thesaurus" in Chapter 5 for a detailed description of the Thesaurus feature in the search engine.

- **Execution And Ranking**   This component is the heart of the query engine. It parses and executes the preprocessed query against the inverted index or the property store or both to find all matching results. It is also responsible for sorting the results if one or more managed properties in the property store have been specified for ascending or descending ordering of results. The standard Search Centers allow users to sort results in descending order by relevancy or last modified date, which translates to the managed properties *Rank* and *Write*, respectively. However, the Query API allows custom search applications to sort results by other managed properties as well. Last, the output of the Execution And Ranking component is simply a sorted list of numeric references to matching entries in the content index, where each entry is identified by a unique number known as the WorkId.

- **Results Assembler**   This is the point where each document reference provided by the Execution And Ranking component is paired with associated metadata in the property store. Only the metadata columns requested in the query are loaded and added to each result object. For example, a query might request the following five columns to be included in each result object: WorkId, Title, Path, Size, and Author. Each column simply refers to the name of a managed property in the property store.

- **Security Trimmer** The Results Assembler also loads the security descriptor—that is, the ACL of each result—if available. The Security Trimmer component checks each security descriptor with the security descriptor of the requesting user. Results that the user does not have permission to view are simply trimmed from the result set. The query engine assumes that it eventually needs to discard half of the result set due to security trimming. Consequently, if the client requests 50 results in the result set, the Execution And Ranking component is internally instructed to find 100 results if possible. If the Security Trimmer ends up removing more results than that, it simply returns control to the Execution And Ranking component and asks it to look for more results.

One of the new features in the Enterprise Search engine of Office SharePoint Server 2007 is the capability to plug in a custom Security Trimmer, which is useful when security trimming is needed against legacy content repositories not using Windows authentication. A custom Security Trimmer runs in managed code outside the query engine, which runs in unmanaged code. It is applied to the search results immediately before they are returned to the client by the Public .NET Query API. See the section "Custom Security Trimmers" later in this chapter for complete coverage of developing custom Security Trimmers.

Recalling the fact that keyword queries and metadata queries are executed differently, let's conclude this discussion of the architecture of the query engine by dissecting some sample queries and seeing how they are executed. This will provide you with a better understanding of what exactly you are asking the query engine to do when developing your own search applications using the Enterprise Search SQL query syntax, as described in Chapter 8. This syntax supports full-text search predicates and non-full-text search predicates targeting the inverted index and the property store, respectively, as outlined in Table 9-1.

TABLE 9-1 Search Predicates and the Part of the Content Index They Target

Search Predicate	Target in Content Index	Supported Data Types
FREETEXT	Inverted index	Text
CONTAINS	Inverted index	Text
LIKE	Property store	Text
=	Property store	Text, Numbers
!= or <>	Property store	Text, Numbers
>	Property store	Numbers, Dates
>=	Property store	Numbers, Dates
<	Property store	Numbers, Dates
<=	Property store	Numbers, Dates
DATEADD	Property store	Dates
IS NULL	Property store	All

The following query expressed using the Enterprise Search SQL query syntax uses only a single full-text predicate in the *WHERE* clause. Consequently, the query engine will need to issue only one query against the inverted index.

```
SELECT WorkId, Rank, Title, Author, Size, Write, SiteName, HitHighlightedSummary
FROM Scope()
WHERE FREETEXT(defaultproperties, 'sharepoint')
ORDER BY Rank
```

The next example uses two full-text predicates, yielding two queries internally to the inverted index. The predicates are joined with the Boolean operator *AND*, which instructs the query engine to return only the intersecting results.

```
SELECT WorkId, Rank, Title, Author, Size, Write, SiteName, HitHighlightedSummary
FROM Scope()
WHERE FREETEXT(defaultproperties, 'sharepoint') AND CONTAINS(Author, ' "Pat Coleman" ')
ORDER BY Rank
```

Using the Boolean operator *OR* instead of *AND* would instruct the query engine to return the union of both queries. The next query searches for the same author using a literal comparison operator instead of the *CONTAINS* predicate. This will again yield two queries internally in the query engine: one against the inverted index and one against the property store. The Boolean operator used to join the predicates will again determine whether the union or the intersection of the combined results will be returned to the client.

```
SELECT WorkId, Rank, Title, Author, Size, Write, SiteName, HitHighlightedSummary
FROM Scope()
WHERE FREETEXT(defaultproperties, 'sharepoint') AND Author = 'Pat Coleman'
ORDER BY Rank
```

The full-text predicate *CONTAINS* can also search textual metadata stored in the inverted index. Using *CONTAINS* for metadata queries has an advantage performance-wise over non-full-text predicates in the sense that each query server receives a local copy of the inverted index, whereas the property store is a shared resource. You should therefore strive to use the *CONTAINS* predicate instead of the *LIKE* and = predicates for textual types of metadata.

IFilters

An *IFilter* is a component that extracts text and properties from documents for placement in the content index. *IFilters* are not a SharePoint-specific technology but rather a general platform technology from Microsoft. They are also used by the Windows Indexing Service, Microsoft SQL Server, Microsoft Exchange Server, and Windows Desktop Search. The name *IFilter* stems from the main C++ interface of the same name. All filters must implement this interface in order to plug in to products relying on this technology to extract content from files.

More Information The official definition of the *IFilter* interface is available on the Microsoft Developer Network (MSDN) at *http://msdn2.microsoft.com/en-us/library/ms691105.aspx*.

The index engine leverages the *IFilter* technology to support the extraction of content from any document format in a uniform manner. Every document format must be backed by an *IFilter* that understands the file format and can extract the text from the content of the file and properties from either the content or the associated properties of the file. To filter a new file format, you simply install a supporting *IFilter* and add the associated file extension or file extensions to the list of included file types at the level of the SSP. See the section "Configuring the Indexer to Support Additional File Types" in Chapter 5 for more information.

Office SharePoint Server 2007 ships with *IFilter*s to support common file formats, including the following:

- Plain-text
- HTML
- XML
- Microsoft Office Word
- Microsoft Office PowerPoint
- Microsoft Office Excel
- E-mail

In December 2007, Microsoft released a new *IFilter* pack for use with different Microsoft products, including Office SharePoint Server 2007. It adds support for the following file formats:

- ZIP (.zip)
- Microsoft Office OneNote
- Microsoft Office Visio

This ZIP *IFilter* will use other *IFilter*s to process the files contained in the ZIP archive. In addition to these filters from Microsoft, the marketplace also offers a rich selection of third-party *IFilter*s that you can install on index servers to add support for file formats, including the following:

- Microsoft Office Project
- Adobe Acrobat PDF
- Autodesk Design Web Format (DWF)

- PostScript
- StarOffice/OpenOffice
- Various multimedia files

Most *IFilter*s come in two versions: a 32-bit version and a 64-bit version. It is necessary simply to compile *IFilter*s separately for the 32-bit and 64-bit Windows platforms, as 32-bit *IFilter*s will not work with 64-bit versions of the products using them. This includes index servers using the 64-bit version of Office SharePoint Server 2007.

> **Tip** Download the Windows Server Platform Software Development Kit (SDK) to view and work with a range of sample *IFilter* implementations in the C++ programming language.

You might need to consider building your own *IFilter* if you are a vendor wanting to provide support for your file format or if you have developed a proprietary file format in your company. The following subsections will introduce you to the internal structure of *IFilter*s and what it takes to develop your own filters.

Building a Custom *IFilter*

*IFilter*s build on an open and well-documented framework from Microsoft, enabling developers to write and plug in custom filters for indexing virtually any file format. The *IFilter* API was conceived by Microsoft many years ago and has not changed fundamentally since. Consequently, older *IFilter*s will continue to work with SharePoint 2007. But registration of filters with the index engine has changed for every release of SharePoint, and installation programs designed for earlier versions of SharePoint will not work with SharePoint 2007. But it is always possible to manually register a filter with the index engine, as you'll see in the section "Installing an *IFilter* on Index Servers" later in this chapter.

> **More Information** The article "How to Write a Filter for Use by SharePoint Portal Server 2003 and Other Microsoft Search-Based Products" on the Microsoft Developer Network (MSDN) at *http://msdn2.microsoft.com/en-us/library/ms916793.aspx* explores a sample *IFilter* implementation in detail. Although the *IFilter* is developed for an earlier version of SharePoint, it will also work with SharePoint 2007. The only issue is installation, as *IFilter*s for SharePoint 2003 and 2007 are registered differently in the Windows registry. Use the guidelines in the section "Installing an *IFilter* on Index Servers" later in this chapter to install the sample *IFilter* on a SharePoint 2007 server.

Building a custom filter requires you to implement some C++ interfaces, and the following subsections will introduce you to these interfaces, along with the data structures referenced by different methods in the interfaces. But in order to successfully develop your own filters, you will first need to be proficient in the following:

- C++ programming language and object-oriented programming techniques
- Windows C++ API
- Multithreaded programming techniques in C++ and Windows
- COM programming techniques
- Constructing and registering a dynamic-link library (DLL)
- Microsoft Visual Studio or a similar development environment

It is additionally an advantage to be familiar with the Active Template Library (ATL), which is a set of template-based C++ classes that simplify the programming of COM objects.

An *IFilter* comes as a DLL file containing a COM-enabled *Filter* class that implements the required *IClassFactory*, *IFilter*, and *IPersistStream* interfaces, as shown in the following illustration. Each *Filter* class must implement two interfaces: the main interface named *IFilter* and the *IPersistStream* interface. The *Filter* class pulls the raw content from a stream provided by the client application through the *IPersistStream* interface. The same client application will in turn pull the extracted content in smaller chunks through the *IFilter* interface. A *Filter* class can alternatively implement the *IPersistFile* or *IPersistStorage* interface instead of *IPersistStream*. But it is recommended to use *IPersistStream* whenever possible, as this will give you the most versatile and secure filter.

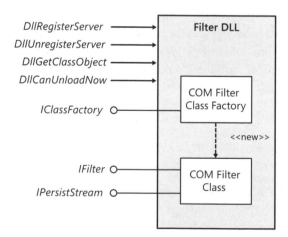

Each filter DLL must also include a COM class implementing the *IClassFactory* interface that provides a class factory responsible for creating and returning new instances of the *Filter* class. In complex scenarios, it is also possible to implement multiple filters within the same DLL.

Last, each DLL must also implement and export the following entry points. They are typically exported using a module definition (.def) file included in the Visual Studio project.

- **DllRegisterServer**   This method is called when running the regsvr32.exe program with the filter DLL file name as argument. The method must in turn add the filter as a persistent handler in the Windows registry. A persistent handler must be registered for the class identifier (CLSID) of the COM *Filter* class as well as for the file extensions supported by the filter. The method can optionally register itself with all the aforementioned Microsoft products, including Office SharePoint Server 2007. Doing so will make installation a breeze for server administrators.

- **DllUnregisterServer**   Removes the persistent handler from the Windows registry. The method is called when running the regsvr32 program with the */u* option.

- **DllGetClassObject**   The content indexing client calls this entry point, through COM, to create a class factory object for the filter and to get a pointer to it.

- **DllCanUnloadNow**   The content indexing client class calls this entry point, through COM, to determine whether it is possible to unload the filter DLL. The filter is unloaded from memory after it has not been used for some time.

A module definition file for a DLL named *SampleFilter* is shown in the following example:

```
LIBRARY     SampleFilter

EXPORTS
        DllCanUnloadNow         PRIVATE
        DllGetClassObject       PRIVATE
        DllRegisterServer       PRIVATE
        DllUnregisterServer     PRIVATE
```

A sample implementation of DLL entry points can be studied in the section "Implementing the Main Module with DLL Registration" later in this chapter. Although this is an implementation for a sample protocol handler DLL, the same technique can be applied to a filter DLL. The following checklist provides you with an overview of the steps you need to follow when implementing your own filters:

1. Use Visual Studio to create a Win32 C++ project with a DLL file as output.

2. Implement and export the DLL entry points as described earlier.

3. Create a COM class that implements the *IClassFactory* interface.

4. Create a COM class that implements the *IFilter* and *IPersistStream* interfaces.

5. Implement both classes as free threaded COM objects to enable client applications to use parallel instances of the filter.

The next section takes a closer look at the interfaces mentioned here.

IFilter Interfaces

The *Filter* class must inherit the *IFilter* interface and one or more derived *IPersist* interfaces. The *Filter* class factory must inherit the *IClassFactory* interface. These interfaces are declared in different header files of the Windows Server Platform SDK. All three interface declarations are shown in this section to illustrate the methods that you need to implement. The purpose of each method is explained only briefly—see the SDK documentation from Microsoft for a detailed description of all methods, their parameters, and their return values.

The *IFilter* Interface   *Filter* classes implementing this interface are responsible for scanning documents for text and properties. The document text should be processed in smaller chunks, filtering out embedded formatting and retaining information about the position of the text. Document properties must be processed as separate chunks. The *IFilter* interface is defined as follows in the filter.h header file of the Platform SDK:

```
/* ID: 89BCB740-6119-101A-BCB7-00DD010655AF */
class IFilter : IUnknown
{
    SCODE Init(
    /* [in] */                          ULONG grfFlags,
    /* [in] */                          ULONG cAttributes,
    /* [in, size_is(cAttributes)] */    FULLPROPSPEC const * aAttributes,
    /* [out] */                         ULONG * pFlags);

    SCODE GetChunk(
    /* [out] */                         STAT_CHUNK * pStat );

    SCODE GetText(
    /* [in, out] */                     ULONG * pcwcBuffer,
    /* [out, size_is(*pcwcBuffer)] */   WCHAR * awcBuffer );

    SCODE GetValue(
    /* [out] */                         PROPVARIANT ** ppPropValue );
}
```

The *Init* method must prepare the filter to start a new filtering session. This method is called first by the Filter Daemon when processing of a new document begins. The job of the *GetChunk* method is to position the filter at the beginning of the first or next chunk and return a descriptor providing the client application with details about the chunk. The descriptor must for instance specify whether the chunk represents a piece of text or a document property. The following C++ code snippet shows an example of filling the *STAT_CHUNK* structure with information about the chunk:

```
pStat->idChunk    = m_ulChunkID;
pStat->breakType  = CHUNK_NO_BREAK;
pStat->flags      = CHUNK_TEXT;
pStat->locale     = 1033;
pStat->attribute.guidPropSet = guidStorage;
pStat->attribute.psProperty.ulKind = PRSPEC_PROPID;
pStat->attribute.psProperty.propid = PID_STG_CONTENTS;
```

```
pStat->idChunkSource   = m_ulChunkID;
pStat->cwcStartSource = 0;
pStat->cwcLenSource    = 0;
```

The *STAT_CHUNK* data structure is described in more detail in the section "*IFilter* Data Structures" later in this chapter. The *GetChunk* method should return the *S_OK* error code as long as chunks are available and return *FILTER_E_END_OF_CHUNKS* when the previous chunk was the last chunk.

The *GetText* method retrieves the text from the current chunk. Client applications will call this method if the *flags* member of the *STAT_CHUNK* structure was set to *CHUNK_TEXT* in the preceding call to the *GetChunk* method. The *GetValue* method retrieves the property value of the current chunk if the *flags* member was set to *CHUNK_VALUE*. The following code snippet shows a sample implementation of the *GetValue* method:

```
STDMETHODIMP CSampleFileFilter::GetValue(PROPVARIANT **ppPropValue)
{
    if (ppPropValue == NULL) return E_POINTER;
    *ppPropValue = (PROPVARIANT *)CoTaskMemAlloc(sizeof(PROPVARIANT));

    if (*ppPropValue == NULL) {
        return E_OUTOFMEMORY;
    }

    PropVariantInit(*ppPropValue);
    PROPVARIANT  pvLocal;
    pvLocal.vt = VT_LPWSTR;    /* Set data type of property value. */
    pvLocal.pwszVal = /* Get text here */;

    return PropVariantCopy(*ppPropValue, &pvLocal);
}
```

In the context of the SharePoint index engine, text chunks go to the inverted index and value chunks go to the property store.

The *IPersistStream* Interface   This interface inherits from the *IPersist* interface and provides methods for saving and loading objects represented as a simple serial byte stream, as shown here:

```
/* ID: 00000109-0000-0000-C000-000000000046 */
class IPersistStream : public IPersist
{
public:
    virtual HRESULT STDMETHODCALLTYPE IsDirty( void) = 0;

    virtual HRESULT STDMETHODCALLTYPE Load(/* [unique][in] */ IStream *pStm) = 0;

    virtual HRESULT STDMETHODCALLTYPE Save(
            /* [unique][in] */  IStream *pStm,
            /* [in] */          BOOL fClearDirty) = 0;

    virtual HRESULT STDMETHODCALLTYPE GetSizeMax(/* [out] */ ULARGE_INTEGER *pcbSize) = 0;
};
```

The only method of interest for an *IFilter* is the *Load* method, which is called to provide *IFilter* with an input stream for the *GetChunk* method of the *IFilter* interface. The input parameter named *pStm* points to an object implementing the *IStream* interface through which the *GetChunk* method can pull content.

The *IClassFactory* Interface   This interface must be implemented for every *Filter* class that you register in the Windows registry and to which you assign a CLSID, as shown in the following code. Client applications that load the filter DLL rely on this implementation to create new instances of the associated *Filter* class.

```
/* ID: 00000001-0000-0000-C000-000000000046 */
class IClassFactory : public IUnknown
{
public:
    virtual /* [local] */          HRESULT STDMETHODCALLTYPE CreateInstance(
             /* [unique][in] */    IUnknown *pUnkOuter,
             /* [in] */ REFIID     riid,
             /* [iid_is][out] */   void **ppvObject) = 0;

    virtual /* [local] */          HRESULT STDMETHODCALLTYPE LockServer(
             /* [in] */            BOOL fLock) = 0;
};
```

The *CreateInstance* method must create a new and uninitialized instance of the associated *Filter* class, as shown here. The *riid* parameter specifies the identifier of the interface that the new object must implement. The Filter Daemon will specify the ID of the *IFilter* interface here. The *ppvObject* parameter points to a pointer variable where the method must provide a pointer to the new instance of the *Filter* class. The method should return *S_OK* on success and *E_NOINTERFACE* if the *riid* input parameter specifies an interface that is not supported.

```
SCODE STDMETHODCALLTYPE CSmpFilterCF::CreateInstance(
    IUnknown * pUnkOuter,
    REFIID riid,
    void  * * ppvObject)
{
    SampleFilter *pIUnknown = 0;

    if (pIUnknown != 0) return CLASS_E_NOAGGREGATION;

    pIUnknown = new SampleFilter();
    if (pIUnknown != 0) {
        if (SUCCEEDED(pIUnknown->QueryInterface(riid , ppvObject))) {
            // Release extra refcount from QueryInterface
            pIUnknown->Release();
        } else {
            delete pIUnk;
            return E_UNEXPECTED;
        }
    } else {
        return E_OUTOFMEMORY;
    }
    return S_OK;
}
```

IFilter Data Structures

The methods of the *IFilter* interface use a number of special data structures as method parameters. This section describes the purpose and the format of each data structure.

FULLPROPSPEC   This data structure specifies a property set and a property set within the property set. It is declared as follows:

```
typedef struct tagFULLPROPSPEC
{
    GUID guidPropSet;
    PROPSPEC psProperty;
} FULLPROPSPEC;
```

The member named *guidPropSet* identifies the property set by its GUID, and the *psProperty* member specifies a property by its property identifier (*propid*) or by the associated string name (*lpwstr*). The embedded *PROPSPEC* data structure has the following format:

```
typedef struct tagPROPSPEC
{
    ULONG ulKind;
    /* [switch_type] */ union
    {
        PROPID propid;
        LPOLESTR lpwstr;
         /* Empty union arm */
    };
} PROPSPEC;
```

The Filter Daemon provides an array of pointers to *FULLPROPSPEC* structures in the filter *Init* method. Each entry in the array identifies a property for which the index engine requests a value, if possible.

STAT_CHUNK   The *STAT_CHUNK* structure describes the characteristics of a chunk isolated by the *GetChunk* method of a filter. The structure is declared in the filter.h file of the Platform SDK as follows:

```
typedef struct tagSTAT_CHUNK
{
    ULONG idChunk;
    CHUNK_BREAKTYPE breakType;
    CHUNKSTATE flags;
    LCID locale;
    FULLPROPSPEC attribute;
    ULONG idChunkSource;
    ULONG cwcStartSource;
    ULONG cwcLenSource;
} STAT_CHUNK;
```

The Filter Daemon provides a pointer to an empty structure upon calling the *GetChunk* method of the *Filter* class that it used for processing of the current document. Table 9-2 descibes the purpose of each member in the structure.

TABLE 9-2 *STAT_CHUNK* **Members**

Member	Description
idChunk	Identifies the chunk by a unique consequtive number. The number must be unique within each instance of the *IFilter* interface. The order in which chunks are numbered should correspond to the order in which they appear in the source document.
breakType	Specifies the type of break that separates the preceding chunk from the current chunk. Possible values are shown here: ❑ *CHUNK_NO_BREAK* No break between the chunks. ❑ *CHUNK_EOW* A word break is placed between the chunks. ❑ *CHUNK_EOS* A sentence break is placed between the chunks. ❑ *CHUNK_EOP* A paragraph break is placed between the chunks. ❑ *CHUNK_EOC* A chapter break is placed between the chunks.
flags	Indicates whether the chunk contains text or a property value. Possible values are shown here: ❑ *CHUNK_TEXT* The current chunk contains text. ❑ *CHUNK_VALUE* The current chunk contains a property value.
locale	Specifies the language and sublanguage of the text contained in the chunk. The locale is used by the index engine to perform language-dependent word breaking of text.
attribute	Specifies the property to be applied to the chunk. If a filter needs to provide the same text to multiple properties, it needs to emit the text once for each property in separate chunks.
idChunkSource	The identifier of the source of a chunk. If the chunk is a text-type chunk, the value of this member must be the same as the value of the *idChunk* member. If the chunk is a value-type chunk derived from textual content, the value must equal the ID of the text chunk from which it was derived.
cwcStartSource	The offset of the chunk with respect to the source text.
cwsLenSource	The length in characters of the source text from which the current chunk was derived.

PROPVARIANT   The Filter Daemon provides a pointer to an instance of this data structure when calling the *GetValue* method on the *Filter* class. The *GetValue* method must in turn fill the data structure with the property value that should be propagated to the content index. The filter.h header file of the Platform SDK declares the data structure as follows:

```
typedef struct PROPVARIANT
{
    VARTYPE vt;
    WORD wReserved1;
    WORD wReserved2;
    WORD wReserved3;
    union {
        CHAR cVal; UCHAR bVal;
        SHORT iVal; USHORT uiVal;
        LONG lVal; ULONG ulVal;
        INT intVal; UINT uintVal;
        LARGE_INTEGER hVal; ULARGE_INTEGER uhVal;
        FLOAT fltVal; DOUBLE dblVal;
        DATE date; FILETIME filetime;
        BLOB blob;
        LPSTR pszVal; LPWSTR pwszVal;
        IStream* pStream;
        CHAR* pcVal; UCHAR* pbVal;
        SHORT* piVal; USHORT* puiVal;
        LONG* plVal; ULONG* pulVal;
        INT* pintVal; UINT* puintVal;
        FLOAT* pfltVal; DOUBLE* pdblVal; DECIMAL* pdecVal;
        PROPVARIANT* pvarVal;
        ...   // The rest omitted for simplicity.
    };
} PROPVARIANT;
```

The union of different data types enables the *GetValue* method to return property values of different types.

IFilter Error Messages

Table 9-3 lists the error codes that are specific to *IFilter*s. They are all defined in the filterr.h header file of the Platform SDK.

TABLE 9-3 Special Error Codes That *IFilters* Can Return to the Filter Daemon

Value	Description
FILTER_E_END_OF_CHUNKS (0x80041700L)	No more chunks available for the current document.
FILTER_E_NO_MORE_TEXT (0x80041701L)	No more text available in the chunk.
FILTER_E_NO_MORE_VALUES (0x80041702L)	No more property values available in the chunk.
FILTER_E_ACCESS (0x80041703L)	Unable to access the object.

Value	Description
FILTER_E_NO_TEXT (0x80041705L)	No text in the current chunk.
FILTER_E_NO_VALUES (0x80041706L)	No values in the current chunk.
FILTER_E_EMBEDDING_ UNAVAILABLE (0x80041707L)	Unable to bind *IFilter* for the embedded object.
FILTER_S_LAST_TEXT (0x00041709L)	Indicates the last text in the current chunk.
FILTER_S_LAST_VALUES (0x0004170AL)	Indicates the last value in the current chunk.
FILTER_E_PASSWORD (0x8004170BL)	The file was not filtered because of password protection.
FILTER_E_UNKNOWNFORMAT (0x8004170CL)	The document format is not recognized by the filter.

Interacting with the Filter Daemon

The Filter Daemon of the index engine interacts with protocol handlers and *IFilters*. Protocol handlers are employed to fetch documents from content repositories, and *IFilters* are used to extract text and properties from these documents. The following Unified Modeling Language (UML) diagram outlines the interaction between the Filter Daemon, protocol handlers, and *IFilters*. The interaction with protocol handlers has been greatly simplified here for brevity and also because the full interaction sequence is outlined in a separate sequence diagram in the section "Program Flow of the Sample Protocol Handler" later in this chapter.

The Filter Daemon starts processing when the Gather Manager directs it to index content from a specific URL location. From the URL scheme, it identifies the proper protocol handler to use for fetching the content. The protocol handler is loaded and initialized on first usage. Thereafter, the Filter Daemon just calls the *CreateAccessor* method for every URL it is requested to process. The *GetDocFormat* method provides the protocol handler with an opportunity to influence the choice of *IFilter* for parsing the document. Otherwise, the Filter Daemon uses the file extension of the document to look up the proper *IFilter*.

Next, the Filter Daemon calls the *BindToStream* method, asking the protocol handler to open and return a stream to the document. The stream is subsequently passed along to the *IFilter* through a call to the *Load* method defined by the *IPersistStream* interface. But before that, the Filter Daemon makes sure to call the *Init* method to prepare the filter for a new session. If this is the first session for the *IFilter*, it is first loaded from the DLL and created from a call to the *CreateInstance* method on the *Filter* class factory in the same DLL.

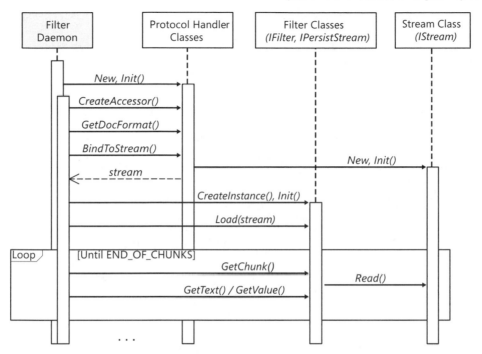

Once the stream has been successfully provided to the *Filter* class, the Filter Daemon enters a loop to retrieve chunks of text and properties from the filter. Each call to the *GetChunk* method is followed by a call to the *GetText* method or the *GetValue* method, depending on the chunk type. The loop ends when the *GetChunk* method returns the error code *FILTER_E_ END_OF_CHUNKS* or an error occurs.

Installing an *IFilter* on Index Servers

IFilters must be installed on all servers with the index server role in the farm. The steps required to install a new filter include copying the DLL file to the server and registering it with the Filter Daemon through the Windows registry. All filters should include the logic to register themselves via the Windows regsvr32.exe program. This enables server administrators to register the DLL from a Windows command-line prompt, as follows:

```
regsvr32 SampleFilter.dll
```

Unregistering a filter again is just as simple, as follows:

```
regsvr32 /u SampleFilter.dll
```

Manual registration is also possible by following these steps:

1. Log in as a local administrator on the index server.

2. Open the Windows Registry Editor by typing **regedit** in the Run menu available from the Windows Start menu.

3. Locate the CLSID of the filter. This would be the GUID of the COM object.

4. Open Notepad, and type or copy the following text into it. (Comment lines starting with a semicolon can be omitted.) This example assumes the CLSID to be {03110E71-AD6F-4304-9487-0A5181129154}.

```
Windows Registry Editor Version 5.00

; Create root key for COM object.
[HKEY_CLASSES_ROOT\CLSID\{03110E71-AD6F-4304-9487-0A5181129154}]
@="SampleFilter Class "

; Specify full path to the Filter DLL, and set the COM threading model to Both.
[HKEY_CLASSES_ROOT\CLSID\{03110E71-AD6F-4304-9487-0A5181129154}\InprocServer32]
@="C:\\WINDOWS\\SYSTEM32\\SampleFilter.dll"
"ThreadingModel"="Both"

; Register the Filter with the index engine of Microsoft Office SharePoint Server
2007. [HKEY_LOCAL_MACHINE\SOFTWARE\Microsoft\Office Server\12.0\Search\Setup\
ContentIndexCommon\Filters\Extension\.smp]
@="03110E71-AD6F-4304-9487-0A5181129154"
```

The value of the *ThreadingModel* entry can also be set to *Apartment* instead of *Both* if the filter is not multithread safe, but doing so will significantly slow down indexing with this particular filter.

> **Note** Installing and registering *IFilters* on a Microsoft SharePoint Portal Server 2003 index server is with one exception identical to the procedure described here. The exception is the key HKEY_LOCAL_MACHINE\SOFTWARE\Microsoft\Office Server\12.0\Search \Setup\ ContentIndexCommon\Filters\Extension, which must simply be replaced with the key HKEY_LOCAL_MACHINE\SOFTWARE\Microsoft\SPSSearch\ContentIndexCommon\ Filters\ Extension.

5. Save the file in Notepad using the file name install.reg or any other file name with the .reg file extension.

6. In Windows File Explorer, double-click the install.reg file created in step 5. This will merge the keys and values in the file with the Windows registry.

7. If the Open File—Security Warning dialog box appears, click Run.

Note *IFilters* cannot be deployed to index servers via the new solution deployment framework in Windows SharePoint Services 3.0. This framework is designed to help SharePoint application developers install and deploy custom applications to all servers in a farm. But it is designed to handle only .NET Framework assemblies, SharePoint Web Parts, SharePoint feature files, SharePoint site template files, and other files that are typically included in custom SharePoint applications. The framework simply does not offer any special support for *IFilters* and cannot handle the necessary registration of the filters in the Windows registry.

Protocol Handlers

Protocol handlers are used by the index engine to enumerate and download content from different types of content repositories in a uniform manner. The name *protocol handler* stems from the scheme part of a Uniform Resource Identifier (URI), which is also referred to as the *protocol*. Some examples of different protocols are HTTP, HTTPS, and file. A protocol handler is specifically responsible for the following tasks:

- **Connecting to content repositories**   Each protocol handler must specify and implement the method by which it connects to and communicates with content repositories. Possible connection methods include but are not limited to Web, file systems, Web services, databases, and I/O ports.

- **Authenticating itself with content repositories**   When access to a content repository is protected, a protocol handler will need to authenticate itself with a user name and password the way a normal user would. Authentication credentials are provided to the protocol handler by the index engine from the default content access account setting or an active crawl rule. See the section "The Default Content Access Account" in Chapter 5 for more information about configuring the authentication credentials.

- **Downloading content**   Through the Filter Daemon, the Gather Manager will continuously provide protocol handlers with the URL of the content item to download. The protocol handler must in turn open a stream to the content, which the Filter Daemon then reads. The downloaded content is then sent to the Indexing Pipeline through an appropriate *IFilter*.

- **Getting content metadata**   It is the responsibility of the protocol handler to help index metadata that resides outside the content data stream. For file systems, this includes file name, file size, file dates, and file attributes, plus any custom metadata associated with the file. Protocol handlers must in fact implement an internal *IFilter* to enumerate the metadata associated with the content. Metadata emitted by the protocol handler ends up as crawled properties in the index.

- **Enumerating content**   Protocol handlers are also responsible for enumerating or discovering additional content from the URLs provided by the index engine. The discovered URLs are fed back to the crawl queue of the index engine. For a file system, this would require the protocol handler to enumerate files in directories. For the Web, this would require the protocol handler to return the URLs found on each page.

- **Implementing an incremental crawl strategy**   Different content repositories often call for different strategies for performing incremental crawls as efficiently as possible. Consequently, it is also the responsibility of the protocol handler to support this strategy. However, it is not a requirement to support incremental crawls, but it is highly recommended when indexing highly dynamic content repositories where users frequently add and modify content.

- **Getting security descriptors**   Security trimming of search results in the query engine works only when protocol handlers provide the index with an ACL—that is, a Windows security descriptor for each content item. This is fairly easy when indexing Microsoft content repositories like Windows file systems and SharePoint sites, as they have native support for ACLs. Security descriptors from other content repositories like Lotus Notes databases must be mapped to ACLs to enable security trimming when searching these repositories. Mapping these security descriptors is also a responsibility of the protocol handler.

The Enterprise Search engine of Office SharePoint Server 2007 includes several protocol handlers to support the crawling of common content repositories, including SharePoint itself. Adding support for other kinds of content repositories requires you to install and register new protocol handlers with the index engine. Fortunately, the marketplace offers many prebuilt protocol handlers for virtually any brand of content repository, as listed in the section "Managing Content Sources" in Chapter 5. But you can also build your own protocol handlers if necessary, and this section will show you how.

More Information See the article "Developing Protocol Handlers" on the Microsoft Developer Network (MSDN) at *http://msdn2.microsoft.com/en-us/library/bb266531.aspx*.

Built-In Protocol Handlers

You can use Office SharePoint Server 2007 out-of-the-box to index SharePoint 2.0/3.0 sites, Web sites, file shares, Exchange Server public folders, and line-of-business (LOB) data. Table 9-4 lists all the supported protocols, along with the name of the DLL in which the code of the associated protocol handler resides. The DLL files are by default all located in the folder C:\Program Files\Microsoft Office Servers\12.0\Bin on SharePoint servers.

TABLE 9-4 Protocols Supported Out-of-the-Box

Protocol	DLL	Description
BDC	*BdcSearchProtocolHandler. dll*	Business Data Catalog. Available only in the Enterprise edition of Office SharePoint Server 2007.
BDC2	*BdcSearchProtocolHandler. dll*	Business Data Catalog URLs (internal protocol).
File	*Mssph.dll*	File shares.
HTTP	*Mssph.dll*	Web sites.
HTTPS	*Mssph.dll*	Web sites over Secure Sockets Layer (SSL).
RB	*Pkmexsph.dll*	Exchange Server public folders.
RBS	*Pkmexsph.dll*	Exchange Server public folders over SSL.
SPS	*Mssph.dll*	People profiles from Windows SharePoint Services 2.0 server farms.
SPS3	*Mssph.dll*	People profiles from Windows SharePoint Services 3.0 server farms only.
SPS3S	*Mssph.dll*	People profiles from Windows SharePoint Services 3.0 server farms only over SSL.
SPSIMPORT	*Spsimportph.dll*	People profile import.
SPSS	*Mssph.dll*	People profile import from Windows SharePoint Services 2.0 farms over SSL.
STS	*Mssph.dll*	Windows SharePoint Services 3.0 root URLs (internal protocol).
STS2	*Mssph.dll*	Windows SharePoint Services 2.0 sites.
STS2S	*Mssph.dll*	Windows SharePoint Services 2.0 sites over SSL.
STS3	*Mssph.dll*	Windows SharePoint Services 3.0 sites.
STS3S	*Mssph.dll*	Windows SharePoint Services 3.0 sites over SSL.
Notes	*NotesPH.dll*	Lotus Notes databases. Requires special configuration steps before it is available for use. See the section "Indexing Lotus Notes Databases" in Chapter 5 for more information about this topic.

Notice that SharePoint sites are not indexed using the HTTP protocol handler as other Web sites are. They are instead indexed using the STS protocol handler that connects to the Site Data Web service available at *http://servername/_vti_bin/sitedata.asmx*. The SPS protocol handler that is used to index user profiles connects to the SPS Crawl Web service available at *http://servername/_vti_bin/spscrawl.asmx*.

Building a Custom Protocol Handler

The protocol handler framework of the index engine enables developers to write and plug in protocol handlers for indexing of custom content repositories. The protocol handler API has not changed fundamentally since the release of SharePoint Portal Server 2001. Consequently, protocol handlers developed for SharePoint 2001 and SharePoint 2003 will continue to work with SharePoint 2007. Registration of protocol handlers with the index engine has changed for every release of SharePoint, and installation programs designed for earlier versions of SharePoint will not work with the 2007 release, however. But it is always possible to manually register a protocol handler with the index engine, as you'll see in the section "Installing a Protocol Handler on Index Servers" later in this chapter.

Building a custom protocol handler requires you to implement the C++ interfaces provided by the protocol handler API. The following subsections will introduce you to these interfaces, along with some special data structures referenced by different methods in the interfaces. To successfully develop your own protocol handlers, you will first need to be proficient in the following:

- The C++ programming language and object-oriented programming techniques

- The Windows C++ API

- Multithreaded programming techniques in C++ and Windows

- COM programming techniques

- Constructing and registering a DLL

- Office SharePoint Server 2007

- Visual Studio or a similar development environment

It is additionally an advantage to be familiar with the ATL, which is a set of template-based C++ classes that simplify the programming of COM objects. When developing a custom protocol handler, you must also decide whether to compile it for the 32-bit or the 64-bit Windows platform, or both. This is important because a 32-bit protocol handler will not work on an index server with the 64-bit version of Office SharePoint Server 2007 installed.

Protocol Handler Interfaces

The Filter Daemon uses the schema of each URL received from the Gather Manager to determine which protocol handler to use to access the content represented by the URL. Each protocol handler available to support different URL schemes must be a free-threaded COM object implementing the *ISearchProtocol* interface.

The *ISearchProtocol* Interface   The Filter Daemon calls methods from this interface when processing URLs from the Gather Manager. The interface is defined as follows:

```
/* ID: c73106ba-ac80-11d1-8df3-00c04fb6ef4f */
class ISearchProtocol : IUnknown
{
public:
    virtual HRESULT Init(
    /* [in] */    TIMEOUT_INFO *pTimeoutInfo,
    /* [in] */    IProtocolHandlerSite *pProtocolHandlerSite,
    /* [in] */    PROXY_INFO *pProxyInfo) = 0;

    virtual HRESULT CreateAccessor(
    /* [in] */     LPCWSTR pcwszURL,
    /* [in] */     AUTHENTICATION_INFO *pAuthenticationInfo,
    /* [in] */     INCREMENTAL_ACCESS_INFO *pIncrementalAccessInfo,
    /* [in] */     ITEM_INFO *pItemInfo,
    /* [out] */    IUrlAccessor **ppAccessor) = 0;

    virtual HRESULT CloseAccessor(
    /* [in] */     IUrlAccessor *pAccessor) = 0;

    virtual HRESULT Shutdown() = 0;
}
```

The *Init* method is called once by the Filter Daemon when it loads the protocol handler. The input parameters *pTimeoutInfo* and *pProxyInfo* of this method provide the protocol handler with information about connection timeouts and proxy settings necessary for accessing items in the content source. The *pProtocolHandler* parameter provides an implementation of the *IProtocolHandlerSite* interface that provides a way for a protocol handler to access *IFilter* objects.

The *CreateAccessor* method is called separately for each URL that the Filter Daemon is asked to process. The method must, through the output parameter *ppAccessor*, return a pointer to an object that implements the *IUrlAccessor* interface. The input parameters provide the following information for the initialization of the *UrlAccessor* object:

- **pcwszURL**   Pointer to a null-terminated Unicode string containing the URL of the item being accessed.

- **pAuthenticationInfo**   Pointer to an *AUTHENTICATION_INFO* structure that contains the authentication information needed to accesses the content.

- **pIncrementalAccessInfo**   Pointer to an *INCREMENTAL_ACCESS* structure that contains access information such as the last time the URL was accessed by the crawler.

- **pItemInfo**   Pointer to an *ITEM_INFO* structure containing information about the item.

Only one crawl URL is processed for each call to the *CreateAccessor* method, but there can be multiple simultaneous calls to this method. As a result, multiple threads can be working in parallel.

The *CloseAccessor* method is called when the Filter Daemon has finished using the *UrlAccessor* object returned by the *CreateAccessor* method. Use this method to release any resources associated with the *UrlAccessor* object. The Filter Daemon will release the object itself once this method returns. The *ShutDown* method is called when a Filter Daemon is shut down. Finally, all methods should upon success return the *S_OK* error code.

The *IProtocolHandlerSite* Interface   An object implementing this interface is provided by the Filter Daemon when it initializes the protocol handler by calling the *Init* method on the object implementing the *ISearchProtocol* interface. The interface is defined as follows:

```
/* ID: 0b63e385-9ccc-11d0-bcdb-00805fccce04 */
class IProtocolHandlerSite : public IUnknown
{
public:
    virtual HRESULT STDMETHODCALLTYPE GetFilter(
        /* [in] */   CLSID *pclsidObj,
        /* [in] */   LPCWSTR pcwszContentType,
        /* [in] */   LPCWSTR pcwszExtension,
        /* [out] */  IFilter **ppFilter) = 0;
};
```

The interface declares the *GetFilter* method that a protocol handler can call only to obtain the appropriate *IFilter* for an embedded document. The method queries the Filter Daemon for an *IFilter* based on the file extension of the content item (*pcwszExtension* parameter), the CLSID of the *IFilter* (*pclsidObj* parameter), or the Multipurpose Internet Mail Extensions (MIME) type of the content item (*pcwszContentType* parameter). You will need to provide only one of these three input parameters, which are tested in the following order:

- *pcwszContentType*

- *pclsidObj*

- *pcwszExtension*

The Filter Daemon will in turn provide a pointer to the appropriate *IFilter* through the output parameter *ppFilter*.

The *IUrlAccessor* Interface   This interface provides methods for the Filter Daemon to access and process the content of a single item. The URL of the item is provided in the call to the *CreateAccessor* method of the *ISearchProtocol* interface. The *IUrlAccessor* interface is defined as follows:

```
/* ID: 0b63e318-9ccc-11d0-bcdb-00805fccce04 */
class IUrlAccessor: IUnknown
{
public:
    virtual HRESULT STDMETHODCALLTYPE AddRequestParameter(
    /* [in] */     PROPSPEC *pSpec,
    /* [in] */     PROPVARIANT *pVar) = 0;

    virtual HRESULT GetCLSID(
    /* [out] */   CLSID* pClsid) = 0;
```

```
virtual HRESULT STDMETHODCALLTYPE GetHost(
/* [size_is][length_is][out] */  WCHAR wszHost[],
/* [in] */     DWORD dwSize,
/* [out] */    DWORD *pdwLength) = 0;

virtual HRESULT STDMETHODCALLTYPE IsDirectory(void) = 0;

virtual HRESULT STDMETHODCALLTYPE GetFileName(
/* [size_is][length_is][out] */   WCHAR wszFileName[],
/* [in] */     DWORD dwSize,
/* [out] */    DWORD *pdwLength) = 0;

virtual HRESULT GetDocFormat(
/* [out, length_is(*pdwLength), size_is(dwSize)] */   WCHAR wszDocFormat[],
/* [in] */     DWORD dwSize,
/* [out] */    DWORD *pdwLength) = 0;

virtual HRESULT GetLastModified(
/* [out] */    FILETIME *pftLastModified) = 0;

virtual HRESULT GetSecurityDescriptor(
/* [out, size_is(dwSize)] */  BYTE *pSD,
/* [in] */     DWORD dwSize,
/* [out] */    DWORD *pdwLength) = 0;

virtual HRESULT STDMETHODCALLTYPE GetRedirectedURL(
/* [size_is][length_is][out] */   WCHAR wszRedirectedURL[],
/* [in] */     DWORD dwSize,
/* [out] */    DWORD *pdwLength) = 0;

virtual HRESULT STDMETHODCALLTYPE GetSecurityProvider(
/* [out] */    CLSID *pSPClsid) = 0;

virtual HRESULT BindToStream(
/* [out] */    IStream **ppStream) = 0;

virtual HRESULT BindToFilter(
/* [out] */    IFilter **ppFilter) = 0;

virtual HRESULT GetSize(
/* [out] */    ULONGLONG* pllSize) = 0;
};
```

The index engine supports only a subset of the methods declared by this interface. The un-supported methods are used by other Microsoft products such as Windows Desktop Search that also rely on protocol handlers for indexing. The supported methods include:

- **GetCLSID**   Gets the registry CLSID of the document type. This method is used for items with special filter associations to indicate the appropriate *IFilter* to use for break-ing the document into chunks.

- **IsDirectory**   Determines whether the URL points to a directory.

- **GetFileName**   Gets the full path of the current item in Universal Naming Convention (UNC) format. It is recommended not to implement this method, as it overrides the *BindToStream* method.

- **GetDocFormat**   Gets the document format represented as a MIME string. The output parameter *wszDocFormat* must contain the document MIME type as a null-terminated Unicode string.

- **GetLastModified**   Gets the timestamp when the content item was last modified. The Filter Daemon calls this method and passes the value of *pftLastModified* along to the index for use with incremental crawls. If this method is not implemented, the protocol handler is limited to participate only in full crawls.

- **GetSecurityDescriptor**   The Filter Daemon calls this method in an attempt to obtain a security descriptor for the content item. Implement this method if an ACL is available for the item and if the security information should be respected by the query time security trimmer. The ACL must represent Windows domain groups or users. Only security for read access to the item is of interest here.

- **GetRedirectedURL**   Gets the redirected URL for the current item. If you implement this method, the URL passed to the *CreateAccessor* method is redirected to the value returned by this method for the *wszRedirectedURL* parameter. This method applies only to Web content, and all subsequent relative URL links are processed based on the redirected URL.

- **BindToStream**   Binds the item being processed to a data stream and returns a pointer for that stream to the Filter Daemon.

- **BindToFilter**   Binds the appropriate *IFilter* object for the current item and returns a pointer to it.

- **GetSize**   Gets the size in bytes of the content item designated by the URL.

As a result, the methods *AddRequestParameter*, *GetHost*, and *GetSecurityProvider* are never called by the Filter Daemon. All methods should upon success return the *S_OK* error code.

It is optional to implement the methods *GetCLSID* and *GetDocFormat*, as the Filter Daemon can automatically make the association between the file extension in the URL and the appropriate *IFilter*. It is only necessary to implement at least one of these methods if you are indexing files with formats different from those indicated by the file extensions. For example, if .doc files in your content source are not Microsoft Office Word files, let the *GetCLSID* method return the registry CLSID of the appropriate *IFilter*, or let the *GetDocFormat* method return the MIME type of the file.

To be useful, a protocol handler must implement at least one of the methods *BindToStream* and *BindToFilter*. It can also implement both. For example, protocol handlers can use the *BindToFilter* method to return an implementation of the *IFilter* interface that emits the metadata associated with content items and use the *BindToStream* method to retrieve the actual content of the item. The sample protocol handler presented in the section "Sample Protocol Handler for Indexing a File Share" later in this chapter implements both methods.

The *IStream* Interface   This is a standard Windows interface for reading and writing data to a stream object. Protocol handlers implementing the *BindToStream* method of the *IUrlAccessor* interface must also return an object implementing the *IStream* interface. The Filter Daemon will in turn read data from the stream and loop it through the appropriate *IFilter* for further processing. The *IStream* interface is defined as follows in the Windows API:

```
/* ID: 0000000c-0000-0000-C000-000000000046 */
public class IStream : public ISequentialStream
{
public:
    virtual /* [local] */ HRESULT STDMETHODCALLTYPE Seek(
            /* [in] */      LARGE_INTEGER dlibMove,
            /* [in] */      DWORD dwOrigin,
            /* [out] */     ULARGE_INTEGER *plibNewPosition) = 0;

    virtual HRESULT STDMETHODCALLTYPE SetSize(
            /* [in] */      ULARGE_INTEGER libNewSize) = 0;

    virtual /* [local] */ HRESULT STDMETHODCALLTYPE CopyTo(
            /* [unique][in] */   IStream *pstm,
            /* [in] */      ULARGE_INTEGER cb,
            /* [out] */     ULARGE_INTEGER *pcbRead,
            /* [out] */     ULARGE_INTEGER *pcbWritten) = 0;

    virtual HRESULT STDMETHODCALLTYPE Commit(
            /* [in] */      DWORD grfCommitFlags) = 0;

    virtual HRESULT STDMETHODCALLTYPE Revert(void) = 0;

    virtual HRESULT STDMETHODCALLTYPE LockRegion(
            /* [in] */      ULARGE_INTEGER libOffset,
            /* [in] */      ULARGE_INTEGER cb,
            /* [in] */      DWORD dwLockType) = 0;

    virtual HRESULT STDMETHODCALLTYPE UnlockRegion(
            /* [in] */      ULARGE_INTEGER libOffset,
            /* [in] */      ULARGE_INTEGER cb,
            /* [in] */      DWORD dwLockType) = 0;

    virtual HRESULT STDMETHODCALLTYPE Stat(
            /* [out] */     __RPC__out STATSTG *pstatstg,
            /* [in] */      DWORD grfStatFlag) = 0;

    virtual HRESULT STDMETHODCALLTYPE Clone(
            /* [out] */     __RPC__deref_out_opt IStream **ppstm) = 0;
};
```

The *IStream* interface inherits from the *ISequentialStream* interface, which is defined as follows:

```
[uuid(0c733a30-2a1c-11ce-ade5-00aa0044773d)]
ISequentialStream : public IUnknown
{
public:
    virtual /* [local] */ HRESULT STDMETHODCALLTYPE Read(
            /* [length_is][size_is][out] */  void *pv,
            /* [in] */      ULONG cb,
            /* [out] */     ULONG *pcbRead) = 0;

    virtual /* [local] */ HRESULT STDMETHODCALLTYPE Write(
            /* [size_is][in] */  const void *pv,
            /* [in] */      ULONG cb,
            /* [out] */     ULONG *pcbWritten) = 0;

    ...
};
```

The Filter Daemon will call the *Read* method only to pull data from the stream.

Protocol Handler Data Structures

The methods of the *ISearchProtocol* interface use a number a special data structures as method parameters. This section describes the purpose and the format of each data structure.

AUTHENTICATION_INFO This data structure contains authentication information such as user name and password, as shown here:

```
typedef struct _AUTHENTICATION_INFO
{
    DWORD dwSize;
    AUTH_TYPE atAuthenticationType;
    LPCWSTR pcwszUser;
    LPCWSTR pcwszPassword;
} AUTHENTICATION_INFO;
```

The *dwSize* member specifies the actual size in bytes of the structure. The authentication type is specified by the *stAuthenticationType* enumeration member, which can assume one of the following values:

- *eAUTH_TYPE_ANONYMOUS*

- *eAUTH_TYPE_NTLM*

- *eAUTH_TYPE_BASIC*

Other authentication types like Kerberos are not supported by protocol handlers. See the section "Crawler Authentication Schemes" in Chapter 5 for a detailed discussion of how the crawler can authenticate with content sources. The *pcwszUser* member represents the user name, including the domain to use for accessing content—for example, *LITWAREINC\ spcrawler*. The *pcwszPassword* represents the password for the user name.

INCREMENTAL_ACCESS_INFO   This data structure contains information for use in incremental crawls, as shown here:

```
typedef struct _INCREMENTAL_ACCESS_INFO
{
    DWORD dwSize;
    FILETIME ftLastModifiedTime;
} INCREMENTAL_ACCESS_INFO;
```

The member named *ftLastModifiedTime* specifies the date and time when the current content item was last modified. The value of the *dwSize* member specifies the actual size in bytes of the structure.

ITEM_INFO   This data structure contains information about the current item, such as the application name and catalog name, as shown here:

```
typedef struct _ITEM_INFO
{
    DWORD dwSize;
    LPCWSTR pcwszFromEMail;
    LPCWSTR pcwszApplicationName;
    LPCWSTR pcwszCatalogName;
    LPCWSTR pcwszContentClass;
} ITEM_INFO;
```

The member named *pcwszFromEmail* contains the e-mail address of the person who should be notified in case of an error. The *pcwszApplicationName* member specifies the name of the search application, which for Office SharePoint Server 2007 is the application ID of the SSP defining the content source being crawled. The value of the next member, named *pcwszCatalogName*, represents the name of the physical index. For Office SharePoint Server 2007, the value of this member is always *Portal_Content*. Earlier versions of SharePoint had the ability to provide different values here, as they also supported multiple content indexes for each search application. Avoid using the *pcwszContentClass* member.

PROXY_INFO   This data structure contains information about proxy settings when the protocol handler is required to access content through a proxy, as shown here:

```
typedef struct _PROXY_INFO
{
    DWORD dwSize;
    LPCWSTR pcwszUserAgent;
    PROXY_ACCESS paUseProxy;
    BOOL fLocalBypass;
    DWORD dwPortNumber;
    LPCWSTR pcwszProxyName;
    LPCWSTR pcwszBypassList;
} PROXY_INFO;
```

The *pcwszUserAgent* member identifies the protocol handler to the proxy. The *paUseProxy* member is an enumeration that tells the protocol handler what proxy settings it should use. The enumeration can assume one of the following values:

- **PROXY_ACCESS_PRECONFIG**   Use proxy settings defined in Internet Explorer.
- **PROXY_DIRECT_ACCESS**   Do not connect through a proxy.
- **PROXY_ACCESS_PROXY**   Use the supplied proxy settings.

The Boolean member *fLocalBypass* specifies whether the protocol handler should bypass the proxy for the local addresses listed by the *pcwszBypassList* member. The members *pcwszProxyName* and *dwPortNumber* specify the network address and port number of the proxy to use.

TIMEOUT_INFO   This data structure contains information about timeout settings for connecting to and retrieving data from content sources, as shown here:

```
typedef struct _TIMEOUT_INFO
{
    DWORD dwSize;
    DWORD dwConnectTimeout;
    DWORD dwDataTimeout;
} TIMEOUT_INFO;
```

The *dwConnectTimeout* member specifies the maximum number of seconds to wait for a connection to a content source to be established. The *dwDataTimeout* member specifies the maximum number of seconds to wait before data is received from a content source. The default value for both timeout settings is 20 seconds. If this time elapses without response, the process hosting the Filter Daemon is terminated. A Filter Daemon might stop responding if a custom *IFilter* or custom protocol handler caused an unexpected error. The automatic shutdown of nonresponsive Filter Daemon processes plus the automatic launch of new processes gives the index engine a chance to recover from such errors.

Protocol Handler Error Messages

A lot of things can go wrong when content is crawled. Content servers subject to the crawl might not respond because of server or network errors, or they might deny access to the content. Protocol handlers must handle possible error conditions and report the correct error code back to the index engine. Legal error codes include special protocol handler error codes plus standard Windows error codes like *S_OK*, *E_INVALIDARG*, *E_OUTOFMEMORY*, and so forth. Table 9-5 lists the error codes that are specific to protocol handlers.

TABLE 9-5 Special Error Codes That Protocol Handlers Can Return to the Index Engine

Value	Description
PRTH_E_ACCESS_DENIED (0x80041205L)	Access is denied. Make sure that the account used to access this URL is the correct account. The ACL of the item does not allow the content access account to read it.
PRTH_E_ACL_TOO_BIG (0x80041211L)	Search will not index the item because its ACL exceeded 64 KB. Make sure that the item has a valid ACL.
PRTH_E_BAD_REQUEST (0x80041212L)	The request was not valid because of an error in the URL.
PRTH_E_COMM_ERROR (0x80041208L)	A communication/server error occurred. If a high volume of these errors occurs, the crawler will mark the server as unavailable.
PRTH_E_NOT_REDIRECTED (0x80041200L)	The redirected URL does not exist.
PRTH_E_OBJ_NOT_FOUND (0x80041207L)	The object was not found. This tells the crawler to delete the document if it is not found during an incremental crawl.
PRTH_E_REQUEST_ERROR (0x80041201L)	The options used are not supported.
PRTH_E_SERVER_ERROR (0x80041202L)	A communication/server error occurred. If a high volume of these errors occurs, the crawler will mark the server as unavailable.
PRTH_S_ACL_IS_READ_EVERYONE (0x80041206L)	The ACL was changed so that the item is readable by everyone. Used in the GetSecurityDescriptor method of the IUrlAccessor interface.
PRTH_S_NOT_ALL_PARTS (0x8004121BL)	Parts of the content item cannot be accessed.
PRTH_S_NOT_MODIFIED (0x00041203L)	The content has not changed. Provides support for incremental crawls.

Sample Protocol Handler for Indexing a File Share

This section demonstrates the development of a sample protocol handler designed to index file shares. The protocol handler presented here is identical to the one included in the Office SharePoint Server 2007 SDK; the handler can be downloaded from the Microsoft Developer Network (MSDN) at *http://msdn2.microsoft.com/en-us/library/bb266531.aspx*.

Note Most of the C++ source code of the protocol handler has been included in this section with rich inline comments not found in the SDK.

Sample Protocol Handler Files

The sample protocol handler included in the Microsoft SDK includes all of the files listed in Table 9-6.

TABLE 9-6 Sample Protocol Handler Files Included in the Microsoft SDK

File Name	Description
SampleProtocolHandler.vcproj	The main Microsoft Visual Studio C++ project file.
SampleProtocolHandler.idl	This file contains the Interface Definition Language (IDL) definitions of the type library, the interfaces, and the classes defined in the project. It will be processed by the Microsoft IDL (MIDL) compiler to generate the following: ❑ *SampleProtocolHandler.h* C++ interface definitions and GUID declarations ❑ *SampleProtocolHandler_i.c* GUID definitions ❑ *SampleProtocolHandler.tlb* A type library ❑ *SampleProtocolHandler_p.c* and *dlldata.c* Marshalingcode
SampleProtocolHandler.h	Contains the C++ interface definitions and GUID declarations of the items defined in SampleProtocolHandler.idl. It will be regenerated by MIDL during compilation.
SampleProtocolHandler.cpp	Contains the object map and the implementation of the DLL exports.
SampleProtocolHandler.rc	Defines all the Microsoft Windows resources that the program uses.
SampleProtocolHandler.def	This module definition file provides the linker with information about the exports required by the DLL. It contains exports for the following: ❑ DllGetClassObject ❑ DllCanUnloadNow ❑ GetProxyDllInfo ❑ DllRegisterServer ❑ DllUnregisterServer
SampleProtocolHandler.rgs	Contains the registration script that registers the protocol handler in the Windows registry.
StdAfx.h StdAfx.cpp	These files are used to build a precompiled header (.pch) file named SampleProtocolHandler.pch and a precompiled type file named StdAfx.obj.
Resource.h	This is the standard header file that defines resource IDs.

File Name	Description
SampleProtocolHandlerps.vcproj	This file is the Visual Studio project file for building a proxy/stub DLL if necessary. The IDL file in the main project must contain at least one interface, and you must first compile the IDL file before building the proxy/stub DLL. This process generates dlldata.c, SampleProtocolHandler_i.c, and SampleProtocolHandler_p.c, which are required to build the proxy/stub DLL.
SampleProtocolHandlerps.def	This module definition file provides the linker with information about the exports required by the proxy/stub DLL.
FileStream.h FileStream.cpp	Source files for the *CFileStream* class that implements the *IStream* interface for a file.
Filter.idl	This file contains the IDL definitions of the *IFilter* interface.
Filter.h	This file contains the C++ interface definitions of the items defined in the Filter.idl file. It will be regenerated by MIDL during compilation.
Filterr.h	*IFilter* error codes.
Prterr.h	Protocol handler error codes.
Sampleacc.hxx Sampleacc.cxx	Source files for the *CSampleAccessor* class that implements the *IUrlAccessor* interface for accessing a Windows file system.
Sampledirfltr.hxx Sampledirfltr.cxx	Source files for the *CSampleDirFilter* class that inherits from the *CSampleFileFilter* class. The *CSampleDirFilter* class implements logic to traverse hierarchical file folder structures and enumerate the files of each folder.
Samplefilefltr.hxx samplefilefltr.cxx	Source files for the *CSampleFileFilter* class that implements the *IFilter* interface. This class implements logic to enumerate all properties of a single file.
Samplehndlr.hxx Samplehndlr.cxx	Source files for the *CSampleProtocolHandler* class that implements the *ISearchProtocol* interface.

The default location of the sample protocol handler files when installing the SDK is C:\Program Files\2007 Office System Developer Resources\Samples\Search\Sample Protocol Handler\SampleProtocolHandler.

Program Flow of the Sample Protocol Handler

Before diving into the raw source code in the next section, let's first examine the key classes and the overall program flow of the sample protocol handler. This knowledge will make it much easier to follow what is going on in each line of code. The key C++ classes implementing the protocol interfaces include the following:

- *CSampleProtocolHandler*   This class implements the *ISearchProtocol* interface and is primarily responsible for delivering objects implementing the *IUrlAccessor* interface to the Filter Daemon.

- *CSampleAccessor*   This class implements the *IUrlAccessor* interface and contains the logic required to process a single URL received from the Filter Daemon.

- *CFileStream*   This class implements the Windows *IStream* interface and is used to open a stream to a single file on a file share.

- *CSampleFileFilter*   This class implements the *IFilter* interface and is responsible for enumerating and returning all properties of a single file.

- *CSampleDirFilter*   This class is an inherited class of *CSampleFileFilter* and is responsible for enumerating all files and folders on a file share. In other words, it is used to discover all files on the file share from the start address of the content source.

The program flow starts when the Filter Daemon receives a URL from the Gather Manager, as shown in the following illustration. The Filter Daemon reads the scheme of the URL and attempts to locate the protocol handler associated with the scheme. Assuming that the sample protocol handler is installed and that the URL scheme equals *sample*, the Filter Daemon will load and instantiate the *CSampleProtocolHandler* class. Subsequently, it calls the *Init* method on the class to initialize the protocol handler. However, loading and initialization of the protocol handler occur only on the first URL with a matching scheme.

For each URL the Filter Daemon receives from the Gather Manager, it calls the *CreateAccessor* method on the *CSampleProtocolHandler* class to obtain a handle to an object implementing the *IUrlAccessor* interface. The *CreateAccessor* method of the sample protocol handler simply returns a new instance of the *CSampleAccessor* class. As mentioned earlier, the Filter Daemon works with many parallel I/O requests to speed crawling. Consequently, it also makes several concurrent calls to the *CreateAccessor* method.

Once the Filter Daemon receives a handle to a *CSampleAccessor* object, it calls the *GetDocFormat* and *GetCLSID* methods on it to determine what *IFilter* to use for breaking a document into text chunks. It will also call the *IsDirectory* method to determine whether the current URL represents a file or a directory. If the URL represents a file, the *GetSize* and *GetLastModified* methods are called to obtain the file size and last modified date, respectively. Next, the *BindToStream* method is called to open and retrieve an *IStream* handle to the file. The *BindToStream* method implemented by the *CSampleAccessor* class responds by instantiating and returning a new instance of the *CFileStream* class.

The Filter Daemon will subsequently start calling the *Read* method on the *IStream* handle to download the contents of the file. The *Read* method is called multiple times to download the document in smaller chunks until the end-of-file (EOF) marker is reached. Each chunk is in turn passed through an appropriate *IFilter* that extracts all text and properties contained in the document. The output of the *IFilter* is then sent into the Indexing Pipeline for further processing. The file stream is closed when the download has completed.

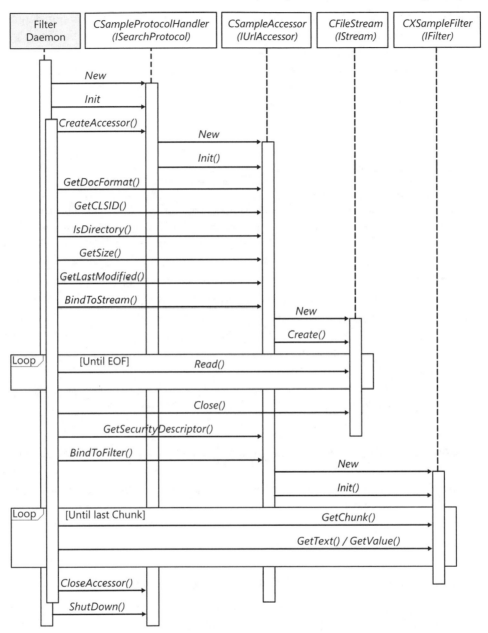

Next, the Filter Daemon calls the *GetSecurityDescriptor* method in an attempt to retrieve an ACL for the file. When indexing an NT File System (NTFS) file share, this method of the *CSampleAccessor* class simply loads and returns the ACL directly from the file system.

The next step for the Filter Daemon is to ask the protocol handler for additional information such as file properties or additional URLs for the crawl queue. It does so by calling the *BindToFilter* method on the *IUrlAccessor* handle. The *CSampleAccessor* implementation will respond in one of two ways, depending on whether the current URL represents a file or a directory. It returns an instance of the *CSampleFileFilter* class if the URL is a file and an instance of the *CSampleDirFilter* class if the URL is a directory.

> **Note** It is optional for a protocol handler to implement the *BindToFilter* method if it implements the *BindToStream* method, and vice versa. If the sample protocol handler did not implement the *BindToStream* method, its *BindToFilter* method implementation would also need to implement the loop that reads chunks from the file stream and loops them through the appropriate *IFilter*. It could in that case use the *IProtocolHandlerSite* handle to retrieve an *IFilter* handle based on the file extension or the file MIME type. The *IProtocolHandlerSite* handle is provided to the protocol handler by the Filter Daemon as a parameter in the *Init* method of the *ISearchProtocol* interface.

If the *BindToFilter* method returns a valid *IFilter* handle, the Filter Daemon enters a new loop, where it first calls the *GetChunk* method. Depending on the type of the chunk returned by the *IFilter*, it then calls the *GetText* method or the *GetValue* method. It stays in the loop as long as the *GetChunk* method returns the Windows error code *S_OK*. The *GetChunk* method of the *CSampleFileFilter* class returns the *IFilter* error code *FILTER_E_END_OF_CHUNKS* once it has returned all file properties. The *CSampleDirFilter* implementation of the *GetChunk* method returns the same error code after it has returned the URL of all files and subfolders of the current directory URL.

Last, after the Filter Daemon completes the processing of the current URL, it calls the *CloseAccessor* method, which provides an opportunity for the protocol handler to free any resources allocated by the accessor. The sample protocol handler does not do anything at this point, however, as it uses auto pointers to ensure proper cleanup of all objects once they are no longer referenced. The *ShutDown* method is called when the index engine terminates the Filter Daemon process. It will do so if the Search service is stopped or if a custom protocol handler or *IFilter* running in the process is not responding.

Implementing the Main Module with DLL Registration

The sample protocol handler is compiled to a DLL file, and the main module discussed here contains the DLL entry point that is called when the Filter Daemon loads the DLL into memory for the first time. The main module of the sample protocol handler is implemented as a class named *CSampleProtocolHandler* that inherits from the ATL template class named *CAtlDllModuleT*. The ATL base class simplifies the implementation of the COM object. The main module is implemented by the files SampleProtocolHandler.h and SampleProtocolHandler.cpp.

The SampleProtocolHandler.h file includes the following lines of code that declare the GUID of the COM class that represents the protocol handler:

```
class DECLSPEC_UUID("195e97b5-8401-460c-804e-06a0416d032b")
CSampleProtocolHandler;
```

This GUID ultimately tells the Filter Daemon which COM object in the DLL implements the sample protocol handler. The SampleProtocolHandler.cpp file defines the *CSampleProtocolHandlerModule* class as follows:

```
class CSampleProtocolHandlerModule : public CAtlDllModuleT<CSampleProtocolHandlerModule> {};

CSampleProtocolHandlerModule _AtlModule;

// DLL Entry Point
extern "C" BOOL WINAPI DllMain(HINSTANCE hInstance, DWORD dwReason, LPVOID lpReserved) {
    hInstance;
    return _AtlModule.DllMain(dwReason, lpReserved);
}

// Used to determine whether the DLL can be unloaded by OLE
STDAPI DllCanUnloadNow(void) {
    return _AtlModule.DllCanUnloadNow();
}

// Returns a class factory to create an object of the requested type
STDAPI DllGetClassObject(REFCLSID rclsid, REFIID riid, LPVOID* ppv) {
    return _AtlModule.DllGetClassObject(rclsid, riid, ppv);
}

// DllRegisterServer - Adds entries to the system registry
STDAPI DllRegisterServer(void) {
    // registers object, typelib and all interfaces in typelib
    HRESULT hr = _AtlModule.DllRegisterServer();
    return hr;
}

// DllUnregisterServer - Removes entries from the system registry
STDAPI DllUnregisterServer(void) {
    HRESULT hr = _AtlModule.DllUnregisterServer();
    return hr;
}
```

The *DllRegisterServer* method is called when the protocol handler is installed using the regsvr32.exe tool, as described in the section "Installing a Protocol Handler on Index Servers" later in this chapter. It executes code that registers the protocol handler with Office SharePoint Server 2007 through the Windows registry. The *DllRegisterServer* method of the ATL template uses the following Windows registry commands defined in the SampleProtocolHandler.rgs file to register the protocol handler:

```
HKCR {
  SampleProtocolHandler.SampleProtocolHandler.1 = s 'SampleProtocolHandler Class' {
    CLSID = s '{195e97b5-8401-460c-804e-06a0416d032b}'
  }

  SampleProtocolHandler.SampleProtocolHandler = s 'SampleProtocolHandler Class' {
    CLSID = s '{195e97b5-8401-460c-804e-06a0416d032b}'
    CurVer = s 'SampleProtocolHandler.SampleProtocolHandler.1'
  }

  NoRemove CLSID {
    ForceRemove {195e97b5-8401-460c-804e-06a0416d032b} = s 'SampleProtocolHandler Class' {
      ProgID = s 'SampleProtocolHandler.SampleProtocolHandler.1'
      VersionIndependentProgID = s 'SampleProtocolHandler.SampleProtocolHandler'
      ForceRemove 'Programmable'
      InprocServer32 = s '%MODULE%' {
        val ThreadingModel = s 'Both'
}}}}

HKLM {
  NoRemove Software {
    NoRemove Microsoft {
      NoRemove 'Office Server' {
        NoRemove 12.0 {
          NoRemove Search {
            NoRemove Setup {
              NoRemove ProtocolHandlers {
                val sample = s 'SampleProtocolHandler.SampleProtocolHandler.1'
}}}}}}}}
```

The *%MODULE%* parameter is automatically replaced with the full path of the DLL file. The SampleProtocolHandler.rc resource file contains the following entry telling ATL where to look for the registration commands:

```
IDR_SAMPLEPROTOCOLHANDLER    REGISTRY        "SampleProtocolHandler.rgs"
```

The *DllUnregisterServer* method simply reverses the registration actions.

Implementing the *ISearchProtocol* Interface

The *ISearchProtocol* interface is implemented by the COM class *CSampleProtocolHandler* defined in the samplehandlr.hxx header file and implemented in the samplehandlr.cxx file. The header file defines the class in the following way:

```
class ATL_NO_VTABLE CSampleProtocolHandler :
    public CComObjectRootEx<CComMultiThreadModel>,
    public CComCoClass<CSampleProtocolHandler, &CLSID_CSampleProtocolHandler>,
    public ISearchProtocol
{
```

```
public:
    CSampleProtocolHandler() {}
    ~CSampleProtocolHandler() {}

DECLARE_REGISTRY_RESOURCEID(IDR_SAMPLEPROTOCOLHANDLER)
BEGIN_COM_MAP(CSampleProtocolHandler)
    COM_INTERFACE_ENTRY(ISearchProtocol)
END_COM_MAP()
DECLARE_PROTECT_FINAL_CONSTRUCT()
    HRESULT FinalConstruct() { return S_OK; }
    void FinalRelease() {}

public:
    STDMETHOD(Init)(/*[in]*/  TIMEOUT_INFO *pTimeoutInfo,
                    /*[in]*/  IProtocolHandlerSite *pProtocolHandlerSite,
                    /*[in]*/  PROXY_INFO *pProxyInfo);

    STDMETHOD(CreateAccessor)(/*[in]*/    LPCWSTR pcwszURL,
                              /*[in]*/    AUTHENTICATION_INFO *pAuthenticationInfo,
                              /*[in]*/    INCREMENTAL_ACCESS_INFO *pIncrementalAccessInfo,
                              /*[in]*/    ITEM_INFO *pItemInfo,
                              /*[out]*/   IUrlAccessor **ppAccessor);

    STDMETHOD(CloseAccessor)(/*[in]*/  IUrlAccessor *pAccessor);

    STDMETHOD(ShutDown)() { return S_OK; }
};
```

The implementation of the *CreateAccessor* method shown here instantiates and returns a new object instance of the *CSampleAccessor* class:

```
HRESULT CSampleProtocolHandler::CreateAccessor(
        /* [in] */    LPCWSTR pcwszURL,
        /* [in] */    AUTHENTICATION_INFO *pAuthenticationInfo,
        /* [in] */    INCREMENTAL_ACCESS_INFO *pIncrementalAccessInfo,
        /* [in] */    ITEM_INFO *pItemInfo,
        /* [out] */   IUrlAccessor **ppAccessor)
{
    *ppAccessor = NULL;
    HRESULT hr = S_OK;

    // Create a new instance of the CSampleAccessor class. Wrap it with a
    // smart pointer for automatic memory cleanup when it is no longer referenced.
    CComPtr<CSampleAccessor> pAccessor;
    pAccessor = new CComObject<CSampleAccessor>;
    if (pAccessor == NULL) hr = E_OUTOFMEMORY;

    if (SUCCEEDED(hr)) {
        // Initialize the new accessor by calling the Init method of the accessor.
        hr = pAccessor->Init(pcwszURL,
                             pAuthenticationInfo,
                             pIncrementalAccessInfo,
                             pItemInfo,
                             this);
```

```
            if (SUCCEEDED(hr)) {
                pAccessor->GetUnknown()->AddRef();
                *ppAccessor = pAccessor;     // Return the new accessor to the Filter Daemon
            }
        }

    return hr;
}
```

The implementation of the other three *ISearchProtocol* methods does nothing and simply
returns the *S_OK* error code.

Implementing the *IUrlAccessor* Interface

The *IUrlAccessor* interface is implemented by the COM class named *CSampleAccessor* defined
in the sampleacc.hxx header file and implemented in the sampleacc.cxx file. The class is
defined in the header file by the following lines of code:

```
class ATL_NO_VTABLE CSampleAccessor :
    public CComObjectRootEx<CComMultiThreadModel>,
    public IUrlAccessor
{
public:
    CSampleAccessor() : m_fIsDirectory(FALSE), m_fValidLastModified(FALSE), m_pHandler(0),
                        m_dwAttributes(0), m_hFile(INVALID_HANDLE_VALUE)
    {
        m_SecurityDescriptor.cbSize = 0;
        m_SecurityDescriptor.pBlobData = NULL;
    }

    ~CSampleAccessor() {
        if (m_hFile != INVALID_HANDLE_VALUE)  {
            CloseHandle(m_hFile);
        }
        if (m_SecurityDescriptor.cbSize) {
            CoTaskMemFree(m_SecurityDescriptor.pBlobData);
        }
    }

    HRESULT Init(LPCWSTR pcwszURL,
                 AUTHENTICATION_INFO *pAuthenticationInfo,
                 INCREMENTAL_ACCESS_INFO *pIncrementalAccessInfo,
                 ITEM_INFO *pItemInfo,
                 CSampleProtocolHandler *pHandler);
    HRESULT Reset();

BEGIN_COM_MAP(CSampleAccessor)
    COM_INTERFACE_ENTRY(IUrlAccessor)
END_COM_MAP()
```

```
// IUrlAccessor
public:
    STDMETHOD(AddRequestParameter)(PROPSPEC *pSpec, PROPVARIANT *pVar);
    STDMETHOD(GetDocFormat)(WCHAR wszDocFormat[], DWORD cwchDocFormat, DWORD *pdwLength);
    STDMETHOD(GetCLSID)(CLSID *pClsid);
    STDMETHOD(GetHost)(WCHAR wszHost[], DWORD cwchHost, DWORD *pdwLength);
    STDMETHOD(IsDirectory)();
    STDMETHOD(GetSize)(ULONGLONG *pllSize);
    STDMETHOD(GetLastModified)(FILETIME *pftLastModified);
    STDMETHOD(GetFileName)(WCHAR wszFileName[], DWORD cwchFileName, DWORD *pdwLength);
    STDMETHOD(GetSecurityDescriptor)(BYTE *pSD, DWORD dwSize, DWORD *pdwLength);
    STDMETHOD(GetRedirectedURL)(WCHAR wszRedirectedURL[], DWORD dwSize, DWORD *pdwLength);
    STDMETHOD(GetSecurityProvider)(CLSID *pSPClsid);
    STDMETHOD(BindToStream)(IStream **ppStream);
    STDMETHOD(BindToFilter)(IFilter **ppFilter);
    static HRESULT GetFileTimes(LPCWSTR wstrFileName,
                                const HANDLE hFile,
                                DWORD& dwAttr,
                                FILETIME* pftWriteTime,
                                FILETIME* pftCreateTime,
                                FILETIME* pftAccessTime,
                                FILETIME* pftChangeTime);
private:
    WCHAR                       m_url[MAX_PATH];
    LPWSTR                      m_pwszPath;
    BOOL                        m_fIsDirectory;
    BOOL                        m_fIsDocument;
    BOOL                        m_fValidLastModified;
    FILETIME                    m_ftWrite;
    FILETIME                    m_ftCreate;
    FILETIME                    m_ftAccess;
    FILETIME                    m_ftChange;
    HANDLE                      m_hFile;
    CSampleProtocolHandler      *m_pHandler;
    DWORD                       m_dwAttributes;
    BLOB                        m_SecurityDescriptor;
};
```

The implementation of the *Init* method called from the *CreateAccessor* method of the *CSampleProtocolHandler* class handles several initialization tasks, including the following:

- Validation of the URL received from the Filter Daemon

- Directory or file detection

- Creation of a handle to the file or directory

- Retrieval of file times, including creation time, last write time, last modified time, and last accessed time

- Loading of the file's security descriptor

- Checking whether the file has changed since the last crawl

The method will return *S_OK* if all initialization tasks succeeded. To support incremental crawls, it returns the error code *PRTH_S_NOT_MODIFIED* if the file has not been modified since the last crawl. The following lines of code present the concrete implementation of the *Init* method:

```
HRESULT CSampleAccessor::Init(LPCWSTR pcwszURL,
                    AUTHENTICATION_INFO *pAuthenticationInfo,
                    INCREMENTAL_ACCESS_INFO *pIncrementalAccessInfo,
                    ITEM_INFO *pItemInfo,
                    CSampleProtocolHandler *pHandler)
{
    m_pHandler = pHandler;
    DWORD dwAttributes = 0;
    int iUrlLen = lstrlen(pcwszURL);

    // Fail on short and long URLs.
    if (iUrlLen >= MAX_PATH) return HRESULT_FROM_WIN32(ERROR_FILENAME_EXCED_RANGE);
    if (iUrlLen < 7) return E_INVALIDARG;

    // Fail if the accessor URL does not specify the sample:// protocol.
    if (memcmp(pcwszURL, L"sample:", 14)) return E_INVALIDARG;

    HRESULT hr = StringCchCopy(m_url, MAX_PATH, pcwszURL);

    // Replace all forward slashes with back slashes.
    for (int i = 0; i<iUrlLen; i++) {
        if (m_url[i] == L'/') m_url[i] = L'\\';
    }

    if (SUCCEEDED(hr)) {
        m_pwszPath = m_url + 7;
        dwAttributes = GetFileAttributes(m_pwszPath);
        if(dwAttributes == 0xFFFFFFFF)
            hr = HResultFromFileStatus(GetLastError());
    }

    if (SUCCEEDED(hr)) {
        m_dwAttributes = dwAttributes;

        if (dwAttributes & FILE_ATTRIBUTE_ENCRYPTED)
            return GTHR_E_URL_EXCLUDED;

        // Detect if the URL represents a directory and not a file as first assumed.
        if (dwAttributes & FILE_ATTRIBUTE_DIRECTORY)
            m_fIsDirectory = TRUE;

        if (!m_fIsDirectory) {
            // Obtain a handle to the file.
            m_hFile = CreateFile(m_pwszPath,
                            GENERIC_READ,
                            FILE_SHARE_READ,
                            NULL,
```

```
                                    OPEN_EXISTING,
                                    FILE_ATTRIBUTE_NORMAL,
                                    NULL);

        if (m_hFile == INVALID_HANDLE_VALUE) {
            hr = HResultFromFileStatus(GetLastError());
        }
    } else {
        // Obtain a handle to the directory.
        m_hFile = CreateFile(m_pwszPath,
                FILE_READ_ATTRIBUTES | FILE_LIST_DIRECTORY | SYNCHRONIZE,
                FILE_SHARE_READ | FILE_SHARE_WRITE | FILE_SHARE_DELETE,
                NULL,
                OPEN_EXISTING,
                FILE_FLAG_BACKUP_SEMANTICS,
                NULL);
    }
}

const DWORD kcbFirstBufferSize = 1024;

if (SUCCEEDED(hr)) {
    // Allocate memory for the security descriptor.
    m_SecurityDescriptor.pBlobData = (BYTE*)CoTaskMemAlloc(kcbFirstBufferSize);
    if (m_SecurityDescriptor.pBlobData == NULL)
        hr = E_OUTOFMEMORY;
}

if (SUCCEEDED(hr)) {
    // Get the file security descriptor.

    m_SecurityDescriptor.cbSize = kcbFirstBufferSize;
    DWORD dwSDLength = 0;

    // We are assuming that GetFileSecurity supports prefix "\\?\"
    // for long path name, although it is not stated explicitly
    // in the documentation.
    if (GetFileSecurity(m_pwszPath, OWNER_SECURITY_INFORMATION |
        GROUP_SECURITY_INFORMATION | DACL_SECURITY_INFORMATION,
        m_SecurityDescriptor.pBlobData, m_SecurityDescriptor.cbSize, &dwSDLength) == 0)
    {
        hr = HResultFromFileStatus(GetLastError());
    }

    if (hr == HRESULT_FROM_WIN32(ERROR_INSUFFICIENT_BUFFER)) {
        //rare case
        m_SecurityDescriptor.pBlobData =
          (BYTE*)CoTaskMemRealloc(m_SecurityDescriptor.pBlobData, dwSDLength);

        if (m_SecurityDescriptor.pBlobData == NULL) hr = E_OUTOFMEMORY;
    }
```

```
        if (SUCCEEDED(hr)) {
            if (GetFileSecurity(m_pwszPath, OWNER_SECURITY_INFORMATION |
                GROUP_SECURITY_INFORMATION | DACL_SECURITY_INFORMATION,
                m_SecurityDescriptor.pBlobData, m_SecurityDescriptor.
                cbSize, &dwSDLength) == 0)
            {
                hr = HResultFromFileStatus(GetLastError());
            }
        }

        if (SUCCEEDED(hr)) {
            dwSDLength = GetSecurityDescriptorLength(m_SecurityDescriptor.pBlobData);
            m_SecurityDescriptor.cbSize = dwSDLength;
        }
    }

    if (SUCCEEDED(hr)) {
        // Get file times.

        DWORD dwAttr;
        if (SUCCEEDED(GetFileTimes(m_pwszPath,
                                   m_hFile,
                                   dwAttr,
                                   &m_ftWrite,
                                   &m_ftCreate,
                                   &m_ftAccess,
                                   &m_ftChange )))
        {
            m_fValidLastModified = TRUE;
        } else {
            m_fValidLastModified = FALSE;
            hr = HResultFromFileStatus(GetLastError());
        }
    }

    if (SUCCEEDED(hr)) {
        // Support for incremental crawls.

        if(!m_fIsDirectory && m_fValidLastModified &&
            (pIncrementalAccessInfo->ftLastModifiedTime.dwLowDateTime != 0 ||
                pIncrementalAccessInfo->ftLastModifiedTime.dwHighDateTime != 0))
        {
            if (CompareFileTime(&m_ftChange,
                                &pIncrementalAccessInfo->ftLastModifiedTime) <= 0)
            {
                hr = PRTH_S_NOT_MODIFIED;
            }
        }
    }

    return hr;
}
```

The *Init* method does all the hard work of loading the security descriptor of the file. Consequently, all the *GetSecurityDescriptor* method has to do is return the security descriptor, as the following implementation suggests:

```
STDMETHODIMP CSampleAccessor::GetSecurityDescriptor(
                              BYTE *pSD, DWORD dwSize, DWORD *pdwLength)
{
    if (pSD == NULL || pdwLength == NULL) return E_POINTER;
    HRESULT hr = S_OK;

    //NTFS
    *pdwLength = m_SecurityDescriptor.cbSize;
    if (dwSize < m_SecurityDescriptor.cbSize) {
        hr = HRESULT_FROM_WIN32(ERROR_INSUFFICIENT_BUFFER);
    } else {
        CopyMemory(pSD, m_SecurityDescriptor.pBlobData, m_SecurityDescriptor.cbSize);
    }

    return hr;
}
```

The implementation of the *BindToStream* method shown here instantiates and returns a new object instance of the *CFileStream* class if the current URL represents a file. The error code *E_NOTIMPL* is returned if the URL represents a directory.

```
STDMETHODIMP CSampleAccessor::BindToStream(IStream **ppStream)
{
    if(ppStream == NULL) return E_POINTER;

    HRESULT hr = E_FAIL;
    CComPtr<CFileStream> pfs;

    // Do not bind to a stream if the current URL represents a directory.
    hr = m_fIsDirectory ? E_NOTIMPL : S_OK;

    if (SUCCEEDED(hr)) {
        pfs = new CComObject<CFileStream>;
        hr = (pfs == NULL) ? E_OUTOFMEMORY : S_OK;
    }

    if(SUCCEEDED(hr)) {
        // Open the stream by calling the Create method on the new CFileStream object.
        hr = pfs->Create(m_pwszPath, GENERIC_READ, FILE_SHARE_READ, NULL,
            OPEN_EXISTING, FILE_ATTRIBUTE_NORMAL, NULL);
    }

    if (SUCCEEDED(hr)) {
        pfs->GetUnknown()->AddRef();
        *ppStream = static_cast<IStream *>(pfs);
    }

    if(FAILED(hr)) *ppStream = NULL;

    return hr;
}
```

The sample protocol handler also implements the *BindToFilter* method. It returns a new object instance of the *CSampleFileFilter* class if the current URL represents a file. If the URL represents a directory, the method returns a new object instance of the *CSampleDirFilter* class. These actions are implemented as follows:

```
STDMETHODIMP CSampleAccessor::BindToFilter(IFilter **ppFilter)
{
    if(ppFilter == NULL) return E_POINTER;
    HRESULT hr = E_FAIL;

    CComPtr<CSampleDirFilter> pdf;
    CComPtr<CSampleFileFilter> pff;

    if(m_fIsDirectory) {
        pdf = new CComObject<CSampleDirFilter>;
        hr = (pdf == NULL) ? E_OUTOFMEMORY : S_OK;
        if (SUCCEEDED(hr))
            hr = pdf->Init(m_pwszPath, m_hFile, m_dwAttributes, m_ftWrite,
                        m_ftCreate, m_ftAccess, m_ftChange);

        if (SUCCEEDED(hr)) {
            pdf->GetUnknown()->AddRef();
            *ppFilter = static_cast<IFilter *>(pdf);
        }
    } else {
        pff = new CComObject<CSampleFileFilter> ;
        hr = (pff == NULL)? E_OUTOFMEMORY : S_OK;

        if (SUCCEEDED(hr))
            hr = pff->Init(m_pwszPath, m_hFile, m_dwAttributes, m_ftWrite,
                        m_ftCreate, m_ftAccess, m_ftChange);

        if (SUCCEEDED(hr)) {
            pff->GetUnknown()->AddRef();
            *ppFilter = static_cast<IFilter*>(pff);
        }
    }

    if(FAILED(hr)) *ppFilter = NULL;

    return hr;
}
```

The implementation of the methods *GetSize* and *GetLastModified* is fairly straightforward and will not be discussed in detail here. The remaining *AddRequestParameter*, *GetDocFormat*, *GetCLSID*, *GetHost*, *GetFilename*, and *GetSecurityProvider* methods all return an error code signaling that the Filter Daemon cannot use them.

Implementing the *IStream* Interface

The Windows *IStream* interface is implemented by the COM class named *CFileStream* defined in the FileStream.h header file and implemented in the FileStream.cpp file. The header file defines the class through the following lines of code:

```
class CFileStream:
        public CComObjectRootEx<CComMultiThreadModelNoCS>,
        public IStream
{
public:
    CFileStream() {}
    ~CFileStream() {}

    BEGIN_COM_MAP(CFileStream)
            COM_INTERFACE_ENTRY(IStream)
    END_COM_MAP()

    void operator =(const CFileStream &rFileStream) {
        if(m_hFile != INVALID_HANDLE_VALUE) {
            CloseHandle(m_hFile);
            Duplicate(rFileStream);
        }
    }

    BOOL IsValid() const { return (m_hFile != INVALID_HANDLE_VALUE) ? TRUE : FALSE; }

    void Close() { if (m_hFile != INVALID_HANDLE_VALUE) CloseHandle(m_hFile); }

    STDMETHOD(Create)(LPCWSTR lpFileName,
                      DWORD dwDesiredAccess,
                      DWORD dwShareMode,
                      LPSECURITY_ATTRIBUTES lpSecurityAttributes,
                      DWORD dwCreationDisposition,
                      DWORD dwFlagsAndAttributes,
                      HANDLE hTemplateFile);

    STDMETHOD(Attach)(HANDLE hFile) {
        if (m_hFile != INVALID_HANDLE_VALUE) CloseHandle(m_hFile);
        m_hFile = hFile;
        return S_OK;
    }

    STDMETHOD(Read)(void *pv, ULONG cb, ULONG  *pcbRead);
    STDMETHOD(Write)(const void  *pv, ULONG cb, ULONG *pcbWritten);
    STDMETHOD(Seek)(LARGE_INTEGER dlibMove, DWORD dwOrigin,ULARGE_INTEGER *plibNewPosition);
    STDMETHOD(SetSize)(ULARGE_INTEGER libNewSize);
    STDMETHOD(CopyTo)(IStream  *pstm,
                      ULARGE_INTEGER cb,
                      ULARGE_INTEGER  *pcbRead,
                      ULARGE_INTEGER  *pcbWritten);
    STDMETHOD(Commit)(DWORD grfCommitFlags);
    STDMETHOD(Revert)();
    STDMETHOD(LockRegion)(ULARGE_INTEGER libOffset, ULARGE_INTEGER cb, DWORD dwLockType);
    STDMETHOD(UnlockRegion)(ULARGE_INTEGER libOffset, ULARGE_INTEGER cb, DWORD dwLockType);
```

```
        STDMETHOD(Stat)(STATSTG  *pstatstg, DWORD grfStatFlag);
        STDMETHOD(Clone)(IStream  **ppstm);

protected:
    HANDLE m_hFile;
    DWORD m_dwAccessMode;
};
```

The implementation of the *Create* method opens the file specified in the *lpFileName* parameter and stores the handle to the file in the member variable named *m_hFile*, as shown here:

```
STDMETHODIMP CFileStream::Create(LPCWSTR lpFileName,
                                 DWORD dwDesiredAccess,
                                 DWORD dwShareMode,
                                 LPSECURITY_ATTRIBUTES lpSecurityAttributes,
                                 DWORD dwCreationDisposition,
                                 DWORD dwFlagsAndAttributes,
                                 HANDLE hTemplateFile)
{
    if (lpFileName == NULL) return E_POINTER;

    m_dwAccessMode = dwDesiredAccess;

    m_hFile = CreateFile(lpFileName,
                         dwDesiredAccess,
                         dwShareMode,
                         lpSecurityAttributes,
                         dwCreationDisposition,
                         dwFlagsAndAttributes,
                         hTemplateFile);

    if (m_hFile == INVALID_HANDLE_VALUE)
        return HRESULT_FROM_WIN32(GetLastError());

    return S_OK;
}
```

The only other method worth looking at in the *CFileStream* class is the *Read* method, which the Filter Daemon calls to read a chunk of bytes from the file stream, as shown here:

```
STDMETHODIMP CFileStream::Read(void *pv, ULONG cb, ULONG  *pcbRead) {
    DWORD dwBytesRead = 0;
    if (pv == NULL) return E_POINTER;

    if (cb) {
        if (ReadFile(m_hFile, pv, cb, &dwBytesRead, NULL) == FALSE)
            return HRESULT_FROM_WIN32(GetLastError());
    }

    if (pcbRead) *pcbRead = dwBytesRead;

    return S_OK;
}
```

The remaining methods are never called by the Filter Daemon.

Implementing the *IFilter* Interface

Protocol handlers that implement the *BindToFilter* method of the *IUrlAccessor* interface must also provide an implementation for the *IFilter* interface. The sample protocol handler presented here provides two implementations for this interface: one for enumerating the properties of a single file and one for enumerating the files and subfolders of a directory on the file system being indexed.

The first implementation for enumerating file properties is represented by the COM class named *CSampleFileFilter*. It is defined in the samplefilefltr.hxx header file as follows:

```
class ATL_NO_VTABLE CSampleFileFilter:
        public CComObjectRootEx <CComMultiThreadModel>,
        public IFilter
{
public:
    CSampleFileFilter() : m_dwAttributes(0xFFFFFFFF), m_ulChunkId(0), m_dwState(stFirst) {}
    ~CSampleFileFilter() {}


    HRESULT Init(LPCWSTR pwszFileName, HANDLE hFile, DWORD dwAttributes,
                const FILETIME &ftLastWrite,
                const FILETIME &ftCreate,
                const FILETIME &ftAccess,
                const FILETIME &ftChange);


BEGIN_COM_MAP(CSampleFileFilter)
        COM_INTERFACE_ENTRY(IFilter)
END_COM_MAP()

public:    // IFilter
    STDMETHOD(Init)(ULONG grfFlags,
                    ULONG cAttributes,
                    FULLPROPSPEC const * aAttributes,
                    ULONG * pFlags);
    STDMETHOD(GetChunk)(STAT_CHUNK * pStat);
    STDMETHOD(GetText)(ULONG * pcwcBuffer, WCHAR *awcBuffer);
    STDMETHOD(GetValue)(PROPVARIANT ** ppPropValue);
    STDMETHOD(BindRegion)(FILTERREGION origPos, REFIID riid, void ** ppunk);

private:
    DWORD       m_dwAttributes;
    ULONG       m_ulChunkId;
    LCID        m_lcid;

    enum {
      stAttrib=0, stLastWrite, stCreate, stAccess,
      stChange, stEnd, stFirst = 0xFF
    } m_dwState;
```

```
                // Write time gets emitted by protocol handler
    FILETIME    m_ftLastWrite;
    FILETIME    m_ftCreate;
    FILETIME    m_ftAccess;
    FILETIME    m_ftChange;
};
```

The *GetChunk* method will enumerate file properties one by one, including the file attributes and the file times. The method uses the member variable *m_dwState* to keep track of the last chunk in the enumeration and returns the error code *FILTER_E_END_OF_CHUNKS* when the last chunk has been processed, as shown here:

```
STDMETHODIMP CSampleFileFilter::GetChunk(STAT_CHUNK * pStat) {
    if (pStat == NULL) return E_POINTER;

    HRESULT hr = S_OK;
    PROPID propid = PID_STG_ATTRIBUTES;
    BOOL fHaveValue = FALSE;

    do {
        switch (m_dwState) {
        case stFirst:
            propid = PID_STG_ATTRIBUTES;
            m_dwState = stAttrib;
            fHaveValue = TRUE;
            break;

        case stAttrib:
            m_dwState = stLastWrite;
            if ((m_ftLastWrite.dwLowDateTime != 0) || (m_ftLastWrite.dwHighDateTime != 0)) {
                propid = PID_STG_WRITETIME;
                fHaveValue = TRUE;
            }
            break;

        case stLastWrite:
            m_dwState = stCreate;
            if ((m_ftCreate.dwLowDateTime != 0) || (m_ftCreate.dwHighDateTime != 0)) {
                propid = PID_STG_CREATETIME;
                fHaveValue = TRUE;
            }
            break;

        case stCreate:
            m_dwState = stAccess;
            if ((m_ftAccess.dwLowDateTime != 0) || (m_ftAccess.dwHighDateTime != 0)) {
                propid = PID_STG_ACCESSTIME;
                fHaveValue = TRUE;
            }
            break;

        case stAccess:
            m_dwState = stChange;
            if ((m_ftChange.dwLowDateTime != 0) || (m_ftChange.dwHighDateTime != 0)) {
```

```
                    propid = PID_STG_CHANGETIME;
                    fHaveValue = TRUE;
                }
                break;

            case stChange:
                hr = FILTER_E_END_OF_CHUNKS;
                m_dwState = stEnd;
                break;

            case stEnd:
                hr = FILTER_E_END_OF_CHUNKS;
                break;
        }
    } while(SUCCEEDED(hr) && !fHaveValue);

    if (SUCCEEDED(hr)) {
        pStat->idChunk = ++m_ulChunkId;
        pStat->breakType = CHUNK_EOS;
        pStat->flags = CHUNK_VALUE;
        pStat->locale = m_lcid;
        pStat->attribute.guidPropSet = PsGuidStorage ;
        pStat->attribute.psProperty.ulKind = PRSPEC_PROPID;
        pStat->attribute.psProperty.propid = propid;
        pStat->idChunkSource = 0;
        pStat->cwcStartSource = 0;
        pStat->cwcLenSource = 0;
    }

    return hr;
}
```

The Filter Daemon will follow each call to the *GetChunk* method with a call to the *GetValue* method to retrieve the property value of the chunk, as shown here. The *GetValue* method reads the member variable *m_dwState* set by the *GetChunk* method to determine the value it should return.

```
STDMETHODIMP CSampleFileFilter::GetValue( PROPVARIANT **ppPropValue) {
    if (NULL == ppPropValue) return E_POINTER;

    *ppPropValue = (PROPVARIANT *)CoTaskMemAlloc(sizeof(PROPVARIANT));
    if (*ppPropValue == NULL) return E_OUTOFMEMORY;

    PropVariantInit(*ppPropValue);
    PROPVARIANT pvLocal;
    pvLocal.vt = VT_FILETIME;

    switch (m_dwState) {
        case stAttrib:
            pvLocal.vt = VT_UI4;
            pvLocal.ulVal = m_dwAttributes;
            break;
```

```
        case stLastWrite:
            pvLocal.filetime = m_ftLastWrite;
            break;

        case stCreate:
            pvLocal.filetime = m_ftCreate;
            break;

        case stAccess:
            pvLocal.filetime = m_ftAccess;
            break;

        case stChange:
            pvLocal.filetime = m_ftChange;
            break;

        default:
            return E_UNEXPECTED;
    }

    return PropVariantCopy(*ppPropValue, &pvLocal);
}
```

The second implementation of the *IFilter* interface for enumerating files and folders is represented by the COM class named *CSampleDirFilter*, which inherits from the *CSampleFileFilter*
class. The class is defined as follows in the header file sampledirfltr.hxx:

```
class ATL_NO_VTABLE CSampleDirFilter : public CSampleFileFilter
{
public:
    CSampleDirFilter() : m_fFoundFile(FALSE), m_fHaveName(FALSE), m_ulChunkId(0),
                         m_dwDirLen(0), m_dwPathLen(0), m_dwFileNameLen(0),
                         m_fBaseFilter(TRUE), m_hFind(INVALID_HANDLE_VALUE)
    {}

    ~CSampleDirFilter() {
        if (m_hFind != INVALID_HANDLE_VALUE) FindClose(m_hFind);
    }

    HRESULT Init(LPCWSTR pwszPath, HANDLE hDir, DWORD dwAttributes,
                 const FILETIME &ftLastWrite,
                 const FILETIME &ftCreate,
                 const FILETIME &ftAccess,
                 const FILETIME &ftChange);

BEGIN_COM_MAP(CSampleDirFilter)
        COM_INTERFACE_ENTRY(IFilter)
END_COM_MAP()

public:    // IFilter
    STDMETHOD(Init)(ULONG grfFlags,
                    ULONG cAttributes,
                    FULLPROPSPEC const * aAttributes,
                    ULONG * pFlags);
```

```
    STDMETHOD(GetChunk)(STAT_CHUNK * pStat);
    STDMETHOD(GetText)(ULONG * pcwcBuffer, WCHAR *awcBuffer);
    STDMETHOD(GetValue)(PROPVARIANT ** ppPropValue);
    STDMETHOD(BindRegion)(FILTERREGION origPos, REFIID riid, void ** ppunk);

private:
    HRESULT FindNext(BOOL fFindFirst);

    HANDLE m_hFind;
    WIN32_FIND_DATA m_FindFileData;
    BOOL m_fFoundFile;
    BOOL m_fHaveName;
    ULONG m_ulChunkId;
    LCID m_lcid;
    HANDLE m_hNtFile;
    BOOL m_fBaseFilter;
    WCHAR m_wszPath[MAX_PATH];
    WCHAR m_wszDir[MAX_PATH];
    DWORD m_dwPathLen;
    DWORD m_dwDirLen;
    WCHAR m_wszFileName[MAX_PATH];
    DWORD m_dwFileNameLen;

    enum { FINDFIRST_SIZE = 0x1000 };
};
```

The *Init* method implemented in the sampledirfltr.cxx file is called from the *BindToFilter* method of the *CSampleAccessor* class to initialize the new *CSampleDirFilter* object, as shown here. The method basically attempts to find the first file or subdirectory from the level of the current directory.

```
HRESULT CSampleDirFilter::Init(LPCWSTR pwszPath, HANDLE hDir, DWORD dwAttributes,
                              const FILETIME &ftLastWrite,
                              const FILETIME &ftCreate,
                              const FILETIME &ftAccess,
                              const FILETIME &ftChange)
{
    // Call Init method of the base class
    HRESULT hr = CSampleFileFilter::Init(pwszPath, hDir, dwAttributes,
                                        ftLastWrite, ftCreate, ftAccess, ftChange);
    if (FAILED(hr)) return hr;

    m_lcid = GetSystemDefaultLCID();
    hr = StringCchCopy(m_wszPath, MAX_PATH, pwszPath);
    if (SUCCEEDED(hr)) {
        StringCchCopy(m_wszDir, MAX_PATH, L"sample:");
        hr = StringCchCopy(m_wszDir + 7, MAX_PATH - 7, pwszPath);
    }

    if (SUCCEEDED(hr)) {
        m_dwPathLen = lstrlen(pwszPath);
        m_dwDirLen = m_dwPathLen + 7;
```

```
        for(unsigned i = 0u; i < m_dwDirLen; i++) {
            if (m_wszDir[i] == L'\\')
                m_wszDir[i] = L'/';
        }

        if (m_dwPathLen + 2 >= MAX_PATH)
            return HRESULT_FROM_WIN32(ERROR_FILENAME_EXCED_RANGE);
    }

    if (m_wszPath[m_dwPathLen - 1] == L'\\') {
        m_wszPath[m_dwPathLen] = L'*';
        m_dwPathLen++;
        m_wszPath[m_dwPathLen] = 0;
    } else {
        m_wszPath[m_dwPathLen] = L'\\';
        m_wszPath[m_dwPathLen+1] = L'*';
        m_wszDir[m_dwDirLen] = L'/';
        m_dwPathLen += 2;
        m_dwDirLen++;
        m_wszPath[m_dwPathLen] = 0;
        m_wszDir[m_dwDirLen] = 0;
    }

    // Find the first file in the current directory, and save the handle.
    m_hFind = FindFirstFile(m_wszPath, &m_FindFileData);
    hr = (m_hFind == INVALID_HANDLE_VALUE) ?
            HResultFromFileStatus(GetLastError()) : S_OK;

    // Skip the current and the parent directory.
    while (SUCCEEDED(hr) && (lstrcmp(m_FindFileData.cFileName, L".") == 0 ||
                            lstrcmp(m_FindFileData.cFileName, L"..") == 0))
    {
        if (FindNextFile(m_hFind, &m_FindFileData)) {
            m_fFoundFile = TRUE;
        } else {
            m_fFoundFile = FALSE;
            hr = HResultFromFileStatus(GetLastError());
        }
    }

    if (SUCCEEDED(hr)) {
        m_fFoundFile = TRUE;
    }

    if (hr == HRESULT_FROM_WIN32(ERROR_NO_MORE_FILES)) {
        m_fFoundFile = FALSE;
        hr = S_OK;
    }

    return hr;
}
```

The Filter Daemon then starts calling the *GetChunk* method, which continues the enumeration started in the *Init* method, as shown here:

```
STDMETHODIMP CSampleDirFilter::GetChunk(STAT_CHUNK *pStat) {
    if (pStat == NULL) return E_POINTER;
    HRESULT hr = S_OK;

    // Enumerate file properties first by calling the GetChunk
    // method of the base filter first.
    if (m_fBaseFilter) {
        hr = CSampleFileFilter::GetChunk(pStat);
        if (hr == FILTER_E_END_OF_CHUNKS) {
            m_fBaseFilter = FALSE;
            hr = S_OK;
        } else {
            return hr;
        }
    }

    // Did we find a file in the Init method or during the last run
    // of the GetChunk method here?
    if (m_fFoundFile) {
        pStat->idChunk = ++m_ulChunkId;
        pStat->breakType = CHUNK_EOS;
        pStat->flags = CHUNK_TEXT;
        pStat->locale = m_lcid;;
        pStat->attribute.guidPropSet = PsGuidGatherer;
        pStat->attribute.psProperty.ulKind = PRSPEC_PROPID;
        pStat->attribute.psProperty.propid = PID_GTHR_DIRLINK;
        pStat->idChunkSource = 0;
        pStat->cwcStartSource = 0;
        pStat->cwcLenSource = 0;

        hr = StringCchCopy(m_wszFileName, MAX_PATH, m_FindFileData.cFileName);
        if (SUCCEEDED(hr)) m_dwFileNameLen = lstrlen(m_wszFileName);

        if (m_FindFileData.dwFileAttributes & FILE_ATTRIBUTE_DIRECTORY) {
            m_wszFileName[m_dwFileNameLen] = L'/';
            m_dwFileNameLen++;
        }

        m_fHaveName = TRUE;
        hr = S_OK;
    } else {
        m_fHaveName = FALSE;
        hr = FILTER_E_END_OF_CHUNKS;
    }

    if (SUCCEEDED(hr)) {
        // Continue the enumeration of files.
        if (FindNextFile(m_hFind, &m_FindFileData)) {
            m_fFoundFile = TRUE;
```

```
        } else {
            m_fFoundFile = FALSE;
            DWORD dwError = GetLastError();
            if (dwError == ERROR_NO_MORE_FILES) {
                hr = S_OK;
            } else {
                hr = HResultFromFileStatus(dwError);
            }
        }
    }
}

return hr;
}
```

The following piece of code shows how the *GetValue* method of the *CSampleDirFilter* class simply calls the *GetValue* method of the base class *CSampleFileFilter*:

```
STDMETHODIMP CSampleDirFilter::GetValue(PROPVARIANT **ppPropValue) {
    if (m_fBaseFilter) {
        return CSampleFileFilter::GetValue(ppPropValue);
    }
    return FILTER_E_NO_VALUES;
}
```

The primary purpose of the *GetText* method implementation in the *CSampleDirFilter* class is to return all the text contained in the full path of the current item in the enumeration process, as shown in the following code. This is very important in order to enable free-text searching for keywords occurring in the URL.

```
STDMETHODIMP CSampleDirFilter::GetText(ULONG *pcwcBuffer, WCHAR *awcBuffer) {
    if (pcwcBuffer == NULL || awcBuffer == NULL) return E_POINTER;

    HRESULT hr = S_OK;

    if (m_fBaseFilter) {
        hr = CSampleFileFilter::GetText(pcwcBuffer, awcBuffer);
        return hr;
    }

    hr = m_fHaveName ? S_OK : FILTER_E_NO_TEXT;
    DWORD dwRequiredLength = m_dwFileNameLen + m_dwDirLen;

    if (SUCCEEDED(hr)) {
        if (*pcwcBuffer < dwRequiredLength) {
            *pcwcBuffer = dwRequiredLength;
            hr = HRESULT_FROM_WIN32(ERROR_INSUFFICIENT_BUFFER);
        }
    }

    m_wszDir[m_dwDirLen] = 0;

    if (SUCCEEDED(hr)) {
        hr = StringCchCopy(m_wszDir + m_dwDirLen, MAX_PATH - m_dwDirLen, m_wszFileName);
```

```
    if (SUCCEEDED(hr)) {
        CopyMemory(awcBuffer, m_wszDir,
                   (m_dwDirLen + m_dwFileNameLen + 1) * sizeof(WCHAR));
        *pcwcBuffer = m_dwDirLen + m_dwFileNameLen;
    }

    m_fHaveName = FALSE;
}

return hr;
}
```

The last method of the *IFilter* interface, *BindRegion*, is not used in this context.

Installing a Protocol Handler on Index Servers

Protocol handlers must be installed on all servers with the index server role in the farm. The steps required to install a new protocol handler include copying the DLL file to the server and registering it with the Filter Daemon through the Windows registry. All protocol handlers should include the logic to register themselves via the Windows Regsvr32.exe tool. The sample protocol handler presented earlier includes this logic and can be registered from a Windows command-line prompt, as follows:

```
regsvr32 SampleProtocolHandler.dll
```

Unregistering the protocol handler again is just as simple, as shown here:

```
regsvr32 /u SampleProtocolHandler.dll
```

Manual registration of the protocol handler is also possible by following these steps:

1. Log in as a local administrator on the index server.

2. Open the Windows Registry Editor by typing **regedit** in the Run menu available from the Windows Start menu.

3. Locate the CLSID of the protocol handler. This would be the GUID of the COM object—for example, {195e97b5-8401-460c-804e-06a0416d032b}, which is the GUID of the sample protocol handler.

4. Open Notepad, and type or copy the following text into it. (Comment lines starting with a semicolon can be omitted.)

```
Windows Registry Editor Version 5.00

; Create root key for COM object.
[HKEY_CLASSES_ROOT\CLSID\{195e97b5-8401-460c-804e-06a0416d032b}]
@="SampleProtocolHandler Class "
```

```
; Specify full path to the protocol handler DLL, and set the
; COM threading model to Both.
[HKEY_CLASSES_ROOT\CLSID\{195e97b5-8401-460c-804e-06a0416d032b }\InprocServer32]
@="C:\\PROGRA~1\\Microsoft Office Servers\\12.0\\Bin\\SampleProtocolHandler.dll"
"ThreadingModel"="Both"

; Create a program identifier for the COM object.
[HKEY_CLASSES_ROOT\CLSID\{195e97b5-8401-460c-804e-06a0416d032b }\ProgID]
@="SampleProtocolHandler.SampleProtocolHandler.1"

; Create a version-independent program identifier for the COM object.
[HKEY_CLASSES_ROOT\CLSID\{195e97b5-8401-460c-804e-06a0416d032b }\
VersionIndependentProgID]
@="SampleProtocolHandler.SampleProtocolHandler"

; Register the protocol handler with the index engine of
; Microsoft Office SharePoint Server 2007, and associate it
; with the URL scheme Sample://.
[HKEY_LOCAL_MACHINE\SOFTWARE\Microsoft\Office Server\12.0\Search\Setup\
ProtocolHandlers]
"Sample"="SampleProtocolHandler.SampleProtocolHandler.1"
```

The value of the *ThreadingModel* entry can also be set to *Apartment* instead of *Both* if the protocol handler is not multithread safe, but this will significantly slow indexing with this particular protocol handler.

> **Note** Installing and registering a protocol handler on a SharePoint Portal Server 2003 index server are with one exception identical to the procedure described here. The exception is the key HKEY_LOCAL_MACHINE\SOFTWARE\Microsoft\Office Server\12.0\ Search\Setup\ProtocolHandlers, which must simply be replaced with the key HKEY_LOCAL_ MACHINE\SOFTWARE\Microsoft\SPSSearch\ProtocolHandlers.

5. Save the file in Notepad with the file name install.reg or any other file name with the .reg file extension.

6. In Windows File Explorer, double-click the install.reg file created in step 5. This will merge the keys and values in the file with the Windows registry.

7. If the Open File—Security Warning dialog box appears, click Run.

These steps register the protocol handler only for use with future SSPs. It must also be registered explicitly with all existing SSPs that intend to use it. The Windows registry settings for a single SSP are stored under the key HKEY_LOCAL_MACHINE\SOFTWARE\Microsoft\Office Server\12.0\Search\Applications\<SSP GUID>. The SSP GUID is easily identified in the registry if your farm has only one SSP. Finding the GUID of a specific SSP among many is explained in the section "Detecting the Search Application Name for an SSP" in Chapter 5. Registering the sample protocol handler with an SSP can be accomplished by adding the following lines to the install.reg file described in step 4 of the preceding manual registration procedure:

```
Windows Registry Editor Version 5.00
[HKEY_LOCAL_MACHINE\SOFTWARE\Microsoft\Office Server\12.0\Search\Applications\{SSP GUID}\
Gather\Portal_Content\Protocols\Sample\0]
"Included"=dword:00000001
"ExtExclusionsUsed"=dword:00000001
"PrefixName"=""
"ProgIdHandler"="SampleProtocolHandler.SampleProtocolHandler.1"
```

These keys and values are automatically created for new SSPs from the template settings registered under the key HKEY_LOCAL_MACHINE\SOFTWARE\Microsoft\Office Server\12.0\ Search\Setup\ProtocolHandlers.

> **Note** Protocol handlers, like *IFilters*, also cannot be deployed to index servers via the new solution deployment framework in Windows SharePoint Services 3.0. Again, the framework is not designed to handle the registration of protocol handlers in the Windows registry.

Creating a Custom Content Source

After you have developed and installed a custom protocol handler, the next step is to configure a custom content source for an SSP. But this can be done only programmatically, as the administration user interface of the SSP search settings does not support it. Create a small tool from the C# code snippet shown here to add a custom content source named *SampleCustomContentSource*. In this example, the content source is added to the SSP associated with the site collection at *http://moss.litwareinc.com* and is given the start address *sample://moss/fileshare*.

```
// Configuration parameters
string contentSourceName = "SampleCustomContentSource";
string siteUrl = "http://moss.litwareinc.com";
Uri startAddress = new Uri("sample://moss/fileshare");
string scheme = startAddress.Scheme;

using (SPSite site = new SPSite(siteUrl))
{
    // Find the SSP associated with the portal.
    SearchContext searchapp = SearchContext.GetContext(site);

    Content content = new Content(searchapp);

    // Create a new custom content source.
    CustomContentSource cs =
        (CustomContentSource)content.ContentSources.Create(typeof(CustomContentSource),
                                                            contentSourceName);
```

```
// Configure it.
cs.FollowDirectories = true;
cs.StartAddresses.Add(startAddress);

// Save it to the database.
cs.Update();

// Check if the protocol handler has been registered with the SSP.
RegistryKey csprotocol = Registry.LocalMachine.OpenSubKey(
    "SOFTWARE\\Microsoft\\Office Server\\12.0\\Search\\Applications\\" +
    searchapp.Name +
    "\\Gather\\Portal_Content\\Protocols", true);

// Abort if it has.
if (csprotocol.OpenSubKey (scheme) != null) return;

// Otherwise, register the sample protocol handler with the specified SSP.
RegistryKey setuproto = Registry.LocalMachine.OpenSubKey(
    "SOFTWARE\\Microsoft\\Office Server\\12.0\\Search\\Setup\\ProtocolHandlers");
string handler = setuproto.GetValue(scheme).ToString();

using (RegistryKey cskey = csprotocol.CreateSubKey(scheme),
                           cssubkey = cskey.CreateSubKey("0"))
{
    cssubkey.SetValue ("ExtExclusionsUsed", 1);
    cssubkey.SetValue ("Included", 1);
    cssubkey.SetValue ("PrefixName", "");
    cssubkey.SetValue ("ProgIdHandler", handler);
}
}
```

Notice that this code updates the Windows registry after the *cs.update* statement to ensure that the sample protocol handler is properly registered with the SSP associated with the specified site. Running the code will add the content source and make it available to SSP administrators, as shown in Figure 9-1.

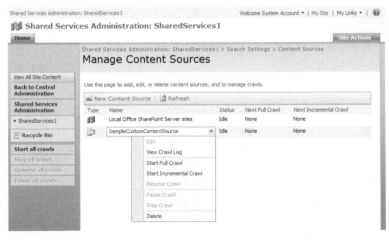

FIGURE 9-1 Custom content source

If you are an SSP administrator, you can use the SharePoint context menu on the content source to initiate full crawls as well as incremental crawls. But as mentioned earlier, you cannot make any changes to the content source from here, as evidenced by the fact that the Edit item on the menu is disabled. Consequently, configuring a crawl schedule for the new content source must also be done programmatically. See the section "Configuring the Crawling of a Content Source" in Chapter 8 for a detailed description of programmatically adding a crawl schedule to a content source.

Testing the Sample Protocol Handler

We are now ready to start a full crawl of the file share specified for the custom content source in the preceding section. Navigate to the search settings at the level of the SSP, initiate a full crawl from the context menu shown in Figure 9-1, and then wait until the crawl completes. Then navigate to a Search Center on a site associated with the SSP, and try searching for a keyword that should yield results from the file share. Figure 9-2 shows an example of a search returning four documents from a file share crawled with the sample protocol handler.

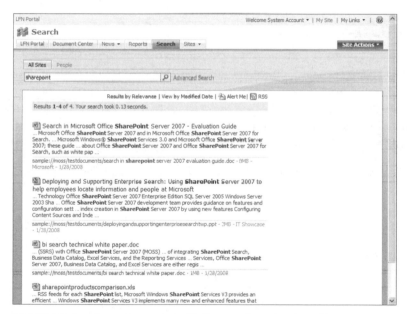

FIGURE 9-2 Search results crawled with the sample protocol handler

If you do not find the expected results, most likely an error occurred in the protocol handler during the crawl. Check the crawl log to determine whether this was the case.

Clicking one of the search results shown in Figure 9-2 will yield an error in the Web browser because the sample URL scheme is not associated with any application. There are two ways to get around this problem. First, the URLs could be mapped to another URL scheme—for example, the file scheme—using server name mappings. See the section "Server Name

Mappings" in Chapter 5 for more information about creating server name mappings. Second, an application could be registered in the Windows registry for the sample scheme. The application must be installed and registered on all client machines where the user would expect it to work. The following registration file demonstrates how a Sample.exe application can be associated with the *Sample* URL scheme in the Windows registry:

```
Windows Registry Editor Version 5.00
[HKEY_CLASSES_ROOT\Sample]
@="URL:Sample Protocol"
"URL Protocol"=""

[HKEY_CLASSES_ROOT\Sample\DefaultIcon]
@="Sample.exe"

[HKEY_CLASSES_ROOT\Sample\shell]
@="open"

[HKEY_CLASSES_ROOT\Sample\shell\open]
[HKEY_CLASSES_ROOT\Sample\shell\open\command]
@="\"C:\\Program Files\\Sample Application\\Sample.exe\" \"%1\""
```

Debugging Tips

Developing a custom protocol handler is not easy, and problems can easily surface when you are about to test it. The crawl log will tell you only that an error occurred and the error code that was returned from the protocol handler. Finding the exact spot in the code where the bug is can be difficult. To locate the bug, you can try to log detailed trace information, or you can use the Visual Studio debugger to debug the code. It is recommended that you adopt the following guidelines when debugging a protocol handler:

- Set the *DebugFilters* registry key to *1* by running the following command from a Windows command-line prompt:

  ```
  Reg ADD "HKLM\SOFTWARE\Microsoft\Office Server\12.0\Search\Global\Gathering Manager"
  /v DebugFilters /t REG_WORD /d 1 /f
  ```

  Change the *1* to *0* to disable debug mode again.

- Set a breakpoint at the *CreateAccessor* method.

- Create a content source with the URL of a single document, and crawl it.

Setting the *DebugFilters* key to the value *1* directs the Filter Daemon to disable timeouts on method calls to the protocol handler.

Custom Security Trimmers

As you've seen in various chapters in this book, by default, users will not see the search results originating from the SharePoint sites or shared folders for which they do not have the appropriate permissions. The index engine, while crawling, collects and stores the information from the ACL defined for the resource or container where the resource is stored. When users are searching, this information is used by the Search service, thus filtering the search results. But this is not the case for all of the types of content sources that administrators can create. For example, there is no security trimming for the results coming out of normal, non-SharePoint Web sites or for the business data indexed. If no additional custom security trimming is applied after the execution of the search query, the users might get to see information that is not appropriate for them or even information that they should not be allowed to see. This is of course quite important when the search results include business data that originates from LOB systems, which often store sensitive enterprise data.

You might also have a business requirement to trim the results based on more than security-related information. Imagine, for example, a salesperson who is responsible for a specific sales region. When she searches within the orders that are stored in an SAP system, say, the search results could be filtered based on information that is stored within the user profile of the salesperson. Handling this type of dynamic criterion is often very hard to achieve by simply using custom search scopes, as described in the section "Search Scopes" in Chapter 5. Custom assemblies that are deployed and filter the results before the users see them in the user interface might be a better option to accomplish this task.

> **More Information** See the article "Custom Security Trimming for Enterprise Search Results Overview" on the Microsoft Developer Network (MSDN) at *http://msdn2.microsoft.com/en-us/ library/aa981236.aspx*.

The *ISecurityTrimmer* Interface

Building and configuring custom security trimmers is a developer-oriented task, not an option that is exposed on the administration pages for the index and search infrastructure in the site of the SSP. The procedure involves building a .NET Framework class library project containing a class that implements the *ISecurityTrimmer* interface. The project has at least a reference to the *Microsoft.Office.Server.Search.dll*.

The *ISecurityTrimmer* interface is defined in the *Microsoft.Office.Server.Search.Query* namespace. The skeleton of such a class is as follows:

```
using System;
using System.Collections.Generic;
using System.Text;
using Microsoft.Office.Server.Search.Query;

namespace InsideSearch
{
    public class ISCustomSecurityTrimmer: ISecurityTrimmer
    {
        #region ISecurityTrimmer Members
        public System.Collections.BitArray CheckAccess
            (IList<string> documentCrawlUrls,
             IDictionary<string, object> sessionProperties)
        {
            throw new Exception("The method or operation is not implemented.");
        }
        public void Initialize
          (System.Collections.Specialized.NameValueCollection staticProperties,
           Microsoft.Office.Server.Search.Administration.SearchContext searchContext)
        {
            throw new Exception("The method or operation is not implemented.");
        }
        #endregion
    }
}
```

Two methods have to be implemented: the *Initialize* method and the *CheckAccess* method.

The *Initialize* Method

This method is called at the time that the .NET Framework assembly is loaded into the worker process. This means that the code written here is executed only once. The method is called again when the worker process is recycled.

Because the method is called only once, it is not the place to include the business logic that implements your custom trimming logic. It is typically the place where you process the values for some of the configuration properties that are provided at the time you register the custom security trimmer using the *STSADM* command-line utility. The details of how to register are explained in the section "Registering the Custom Security Trimmer" later in this chapter.

There are two parameters of importance here:

- **staticProperties** This is an object of type *System.Collections.Specialized. NameValueCollection*, containing the configuration properties specified for the security trimmer at registration time.

- **searchContext** This is an object of type *SearchContext*, representing the Search service of the SSP.

Assume, for example, that you want to limit the number of search results that are processed at run time within the *CheckAccess* method. To start, you define a small variable within your class, and in the *Initialize* method, you retrieve the value that is set at registration time from the *NameValueCollection* and store the value in the variable. The following code is an example of this:

```
private int trimmerLimit = 100;

public void Initialize
    (System.Collections.Specialized.NameValueCollection staticProperties,
     Microsoft.Office.Server.Search.Administration.SearchContext searchContext)
{
    if (staticProperties["TrimmerLimit"] != null)
        trimmerLimit = Convert.ToInt32(staticProperties["TrimmerLimit"]);
}
```

The properties you configure here can then be used in the *CheckAccess* method that is called for each of the search results. For example, for performance reasons, you might want to limit the number of crawled URLs to be processed by your custom security trimming code. When users perform a search query, thousands of search results can be returned. If you are going to apply custom business logic for each of these search results before they are displayed to the user, you'll risk slowing the whole process. You might want to let the administrator set a limit on the number of URLs that need to be checked and then use that information before you execute the business logic. If there are too many URLs to check, you might want to notify the user that the search query needs to be refined.

The *CheckAccess* Method

This method is where all of your business logic that will trim the search results ends up. It is called each time a query is performed. All of the crawled URLs are passed as an instance of a *System.Collections.Generic.IList*. It is possible that the method is called multiple times per search session, depending on the number of search results returned. This is why you might want to limit the number of results, as mentioned earlier. The second parameter that is passed to the method contains information that can be used to track information across multiple *CheckAccess* method calls for the same search query.

A typical flow within the method is to first retrieve information about the currently logged on user and any additional information as needed, such as the associated user profile values. All of this can be used while the search results are processed; you have to direct Office SharePoint Server to display the result, yes or no, on the results page. For that reason, you'll notice a return value of type *System.Collections.BitArray* that contains a *true* or *false* value for every search result. Your job is to set this flag in the loop based on the outcome of your business logic.

The format of the URL of an item in the *documentCrawlUrls* array depends on the type of the search result and the protocol handler used to access it. The following code is the representation of a list item that comes from a list in a SharePoint site. As you'll notice, the URL contains all of the necessary pieces to retrieve more information about the item, but it will require a bit of parsing.

```
sts3://moss/siteurl=/siteid={86051521-13de-4dac-80d1-231406b51b57}
/weburl=/webid={e67908fc-024b-4689-b854-4837d0d32abb}
/listid={30dc794a-c5b6-4c86-97f6-2ed65133149d}/viewid={efc86211-
96e2-4443-9dfc-5d8e42daf285}
```

A page in a crawled normal Web site is represented just with its URL. That is far easier to process than the preceding example. In all cases, you'll have to do something in the *CheckAccess* method with the results. Assume, for example, the scenario within your company where an internal Web site is part of the content index. As defined earlier, no security information is collected for non-SharePoint Web sites during the crawling. It could be that there are pages in one of the subsites that should be accessible only if you work for the IT department. Employees working for other departments do not have to see search results for those pages.

The code in the *CheckAccess* method can be the following:

```
public System.Collections.BitArray CheckAccess
          (IList<string> documentCrawlUrls,
           IDictionary<string, object> sessionProperties)
{
    BitArray retArray = new BitArray(documentCrawlUrls.Count);
    string user = WindowsIdentity.GetCurrent().Name.ToLower();
    for (int i = 0; i < documentCrawlUrls.Count; i++)
    {
        retArray[i] = CheckSecurityRule(documentCrawlUrls[i], user);
    }
    return retArray;
}
```

The return value of type *BitArray* is populated with a *true* or *false* value, depending on the return value of the *CheckSecurityRule* procedure. This is an internal custom procedure in your class that implements the check that you want to apply on the crawled URL for the currently logged on user. Remember that you want to make the code in that procedure as fast as possible. Caching of the data that is underlying your decision is a very good idea. Talking every time to a Web service or performing a database call is often not a good idea.

To incorporate the limitation on the number of results that need to be trimmed as it was set in the *Initialize* method, you'll have to add a small check while processing the URLs of the crawled items. If the number of items exceeds the value indicated by the administrator during the registration of the security trimmer, you can throw an exception. The exception you throw is of type *PluggableAccessCheckException*, as shown here:

```
if (i > trimmerLimit)
    throw (new PluggableAccessCheckException
        ("Too many results, please refine your search query..."));
```

Raising this type of exception will ensure that the user is notified in a friendly way on the search results page, as shown in Figure 9-3.

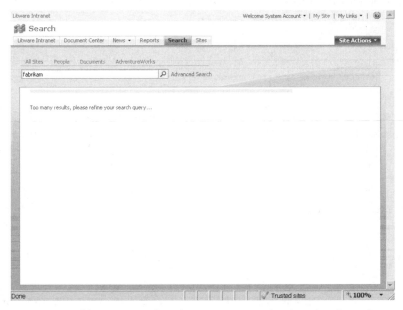

FIGURE 9-3 Raising an error when there are too many results to be trimmed

All of the code in your .NET Framework assembly must be signed and compiled because these types of assemblies need to be installed in the Global Assembly Cache (GAC).

Registering the Custom Security Trimmer

The custom security trimmer must be registered before SharePoint takes it into consideration. Before you can actually do that, you must have a crawl rule defined that covers one or more of the content sources that are indexed and for which you want to have the security trimming applied. Once that is done, you can make the following call to the *STSADM* command-line utility that will register the trimmer:

```
Stsadm.exe -o registersecuritytrimmer -ssp SharedServices1 -id 1 -typeName
"InsideSearch.ISCustomSecurityTrimmer, InsideSearch.CustomSecurityTrimmerSample,
Version=1.0.0.0, Culture=neutral, PublicKeyToken=0b90369978b3b6d8" -rulepath
http://smb.litwareinc.com/*
```

The option *registersecuritytrimmer* does the trick if you give it the name of the SSP as the value for the *ssp* parameter. Custom security trimmers are internally registered with a unique ID. Next, the value for the *typeName* parameter is a comma-delimited string, with the first part being the full name of the class (that is, the namespace followed by the name of the class) and the second part being the full strong name of the assembly. The last parameter, *rulepath*, is the one you assign the crawl rule to.

If you need to pass the value for a configuration property, you simply append it to the line as the value for the *configprops* parameter, as shown here. Notice the special format for the value of the parameter. The name-value pairs that specify the configuration properties must be in the format *Name1~Value1~Name2~Value2~....*

```
stsadm -o registersecuritytrimmer -ssp SharedServices1 -id 1 -typeName
"InsideSearch.ISCustomSecurityTrimmer, InsideSearch.CustomSecurityTrimmerSample,
Version=1.0.0.0, Culture=neutral, PublicKeyToken=0b90369978b3b6d8" -rulepath
http://smb.litwareinc.com/* -configprops trimmerLimit~50
```

Note that you can of course also unregister your custom security trimmer using *STSADM*. Here is the line to do that:

```
Stsadm.exe -o unregistersecuritytrimmer -ssp SharedServices1 -id 1
```

The *unregistersecuritytrimmer* option requires only the name of the SSP and the *id* value for the registered security trimmer.

Testing the Security Trimmer

The custom security trimmer will be applied only if you delete the content source you want to target and then re-create the content source and follow up with a full crawl on it. If there are problems with the trimmer, you can always attach your Visual Studio to the worker process, identified as *w3wp.exe*, and debug your code.

Faceted Search

The last topic we'll cover in this chapter is the support for Faceted Search that you can add to the search infrastructure delivered with Office SharePoint Server 2007 or Search Server 2008 by downloading and installing an open-source solution that is available from CodePlex. The solution has been developed by a Microsoft field consultant named Leonid Lyublinski, and at the time of this writing, version 2.0 is available for download from *http://www.codeplex.com/ facetedsearch*.

What Is Faceted Search?

As you've seen throughout this book, metadata is important for delivering a rich end-user search experience. During the crawling of SharePoint content and content that is accessible through the BDC, many custom metadata fields are collected and stored in the Search database so that administrators can map them to managed properties that are exposed in various ways to the users when they start executing their search queries. Chapter 3, "Customizing the Search User Interface," demonstrated how an administrator and a developer can, for example, tweak the Search Core Results Web Part so that the extra metadata is displayed within the details of a search result item. Many times, however, this preconfigured display is not flexible enough for users, who might attribute different meanings to the metadata, depending on the context, the type of search, and the expectations they have regarding the search results.

Consider, for example, the metadata collected for a catalog of products that is indexed. The metadata can include values for the category of the product, the price, the details concerning the physical shape of the product such as the weight and the size, the list of customers that have bought the product, and so forth. A technical engineer typically wants to see a different facet than a salesperson might be interested in. Instead of creating a common search configuration for all users, it is better to let the users choose how they want to see the search results and not confine them to a preconfigured experience. This is exactly what the Faceted Search add-on can provide for them.

Office SharePoint Server 2007 Faceted Search

The CodePlex solution is basically a collection of Web Parts that can be configured to expose the multiple facets of the metadata in the search results so that the user can see all of the refinement options at any time. The user is given the option to decide how to display the data. The user can decide to skip the entry of a search query and to use a more structured approach of drilling down to the information that is required. In other words, instead of taking a search-based approach, users can take a metadata-browsing approach to finding the results they seek.

Here is a list of the key features that are supported with Office SharePoint Server 2007 Faceted Search:

- Aspects of the current result set can be displayed in multiple categorization schemes.
- The user sees only categories that have a result set. Links leading to dead ends or empty result sets are not shown.
- For users, it can be important to immediately have a clue about the size of the result set to expect if they choose a specific facet. Displaying a count of the contents for each category is helpful for this.
- Users are able to generate groupings on the fly, such as size, price, or date.
- Users are able to drill down by facet. The technical engineer can immediately drill down in the more engineering-related facets, while the salesperson probably is going to have a closer look at another branch of the taxonomy.

- Plenty of configuration options are available, such as the addition of custom facets within categories so that more structure can be added to the taxonomy that is exposed.

Installing Faceted Search

The installation of the support for Faceted Search in your Office SharePoint Server 2007 farm is very straightforward. After you have downloaded the package and extracted it, you'll be able to deploy it as a SharePoint solution in the server farm. The solution is installed using the SharePoint Solution Installer, another community tool that is available from CodePlex. Figure 9-4 displays the first page of the Faceted Search Setup Wizard that guides you through the steps of the deployment.

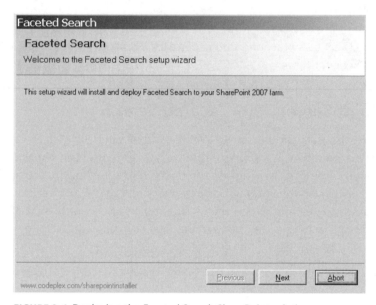

FIGURE 9-4 Deploying the Faceted Search SharePoint solution

In the next step, various checks are performed to determine whether your environment is ready for the solution deployment. After that, you'll see the end-user license agreement, and you'll have to indicate the list of IIS Web applications you want to target with the solution. After you have answered all of the questions, the wizard will start the installation process that adds the solution to the SharePoint configuration database of the server farm and deploy it to the selected IIS Web applications on all Web front-end servers in the farm.

If you open SharePoint 3.0 Central Administration and navigate to the Solution Properties page, available from the Operations tab, you'll see the Faceted Search SharePoint solution listed as one of the deployed solutions. Figure 9-5 shows this page.

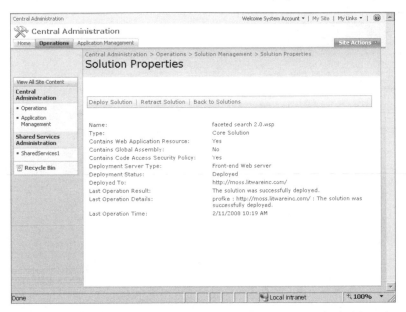

FIGURE 9-5 The Solution Properties page in SharePoint 3.0 Central Administration, indicating the successful deployment of the Faceted Search 2.0 solution in the server farm

The collection of Web Parts that make up the Faceted Search solution are made available in the targeted IIS Web applications via a Feature that you have to activate for the site collection where you want to use them. Notice that there is internally an activation dependency defined with the Office SharePoint Server 2007 Search Web Parts Feature. This means that you first have to make sure that this Feature is activated in your site collection. This is not a problem when you work in a collaboration portal, since the Office SharePoint Server 2007 Search Web Parts Feature is activated by default within a collaboration portal. To activate the Office SharePoint Server Faceted Search Web Parts Feature, you open the Site Settings page via the Site Actions menu and then navigate to the Site Collection Features page by clicking the corresponding link under the Site Collection Administration group. On the Site Collection Features page, shown in Figure 9-6, you'll see the Office SharePoint Server Faceted Search Web Parts Feature listed, and you can click the Activate button to make the new Web Parts available.

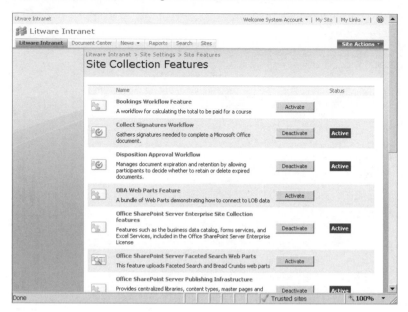

FIGURE 9-6 The Office SharePoint Server Faceted Search Web Parts available as part of the site collection Features

Now you are ready to configure the Search Center with the newly available Web Parts.

Adding Faceted Search to the Search Center

The Office SharePoint Server 2007 Faceted Search Web Parts are typically added to the search results page that is part of the Search Center in the collaboration portal. In the Search Center, enter a query so that you end up on the search results page. Edit the page by clicking Site Actions on the Edit Page menu. A lot of the out-of-the-box Office SharePoint Server 2007 Search Web Parts are already available on the page. A good zone in which to add the Faceted Search Web Parts is the right zone, which already includes the Best Bets Web Part. Click the Add A Web Part button to open the Add Web Parts dialog box. As shown in Figure 9-7, two new Web Parts are now included in the list of suggested Web Parts. Let's start with the addition of the most important one, the Search Facets Web Part.

Most likely, the Web Part will immediately show a number of facets that it has discovered from the metadata that is currently displayed or available in the context of the search query you have executed. Figure 9-8 shows an example of this after the search results page has been published again and the modifications saved.

By default, the Search Facets Web Part picks up the names of the authors, the content sources where the search results originate from, and the various content types that underlie the items in the search results. Of course, you have the option to configure all of this, as you'll learn in the next section.

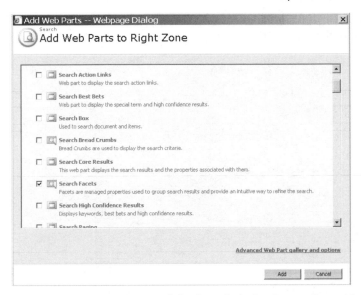

FIGURE 9-7 The Add Web Parts dialog box, displaying the new Faceted Search Web Parts

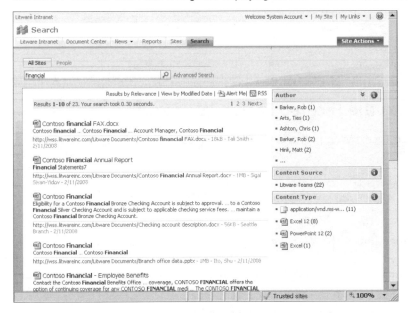

FIGURE 9-8 The Search Facets Web Part on the search results page

The Search Facets Web Part is not the only new Web Part that you can add to the search results page. The Search Bread Crumbs Web Part, when added to the page in the bottom zone, for example, will display information about the search criteria and the path that has been followed as you drill down in the search results. Figure 9-9 shows the Search Bread Crumbs Web Part in action after a drill-down in the results for all of the documents authored by Rob Barker. The Web Part displays the selected facet and allows for the removal of it. You can reset all the facets if the drill-down has more than one, and you can also reset the search, resulting in a clearance of the search query and the search results.

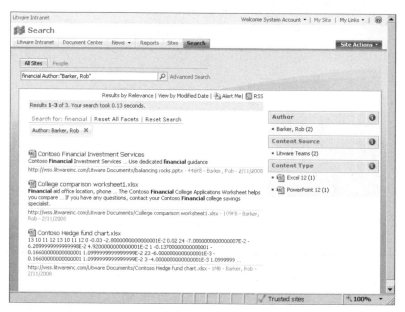

FIGURE 9-9 The Search Bread Crumbs Web Part on the search results page

Configuring the Faceted Search Web Parts

Both the Search Facets Web Part and the Search Bread Crumbs Web Part can be configured in a number of ways.

Configuring the Search Bread Crumbs Web Part

You might first want to configure the display of friendly names in the Search Bread Crumbs Web Part. As mentioned, this Web Part displays the path you followed when drilling down in the facets. Many times, the name displayed in the Web Part will be an internal name that is not really very meaningful to the user. Consider, for example, the page shown in Figure 9-10. This is the result of clicking the *Excel 12* content type facet. As you'll notice, the Search Bread Crumbs Web Part shows the string *application/vnd.ms-excel.12* instead of the name of the facet as it is displayed in the Search Facets Web Part.

To improve the user experience here, you can connect the Search Bread Crumbs Web Part with the Search Facets Web Part. Connecting Web Parts is one of the many tasks you can accomplish in the Windows SharePoint Services 3.0 Web Part infrastructure. To start the connection, switch the search results page back into edit mode. Next, on the Edit menu of the Search Bread Crumbs Web Part, select the Connections option to direct the Web Part to get the facet settings from the Search Facets Web Part, as shown in Figure 9-11.

FIGURE 9-10 The Search Bread Crumbs Web Part, displaying the internal value of the selected content type facet

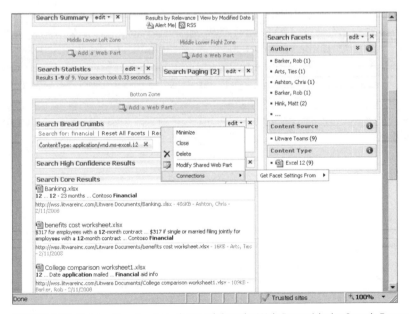

FIGURE 9-11 Connecting the Search Bread Crumbs Web Part with the Search Facets Web Part

Once the connection is established between the two Web Parts, the Search Bread Crumbs Web Part immediately picks up the display name of the selected facet. Figure 9-12 shows the result for the *Excel 12* content type.

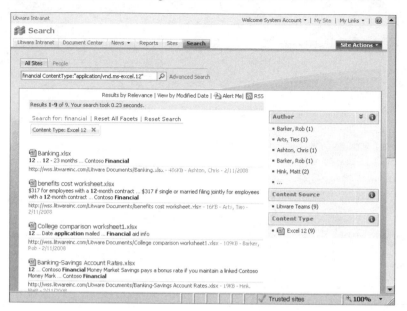

FIGURE 9-12 The Search Bread Crumbs Web Part, displaying the proper name of the selected facet after being connected to the Search Facets Web Part

This is of course not the only configuration that you can set for this Web Part. A number of properties are exposed in the tool pane that allow you to customize the display of the content of the Search Bread Crumbs Web Part. Several cascading style sheets (CSS) classes are used by default, but you have the option to deploy your own style sheet and refer to the classes you make available within it. Figure 9-13 displays the properties for the Search Bread Crumbs Web Part that you can connect to your own CSS class. Please refer to the document available from the CodePlex site describing the different styles if you decide to change the look and feel of this Web Part.

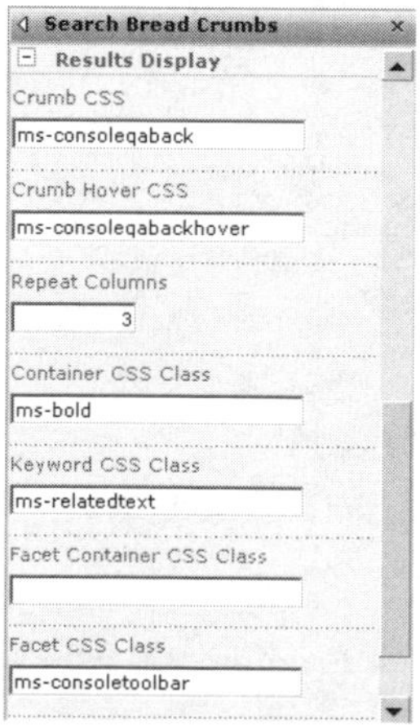

FIGURE 9-13 Properties exposed for the Search Bread Crumbs Web Part

Configuring the Search Facets Web Part

The Search Facets Web Part also exposes a collection of properties for modifying the display style; again, please refer to the same style guide, downloadable from the CodePlex site, for more information.

Figure 9-14 shows the exposed properties, including a number of properties that are not directly related to the styling. One of these is the *SelectColumns* property, which is displayed here as the Select Columns For Facets option.

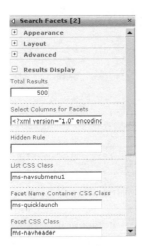

FIGURE 9-14 Properties exposed by the Search Facets Web Part

The property contains an XML string defining the facets to be displayed and optional mappings for a customized display of a possible match, as shown here:

```xml
<?xml version="1.0" encoding="utf-8" ?>
<root xmlns:xsi="http://www.w3.org/2001/XMLSchema-instance">
  <Columns OrderBy="Name" >
    <Column Name="Author" OrderBy="Name" TotalResults="5" />
    <Column Name="ContentType" OrderBy="Hits" TotalResults="5"
     DisplayName="Content Type" DefaultImage="STS_ListItem16.gif" >
      <Mappings>
          <Mapping Match="message/rfc822" DisplayName="Email" Image="iceml.gif" />
          <Mapping Match="message" Image="icmsg.gif" />
          <Mapping Match="application/octet-stream" DisplayName="Message"
           Image="ICMSG.gif" />
          <Mapping Match="text/html" DisplayName="Html" Image="html16.gif" />
          <Mapping Match="text/plain" DisplayName="Text" Image="ictxt.gif" />
          <Mapping Match="text/xml" DisplayName="Xml" Image="ICXML.gif" />
          <Mapping Match="application/xml" DisplayName="Rss" Image="ICXML.gif" />
          <Mapping Match="application/vnd.ms-powerpoint.presentation.12"
           DisplayName="PowerPoint 12" Image="icpptx.gif" />
          <Mapping Match="application/vnd.ms-powerpoint "
           DisplayName="PowerPoint" Image="icppt.gif" />
```

```
            <Mapping Match="application/vnd.ms-excel.12" DisplayName="Excel 12"
             Image="icxlsx.gif"/>
            <Mapping Match="application/vnd.ms-excel" DisplayName="Excel"
             Image="icxls.gif"/>
            <Mapping Match="application/msword" DisplayName="Word" Image="icdoc.gif"/>
            <Mapping Match="application/vnd.ms-word" DisplayName="Word 12"
             Image="icdocx.gif"/>
            <Mapping Match="application/vnd.visio" DisplayName="Visio" Image="icvsd.gif"/>
        </Mappings>
      </Column>
      <Column Name="ContentSource" OrderBy="Hits" TotalResults="5"
       DisplayName="Content Source"    >
        <Mappings>
            <Mapping Match="Internet site" Image="csWeb.gif" />
            <Mapping Match="Network share" Image="csFlshr.gif" />
            <Mapping Match="Exchange folder" Image="csExch.gif" />
            <Mapping Match="Local Office SharePoint Server sites" Image="stsicon.gif" />
        </Mappings>
      </Column>
    </Columns>
</root>
```

Facets are basically metadata that you expose to the user for drill-down operations. To create a new facet, you thus have to start by making sure that you have a managed property exposing the metadata. Consider, for example, the page shown in Figure 9-15.

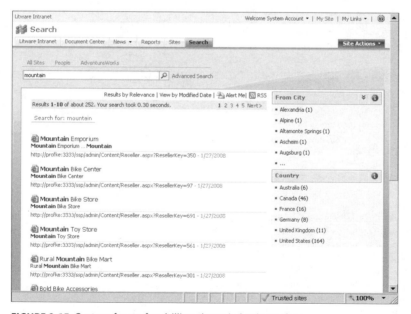

FIGURE 9-15 Custom facets for drilling down in business data

The Search Facets Web Part on this page is configured with the following value for the *SelectColumns* property:

```
<root xmlns:xsi="http://www.w3.org/2001/XMLSchema-instance">
  <Columns OrderBy="Name" >
    <Column Name="ResellerCountry" DisplayName="Country"
        OrderBy="Name" TotalResults="10" />
    <Column Name="ResellerCity" DisplayName="From City"
        OrderBy="Name" TotalResults="5" />
  </Columns>
</root>
```

Two managed properties, *ResellerCountry* and *ResellerCity*, are exposed as facets in the Web Part. There is the additional option of adding *Mapping* elements for each column if needed. Each mapping element can, for example, replace a string with an image or a more user-friendly name. You might associate an icon displaying the flag of each of the countries picked by the Search Facets Web Part this way.

When clicking a country, you filter the list of search result items on the selected country and immediately also refresh the matches picked up by the *ResellerCity* facet. This way, the user can quickly fine-tune the search results to a specific country and city in our example.

The Faceted Search solution is a very nice example of the type of customizations you, as a developer, can add to the indexing and search infrastructure that is delivered with Office SharePoint Server 2007.

Summary

This concludes our exploration of the advanced topics of the Enterprise Search engine. Starting with a detailed overview of the internal architecture of the search engine, this chapter then introduced you to the development of *IFilters* and protocol handlers using the C++ programming language. The development of such components is truly one of the most advanced challenges you can possibly face as a SharePoint developer. Fortunately, it is rarely necessary to enter into such an endeavor. If you find yourself in a situation where these components seem necessary, it is highly recommended to seek professional assistance unless you are already highly familiar with the technology. Solution specialists can be found who have significant experience with this end of SharePoint and who have chosen to offer their expertise to clients with a need to develop their own protocol handlers and *IFilters*. You are welcome to contact the authors of this book for recommendations of specialists. The last sections of this chapter covered the development of custom security trimmers and the deployment of a Faceted Search add-on. Installing the Faceted Search add-on is well worth the effort. Your end users will appreciate Faceted Search mainly because it offers a more user friendly and intuitive way of narrowing the scope of the result set than the advanced search form does. The next and last chapter in this book covers the Search API and administration of the limited search engine included in Windows SharePoint Services 3.0.

Chapter 10
Searching with Windows SharePoint Services 3.0

After completing this chapter, you will be able to

- Understand that the search support in Windows SharePoint Services 3.0 is similar to the search support in Microsoft Office SharePoint Server 2007.

- Execute search queries programmatically using the Query object model and the Windows SharePoint Services 3.0 Query Web service.

- Configure the few options within the SharePoint Central Administration pages for Windows SharePoint Services 3.0 indexing and searching.

This final chapter is a short one, not because we've run out of things to say, but because Microsoft has replaced the Windows SharePoint Services–specific search infrastructure that was at the core of the earlier version of Office SharePoint Server with an infrastructure that is similar to the one we've examined throughout this book. Windows SharePoint Services 3.0 uses the same SharePoint search technology used by Enterprise Search in Microsoft Office SharePoint Server 2007 rather than relying on Microsoft SQL Server full-text searching, as earlier versions of Windows SharePoint Services did.

There are a number of important restrictions when you operate in a server farm that runs only Windows SharePoint Services 3.0. To start, the end-user search experience is limited to a single site collection. The scope is dependent on the level in that site collection where you execute the search query. If you execute the search in the top-level site, you'll get search results including content from the site and all of the subsites under it. The execution of a search query at a lower level, that of a subsite, will include only search results from that subsite and its subsites, not from the parent site or other sites.

In addition to this, only SharePoint content in the site collection can be crawled. You cannot configure the Search service to crawl databases, mail servers, application servers, or Web sites and file shares outside the site collection. In a deployment with more than one site collection, each site collection supports searching only for content on that site collection, and there is no aggregation of search results across site collections.

Apart from these limitations, the components in the index and search architecture are the same, as is the approach you take as a developer when there is a need for a programmatic execution of a search query in, for example, a Web Part on one of the Web Part pages in a SharePoint team site.

The Windows SharePoint Services 3.0 Search Object Model

The developer support in Windows SharePoint Services 3.0 for search operations is delivered by the Query object model. As you saw in Chapter 8, "Search APIs," the execution of a search query can also be performed remotely through a call to the Query Web service. The approach in Windows SharePoint Services 3.0 is similar, but the physical assemblies are different from the search support for developers working in Office SharePoint Server 2007.

Building Search Queries

Three ways of formulating a search query are supported in Windows SharePoint Services 3.0. These three types of search syntaxes are

- **Keyword query**   Useful for short and simple queries that are passed directly to the Search service. Users formulate their queries in the keyword query syntax when they work with the small Search Box that is found on the home pages of their SharePoint collaboration sites, such as the team sites and the document workspaces.

- **SQL syntax**   This syntax is not directly exposed in the end-user search experience. It is generally used when the query is executed in code, as in a custom Search Web Part.

- **URL syntax**   The search parameters are encoded in a URL and posted directly to the search page.

The Query Object Model

Chapter 8 covered the Query object model included in *Microsoft.Office.Server.Search.dll*. This assembly is not available if you have only Windows SharePoint Services 3.0 installed in your server farm. But don't worry, the required classes to programmatically execute search queries are also part of *Microsoft.SharePoint.Search.dll*, and you can find the classes within the *Microsoft.SharePoint.Search.Query* namespace. You'll notice if you browse through these classes that the Query object model for Windows SharePoint Services 3.0 provides the same types of classes as you use within Office SharePoint Server 2007. This is a major improvement for developers who have to target both possible environments. Only one application programming interface (API) must be learned to accomplish the same results.

There are, however, some slight differences that will be discussed in the following sections. As we've done for most of the topics covered in this book, the use of the classes that are part of the Query object model are illustrated with a sample project named WSSSearchKeywords. The sample project is part of the download package available from the companion Web site. Figure 10-1 shows this application in action.

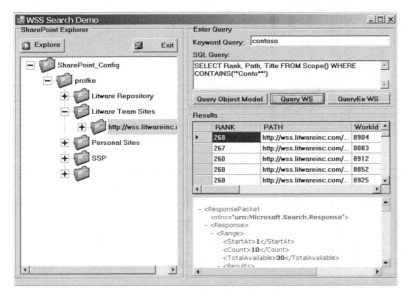

FIGURE 10-1 Sample application, executing search queries with the Windows SharePoint Services 3.0 Query object model and the Windows SharePoint Services 3.0 Query Web service

On the left in Figure 10-1 is a tree view that displays everything available in the server farm. The top node represents the farm, and under that is the servers. For each server, the application displays the IIS Web applications that host SharePoint sites. The site collections and individual sites contained within them are displayed as subnodes. On the right is the option to enter a keyword query or formulate the query using the SQL syntax. The query can be executed by instantiating objects from the two available classes in the Query object model. There is also the option to pass the query to the Query Web service that is available within Windows SharePoint Services 3.0.

The tree of nodes is built using the following code in the *Click* event handler of the Explore button and one recursive function for the display of the subnodes representing each site in the site collection:

```
private void buttonExplore_Click(object sender, EventArgs e)
{
  //-- access the farm and add node
  SPFarm myFarm = SPFarm.Local;
  TreeNode farmNode = treeViewItems.Nodes.Add(myFarm.DisplayName);
  farmNode.Tag = myFarm;
  farmNode.ImageIndex = 0;
  farmNode.SelectedImageIndex = 0;
  //-- show all servers
  foreach (SPServer aServer in myFarm.Servers)
  {
    TreeNode serverNode = farmNode.Nodes.Add(aServer.DisplayName);
    serverNode.Tag = aServer;
```

```
            serverNode.ImageIndex = 0;
            serverNode.SelectedImageIndex = 0;
            //-- add all IIS Web applications
            SPWebService wsi = null;
            foreach (SPServiceInstance si in aServer.ServiceInstances)
            {
                if (si.Service is SPWebService)
                {
                    wsi = (SPWebService)si.Service;
                    foreach (SPWebApplication webApp in wsi.WebApplications)
                    {
                        // -- add only if Windows SharePoint Services only site
                        // -- collections are hosted
                        bool flagAdd = true;
                        foreach (SPSite sitecollection in webApp.Sites)
                        {
                            if (sitecollection.Features
                              [new Guid("F6924D36-2FA8-4f0b-B16D-06B7250180FA")] != null)
                            {
                                flagAdd = false;
                                break;
                            }
                        }
                        if (flagAdd)
                        {
                            TreeNode webAppNode = serverNode.Nodes.Add(webApp.Name);
                            webAppNode.Tag = webApp;
                            webAppNode.ImageIndex = 0;
                            webAppNode.SelectedImageIndex = 0;
                            //-- add all site collections
                            foreach (SPSite sitecol in webApp.Sites)
                            {
                                TreeNode sitecolAppNode = webAppNode.Nodes.Add(sitecol.Url);
                                sitecolAppNode.Tag = sitecol;
                                sitecolAppNode.ImageIndex = 0;
                                sitecolAppNode.SelectedImageIndex = 0;
                                //-- add root site
                                SPWeb rootWeb = sitecol.RootWeb;
                                TreeNode webNode = sitecolAppNode.Nodes.Add(rootWeb.Title);
                                webNode.Tag = rootWeb;
                                webNode.ImageIndex = 0;
                                webNode.SelectedImageIndex = 0;
                                //-- recursively add sub sites
                                AddSubSiteNodes(webNode, rootWeb);
                            }
                        }
                    }
                }
            }
        }
```

```
private void AddSubSiteNodes(TreeNode parentNode, SPWeb web)
{
  foreach (SPWeb subWeb in web.Webs)
  {
    TreeNode webNode = parentNode.Nodes.Add(subWeb.Title);
    webNode.Tag = subWeb;
    webNode.ImageIndex = 0;
    webNode.SelectedImageIndex = 0;
    AddSubSiteNodes(webNode, subWeb);
  }
}
```

This code illustrates the powerful options that are available in the *Microsoft.SharePoint* and *Microsoft.SharePoint.Administration* namespaces to retrieve information about the farm topology and the content that is part of it. These classes can come in handy when you have to build your custom SharePoint solutions such as Web Parts, custom site and application pages, event handlers, and so forth.

The *Query* Class

The Query object model has one top-level class named *Query*. This is the base class for the two classes that you'll actually program with: the *KeywordQuery* class and the *FullTextSqlQuery* class. The *Query* class delivers the base functionality for these two classes and is not needed directly in your code. All of the properties and methods reviewed for this class in Chapter 8, in the section titled "The Query Object Model," are also part of the interface for the *Query* class here in *Microsoft.SharePoint.Search.dll*.

The *KeywordQuery* Class

As its name implies, the *KeywordQuery* class is instantiated whenever there is the need to to execute a search query formulated using the keyword syntax. There are four stages to working with this class, as illustrated in the WSSSearchKeywords sample project.

To start, you create an instance of the class. The constructor of the class can accept two possible values: an object of type *SPSite* or the name of a site. Remember that this is important for the results returned. If you decide to use an *SPSite* instance, the search results will include items from all of the sites within the site collection. If you create the object by passing the name of a site, the search results will originate out of that site and the subsites that are available under it. Here is the code for creating the instance of the *KeywordQuery* class:

```
using (KeywordQuery qry = new KeywordQuery(sitecol))
{
}
```

It is a good practice to create a *using* block so that the *KeywordQuery* instance is disposed of automatically at the end of the code block.

The second stage is the preparation of the execution of the query. This is again done by setting values for the various properties that are exposed with the *KeywordQuery* class, as shown in the following code. All of these properties are discussed in Chapter 8. One note about the *ResultTypes* property: Only relevant results are returned for a Windows SharePoint Services 3.0 search query. There is no inclusion of other types of search results, such as high confidence search results.

```
qry.EnableStemming = true;
qry.StartRow = 0;
qry.RowLimit = 100;
qry.QueryText = textBoxKeywordQuery.Text;
qry.ResultTypes = ResultType.RelevantResults;
```

The third stage is the actual execution of the query. For this, the *Execute* method is called, and the result is an instance of the *ResultTableCollection* type. In there, you'll find the one and only *ResultTable* storing the search results.

```
ResultTableCollection results = qry.Execute();
if (results.Count > 0)
{
    ResultTable result = results[ResultType.RelevantResults];
}
```

The last stage is of course the processing of the results. The results can be loaded in a Microsoft ADO.NET *DataTable* for binding with one of your user controls in a Windows-based or Web application, as shown in the following code. Another approach is the generation of an XML string that can be transformed using an XSL in HTML that is possibly displayed as part of the page in the SharePoint environment.

 More Information A sample project, SQLSearchQueriesSample, demonstrating the processing of the search results within an XML string is included in the download package available from the companion Web site. This is the demo application that was used in the section "Enterprise Search SQL Query Syntax" in Chapter 8.

```
if (results.Count > 0)
{
    ResultTable result = results[ResultType.RelevantResults];
    DataTable tbl = new DataTable();
    tbl.Load(result, LoadOption.OverwriteChanges);
    dataGridViewResults.DataSource = tbl;
}
```

The *FullTextSqlQuery* Class

You instantiate an object of the *FullTextSqlQuery* class when the query uses the SQL syntax. There is no difference in the use of this class compared with the *KeywordQuery* class. You can also identify four stages: creation of the instance and preparation, execution, and processing of the search results. In the sample application, the following code is executed for a search query using the SQL syntax:

```
using (FullTextSqlQuery qry = new FullTextSqlQuery(sitecol))
{
  qry.EnableStemming = true;
  qry.StartRow = 0;
  qry.RowLimit = 100;
  qry.QueryText = textBoxSQLQuery.Text;
  qry.ResultTypes = ResultType.RelevantResults;
  ResultTableCollection results = qry.Execute();
  if (results.Count > 0)
  {
    ResultTable result = results[ResultType.RelevantResults];
    DataTable tbl = new DataTable();
    tbl.Load(result, LoadOption.OverwriteChanges);
    dataGridViewResults.DataSource = tbl;
  }
}
```

The Query Web Service

Windows SharePoint Services 3.0 exposes a Query Web service that allows you to execute search queries remotely in client applications such as Windows-based applications, mobile applications, or extensions loaded within the Microsoft Office system products. The Web service is exposed as the spsearch.asmx. The endpoint URL to communicate with in the client applications is shown here:

```
http:// <Site_Name> /_vti_bin/spsearch.asmx
```

Four Web methods are exposed by the Web service:

- *Query*   This method is called when you want to have the results returned in XML format, ready to be transformed using an XSL. The *Query* method accepts both a query formulated using the keyword syntax and a query using the SQL syntax.

- *QueryEx*   This method behaves like the *Query* method, but it returns the search results as a serialized ADO.NET *DataSet*. *DataSet* objects can immediately be set as the value for the *DataSource* property of many of the user controls that are added to Windows-based forms or Microsoft ASP.NET pages.

- *Registration*   The spsearch.asmx complies with the schemas that need to be implemented in a Web service to make it a Microsoft Office system Research service. This is similar to what was described in the section "The Query Web Service" in Chapter 8. The *Registration* method is called when the research pane in the Microsoft Office system is configured to include the Web service, as shown in Figure 10-2.

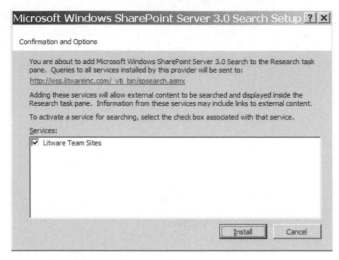

FIGURE 10-2 Registering the spsearch.asmx as a Research service in Microsoft Office Word 2007

- *Status* This method returns status information regarding the search support in Windows SharePoint Services 3.0.

To use the Query Web service in a Microsoft Visual Studio project, you first add a Web reference to your project, as shown in Figure 10-3.

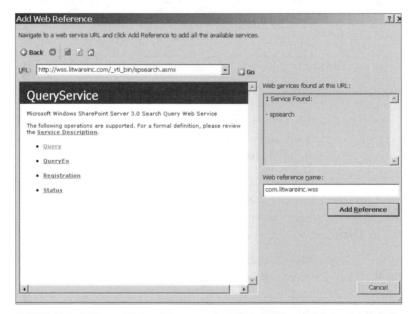

FIGURE 10-3 Adding a Web reference to the Windows SharePoint Services 3.0 Query Web service

The execution of the query using either the *Query* or the *QueryEx* Web method must be prepared by encapsulating the actual search query in a *QueryPacket* XML string. The format of this XML is similar to the XML that must be delivered to the *Query* or *QueryEx* Web method of the Query Web service (search.asmx) that is part of Office SharePoint Server 2007. The section "The Query Web Service" in Chapter 8 covers the format of the XML for constructing the request as well as the returned response packet.

Remember that the choice of the *SPSite* or the individual site in the site collection is very important when you execute a Windows SharePoint Services 3.0 search. You get results only from that site and the subsites. This is why you'll notice in the sample application that the first lines of code create the instance of the generated Web service proxy and then immediately set the proper URL value based on the selection made in the left panel in the tree view. The variable *sitecol* in this code is the instance of the *SPSite*. Don't forget to also pass the proper credentials to the Web service. Two options are available: passing the credentials of the currently logged user, as done in the code, or passing a new instance of the *System.Net. NetworkCredential* class with custom set credentials. And you might want to preauthenticate before actually calling the *Query* or *QueryEx* method. Preauthenticating causes the credentials to be sent to the server, even when the server does not ask for them. This is an optimization option that can save a roundtrip after receiving a 401 error. The code illustrating all of this is shown here:

```
com.litwareinc.wss.QueryService ws =
    new EventHandlerExplorer.com.litwareinc.wss.QueryService();
ws.Url = sitecol.OpenWeb().Url + "/_vti_bin/spsearch.asmx";
ws.Credentials = System.Net.CredentialCache.DefaultCredentials;
ws.PreAuthenticate = true;
```

The *QueryPacket* for a keyword query is as follows:

```
string keywordQryPacket =
    "<QueryPacket xmlns='urn:Microsoft.Search.Query'>"+
    "<Query><SupportedFormats><Format revision='1'>"+
    "urn:Microsoft.Search.Response.Document:Document</Format>"+
    "</SupportedFormats><Context><QueryText language='en-US' type='STRING'>"+
    keywordQry + "</QueryText></Context></Query></QueryPacket>";
```

If the query is formulated using the SQL syntax, the query packet should be the following:

```
string sqlQryPacket = "<QueryPacket xmlns='urn:Microsoft.Search.Query'>"
    + "<Query><SupportedFormats><Format Revision='1'>"
    + "urn:Microsoft.Search.Response.Document:Document</Format>"
    + "</SupportedFormats><Context><QueryText language='en-US' type='MSSQLFT'>"
    + fulltextQry + " --</QueryText></Context></Query></QueryPacket>";
```

Important Due to a bug in the Query Web service, you must append the two dashes (--) to your SQL query. If you do not append the dashes, you'll always get the *Your query is malformed, please rephrase your query* error from the Query Web service. When your query is internally executed, a keyword property is appended automatically to the query for the site context. Adding the dashes will make this an SQL comment, and as such it will be ignored, resulting in your query being executed properly.

If you decide to execute the query using the *Query* method, you'll get the results in XML, and you can process them as follows:

```
string results = string.Empty;
if (keywordQry != string.Empty)
    results = ws.Query(keywordQryPacket);
else
    results = ws.Query(sqlQryPacket);
if (results != string.Empty)
    XmlDocument doc = new XmlDocument();
    doc.LoadXml(results);
    StreamWriter file = new StreamWriter(@"c:\tmp.xml", false);
    file.Write(doc.OuterXml);
    file.Flush();
    file.Close();
    webBrowser1.Navigate(@"c:\tmp.xml");
}
```

If the query is executed using the *QueryEx* method, you'll get a *DataSet* back from the proxy that can immediately be bound to the *DataGridView* control in the application, as shown here:

```
DataSet ds = null;
if (keywordQry != string.Empty)
    ds = ws.QueryEx(keywordQryPacket);
else
    ds = ws.QueryEx(sqlQryPacket);
if (ds != null)
{
    dataGridViewResults.DataSource = ds.Tables[0];
}
```

Windows SharePoint Services 3.0 Search Administration

As mentioned at the beginning of this chapter, the search infrastructure that is part of Windows SharePoint Services 3.0 relies on the same infrastructure that is included in Office SharePoint Server 2007. Chapter 5, "Search Administration," covered many of the topics that administrators within the server farm should know about when it comes to the configuration and management of the indexing and search engines within an Office SharePoint Server 2007 server farm. When working in a server farm with only Windows SharePoint Services 3.0, however, few administration details and configuration options are exposed to the administrators in the browser.

All of the configuration for indexing and searching in Windows SharePoint Services 3.0 is handled automatically behind the scenes by the platform. There is one content source that is automatically created when you install Windows SharePoint Services 3.0. This content source is for all user-content Web applications. New sites that are added to the server farm are immediately added to the start address for this content source. There is no exposure of this content source in the user interface of Windows SharePoint Services 3.0 for the administrators. A second content source for the SharePoint 3.0 Central Administration Web application is also available, although this content source is not especially useful in the real world because users typically will not start a query for content that is made available within this administrator-focused Web application.

The crawling of these content sources is dependent on the crawl schedule as configured by the administrator in the SharePoint 3.0 Central Administration Web application. To access this configuration page, you open the SharePoint 3.0 Central Administration site, and on the Operations page, you click the Services On Server link in the Topology And Services group. Figure 10-4 displays the page, with all of the services that are running within the farm.

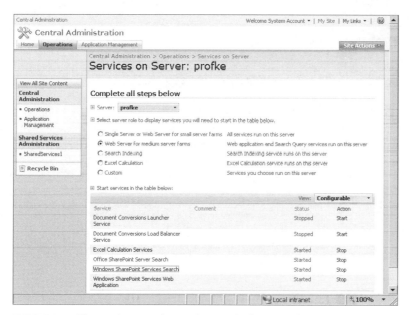

FIGURE 10-4 The services running on a server in the server farm

If you click the Windows SharePoint Services Search link, you'll be redirected to the configuration page shown in Figures 10-5 and 10-6.

Figure 10-5 shows the first two sections on the page, which allow for the setting of the service account and the content access account. The service account is the account that is used to run the Windows SharePoint Services Search service. The content access account is the account that is used to crawl the content. You can assign here any existing domain account. The account will be given the required Full Read policy to all of the start addresses that are included in the content sources that have to be crawled.

FIGURE 10-5 Configuring the service account and the content access account

The second part of the configuration page is shown in Figure 10-6. Here you have the option as an administrator to set the database server and the name of the database that will store all of the search configuration details as well as the crawled metadata. The last section is the configuration of the crawl schedule.

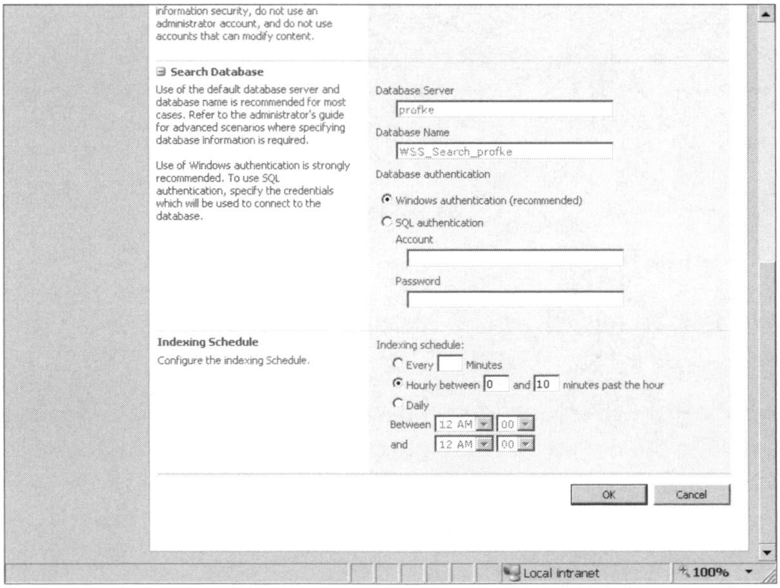

FIGURE 10-6 Configuring the search database and the crawl schedule

The preceding configurations are for the most part the only possible options for the administrators to configure the Windows SharePoint Services 3.0 search infrastructure.

Summary

Key information to take away from this chapter is that the support for search in a server farm that has only Windows SharePoint Services 3.0 installed is similar to the support offered by Microsoft Office SharePoint Server 2007. This is a very good thing, because you can reuse many of the programming techniques covered in the previous chapters in this book within Windows SharePoint Services 3.0 server farms. Keep in mind, however, that you will be able to have only SharePoint content included in the search results and that the scope is dependent on the site that you navigate to or reference in code.

Conclusion

We hope that you have enjoyed reading this book as much as we had fun writing all of the content, and you'll make us very happy if you found the answers you were looking for. Enterprise Search is a big subject to cover, and we've done our best to explain the various topics that are important for both administrators and developers. When we started in the summer of 2007 laying out the table of contents for this book, we knew that there was a lot to write about this collection of technologies. As we progressed and researched some of the topics, we started to get a good feeling about the contents of the book and recognized that all of it would be very useful to many people. We hope that we did not disappoint you in this.

Remember the wise words of Samuel Johnson from Chapter 1: "Knowledge is of two kinds: we know a subject ourselves, or we know where we can find information upon it." As a human being, you want to know as much as possible, and it can be frustrating to experience that this is not really possible anymore. We work in a world where information rules, and we can't survive without the proper tools to support us in our quest for the data that we can transform into information and ultimately into knowledge. We believe that Microsoft holds a strong position as a provider of these tools and the underlying infrastructure that enables its partners to build their own solutions on top of it. We knew this before writing this book—it was in fact the main motivation for writing the book—and we are even more convinced now that we have completed it. We see the many investments that are made in the search space today and the plans for tomorrow, and we are convinced that Microsoft is and will continue to be a big player in the Enterprise Search space.

What are the reasons behind this thinking? First, Microsoft understands how information workers want to see their tasks supported and how they'd like to see search integrated into their daily work environment. There is of course always room for improvement, but tools such as the Microsoft Office system products, Windows SharePoint Services 3.0, and Microsoft Office SharePoint Server 2007 are being adopted at a high speed within the organizations of today. Key for information workers is quick access to information—that is, the most correct and up-to-date information, information that matters to them with the most important parts highlighted, and information that can immediately be processed within their daily work environments without the need for a scribble on a page, a copy and paste, or other arcane ways of processing. Does Microsoft deliver all this? To be honest, not yet... But they are on their way, and they do make available the platform so that in-house developers, consultants, and independent software vendors (ISVs) can jump in and add the missing pieces. Many vendors have done so in the past, and there will always be a place for them in the future. A large part of this book covers the many options you have as a developer to integrate with, extend, or even completely replace the different components that make up the end-user search experience. You also learned how to accomplish this as a developer to support the administrators by using the new administration object model, which we explored in depth. One conclusion that we hope you have reached is that Windows SharePoint Services 3.0 and Microsoft Office SharePoint Server 2007 ought to be seen as development platforms that you can use to build solutions for information workers. Many of these solutions will incorporate search functionality. As developers, you don't have to worry about the underlying plumbing for the indexing and the execution of the search queries. That is part of the platform just like many other features that are delivered with SharePoint. Take as a comparable example the Windows Workflow Foundation (WF). In WF, all of the complexity is nicely encapsulated in the platform and exposed through rich application programming interfaces (APIs) that you as a developer can benefit from when you have to build your own custom workflow templates. Shifting your perspective from viewing Windows SharePoint Services 3.0 and Office SharePoint Server 2007 as finished products that will solve all of your problems in your organization to a more realistic perspective in which you view these as platforms for building or buying these types of solutions was one of our major goals in this book.

Another important factor that we think makes Microsoft's position very strong is the scalability of the search and indexing infrastructure. Microsoft invests a lot in the building of one core architecture for the indexing and searching of data, no matter what level you are working at: desktop, Internet, small teams, medium-size organization, or large to very large organizations. What you do, how you do it, and how you manage it will be done in the same manner no matter what level you are currently working at. The search topology is very flexible, and administrators have many ways to install, configure, and manage the different players within the infrastructure. And you don't have to have it exactly right the first time. You can start small and grow big. The search topology can grow and scale with the organization if there is a need for more indexing and more search support or the need to have the information organized and configured in different ways because of changing needs in your organization.

As authors of a book on an important topic like this, we have had close contact with many people in Redmond who are working on the new generation of SharePoint and Enterprise Search products and technologies. One thing is clear: Many enhancements have been added to the indexing and search support within Microsoft Office SharePoint Server 2007. The launch of Microsoft Search Server 2008 definitely opens up new worlds for in-house developers, administrators, consultants, and product developers, with more integration points and opportunities to deliver a better and more optimized search experience for users. Some of the topics covered in this book might become obsolete as the technology evolves, but the core techniques described will remain the same in the next versions, and the effort, time, and investment in this book will be beneficial as a good foundation when you are about to dive deeper into the new versions. And perhaps by then, we'll be able to provide you with an update of this book. Once again, thanks for your time reading the book, and we wish you the best in your quest, whatever that might be.

Index

Symbols

< predicate, SQL queries, 510
< > predicate, SQL queries, 510
<= predicate, SQL queries, 510
> predicate, SQL queries, 510
>= predicate, SQL queries , 510
* for wildcard searching, 45
  with CONTAINS predicate (SQL), 435
!= predicate, SQL queries, 510
[ ] (brackets) in SQL queries, 429
^ (caret) in SQL queries, 429
: (colon) in search queries. *See* property filters
$ in XSL strings , 120
 in search queries, 46, 426
% (percent sign) in SQL queries, 429
+ (plus sign) in search queries, 46, 426
_ (underscore) in SQL queries, 429

A

<a> element, XML usage package, 186
accented characters in search. *See* diacritic-sensitive search
Account element (application definition files), 314, 345
accounts
  crawler authentication. *See* default content access
     account
  crawling business data, 312, 337
  for crawling specific paths, 403
  farm Search service, 211, 361
  search service account, 211, 361, 597
ACLs for search results, 510
Acrobat PDF format
  configuring indexer to support, 245, 247
  exporting usage data to, 202
Action element (ResponsePacket), 489
action links. *See also* Search Action Links Web Part
  custom, 150
  extending list of, 150
  hiding or displaying, 101
  layout for, 149-150
Active Directory service, populating user profiles with, 59
Add Content Source page, 19
add-in for Microsoft Word 2007 (example), 492-497
Add LOB System option (BDC Definition Editor), 310
Add method
  PublishingPage class, 161
  ScopeDisplayGroup class, 412
Add Property Restrictions area (Advanced Search), 62, 255
Add To My Colleagues link, 67
  rendering, XSL for, 145
Add Web Parts dialog box, 26
  adding to queries, 88
Additional Query Terms property (search box), 88
AddWebPart method (SPWebpartManager), 164
Administration Bar (Search Server 2008), 17
administration object model, 390-425. *See also* Search
    Administration API
  BDC (Business Data Catalog), 306, 308

content sources, 395-403
keywords, definitions, and best bets, 423-425
managed properties, 413-420
relevance tuning, 420-423
search scopes, 404-413
compiling, 407, 408
  creating, 408
  creating scope rules, 409
  deleting, 408
  listing display groups, 411
  listing search scopes, 406
  managing display groups, 412
SearchContext class, 393
ServerContext class, 392-393
administrative tasks in Search Center, 78-118
  configuring Search Web Parts, 85-118
  creating custom pages, 79-82
  creating custom tabs, 83-84
Adobe Acrobat PDF format
  configuring indexer to support, 245, 247
  exporting usage data to, 202
ADO.NET, 305
advanced installation, Search Server Express, 16
Advanced Search Box Web Part, 77, 114-118
  developer view of, 162-164
Advanced Search display group, 285
Advanced Search link (in Search Box), 42
Advanced Search page, 60-62
  configuring link to, 90
  exposing managed properties in, 262
  hiding/displaying link to, 91
  navigating to. *See* Advanced Search link
Advanced Search Page layout (AdvancedSearchLayout.
    aspx), 76
Advanced Search Web Part, 60
AdvancedSearchPageURL property (Search Box), 166
Alert Me link, 65
  hiding or displaying, 101
AlertNotificationFormat property (SearchContext), 394
alerts, document libraries, 225
alerts, search-based, 65, 68, 272-273
  e-mail message format, 394
  logical limits (software boundaries), 379
  resetting content index and, 274
aliases in SQL queries, 428
All Content rules (search scope), 252
All Sites search scope, 257
All Sites tab (Search Center With Tabs), 57, 75
  scoping of, 249
AllCategories property (Schema), 414
AllContentScopeRule class, 407, 411
AllDisplayGroups property (Scopes), 412
AllKeywords property (Keywords), 424
AllManagedProperties property (Schema), 410, 416
Allow This Property To Be Used In Scopes option, 255
All_Results/DiscoveredDefinitions template, 127
AllScopes property (Scopes), 406
AllUsersWebPart element (ONET.XML), 72, 163
alternate access mappings, 243
AlwaysCompile option (scopes), 408
analyzing search usage. *See* search usage reporting

G

H

I

Z

Patrick Tisseghem

Patrick Tisseghem is a Microsoft MVP for Office SharePoint Server 2007, and he teaches and develops courseware for SharePoint Products and Technologies. He is a managing partner of U2U nv/sa, a Microsoft Certified Partner for learning solutions, and the author of *Inside Microsoft Office SharePoint Server 2007*.

Lars Fastrup

Lars Fastrup is an independent contractor offering software development and advisory services for SharePoint Products and Technologies, the .NET framework and Microsoft SQL Server. Until the end of 2007, he worked for the search technology company Mondosoft where he headed the conception and development of the popular Ontolica search add-ons for SharePoint Portal Server 2003 and SharePoint Server 2007.

What do you think of this book?

We want to hear from you!

Do you have a few minutes to participate in a brief online survey?

Microsoft is interested in hearing your feedback so we can continually improve our books and learning resources for you.

To participate in our survey, please visit:

www.microsoft.com/learning/booksurvey/

...and enter this book's ISBN-10 or ISBN-13 number (located above barcode on back cover*). As a thank-you to survey participants in the United States and Canada, each month we'll randomly select five respondents to win one of five $100 gift certificates from a leading online merchant. At the conclusion of the survey, you can enter the drawing by providing your e-mail address, which will be used for prize notification only.

Thanks in advance for your input. Your opinion counts!

* Where to find the ISBN on back cover

ISBN-13: 000-0-0000-0000-0
ISBN-10: 0-0000-0000-0

Example only. Each book has unique ISBN.

Microsoft®
Press